Lecture Notes in Computer Science 12318

More information about this series at http://www.springer.com/series/7409

Xin Wang · Rui Zhang ·
Young-Koo Lee · Le Sun ·
Yang-Sae Moon (Eds.)

Web and Big Data

4th International Joint Conference, APWeb-WAIM 2020
Tianjin, China, September 18–20, 2020
Proceedings, Part II

 Springer

Editors
Xin Wang (iD)
Tianjin University
Tianjin, China

Young-Koo Lee (iD)
Kyung Hee University
Yongin, Democratic People's Republic
of Korea

Yang-Sae Moon (iD)
Kangwon National University
Chunchon, Korea (Republic of)

Rui Zhang (iD)
University of Melbourne
Melbourn, NSW, Australia

Le Sun
Nanjing University of Information Science
and Technology
Nanjing, China

ISSN 0302-9743   ISSN 1611-3349   (electronic)
Lecture Notes in Computer Science
ISBN 978-3-030-60289-5   ISBN 978-3-030-60290-1   (eBook)
https://doi.org/10.1007/978-3-030-60290-1

LNCS Sublibrary: SL3 – Information Systems and Applications, incl. Internet/Web, and HCI

This Springer imprint is published by the registered company Springer Nature Switzerland AG
The registered company address is: Gewerbestrasse 11, 6330 Cham, Switzerland

Preface

This volume (LNCS 12317) and its companion volume (LNCS 12318) contain the proceedings of the 4th Asia-Pacific Web (APWeb) and Web-Age Information Management (WAIM) Joint Conference on Web and Big Data (APWeb-WAIM 2020). This joint conference aims at attracting professionals from different communities related to Web and big data who have common interests in interdisciplinary research to share and exchange ideas, experiences, and the underlying techniques and applications, including Web technologies, database systems, information management, software engineering, and big data.

APWeb-WAIM 2020 was held in Tianjin, China, during September 18–20, 2020. APWeb and WAIM are two separate leading international conferences on research, development, and applications of Web technologies and database systems. Previous APWeb conferences were held in Beijing (1998), Hong Kong (1999), Xi'an (2000), Changsha (2001), Xi'an (2003), Hangzhou (2004), Shanghai (2005), Harbin (2006), Huangshan (2007), Shenyang (2008), Suzhou (2009), Busan (2010), Beijing (2011), Kunming (2012), Sydney (2013), Changsha (2014), Guangzhou (2015), and Suzhou (2016). Previous WAIM conferences were held in Shanghai (2000), Xi'an (2001), Beijing (2002), Chengdu (2003), Dalian (2004), Hangzhou (2005), Hong Kong (2006), Huangshan (2007), Zhangjiajie (2008), Suzhou (2009), Jiuzhaigou (2010), Wuhan (2011), Harbin (2012), Beidaihe (2013), Macau (2014), Qingdao (2015), and Nanchang (2016). Starting in 2017, the two conference committees agreed to launch a joint conference. The first APWeb-WAIM conference was held in Beijing (2017), the second APWeb-WAIM conference was held in Macau (2018), and the third APWeb-WAIM conference was held in Chengdu (2019). With the increased focus on big data, the new joint conference is expected to attract more professionals from different industrial and academic communities, not only from the Asia Pacific countries but also from other continents.

The high-quality program documented in these proceedings would not have been possible without the authors who chose APWeb-WAIM for disseminating their findings. After the double-blind review process (each paper received at least three review reports), out of 259 submissions, the conference accepted 68 regular papers (acceptance rate 26.25%), 29 short research papers, and 8 demonstrations. The contributed papers address a wide range of topics, such as big data analytics, data and information quality, data mining and application, graph data and social networks, information extraction and retrieval, knowledge graph, machine learning, recommender systems, storage, indexing and physical database design, text analysis, and mining. We are deeply thankful to the Program Committee members for lending their time and expertise to the conference. The technical program also included keynotes by Prof. James Hendler (Rensselaer Polytechnic Institute, USA), Prof. Masaru Kitsuregawa (The University of Tokyo, Japan), Prof. Xuemin Lin (University of New South Wales, Australia), and Prof. Xiaofang Zhou (The University of Queensland, Australia). We are grateful to these distinguished scientists for their invaluable contributions to the conference program.

We thank the honorary chairs (Masaru Kitsuregawa and Keqiu Li) and the general co-chairs (Xiaofang Zhou and Zhiyong Feng) for their guidance and support. Thanks also go to the workshop co-chairs (Qun Chen and Jianxin Li), panel co-chairs (Bin Cui and Weining Qian), tutorial co-chairs (Yunjun Gao and Leong Hou U), demo co-chairs (Xin Huang and Hongzhi Wang), industry co-chairs (Feifei Li and Guoliang Li), publication co-chairs (Le Sun and Yang-Sae Moon), and publicity co-chairs (Yi Cai, Yoshiharu Ishikawa, and Yueguo Chen).

We hope you enjoyed the exciting program of APWeb-WAIM 2020 as documented in these proceedings.

August 2020   Xin Wang
                                                           Rui Zhang
                                                   Young-Koo Lee

Organization

Honorary Chairs

Masaru Kitsuregawa	The University of Tokyo, Japan
Keqiu Li	Tianjin University, China

General Chairs

Xiaofang Zhou	The University of Queensland, Australia
Zhiyong Feng	Tianjing University, China

Program Committee Chairs

Xin Wang	Tianjin University, China
Rui Zhang	The University of Melbourne, Australia
Young-Koo Lee	Kyunghee University, South Korea

Panel Chairs

Bin Cui	Peking University, China
Weining Qian	East China Normal University, China

Workshop Chairs

Qun Chen	Northwestern Polytechnical University, China
Jianxin Li	Deakin University, Australia

Tutorial Chairs

Yunjun Gao	Zhejiang University, China
Leong Hou U.	University of Macau, Macau

Demo Chairs

Xin Huang	Hong Kong Baptist University, Hong Kong
Hongzhi Wang	Harbin Institue of Technology, China

Industry Chairs

Feifei Li	University of Utah, USA, and Alibaba, China
Guoliang Li	Tsinghua University and Huawei, China

Publication Chairs

Le Sun   Nanjing University of Information Science
                            and Technology, China
Yang-Sae Moon   Kangwon National University, South Korea

Publicity Chairs

Yi Cai   South China University of Technology, China
Yoshiharu Ishikawa   Nagoya University, Japan
Yueguo Chen   Renmin University of China, China

APWeb-WAIM Steering Committee Representative

Yanchun Zhang   Victoria University, Australia

Senior Program Committee

Wolf-Tilo Balke   TU Braunschweig, Germany
K. Selçuk Candan   Arizona State University, USA
Reynold Cheng   The University of Hong Kong, Hong Kong
Byron Choi   Hong Kong Baptist University, Hong Kong
Saiful Islam   Griffith University, Australia
Mizuho Iwaihara   Waseda University, Japan
Peer Kroger   Ludwig Maximilian University of Munich, Germany
Byung Suk Lee   University of Vermont, USA
Bohan Li   Nanjing University of Aeronautics and Astronautics,
                            China
Guoliang Li   Tsinghua University, China
Sebastian Link   The University of Auckland, New Zealand
Makoto Onizuka   Osaka University, Japan
Wookey Lee   Inha University, South Korea
Demetrios   University of Cyprus, Cyprus
   Zeinalipour-Yazti
Xiangliang Zhang   King Abdullah University of Science and Technology,
                            Saudi Arabia
Ying Zhang   University of Technology Sydney, Australia
Xiang Zhao   National University of Defence Technology, China
Shuigeng Zhou   Fudan University, China

Program Committee

Toshiyuki Amagasa   University of Tsukuba, Japan
Wolf-Tilo Balke   University of Hannover, Germany
Zhifeng Bao   RMIT University, Australia
Ilaria Bartolini   University of Bologna, Italy

Ladjel Bellatreche   ISAE-ENSMA, France
Zouhaier Brahmia   University of Sfax, Tunisia
Yi Cai   School of Software Engineering, China
Tru Hoang Cao   Ho Chi Minh City University of Technology, Vietnam
Xin Cao   University of New South Wales, Australia
Hong Chen   Renmin University of China, China
Lisi Chen   Hong Kong Baptist University, Hong Kong
Lu Chen   Aalborg University, Denmark
Qun Chen   Northwestern Polytechnical University, China
Shimin Chen   Chinese Academy of Sciences, China
Jiangtao Cui   Xidian University, China
Lizhen Cui   Shandong University, China
Maria Luisa Damiani   University of Milano, Italy
Alex Delis   University of Athens, Greece
Lei Duan   Sichuan University, China
Amr Ebaid   Purdue University, USA
Markus Endres   University of Augsburg, Germany
Ju Fan   Renmin University of China, China
Yaokai Feng   Kyushu University, Japan
Jun Gao   Peking University, China
Yunjun Gao   Zhejiang University, China
Tingjian Ge   University of Massachusetts, USA
Zhiguo Gong   University of Macau, Macau
Yu Gu   Northeastern University, China
Giovanna Guerrini   Universita di Genova, Italy
Jialong Han   Tencent AI Lab, China
Tanzima Hashem   Bangladesh University of Engineering and Technology,
                            Bangladesh
Xiaofeng He   East China Normal University, China
Zhenying He   Fudan University, China
Liang Hong   Wuhan University, China
Haibo Hu   Hong Kong Polytechnic University, Hong Kong
Jilin Hu   Inception Institute of Artificial Intelligence, UAE
Jianbin Huang   Xidian University, China
Chih-Chieh Hung   Tamkang University, Taiwan
Dawei Jiang   Zhejiang University, China
Cheqing Jin   East China Normal University, China
Peiquan Jin   Universiity of Science and Technology of China, China
Tung Kieu   Aalborg University, Denmark
Carson K. Leung   University of Manitoba, Canada
Bohan Li   Nanjing University of Aeronautics and Astronautics,
                            China
Cuiping Li   Renmin University of China, China
Feifei Li   The University of Utah, USA
Hui Li   Xiamen University, China
Jianxin Li   Deakin University, Australia

Jingjing Li	University of Electronic Science and Technology of China, China
Lin Li	Wuhan University of Technology, China
Ronghua Li	Shenzhen University, China
Tianrui Li	School of Information Science and Technology, China
Yafei Li	Zhengzhou University, China
Yu Li	Hangzhou Dianzi University, China
Zheng Li	Amazon, USA
Zhixu Li	Soochow University, China
Defu Lian	Big Data Research Center, China
Xiang Lian	Kent State University, USA
Guoqiong Liao	Jiangxi University of Finance and Economics, China
An Liu	Soochow University, China
Guanfeng Liu	Macquarie University, Australia
Hailong Liu	Northwestern Polytechnical University, China
Hongyan Liu	Tsinghua University, China
Yu Liu	Huazhong University of Science and Technology, China
Lizhen Wang	Yunnan University, China
Hua Lu	Aalborg University, Denmark
Wei Lu	Renmin University of China, China
Jizhou Luo	Harbin Institute of Technology, China
Mihai Lupu	Vienna University of Technology, Austria
Zakaria Maamar	Zayed University, UAE
Sanjay Kumar Madria	Missouri University of Science and Technology, USA
Yang-Sae Moon	Kangwon National University, South Korea
Mirco Nanni	ISTI-CNR, Italy
Wee Ng	Institute for Infocomm Research, Singapore
Baoning Niu	Taiyuan University of Technology, China
Hiroaki Ohshima	University of Hyogo, Japan
Vincent Oria	NJIT, USA
P. Krishna Reddy	International Institute of Information Technology, Hyderabad, India
Haiwei Pan	Harbin Engineering University, China
Sanghyun Park	Yonsei University, South Korea
Yuwei Peng	Wuhan University, China
Jianzhong Qi	The University of Melbourne, Australia
Tieyun Qian	Wuhan University, China
Lu Qin	University of Technology Sydney, Australia
Yanghui Rao	Sun Yat-sen University, China
Daniele Riboni	University of Cagliari, Italy
Chuitian Rong	Tiangong University, China
Dimitris Sacharidis	TU Wien, Austria
Aviv Segev	University of South Alabama, USA
Shuo Shang	University of Electronic Science and Technology of China, China

Junming Shao	University of Electronic Science and Technology of China, China
Yingxia Shao	Beijing University of Posts and Telecommunications, China
Derong Shen	Northeastern University, China
Wei Shen	Nankai University, China
Victor S. Sheng	Texas Tech University, USA
Yongpan Sheng	Tsinghua University, China
Kyuseok Shim	Seoul National University, South Korea
Lidan Shou	Zhejiang University, China
Shaoxu Song	Tsinghua University, China
Wei Song	Wuhan University, China
Han Su	Big Data Research Center, China
Le Sun	Nanjing University of Information Science and Technology, China
Weiwei Sun	Fudan University, China
Chih-Hua Tai	National Taipei University, Taiwan
Yong Tang	South China Normal University, China
Bo Tang	Southern University of Science and Technology, China
Xiaohui Tao	University of Southern Queensland, Australia
Yongxin Tong	Beihang University, China
Goce Trajcevski	Iowa State University, USA
Leong Hou U.	University of Macau, Macau
Kazutoshi Umemoto	The University of Tokyo, Japan
Hongzhi Wang	Harbin Institute of Technology, China
Hua Wang	Victoria University, Australia
Jianguo Wang	University of California San Diego, USA
Jin Wang	University of California Los Angeles, USA
Junhu Wang	Griffith University, Australia
Meng Wang	Southeast University, China
Peng Wang	Fudan University, China
Senzhang Wang	Nanjing University of Aeronautics and Astronautics, China
Sheng Wang	New York University, USA
Wei Wang	University of New South Wales, Australia
Xin Wang	Tianjin University, China
Yangtao Wang	Huazhong University of Science and Technology, China
Yijie Wang	National University of Defense Technology, China
Raymond Chi-Wing Wong	Hong Kong University of Science and Technology, Hong Kong
Shengli Wu	Jiangsu University, China
Xiaokui Xiao	National University of Singapore, Singapore
Yanghua Xiao	Fudan University, China
Qing Xie	Wuhan University of Technology, China
Xike Xie	University of Science and Technology of China, China

Jiajie Xu	Soochow University, China
Jianliang Xu	Hong Kong Baptist University, Hong Kong
Jianqiu Xu	Nanjing University of Aeronautics and Astronautics, China
Xinshun Xu	Shandong University, China
Zhouming Xu	Hohai University, China
Dingyu Yang	Shanghai Dianji University, China
Lianghuai Yang	Zhejiang University of Technology, China
Shiyu Yang	East China Normal University, China
Yajun Yang	Tianjin University, China
Junjie Yao	East China Normal University, China
Hongzhi Yin	The University of Queensland, Australia
Jian Yin	Sun Yat-sen University, China
Xiaohui Yu	Shandong University, China
Kai Zeng	Microsoft, USA
Dongyang Zhang	University of Electronic Science and Technology of China, China
Haiwei Zhang	Nankai University, China
Meihui Zhang	Beijing Institute of Technology, China
Wen Zhang	Wuhan University, China
Xiaowang Zhang	Tianjin University, China
Yong Zhang	Tsinghua University, China
Yongqing Zhang	Chengdu University of Information Technology, China
Yuxiang Zhang	Civil Aviation University of China, China
Zheng Zhang	Harbin Institute of Technology, China
Zhiqiang Zhang	Zhejiang University of Finance and Economics, China
Zhiwei Zhang	Hong Kong Baptist University, Hong Kong
Lei Zhao	Soochow University, China
Xiang Zhao	National University of Defence Technology, China
Xujian Zhao	Southwest University of Science and Technology, China
Bolong Zheng	Huazhong University of Science and Technology, China
Kai Zheng	University of Electronic Science and Technology of China, China
Weiguo Zheng	Fudan University, China
Xiangmin Zhou	RMIT University, Australia
Xuan Zhou	Renmin University of China, China
Feida Zhu	Singapore Management University, Singapore
Xingquan Zhu	Florida Atlantic University, USA
Lei Zou	Peking University, China
Zhaonian Zou	Harbin Institute of Technology, China

Contents – Part II

Text Analysis and Mining

Spatial, Temporal and Multimedia Databases

Database Systems

Contents – Part I

Knowledge Graph

Recommender Systems

Information Extraction and Retrieval

Machine Learning

Blockchain

DHBFT: Dynamic Hierarchical Byzantine Fault-Tolerant Consensus Mechanism Based on Credit

Fengqi Li[✉], Kemeng Liu, Jing Liu, Yonggang Fan, and Shengfa Wang

School of Software Technology, Dalian University of Technology, Dalian, China
lifengqi@dlut.edu.cn

Abstract. It is significant to improve Practical Byzantine Fault Tolerance algorithm (PBFT) in consortium blockchain. At present, the serial verification process of transactions in the primary and backups greatly affects consensus efficiency. Meanwhile, the lack of reasonable valuation mechanism in PBFT makes it difficult to motivate existing reliable nodes. Moreover, consensus nodes work in an enclosed environment, where nodes cannot join and exit dynamically.

To solve the shortcomings stated above, we propose a dynamic hierarchical Byzantine fault-tolerant consensus mechanism based on credit (DHBFT). Firstly, we design a hierarchical-parallel scheme composed of consensus nodes, candidate nodes, and ordinary nodes. We realize parallel transaction logic verification in the primary and backups by delegating candidate nodes to verify the validity of transactions preliminarily. Secondly, we create a reward-punishment scheme. The consensus nodes with better performances are assigned higher credit value and have higher probability to become the primary. Thirdly, we propose a dynamic promotion-demotion scheme. It enables faulty nodes to be excluded from the consensus set and reliable candidate nodes to join.

Experimental results show that DHBFT has better efficiency and higher stability. Compared with PBFT, the overall throughput of transactions is increased by 16%, and the average delay is reduced by 12%. Moreover, the proportion of abnormal nodes is basically 0 and much lower than that of PBFT.

Keywords: Consortium blockchain · Consensus mechanism · Dynamic-hierarchical scheme · Reward-punishment scheme · Promotion-demotion scheme

1 Introduction

Blockchain technology is a secure, reliable, and decentralized network system [1]. The consensus mechanism is the key to guarantee the sustainable operation of a robust blockchain. There are now three consensus mechanisms based on proof, stake, and voting. The first two consensus mechanisms are usually utilized in public blockchain [2]. They compete for accounting right by means of computing resources or the stake of

Supported by The Fundamental Research Funds for the Central Universities (NO. DUT19ZD209).

© Springer Nature Switzerland AG 2020
X. Wang et al. (Eds.): APWeb-WAIM 2020, LNCS 12318, pp. 3–17, 2020.
https://doi.org/10.1007/978-3-030-60290-1_1

cryptocurrency which is not suitable for the consortium blockchain due to low throughput and high delay. For the consortium blockchain, the consensus mechanism should meet the requirements of high throughput, low delay, and Byzantine fault-tolerance (BFT). Thus, BFT state machine replication algorithm appears in public.

The first practical BFT state machine replication algorithm is PBFT [3]. The algorithm provides both safety and liveness, but in all n replicas, at most $\lfloor \frac{n-1}{3} \rfloor$ replicas are faulty simultaneously. The non-faulty replicas will reach a consensus through several rounds of mutual voting. However, there are still some fatal problems to be solved [4]. Firstly, the serial transaction verification process of the primary and backups, especially the verification of signature and version dependency for lots of transactions, takes up most of the consensus time, which reduces the overall efficiency of consensus greatly. Secondly, all consensus nodes are equal and have the same opportunity to be the primary, which is not in line with the fact that more reliable nodes should play a greater role in the actual scenario [5]. Furthermore, the primary is generated in rotation, which causes it to be more vulnerable. Thirdly, the replicas are fixed, working in an enclosed environment. The system can only "punish" the primary by view-change protocol, can hardly detect faulty backups or exclude any faulty replicas, which reduces the security and stability of the system. It will be crashed when the number of faulty replicas exceeds $\lfloor \frac{n-1}{3} \rfloor$.

To solve the problems mentioned above, we propose DHBFT. Like PBFT, it is also a protocol based on week synchrony assumptions. At first, we design a hierarchical-parallel scheme. The candidate nodes execute *"read"* transactions, which makes consensus nodes invest more resources to process *"write"* transactions. We also realize parallel transaction logic verification of the primary and backups in each round of consensus by delegating candidate nodes to verify the validity of transaction in advance, which improves the overall efficiency of consensus. Secondly, we create a reward-punishment scheme. This scheme monitors the state of consensus nodes in real-time, rewards reliable consensus nodes and punishes abnormal nodes by increasing or decreasing their credit value. We also eliminate the view-change protocol and propose a self-adapting primary selection protocol to guarantee that the nodes with higher credit value gain a greater probability to become the primary, which enhances the stability of the system. Thirdly, we propose a dynamic promotion-demotion scheme. It can exclude faulty consensus nodes, and add reliable candidate nodes to consensus set with no downtime, which breaks the enclosed running environment of PBFT and further enhances the stability and security of the system.

This paper is organized as follows. We introduce the basic ideas of PBFT in Sect. 2. We describe the system model and consensus process in Sect. 3 and Sect. 4. The analysis and experimental results are described in Sect. 5 and Sect. 6. Finally, we list related work and conclude this paper in Sect. 7 and Sect. 8, respectively.

2 The Basic Ideas of PBFT

PBFT is a state machine replication protocol, that is, the service is modeled as a state machine. The state machine replicates on different replicas in a distributed system. The replicas execute the same operations and maintain the consistency state of services. PBFT offers both safety and liveness when the number of faulty replicas does not exceed $\lfloor \frac{n-1}{3} \rfloor$. The concepts of safety and liveness are defined as follows.

Safety: all non-faulty replicas agree on the sequence numbers of requests that commit locally.

Liveness: clients eventually receive replies to their requests.

2.1 Consistency Protocol

PBFT uses the consistency protocol to ensure that each operation request has a unique sequence number, and at least $2f + 1$ replicas reach a consensus, where f is the maximum number of Byzantine replicas. There are two kinds of nodes in the consistency protocol: the primary and backups, and three phases: pre-prepare, prepare, and commit, as shown in Fig. 1. The primary is responsible for ordering requests of the client. The backups verify the validity of requests provided by the primary in order.

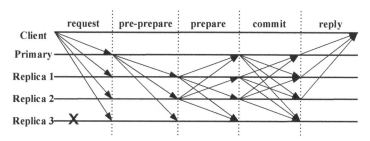

Fig. 1. PBFT normal case operation.

- *Pre-prepare phase*: after receiving the operation request, the primary assigns a sequence number to the request, and multicasts a pre-prepare message to backups. If a backup receives and recognizes the pre-prepare message, it will enter the prepare phase by multicasting a prepare message to all other replicas.
- *Prepare phase*: once the replica collects a quorum of $2f$ (including its own) prepare messages that match the pre-prepare message, it will multicast a commit message to other replicas and turns into the commit phase.
- *Commit phase*: the replica collects a quorum of $2f + 1$ commit messages to ensure that the operation request has been recognized by enough replicas. Finally, the replicas send reply messages containing the result of the request to the client.

2.2 View-Change and Checkpoint Protocol

According to the consistency protocol, PBFT relies on the primary to multicast a valid pre-prepare message to guarantee the algorithm working successfully. Therefore, when the primary is faulty, the view-change protocol will be executed to select another replica to replace it. The view-change process is equivalent to an additional round of consensus, which is quite time-consuming.

To save resources and correct system state in time, PBFT designs a checkpoint protocol. In the consensus process, there are lots of logs generated by replicas. To save memory and prevent system failure, when every k requests are executed, the replica records the current state and multicasts a checkpoint message to other replicas. If the replica collects $2f + 1$ valid checkpoint messages with the same state, it will clear the local logs of these k requests.

3 System Model

DHBFT is a dynamic hierarchical consensus mechanism. There are three kinds of nodes, consensus nodes, candidate nodes, and ordinary nodes, as shown in Fig. 2. The candidate nodes are responsible for executing "*read*" transactions and preliminarily verifying the validity of "*write*" transactions sent by clients, while the consensus nodes are only responsible for consensus on "*write*" transactions. In a round of consensus, the primary orders "*write*" transactions in chronological order and packs them into a new block. It will reach a consensus if the block is verified valid by most backups. All nodes append the valid block broadcasted by consensus nodes to their local blockchain.

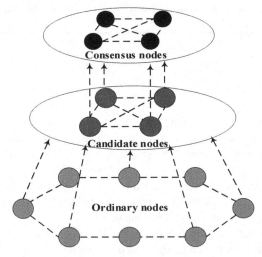

Fig. 2. DHBFT model for a consortium blockchain system.

Malicious attacks and software errors are becoming more common [3], which cause faulty nodes to exhibit arbitrary behaviors [6]. Moreover, to recognize each other in a distributed network, a trusted key generation center (KGC) is necessary. To guarantee Byzantine fault-tolerance and validate identity each other in a distributed network, we make the following assumptions.

Assumption 1: we assume that the number of consensus nodes and candidate nodes are both n, the number of faulty consensus nodes and faulty candidate nodes are both no more than $\lfloor \frac{n-1}{3} \rfloor$.

Assumption 2: KGC generates private key $x_i \in [1, p-1]$ and public key $y_i = g^{x_i} \bmod p$ for every node and discloses the system parameters p, g *and* H, where p is a big prime number, g is the generator of $GF(p)$, and H is a secure hash function.

Finally, every node has three lists, consensus node list (C_0NL), candidate node list (C_1NL), and ordinary node list (ONL). These record IP address/port, public key, credit value, and sequence number of three types of nodes.

4 The Basic of DHBFT

4.1 Consensus Process

The consensus process of DHBFT is shown in Fig. 3. It is a classic three-phase protocol and replies correct results to the client. The difference between PBFT is that consensus nodes initialize a local state list *SL* at the beginning of each round of consensus [6]. We define $SL_i[j]$ that the consensus node i saves the digest of the block in pre-prepare message when the node j is the primary or the digest of the prepare message from the backup j. After a round of consensus, consensus nodes will compute and update their credit value according to the state list.

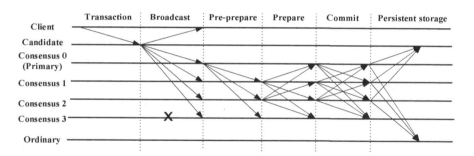

Fig. 3. Consensus process of DHBFT.

Then, we will introduce more details about DHBFT in the following steps.

1. The client sends a transaction request $\langle TRANSACTION, tx, ty, [ver], t, c_j \rangle \sigma_{cj}$ to a candidate node, where tx is a transaction, ty is the transaction type, ver is the version dependency of the transaction and is optional, t is the current timestamp, c_j is the sequence number of the client, and $<> \sigma_{cj}$ is the signature of the client.

2. When the candidate node i receives a transaction request, it verifies the validity of the transaction by its signature and format, and pre-executes transaction to verify the validity of version dependency. Then, the candidate node i multicasts the valid transaction to other candidate nodes. If the transaction is a *"read"* transaction, they will return the reply message $\langle REPLY, tx, ty, [ver], t, r, l \rangle \sigma_l$ to the client, where r is the result of the *"read"* transaction and l is the sequence number of candidate node l. When the client collects $f+1$ valid reply messages with the same result, it acknowledges this result. If the transaction is a *"write"* transaction, other candidate nodes will verify the validity of the transaction again by its signature, format and version dependency, and send the signature $\langle s_l, r_l \rangle \sigma_l$ for the valid transaction to candidate node i, where $s_l = H(m)x_l - r_l k_l \bmod \varphi(p)$ is the signature result of candidate node l for transaction m, $r_l = g^{k_l} \bmod p$ and $k_l \in [1, p-1]$ is a random number.

3. When the candidate node i receives $2f + 1$ valid signature results, it generates a multi-signature $\langle S, R \rangle \sigma_l$ by [12], where $S = R \times \left(\sum_{l=1}^{2f+1} s_l \right) \bmod \varphi(p)$ and $R = \prod_{l=1}^{2f+1} r_l^{r_l} \bmod p$. Then, the candidate node i multicasts "write" transaction proposal $\langle \langle TRANSACTION, tx, ty, [ver], t, c_j \rangle \sigma_{cj}, \langle R, S, U = \{u_1, \ldots, u_{2f+1}\} \rangle \sigma_l \rangle$ to consensus nodes, where U is a set containing $2f + 1$ sequence numbers of signers.

4. When consensus nodes receive the transaction proposal, they calculate the verification public key $Y = \prod_{l=1}^{2f+1} y_l \bmod p$ to verify the validity of multi-signature for this transaction. If the transaction is valid, it will be stored in the local transaction pool, otherwise, it will be abandoned. When the timer or the number of transactions reaches a specific threshold, the primary orders and packs transactions into a new block embedded in the current timestamp.

5. In the pre-prepare phase, the primary generates and multicasts a pre-prepare message $\langle \langle PRE - PREPARE, h, d, p \rangle \sigma_p, B \rangle$ with block piggybacked to other consensus nodes, where B is the new block, h is the height of B, d is the digest of B, and p is the sequence number of the primary.

6. If consensus node i receives the pre-prepare message, it verifies the identity of the primary and validity of the block, and records d at $SL_i[p]$, whether the block is valid or not. Then, the primary and consensus nodes verify the validity of transaction logic in parallel to guarantee that the version dependency of all transactions does not conflict and duplicate transactions do not exist. If they are all valid, it enters prepare phase by multicasting a prepare message $\langle PREPARE, h, d, i \rangle \sigma_i$ to other consensus nodes.

7. The consensus node i receives prepare messages sent by other nodes and adds them to its local log. Then, it records the digest of prepare message received from consensus node j at $SL_i[j]$. When the consensus node i receives $2f + 1$ prepare messages matching the pre-prepare message, it enters commit phase and multicasts a commit message with state list piggybacked to other consensus nodes. The message has the form $\langle \langle COMMIT, h, d, i \rangle \sigma_i, \langle SL_i \rangle \sigma_i \rangle$.

8. When consensus node i receives commit messages sent by other nodes, it verifies the validity of message. If consensus nodes collect $2f + 1$ valid commit messages, their consensus state becomes commit-local. Then, consensus nodes enter persistent storage phase and multicast the new block to candidate and ordinary nodes. At the same time, consensus nodes update the credit value according to the state list based on reward-punishment scheme and select a new primary based on self-adapting primary selection protocol to start a new round of consensus.

9. In persistent storage phase, after verifying the validity of the block, all nodes append the new block to their local blockchain and execute transactions contained in the block. Then consensus nodes clean up transactions in the transaction pool and logs which have already been stored into the blockchain.

In the actual scenario, there are usually thousands of transactions in a block, so it is important to optimize the transaction verification process to improve consensus efficiency. Based on the hierarchical-parallel scheme, DHBFT delegates the candidate nodes to verify the validity of transaction signature, format, and version dependency preliminarily, so the primary need not verify the validity of each transaction when packing a block. The primary and backups just need verify transaction logic in parallel in prepare phase, which decreases consensus time from $2(t + t') + t''$ to $t' + t''$, where t is the verification time of transaction signature, format, and version dependency, t' is the verification time of transaction logic, and t'' is the other times in the consensus process.

4.2 Reward and Punishment Scheme

We require that all consensus nodes have to multicast SL to each other when they reach prepared state or this round of consensus is timeout. Consensus nodes can compare with each other to detect all abnormal nodes. There are three states: *benign*, *absent*, and *evil*. Benign state means that the primary generates a valid block and eventually reaches a consensus or the backup multicasts consistent messages and agrees with the majority. Absent state means that the primary does not generate a new block or the backup does not multicast messages due to crash. Evil state means that the primary generates an invalid block or the backup multicasts inconsistent messages or disagrees with the majority.

We update the credit value of consensus nodes according to their state. In DHBFT, $C(i)$ is the credit value of the consensus node i, where $0 \leq C(i) \leq 1$, and the highest credit value is 1. The credit value of consensus nodes is initialized with $C_{init} = 0.5$, while the credit value of candidate nodes and ordinary nodes are initialized with 0.2. Since the behavior of the primary and backups affects the result of consensus in varying degree, we utilize different formulas to calculate the credit value separately. We define $C(i, r - 1)$ as the credit value of the node i during the $(r - 1)$ th round of consensus, then $C(i, r)$ can be specified as follows.

- If node i is the primary, then

$$C(i, r) = \begin{cases} \min(C(i, r - 1) + \varepsilon_p, 1), & State_i = benign \\ \max(C(i, r - 1) - ReD_p, 0), & State_i = absent \\ 0, & State_i = evil \end{cases}.$$

- If node i is the backup, then

$$C(i, r) = \begin{cases} min(C(i, r - 1) + \varepsilon_b, 1), & State_i = benign \\ max(C(i, r - 1) - ReD_b, 0), & State_i = absent \\ C_{init} & State_i = init \text{ or } (end \text{ of} \\ & punishment \text{ } period) \\ 0, & State_i = evil \text{ or } (the \text{ } node \text{ } is \text{ } in \text{ } the \\ punishment \text{ } period \text{ } and \text{ } State_i = absent) \end{cases}$$

Where ε_p and ε_b are the credit value increment of the primary and backups, ReD_p and ReD_b are the credit value reduction of the primary and backups respectively. Usually, $0 < \varepsilon_b < \varepsilon_p < 0.1$, $0 < ReD_b < ReD_p < 0.27$, and they can be adjusted according to the actual scenario.

In DHBFT, we propose a concept of *punishment period* to punish abnormal (*absent* or *evil*) consensus nodes. We define that a round of consensus time threshold is τ, then the node i must experience the punishment period of at least $\theta_i \tau$ in which it is limited to be the primary. The value of θ_i is related to the behavior of node i in the $(r-1)$ th round of consensus. The formula for calculating θ_i is as follows.

$$\theta_i = log_\alpha \left\{ \frac{min(C(i, r-1) + \varepsilon_n, 1)}{C(i, r)} \right\} \tag{1}$$

Where $\alpha > 1$ is a punishment factor, the smaller the α, the greater the θ_i. According to the state of consensus nodes, we can get different punishment period.

- If the node state is benign, then $\frac{min(C(i,r-1)+\varepsilon_n,1)}{C(i,r)} = 1, \theta_i = 0$, it need not enter a punishment period, and is qualified to be the primary in subsequent consensus process.
- If the node state is absent, then $\frac{min(C(i,r-1)+\varepsilon_n,1)}{C(i,r)} > 1, \theta_i > 0$, its punishment period is $\lceil \theta_i \rceil \tau$. This node is limited to be the primary in the punishment period.
- If the node state is evil, then $\frac{min(C(i,r-1)+\varepsilon_n,1)}{C(i,r)} \to +\infty, \theta_i \to +\infty$, its punishment period $\lceil \theta_i \rceil \tau$ is infinite. This node will be replaced by the candidate node with the highest credit value based on dynamic promotion-demotion scheme.

4.3 Self-adapting Primary Selection Protocol

In DHBFT, we use self-adapting primary selection protocol to ensure the nodes with higher credit value gain a greater probability to become the primary, and the selection result is unpredictable. We calculate the probability that the benign node i is selected as the new primary by the following formula.

$$P(i, r) = \frac{C(i, r)^\lambda}{\sum_{j=1}^{N} C(j, r)^\lambda} \tag{2}$$

Where N is the number of benign consensus nodes, and the power exponent λ is given by the following formula.

$$\lambda = \frac{k}{\frac{C_{max}}{\overline{C}} - 1} \tag{3}$$

Where C_{max} and $\overline{C}$ are the maximum and average credit value of benign nodes, and k is a coefficient. Then, we calculate the cumulative probability of each node in the order of probability value from low to high. If the probabilities of two nodes are equal, the node with a smaller sequence number will be placed in front of another.

$$q_i = \sum_{j=1}^{i} P(j, r) \tag{4}$$

To ensure the unpredictability of the primary selection process, a random number RN distributed over the interval $[0, 1]$ should be generated. We hash the block head of the latest block by SHA256 to generate RN.

$$RN = StrToInt(SHA256(blockhead)) mol \, N \tag{5}$$

According to the cumulative probability of each node, the primary in the new round of consensus will be finally determined. If the consensus node i is identified as the primary, it needs to meet the following condition.

$$q_{i-1} < min\left(1, \frac{RN}{N} + \varepsilon\right) \le q_i \qquad (6)$$

Where ε is a constant between 0 and 1, we can ensure that the reliable nodes have a higher probability to become the primary by adjusting the value of ε.

4.4 Dynamic Promotion and Demotion Scheme

In PBFT, consensus nodes work in an enclosed environment. The system cannot exclude any faulty nodes, so it will be crashed when the number of faulty nodes exceeds $\lfloor \frac{n-1}{3} \rfloor$, which reduces the security and stability of the blockchain system. Besides, reliable nodes cannot join consensus set either. To realize that nodes join and exit consensus set dynamically, we propose the change protocol, as shown in Fig. 4.

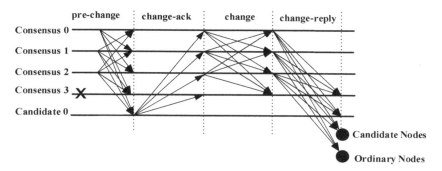

Fig. 4. Change protocol.

1. After a round of consensus, if the state of consensus node j is evil, non-faulty consensus nodes, such as node i, will multicast a pre-change message $\langle PRE - CHANGE, h, t, j, k, i \rangle \sigma_i$ to other consensus nodes and the candidate node with the highest credit value, where h is the height of the current block, t is the effective time of message that is generally the time of a round of consensus, j is the sequence number of evil node, k is the sequence number of the candidate node with the highest credit value. If there are two nodes with highest credit value, the node with a smaller sequence number will be selected.

2. When the candidate node k receives $2f + 1$ valid pre-change messages, it generates and multicasts a change-ack message to consensus nodes. The form of change-ack message is $\langle CHANGE - ACK, h, t, j, k \rangle \sigma_k$.

3. When consensus nodes receive a change-ack message, they verify whether the signature is correct and message time is timed out, and compare the change-ack message with pre-change message. If change-ack message is valid, consensus nodes will multicast a change message $\langle CHANGE, h, j, k, i \rangle \sigma_i$ to each other. When consensus nodes collect

$2f + 1$ valid change messages, they will multicast a change-reply message to the evil consensus node j, all candidate nodes and ordinary nodes. The form of change-reply message is $\langle CHANGE - REPLY, h, j, k, i \rangle \sigma_i$.

4. Then, all nodes update their C_0NL, C_1NL and ONL which means that the candidate node k joins consensus set successfully and its state and credit value are initialized to benign and 0.5 respectively, and the consensus node j to be an ordinary node. Finally, the consensus node with highest credit value sends transactions in its transaction pool to the newly joined node, and the newly joined node can also ask others to get transactions.

At the same time of starting a new round of consensus, candidate nodes will multicast a join message to the ordinary node with the highest credit value to join candidate set ensuring the number of candidate nodes required. the process is similar with candidate node joining consensus set.

5 Analysis

5.1 Safety

In DHBFT, we define the safety of algorithm as all benign consensus nodes agree on the same block that commits locally.

In PBFT, there are three predicates, $prepared(m, v, n, i)$, $committed(m, v, n)$ and $committed-local(m, v, n, i)$ to ensure that two non-faulty replicas agree on the sequence number of requests that commit locally in the same view at two replicas. And the view-change protocol ensures that non-faulty replicas also agree on the sequence number of requests that commit locally in different views at different replicas.

As we cancel the view-change protocol, we need to define new predicates.

- $prepared(B, h, SL_i, i)$ is true if and only if the node i has inserted a new block B, a pre-prepare message for B with height h, $2f + 1$ valid prepare messages that match the pre-prepare message, and SL_i recording the digest of B from pre-prepare and prepare messages received by node i, in its local log.
- $committed(B, h, n)$ is true if and only if $prepared(B, h, SL_i, i)$ is true for each node i in a set of $f + 1$ non-faulty consensus nodes.
- $committed-local(B, h, i)$ is true if and only if $prepared(B, h, SL_i, i)$ is true and node i has received $2f + 1$ commits from different nodes that match the pre- prepare message for B.

In DHBFT, if $prepared(B, h, SL_i, i)$ is true, $prepared(B', h, SL_i, j)$ is false for any non-faulty consensus node j (including $i = j$) and any B' such that $D(B') \neq D(B)$, where $D(B)$ is the digest of the block B. This implies that two benign consensus nodes agree on the block with height h that commits locally in a round of consensus. Then, as we cancel the view-change protocol, we need new scheme to ensure the block prepared reaches a consensus with the same h. As we have described in the consensus process, if non-faulty consensus nodes do not reach a consensus on a new block in a round of consensus, the non-faulty nodes will multicast SL to each other. Assuming that node i have reached prepared state, if node k and node i find that there are differences in $SL_k[j]$ and $SL_i[j]$, they will exchange prepare message received from node j to each other. So, the node

k will receive at least $2f + 1$ valid prepare messages through node i. Then the node k reaches commit-local state and know that other non-faulty consensus nodes will also reach commit-local state. Finally, all non-faulty consensus nodes will reach a consensus on the block with prepared state, which ensures the block consistency in the system.

5.2 Liveness

In DHBFT, we define the liveness of the algorithm that consensus nodes must move to a new round of consensus when they cannot reach a consensus, and at least $2f + 1$ benign nodes can move to the same round of consensus in a long enough time.

First, when consensus nodes do not reach a consensus on a new block, they multicast their SL to each other, and start a timer to expire after some time T. If the timer expires before consensus nodes receives all valid SL, for example, the consensus node j does not receive the SL of node i, it will multicast a message to other nodes for requesting SL_i but this time it will wait $2T$. These avoid starting a new consensus too soon.

Second, when a consensus node receives a message from consensus node j for requesting SL_i, it will send SL_i to the consensus node j. If the timer expires before node j receives $2f + 1$ replies, it will mark the state of the node i as absent. In addition, when a consensus node finds that other nodes are faulty because they send inconsistent SL, it multicasts the information of faulty nodes and corresponding evidence found in this round to other consensus nodes. These prevent staring a new consensus too late.

Third, it is infeasible for malicious consensus nodes to attack the system by forging SL. That is because SL_i is signed by its private key of consensus node i, other consensus nodes cannot forge valid SL_i. Moreover, only when consensus nodes receive all the SL in the consensus set or there are evidences that some nodes are absent or faulty, they will enter the next round consensus.

The above measures ensure the liveness of DHBFT and the sustainable operation of the blockchain system.

6 Performance Evaluation

To analyze the performance of DHBFT, we implemented a consortium blockchain system whose consensus algorithm is encapsulated by PBFT and DHBFT respectively. We created multiple servers to simulate different nodes running on a four-core machine, with Intel Core i5-6300HQ, 2.30 GHz and 8 GB RAM. To continuously generate transactions, we create five accounts with enough balance, and just trade 1 in each transaction. In the following experiments, we evaluate the performance of DHBFT in two aspects, including the efficiency and stability of the system.

Throughput and delay are two main metrics used to evaluate the efficiency of a blockchain system. The throughput is usually represented by TPS, and the delay indicates the running time from a new block generation to confirmation. Suppose that block generation time is $T_{packing}$, consensus algorithm execution time is $T_{consensus}$, and block broadcast time among consensus nodes is $T_{broadcast}$, then delay can be defined as follows.

$$Delay = T_{packing} + T_{consensus} + T_{broadcast} \qquad (7)$$

The proportion of abnormal nodes is the ratio of the number of abnormal (*absent* or *evil*) nodes to the total number of consensus nodes, which is an important index to measure the security and stability of the system. The lower the proportion of abnormal nodes, the safer and more stable the blockchain system.

6.1 The Relationship Between Efficiency and the Number of Consensus Node, the Number of Transaction

We evaluate the throughput and delay of transactions with different number of nodes and transaction packing threshold. The number of consensus nodes and candidate nodes is 4, 7, 10, and 13 respectively, and the number of faulty nodes in consensus set is 1, 2, 3, and 4 correspondingly. The number of transactions in a block increases from 500 to 2000. Figures 5 and 6 illustrate the experimental results.

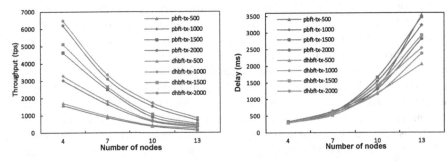

Fig. 5. The throughput of transactions.   **Fig. 6.** The delay of transactions.

With the same number of consensus nodes and the transaction packing threshold, the throughput of DHBFT is always higher than that of PBFT, and the delay of DHBFT is always lower than that of PBFT. Besides, the maximum throughput of DHBFT reaches 6500 tps, and the delay is just between 250 ms and 300 ms. On average, the throughput of DHBFT is 16% higher than that of PBFT. The delay of DHBFT is 12% lower than that of PBFT. That's because the primary and backups only verify the transaction logic parallelly in DHBFT, while they verify transaction signature, format, version dependency, and logic serially in PBFT.

6.2 The Relationship Between Consensus Efficiency and Running Time

To reflect the general situation, we evaluate the efficiency of the overall system over time with 2000 transaction packing threshold, 7 consensus nodes and 2 faulty nodes.

As shown in Figs. 7 and 8, the throughput of PBFT is stable at about 3000 tps, while the throughput of DHBFT is 2350 tps at the beginning, which is less than that of PBFT. In the 2nd round of consensus, the throughput of DHBFT continues to decrease, because it detects and excludes faulty consensus nodes and make reliable candidate nodes join the consensus set, which brings additional overhead. After the 3rd round of consensus, the throughput of DHBFT is higher than that of PBFT. Subsequently, it is stable at about 3500 tps, which is higher than that of PBFT.

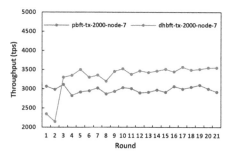

Fig. 7. The change of throughput over time.

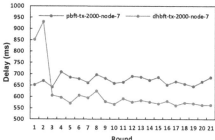

Fig. 8. The change of delay over time.

The delay of PBFT is stable at about 670 ms at the beginning, while the delay of DHBFT is 850 ms, and reaches 930 ms in the 2nd round of consensus. Then the delay of DHBFT decreases and finally reaches about 570 ms, which is less than that of PBFT.

6.3 The Relationship Between Stability and Running Time

To evaluate the stability of the DHBFT and PBFT, we analyze the proportion of abnormal nodes over time with 2000 transaction packing threshold, 13 consensus nodes, 13 candidate nodes, and 4 abnormal nodes (2 absent nodes and 2 evil nodes).

As shown in Fig. 9, initially, there are both 4 abnormal nodes in DHBFT and PBFT, the proportion of abnormal nodes for DHBFT and PBFT are both 30.78% (approximately equal to 33.33%). In PBFT, consensus nodes are fixed and cannot exclude any abnormal nodes, so the proportion of abnormal node is always 30.78% over time. However, based on the dynamic promotion-demotion scheme, DHBFT can update evil nodes with reliable candidate nodes at the end of the first round of consensus. So, in the 2nd round of consensus, there are only 2 absent nodes, and the proportion of abnormal nodes reduces to 15.38% (approximately equal to 16.67%). Then, since 2 absent nodes are absent in two successive rounds of consensus, their credit value will be set to 0 and they will be excluded from consensus set. Therefore, in the 3rd round of consensus, there are no abnormal nodes in consensus set and the proportion of abnormal nodes reduces to 0. After that, only in the 6th round of consensus, one node goes down. After a period of stable running of the system, the proportion of abnormal nodes in DHBFT is always 0, and the system maintains high stability and security.

7 Related Work

PBFT is a practical Byzantine state-machine replication algorithm in distributed fields, as time goes by, there are many improvements to PBFT. Cowling et al. proposed HQ [7] to improve the performance of PBFT. HQ cancels the two-way interactions of consistency verification process among servers when there is no conflict. Although this method reduces the secondary cost of communication between replicas, the cost of communication between copies cannot provide a generic model because the PBFT protocol is still executed once the clients compete to send requests. Then Dahlin et al. proposed

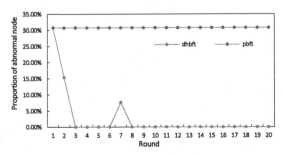

Fig. 9. The change of the proportion of abnormal nodes over time.

Zyzzyva [8] protocol which utilizes speculation technology to reduce cost and simplifies the consensus process. This method can improve the efficiency of PBFT. However, this algorithm requires client to determine whether servers reach a consensus or not, it is not suitable for peer to peer networks in consortium blockchain. In addition, Wood et al. proposed ZZ [9], a protocol widely applicable to current Byzantine state-machine system. Its characteristic is that the number of servers requesting Byzantine state-machine protocol execution is reduced from $2f + 1$ to $f + 1$ by virtualization technology. When the server fails, the client quickly starts other servers to replace the faulty servers. Although the stability of the system is improved by replacing the faulty nodes, it still depends on the client to determine the state of the server.

When it is applied to blockchain domain, PBFT still needs to be further improved. Recently, many studies have begun to improve the efficiency and stability of the PBFT in consortium blockchain. Lei et al. propose RBFT [6]. Nodes with high reputation value have higher discourse rights to participate in consensus. It will reach a consensus when the discourse rights exceed 2/3 not the number of nodes. Although this algorithm improves the efficiency of PBFT, with the operation of the system, the discourse rights will be concentrated in a few nodes which results in centralization reducing the stability and security of system. Wang et al. propose CDPBFT [10]. It reduces the participation of abnormal nodes in the consensus process, but it cannot eliminate the faulty nodes or detect faulty backups. Xu et al. proposed Dynamic PBFT [11] to improve the stability of PBFT that allows nodes to join and exit dynamically. However, it introduces a centralized node *NodeCA*, which reduces the security of the system due to the centralized node. Furthermore, these studies do not change the serial verification of transactions in the primary and backups, so the efficiency is not much improved compared with the original PBFT.

8 Conclusion

In this paper, we propose a novel consensus mechanism DHBFT for consortium blockchain. We first design a hierarchical-parallel scheme to improve the efficiency of the system. We also realize parallel transaction logic verification in the primary and backups. To stimulate enthusiasm of reliable nodes and punish faulty nodes, we create a reward-punishment scheme. The abnormal nodes get lower credit value entering punishment period and the reliable nodes gain higher credit value with a greater probability to become the primary. Since consensus nodes in PBFT work in an enclosed environment, we also propose a dynamic promotion-demotion scheme to improve the stability of system, which realizes nodes join and exit consensus set dynamically. Finally, our experiments demonstrate that DHBFT has higher efficiency, higher reliability, and higher stability especially in complex environments.

References

1. Nakamoto, S.: Bitcoin: a peer-to-peer electronic cash system. https://bitcoin.org/bitcoin.pdf. Accessed 10 May 2020
2. Bentov, I., et al.: Proof of activity: extending bitcoin's proof of work via proof of stake. ACM SIGMETRICS Perform. Eval. Rev. **42**(3), 34–37 (2014)
3. Castro, M., Liskov, B.: Practical byzantine fault tolerance and proactive recovery. ACM Trans. Comput. Syst. **20**(4), 398–461 (2002)
4. Zhang, L., Li, Q.: Research on consensus efficiency based on practical byzantine fault tolerance. ICMIC **2018**, 1–6 (2018)
5. Miller, A. et al.: The honey badger of BFT protocols. In: ACM SIGSAC Conference on Computer and Communications Security, pp. 31–42 (2016)
6. Lei, K., et al.: Reputation-based byzantine fault-tolerance for consortium blockchain. In: ICPADS, pp. 604–611 (2019)
7. Cowling, J., et al.: HQ replication: a hybrid quorum protocol for byzantine fault tolerance. In: 7th symposium on Operating system Design Implement, pp. 13–23 (2006)
8. Reiser, H.P., et al.: Hypervisor-based efficient proactive recovery. In: 26th IEEE International Symposium on Reliable Distributed Systems, pp. 83 − 92 (2007)
9. Wood, T., et al.: ZZ and the art of practical BFT execution. In: 6th Conference on Computer Systems, pp. 123–138 (2011)
10. Wang, Y., et al.: Study of blockchains's consensus mechanism based on credit. IEEE Access **7**, 10224–10231 (2019)
11. Hao, X., et al.: Dynamic practical byzantine fault tolerance. In: IEEE Conference on Communications and Network Security, pp. 1–8 (2018)
12. Zhang, Q., et al.: Multisignature scheme with threshold value. Comput. Eng. **33**(2), 15–17 (2007)

MaSRChain: A Trusted Manuscript Submission and Review System Based on Blockchain

Fengqi Li[✉], Kemeng Liu, Haoyu Wu, and Xu Zhang

School of Software Technology, Dalian University of Technology, Dalian, China
lifengqi@dlut.edu.cn

Abstract. Manuscript submission and review (MaSR) systems play an important role in scholarly publishing. However, there are some problems to be solved. Authors cannot gain an authoritative copyright certificate of manuscripts. Journals and conferences cannot achieve effective detection of multiple contributions with one manuscript. Reviewers may intentionally submit malicious evaluations due to competition. In this paper, we propose a trusted decentralized manuscript submission and review system based on blockchain (MaSRChain) to solve problems above. At first, we use blockchain and Attribute-Based Encryption (ABE) to protect manuscript copyright and realize access control of manuscripts for authors. Secondly, we utilize blockchain to realize manuscript sharing that encrypted by Locality Sensitive Hash (LSH), which can achieve multiple contributions detection among different institutions. Thirdly, we apply Ring Signature to realize authentication of review evaluations, while providing some anonymity to reviewers. Finally, we conduct experiments based on Hyperledger Fabric and experimental results demonstrate the effectiveness and efficiency of the system.

Keywords: Manuscript submission and review system · Blockchain · Copyright protection · Multiple contributions detection · Anonymous peer review

1 Introduction

MaSR systems have become a central fixture in scholarly publishing. However, current centralized systems bring lots of risks for all parties. At first, after the submission, authors lose the control of manuscripts. When dishonest program committee members or peer reviewers plagiarize unpublished work [1], it is difficult for authors to prove their ownership of the work. Moreover, some dishonest authors submit one manuscript to multiple institutions [2]. However, it is impossible to detect multiple contributions because they cannot share unpublished manuscripts. Finally, reviewers may deliberately submit negative review evaluations due to the lack of effective constraints [3].

To solve these problems, we propose MaSRChain. Firstly, we design a manuscript copyright protection protocol based on the tamper-proof infrastructure of blockchain and ABE. The manuscript encrypted by ABE is recorded into the blockchain, which

Supported by The Fundamental Research Funds for the Central Universities (NO. DUT19ZD209).

X. Wang et al. (Eds.): APWeb-WAIM 2020, LNCS 12318, pp. 18–26, 2020.
https://doi.org/10.1007/978-3-030-60290-1_2

realizes copyright protection and access control to manuscripts for authors. Secondly, we propose a detection method of multiple contributions based on the distributed features of blockchain and LSH. The manuscript hashed by LSH can be shared among different institutions. So, the multiple contributions can be detected on the premise of protecting the confidentiality of manuscript. Finally, we realize accountable and anonymous review protocol based on blockchain and Ring Signature. The tamper-proof storage of review evaluations restricts reviewers to review manuscripts more fairly, while Ring Signature helps authors verify the authenticity of evaluations anonymously.

The paper is organized as follows. The preliminary is introduced in Sect. 2. Section 3 describes the system model. The system analysis and experiment are described in Sect. 4 and Sect. 5. We list related work and conclude this paper in Sect. 6 and Sect. 7.

2 Preliminary

2.1 Distributed Ledger Technology

MaSRChain is built on the Hyperledger Fabric [4]. In Fabric, *Peer* interfaces with applications, executes smart contracts. *Orderer* sorts transactions, and ensures data consistency of the whole network. Inter Planetary File System (IPFS) is a peer-to-peer distributed file system [5]. it is high-capacity, content-addressable and allocates a unique identifier for stored file, which makes up for the limited storage space of blockchain.

2.2 Locality Sensitive Hash

we utilize Simhash [6] and Perceptual Hash (PHash) [7] to detect the similarity of text and figures in different manuscripts respectively. After tokenizing, hashing, weighting, summation and dimensionality reduction, we get the Simhash value of the text with N bits length. In addition, after reducing size, simplifying color, getting lowest frequency matrix and calculating average, we get the PHash value of figures. Finally, the algorithm uses Hamming distance to judge the similarity of text and figures in manuscripts.

2.3 Attribute-Based Encryption

we use DPUPH-CP-ABE [8] to realize protection and access control of manuscripts for authors. The DPUPH-CP-ABE consists of five algorithms.

Set(1^λ, U)→pk, msk. Inputs are security parameter λ and attribute universe description U. It outputs public key pk and master key msk.

Encr(pk, M, $\mathbb{A}$)→ct. Inputs are pk, a message M and access structure $\mathbb{A}$. It outputs ciphertext ct and E_{info} which is encrypted information about message M.

KeyG(pk, msk, S)→sk. Inputs are pk, msk and attributes S. It outputs secret key sk.

Decr(pk, sk, ct)→M. Inputs are pk, sk and ct. It outputs the message M.

Update(E_{info}, $C_i^{(2)'}$)→ct'. Inputs are E_{info} and $C_i^{(2)'}$ which is calculated from $C^{(2)}$ in ct. It outputs a new ciphertext ct'.

2.4 Ring Signature

Ring Signature [9] allows the authorization of a collection of identities to perform an action, while maintaining the privacy of the specific identity that performed the action. The Ring signature consists of three algorithms.

RKeyGen(P)→x_i, y_i. Inputs is a big prime number P. It outputs the public key y_i and secret key x_i for reviewers.

RSign(m, L, x_i)→σ. Inputs are the message m, a public key set L of n no-signers and the secret key x_i of the actual signer. It outputs the signature result σ.

RVeri(m, σ)→{1|0}. Inputs are m and σ. It outputs the verification result.

3 System Overview

3.1 Overview

MaSRChain aims to provide a distributed, tamper-proof and verifiable solution for manuscript copyright protection, multiple contributions detection, and accountable and anonymous peer review. As shown in Fig. 1, there are five entities in system: *authors*, *editors*, *reviewers*, *permissioned blockchain* and *external storage*. The permissioned blockchain consists of publishers, journals and conference agents based on Fabric. The publishers are *orderer*, while journals and conference agents are *peer* in different *organizations*. The solution can be divided into five phases.

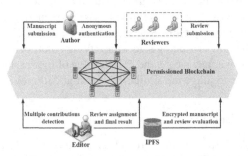

Fig. 1. Overview of MaSRChain system.

Manuscript Submission. Authors upload manuscripts encrypted by DPUPH-CP-ABE to IPFS and blockchain. Then, the system provides a copyright certificate to authors.

Multiple Contributions Detection. When journals or conferences receive manuscript, the editor executes multiple contributions detection to avoid wasting review resources.

Review Assignment. The editor submits review assignment to the blockchain. Then, the author chooses capable reviewers in this scope to review this manuscript.

Review Submission. The reviewers submit evaluations signed by Ring Signature to IPFS and Blockchain. The tamper-proof storage of evaluations can restrict reviewers to review more fairly.

Final Notification and Anonymous Authentication. The editor sends final notification to authors. The author can verify the authenticity and creditability of evaluations.

3.2 Manuscript Copyright Protection Protocol

To realize copyright protection and access control to manuscripts for authors, we design a manuscript copyright protection protocol based blockchain and DPUPH-CP-ABE. Next, we will explain this protocol in detail by submitting a manuscript in Fig. 2.

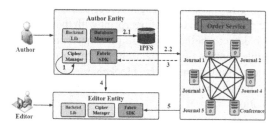

Fig. 2. The process of submitting a manuscript.

- **Step 1.** Before submitting a manuscript, the author entity runs $Setup(1^\lambda, U)$ algorithm to generate pk and msk and encrypts the manuscript by $Encrypt(pk, M, \mathbb{A})$ algorithm to generate the ciphertext of the manuscript $ct = \left(C, C^{(1)}, \{C^{(2)}\}_{i \in [1,l_s]}, C^{(3)}\right)$.
- **Step 2.** Then, the author entity submits ct to IPFS and submits manuscript information (including title, unique identifier returned by IPFS and the fingerprint of manuscript) to the blockchain by invoking manuscript submission smart contract (SC).
- **Step 3.** If the fingerprint of manuscript is not similar with the published manuscripts, the blockchain will provide a copyright certificate to the author.
- **Step 4–5.** Finally, the author entity sends pk and msk to the editor, and the system will send submission notice to the editor.

3.3 Multiple Contributions Detection and Review Assignment Protocol

To realize multiple contributions detection and choose suitable reviewers to review manuscripts, we propose a multiple contributions detection and review assignment protocol. Next, we will explain this protocol in detail in Fig. 3.

- **Step 1.** Editor invokes viewing manuscript SC to get the manuscript information. Then, the editor gets the ciphertext of manuscript through unique identifier from IPFS.

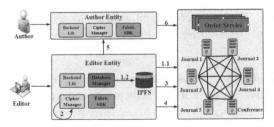

Fig. 3. The process of multiple contributions detection and review assignment.

- **Step 2.** The editor runs **keyGen**(**pk**, **msk**, **S**) algorithm generate the private key sk, and runs **Decrypt**(**pk**, **sk**, **ct**) algorithm to get the plaintext of manuscript.
- **Step 3.** Subsequently, the editor invokes multiple contributions detection SC to detect multiple contributions. The system calculates the fingerprint $f = (h_s, h_p)$ of manuscript containing Simhash and PHash value. Then, MaSRChain compares the Hamming distance $dis = (f_x, f_y)$ of the fingerprint with that of submitted manuscripts in the blockchain to detect whether it is multiple contributions.
- **Step 4.** After multiple contributions detection, the editor invokes review assignment SC to submit review assignment to the blockchain, which contains 5 reviewers' pseudonymous identity attributes and brief introduction to reviewers but no personally identifiable information.
- **Step 5.** The editor informs author to choose 3 reviewers as he thinks suitable to review his manuscript.
- **Step 6.** Then, the author gets pseudonymous identity attributes of reviewers he chose from blockchain and runs **Update**$\left(E_{info}, C_i^{(2)\prime}\right)$ to update access policy and generate new ciphertext ct', Finally, the author submits new ciphertext to IPFS and blockchain.

3.4 Accountable and Anonymous Review Protocol

To restrict reviewers to review manuscripts more fairly, and verify the authenticity and creditability of evaluations on the premise of anonymity, we design an accountable and anonymous review protocol based blockchain and Ring Signature as shown in Fig. 4.

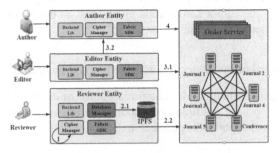

Fig. 4. The process of review evaluations submission and anonymous authentication.

- **Step 1.** When reviewers finish review evaluations, they run **RKeyGen**(P) algorithm to generate temporary secret key σ_i and temporary public key y_i. Then, the signer runs **RSign**(m, L, x_i) to generate the Ring Signature result σ.
- **Step 2.** The reviewer submits the review evaluation to the IPFS and uploads unique identifier, and Ring Signature result σ to the blockchain.
- **Step 3.** When all reviewers have uploaded their evaluations, the editor invokes submitting final notification SC to upload the final review result of this manuscript, and informs the author final decision through the system.
- **Step 4.** When the author receives the final review result of manuscript, he runs **RVerify**(m, σ) to verify the authenticity and creditability of evaluations that submitted by the reviewers of his choice under the condition of anonymity.

4 Security and Privacy Analysis

It is important to protect the copyright and content of manuscript. The timestamp and tamper-proof infrastructure of blockchain prove that the author begins to own this manuscript at a specific time. Moreover, the manuscript is encrypted by DPUPH-CP-ABE to protect the content of manuscript, and DPUPH-CP-ABE is indistinguishable under chosen plaintext attack, which meets the security requirement in scholarly publishing.

Now, double blind reviews are becoming more and more common. The anonymity of author can be achieved simply by hiding authors' identity information. In MaSR-Chain, the author needs to authorize reviewers to access the manuscript. To prevent the author from getting reviewers' identity information, we utilize pseudonymous identity attributes of reviewers to construct DPUPH-CP-ABE cryptosystem, which realizes access authorization without knowing reviewers' identity.

5 Performance Evaluation

MaSRChain is built on Fabric 1.2, which is composed of ten computers running Ubuntu 16.04 and equipped with I7-6700 processor with 3.4 GHz and 8 GB memory. There are four *orderer* and six *organizations*. To fully reflect the performance of the system, we have tested the performance of algorithms utilized in this paper and blockchain system.

5.1 Evaluation of Main Algorithm

we test the performance of DPUPH-CP-ABE with 2 attributes, the performance of Simhash and PHash algorithm with 64 bits length, and the performance of Ring Signature with 5 users. The size of manuscript ranges from 0.5 MB to 5 MB, while the size of figure is 64×64, 128×128, 256×256, 512×512, and 1024×1024 pixels respectively.

Figure 5 shows that the time consumed by **Encrypt**, **Decrypt** and **Update** algorithms in DPUPH-CP-ABE increases gradually with the change of data size. The average consumption time is about 72 ms, 31 ms and 6 ms respectively.

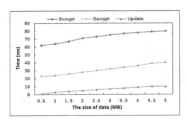
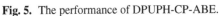

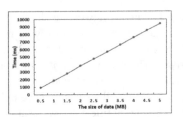

Fig. 5. The performance of DPUPH-CP-ABE.   **Fig. 6.** The performance of Simhash.

Figure 6 and Fig. 7 show that the time consumed by Simhash increases linearly from 900 ms to 9500 ms, and the time consumed by PHash increases exponentially from 10 ms to 210 ms with the change of data size. Although Simhash takes some time, it is tolerated in manuscript submission scenario.

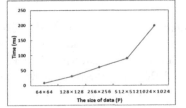

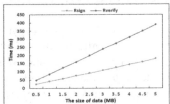

Fig. 7. The performance of PHash.   **Fig. 8.** The performance of Ring Signature.

Figure 8 shows that the time consumed by **Rsign** and **Rverify** algorithms in Ring Signature increase linearly with the change of data size. The average consumption time is about 218 ms and 101 ms respectively, which meets system requirements.

5.2   Evaluation of Query and Submit Operation

In MaSRChain, there are two types of operations: *query* operation from blockchain and *submit* operation to blockchain. Next, we test the transaction response time and confirmation time with the different number of concurrent transactions per second. Moreover, the consensus mechanism is *Kafka*, batch timeout is 2 s, and block size is 32 KB.

Figure 9 depicts the relationship between response time of *query* operation and number of concurrent transactions. The response time increases slowly at beginning until throughput reaches 300 tps. After that, the response time increases rapidly, higher the number of concurrent transactions brings higher response time duo to processing bottleneck.

Figure 10 shows the relationship between transaction conformation time *submit* operation and the number of concurrent transactions. When the number of concurrent transactions is small, the system needs to wait for batch time to pack a new block. Then, the transaction confirmation time decreases gradually with the change of throughput from 100 tps to 300 tps. This is because the threshold of block size is met, and a new block will be generated before the predefined batch time. As the number of concurrent transactions continues to increase, it exceeds processing capability and transactions cannot be confirmed in time which causes transaction confirmation time increases gradually.

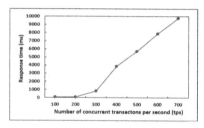
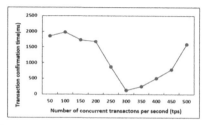

Fig. 9. The performance of *query* operation.   **Fig. 10.** The performance of *submit* operation.

6   Related Work

Some researchers propose decentralized MaSR systems based on blockchain. Bela G et al. propose CryptSubmit [10]. It uses the trusted timestamp of Bitcoin to provide authors with a reliable certificate. However, to reduce cost, CryptSubmit collects submitted manuscripts from one day, and submits the hashes of manuscripts together to Bitcoin, which prevents it from realizing copyright confirmation in real time. To realize multiple contributions detection, Nitesh E et al. propose a blockchain-based solution that all journals or conferences implement a shared ledger to share the title of submitted manuscripts [11]. However, these solutions are useless because it is easy to change the title of the manuscript and submits to other institutions. Then, For the accountable review mechanism, there are some decentralized publication systems for open science can record review evaluations into blockchain [12]. Although evaluations that are stored in the blockchain cannot be tampered with, authors cannot ensure that the evaluations received are from responsible peer reviewers.

7   Conclusion

In this paper, we proposed MaSRChain to solve common academic misconduct. It can realize manuscript copyright protection, multiple contributions detection, and accountable and anonymous peer review at the same time on the premise of protecting the confidentiality of the manuscript and not affecting the fairness of review. Besides, experimental results demonstrate the performance of system meets the actual requirement.

References

1. Dansinger, M.: Dear plagiarist: a letter to a peer reviewer who stole and published our manuscript as his own. Ann. Intern. Med. **166**(2), 143 (2017)
2. Tie-cheng, J.I.N.: A review on the research of phenomenon of multiple contributions with one manuscript of journal. J. Henan Univ. Technol. (2005)
3. Lee, C.J., et al.: Bias in peer review. J. Am. Soc. Inf. Sci. Technol. **64**(1), 2–17 (2013)
4. Androulaki, E., et al.: Hyperledger fabric: a distributed operating system for permissioned blockchains. In: Proceedings of the Thirteenth EuroSys Conference, pp. 1–15 (2018)
5. Benet, J.: Ipfs-content addressed, versioned, p 2p file system. arXiv preprint arXiv 1407, 3561 (2014)

6. Manku, G.S., et al.: Detecting near-duplicates for web crawling. In: Proceedings of the 16th International Conference on World Wide Web, pp. 141–150 (2007)

7. Venkatesan, R., et al.: Robust image hashing. In: Proceedings 2000 International Conference on Image Processing, pp. 664–666. IEEE (2000)

8. Ying, Z.B., et al.: Partially policy hidden CP-ABE supporting dynamic policy updating. J. Commun. **36**(12), 178–189 (2015)

9. Rivest, R.L., Shamir, A., Tauman, Y.: How to Leak a Secret. In: Boyd, C. (ed.) ASIACRYPT 2001. LNCS, vol. 2248, pp. 552–565. Springer, Heidelberg (2001). https://doi.org/10.1007/3-540-45682-1_32

10. Gipp, B., et al.: Cryptsubmit: introducing securely timestamped manuscript submission and peer review feedback using the blockchain. In: JCDL2017, pp. 1–4. IEEE (2017)

11. Emmadi, N., Maddali, L.P., Sarkar, S.: MaRSChain: framework for a fair manuscript review system based on permissioned blockchain. In: Mencagli, G., et al. (eds.) Euro-Par 2018. LNCS, vol. 11339, pp. 355–366. Springer, Cham (2019). https://doi.org/10.1007/978-3-030-10549-5_28

12. Tenorio-Fornés, A., et al.: Towards a decentralized process for scientific publication and peer review using blockchain and IPFS. In: Proceedings of the 52nd Hawaii International Conference on System Sciences (2019)

Enabling Efficient Multi-keyword Search Over Fine-Grained Authorized Healthcare Blockchain System

Yicheng Ding, Wei Song[✉] [iD], and Yuan Shen

School of Computer Science, Wuhan University, Wuhan, Hubei, China
{2019282110239,songwei,yuanshen}@whu.edu.cn

Abstract. As a new emerging technology, blockchain is attracting the attention from academic and industry and has been widely exploited to build the large-scale data sharing and management systems, such as healthcare database or bank distributed database system. The health records contain a lot of sensitive information, so putting these health records into blockchain can solve the security and privacy issues while uploading them to an untrustworthy network. In a typical health record management system, there are escalating demands for users including the patients and the doctors to execute multi-keyword search over the huge scale of healthcare records. In the meantime, they can authorize some part of their personal treatments to others according to personalized needs of the patients. In literatures, there is not an existing blockchain solution can satisfy these two requirements at the same time. These issues become prominent since it's more inconvenient to adjust a blockchain-based system to support efficient multi-keyword search and fine-grained authorization comparing to traditional RDBMS. To overcome the two challenges, we propose a novel multi-keyword searching scheme by establishing a set of Bloom Filters within the health record blockchain system to accelerate the searching process on service provider (SP). Moreover, we reduce the overhead of key derivation by proposing a Healthcare Data Key Derivation Tree (HDKDT) stored locally on the user's side. Putting our proposed scheme on the medical blockchain can speed up the multi-keyword search [3, 12] processes and reduce the key storage space to certain extent. At the end of this article, we formally prove the security of the proposed scheme and implement a prototype system to evaluate its performance. The experimental results validate our proposed scheme in this paper is a secure and efficient approach for the health record management scenario.

Keywords: Multi-keyword search · Fine-grained authorization · Blockchain in healthcare

1 Introduction

It has been a decade since cryptocurrency such as Bitcoin and Ethereum has a great impact on trading and data sharing [11]. The underlying technology behind these networks is

© Springer Nature Switzerland AG 2020
X. Wang et al. (Eds.): APWeb-WAIM 2020, LNCS 12318, pp. 27–41, 2020.
https://doi.org/10.1007/978-3-030-60290-1_3

called blockchain which is a distributed ledger. In blockchain, recording transactions and tracking assets don't rely on any intermediaries by building a chain of block. Combing with the consensus protocols such as proof of work (POW) [2] in Bitcoin and proof of stake in Ethereum, blockchain ensures all the loyal nodes within the peer-to-peer network to own the same copy of data. Blockchain is essentially an append-only data structure with ascending timestamp data that sorted by the timestamp and query data on top of it since it's immutable. Tampering data on blockchain needs to corrupt the entire system in a certain degree.

Based on the immutable nature of blockchain technology, it becomes the ultimate use to improve medical record management, accelerating clinical and biomedical research and advanced health record ledger in the field of healthcare. In the field of healthcare, the integrity and security of data such as the case history of patients are the first priority for medical institutions or hospitals. They don't want to share their own data with counterparts if the shared data can't guarantee to be authenticated. That's what blockchain does, it fills the gap of distrust among the patients and the medical institutions.

Thus, there have been a larger number of blockchain applications for the medical data management scenarios such as Doc.AI nowadays. For example, disease researchers are likely interested in a certain kind of diseases, which majority of them have some common features such as breast tumors usually have some symptoms like growing out a lump around the breast, so these researchers may search for {"tumor", "lump", "early"} on the blockchain to fetch the health records that are relevant to those keywords. On the other hand, sharing data among peers in the network requires a huge number of keys to maintain the confidentiality. Thus, we need an efficient multi-keyword algorithm and a fined-grained authorization to elegantly solve these problems.

However, there is not an existing blockchain solution can well support these two fundamental operations for the real-world healthcare data management system. To address this issue, we propose a novel multi-keyword searching scheme by establishing Bloom Filter [6] within the health record blockchain system. Moreover, we design a Healthcare Data Key Derivation Tree (HDKDT) to achieve the fine-grained authorization and reduce the overhead of key derivation. The main contributions of this paper can be summarized as follow:

- We propose a novel multi-keyword search scheme on the blockchain in healthcare system to optimize the performance of search request. It reduces the times of the interaction among the clients (patients) and servers (services provider) by completing search request from the clients within one send/receive and speeding up search process with a probabilistic called Bloom filter.
- We propose a key derivation management scheme called HDKDT to enable fine-grained authorization among patients and research institutions with reducing key storage space and shortening the key derivation path.
- We theoretically analyze the security of the proposed blockchain scheme, moreover, we evaluate the performance against the state-of-the-art solutions. The experimental results show that our model is an efficient and secure solution for the healthcare records management.

The rest of the paper is organized as follow, in the next section, we discuss the related work. And Sect. 3 introduces the system model of the medical chain network and explains the motivation of optimizing multi-keyword search and enabling fine-grained authorization. Then, we introduce several preliminaries in Sect. 4. Section 5 details our work which is followed by the security analysis in Sect. 6. Experimental parameters and results are reported in Sect. 7. Finally, we conclude our paper and provide directions of future work in Sect. 8.

2 Related Work

The main motivation of our work is to design a practical blockchain scheme for the medical data management. In this section, we review the relevant work for this scenario, including the multi-keyword search over encrypted data on blockchain and fine-grained authorization with Attribute-Based Encryption (ABE) [16] scheme.

2.1 Multi-keyword Search Over Encrypted Data on Blockchain

Recent years, many efforts have been done to enable multi-keyword search on blockchain. Shan et al. [4] have developed a fine-grained searching scheme that can fetch all the matched results from the SP within one round communication. They put some auxiliary spaces into both the client and the SP to speed up multi-keyword search on the blockchain. Zhang et al. [13] proposed a novel authenticated data structure (ADS) [9], called GEM^2-tree, which is not only gas-efficient but also effective in supporting authenticated queries. To further reduce the ADS maintenance cost without sacrificing much query performance, Hu et al. [14] introduced a scheme by designing a new smart contract for a financially-fair search construction, in which every participant (especially in the multiuser setting) is treated equally and incentivized to conform to correct computations. Ruan et al. [15] proposed an ADS called LineageChain provides a skip list index designed for supporting efficient provenance query processing. Niu et al. [17] proposed a multi-keyword search scheme under the assumption of decisional bilinear Diffie-Hellman exponent (q-BDHE) and decisional Diffie-Hellman (DDH) in the selective security model.

Cheng et al. [5] builds index inside each block called intra-block index and the other among all the blocks called inter-block index. The intra-block index skips some of the mismatched attributes rapidly by creating an ADS that unions by every data set within the block. The inter-block index skips some of the mismatched block by using SkipList.

These schemes we described above are not likely fix into blockchain in healthcare system to support multi-keyword search in a large scale since none of them can strictly reduce the time complexity with multi-keyword search. Thus, we propose a novel multi-keyword search scheme based on a set of Bloom filter [8] that can always guarantee to acquire relatively good performance on the worst case time scenario.

2.2 Authorization with Attribute-Based Encryption Scheme

Vasilios et al. [18] proposed a new type of OAuth 2.0 token backed by a distributed ledger. Their construction is secure, and it supports proof-of-possession, auditing, and accountability. Zhang et al. [19] discussed the potentials of the proposed approach to effectively address certain vulnerabilities in current OAuth-like authorization and authentication services with tolerable performance. Rashid et al. [20] proposed a multi-layer security network model for IoT network based on blockchain technology for authentication and authorization purpose within each cluster handed by each Cluster Head. Yamauchi et al. [21] pointed out a new issue by abusing published information with relation to recipients on blockchain. Then, they proposed a solution to their discovered issue. Widick et al. [22] proposed a novel authentication and authorization framework based on blockchain technologies to control access to the resources of an IoT device.

However, all the schemes above are restricted by the key storage space for user to manage their own keys for authorization. It is not practical enough for the medical data sharing scenario. Thus, we extend GLHG [1] to enable a key derivation path in a graph for the data owner to calculate derived key while the data owner only needs to hold the source key at all time, which cost relatively small space to implement this scheme for the clients.

3   Problem Definition

3.1   System Model

Figure 1 shows the system model in this paper which is the primary structure of healthcare system. There are two entities in our system model, light node only stores the block header while full node stores a full copy of the entire medical chain.

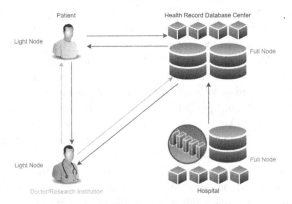

Fig. 1. A Blockchain Network in healthcare

More specifically, the clients, patients, Doctor or research institutions represented as light node, the service providers, healthcare database center and hospitals represented as full node. The light node can send their request to the SP such as health record database center and receive the corresponding result set. The light node such as the patients can also agree to authorize some of their health records by sending corresponding derived key to doctors or research institutions if they want to trade for their data. Once these doctors or institutions get the key, they are allowed to search and look up the health records of these patients from the SP. On the other hand, Full node such as hospitals pack up a number of health records of different patients from the mining pool and create a new block after these patients commit to pay the gas after every loyal node in the network have verified and accepted this new block (reach consensus).

3.2 Design Goals

In the business related to the healthcare, the patients can be seen as the original owners of their own health records. It's somehow a certain kind of assets which they are eligible to acquire a full control over these pieces of data even if they don't realize about this. To let them be aware of this situation, companies like **Medicalchain** start to build their own blockchain for storing and securing their electronic health records. Legally, the patients can sell all or some of their data to other research institutions, medical big data companies and healthcare sectors by authorizing them to be one of their authorized users and get paid through the medical chain. And the authorized users such as the doctors can perform multi-keyword search on the chain to look up the some of the owner's health records. The design goals of our paper include the multi-keyword search and the fine-grained authorization over medical blockchain.

Definition 1: *Multi-keyword Search Over Blockchain:* Given a client C and a set of keywords $K = \{k_1, k_2 \ldots k_n\}$, C asks the SP to retrieve the health records according to K. Based on the protocol, the SP executes the multi-keyword search for C over the blockchain and returns the result $R = \{r_1, r_2 \ldots r_m\}$. For each $r_i \in R$, r_i contains all the keywords in K.

Suppose the clients sends three keywords $K = \{$"triple-negative breast cancer", "positive", "early"$\}$ to the SP. Once SP receive these three keywords, it will search on all the health records on the entire blockchain to see if there exist some health records that match to these three keywords. e.g. {"Nasopharyngeal Carcinoma", "positive", "early", "chemotherapy three months ago"} is not a match, but {"triple-negative breast cancer", "positive", "early", "radiation therapy 1 month ago"} is a match.

Definition 2: *Fine-Grained Authorization Among Clients:* Given a client Alice and other client Bob, Alice asks Bob to authorize her a set of a set of encrypted derived keys $DK = dk_1, dk_2 \ldots dk_n\}$ based on the key exchange protocol, then Bob calls the key derivation function (KDF) [10] to generate the corresponding DK and send back to Alice. After that, Alice can send search request to SP to look up some of the Bob's health records.

Usually, Multi-keyword search aka data provenance or lineage takes linear time to achieve since demanding search operation and constructing ADS directly on blockchain are limited by the native hash pointer that forms the chain. More importantly, each health record may be encrypted by a group of symmetric key using PRF for different attributes (e.g. treatment program, condition description or body index) within it since medical chain needs to enable fine-grained authorization for the client to trade some part of their health record with other peers in the network. It increases the difficulty level of applying efficient multi-keyword search and arranging cumulative key storage space. Hence, we add a set of bloom filters [6–8] to the blockchain to support multi-keyword search and avoid mismatched attributes by using owner's key as the index to shorten the search path while we're doing binary search on the top of the bloom filter. Combing with this scheme, we propose encryption scheme the Healthcare Data Key Derivation Tree (HDKDT) to dynamically derive and create new encryption key from owner's original key to satisfy the requirement of fine-grained authorization for encrypting different contents.

4 Preliminaries

4.1 Bloom Filter

It's a space-efficient probabilistic data structure conceived by Burton Howard Bloom in 1970 that determine if an element is in a set and save a large amount of time and space comparing to hash table when the server needs to deal with massive data. The mechanism behinds the bloom filter is suppose we have an array of hash function [7] $\{h_0, h_1, h_2, \ldots, h_{k-1}\}$ where k is the number of hash function, then we can apply each h_i to an element to get an array of index $IS_1 = \{i_{00}, i_{10}, i_{20}, \ldots, i_{(k-1)0}\}$ and another element to get $IS_2 = \{i_{01}, i_{11}, i_{21}, \ldots, i_{(k-1)1}\}$. The best part of these two arrays is they are unlikely to be the same. Also, it's relatively hard to find a collusion array IS_3 that equals to IS_1 or IS_2 or any other IS_i that forms by arbitrary string. In this case, the server has three variables, the size of bloom filter array m, the number of hash function k, the expected number of data n and defining error rate as er, then we have the formula below for the server to choose the most appropriate size of bloom filter and the number of hash function:

$$m = \frac{n ln(er)}{(ln2)^2} \quad k = \frac{m}{n} ln2$$

Once the server picks up the number m and k that is close or satisfy the formula, it gets better performance on solving this problem.

4.2 Access Control Based on Global Logical Hierarchical Graph (GLHG)

To enable fine-grain authorization on the medical chain, the client has to generate its own key pair and regenerate derived keys based on the original key pair. The process of the data owners authorizing other users to access the data is essentially an authorized sharing of some of their own data key. In the meantime, to allow the data owners are able to perform selective data authorization access to different users, the data owners need to encrypt different parts of their data with different keys. As the time goes on, the number of keys will grow rapidly with the escalating amount of data, and users will suffer from storing a large scale of redundant keys in their own disk or memory.

Thus, a secure, efficient and flexible support for accessing authorization control key management methods are critical for sharing data. According to Peng et al. [1], users can apply a fine-grained key management scheme based on Global Logical Hierarchical Graph (GLHG) as $G[R, V, E, T]$, which greatly release the redundant space for storing derived keys. Here is some of the definition about GLHG:

Definition 3: The GLHG key derivation graph $G[R, V, E, T]$ satisfies the full coverage of the key derivation path iff the following condition hold: for$\{\forall v | v \in V, v.level > 2\}$, such that $\cup \{v_i.acl\!, v_i \in V, (v_i, v) \in E\} = v.acl$.

Definition 4: The GLHG key derivation graph $G[R, V, E, T]$ satisfies the key derivation path that is not redundant iff the following conditions are true: for $\{\forall v | v \in V, v.level > 2\}$ and $\{\forall v_i | v_i \in V, (v_i, v) \in E\}, \exists u \in v_i.acl$, such that $u \notin \{\forall v_l.acl | v_l \in V, (v_l, v) \in E, v_l \neq v_i\}$.

5 Efficient Multi-keyword Search Algorithm Over Blockchain

5.1 Constructions of the Bloom Filter Index

To obtain multi-keyword search functionality on medical chain whether it's encrypted or not, we essentially need to avoid mismatched case as best we can. Hence, the hospital can establish a set of bloom filter denoted as $BF_i = \{bf_{i0}, bf_{i1}, bf_{i2} \ldots bf_{i(n-1)}\}$ during the creation of a block, where i indicates the index of the block and 2^n gives an upper bound on the size of the blockchain, then the hospital uses multiple sets of hash functions $\{[h_{00}, h_{01} \ldots h_{0(k0)}], [h_{10}, h_{11} \ldots h_{1(k1)}], [h_{20}, h_{21} \ldots h_{2(k2)}] \ldots [h_{(n-1)0}, h_{(n-1)1} \ldots h_{(n-1) \cdot (k(n-1))}]\}$ to build Bloom filter, where both $[h_{j0}, h_{j1} \ldots h_{j(kj)}]$ and the number of hash function denoted as $k_j + 1$ belong to bf_{ij} ($0 <= j <= n$).

Assuming the hospital wants to pack and verify a set of health records $\{hr_0, hr_1, hr_2 \ldots hr_{m-1}\}$ into a new block, where hr_j contains a set of attribute values $\{a_0, a_1, a_2 \ldots a_{p-1}\}$. Some of these attributes may be encrypted by its owner's key and some of them may not. And the client put one secret number $shift_{ii}$ into each attribute value a_{ii} of each health record before the client adds to the mining pool where $0 <= ii <= p$, then hospitals use $[h_{j0}, h_{j1} \ldots h_{j(kj)}]$ to calculate a set of index position $ps_j = \{l_{j0}, l_{j1}, l_{j2} \ldots l_{j(kj)}\}$ for a_0 by setting $l_{j(jj)} = h_{j(jj)}(a_0) + shift_0$ ($0 <= jj <= k_j$) and put them into bf_{ij}, then hospitals calculate ps_{j+1} for $bf_{i(j+1)}$ using $[h_{(j+1)0}, h_{(j+1)1} \ldots h_{(j+1)k(j+1)}]$ and so on. The equation below shows this process in detail:

$$\bullet ps_0 = \{l_{00} = h_{00}(a_0) + shift_0, l_{01} = h_{01}(a_0) + shift_0 \ldots l_{0(k0)} = h_{0(k0)}(a_0) + shift_0\}$$
$$\bullet ps_1 = \{l_{10} = h_{10}(a_0) + shift_0, l_{11} = h_{11}(a_0) + shift_0 \ldots l_{1(k1)} = h_{1(k1)}(a_0) + shift_0\}$$
$$\cdots \quad \cdots \quad \cdots \quad \cdots$$
$$\bullet ps_i = \{l_{i0} = h_{i0}(a_0) + shift_0, l_{i1} = h_{i1}(a_0) + shift_0 \ldots l_{i(ki)} = h_{i(ki)}(a) + shift_0\}$$
$$\cdots \quad \cdots \quad \cdots \quad \cdots$$
$$\bullet ps_{n-1} = \{l_{n0} = h_{n0}(a) + shift_0, l_{n1} = h_{n1}(a) + shift_0 \ldots l_{i(k(n-1))} = h_{i(k(n-1))}(a) + shift_0\}$$

Intuitively, hospitals continue to calculate all the index positions for $a_1, a_2 \ldots a_{p-1}$. The secret number $shift$ that belongs to each attribute value of each health record is based on the identifier id that equals to the hash h_{sk} of the symmetric key (SK) of its owner if the attribute is encrypted by that SK. SK is created by key derivation scheme that we will discuss later. We define $shift = h_{sk}(SK) + flag$, where the number $flag$ reveals which direction of each binary search case will go to (left, right or both) when SP starts this binary search on the top of the bloom filter to find matches. If the hospitals set $flag = +1$ during the creation step of a new block, then SP will go to block $2^{n-1}+1$ to block 2^n to find the matched attributes of the given keyword that are encrypted by the SK of the owner and set $flag = -1$ means go to block$_0$ to block 2^{n-1}. If an attribute within a health record is not encrypted, then we simply set $h_{sk}(SK)$ to be 0 since there is no encryption key. And the miner set $flag = 0$ to imply it's the end of the recursion call.

5.2 Search Phase

Before enabling efficient multi-keyword search on the bloom filter, the client needs to send a map denoted as $KI = \{(key_0, id_0), (key_1, id_1) \ldots (key_{s-1}, id_{s-1})\}$ that contains multiple keyword-identifier pair (key_r, id_r) where $0 <= r <= s$. Then the client uses the same SK_r to compute id_r ($id_r = h_{sk}(SK_r)$) and some of them may not. At the first step, SP can start a binary search on the bloom filter bf_{n-1} to determine if there exist some attributes from $block_0$ to block 2^{n-1} or block $2^{n-1}+1$ to block 2^n or both that match to key_r while SP know the corresponding value of id_r. Once every decision of the next direction for every key_r is made, SP simply takes an intersection of them and apply recursions on the final decision set ds. (e.g. $ds = \{left\}$ if the global decision set $gs = \{[left, right], [left], [left]\}$ or $gs = \{\emptyset\}$ if $ds = \{[left, right], [left], [right]\}$). To sustain this optimization with binary search, we need $n\log(n)$ bloom filters to redirect instead of n. Because each block only store part of the bloom filter array that contains its attributes (e.g. in Fig. 2). And merging bf_{100} and bf_{101} forms a greater bloom filter with size of 26 denoted as bf_{10}. With this data structure below, SP can locate all the health records where one or more attributes in these records matches to each key_r. At last, SP will find all the exact health records that matches the KI and takes a union of all matched result sets found from different block that contains multiple health records and sends it back to the client.

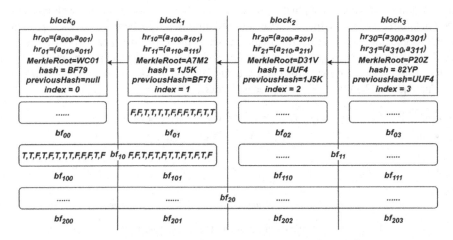

Fig. 2. Bloom Filter index structure on the Medical Chain

Notice that in Fig. 2, for attribute a_{110}, these three subscript numbers indicate the index of the block in the medical chain, the index of health record in the block and the index of the attribute in health record. And for bf_{101}, these numbers indicate the level (starting from 0) or index idx_1 of the bloom filter set BF_1 in the global bloom filter set BF, the index idx_2 of the bloom filter BF_2 in the set BF_1 and the index of the subarray (a part of BF_2) in BF_2.

In Fig. 2, we have: (h_{ij0}, h_{ij1}) belongs to bf_{ij} and the length of each chunk of bf_{ij} equals 13. Specifically, we calculate the index position for each attribute by using $(h_{ijk}(a_{xyz})$

$+ h_{sk}(SK_{xyz}) +$ direction) $\%$ len($n * 13$), then the true or false elements in bf_{01} is determined by the union of all the index positions ip we have calculated for $\{a_{100}, a_{101}, a_{110}, a_{111}\}$. If we assume $ip = \{\{3,11\}, \{2,5\}, \{9,2\}, \{4,12\}\}$, then the elements in bf_{01} is shown above. In this case, the direction number is 0.

Other cases such as bf_{10} follows the same step as we state above, remembering that the index position hospitals calculate for each attribute may reside in different chunks of bf, thus the client needs to wait for the creation of new blocks until this chunk is created together with the corresponding new block. If hospitals calculate all the index positions of a_{000} in bf_{10} is $\{0, 15\}$ which means the first element in bf_{100} and the third element in bf_{101} will set to be true. However, if $block_1$ has not created yet, the hospitals only set the first element bf_{100} to be true and bf_{10} is not available now since hospitals only have $block_0$ and only have the left half of bf_{10} which is bf_{100}. If the hospitals get the index positions for $\{a_{000}, a_{001}, a_{010}, a_{011}, a_{100}, a_{101}, a_{110}, a_{111}\}$ is $\{\{0,15\}, \{5,17\}, \{6,20\}, \{1,11\}, \{24,7\}, \{20,3\}, \{3,6\}, \{19,22\}\}$, then the element in bf_{10} is shown above.

Other factor that can have influence on the performance of bloom filter is the choice of hash function. Fast simple non-cryptographic hashes with collision resistant fashion which are independent enough for bloom filter to use can be FNV series such as FNV-1 and FNV-1a. BKDR hash (hash function of Hashmap in Java) also works fine, but it takes longer time to calculate the index since it combines the output index of each character of a string by simply adding them with Horner's rule while FNV does bitwise XOR. We can also set the size of the bloom filter to be power of 2 to accelerate the mod operation by using bitwise AND between the index and size - 1. We also put different prime number to distinguish these hash functions in each bloom filter while doing $hash = hash * prime$ $\hat{\ } byte\_of\_data$.

In real case, suppose Alice wants to see Bob's health records, then before this transaction proceed and executed by smart contract, it needs to check Alice's balance to see if she has sufficient money to spend. The only way to get balance for the smart contract is to look up the entire chain and sum up the balance. The only way to get balance for the smart contract is to look up the entire chain and sum up the balance. This procedure can be done efficiently by the scheme about it's transparent to the smart contract and accelerate the searching.

5.3 Key Derivation and Fine-Grained Authorization

In Sect. 4.2, we introduce a key derivation scheme called GLHG. It allows different data owned by different users can be encrypted with the same key under the premise of they share some common derived keys which means they share the same group of authorized users. For data owners, they don't need allocate a linear key storage space to keep track which key belongs to whom by creating key and authorized user entries and put them into an unsorted map. Because they can derive all the keys if there exists a derivation path from the key they're holding to these keys in the GLHG.

We believe that medical data is a personal asset and should be authorized by the patient himself. However, due to the lack of professional knowledge of individuals, complete autonomous authorization will make it difficult to control the scope of data sharing and lead to the inevitable privacy leaks. Therefore, we design a HDKDT to achieve practical and fine-grained authorization for the medical data management scenarios. Generally, it extends GLHG by restricting the authorization of the patients with building an authorization tree of the patients (data owners) shown as following.

The structure of HDKDT is illustrated in Fig. 3, which contains two parts, i.e., the disease classification tree, and the level hierarchical structure. If the patient c upload two health records denoted as A and B to the HDKDT, and then authorize two doctors denoted as Doctor A and Doctor B with the corresponding keys. The doctor B at chief physician level can decrypt both records in terms of holding the corresponding symmetric key. For doctor B, it's impossible for him to calculate any derivation path to get the key that can decrypt the health record A.

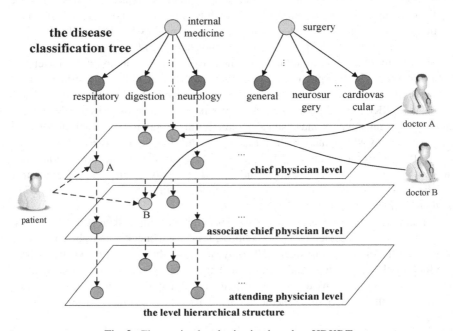

Fig. 3. Fine-grained authorization based on HDKDT

Instead of enabling the patients to randomly authorize their derived key to any other untrustworthy parties, we only allow the patients to authorize the derived key to other trusted third party such as a chief physician of Oncology in some surgical department. Hence, we can cut off lots of unnecessary authorization between the data owners and some anonymous users by managing the limit of authorization. Moreover, by setting up these restrictions, it turns out to be a tree data structure instead of a graph, which means it will be less redundant pointers. Our method can adapt to the fine-grained authorization scenario of medical data since it perfectly fit the classification of any hospital departments.

6 Performance and Security Analysis

6.1 Performance Analysis

By enabling a binary search on the top of blockchain with Bloom Filter, we can speed up the search process with $O(\log(N))$ where $N = 2^n$ is the number of blocks in the chain at worst case scenario. Theoretically, its performance gets better than those ADS in [4] and [5], since those ADS are not strictly $O(\log(N))$. Although we need some auxiliary spaces to store the number of $\log(n)$ Bloom filter with each block, which increases the space complexity to $O(N\log(N))$, it's still worthy to get $\log(N)$ on search process. On the other hand, with extending HDKDT instead of using traditional key derivation function such as PBKDF2 to establish the key management system, the data owners can reduce the key storage space by simply storing the source key and using it to derive all the authorized keys on the derivation paths within HDKDT.

6.2 Security Analysis

We can implement the global user access authorization policy $A[U][D]$ [1] based on the HDKDT key derivation mechanism G [R, V, E, T]. Its security and unforgeability are achieved by the following guarantees:

1. The security of the key derivation function. The unidirectionality and security of the derivation process have been analyzed in detail in [4, 5].
2. Uniqueness of user's key. For $\forall\ v_i.key, v_j.key \in UKey$, such that $v_i.key \neq v_j.key$.
3. The correctness and completeness of the key derivation path. *1)* **correctness:** for $\forall\ u_i \in U$, if $\exists\ v \in V$, $\exists\ (v, v_j) \in E$ and $u_i \in v.acl$, such that $u_i \in v_j$, that is $\{v.key, v_j.key\} \in \varphi^*(u_i)$; 2) **completeness:** see Definition 1.
4. The equivalence between $A[U][D]$ and G [R, V, E, T]. 1) **correctness:** for $\forall\ v \in V$, if $\exists\ u_i \in U$, $\exists\ d_j \in D$, such that $\varphi(d_j) = v.key \in \varphi^*(u_i)$, then we have $d_j \in v.data$ and $u_i \in v.acl = acl(d_j)$, which is $A[u_i][d_j] = 1$. 2) **completeness:** for $\forall\ u_i \in U$, $\forall\ d_i \in D$, if $A[u_i][d_j] = 1$, then we have $u_i \in acl(d_j)$ and $\exists\ v \in V$, such that $d_j \in v.data$ and $u_i \in v.acl = acl(d_j)$, which is $\varphi(d_j) = v.key \in \varphi^*(u_i)$.

The properties **1.** and **2.** ensures that any user can derive any other key pairs that can be derived iff these users has the original key pair. And the properties **3.** and **4.** ensures that any user can only obtain the key of the data that he has access to through the HDKDT key derivation map.

7 Performance Evaluation

We conduct our experiments by creating two different data sets and put them into a blockchain-based system to restore the real scenario of medical chain, then simulating the operations of creating new block with Bloom filter, starting multi-keyword search, building HDKDT and authorizing derived key between the virtual clients by on that. We run both data sets on one laptop running Ubuntu 18.04.4 with 64 GB DDR4 2933 MHz

XMP RAM and one Intel i9-9900K core. The SP forms a local simulated medical chain network and receive the query request from the virtual clients.

To aim on the real performance of our schemes, we set the difficulty of mining to less than 5 to accelerate our experiments since the mechanism of the complex network topology such as consensus protocol and malicious node are not taken into account. We also set network latency to be a constant number from 100–1000 ms. After setting up our experimental environment, we perform a multi-keyword search using a number of keywords about 236K from the *The Lancet* journal. Most of the keywords are related to treatment analysis, medical terms and disease description made up by key and value pairs such as {"name": "Alice", "Pathological grade":2, "Local lymph node size: "2 cm", "Liver ultrasound": "metastasis"...}.

7.1 Performance of Multi-keyword Search

We stimulate a virtual environment while the hospital node creates new blocks and the patient node performs multi-keyword search. We encrypt these keywords with the associated keys that hold by different owners. By this means, we get a medical chain network with about 50–120 nodes, 10 health records in each book, 5 to 10 attributes in each health record and a block size of 100 to 3000 and 1000–10000 nodes (short chain), 40–80 health records in each block, 20–30 attributes in each health record and a block size of 5000–15000 (long chain). Notice that there may exist false positive error during the search step of SP. These errors may lead to some mismatched case that should be cutting out before, but it will never miss any matched attribute since there is not true negative error in bloom filter. We take an average search overhead per second and draw the following graph that reveals the performance by applying different schemes such as traditional method with repeating single-keyword search multiple time. Figure 4 shows our experimental results.

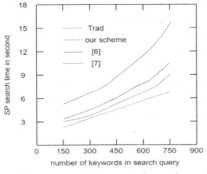

(a) perform Multi-keyword searches on short chain between SP and client

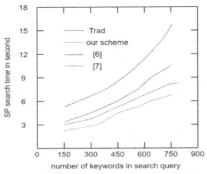

(b) perform Multi-keyword searches on long chain between SP and client

Fig. 4. performance test on multi-keyword search scheme

The running time overhead of traditional method is significantly affected by the number of keywords even if we have not count for network latency and packet loss may occurred in the real network. And sending single-word search request multiple time increases the chance of network failure. Overall, the computational cost of our scheme speed up about 32% when the number of keys increases from 2–20 since we use bloom filter to locate the results and only need one send/receive for each search request.

7.2 Performance of Authorization

For enabling fine-grained authorization, we use PBKDF2 as the traditional method comparing to HDKDT. The virtual clients arbitrarily send 5–50 of their derived keys to other clients and generate their own health records with $h_{sk}(SK)$ and put them into the mining pool. We take the average memory cost and draw two curves based on them to the graph in Fig. 5.

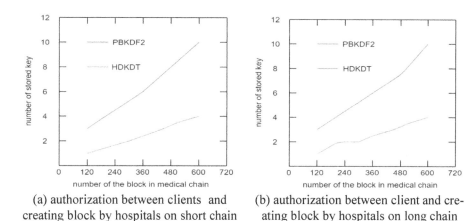

(a) authorization between clients and creating block by hospitals on short chain

(b) authorization between client and creating block by hospitals on long chain

Fig. 5. performance test of HDKDT

From the graph about, we see as the number of authorized user increased, the volume of stored key is about 35% by implementing HDKDT comparing to PBKDF2. Because with HDKDT, we can avoid to store majority of the derived keys in local disk since we are able to calculate the specific key by following the corresponding derivation path with HDKDT.

8 Conclusion

In this paper, we propose both the multi-keyword search scheme and the fine-grained authorization scheme on the healthcare system. The technique to combine bloom filter with original blockchain-based system enables a fast search operation on the medical chain. The critical contribution lies in using hash function to redirect the direction of next recursion case for binary search, which greatly increases the possibility of skipping mismatched health records even if there exists some false positive case during the searching step.

On the client side, the memory cost of building key management system reduces dramatically by eliminating redundant derived key space using the HDKDT comparing to traditional method. Adopting the HDKDT to manage all the keys, and on the premise of ensuring the security and unforgeability of the derived key, we minimize the overhead of calculation, transmission during the authorization step.

For later optimization, we attempt to build an ADS within each block to further reduce the computation overhead of search and key storage space within some authentication data structure such as Merkle Hash Tree.

Acknowledgement. This work is supported by the National Natural Science Foundation of China (No. 62072349, U1811263, 61572378), the major technical innovation project of Hubei Province (No. 2019AAA072), the Science and Technology Project of State Grid Corporation Of China (No. 5700-202072180A-0-0-00), the Teaching Research Project Of Wuhan University (No. 2018JG052), and the Natural Science Foundation Of Hubei Province (No. 2017CBF420).

References

1. Fangquan, C., Zhiyong, P., Wei, S., Shulin, W., Yihui, C: Key management for access control in trusted cloud storages. J. Comput. Res. Dev. **50**(8), 1613–1627 (2013)
2. Porat, A., Pratap, A., Shah, P., Adkar, V: Blockchain Consensus: An analysis of Proof-of-Work and its Applications
3. Song, W., et al.: A privacy-preserved full-text retrieval algorithm over encrypted data for cloud storage applications. J. Parallel Distrib. Comput. **99**, 14–27 (2017)
4. Jiang, S., et al.: Privacy-preserving and efficient multi-keyword search over encrypted data on blockchain. In: Blockchain conference, pp. 405–410 (2019)
5. Xu, C., Zhang, C., Xu, J: vChain: enabling verifiable boolean range queries over blockchain databases. In: Proceedings of International Conference on Management of Data, Proceedings of SIGMOD Conference, pp. 141–158 (2019)
6. Bloom, B.: Space/time tradeoffs in in hash coding with allowable errors. Commun. ACM **13**(7), 422–426 (1970)
7. Carter, J.L., Wegman, M.N.: Universal classes of hash functions. J. Comput. Syst. Sci. **18**, 143–154 (1979)
8. Ramakrishna, M.V.: Practical performance of Bloom filters and parallel free-text searching. Commun. ACM **32**(10), 1237–1239 (1989)
9. Tamassia, R.: Authenticated data structures. In: Di Battista, G., Zwick, U. (eds.) ESA 2003. LNCS, vol. 2832, pp. 2–5. Springer, Heidelberg (2003). https://doi.org/10.1007/978-3-540-39658-1_2
10. Papamanthou, C., Tamassia, R., Triandopoulos, N.: Optimal verification of operations on dynamic sets. In: Rogaway, P. (ed.) Advances in Cryptology – CRYPTO 2011. CRYPTO 2011. Lecture Notes in Computer Science, vol. 6841, pp. 91–110. Springer, Berlin, Heidelberg (2011). https://doi.org/10.1007/978-3-642-22792-9_6
11. Clifton, C., Doan, A., Elmagarmid, A., Kantarcıoglu, M.: Gunther Schadow. Jaideep Vaidya, privacy-preserving data integration and sharing. DMKD, Dan Suciu (2004)
12. Song, W., Wang, B., Wang, Q., Shi, C., Lou, W., Peng, Z.: Publicly Verifiable Computation of Polynomials over Outsourced Data with Multiple Sources. IEEE Trans. Inf. Forensic. Secur. **12**(10), 2334–2347 (2017)
13. Zhang, C., Xu, C., Xu, J., Tang, Y., Choi, B: GEM^2-Tree: a gas efficient structure for authenticated range queries in blockchain. In: ICDE, pp. 842–853 (2019)

14. Hu, S., et al.: Searching an encrypted cloud meets blockchain: a decentralized reliable and fair realization. In: INFOCOM (2018)
15. Ruan, P., et al.: Fine-grained, secure and efficient data provenance on blockchain systems. Proc. VLDB Endow. **12**(9), 975–988
16. Wang, S., Zhao, D., Zhang, Y.: Searchable attribute-based encryption scheme with revocation in cloud storage. PLOS One, pp. 210–223 (2018)
17. Niu, J., Li, X., Gao, J., Han, Y.: Blockchain-based anti-key-leakage key aggregation searchable encryption for IoT. Int. Things J. **7**(2), 1502–1518 (2020)
18. Siris, V.A., et al.: OAuth 2.0 meets blockchain for authorization in constrained IoT environments. In: Proceedings of IEEE World Forum on Internet of Things (3), pp. 64–367 (2019)
19. Zhang, A., Bai, X.: Decentralized authorization and authentication based on consortium blockchain. In: Zheng, Z., Dai, H.N., Tang, M., Chen, X. (eds.) Blockchain and Trustworthy Systems. BlockSys 2019. Communications in Computer and Information Science, vol. 1156, pp. 267–272. Springer, Singapore (2019). https://doi.org/10.1007/978-981-15-2777-7_22
20. Rashid, M.A., Pajooh, H.H.: A security framework for IoT authentication and authorization based on blockchain technology. In: BigDataSE, pp. 264–271 (2019)
21. Yamauchi, R., Kamidoi, Y., Wakabayashi, S: A protocol for preventing transaction commitment without recipient's authorization on blockchain. In: COMPSAC, pp. 934–935 (2019)
22. Widick, L., Ranasinghe, I., Dantu, R., Jonnada, S: Blockchain based authentication and authorization framework for remote collaboration systems. In: WOWMOM, pp. 1–7 (2019)

Data Mining

Debiasing Learning to Rank Models
with Generative Adversarial Networks

Hui Cai[1], Chengyu Wang[1], and Xiaofeng He[2(✉)]

[1] School of Software Engineering, East China Normal University, Shanghai, China
huicai.me@gmail.com, chywang2013@gmail.com
[2] School of Computer Science and Technology, East China Normal University,
Shanghai, China
hexf@cs.ecnu.edu.cn

Abstract. Unbiased learning to rank aims to generate optimal orders for candidates utilizing noisy click-through data. To deal with such problem, most models treat the biased click labels as combined supervision of relevance and propensity, which pay little attention to the uncertainty of implicit user feedback. We propose a semi-supervised framework to address this issue, namely ULTRGAN (Unbiased Learning To Rank with Generative Adversarial Networks). The unified framework regards the task as semi-supervised learning with missing labels, and employs adversarial training to debias click-through datasets. In ULTRGAN, the generator samples potential negative examples combined with true positive examples for the discriminator. Meanwhile, the discriminator challenges the generator for better performances. We further incorporate pairwise debiasing to generate unbiased labels diffusing from the discriminator to the generator. Experimental results over both synthetic and real-world datasets show the effectiveness and robustness of ULTRGAN.

Keywords: Unbiased Learning to Rank · Inverse propensity weighting · Generative Adversarial Networks · Semi-supervised learning

1 Introduction

Learning To Rank (LTR) [19] is a family of machine learning models, used in a wide range of applications in Information Retrieval (IR), such as Web search, recommender systems and question answering. Given a query and the potential candidates, LTR maps query-document feature vectors to relevance scores for the generation of optimal orders. Existing LTR models optimize scoring functions over individual documents [11], document pairs [5,6] or the whole ranked list [7] in the setting of supervised learning.

Human-labeled relevance scores are necessary for the training of supervised LTR models, which requires the time-intensive manual work to curate. In some special scenarios such as personalized search, manual annotations are even inaccessible due to privacy restrictions [29,30]. More severely, real user preferences

© Springer Nature Switzerland AG 2020
X. Wang et al. (Eds.): APWeb-WAIM 2020, LNCS 12318, pp. 45–60, 2020.
https://doi.org/10.1007/978-3-030-60290-1_4

can not be precisely annotated, which are dynamic and context-aware. In modern IR systems, click-through data can be collected in massive amount as the substitute for relevance scores [16]. However, such data is heavily biased. For example, position bias is a typical noise that people tend to click on the results presented in higher positions [17]. If LTR models directly consider the click and non-click signals as positive and negative, they actually learn the user bias instead of the inherent relevance between queries and candidate documents.

Unbiased Learning To Rank (ULTR) [2,21] tries to solve the problem with the biased click data. Counterfactual LTR is a popular solution, which mostly consists of two types of methods, i.e., click models [10] and randomization experiments [18,29]. Click models make assumptions about user behaviors and maximize the received click likelihood. Randomization experiments extract propensities for each position by presenting documents in random orders. These models split ULTR into two separate stages: i) label debiasing and ii) relevance learning. Hence, the prevalent techniques could introduce uncertainty to the follow-up work when the bias is not completely rectified. With the rapid advancement of counterfactual LTR, end-to-end algorithms are proposed [1,15,30], in order to improve ranking performances and to make inferences about selection bias.

Despite the success made in recent years, we observe that existing approaches utilize the inverse propensity weighting technique to discriminate against all the candidates [1,15,18,29,30]. It should be noted that in the task of relevance prediction, only part of labels generated by such approaches (especially head exposures) are valid, non-clicks (mostly presented in tail candidates) do not necessarily reflect irrelevance [17]. Therefore, the selection bias of these supervised ULTR models is still avoidable, resulting from the neglect of sampling competitive document pairs. This problem naturally motivates us to treat ULTR as a semi-supervised learning problem, with a large number of missing labels. It is also similar to a causal inference problem of selection bias [25].

In this paper, we propose a new framework named ULTRGAN (Unbiased Learning To Rank with Generative Adversarial Networks) to further improve the performance of ULTR. It is built upon the minimax game from Generative Adversarial Network (GAN) [14], and optimizes rankings with limited labels [28]. Specifically, in ULTRGAN, a generator plays as a sampler to generate hard negative results (i.e., less irrelevant candidates) for the discriminator, while the discriminator challenges the generator for better performances. Meanwhile, we incorporate the label debiasing technique [15] during the training of the discriminator, which enables true relevance to propagate from the discriminator to the generator. Experimental results demonstrate the advantages of ULTRGAN. In summary, we make the following major contributions:

- We formulate the ULTR problem in a semi-supervised setting, and propose the ULTRGAN framework to improve ULTR based adversarial learning.
- We design the minimax game between the two components in ULTRGAN, and incorporate the pairwise debiasing technique to the discriminator.
- We experimentally show the effectiveness and robustness of ULTRGAN over both synthetic and real-world datasets.

The rest of this paper is organized as follows. In Sect. 2, we review the prior related literature. Section 3 and Sect. 4 give the theoretical analysis on ULTR and describe the proposed model ULTRGAN, respectively. Experimental setups and result analysis are described in Sect. 5. Finally, we conclude the paper and discuss the future work in Sect. 6.

2 Related Work

In this section, we give a brief overview on the related work of LTR, ULTR and adversarial learning techniques for IR.

2.1 LTR and ULTR

In classical IR research, LTR [19] is mostly considered as a supervised learning problem which optimizes the ranking function, mapping from feature vectors to relevance scores. Typically, human annotations in TREC style [8] are used as supervision, which are expensive and unpractical under certain circumstances [29,30]. Click data is a resource that implies real user preferences without privacy restrictions. However, the heavy inherent bias in the click data is a critical concern for designing IR models, such as position bias [17], presentation bias [33] and trust bias [23]. To infer true preferences, early attempts apply result interleaving and heuristic rules. For example, Joachims [16] proposes the "skip-above" strategy to filter pairs with high confidence. However, these methods either bring in instability nor are limited to identified counterfactual samples.

ULTR [2,21] optimizes relevance prediction functions with noisy click data. As summarized in [21], two types of techniques have been proposed for the problem. The first one is online LTR, which directly interacts with users and adjusts to immediate feedbacks [22,32]. Another is called counterfactual LTR, performing offline training with historical data, which is the focus of this work.

Click models [10] are a collection of counterfactual LTR methods, which employ Bayesian graph models to simulate user behaviors. The Position-Based Model (PBM) [24] assumes that the click probability only relates to that of relevance and observation. The Cascade Model (CM) [12] believes that users examine results from head to tail and click only once. The User Browsing Model (UBM) [13] allows for multiple clicks and considers former-click effects. Recently, the neural click model is proposed in [4]. These models rely on various assumptions to justify user behaviors. Another type of solutions is called randomization experiments [18,29]. According to observational studies on causal inference [25], we consider whether a user examines the result as the treatment, and the user's action (click or non-click) as the outcome. However, user behaviors are influenced by surfing habits and presentation orders (i.e., the selection bias). By presenting results in random orders at the cost of user experiences, the bias can be eliminated in a theoretically principal way [18,29].

Above methods share a common thinking of estimating the selection bias in advance, which has negative effects on the final ranking if propensities are not accurately estimated. Recent studies [1,15,30] differ from the above methods in an end-to-end way. Wang et al. [30] propose a novel regression-based EM algorithm for propensity and relevance estimation simultaneously. Ai et al. [1] propose a dual learning algorithm for deep ranking models. Hu et al. [15] extend pointwise learning to pairwise and apply to LambdaMart [6]. Our proposed approach is different from above algorithms for treating click labels as semi-supervised signals and sampling pairs for discriminative learning.

2.2 Adversarial Learning in IR

Adversarial learning has been leveraged for designing various IR systems. For example, GAN-related models have been utilized to deal with semi-supervised learning [20,28] and Positive-Unlabeled (PU) learning [3] problems in IR. Unlike the original GAN [14] which generates continuous data such as images, these models select discrete documents or words from candidates. The discriminator tries to distinguish positive instances from selected negative instances by the generator, while the generator aims to estimate real data distribution. The usage of adversarial learning in ULTR differs from existing models in the need to alleviate the propensity of examination from click labels.

3   Theoretical Analysis

In this section, we present the definition of ULTR, and give theoretical analysis on debiasing pairwise LTR. Table 1 summaries the important annotations.

Table 1. A summary of notations.

$\mathbf{Q}$, Q, q	The universal set of queries $\mathbf{Q}$, a sample set Q, a query instance q
π_q, x, i, y	A ranked list π_q of query q produced by ranking system, a document x in the ith position and its relevance y
$o_q^{x,i}$ (o_i^+, o_i^-), $c_q^{x,i}$ (c_i^+, c_i^-), $r_q^{x,i}$ (r_i^+, r_i^-)	Bernoulli variables that represent whether a document x in the ith position of the ranked list π_q is observed ($o_q^{x,i}$), clicked ($c_q^{x,i}$), or perceived as relevant ($r_q^{x,i}$)
G, θ, D, ϕ	A generator G with parameters θ, a discriminator D with parameters ϕ
$g_\theta(x,q)$, $f_\phi(x,q)$	The generative and discriminative retrieval functions of G and D for document x given query q
t_i^+, t_j^-	The positive position ratio for a clicked item in the ith position and the negative position ratio for an unclicked item in the jth position

3.1   Preliminaries of ULTR

The goal of LTR is to learn the ranking function f that minimizes the global loss. In reality, it is impractical to obtain the universal set of queries $\mathbf{Q}$. Given a subset of queries Q, the normalized loss is defined as: $\hat{L}(f) = \frac{1}{|Q|}\sum_{q\in Q} l(f,q)$, where $l(f,q)$ is the individual ranking loss. The empirical loss function measures the distance between the relevance score y and the predicted score $f(x,q)$ for document x given query q. For IR, the ranking matrices (Mean Average Precision (MAP), normalized Discounted Cumulative Gain (nDCG), etc.) pay the most attention to relevant documents. Hence, the individual loss is defined to approximate the evaluation matrices:

$$l_{rel}(f,q) = \sum_{x\in\pi_q, y=1} l(f(x,q), y)$$

Under the setting of ULTR, the relevance score y is not available. For document x related to query q presented in the position i, let $c_q^{x,i}$, $o_q^{x,i}$ and $r_q^{x,i}$ denote the click, observation and intrinsic relevance respectively. The basic assumption of ULTR is that the probability of being clicked is related to that of being examinated and perceived relevance. Therefore, we need to alleviate selection bias $P(o_q^{x,i})$, with the click-based unbiased loss function as:

$$l_{IPW}(f,q) = \sum_{x\in\pi_q, y=1\wedge o_q^{x,i}=1} \frac{l(f(x,q), y)}{P(o_q^{x,i}=1)} = \sum_{x\in\pi_q, c_q^{x,i}=1} \frac{l(f(x,q), y)}{P(o_q^{x,i}=1)}$$

As proved in [18], the expectation of $l_{IPW}(f,q)$ is equal to the initial LTR loss, i.e., $\mathbb{E}_{o_q}[l_{IPW}(f,q)] = l_{rel}(f,q)$.

3.2 Pairwise ULTR

Hu et al. [15] extend the previous function to the pairwise setting. Assume that:

$$P(c_i^+ \mid x_i) = t_i^+ P(r_i^+ \mid x_i) \quad P(c_j^- \mid x_j) = t_j^- P(r_j^- \mid x_j)$$

Given the basic assumption $P(c_i^+ \mid x_i) = P(r_i^+ \mid x_i) \cdot P(o_i^+ \mid x_i)$, we directly transform the position ratios as follows:

$$t_i^+ = P(o_i^+ \mid x_i)$$

$$t_j^- = \frac{1 - P(c_j^+ \mid x_j)}{1 - P(r_j^+ \mid x_j)} = \frac{1 - P(r_j^+ \mid x_j) \cdot P(o_j^+ \mid x_j)}{1 - P(r_j^+ \mid x_j)}$$

Therefore, the positive position ratio implies the probability of observation, which is supposed to decrease with position increasing. The negative position ratio is the combination of average relevance probability and observation probability, which depends on the initial ranker.

In pairwise LTR, the empirical ranking loss is defined over the set of document pairs (x_i, x_j) where x_i is relevant and x_j is irrelevant [5,6]. The pairwise loss concentrates on the relative order between two documents, shown as follows:

$$l_{rel}(f,q)^{pair} = \sum_{x_i, x_j \in \pi_q, r_i^+ \wedge r_j^-} l(f(x_i,q), r_i^+, f(x_j,q), r_j^-)$$

We prove that the ranking model based on our assumption produces unbiased ranking. In ULTR, there exists a set of document pairs (x_i, x_j) in the ith position and jth position where x_i is clicked and x_j is unclicked. The pairwise loss function can be derived as follows:

$$
\begin{aligned}
l_{unbiased}(f,q)^{pair} &= \mathbb{E}_{c_i^+, c_j^-} \left[\sum_{x_i, x_j \in \pi_q, c_i^+ \wedge c_j^-} \frac{l(f(x_i,q), r_i^+, f(x_j,q), r_j^-)}{t_i^+ \cdot t_j^-} \right] \\
&= \sum_{x_i, x_j \in \pi_q} \frac{\mathbb{E}_{c_i^+, c_j^-}[c_i^+ \cdot c_j^-] \cdot l(f(x_i,q), r_i^+, f(x_j,q), r_j^-)}{\frac{P(c_i^+|x_i)P(c_j^-|x_j)}{P(r_i^+|x_i)P(r_j^-|x_j)}} \\
&= \sum_{x_i, x_j \in \pi_q} \frac{P(c_i^+ \mid x_i)P(c_j^- \mid x_j)l(f(x_i,q), r_i^+, f(x_j,q), r_j^-)}{\frac{P(c_i^+|x_i)P(c_j^-|x_j)}{P(r_i^+|x_i)P(r_j^-|x_j)}} \\
&= \sum_{x_i, x_j \in \pi_q} P(r_i^+ \mid x_i)P(r_j^- \mid x_j)l(f(x_i,q), r_i^+, f(x_j,q), r_j^-) \\
&= \sum_{x_i, x_j \in \pi_q, r_i^+ \wedge r_j^-} l(f(x_i,q), r_i^+, f(x_j,q), r_j^-)
\end{aligned}
$$

(1)

Therefore, it is easy to see that $l_{unbiased}(f,q)^{pair} = l_{rel}(f,q)^{pair}$. Based on this conclusion, in the next part, we introduce the model ULTRGAN in detail.

4 The Proposed Approach

In this section, we formally present the ULTRGAN framework, followed by the model details and optimization methods.

4.1 The ULTRGAN Framework

Before deriving our approach for ULTR, we firstly review current problems. Existing ULTR models [1,15,18,29,30] focus on label debiasing to better conduct supervised learning, making all the unclicked documents contribute to discriminative function. However, unclicked samples are composed of true negative (irrelevant) and skipped positive (relevant) results [16,24]. Even with propensity weighting, relevance is still hard to discriminate especially for tail exposures. Therefore, we regard ULTR as a task of semi-supervised, with a small amount oflabeled dataand a large amount of unlabeled data. Additionally, current adversarial learning models for search problems [20,28] have not employed propensity weighting to deal with labels that are missing not at random (MNAR) [26,31], possibly due to the ignorance of making good use of the side information (e.g. initial presentation orders).

Based on the above considerations, we design a general framework for adversarial ULTR. It is composed of a discriminator, a generator and a bias estimator as shown in Fig. 1: i) The minimax game between the two players naturally provides the most difficult cases for each other; ii) The bias estimator fully utilizes propensity-related information for pairwise debiasing. The three elements are introduced as follows:

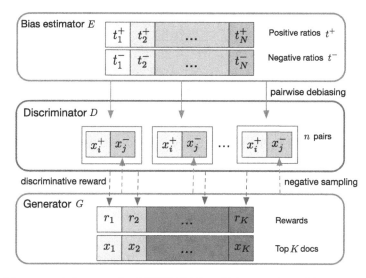

Fig. 1. The general framework of ULTRGAN, which contains a bias estimator E, a discriminator D and a generator G.

- **Bias estimator E:** It learns the top N position ratios of t^+, t^- to eliminate selection bias induced by presentation orders for the discriminator.
- **Discriminator D:** It learns the classifier $f_\phi(x, q)$, which tries to discriminate between relevant and irrelevant documents. By providing discriminative reward for generated (or selected) documents, it also retrains the generator.
- **Generator G:** It learns the distribution $p_\theta(x, q)$, which tries to generate (or select) the K-most relevant documents from candidate pool. It also plays as a dynamic sampler, selecting a less irrelevant document x_j^- for each relevant instance x_i^+ to push the discriminator to its limit.

4.2   Model Details

ULTRGAN is a minimax game played by the generator and discriminator, together with the estimation of position ratios. The discriminator tries to maximize the expectation of data distributions of relevant and irrelevant documents. The generator tries to fit the distribution of true relevant documents by minimizing the refined objective function. Our model considers click propensity for instances respectively in positive and negative groups. It can also be explained as a reweighting method of inverse propensity.

In Web search, for query q, the true data distribution can be described as $p_{true}(x, c_q^{x,i})$, which consists of query-document feature vectors and user clicks. The overall loss function is:

$$
\begin{aligned}
J^{G^*, D^*} &= \min_\theta \max_\phi \sum_{q \in Q} \mathbb{E}_{x_i \sim p_{true}(x, c_q^{x,i}=1)} \left[\frac{log(f_\phi(x_i, q))}{t_i^+} \right] \\
&+ \mathbb{E}_{x_j \sim p_\theta(x, c_q^{x,j}=0)} \left[\frac{log(1 - f_\phi(x_j, q))}{t_j^-} \right] \\
&= \min_\theta \max_\phi \sum_{q \in Q} \mathbb{E}_{x_i^+} \left[\frac{log(f_\phi(x_i^+, q))}{t_i^+} \right] + \mathbb{E}_{x_{j,\theta}^-} \left[\frac{log(1 - f_\phi(x_{j,\theta}^-, q))}{t_j^-} \right]
\end{aligned}
$$

where x_i^+ represents a clicked document for query q in the position i, and $x_{j,\theta}^-$ represents an unclicked document for query q in the position j, sampled by the generator with parameters θ. Our model selectively learns debiased preferences over competitive document pairs, which is different from previous work.

Optimizing Discriminator: In the overall loss, the objective for the discriminator is to find optimal parameters ϕ that maximize the log-likelihood of correctly distinguishing the true and selected relevant documents as follows:

$$
\phi^* = argmax_\phi \sum_{q \in Q} \mathbb{E}_{x_i^+} \left[\frac{log(f_\phi(x_i^+, q))}{t_i^+} \right] + \mathbb{E}_{x_{j,\theta}^-} \left[\frac{log(1 - f_\phi(x_{j,\theta}^-, q))}{t_j^-} \right] \tag{2}
$$

Pairwise risk function has been proved to be unbiased in Eq. (1), which pays more attention to the relative order between document pairs. Therefore, we can easily extend Eq. (2) with pairwise loss function L:

$$
\begin{aligned}
\phi^* &= argmax_\phi \sum_{q \in Q} \mathbb{E}_{x_i^+, x_{j,\theta}^-} \left[\frac{L(f_\phi(x_i^+, q) - f_\phi(x_{j,\theta}^-, q))}{t_i^+ \cdot t_j^-} \right] \\
&= argmin_\phi \sum_{q \in Q} \mathbb{E}_{x_i^+, x_{j,\theta}^-} \left[\frac{L(-(f_\phi(x_i^+, q) - f_\phi(x_{j,\theta}^-, q)))}{t_i^+ \cdot t_j^-} \right]
\end{aligned} \tag{3}
$$

Note that in Eq. (3), the discriminator parameters ϕ, positive ratio t_i^+ and negative ratio t_j^- are unknown. We follow the work [15] to estimate t_i^+ and t_j^-. Denote the discriminative objective function as follows:

$$
\mathbb{L} = \sum_{q \in Q} \sum_{i,j: x_i^+ \wedge x_{j,\theta}^-} \left[\frac{L(-(f_\phi(x_i^+, q) - f_\phi(x_{j,\theta}^-, q)))}{t_i^+ \cdot t_j^-} \right] + \lambda \|t^+\|_p^p + \lambda \|t^-\|_p^p \tag{4}
$$

Here, $\lambda \|\cdot\|_p^p$ is L_p regularization term, with parameter $p > 0$ and $\lambda > 0$ controlling the degree of imposed regularization. We can optimize ϕ, t_i^+ and t_j^- iteratively. In each iteration, when the optimal parameters ϕ^* have been computed for several times, we fix ϕ and estimate the values of t_i^+ and t_j^- by partial derivative of the objective function in Eq. (4):

$$t_i^+ = \left[\frac{\sum_q \sum_{j:x_i^+,x_j^-} \left(L(-(f_{\phi^*}(x_i^+,q) - f_{\phi^*}(x_{j,\theta}^-,q)))/(t_j^-)^* \right)}{\sum_q \sum_{k:x_1^+,x_k^-} \left(L(-(f_{\phi^*}(x_1^+,q) - f_{\phi^*}(x_{k,\theta}^-,q)))/(t_k^-)^* \right)} \right]^{\frac{1}{p+1}} \quad (5)$$

$$t_j^- = \left[\frac{\sum_q \sum_{i:x_i^+,x_j^-} \left(L(-(f_{\phi^*}(x_i^+,q) - f_{\phi^*}(x_{j,\theta}^-,q)))/(t_i^+)^* \right)}{\sum_q \sum_{k:x_k^+,x_1^-} \left(L(-(f_{\phi^*}(x_k^+,q) - f_{\phi^*}(x_{1,\theta}^-,q)))/(t_k^+)^* \right)} \right]^{\frac{1}{p+1}} \quad (6)$$

The results calculated by Eqs. (5) (6) are normalized to make the position bias at the first position to be 1. The pairwise function $L(-(f_\phi(x_i^+,q) - f_\phi(x_{j,\theta}^-,q)))$ is implemented as $log(1+exp(-(f_\phi(x_i^+,q)-f_\phi(x_{j,\theta}^-,q))))$ in our experiments. Then we use the updated ratios to optimize parameters ϕ. To speed up the training of the discriminator, we update the discriminator e-step times and update the position ratios once. This process iterates until convergence. The optimization algorithm of the discriminator is shown in Algorithm 1.

Optimizing Generator: In the minimax game, the generator is expected to minimize the objective function, fitting in the underlying relevance distribution via the signals from the discriminator:

$$J^{G^*} = \underset{\theta}{minmax} \underset{\phi}{\sum_{q \in Q}} \mathbb{E}_{x_i \sim p_{true}(x,c_q^{x,i}=1)}[log(f_\phi(x_i,q))]$$
$$+ \mathbb{E}_{x_j \sim p_\theta(x,c_q^{x,j}=0)}[log(1 - f_\phi(x_j,q))]$$

which can be converted into the following maximization function:

$$\theta^* = \underset{\theta}{argmin} \sum_{q \in Q} \mathbb{E}_{x_j \sim p_\theta(x,c_q^{x,j}=0)}[log(1 - f_\phi(x_j,q))]$$
$$= \underset{\theta}{argmax} \sum_{q \in Q} \mathbb{E}_{x_j \sim p_\theta(x)}[log(f_\phi(x_j,q))]$$

Inspired by the work IRGAN [28], we employ the policy gradient algorithm [27] for optimization. Following [28], we also constrain the reward function $D(x,q)$ in $(-1,1)$: $D(x,q) = 2\sigma(f_\phi(x,q)) - 1$. The gradient of the loss function is derived as:

$$\nabla_\theta J^G(q) \simeq \frac{1}{K} \sum_{k=1}^{K} \nabla_\theta logp_\theta(x_k)log(D(x_k,q)) \quad (7)$$

The true relevance distribution $p_{true}(x, c_q^{x,i})$ is dynamic and uncertain, which makes the equilibrium between the discriminator and the generator comparatively hard to reach. Convergence analysis in this problem is still an open question in current research literature [14,28]. We summarize the overall learning algorithm of ULTRGAN in Algorithm 1.

5   Experiments

In this section, we conduct extensive experiments to evaluate ULTRGAN.[1] Specifically, we aim to answer the following research questions:

RQ1: Can ULTRGAN effectively and robustly estimate inherent relevance?

RQ2: Does ULTRGAN have a better performance, compared to other pairwise debiasing models?

5.1   Experiments over Synthetic Dataset

Dataset and Experimental Settings. To our knowledge, the Yahoo! learning-to-rank challenge [8] is one of the largest datasets for LTR, which has been divided into training, valuation and test sets. In this dataset, each record contains a query-document identifier followed by a 700-dimension feature vector. The corresponding human-annotated relevance labels include Perfect (4), Excellent (3), Good (2), Fair (1) and Bad (0).

We follow the same settings as [1,15,18] to simulate exposures and clicks. A weak Ranking SVM model trained with 1% of the training data is used to create initial ranked list. Then clicks can be generated by simulating user behaviors based on the pre-defined click models [10]. Specifically, we use the position-based model [24] as follows:

$$P(c_i^+) = P(o_i^+) \cdot P(r_i^+)$$

Algorithm 1: ULTRGAN

    Input: click dataset $\mathbb{D} = \{q, \pi_q, c_q\}$, discriminator f_ϕ, generator p_θ;
    Output: ϕ, θ, t^+, t^-;

1   Initialize ϕ, θ, $t^+ \Leftarrow 1$, $t^- \Leftarrow 1$;
2   **repeat**
3 | **for** *d-step* **do**
4 | | Prepare training set $\mathbb{S} = \{(x_i^+, x_j^-)\}$ by using current p_θ to select x_j^- from unclicked documents for each clicked document x_i^+;
5 | | Update f_ϕ with t^+, t^- on $\mathbb{S}$ with Eq.(3);
6 | | **if** *d-step mod e-step = 0* **then**
7 | | | Update position ratios t^+, t^- by with Eq.(5)(6);
8 | | **end**
9 | **end**
10 | **for** *g-step* **do**
11 | | Use current p_θ to select most relevant K documents for each q;
12 | | Update p_θ via policy gradient with Eq.(7);
13 | **end**
14   **until** *ULTRGAN converges*;

---

[1] Code is available at https://github.com/April-Cai/Debiasing-Learning-to-Rank-Models-with-GANs.

$P(o_i^+)$ is the probability of a document being observed in the position i with $P(o_i^+) = \rho_i^\eta$ where ρ_i is derived from empirical results [18], and η controls the severity of position bias. We set $\eta = 1$ for the main experiment. The perceived relevance probability $P(r_i^+)$ is computed as:

$$P(r_i^+) = \epsilon + (1 - \epsilon)\frac{2^y - 1}{2^{y^{max}} - 1}$$

where $y \in \{0, 1, 2, 3, 4\}$ and y^{max} equals to 4 as the highest relevance score. The severity of relevance bias is controlled by ϵ. By default, we set ϵ as 0.1.

The discriminator and generator are implemented with deep neural networks (DNNs) that work with stochastic gradient decent (SGD). The hidden layers are 512, 256, 128 in size, remain consistent with [1]. Given input feature vector $\mathbf{x}$, the discriminative function $f_\phi(\mathbf{x})$ can be derived from the output of network a_4:

$$a_0 = \mathbf{x}; a_n = leakyReLU(W_{n-1}a_{n-1} + b_{n-1}), n = 1, 2, 3, 4$$

The generative function $p_\theta(\mathbf{x})$ can be derived from the output of network h_4:

$$h_0 = \mathbf{x}; h_n = leakyReLU(W_{n-1}h_{n-1} + b_{n-1}), n = 1, 2, 3$$
$$h_4 = tanh(W_3 h_3 + b_3)$$

Here, $leakyReLU$ and $tanh$ are commonly-used activation functions. Scalers a_4 and h_4 indicate predicted relevance score. For both networks, we set the learning rate as 0.05, the batch size as 256, and the weight decay as 1e-4. The parameter p is 0.05 and λ is 1 in Eq. (4). The number of sampled documents K is set as 5. We train the model with d-step as 100, g-step as 50 and e-step as 10 in Algorithm 1.

Baselines. We consider the following debiasing methods as baselines:

- *No Correct*: Directly treat clicks as labels, used as the lower bound.
- *Randomization*: The randomization-based model [18] for bias elimination.
- *Regression-EM*: A regression-based EM algorithm proposed in [30].
- *Dual Learning*: The dual learning algorithm (DLA) implemented in DNN [1].[2]
- *Pairwise Debiasing*: The pairwise debiasing model [15] for LambdaMart [6].[3]

In the experiments, Regression-EM and Randomization are implemented in three rankers (RankSVM, LambdaMart and DNN). DLA is bound to DNN only. Pairwise debiasing has only been employed in LambdaMart. Following [1,15], we use MAP and nDCG as the evaluation matrices. MAP and nDCG at 1, 3, 5 and 10 are reported.

Effectiveness Analysis. As shown in Table 2, our model outperforms all the baselines, and is as effective as (if not better than) the pairwise debiasing [15] of LambdaMart. We can observe that LambdaMart is the most effective base model when no corrections are conducted. However, ULTRGAN is superior to basic

---

[2] https://github.com/QingyaoAi/Unbiased-Learning-to-Rank-with-Unbiased-Propensity-Estimation.
[3] https:// github. com/ acbull/ Unbiased_LambdaMart.

DNN, indicating that the combination of generative and discriminative retrieval models makes it possible to exceed the limit of the base model. Meanwhile, ULTRGAN is completely end-to-end, enhancing the discriminative function by sampling negative documents and updating position ratios dynamically. The estimated ratios are in accordance with former analysis shown in Fig. 2. These factors give ULTRGAN an advantage over state-of-the-art debiasing methods.

Robustness Analysis. For fair comparison, we perform experiments on different debiasing methods implemented in DNN. The robustness of these models can be evaluated by varying η from 0.2 to 1.8. As shown in Fig. 3, the overall ranking approaches become less effective with the bias getting much severer, which is in accordance with assumption. We can observe that our method provides robust performances compared with baselines. This indicates that ULTRGAN scales well and could be adapted to real-world conditions.

Table 2. Comparisons of different unbiased learning-to-rank models.

Ranker	Debiasing method	MAP	NDCG@1	NDCG@3	NDCG@5	NDCG@10
RankSVM	Regression-EM	0.815	0.629	0.648	0.674	0.705
	Randomization	0.814	0.628	0.644	0.672	0.707
	No correct	0.811	0.614	0.629	0.658	0.697
LambdaMart	Pairwise Debiasing	0.836	0.717	0.716	0.728	0.764
	Regression-EM	0.830	0.685	0.684	0.700	0.743
	Randomization	0.827	0.669	0.678	0.690	0.728
	No Correct	0.820	0.658	0.669	0.672	0.716
DNN	Dual Learning	0.828	0.674	0.683	0.697	0.734
	Regression-EM	0.829	0.676	0.684	0.699	0.736
	Randomization	0.825	0.673	0.679	0.693	0.732
	No correct	0.819	0.637	0.651	0.667	0.711
GAN	ULTRGAN	**0.842**	**0.722**	**0.718**	**0.730**	**0.766**

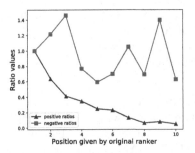

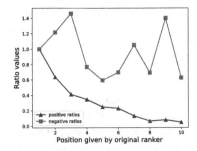

Fig. 2. Position biases (ratios) estimated by ULTRGAN.

Fig. 3. The performances of different debiasing methods when η varies.

5.2   Experiments over Real-World Dataset

Dataset and Experimental Settings. We perform experiments on a real-world dataset named TianGong-ST [9]. It was collected from a commercial web search engine on a 18-day span search log, which contains 147,155 refined search sessions in total with clicks and positions. This dataset also provides a corpora covered over 90% web pages. For evaluation purpose, a test set of 2000 queries each with top 10 documents is attached, labeled manually in TREC style.

As in [1], we employ content-based algorithms to extract features based on the text of queries and documents. We use Lucene [4] to index and search. The 29 features extracted are as follows: the average term frequency (TF), the average inverse document frequency (IDF), the average $tf \cdot idf$ scores, the BM25 scores, the language model (LM) with Dirichlet smoothing and with Jelinek-Mercer scores [34], the number of terms, each feature calculated in title, URL, content and the whole document, together with the number of slashes in URL.

We do stratified sampling by session lengths and acquire 13,484 ranked lists. For each query in the training and test sets, we remove candidates that are invalid or cannot be reached. We evaluate the ranking performances over the test set. The length of initial ranked list is 10 at most, therefore we report nDCG at 1, 3 and 5, respectively. As to the experimental settings, we vary the sizes of hidden layers to 16, 8. The d-step is set as 50, g-step as 10 and e-step as 10.

Baselines. We compare ULTRGAN against the following pairwise debiasing approaches:

- *No Correct*: Directly use clicks as labels in LambdaMart [6].
- *Unbiased LambdaMart*: Pairwise debiasing [15] in LambdaMart.
- *Unbiased DNN*: Pairwise debiasing in DNN.

Comparison and Analysis. As shown in Table 3, our model achieves the best performances compared to Unbiased LambdaMart [15] and Unbiased DNN, implying that our method has the advantage of sampling informative unlabeled instances instead of using all candidates to further optimize the ranking function.

Out of concern for the unstable training of GAN, we outline the learning curve of the discriminator as shown in Fig. 4. Here, we only report the performances measured by nDCG@5, other matrices exhibit the similar trend. After training for 50 epochs, the model converges and consistently outperforms baselines. The results imply that our method can steadily achieve a high level of performance that is promising to be applied in production.

---

[4] https:// lucene. apache. org/.

Table 3. Performances of different pairwise debiasing models on TianGong-ST.

Ranker	NDCG@1	NDCG@3	NDCG@5
No correct	0.663	0.715	0.771
Unbiased LambdaMart	0.674	0.725	0.776
Unbiased DNN	0.693	0.736	0.788
ULTRGAN	**0.698**	**0.749**	**0.798**

Fig. 4. Learning curves on TianGong-ST.

6   Conclusion and Future Work

In this paper, we formulate ULTR as a ranking problem under the semi-supervised setting. The incorporation of pairwise debiasing into generative adversarial networks better employs competitive negative instances for discriminative learning, which enables unbiased relevance supervision to propagate from the discriminator to the generator. In this way, propensity estimation and relevance learning can be performed at the same time. Empirical results demonstrate effectiveness and robustness of our approach.

This work represents an initial attempt to combine adversarial training mechanism with counterfactual learning and there are still many problems. For example, the sampling strategy is relatively inefficient and the equilibria could not be reached easily. In the future, we plan to investigate other conditions such as pointwise and listwise ranking functions that could be extended to this framework. Model pre-training may bring in benefits, which is also left for future studies.

Acknowledgements. This work is supported by the National Key Research and Development Program of China under Grant No. 2016YFB1000904. We thank the anonymous reviewers for their careful reading and insightful comments on our manuscript.

References

1. Ai, Q., Bi, K., Luo, C., Guo, J., Croft, W.B.: Unbiased learning to rank with unbiased propensity estimation. In: SIGIR, pp. 385–394 (2018)
2. Ai, Q., Mao, J., Liu, Y., Croft, W.B.: Unbiased learning to rank: theory and practice. In: CIKM, pp. 2305–2306 (2018)
3. Bekker, J., Davis, J.: Learning from positive and unlabeled data: a survey. Mach. Learn. **109**, 719–760 (2020)
4. Borisov, A., Markov, I., De Rijke, M., Serdyukov, P.: A neural click model for web search. In: WWW, pp. 531–541 (2016)
5. Burges, C., et al.: Learning to rank using gradient descent. In: ICML, pp. 89–96 (2005)

6. Burges, C.J.: From ranknet to lambdarank to lambdamart: an overview. Learning **11**(23–581), 81 (2010)
7. Cao, Z., Qin, T., Liu, T.Y., Tsai, M.F., Li, H.: Learning to rank: from pairwise approach to listwise approach. In: ICML, pp. 129–136 (2007)
8. Chapelle, O., Chang, Y.: Yahoo! learning to rank challenge overview. In: Proceedings of the Learning to Rank Challenge, pp. 1–24 (2011)
9. Chen, J., Mao, J., Liu, Y., Zhang, M., Ma, S.: TianGong-ST: a new dataset with large-scale refined real-world web search sessions. In: CIKM, pp. 2485–2488 (2019)
10. Chuklin, A., Markov, I., de Rijke, M.: Click models for web search. Synth. Lect. Inf. Concepts Retr. Serv. **7**(3), 1–115 (2015)
11. Cossock, D., Zhang, T.: Subset ranking using regression. In: Lugosi, G., Simon, H.U. (eds.) COLT 2006. LNCS (LNAI), vol. 4005, pp. 605–619. Springer, Heidelberg (2006). https://doi.org/10.1007/11776420_44
12. Craswell, N., Zoeter, O., Taylor, M., Ramsey, B.: An experimental comparison of click position-bias models. In: WSDM, pp. 87–94 (2008)
13. Dupret, G.E., Piwowarski, B.: A user browsing model to predict search engine click data from past observations. In: SIGIR, pp. 331–338 (2008)
14. Goodfellow, I., et al.: Generative adversarial nets. In: NIPS, pp. 2672–2680 (2014)
15. Hu, Z., Wang, Y., Peng, Q., Li, H.: Unbiased lambdamart: an unbiased pairwise learning-to-rank algorithm. In: WWW, pp. 2830–2836 (2019)
16. Joachims, T.: Optimizing search engines using clickthrough data. In: KDD, pp. 133–142 (2002)
17. Joachims, T., Granka, L., Pan, B., Hembrooke, H., Gay, G.: Accurately interpreting clickthrough data as implicit feedback. In: SIGIR, vol. 51, pp. 4–11 (2017)
18. Joachims, T., Swaminathan, A., Schnabel, T.: Unbiased learning-to-rank with biased feedback. In: WSDM, pp. 781–789 (2017)
19. Liu, T.Y.: Learning to rank for information retrieval. Found. Trends Inf. Retr. **3**(3), 225–331 (2009)
20. Lu, S., Dou, Z., Jun, X., Nie, J.Y., Wen, J.R.: PSGAN: a minimax game for personalized search with limited and noisy click data. In: SIGIR, pp. 555–564 (2019)
21. Oosterhuis, H., Jagerman, R., de Rijke, M.: Unbiased learning to rank: counterfactual and online approaches. In: WWW (Companion Volume), pp. 299–300 (2020)
22. Oosterhuis, H., de Rijke, M.: Differentiable unbiased online learning to rank. In: CIKM, pp. 1293–1302 (2018)
23. O'Brien, M., Keane, M.T.: Modeling result-list searching in the world wide web: the role of relevance topologies and trust bias. In: Proceedings of the 28th Annual Conference of the Cognitive Science Society, vol. 28, pp. 1881–1886. Citeseer (2006)
24. Richardson, M., Dominowska, E., Ragno, R.: Predicting clicks: estimating the click-through rate for new ads. In: WWW, pp. 521–530 (2007)
25. Rosenbaum, P.R., Rubin, D.B.: The central role of the propensity score in observational studies for causal effects. Biometrika **70**(1), 41–55 (1983)
26. Steck, H.: Training and testing of recommender systems on data missing not at random. In: KDD, pp. 713–722 (2010)
27. Sutton, R.S., McAllester, D.A., Singh, S.P., Mansour, Y.: Policy gradient methods for reinforcement learning with function approximation. In: NIPS, pp. 1057–1063 (2000)
28. Wang, J., et al.: IRGAN: a minimax game for unifying generative and discriminative information retrieval models. In: SIGIR, pp. 515–524 (2017)
29. Wang, X., Bendersky, M., Metzler, D., Najork, M.: Learning to rank with selection bias in personal search. In: SIGIR, pp. 115–124 (2016)

30. Wang, X., Golbandi, N., Bendersky, M., Metzler, D., Najork, M.: Position bias estimation for unbiased learning to rank in personal search. In: WSDM, pp. 610–618 (2018)
31. Yang, L., Cui, Y., Xuan, Y., Wang, C., Belongie, S., Estrin, D.: Unbiased offline recommender evaluation for missing-not-at-random implicit feedback. In: RecSys, pp. 279–287 (2018)
32. Yue, Y., Joachims, T.: Interactively optimizing information retrieval systems as a dueling bandits problem. In: ICML, pp. 1201–1208 (2009)
33. Yue, Y., Patel, R., Roehrig, H.: Beyond position bias: Examining result attractiveness as a source of presentation bias in clickthrough data. In: WWW, pp. 1011–1018 (2010)
34. Zhai, C., Lafferty, J.: A study of smoothing methods for language models applied to ad hoc information retrieval. In: ACM SIGIR Forum, vol. 51, pp. 268–276. ACM, New York (2017)

An Effective Constraint-Based Anomaly Detection Approach on Multivariate Time Series

Zijue Li[1], Xiaoou Ding[1], and Hongzhi Wang[1,2(✉)]

[1] Harbin Institute of Technology, Harbin, China
{lizijue,wangzh}@hit.edu.cn, dingxiaoou_hit@163.com
[2] Peng Cheng Laboratory, Shenzhen, China

Abstract. With the development of IoT, various sensors are deployed in industry applications. Sensors produce multivariate time series, while error data and abnormal values often exist in the data. Correlation in multivariate time series can be used to identify such anomaly. In this paper, we propose an efficient method to utilize the correlation between multivariate time series with constraint-based anomaly detection. We develop a DP algorithm to execute the detection process, and optimize the algorithm efficiency with 2D range tree. Experiments on real IIoT dataset demonstrate the superiority of our proposed method compared to the prediction based models.

Keywords: Anomaly detection · Temporal data analysis · Data cleaning · Multivariate time series

1   Introduction

With the rapid development of Internet of Things (IoT), various sensors are used in industrial applications. Sensors generate time series, which is one of the most important data in IoT application scenarios. However, the collected time series data often contains dirty values or abnormal values, because of environmental changes, sensor fault, and etc. The hidden anomaly could severely affect the reliability and the effectiveness of data mining and knowledge discovery.

Prediction-based models are widely used in time series anomaly detection [4]. The outlier score of a data point in sequence is always computed as its deviation from the predicted value by a designed model. Statistical methods (*e.g.*, AR-model [5]) have been developed in anomaly detection with customized tasks. Existing studies [1] often predict the value as a median of the value with sliding window. In recent years, constraint-based methods are proposed to detect and repair specific anomaly. Existing work [7] proposed *speed constraint* in stream data to describe the *jump* of values. However, users need to make decisions after

---

This paper was partially supported by NSFC grant U1866602, 61602129, 61772157.

X. Wang et al. (Eds.): APWeb-WAIM 2020, LNCS 12318, pp. 61–69, 2020.
https://doi.org/10.1007/978-3-030-60290-1_5

double-checking the outliers in many cases, instead of repairing the outlier data straight and automatically.

Existing methods usually detect each sequence separately, and fail to address the correlation between multivariate time series. Motivated by the works [6,8] which consider the correlation in the multivariate time series, we model the correlation among sequences and proceed with a collaborative constraint-based detection in the multiple time series. The approach studied in this paper is also applied in the data cleaning system Cleanits [3].

Contribution. Our major contributions are summarized as follows:

(1) We formalize the anomaly detection problem in sequence under speed constraints (SC), and devise a naive dynamic programming algorithm running in $O(n^2)$ time to detect outliers in one sequence, where n is the length of sequence (*i.e.*, the total number of data points).
(2) We transform the anomaly detection problem to a 2D-range-query problem, and employ a 2D-range tree to optimize algorithm efficiency. The proposed optimized DP algorithm runs in $O(n \log^2 n)$ time.
(3) We propose an integrated method to detect outliers in multivariate time series. We design experiments on real-life IIoT data, and demonstrate both the efficiency and effectiveness of the proposed method.

2   Problem Formulation

2.1   Definitions

Considering one sequence $S = (n, s, t)$, where n is the volume of data. $s = s[1], s[2], ..., s[n]$ is the data values, and each $s[i]$ has a timestamp $t[i]$. Referring to [7], a *speed constraint* (SC) $sc_k = (s_{min}, s_{max})$ defined on sequence S_k is a tuple consisting a minimum speed s_{min} and a maximum speed s_{max}. In a sequence S_k, we say that two points $s_k[i]$ and $s_k[j]$ satisfy a speed constraint sc_k, if $s_{min} \leq \frac{s_k[j]-s_k[i]}{t_k[j]-t_k[i]} \leq s_{max}$ holds. S_k is considered to satisfie one SC sc_k, if every two points in S_k satisfy this speed constraint.

It is worth noting that we do not modify values to make a whole sequence satisfy speed constraint. Instead, we employ remove operations and make a sequence satisfy SC after removing some points in sequence. The removed points are treated as abnormal data points as defined in Definition 1.

Definition 1 (Abnormal data points). E_k *is the set of abnormal data point indexes in sequence S_k, if every two points with indexes in $\{1, 2, 3, ..., n_k\} \setminus E_k$ satisfy the speed constraint sc_k. That is, after removing points with indexes in E_k, sequence S_k satisfies the speed constraint sc_k.*

We focus on discovering all abnormal data points in multiple time series. Multiple time series $\mathcal{S} = \{S_1, S_2, ..., S_N\}$ is a group of sequences which are collected by N sensors. The kth sensor generates one sequence $S_k = (n_k, s_k, t_k)$. Suppose that each sequence is highly correlated with at least another one sequence in $\mathcal{S}$.

Time series correlation is computed via Pearson Coefficient on the values with the same timestamp in two sequences S_k and S_l. S_k and S_l are highly correlated if they have a high correlation coefficient, *i.e.*, the absolute value of their coefficient is no less than a given threshold c. Our problem definition is shown in Problem 1.

Problem 1. Given multiple time series $\mathcal{S} = \{S_1, S_2, ..., S_N\}$, each sequence S_k has a speed constraint sc_k, and each sequence is highly correlated with at least one sequence, the anomaly detection problem in multiple time series is to identify the minimum number of outliers in each sequence (*i.e.*, E_k with minimum cardinality) that S_k satisfies sc_k after removing all outlier points.

2.2 Framework Overview

Figure 1 show our method framework, which has three phases: PAA processing, correlation evaluation, and anomaly detection. The PAA processing (Sect. 3.1) is the first step in our method, which helps aggregate values in fixed time intervals and rebuild all sequences. After that, we determine suspect sequences which may have outliers in correlation evaluation phase (Sect. 3.2). We employ correlation as a priori information and evaluate whether correlation changes or not. We finally proceed with a further anomaly detection (Sect. 3.3) on suspect sequences, and employ a 2D range tree to optimize the efficiency.

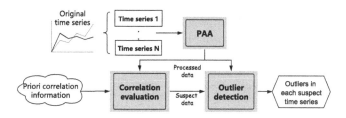

Fig. 1. Method framework

3 Proposed Methods

3.1 PAA Processing

In practical, sensors may not generate data at the same frequency. It affects the accuracy of the correlation calculation in the correlation evaluation phase, as the time series correlation coefficient is computed on the data with the same timestamps. Besides, sensors may collect data in a very short period, and the values may not change fast. As a result, many redundant data are collected, which seriously reduces data processing efficiency.

Algorithm 1: Correlation Evaluation

Input: $\mathcal{S}$, correlation coefficient matrix $\mathcal{C}^{N*N}$, high correlation coefficient
threshold c, correlation coefficient decline threshold d,
suspect threshold θ

Output: Suspect time series set $\mathcal{E}$

1 **foreach** $S_k \in \mathcal{S}$ **do**
2   initialize $correlated \leftarrow 0$ and $declined \leftarrow 0$;
3   **foreach** $S_l \in \mathcal{S}$ **do**
4   **if** $\mathcal{C}_{k,l} \geq c$ **then**
5              $correlated \leftarrow correlated + 1$;
6              $x_k, x_l =$ selected values with same timestampe in S_k and S_l ;
7              $r \leftarrow \frac{\text{cov}(x_k,x_l)}{\sigma_{x_k}\sigma_{x_l}}$;
8   **if** $r < \mathcal{C}_{k,l} - d$ **then**
9                  $declined \leftarrow declined + 1$;
10   **if** $\frac{declined}{correlated} \geq \theta$ **then**
11          $\mathcal{E} \leftarrow \mathcal{E} \cup \{S_k\}$;

12 **return** $\mathcal{E}$

To achieve an efficient detection, we deploy Piecewise Aggregate Approximation (PAA) as a preprocessing step, which is a well-known rebuilding technology
in time series [2]. PAA aggregates the data in each fixed time interval and calculates the mean of data as an approximation value in the interval. After that,
each sequence are aligned with losing little information.

After PAA, the volume of sequence is reduced from n_i to n'_i, where $n'_i \leq n_i$.
We use $S'_i = (n'_i, s'_i, t'_i)$ as the input of the further phases. For brevity, we still
use S_i as processed sequence instead of S'_i below.

3.2 Correlation Evaluation

Note again that the data collected by adjacent sensors are usually similar and
correlated. The correlation in time series can provide pre-detection information.
That is, if the correlation significantly weakens, some sequences probably contain
outliers. This assist to detect anomaly effectively.

Correlation evaluation step aims to identify suspect sequences containing
outliers, as shown in Algorithm 1. We collect correlation coefficients $\mathcal{C}^{N*N}$ as
a priori knowledge. In line 4, the algorithm verifies whether S_k and S_l have a
high correlation in priori correlation information. Then, values with the same
timestamp are selected, and we compute the correlation coefficient (lines 6–7).
We then evaluate whether the correlation coefficient declines significantly. The
algorithm evaluates how many high correlations have changed. If more than θ
percent of high correlations weaken significantly, S_k is considered to contain
outliers and we will execute a further detection on S_k.

Algorithm 2: Naive DP

Input: Sequence S_k, speed constraint sc_k
Output: Outlier point indexes E_k

1 initialize $dp[i] \leftarrow i - 1$ and $trace[i] \leftarrow -1$ for $i \leftarrow 1, ..., n_k$;
2 **for** $j \leftarrow 1, ..., n_k$ **do**
3   **for** $i \leftarrow 1, 2, ..., j - 1$ **do**
4   **if** $s_{min} \leq \frac{s_k[j] - s_k[i]}{t_k[j] - t_k[i]} \leq s_{max}$ and $dp[j] > dp[i] + (j - i - 1)$ **then**
5               $dp[j] \leftarrow dp[i] + (j - i - 1)$;
6               $trace[j] \leftarrow i$;

7 find $index$ with minimum value $dp[index] + (n_k - index)$;
8 $I_k \leftarrow$ trace back indexes using $index \leftarrow trace[index]$;
9 $E_k \leftarrow \{1, 2, 3, ..., n_k\} \setminus I_k$;
10 **return** E_k;

3.3   Anomaly Detection Under Speed Constraint

In this section, we propose a naive dynamic programming algorithm to solve the outlier detection problem in single sequence. We transform the problem to a 2D range query problem and optimize the naive algorithm using a 2D range tree.

Naive Algorithm. Algorithm 2 shows the anomaly detection process in one sequence. Let $dp[i]$ be the minimum number of abnormal data points in sub-sequence $s[1, 2, ..., i - 1]$, where the subsequence $s[1, 2, ..., i]$ satisfies SC after removing $dp[i]$ points. If two points $s[i]$ and $s[j]$ satisfy the speed constraint, we can remove $dp[i]$ points and all points in $s[i + 1, ..., j - 1]$ to make subsequence $s[1, 2, ..., j]$ satisfy the speed constraint. So we have $dp[j] = dp[i] + (j - i - 1)$. Then we need to remove all points in $s[j + 1, ..., n_k]$ to make the whole sequence satisfy the speed constraint.

The time complexity of Algorithm 2 is $O(n^2)$, where n is the number of points in sequence S_k.

Algorithm Optimization. A straight idea for efficiency improvement is to optimize the process of determining the index i in lines 3–6 in Algorithm 2. For every fixed index j, we need to find an index i which satisfies the following conditions: a) $i < j$, b) $s_{min} \leq \frac{s_k[j] - s_k[i]}{t_k[j] - t_k[i]}$, c) $\frac{s_k[j] - s_k[i]}{t_k[j] - t_k[i]} \leq s_{max}$, and d) $dp[i] + (j - i - 1)$ is minimum. Let $X_k[j] = s_k[j] - t_k[j] * s_{min}$, and $Y_k[j] = s_k[j] - t_k[j] * s_{max}$, the condition 2 and 3 can be presented as: $X_k[i] \leq X_k[j]$ and $Y_k[i] \geq Y_k[j]$. Let $f[i]$ denote $dp[i] - i$, then condition 4 is to find the minimum $f[i]$. In this case, the problem is to find an index i which satisfies: a) $i < j$, b) $X_k[i] \leq X_k[j]$, c) $Y_k[i] \geq Y_k[j]$, and d) $f[i]$ is minimum.

The optimization problem is to find a point with minimum value $f[i]$ in a 2D orthogonal area $x \leq X_k[j]$ and $y \geq Y_k[j]$. This problem can be solved in $O(\log^2 n)$ time with $O(n \log n)$ space using a 2D range tree. We modify the 2nd

Algorithm 3: Optimized DP

Input: Sequence S_k, speed constraint sc_k
Output: Outlier point indexes E_k

1 initialize $dp[i] \leftarrow i - 1$ and $trace[i] \leftarrow -1$ for $i \leftarrow 1, ..., n_k$;
2 initialize an empty 2-dimension range tree T.
3 **for** $j \leftarrow 1, ..., n_k$ **do**
4      $X[j] \leftarrow s_k[j] - t_k[j] * s_{min}$ and $Y[j] \leftarrow s_k[j] - t_k[j] * s_{max}$;
5   find i with minimum $f[i]$ in range $x \in (-\infty, X[j]]$ and $y \in [Y[j], \infty)$ in T ;
6   **if** i exists **then**
7          $dp[j] \leftarrow dp[i] + (j - i - 1)$;
8          $trace[j] \leftarrow i$;
9   insert point $(X[j], Y[j])$ into T ;
10 find $index$ with minimum value $dp[index] + (n_k - index)$;
11 $I_k \leftarrow$ trace back indexes using $index \leftarrow trace[index]$;
12 $E_k \leftarrow \{1, 2, 3, ..., n_k\} \setminus I_k$;
13 **return** E_k;

---

dimension range tree to report a minimum value point in a range query. In the 2nd dimension range tree, we store extra information in each node, *i.e.*, the minimum value $f[i]$ in subtree, and the index i with minimum $f[i]$ in subtree. So we can get an *index* with minimum $f[index]$ in that range as the query process progressing, without paying any extra time cost.

Algorithm 3 shows the optimization detection process. For any fixed index j, we execute a query operation and an insert operation. This algorithm runs in $O(n \log^2 n)$ time, where n is the length of input sequence S. The 2D range tree uses $O(n \log n)$ space.

Suppose there are N multiple time series S. Let m be the maximum number of points in one sequence. PAA runs in $O(Nm)$ time, correlation evaluation runs in $O(N^2 m)$ time, and outlier detection phase uses $O(Nm \log^2 m)$ time, so the total time complexity of our framework is $O(N^2 m + Nm \log^2 m)$.

4 Experiment

In this section, we experimentally compare our proposed methods. We first introduce the experiment settings, then we compare the efficiency of optimized DP algorithm. We compare the efficiency and performance of our proposed detection framework with prediction models. All the experiments run on a computer with 2.50 GHz Core i7 CPU and 16 GB RAM.

4.1 Experimental Settings

We employ a real dataset, Wind Turbine dataset. It includes 123 sensors collecting data in 3 days. Sensors produce data points simultaneously in every 7 s.

We intercept $33 \times 30k$ points and use the first $10k$ points as training data for the correlation coefficient matrix and for AR models. The rest $20k$ points are used as testing data. We randomly select some sequences as error series. Then we inject error points into each error series in testing data. We randomly select some data points and replace their values. For each replaced data point, it takes a random value between the minimum and maximum values in the dataset.

We implement all the algorithms in our proposed framework in this paper named SC. Besides, we implement two anomaly detection models for comparative evaluation: WM (Window-median predict model) and AR (AR predict model). All parameters are tuned through a lot of experiments.

The evaluation criteria include a) time cost, b) anomaly detection precision (P), and c) anomaly detection recall (R). We evaluate the efficiency and performance with three parameters: 1) varying error sequence rate, 2) varying error point rate in error sequence, and 3) varying data volume of sequence.

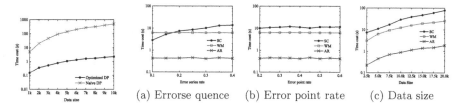

(a) Errorse quence   (b) Error point rate   (c) Data size

Fig. 2. Anomaly detection efficiency evaluation

Fig. 3. Method efficiency evaluation

4.2   Performance for Phases

We evaluate the performance of correlation evaluation phase in our method. We evaluate the precision and recall of suspect sequences selected by this phase. The average performance on the condition that error sequence rate $= 0.3$, error point rate $= 0.5$, and data size $= 5k$ are: $P = 0.88$ and $R = 1$.

We compare the efficiency of naive DP algorithm and optimized DP algorithm in one sequence. On the condition that error point rate is 0.35, Fig. 2 shows the time cost on varying data size from 1k to 10k. Optimized DP has less running time than naive DP algorithm. Besides, with the data size increasing, optimized DP has a lower time cost growth. It does accelerate the whole detection process because we do not need to execute anomaly detection on those normal sequences.

4.3   Performance for Detection Framework

We then report the detection efficiency and performance comparison. The data size is the points in each sequence, so the total data points should be multiplied by 33. In addition to varying conditions, experiments are implemented under the condition that error sequence rate $= 0.3$, error point rate $= 0.35$, and data size $= 5k$.

We compare the efficiency of SC, WM, and AR on the varying parameters in Fig. 3. The proposed SC has a slightly higher time cost than WM, while AR model always costs the least time.

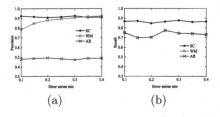
(a)   (b)

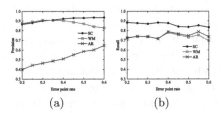
(a)   (b)

Fig. 4. Varying error sequence rate   **Fig. 5.** Varying error point rate

Figure 4 shows that our proposed SC has higher precision in low error sequence rate, and has the highest recall with all error sequence rate. Figure 5 shows that our proposed SC has higher precision in high error point rate, and has the highest recall in all error point rate. All three methods have almost unchanged performance as data size increases, SC has the highest precision and recall, while AR model has the worst performance.

5   Conclusions

We formalize outlier detection problem under speed constraint in one sequence and in multivariate time series. We propose a novelty detection framework consisting of three phases for outlier detection in multivariate time series. Experiments on real dataset show the superiority of our proposed framework. In the future, we will try to optimize the space cost of this algorithm, and design new algorithms for detecting simultaneous outliers in highly correlated series.

References

1. Basu, S., Meckesheimer, M.: Automatic outlier detection for time series: an application to sensor data. Knowl. Inf. Syst. **11**(2), 137–154 (2007)
2. Ding, J., Liu, Y., Zhang, L., Wang, J., Liu, Y.: An anomaly detection approach for multiple monitoring data series based on latent correlation probabilistic model. Appl. Intell. **44**(2), 340–361 (2016)
3. Ding, X., Wang, H., Su, J., Li, Z., Li, J., Gao, H.: Cleanits: a data cleaning system for industrial time series. Proc. VLDB Endowment **12**(12), 1786–1789 (2019)
4. Gupta, M., Gao, J., Aggarwal, C.C., Han, J.: Outlier detection for temporal data: a survey. IEEE Trans. Knowl. Data Eng. **26**(9), 2250–2267 (2013)
5. Hill, D.J., Minsker, B.S.: Anomaly detection in streaming environmental sensor data: a data-driven modeling approach. Environ. Model Softw. **25**(9), 1014–1022 (2010)

6. Sakurada, M., Yairi, T.: Anomaly detection using autoencoders with nonlinear dimensionality reduction. In: Proceedings of the MLSDA 2014 2nd Workshop on Machine Learning for Sensory Data Analysis, pp. 4–11 (2014)
7. Song, S., Zhang, A., Wang, J., Yu, P.S.: Screen: stream data cleaning under speed constraints. In: Proceedings of the 2015 ACM SIGMOD International Conference on Management of Data, pp. 827–841 (2015)
8. Su, Y., Zhao, Y., Niu, C., Liu, R., Sun, W., Pei, D.: Robust anomaly detection for multivariate time series through stochastic recurrent neural network. In: Proceedings of the 25th ACM SIGKDD International Conference on Knowledge Discovery and Data Mining, pp. 2828–2837 (2019)

A Method for Decompensation Prediction in Emergency and Harsh Situations

Guozheng Rao[1,3,5] (ID), Shuying Zhao[1], Li Zhang[2(✉)] (ID), Qing Cong[1] (ID),
and Zhiyong Feng[1,4,5] (ID)

[1] College of Intelligence and Computing, Tianjin University, Tianjin 300350, China
{rgz,chf,zyfeng}@tju.edu.cn, 18322302639@163.com
[2] School of Economics and Management,
Tianjin University of Science and Technology, Tianjin 300222, China
zhangli2006@tust.edu.cn
[3] School of New Media and Communication, Tianjin University, Tianjin 300072, China
[4] Shenzhen Research Institute of Tianjin University, Shenzhen 518000, China
[5] Tianjin Key Laboratory of Cognitive Computing and Applications, Tianjin 300350, China

Abstract. To save more lives, critically ill patients need to make timely decisions or predictive diagnosis and treatment in emergency and harsh conditions, such as earthquakes, medical emergencies, and hurricanes. However, in such circumstances, medical resources such as medical staff and medical facilities are short supply abnormally. So, we propose a method for decompensation prediction in emergency and harsh conditions. The method includes components such as patient information collection, data selection, data processing, and decompensation prediction. Based on this, this paper demonstrates the method using MIMIC-III data. Firstly, we tried a series of machine learning models to predict physiological decompensation. Secondly, to detect patients whose condition deteriorates rapidly under severe and limited circumstances, we try to reduce the essential physiological variables as much as possible for prediction. The experimental results show that the Bi-LSTM-attention method, combined with eleven essential physiological variables, can be used to predict the decompensation of severe ICUs patients. The AUC-ROC can reach 0.8509. Furthermore, these eleven physiological variables can be easily monitored without the need for complicated manual and massive, costly instruments, which meets the real requirements under emergency and harsh conditions. In summary, our decompensation prediction method can provide intelligent decision support for saving more lives in emergency and harsh conditions.

Keywords: Decompensation prediction · Bi-LSTM · Attention mechanism · ICUs

1 Introduction

With the rapid increase of medical data, the collision between medical problems and medical data is also intensifying. It is an essential task in the medical field to determine the

X. Wang et al. (Eds.): APWeb-WAIM 2020, LNCS 12318, pp. 70–84, 2020.
https://doi.org/10.1007/978-3-030-60290-1_6

severity of a patient's condition to assist clinical diagnosis and treatment. In particular, in some emergency and harsh situations, such as earthquakes, emergency medical events, and hurricanes. There is a severe shortage of medical personnel and medical equipment. Under such circumstances, some patients may miss the best opportunity for treatment because they cannot predict the patient's condition in a timely and accurate manner.

Moreover, some patients may miss out on rescue opportunities and even lose their lives. Besides, in emergency medical events, medical equipment often cannot be put in place in one step, and many patients may not be monitored by professional equipment. Usually, physiological data can be used to determine whether a patient is at risk for decompensation before the patient's condition worsens [1]. The current situation of the patient can be obtained through a method calculation based on clinical monitoring data, and intelligently assisted diagnosis and treatment in saving more lives. Therefore, in emergency and harsh situations, how to use artificial intelligence technology to combine with primary medical data in the past to determine the severity of a patient's condition to assist clinical diagnosis and treatment has attracted significant attention from researchers.

In the past applied research on clinical data, most of the study focused on the application of electronic medical records. The directions involved are probably the prediction of mortality, the length of hospitalization, and the triage of patients. There are a large number of early studies using neural networks to predict the length of stay of hospitalized patients [2, 3]. Recently, it was shown that using 13 frequent clinical measurements based on machine learning to classify diagnoses in a pediatric intensive care unit (PICU) [4]. Besides, novel neural structures perform well in predicting inpatient mortality and diagnosing routine Electronic Health Record (EHR) data [5]. However, few studies have focused on monitoring data to predict physiological decompensation, that is, the rapid deterioration of the patient's condition.

In emergency situations, many are in danger, and some even lose their lives. In the Haiti earthquake on January 12, 2010, the official government statistics of the dead and injured totaled 316,000 [6]. With the outbreak of COVID-19, as of May 14, 2020, over 4.33 million confirmed cases were reported all over the world. Over 295 thousand of them were dead [7]. The healthcare systems of some countries have been pushed to the brink. In emergencies, Therefore, the prediction of physiological decompensation is a significant task.

On the one hand, the prediction of physiological decompensation can help doctors to make a decision. On the other hand, the prediction of physical decompensation can relieve the pressure on the medical staff. Moreover, the prophecy of physiological decompensation can give early warning for critical patients under the condition of insufficient medical staff and medical equipment so that timely diagnosis and rescue measures can be taken for essential patients to save more lives.

In this paper, we propose a method for predicting decompensation for emergency medical and decision-making under emergency and harsh situations. The method includes components such as patient information collection, data selection, data processing, and decompensation prediction. We strive to reduce false early warnings of physiological decompensation due to data noise. Also, in the selection of data, we try to choose standard physiological variables that can be monitored without the complicated manual and bulky equipment. Finally, the Multiparameter Intelligent Monitoring in Intensive Care III (MIMIC-III) dataset was selected to verify the effectiveness of the method. Consequently, our main contributions in this paper can be summarized as follows:

(1) We propose a novel method for decompensation prediction in emergency and harsh situations. The method can alert patients whose status is about to worsen based on fundamental physiological values.
(2) We tried a series of machine learning models to predict physiological decompensation. The Bi-LSTM-attention model can pass information across multiple time steps to improve decompensation prediction based on changes before and after physiological values.
(3) We try to reduce the essential physiological variables as much as possible for prediction to detect patients whose condition deteriorates rapidly in emergency and harsh situations. The experimental using MIMIC-III data results show that the Bi-LSTM-attention method, combined with eleven essential physiological variables, can be used to predict the decompensation of severe patients. The AUC-ROC can reach 0.8509. Furthermore, these eleven physiological variables can be easily monitored without the need for complicated manual and massive, costly instruments, which meet the real requirements under emergency and harsh situations.

The remaining part of the paper is organized as follows. In Sect. 2, we review prior works most related to ours. In Sect. 3, we introduced the methods and models we chose. Then we demonstrate the experiments based on a real-world database. Section 5 shows the results obtained. Finally, we give discussion and conclusions.

2 Related Work

There are currently many studies on intelligent assisted medical decision-making. In previous research, six can be used to support clinical care by applying clinical data: high-cost patients, readmission, triage, and decompensation (when the patient's condition worsens), adverse events, and treatment optimization for diseases affecting multiple organ systems [1]. We try to emphasize research and methods that are relevant to us.

For the prediction of decompensation, there has been researched in this area in the early years. Ghali, JK, et al. have explored and found the potential predisposing factors that lead to cardiac decompensation and subsequent hospital admission for heart failure [8]. Ramachandran studied that overlapping infections with hepatitis E can cause severe decompensation in patients with chronic liver disease [9]. Annalisa et al. proved that obesity is an independent risk factor for clinical decompensation in patients with liver cirrhosis [10].

However, most of these early studies used manual calculations of decompensated early warning scores on smaller data sets, and they were usually aimed at predicting disease. Recent studies have proven that we can use the current electronic medical system to effectively use past clinical data to make comprehensive decompensation predictions for patients (that is, predict patients who are about to deteriorate). In particular, new neural structures perform well in predicting decompensation [11]. Feedforward networks [12] and spatiotemporal convolutional networks [13] have been used to predict decompensation based on the clinical time series. For example, large-scale clinical monitoring data and electronic medical records are used to predict decompensation and length of hospital stay for patients [14]. Long Short-Term Memory (LSTM) is a kind of time recurrent neural network. It is specially designed to solve the long-term dependency problem of general RNN (recurrent neural network) [15]. It is also very suitable for solving our current.

The prediction of medical problems with the help of deep learning is inseparable from the construction of standard data sets [16, 17]. Because the raw data of clinical databases are involved, there are a large number of early studies using databases to construct standard data sets [18, 19]. These data sets are used in all aspects of intelligently assisted medical decision making. For example, RNN is used in the detection of electronic medical records of medical events [20]. Recursive networks combined with an attention for diagnostic prediction in healthcare [21].

However, none of these efforts solve the problem of assisting smart medical decision-making through decompensation prediction in emergency and harsh situations. Most studies focus on the availability of adequate medical personnel and medical equipment in ordinary life. In the face of unexpected medical and health events, we are working to find a way to reduce the stress of intensive care and save more lives.

3 Methods and Models

In previous studies, most of them focused on predicting decompensation for patients with a single disease under normal conditions (with adequate medical staff and equipment). Moreover, the alarm is usually a false positive due to the noise of the data. So, some information on decompensation is often incorrectly predicted. Therefore, after collecting patient information, it is necessary to reduce data noise and accurately predict patients with worsening conditions. So, we propose a method for decompensation prediction in emergency and harsh situations. The method includes components such as patient information collection, data selection, data processing, and decompensation prediction. Based on this, the Bi-LSTM-attention model is selected for the prediction of physiological decompensation because the model can capture long-distance dependencies and is suitable for modeling time series.

3.1 Methods

In this section, we introduce the method for decompensation in emergency and harsh situations, and briefly introduce our component settings. As shown in Fig. 1, we show a conceptual diagram of our approach. Under unpredictable earthquakes and difficult-to-control infectious diseases, the number of medical staff and medical equipment is in short supply. Patients may lose their lives because they cannot be treated on time. Therefore, a large number of existing patients need to identify who currently needs to be processed by a doctor. We propose a method to predict decompensation (the patient's condition worsens). In our method, we need to collect patient information through cooperation with hospitals or other means. These patients may be children or adults. Patients of different ages should have different decompensation processes. Our method attempts to use adults as the research object to predict patients who are about to deteriorate.

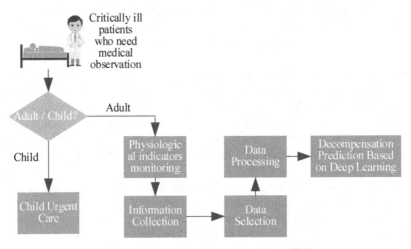

Fig. 1. The method for decompensation prediction.

To make our method suitable for emergency and harsh environments, we should minimize the use of patient information in the process of decompensation prediction. Each less information means less use of a device, a test, or a doctor. The decompensation method is divided into four components. The first step is the patient information collection, the second step is data selection, the third step is data processing, and the fourth step is decompensation prediction. Each step is divided into more detailed sub-processes, and then specific processing operations are selected according to each sub-process. Secondly, according to our goal is that to apply the method to the condition in emergency and harsh and assist intelligent decision-making, we set filtering conditions in the data selection step.

Information Collection. The collection of patient information is the first and most essential step in the method. We want to use the previous medical data to assist intelligent diagnosis and treatment, and we need to collect and select medical information from former patients. At present, most hospitals in the world have adopted electronic systems to record patient information, including diagnosis, medication, electronic medical records, and patient monitoring data in the hospital. These electronic records may appear in the form of text or the kind of tables. With the development and treatment of patients in the hospital period, it has a particular auxiliary medical application value. However, in our method application, these data are certainly not all inputs. Therefore, the first step in our method is to target the source of data (tables or text, etc.) that we need in the electronic system. After locking the required forms and writing in the electronic system, we enter the second component of the method.

Data Selection. Data selection is the second component in the method and the key to the method's suitability for emergency and harsh situations. There is a large amount of data in the records of the hospital electronic system. In the first component, we selected the required data source. However, the data in these data sources are many and complicated. For example, a spreadsheet record may record a series of measurements during the entire hospitalization of a patient from the emergency department. There may be hundreds of monitoring records. About ten essential physiological monitoring records are selected as input data for the final decompensation prediction. These data should have the following characteristics. First, it should be detectable without the need for sufficient professional medical staff. That is because, in some emergencies (earthquakes or medical emergencies, etc.), medical staff is often insufficient. Secondly, it should be able to be monitored without the aid of extremely complex instruments. That is because, in the event of a sudden large-scale health event, professional equipment often cannot meet the demand in a short time.

Data Processing. Data Processing. Data processing is the third component in the method and the cornerstone of final decompensation prediction. In the previous step, we selected essential physiological value monitoring records as input data for the final decompensation prediction. However, previous studies have shown that the data directly extracted from the database will have much noise. So, the probability of real decompensation prediction is about 50% [1]. That means that the direct use of this data often leads to false early warnings of decompensation.

On the one hand, the information is noisy in the original record. For example, the unit of the data is incorrect, or the physiological value is abnormally high or low due to the error; on the other hand, a patient may be admitted to the hospital multiple times due to different diseases, or even transferred to the hospital during the change of the condition. In our method, we propose data processing components to make the data more standardized for our practice. First, because children and adults have different reference ranges for physiological values, we select patients older than 18 in the selection process. Second, we proposed an independent mechanism for multiple inpatient records for the same patient and created different examples of inpatients to avoid inaccurate predictions of compensation due to admission transfers effectively. Then, we clean the data. These operations may include correction of error units, handling of outliers outside the reference range, and so on. Finally, we get a set of standard experimental data for each physiological value.

Decompensation Prediction. Decompensation prediction is the last component in the method and the final decisive component to support intelligent medical decisions. In early studies, patients with abnormal physiological functions would trigger alerts. These warnings were implemented through old warning scores, such as the Modified Early Warning Score (MEWS) [22], the VitalPAC Early Warning Score (ViEWS) [23], and the National Early Warning Score (NEWS) [24]. But these ratings are often manual. The alert score summarizes patient status through an overall score and a trigger summary based on abnormally low values. In an emergency and harsh environment, medical staff and medical equipment are seriously inadequate. Detecting patients who are rapidly deteriorating can reduce the pressure on medical care, and timely warning of decompensation information can enable more patients to be treated in time and save more lives. In our decompensation prediction component, we implement it with a combination of machine learning methods. In the process of predicting decompensation, we have inherited previous research. We describe the decompensation benchmark task as a binary classification problem, where the target label indicates whether the patient died within the next 24 h. We use the area under the receiver operator characteristic curve (AUC-ROC) and area under the precision-recall curve (AUC-PR) as evaluation indicators, which are the two most commonly used indicators in clinical prediction tasks.

3.2   Models

In this section, we used bidirectional LSTM and attention mechanisms to predict the decompensation in Fig. 2. Due to its unique design structure, it is suitable for processing and predicting important events with very long intervals and delays in time series. In our method, the data are monitored values with timestamps. Based on the method, the original monitoring data passes through a series of preprocessing. We discretize the time series into equal durations. The final input sequence is x_t with length T. We will briefly describe the theoretical basis of our method below.

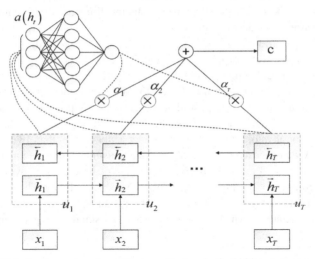

Fig. 2. Bi-LSTM-attention network architecture. Vectors in the hidden state sequence h_t are fed into the learnable function $a(h_t)$ to produce a probability vector α. The vector c is computed as a weighted of h_t, with weighting given by α.

Bi-LSTM. Although a unidirectional LSTM can capture long-term dependency problems, the LSTM can only predict the output of the next moment based on the timing information of the previous moment. However, according to the characteristics of patient physiological monitoring values, the current physiological values may be related to the previous and upcoming ones. Therefore, the output at the present moment is related to not only the former state but also the future state. So, we add-ed a bidirectional LSTM layer. There are two parallel LSTM layers: forward LSTM layer and backward LSTM layer. In this way, the model can learn and store values monitored by specific variables at earlier time steps, such as storing the maximum PH or the minimum blood glucose value.

$$f_t = \sigma\left(W_f\left[h_{t-1}, x_t\right] + b_f\right) \tag{1}$$

$$i_t = \sigma\left(W_i\left[h_{t-1}, x_t\right] + b_i\right) \tag{2}$$

$$o_t = \sigma\left(W_o\left[h_{t-1}, x_t\right] + b_o\right) \tag{3}$$

$$\hat{C}_t = tanh\left(W_C\left[h_{t-1}, x_t\right] + b_C\right) \tag{4}$$

$$C_t = f_t * C_{t-1} + i_t * \hat{C}_t \tag{5}$$

$$h_t = o_t * tanh(C_t) \tag{6}$$

$$\widehat{D_T} = \sigma\left(w^{(D)}h_T + b^D\right) \tag{7}$$

$$p_t = L([u_t; c_t], p_{t-1}) \tag{8}$$

$$q_t = L\left(\left[\overleftarrow{u_t}; \overleftarrow{c_t}\right], q_{t-1}\right) \tag{9}$$

$$u_t = \left[p_t^{(k)}; \overleftarrow{q_t^{(k)}}\right] \tag{10}$$

$$H_t = L(u_t, H_{t-1}) \tag{11}$$

The σ (sigmoid) and tanh functions are applied element-wise. The W matrices and b vectors are the trainable parameters of the LSTM. where L stands for LSTM.

Attention. The attention mechanism is a solution to the problem that mimics human attention and aims to quickly screen out high-value information from a large amount of data. The attention mechanism can solve the problem that it is difficult to obtain a final reasonable representation when the LSTM model input sequence is long. In this article, we also added the attention mechanism and adopted the attention idea of adding the activation function and summing it. The idea is to add a *tanh* activation function after the weight calculation and add it after calculating the weight.

Adam. Adam is a first-order optimization algorithm that can replace the traditional stochastic gradient descent (SGD) process [25]. It can iteratively update neural network weights based on training data.

$$m_t = \beta_1 m_{t-1} + (1 - \beta_1)g_t \tag{12}$$

$$v_t = \beta_2 v_{t-1} + (1 - \beta_2)g_t^2 \tag{13}$$

$$\hat{m}_t = \frac{m_t}{1 - \beta_1^t} \tag{14}$$

$$\hat{v}_t = \frac{v_t}{1 - \beta_2^t} \tag{15}$$

$$W_{t+1} = W_t - \frac{\eta}{\sqrt{\hat{v}_t} + \epsilon} \hat{m}_t \tag{16}$$

Among them, A and B are first-order momentum terms and second-order momentum terms, respectively.

Loss Function. The *loss* functions we use to train these models are:

$$.\mathcal{L}_t = CE\left(D_T, \widehat{D_T}\right) \tag{17}$$

where $CE(y, \hat{y})$ is the binary cross-entropy defined over the C class.

$$CE(y, \hat{y}) = -\left(y \cdot \log(\hat{y}) + (1 - y) \cdot log\left(1 - \hat{y}\right)\right) \tag{18}$$

4 Experiments

In this section, we try to implement our method. First, we introduced the data processing process in the selected database and decompensation method. Then we added our basic ideas and parameter settings in the process of predicting decompensation.

Dataset. To implement our method, we first need to get the data. Because patient information is often kept secret in hospitals, it is not easy to manually collect it. Therefore, we chose the MIMIC-III database-a real-world database [26]. It is the only publicly available critical care database and needs to finish online courses and tests to get access. MIMIC-III contains data associated with 53,423 distinct hospital admissions for adult patients admitted to critical care units between 2001 and 2012. It covers 38,597 distinct adult patients and 49,785 hospital admissions. Moreover, it contains data for 7870 neonates admitted between 2001 and 2008. Given the data richness and authenticity of MIMIC-III, we chose it as our data source for the research.

Information Collection. The MIMIC-III database contains all the information from the patient's emergency department to the discharge. This information is recorded in 26 tables, including physiological measurements, medical records, doctor's orders, discharge summary, disease diagnosis, medication time, etc. However, in our decompensation prediction method, we do not need to collect all the information of patients. That is because, to make our method applicable to emergency and harsh situations, our goal is to select physiological variables that are easy to monitor and use these variables to predict decompensation to assist intelligent medical decision-making. Therefore, we have locked the following tables containing this information in MIMIC-III database. We extracted data for the tables as follows: ADMISSIONS (every unique hospitalization for each patient); PATIENTS (every unique patient); ICUSTAYS (every unique Intensive Care Unit (ICU) stay); D_ICD_DIAGNOSES (dictionary of International Statistical Classification of Diseases and Related Health Problems codes relating to diagnoses); DIAGNOSES_ICD (hospital assigned diagnoses, using the International Statistical Classification of Diseases and Related Health Problems system); CHARTEVENTS (all charted observations for patients); LABEVENTS (laboratory measurements for patients both within the hospital and in outpatient clinics); and OUTPUTEVENTS (output information for patients while in the ICU).

Data Selection. The MIMIC-III database contains monitoring records of more than 40 physiological variables. However, in emergencies (such as earthquakes, infectious diseases), medical equipment is often in short supply. We can't provide all the equipment to every patient in need in a short time. Therefore, we should minimize the types of physiological variables and try to select physiological indicators that can be easily monitored. Based on this, we extracted the physiological variables record from these tables. We decided 11 basics physiological variables. These 11 physiological variables can be easily monitored without the need for complicated manual and massive, costly instruments. The selected physiological variables include the Glasgow coma scale total, PH, Weight, Temperature, Systolic blood pressure, Respiratory rate, Mean blood pressure, Height, Heart Rate, Glucose, and Diastolic blood pressure.

Data Processing. First, due to physiological differences between children and adults, we select the ICU stays where the patients are over 18 years at the time of ICU admission. That is because the proportion of adults in ICU patients is much higher than that of children, and the normal range of physiological values for adults and children is different. Second, for each patient, we only use their single admission without complex and transferred information. That is because each patient may have multiple hospitalization records, and some may cause discontinuity of measurement data during the transfer of the ward. Therefore, we sorted the data and targeted them at their single admission. It was done to prevent possible information interference in the analysis.

To get the final experimental data, we further cleaned the data, including correction and deletion. The data extracted from MIMIC-III database has lots of erroneous entries, including noise, missing values, outlier low, outlier high, and measurement unit error. Our goal is to eliminate as much as possible to avoid false early warning of final physiological decompensation. For missing values, we determine alternative operations for missing values based on different situations (such as calculating the median of the two previous and subsequent measurements within the most recent time of the missing value) or leaving the missing value blank. For outliers, we will delete or correct them. For errors in measurement units, we perform corrective actions. That yields 3,431,000 instances. We briefly describe the data acquisition process in Fig. 3.

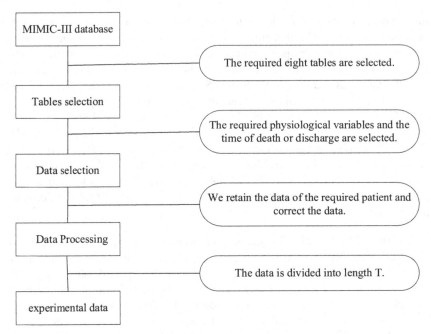

Fig. 3. Experimental data acquisition process using MIMIC-III database as an example.

Decompensation. We have combined our method with the two LSTM-based approaches (LSTM and Bi-LSTM-attention) from the previous chapters. That is because of the nature of the continuous monitoring time series of clinical data, the current state of an instance is closely related to its pre- and post-states and LSTM can learn long-term dependence information. Besides, we also selected a simple baseline model—a multi-nominal logistic regression (LR) model. The goal of our decompensation prediction is to warn patients whether their condition worsens or even die within the next 24 h. We use the data of the same 20% patients of the predefined training set as validation data and train the models on the remaining 80%. When discretizing the data, we set the length of the regular interval to one hour. For the above model, during the development process, we found that applying dropout to embedding can improve the performance of data sets. To prevent overfitting, we used a dropout rate of 30%, and $\beta 1 = 0.9$. We used Adam optimizer with a learning rate of 0.001 and fixed the hyperparameters (i.e., dropout values, learning rate) on the validation set.

5   Results

We demonstrate the method using MIMIC-III data and use the bootstrap method to estimate the confidence interval of the score. The bootstrap method has been used to estimate the standard deviation of the evaluation method, calculate the statistical differences between different models, and report the 95% bootstrap confidence interval of the model. To estimate the 95% confidence interval, we resampled the test set 1000 times.

Calculate the scores of the resampled set; and use 2.5% and 97.5% of these scores as our confidence interval estimates.

The results of the decompensation prediction task are reported in Fig. 4 and Table 1 respectively. Figure 4 is a visualization of the average value of one of the indicators (AUC-ROC). Table 1 is a table listing the result values of all models and the 95% confidence interval obtained by the bootstrap test set.

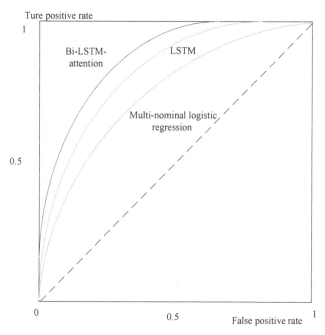

Fig. 4. Schematic diagram of the ROC curve and AUC area results under the three models, the blue represents multi-nominal logistic regression, the yellow represents LSTM, and the red represents Bi-LSTM-attention (Online).

Table 1. Experimental results under different models

Model	AUC-ROC	AUC-PR
LR	0.8336 (0.8303,0.8370)	0.1856 (0.1802,0.1911)
LSTM	0.8417 (0.8395,0.8439)	0.1952 (0.1917,0.1988)
Bi-LSTM-attention	0.8509 (0.8486,0.8531)	0.2078 (0.2052,0.2104)

Experimental results show that these 11 physiological variables can be easily monitored without the need for complicated manual and massive, costly instruments, which meet the real requirements under emergency and harsh situations. Therefore, our method is suitable for saving patients by alerting patients who are about to worsen in the event of a medical emergency.

6 Discussion

We describe a method for decompensation prediction in emergency and harsh situations. Our method can select the most basic physiological variables for clinical monitoring data. These variables are easy to detect and avoid complicated labor. Therefore, in an emergency, early warning of dangerous patients can alleviate the pressure of medical care and save more lives. In the process of implementing the method, we chose a model that can rely on the information before and after learning clinical monitoring data.

However, in our current approach, it is purely data-driven and does not contain human knowledge. In clinical practice, each physiological variable has its normal range, and experts for specific diseases have rich practical experience. Besides, to avoid irregular data, we prevent a small number of children, which limits the scope of our method.

7 Conclusions

In this article, we used large-scale data, explored how to save more lives in emergencies and harsh conditions, and gave our method. With the abnormal shortage of medical staff and medical facilities, our method for predicting physical decompensation is sufficient to alert patients who are at risk of dying within the next 24 h, thereby providing intelligent decision support and saving more lives. With the richness and authenticity of the data, our results are credible. Although specific tasks inspire our method, it has the potential to be generalized to other clinical duties. For example, the prediction of physiological decompensation can be migrated to intelligent diagnosis, which can relieve the pressure of medical care. In future work, on the one hand, the data of pediatric patients can be incorporated into our method, so that the method has a broader scope of application; on the other hand, we will consider integrating human knowledge to get more accurate decompensation result.

Acknowledgement. This work was supported by the National Natural Science Foundation of China (NSFC) under Grant 61373165, 61672377. The work described in this paper is partially supported by Shenzhen Science and Technology Foundation (JCYJ20170816093943197).

References

1. Bates, D.W., Saria, S., Ohno-Machado, L., Shah, A., Escobar, G.: Big data in health care: using analytics to identify and manage high-risk and high-cost patients. Health Aff. 33(7), 1123–1131 (2014)
2. Miwa, M., Sasaki, Y.: Modeling joint entity and relation extraction with table representation. In: Proceedings of the 2014 Conference on Empirical Methods in Natural Language Processing (EMNLP), pp. 1858–1869 (2014)
3. Vaswani, A., Shazeer, N., Parmar, N., Uszkoreit, J,. Jones, L.: Attention is all you need. In: Advances in Neural Information Processing Systems, pp. 5998–6008 (2017)
4. Lipton, Z.C., Kale, D.C., Elkan, C., Wetzel, R.: Learning to Diagnose with LSTM Recurrent Neural Networks, pp. 1–18 (2015)

5. Lample, G., Ballesteros, M., Subramanian, S., Kawakami, K., Dyer, C.: Neural architectures for named entity recognition. In: Proceedings of the 2016 Conference of the North American Chapter of the Association for Computational Linguistics: Human Language Technologies, pp. 260–270 (2016)
6. Daniell, J.E., Khazai, B., Wenzel, F.: Uncovering the 2010 Haiti earthquake death toll. Nat. Hazards Earth Syst. Sci. Discuss. **1**, 1913–1942 (2013).https://doi.org/10.5194/nhessd-1-1913-2013
7. COVID-19 Dashboard by the Center for Systems Science and Engineering (CSSE) at Johns Hopkins University (JHU). https://coronavirus.jhu.edu/map.html. Accessed 14 May 2020
8. Ghali, J.K.: Precipitating factors leading to decompensation of heart failure. Traits among urban blacks. Arch. Int. Med. 1988, **148**(9) (2013)
9. Ramachandran, J.: Hepatitis E superinfection produces severe decompensation in patients with chronic liver disease. J. Gastroenterol. Hepatol. **19**(2), 134–138 (2004)
10. Berzigotti, A., Garcia-Tsao, G., Bosch, J., Grace, N.D.: Obesity is an independent risk factor for clinical decompensation in patients with cirrhosis. Hepatology **54**(2), 555–561 (2011)
11. Harutyunyan, H., Khachatrian, H., Kale, D.C., Steeg, G.V.: Multitask learning and benchmarking with clinical time series data. Scientific Data (2017)
12. Lasko, T.A., Denny, J.C., Levy, M.A.: Computational phenotype discovery using unsupervised feature learning over noisy, sparse, and irregular clinical data. PLoS ONE **8**, e66341 (2013)
13. Razavian, N., Marcus, J. Sontag, D.: Multi-task prediction of disease onsets from longitudinal lab tests. In: 1st Machine Learning for Healthcare Conference (2016)
14. Xu, Y., Biswal, S., Deshpande, S.R., Maher, K.O., Sun, J.: Raim: recurrent attentive and intensive model of multimodal patient monitoring data. In: Proceedings of the 24th ACM SIGKDD International Conference on Knowledge Discovery & Data Mining, pp. 2565–2573 (2018)
15. Hochreiter, S., Schmidhuber, J.: Long short-term memory. Neural Comput. **9**, 1735–1780 (1997)
16. Rao, G., Huang, W., Feng, Z., Cong, Q.: LSTM with sentence representations for documentlevel sentiment classification. Neurocomputing **308**, 49–57 (2018). https://doi.org/10.1016/j.neucom
17. Rao, G., Zhang, Y., Zhang, L., Cong, Q., Feng, Z.: MGL-CNN: a hierarchical posts representations model for identifying depressed individuals in online forums. IEEE Access. **8**, 32395–32403 (2020)
18. Purushotham, S., Meng, C., Che, Z., Liu, Y.: Benchmarking deep learning models on large healthcare datasets. J. Biomed. Inform. **83**, 112–134 (2018)
19. Balbino, A.: Benchmarking with administrative or clinical databases: serious pitfalls. BMJ 7602 (2015)
20. Jagannatha, A.N., Yu, H.: Bidirectional RNN for medical event detection in electronic health records. In: Proceedings of the Conference. Association for Computational Linguistics. North American Chapter. Meeting (2016)
21. Feng, M., et al.: Diagnosis prediction in healthcare via attention-based bidirectional recurrent neural networks. In: Proceedings of the 23rd ACM SIGKDD International Conference on Knowledge Discovery and Data Mining, pp. 1903–1911. ACM (2017)
22. Subbe, C., Kruger, M., Rutherford, P., Gemmel, L.: Validation of a modified early warning score in medical admissions. QJM **94**, 521–526 (2001)
23. Prytherch, D.R., Smith, G.B., Schmidt, P.E., Featherstone, P.I.: Views—towards a national early warning score for detecting adult inpatient deterioration. Resuscitation **81**, 932–937 (2010)
24. Williams, B.: National Early Warning Score (News): Standardizing the Assessment of Acute-Illness Severity in the NHS. The Royal College of Physicians, London (2012)

25. Kingma, D., Ba, J.: Adam: a method for stochastic optimization. arXiv preprint arXiv:1412. 6980 (2014)
26. Johnson, A.E.W., Pollard, T.J., Shen, L., Lehman, L.H., Feng, M., Ghassemi, M., Moody, B., Szolovits, P., Celi, L.A., Mark, R.G.: MIMIC-III, a freely accessible critical care database. Sci. data **3**, 160035 (2016)

Improved Brain Segmentation Using Pixel Separation and Additional Segmentation Features

Afifa Khaled[1] ⓘ, Chung-Ming Own[1] ⓘ, Wenyuan Tao[1]([✉]) ⓘ,
and Taher Ahmed Ghaleb[2] ⓘ

[1] College of Intelligence and Computing, Tianjin University, Tianjin, China
{afifakhaied,chungming.own,taowenyuan}@tju.edu.cn
[2] College of Computing, Queen University, Kingston, Canada
taher.ghaleb@queensu.ca

Abstract. Brain segmentation is key to brain structure evaluation for disease diagnosis and treatment. Much research has been invested to study brain segmentation. However, prior research has not considered separating actual brain pixels from the background of brain images. Not performing such separation may (a) distort brain segmentation models and (b) introduce overhead to the modeling performance. In this paper, we improve the performance of brain segmentation using $3D$, fully Convolutional Neural Network (CNN) models. We use (i) infant and adult datasets, (ii) a multi-instance loss method to separate actual brain pixels from the background and (iii) Gabor filter banks and K-means clustering to provide additional segmentation features. Our model obtains dice coefficients of 87.4%–94.1% (i.e., an improvement of up to 11% to the results of five state-of-the-art models). Unlike prior studies, we consult experts in medical imaging to evaluate our segmentation results. We observe that our results are fairly close to the manual reference. Moreover, we observe that our model is $1.2x$–$2.6x$ faster than prior models. We conclude that our model is more efficient and accurate in practice for both infant and adult brain segmentation.

Keywords: Brain segmentation · Multi-instance loss (MIL) · Gabor filter banks · Convolutional Neural Network (CNN)

1 Introduction

Brain tissues grow rapidly at early stages of human's life. Over the past two decades, brain segmentation has relied on manual segmentation, which is extremely expensive and time consuming [1]. For example, 15–20 images of infant's brain may require 9–11 h to segment. Obtaining accurate tissue segmentation of infant's brain into white matter (WM), gray matter (GM) and cerebrospinal fluid (CSF) is important to (a) measure abnormal early brain development, (b) monitor their progression and (c) evaluate treatment outcomes [2].

© Springer Nature Switzerland AG 2020
X. Wang et al. (Eds.): APWeb-WAIM 2020, LNCS 12318, pp. 85–100, 2020.
https://doi.org/10.1007/978-3-030-60290-1_7

However, due to low contrast and unclear boundaries between WM and GM, it could be difficult to obtain accurate segmentation. Moreover, different experts may produce different segmentation results.

Much research has been invested to perform brain segmentation using automated models, including atlas-based, statistical, and deep learning models. Deep learning models, in particular Convolutional Neural Networks ($CNNs$), have recently been used to perform automated segmentation of infant brain [5]. Previous models have achieved acceptable segmentation performance. However, prior studies have not considered separating actual brain pixels from the background of brain images. Not performing such separation may (a) distort brain segmentation models and (b) introduce overhead to the modeling performance. Therefore, it is important to develop robust models to segment brain regions to improve pathology detection and diseases diagnosis.

In this paper, we improve the performance of brain segmentation using fully CNN models. To this end, we employ (i) a multi-instance loss method to separate actual brain pixels from background and (ii) Gabor filter banks and K-means clustering to provide additional segmentation information to support the machine-learned features. To overcame the lack of medical imaging applications [6], we use full images as input to our model and apply max pooling and mean pooling to process the data. To evaluate our model, we use both infant and adult datasets and measure the performance of our model using dice coefficients. Unlike prior studies, our results are evaluated by the MICCAI iSEG organizers (experts in medical imaging) [4]. Our model obtain dice coefficients ranging between 87.4% and 94.1% (i.e., an improvement of up to 11% to the results obtained by five state-of-the-art models). Moreover, our model is $1.2x$–$2.6x$ faster than prior models. Such results indicate that our model is more efficient and accurate in practice for both infant and adult brain segmentation.

The rest of this paper is organized as follows. Section 2 presents prior studies related to brain segmentation. Section 3 presents the methodologies used in our paper. Section 4 presents our experimental results. Section 5 discusses threats to the validity of our results. Finally, Sect. 6 concludes the conclusion and discusses directions for future work.

2   Related Work

This section presents prior studies related to brain segmentation. The main objective of a brain segmentation model is to solve the problem of having low contrast and unclear boundaries between the white matter and the gray matter in brain images. Some prior models for brain segmentation targeted infantile stages [10] (e.g., using multiple modalities [11]), whereas some other targeted early adult (<12 months). Images used by prior models are either $T1$, or $T2$ MRI images.

Dolz et al. [6] proposed $3D$ and fully CNN for subcortical brain structure segmentation. Later on, Bao and Chung [2] have improved the model proposed by Dolz et al. by using a multi-scale structured CNN with label consistency.

Badrinarayanan et al. [7] have also proposed $CNNs$ models with the use of residual connections to segment white matter hyperintensity from $T1$ and flair images. Their models outperformed previous models with an overall dice coefficients of 0.75% on $H95$ and 27.26% on an average surface distance. Fechter et al. [8] also used fully $CNNs$ for brain segmentation. Using five datasets, they obtained dice coefficient rangin between 0.82 and 0.91 for each dataset. Visser et al. [1] proposed CNN models for brain segmentation using a multimodal method and subcortical segmentation. de Brebisson and Montana [9] proposed a random walker approach driven by a $3D$ fully CNN to different tissue classes. Their model was able to segment the esophagus using CT images.

Despite the research invested on brain segmentation, we observe that previous models were trained using images that contain actual brain pixels intermixed with the image background. Therefore, in our work, we propose to separate brain pixels from background to improve the overall performance of brain segmentation. Then, we use fully CNN model and supply it with additional machine-learned features. In summary, our proposed method:

- speeds up model training;
- produces more accurate segmentation results;
- improves information and gradients flow throughout the entire network; and
- reduces the risk of overfitting.

Furthermore, what distinguishes our work from prior work is that our results are evaluated by the MICCAI iSEG organizers.

3 Methodology

This section presents the methods that we use to process brain images, extract addition features, and construct brain segmentation models. Figure 1 shows an overview of our proposed network.

3.1 The Proposed CNN Model

In our proposed model, we use two paths where each path has six groups of layers, as follows:

- **The 1st group of layers:** consists of two layers, each of which containing 90 filters. Each filter in a layer is applied to the input images. The outcome of this process is known as a feature map. Feature maps are fed into the second group of layers.
- **The 2nd group of layers:** consists of two layers, each of which contains 120 filters. Our kernel size is $3 \times 3 \times 3$, which allows the network to learn more complex features with a reduced risk of overfitting. Feature maps from the second convolutional layers were up-sampled through a deconvolution layer.
- **The 3rd group of layers:** consists of two convolutional layers, each with 120 filters.

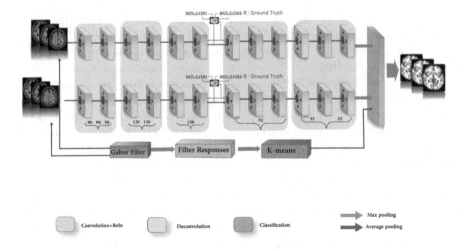

Fig. 1. The proposed fully CNN on multi-instance loss and Gabor filter bank

- **The 4th and 5th groups of layers:** consists of deconvolution layers. Since we employ four classes (i.e., WM, GM, CSF, and background), the last deconvolution layer has four filters (i.e., one filer per class). Convolution layers are used after each deconvolution operation.
- The last layer performs classification with **softmax** units.

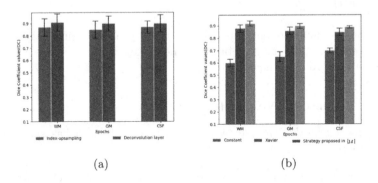

Fig. 2. (a) Two upsampling strategies, (b) Three initialization strategies.

Overfitting is a major problem in deep neural networks. Jonathan et al. [24] reported that deconvolution layers perform upsampling by learning to deconvolve the input feature map. Badrinarayanan et al. [7] reported that index-upsampling uses max pooling indices to upsample feature maps (without learning) and convolves with a bank of trainable filters. We experiment both upsampling strategies using our data and observe, in Fig. 2 (a), that deconvolution layer performs better than index-upsampling. Therefore, we choose to use the deconvolution layer to upsample the input feature map to higher spatial space. After each convolution layer, we use PReLU [13] as an activation function, which (a) introduces a smaller number of extra parameters (equal to the number of channels) and (b) prevents overfitting.

As is the case with deep models, the weights were initialized by random weights. He et al. [14] included *Restricted Boltzmann* machines and showed that the equivalence between RBM's and infinite directed nets with tied weights suggests an efficient learning algorithm for multi-layer networks in which the weights are not tied. Besides, He et al. [14] reported that the deep models can have difficulties to converge and proposed a weights initialization strategy to improve the accuracy of deep neural networks. Figure 2 (b) shows that the initialization strategy proposed by He et al. performs better than two other strategies. Therefore, in our model, we use the initialization strategy proposed by He et al., which employs variant responses in each layer.

A careful selection of a learning rate value can lead to better performance results. However, increasing learning rate makes model training slower due to local optimizations used to update the parameters. To this end, we experiment different learning rates to investigate what suits our data and topology. We start with a learning rate that is taken from a group of comparable models. First, we use multiple runs by changing the learning rate value by alternating factors of 3 or 10 (i.e., 0.01, 0.003, 0.001, 0.0003, and so on). When obtain an acceptable estimate of the sweet spot, where the final digit is tweaked to reach an optimum value. Second, we increase the initial learning rate by a factor of 10 until the model fails to converge to an optimum value. Similarly, we perform experiments to identify the lowest number of epochs needed to train our model. Finally, we initially set the learning rate to 0.01 and then reduce it by a factor of 10 after every 10 epochs.

Dropout and normalization techniques are also used to reduce overfitting in a neural network models and other gradient-related problems [14]. During forward propagation in neural network models, activations are passed from one layer to another. Such activations may not fit a single distribution. In addition, in model training, each layer has to learn a new distribution every time, which slows down the training process (i.e., internal covariate shift). Hence, fixing the distribution of layer inputs eliminates the internal covariate shift and offers faster and better model training. Therefore, in our model, we compute batch mean and batch variance to normalize the inputs/outputs of each layer. In batch normalization, layer outputs are normalized to a fit a single distribution by maintaining a standard deviation of 1 and a mean of 0. Dropout randomly sets the activations of a certain number of neurons (i.e., dropout rate) to 0. That allows neurons to survive and participate in the learning at the next layer. In our model, we applied batch normalization according to the strategy proposed in [13]. We note that we do not preprocess the $T1$ and $T2$ input images.

3.2 Loss Methods

In our proposed model stochastic gradient descent was used with two loss methods:

In our proposed model, we use stochastic gradient descent with two loss methods: (i) Multi-instance loss at the intermediate stages and (ii) Cross-entropy loss at the final stage.

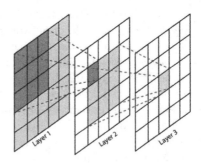

Fig. 3. Pink area marks the receptive field of one pixel in Layer 2. Blue area marks the receptive field of one pixel in Layer 3. (Color figure online)

3.2.1 Multi-Instance Loss

Multi-instance learning is used to describe learning examples in a diverse array. Each learning example contains a bag of instances instead of a single feature vector. Each bag is associated with a label. In the training examples, a single example object has feature vectors (instance). Only one of those feature vectors is responsible for the classification of the object [15]. In traditional supervised learning, the aim was to find a model that predicts the value of a target variable, $y \in \{0, 1\}$, for a given instance, $x \in R^D$). In multi-instance learning, there is a bag of instances instead of a single instance $X = \{x1, ..., x^K\}$ and there is a single label Y associated with the bag, $y^k \in \{0, 1\}$. During the training set, there is no access to the labels as they remain unknown.

Multi-instance loss was inspired by multi-instance learning assumptions. The assumption is that (a) if at least one instance in the bag is positive, then the bag is positive and (b) if all instances in the bag are negative, then the bag is negative. In our model, the third and forth layers can be considered as a multi-instance problem. We use two loss functions: one for positive pixels (i.e., inside the MRI image) and another for negative pixels (i.e., outside the MRI image). The I-loss function (inside the MRI image) is given by the following equation:

$$LOS1 = \sum_{i,j,R_{i,j}=1} \log(1 + \exp(-R_{i,j} * H_{i,j}^m)), \tag{1}$$

where $R_{i,j}$ is the ground truth provided by the dataset organizers. $R_{i,j} = 1$ if pixel (i, j) is inside the MRI image. The novelty here is that pixel (i, j) is in $R_{i,j}$ and such pixel has a receptive field. The receptive field refers to a certain part of an image. If the receptive field has at least one positive pixel (inside MRI image), then (i, j) should be positive. Otherwise, (i, j) is negative. Figure 3 depicts the receptive field where pink area marks the receptive field of one pixel in Layer 2, whereas blue area marks the receptive field of one pixel in Layer 3. A bag-level predictive map $H_{i,j}^m$ represents max pooling from feature maps. Ou-$loss$ functions (outside the MRI image) is given by the following equation:

$$LOS2 = \sum_{i,j,R_{i,j}=-1} \log(1 + \exp(-R_{i,j} * H_{i,j}^a)), \tag{2}$$

where $R_{i,j} = -1$ if pixel (i, j) is outside the MRI image. A bag-level predictive map $H_{i,j}^a$ represents average pooling from feature maps. The total multi-instance loss function is given by the following equation:

$$MIL = LOS1 + \| W \|_2 LOS2, \tag{3}$$

where the MIL ensures a proper differentiation between actual brain pixels and background. $\| W \|_2$ presents the weights in the neural network, which is given by the following equation:

$$\| W \|_2 = \sqrt{W_1^2 + W_2^2 + ... + W_n^2}. \tag{4}$$

3.2.2   Cross-Entropy Loss

Loss functions are crucial in machine learning pipelines. However, knowing which one loss function to use can be challenging. Cross-entropy loss is commonly used as a cost function when training classifiers. Cross-entropy loss is also used to measure the performance of a classification model. In our model, we use the softmax function to convert the output of the classification layer into normalized probability values.

3.3   Gabor Filters

Due to low contrast and lack of clear boundaries between WM and GM, features are not sufficient for accurate segmentation. Gabor filter is a strong tool for the description of textures in images. Figure 4 shows the process of obtaining Gabor filters. Gabor filter can be obtained by convolving the image and applied to our model as human-designed features to improve the segmentation results [23]. The equation is given by:

$$G(x, y; \lambda, \theta, \psi, \sigma, \gamma) = \quad \exp(-((x'^2 + y^2 y'^2)/2\sigma2)) \exp(i(2\pi x'/y + \psi)), \tag{5}$$

where σ is the standard deviation of Gaussian envelope, ψ is the phase shift, λ is the wavelength of the sinusoid, θ is the spatial orientation of the filter and

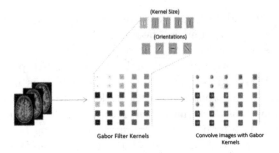

Fig. 4. Gabor filter bank.

γ is the spatial aspect ratio. The terms x' and y' are given by the following equations:

$$x' = xcon(\theta) + ysin(\theta), \tag{6}$$

$$y' = ycos(\theta) - xsin(\theta), \tag{7}$$

where filter sizes are from 0.3 to 1.5 and the wavelength of sinusoid coefficients was 0.8, 1.0, 1.2 and 1.5.

3.4 K-means

K-means is a technique used to split a dataset into k groups. In our model, the filter responses are merged together and apply the K-means clustering algorithm to cluster the pixels with similar features.

4 Experiments

This section presents our experimental design and evaluation.

4.1 Datasets

In our work, we use two different datasets of brain images: the MICCAI iSEG dataset and MRBrains dataset. We describe each of these datasets in the following.

4.1.1 MICCAI iSEG Dataset

The aim of the evaluation framework[1] introduced by the MICCAI iSEG organizers is to compare segmentation models of WM, GM and CSF on $T1$ and $T2$. The MICCAI iSEG dataset contains 10 images, named subject-1 through

---

[1] http://iseg2017.web.unc.edu.

subject-10, subject $T1$: $T1$ -weighted image, subject $T2$: $T2$-weighted, and a 'manual segmentation' label used as a training set. The dataset also contains 13 images, named subject-11 through subject-23, used as a testing set. An example of the MICCAI iSEG dataset ($T1$, $T2$, and manual reference contour) is shown in Fig. 5. The dataset has two different times (i.e., longitudinal relaxation time and transverse relaxation time), which are used to generate $T1$ and $T2$ (Table 1). The dataset has been interpolated, registered, and skull-removed by the MICCAI iSEG organizers. We present the evaluation equations in Subsect. 4.2.

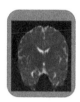

Fig. 5. Example of *MICCAIiSEG* dataset ($T1$, $T2$, manual reference contour)

Table 1. Shows the parameters used to generate $T1$ and $T2$.

Parameters	TR/TE	Flip angle	Resolution
$T1$	1900/4.38 ms	7	$1 \times 1 \times 1$
$T2$	7380/119 ms	150	$1.25 \times 1.25 \times 1.25$

4.1.2   MRBrains Dataset

The MRBrains[2] dataset contains 20 subjects for adults for segmentation of (a) cortical gray matter, (b) basal ganglia, (c) white matter, (d) white matter lesions, (e) peripheral cerebrospinal fluid, (f) lateral ventricles, (g) cerebellum, and (h) brainstem on $T1$, $T2$, and FLAIR. Five (i.e., 2 male and 3 female) subjects are provided to the training set and 15 subjects are provided for the testing set. On the evaluation of the segmentation, these structures merged into gray matter (a–b), white matter (c–d), and cerebrospinal fluid (e–f). The cerebellum and brainstem were excluded from the evaluation.

4.2   Segmentation Evaluation

To better demonstrate the significance of our model, we submitted our results to be evaluated by the MICCAI iSEG organizers [4]. The MICCAI iSEG organizers have used three metrics to evaluate our model.

---

[2] https://mrbrains13.isi.uu.nl/results.php.

4.2.1 Dice Coefficient (DC)

V_{ref} is the reference. V_{auto} is automatic segmentations. The DC is given by the following equation:

$$DC(V_{\text{ref}}, V_{\text{auto}}) = \frac{2|V_{\text{ref}} \cap V_{\text{auto}}|}{|V_{\text{ref}}| + |V_{\text{auto}}|}, \tag{8}$$

DC values are given in this range $[0, 1]$. 1 corresponding to the perfect overlap and 0 indicating the total mismatch.

4.2.2 Modified Hausdorff Distance (MHD)

P_{ref} denote to sets of voxels within the reference and P_{auto} indicate automatic segmentation boundary. MHD is given by the following equation:

$$MHD\left(P_{\text{ref}}, P_{\text{auto}}\right) = \max\left\{ \max_{q \in P_{\text{ref}}} d(q, P_{\text{auto}}), \max_{q \in P_{\text{auto}}} d(q, P_{\text{ref}}) \right\}, \tag{9}$$

$d(q, p_{\text{auto}})$ denote to the point-to-set distance. The equation is given by:

$$d\left(q, p_{\text{auto}}\right) = \min_{p \in P} \|q - p_{\text{auto}}\|, \tag{10}$$

$\|.\|$ indicate the Euclidean distance.

4.2.3 Average Surface Distance (ASD)

The ASD is given by the following equation:

$$ASD\left(P_{\text{ref}}, P_{\text{auto}}\right) = \frac{1}{|(P_{\text{ref}}|} \sum_{P \in P_{\text{ref}}} d(p, P_{\text{auto}}), \tag{11}$$

$|.|$ denote to the cardinality of a set. Due to the limited number of pages, we refer readers to read about the three metrics on [4].

4.2.4 Comparing Our Results with Prior Work

To demonstrate the significance of our model, we compare our obtained results with the results of five state-of-the-art models. We choose these five models because (a) they have been considered as a baseline (i.e., benchmark) to compare segmentation models in the literature to compare brain segmentation models [4,17,19–21] and (b) all implementation details of such models are publicly available.

4.3 Result and Discussion

We train and test our model on two datasets of different ages (i.e., infants and adults). Table 2 presents the results of our model to segment CSF, GM, and

WM using the MICCAI iSEG dataset. Our model obtains a DC values of 94.1% in CSF segmentation. The DC values obtained from segmenting CSF by state-of-the-art models range between 83.5% and 91.5%. The results indicate that our proposed model improves CSF segmentation by 2.6%–10.6%. In addition, our model obtains a DC values of 90.2% and 89.7% in segmenting GM and WM, respectively. The state-of-the-art models, on the other hand, obtain DC values in the ranges of 85.2%–88.6% for GM segmentation and 80.6%–88.7% for WM segmentation. According to the results obtained, we observe that our model achieves a significant improvement of 1.5%–9.6% on segmenting GM and WM. Such results highlight the remarkable efficiency gained by separating actual brain pixels from background and the additional features used in our model.

Table 2. Results for our model provided by $MICCAIiSEG$ organizers [4]. (a) CSF evaluation, (b) WM evaluation, (c) GM evaluation.

(a)				(b)				(c)			
ID	DC	MHD	ASD	ID	DC	MHD	ASD	ID	DC	MHD	ASD
11	0.89	10.8	0.44	11	0.89	7.3	0.44	11	0.89	8.5	0.42
12	0.93	10.2	0.49	12	0.87	6.4	0.49	12	0.87	5.0	0.43
13	0.93	9.5	0.47	13	0.89	7.3	0.47	13	0.89	10.7	0.44
14	0.89	10.9	0.48	14	0.89	5.8	0.48	14	0.88	6.7	0.48
15	0.93	12.2	0.47	15	0.89	6.0	0.47	15	0.89	11.0	0.42
16	0.92	11.8	0.49	16	0.89	8.1	0.49	16	0.89	7.1	0.45
17	0.92	9.00	0.38	17	0.90	10.6	0.38	17	0.90	10.7	0.37
18	0.93	10.8	0.44	18	0.89	7.4	0.44	18	0.89	8.6	0.40
19	0.93	11.1	0.48	19	0.89	8.1	0.48	19	0.89	6.7	0.42
20	0.90	13.2	0.69	20	0.83	8.5	0.69	20	0.83	7.8	0.58
21	0.92	10.8	0.52	21	0.87	8.1	0.52	21	0.87	8.1	0.45
22	0.89	10.1	0.65	22	0.85	8.6	0.65	22	0.85	6.7	0.58
23	0.92	10.6	0.56	23	0.86	7.7	0.56	23	0.86	7.6	0.47
Mean	0.92	10.9	0.2	Mean	0.88	7.69	0.50	Mean	0.89	8.09	0.45
Std	0.01	1.1	0.03	Std	0.02	1.26	0.08	Std	0.01	1.80	0.06

Fig. 6. (a) $T1$, (b) $T2$, (c) manual reference contour, and (d) our model result on the subject used for validation.

Table 3. Segmentation performance in Dice Coefficient (DC) obtained on the $MICCAIiSEG$ dataset. The best performance for each tissue class is highlighted in bold.

Model	Dice Coefficient (DC) Accuracy		
	CSF	GM	WM
[19]	91.2%	86.1%	84.1%
[20]	83.5%	85.2%	86.4%
[17]	90.3%	86.8%	84.3%
[21]	85.5%	87.3%	88.7%
3D, FCN	85.2%	87.6%	80.6%
3D, FCN + MIL	91.5%	88.6%	87.6%
3D, FCN + MIL+G+K	**94.1%**	**90.2%**	**89.7%**

Table 3 compares the results obtained using the `MRBrains` dataset. We observe that our model achieves a DC value of 87.4% on CSF segmentation, 90.6% on GM segmentation, and 90.1% on WM segmentation. Such results are superior to the results obtained using the state-of-the-art models. Therefore, we argue that our mode can perform better on segmenting both infant or adult brain structures.

Figure 6 shows a sample of the results of our model on the subject used for validation set. We observe that our model performs well for brain segmentation, especially for the brain tissues. In Fig. 6, we show an example of our segmentation results and how our result compares to the ground truth. We observe that segmentation results obtained by our model fairly close to the manual reference contour provided by the `MICCAI iSEG` organizers [4]. As expected, much of the improvement by our model is gained at the brain boundary (i.e., between GM and WM). Moreover, we observe that the use of multi-instance loss and Gabor filter banks enabled our model to better handle thin regions than using original brain images. Table 5 presents the execution time (in minutes) for the state-of-art-models and our proposed model. We observe that the execution of our proposed model is faster than the state-of-the-art models. Such results indicate that our model is more efficient and practical to be used in real time systems.

5   Threats to Validity

This section discusses the validity threats of our results and how we address them in our study.

5.1   External Validity

Threats to external validity are related to the generalizability of our results. One could argue that our datasets do not have enough samples. We mitigate such threat by using two datasets that (a) contain both infant and adult brain data and (b) were previously used by prior studies. In addition, we compare our model with five prior models using the same datasets. Furthermore, we use the small-size kernels, deconvolution layer (to upsample the input), PReLU, dropout and normalization methods to reduce the risk of overfitting. Hence, any potential deficiency in the data should affect all the implemented models. Nevertheless, our model obtains higher performance than prior models (Table 4 and Fig. 7).

Table 4. Segmentation performance in Dice Coefficient (DC) obtained on the $MRBRAINS$ datasets. The best performance for each tissue class is highlighted in bold.

Model	Dice Coefficient (DC) Accuracy		
	CSF	GM	WM
[4]	83.9%	88.9%	89.4%
[20]	83.5%	85.4%	88.9%
[21]	82.8%	84.8%	88.5%
[22]	83.7%	84.8%	88.3%
3D, FCN	81.4%	86.1%	85.2%
3D, FCN + MIL	84.3%	87.6%	89.4%
3D, FCN + MIL+G+K	**87.4%**	**90.6%**	**90.1%**

Fig. 7. A sample of our model result on the subject employed for validation. (a) 10 epochs, (b) 20 epochs, (c) 30 epochs.

5.2   Internal Validity

Threats to internal validity are related to experimental errors and bias. Our model is constructed using data extracted from medical images in which contracts might be low. To mitigate such threat, we use the multi-instance loss method to reduce any potential noise in the data by separating actual brain pixels from background. Such method has improved the efficiency and accuracy of our model as well as the accuracy. In addition, our results have been evaluated by the same medical experts (i.e., the organizers of the MICCAI iSEG dataset).

Table 5. Average execution time (in minutes) and standard deviation (SD) in the `MRBrains` dataset

Model	Time (SD)
[19]	15.40 (0.16)
[20]	19.23 (0.20)
[17]	17.6 (0.18)
[21]	18.4 (0.15)
3D, FCNN	7.2 (0.12)
3D, FCNN + MIL	**5.9 (0.11)**
3D, FCNN + MIL+G+K	**5.9 (0.11)**

6   Conclusion and Future Work

In this study, we propose an improved fully Convolutional Neural Network (CNN) model for brain segmentation supported by (i) separating brain pixels from background using the multi-instance loss method and (ii) adding additional features using Gabor filter bank and K-means clustering. Our results have been evaluated by the `MICCAI iSEG` organizers and found to be fairly close to the manual reference. In addition, we compare our model with five baseline state-of-the-art models and observe that our model achieves an improvement of up to 11%. In particular, we obtain dice coefficients that range between 87.4% and 94.1%. Such results indicates that the adoption of the multi-instance loss method and Gabor filter banks has significantly improved segmentation results. We argue that our model is more efficient and accurate in practice for both infant and adult brain segmentation.

Despite the promising results obtained from our proposed model, we believe that further improvements can be achieved in the future. For example, conditional random fields (i.e., statistical modeling methods) can be used to predict sequences in pattern recognition and machine learning. We plan to supply a conditional random field to brain segmentation models to investigate whether it is possible to gain better segmentation performance.

References

1. Visser, E., et al.: Automatic segmentation of the striatum and globus pallidus using mist: multimodal image segmentation tool. NeuroImage **125**, 479–497 (2016)
2. Bao, S., Chung, A.C.: Multi-scale structured CNN with label consistency for brain MR image segmentation. Comput. Methods Biomech. Biomed. Eng. Imaging Vis. **6**(1), 113–117 (2018)
3. Chen, H., Dou, Q., Yu, L., Qin, J., Heng, P.A.: VoxResNet: deep voxelwise residual networks for brain segmentation from 3D MR images. NeuroImage **170**, 446–455 (2018)

4. Wang, L., et al.: Benchmark on automatic 6-month-old infant brain segmentation algorithms: the ISEG-challenge. IEEE Trans. Med. Imaging. **38**(9), 2219–2230 (2019)
5. Bernal, J., et al.: Deep convolutional neural networks for brain image analysis on magnetic resonance imaging. Artif. Intell. Med. **95**, 64–81 (2017)
6. Dolz, J., Desrosiers, C., Ayed, I.B.: 3D fully convolutional networks for subcortical segmentation in MRI: a large-scale study. NeuroImage **170**, 456–470 (2018)
7. Badrinarayanan, V., Kendall, A., Segnet, R.: A deep convolutional encoder-decoder architecture for image segmentation. IEEE Trans. Pattern Anal. Mach. Intell. **39**(12), 2481–2495 (2017)
8. Fechter, T., Adebahr, S., Baltas, D., Ayed, I.B., Desrosiers, C., Dolz, J.: Esophagus segmentation in CT via 3D fully convolutional neural network and random walk. Med. Phys. **44**(12), 6341–6352 (2017)
9. de Brebisson, A., Montana, G.: Deep neural networks for anatomical brain segmentation. In: IEEE Conference on Computer Vision and Pattern Recognition Workshops, pp. 20–28 (2015)
10. Moeskops, P., Viergever, M.A., Mendrik, A.M., de Vries, L.S., Benders, M.J., Isgum, I.: Automatic segmentation of MR brain images with a convolutional neural network. IEEE Trans. Med. Imaging **35**(5), 1252–1261 (2016)
11. Glorot, X., Bengio, Y.: Understanding the difficulty of training deep feedforward neural networks. In: The Thirteenth International Conference on Artificial Intelligence and Statistics, pp. 249–256 (2010)
12. Ioffe, S., Szegedy, C.: Batch normalization: accelerating deep network training by reducing internal covariate shift. arXiv preprint arXiv. 1502.03167 (2017)
13. He, K., Zhang, X., Ren, S., Sun, J.: Delving deep into rectifiers: surpassing human-level performance on imagenet classification. In: IEEE International Conference on Computer Vision, pp. 1026–1034 (2015)
14. He, K., Zhang, X., Ren, S., Sun, J.: Deep residual learning for image recognition. In: IEEE Conference on Computer Vision and Pattern Recognition, pp. 770–778 (2016)
15. Foulds, J., Frank, E.: A review of multi-instance learning assumptions. Knowl. Eng. Rev. **25**(1), 1–25 (2010)
16. Deng, X., Feng, S., Guo, P., Yin, Q.: Fast image recognition with Gabor filter and pseudoinverse learning autoencoders. In: Cheng, L., Leung, A.C.S., Ozawa, S. (eds.) ICONIP 2018. LNCS, vol. 11306, pp. 501–511. Springer, Cham (2018). https://doi.org/10.1007/978-3-030-04224-0_43
17. Kamnitsas, K., et al.: Efficient multi-scale 3D CNN with fully connected CRF for accurate brain lesion segmentation. Med. Image Anal. **36**, 61–78 (2017)
18. Zhang, W., et al.: Deep convolutional neural networks for multi-modality isointense infant brain image segmentation. NeuroImage **108**, 214–224 (2015)
19. Çiçek, Ö., Abdulkadir, A., Lienkamp, S.S., Brox, T., Ronneberger, O.: 3D U-Net: learning dense volumetric segmentation from sparse annotation. In: Ourselin, S., Joskowicz, L., Sabuncu, M.R., Unal, G., Wells, W. (eds.) MICCAI 2016. LNCS, vol. 9901, pp. 424–432. Springer, Cham (2016). https://doi.org/10.1007/978-3-319-46723-8_49
20. Nie, D., Wang, L., Gao, Y., Shen, D.: Fully convolutional networks for multi-modality isointense infant brain image segmentation. In: IEEE 13th International Symposium on Biomedical Imaging (ISBI), pp. 1342–1345 (2016)
21. Mahbod, A., Chowdhury, M., Smedby, O., Wang, C.: Automatic brain segmentation using artificial neural networks with shape context. Pattern Recogn. Lett. **101**, 74–79 (2018)

22. Stollenga, M.F., Byeon, W., Liwicki, M., Schmidhuber, J.: Parallel multi-dimensional with application to fast biomedical volumetric image segmentation. CoRR abs/1506.07452. arXiv:1506.07452 (2018)
23. Hitesh, A., Gupta, A., Raju, A.: Non-linear dimension reduction of Gabor features for noise-robust ASR. In: IEEE International Conference on Acoustics, Speech and Signal Processing (ICASSP), pp. 1715–1719 (2014)
24. Jonathan, L., Evan, S., Trevor, D.: Fully convolutional networks for semantic segmentation. In: IEEE Conference on Computer Vision and Pattern Recognition, pp. 3431–3440 (2015)
25. Xavier, G., Yoshua, B.: Understanding the difficulty of training deep feedforward neural networks. In: The Thirteenth International Conference on Artificial Intelligence and Statistics, pp. 249–256 (2010)

Evaluating Fault Tolerance of Distributed Stream Processing Systems

Xiaotong Wang[1], Cheng Jiang[1], Junhua Fang[2], Ke Shu[3], Rong Zhang[1(✉)],
Weining Qian[1], and Aoying Zhou[1]

[1] School of Data Science and Engineering, East China Normal University,
Shanghai, China
{wxt,jc}@stu.ecnu.edu.cn, {rzhang,wnqian,ayzhou}@dase.ecnu.edu.cn
[2] Soochow University, Suzhou, China
jhfang@suda.edu.cn
[3] PingCAP Ltd., Shanghai, China
shuke@pingcap.com

Abstract. Since failures in large-scale clusters can lead to severe performance degradation and break system availability, fault tolerance is critical for distributed stream processing systems (DSPSs). Plenty of fault tolerance approaches have been proposed over the last decade. However, there is no systematic work to evaluate and compare them in detail. Previous work either evaluates global performance during failure-free runtime, or merely measures throughout loss when failure happens. In this paper, it is the first work proposing an evaluation framework customized for quantitatively comparing runtime overhead and recovery efficiency of fault tolerance mechanisms in DSPSs. We define three typical configurable workloads, which are widely-adopted in previous DSPS evaluations. We construct five workload suites based on three workloads to investigate the effects of different factors on fault tolerance performance. We carry out extensive experiments on two well-known open-sourced DSPSs. The results demonstrate performance gap of two systems, which is useful for choice and evolution of fault tolerance approaches.

Keywords: Fault tolerance · Benchmarking · Stream processing

1 Introduction

Over the last two decades, numerous stream processing systems (SPS) have sprung up from both academia and industry, catering to the increasing requirements of continuous real-time processing from a wide range of scenarios, including stock trading, network monitoring and fraud detection. Aurora [1] starts the work in data stream management system (DSMS, one branch of SPS), which adopt a centralized architecture. Then the growth and intrinsic dispersity of data stream promote the emergence of distributed stream processing systems (DSPS) which provide advanced features. Representatives include Borealis [3].

© Springer Nature Switzerland AG 2020
X. Wang et al. (Eds.): APWeb-WAIM 2020, LNCS 12318, pp. 101–116, 2020.
https://doi.org/10.1007/978-3-030-60290-1_8

Since the prevalence of cloud computing, superior DSPSs have been developed, e.g. Storm [20], Spark Streaming [22] and Flink [5], which are required to provide highly-scalable and highly-available services.

Researchers have put much effort in benchmarking the characteristics (e.g., scalability) and performance (e.g., throughput and latency) of modern DSPSs [2, 4,6,14,18,21], shown in Table 1. We roughly classify these benchmarks into two types based on workloads. One type is to simulate real-world scenario, such as advertisement clicking analysis in Yahoo! StreamingBench [6]; the other type is to compose synthetic operators to evaluate the specific characteristic, e.g. sampling and projection in StreamBench [14]. However current stream benchmarks focus on performance evaluation during failure-free runtime, except that StreamBench introduces a penalty factor for latency and throughout during a failure.

Table 1. The overview of existing stream benchmarks.

Benchmarks	System	Datasets	Workloads	Metrics
LinearRoad [2]	Aurora STREAM	Road and vehicle data	Highway toll monitoring	Throughput
StreamBench [14]	Storm Flink Spark Streaming	Search internet traces	Synthetic sampling work counting, et al.	Latency Throughput Penalty factor
Yahoo! StreamingBench [6]	Storm Flink Spark Streaming	Advertising and user clicking data	Clicking analysis	Latency Throughput
YCSB Extension [9]	Storm Flink Spark Streaming	Advertising and user clicking data	Clicking analysis	Latency Throughput
StreamBench [21]	Storm Flink Spark Streaming	Synthetic data	Synthetic word counting, Clicking, KMeans	Latency Throughput

DSPSs are usually deployed on large-scale clusters of commodity servers, with 24/7 running requirement. Failures are ubiquitous, because failure probability increases with the growing scale of cluster and running time [8]. DSPSs should recover rapidly and accurately enough to minimize performance degradation. A bunch of fault tolerance approaches have been proposed. We group them into three categories: (1) *active* scheme replicates data on multiple nodes as well as the processing; (2) *passive* scheme creates a global snapshot of system; (3) *hybrid* scheme combines the strong points of these two schemes. However, there is no systematic work to quantitatively evaluate the quality of a fault tolerance mechanism, which is necessary to consolidate the state-of-the-art research and to guide the development of strong fault-tolerant DSPSs. We address such a gap in this paper, and make the following contributions:

- We first design an evaluation framework dedicated to compare extra runtime overhead and recovery efficiency of fault tolerance of DSPSs.
- We define measurements of general and fault-tolerance-specific metrics.
- We exploit the design principles of fault tolerance mechanisms in classic DSPSs. In order to study the extra cost during runtime, we dissect workloads

employed in previous work, abstract the common operations and construct five fault-tolerance-sensitive workload suites with a set of configurable knobs.
– We present performance analysis of Flink and Storm through extensive experiments. We conclude with interesting observations and future work.

The rest of this paper is organized as follows: Sect. 2 introduces the basic concepts of stream processing and classifies fault tolerance approaches. The design of evaluation framework is described in Sect. 3. Section 4 presents the experimental results and fault tolerance routines of Flink and Storm. Section 5 discusses related work. We conclude the paper in Sect. 6.

2   Background

2.1   Stream Processing Model

SPSs can be classified into two categories based on processing model: (1) native *continuous-operator* model, such as Flink and Storm; (2) *micro-batch* model, such as Spark Streaming. As Fig. 1(a) shows, data stream is separated with data processing in continuous-operator model. After job submission, user programs are converted into a directed acyclic graph (DAG, a.k.a, topology) of operators connected by data streams. Each operator encapsulates the real computation logic, and consumes(produces) tuples from input(into output) queues. Operators are usually parallelized into multiple instances and run on different nodes for high throughput. On the contrary, as Fig. 1(b) shows, data stream is bundled with data processing in micro-batch model. In this example, there are two operators in the job[1]. Input streams are divided into continuous series of discrete *t-second* micro-batches. User programs are converted into a directed acyclic graph of *stages*. Within each stage, all the parallel instances of an operator are scheduled by a centralized driver, consume the micro-batches and report the size of output results to the driver. Then the driver launches the next state, and sends data information that another operator should fetch. We mainly concern DSPSs with continuous-operator model. DSPSs with micro-batch model, especially Spark Streaming, are almost inherent fault-tolerant owing to the underlying resilient data structures and lineage information [22].

2.2   Fault Tolerance Overview

Fault tolerance in SPSs is realized via replication, either data processing or internal state. We can group them into *active* scheme [3,12,17], *passive* scheme [5,7,11,13,16] and *hybrid* scheme [10,15,19]. In active scheme, each primary node has $k \geq 1$ standby nodes doing the same job. Once a primary node becomes unavailable, one of the standby nodes takes over it instantly. The main challenge of active scheme lies in replica synchronization between primary and standby nodes. On the contrary, in passive scheme, only the primary node consumes the

---

[1] Circles in the same column are the parallel instances of an operator.

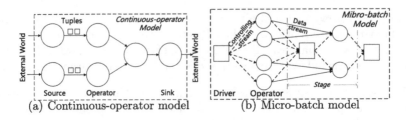

(a) Continuous-operator model   (b) Micro-batch model

Fig. 1. Two common stream processing models.

input stream, but it creates a *checkpoint* of its internal state as well as other information necessary for recovery. Upon failure, operators on the primary node will be relaunched on ≥ 1 standby nodes and rebuild the state from checkpoints. Challenges of passive scheme mainly lie in four aspects: when to do checkpoint, how to coordinate all the operators to create a consistent global snapshot, what data to checkpoint, and where to store checkpoints. Recently, some work proposes hybrid scheme to combine active and passive scheme. But how to find an optimal assignment plan on each node is a key issue.

Table 2. Design goals of fault tolerance.

Runtime overhead	Normal latency	Hardware resource
		CPU, Memory, Network
Recovery efficiency	Recovery latency	Recovery accuracy
		Identical, Duplicated, Disordered, Lost, Incorrect

To measure the quality of fault tolerance, we define *runtime overhead* and *recovery efficiency*, as summarized in Table 2. Obviously, extra overhead is inevitable during failure-free runtime, such as more storage in active scheme, or higher normal latency incurred by checkpointing in passive scheme. Recovery efficiency can be evaluated from two aspects, i.e. recovery latency and degrees of recovery accuracy. These design goals, however have trade-offs between each other. For example, active scheme favors instant recovery at the cost of substantial hardware resource consumption, while passive scheme sacrifices higher recovery latency to save resources, or trades accuracy for lower normal latency by leveraging approximation techniques.

3   Evaluation Framework

Figure 2 shows the overview of our evaluation framework. In-memory *Data Generator (DG)* injects tuple into *Data Broker (DB*, e.g., Kafka[2].) and controls the input rate as well as skew distribution. DSPS under test is isolated from *DG* and

---

[2] http://kafka.apache.org.

DB. It executes workloads, fetches input streams from DB and exports results to DB as well. *Metrics Collector* is integrated into DB to collect metrics.

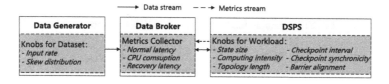

Fig. 2. The evaluation framework.

3.1   Evaluation Metric

Normal Latency (NL). NL is the average time difference (L_t) between each tuple t generated at DG (T_t^{DG}) and all its causally dependent tuples generated at the sink operators (T_t^{Sink}), shown in Eq. 1. T_t^{DG} is also known as *event time* [5], and thus NL is also called as *event-time latency*.

$$L_t = T_t^{DG} - T_t^{Sink}; \quad NL = \overline{\sum L_t} \tag{1}$$

Resource Consumption (CPU). Extra resource overhead often results from (1) scheduling checkpointing procedure and preparing state, which consume CPU cycles; (2) maintaining operator state, which consumes memory; (3) transmitting checkpoints to stable storage, which consumes network bandwidth. During the experiments we observe that the consumption of memory and network bandwidth is proportional to the size of checkpoints. Hence we measure CPU consumption. We monitor CPU every second by `Ganglia`[3], and present both average value and variation trend over time.

Recovery Latency (RL). We define RL from two perspectives: (1) A fine-version RL is defined as the duration from the moment when a failure happens to the moment when DSPS finishes replaying the last tuple. The recovery procedure is composed of rollback phase and replay phase. These two phases execute in sequence and in parallel inside Flink and Storm, respectively. Therefore, we define RL of Flink as the sum of rollback latency and replay latency as shown in Fig. 3(a); we define RL of Storm as the higher one between rollback latency and replay latency. (2) A coarse-version RL can be evaluated indirectly by the evolution of throughput as shown in Fig. 3(b). Once failure happens, throughput fluctuates sharply compared to that during failure-free runtime. Hence, we can measure RL roughly by the duration from the moment when a failure happens to that when throughput comes to be steady.

---

[3] http://ganglia.sourceforge.net/.

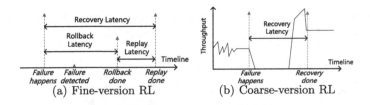

Fig. 3. Two versions of recovery latency.

3.2 Data Generation

We use two kinds of datasets: (1) a collection of real-world English novels crawled from Project Gutenberg[4]; (2) a synthetic dataset with different skew distributions of words. We present knobs for datasets in Table 3. To ensure stable running of each system and avoid backpressure, we keep the data generation at a steady rate 5000 tuples/s. But we lower the input rate down to 500 tuples/s in the last set of experiments on Storm due to its performance bottleneck. Whether barriers are aligned has significant influences on performance, especially when input streams are highly-skewed. Hence, we generate synthetic dataset with uniform (skew $= 0$) and highly-skewed (skew $= 1$) distributions.

Table 3. Configurable knobs for data generation.

Knob	Abbr	Unit	Value
Input rate	*IR*	tuples/s	500, **5000**
Skew distribution	*Skew*	-	**0**,1

3.3 Workloads Design

Workloads. Covering all the streaming workloads is impractical. Hence, we choose and generate three typical workloads as depicted in Fig. 4. (1) In most realistic scenarios, aggregation is one of the basic operations. The widely-used task is streaming *Word Count (WC)* that counts the number of occurrences of each word in continuously arriving sentences. As Fig. 4(a) shows, it contains both stateless (i.e., Spliter) and stateful operators (i.e., Counter). (2) Numerical computation is also common in stream processing, and its amount of computation varies in different stream applications, such as CPU-bound model training in machine learning algorithms. Hence, we create a synthetic *PI Calculation (PI)* topology as shown in Fig. 4(b). Within it, we utilize Gregory-Leibniz series formula for π which can control the amount of computation via n. (3) We generate *Dummy Topologies (DT)* with different numbers of operators to simulate the

---

[4] https://www.gutenberg.org/.

complexity of topology. Each operator in dummy topologies has no real computing task, but receives and sends tuples.

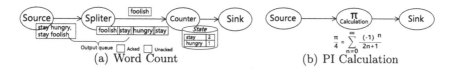

(a) Word Count   (b) PI Calculation

Fig. 4. Three typical workloads.

Workload Suites. After investigating all the fault tolerance approaches of passive scheme, we summarize 6 knobs in Table 4 to compose different workloads
suites, by configuring application characteristics and checkpoint requirements.
State denotes the size in byte of states including in a checkpoint. During the
experiments, we find that if we enable the window mode of operators, checkpointing can happen at any moment within a time window. As a result, *State* of each
checkpoint is of random distribution, which baffles the evaluation of its impacts
on performance. Therefore, we artificially simulate *State* of each operator by
maintaining a string variable and conduct the experiments under full-history
mode. *Computing intensity* controls the computation amount of operators and
is configured as various execution rounds of PI calculation. *Topology length* is
the number of operators in a dummy topology. *Checkpoint interval* defines the
time interval between two consecutive checkpointing requests. *Checkpoint syn-
chronicity* defines whether checkpointing executes synchronously with normal
processing. *Barrier alignment* defines whether barriers are aligned.

The knobs, along with workloads mentioned above, together compose 5 workload suites as listed in Table 5, each of which focuses on distinct effects of knobs
on fault tolerance performance. **Suite 1–3** evaluate extra overhead of each DSPS
incurred by fault tolerance during failure-free runtime. **Suite 4–5** evaluate the
recovery latency of each DSPS after randomly killing worker processes.

Table 4. Configurable knobs for workloads: default value in bold.

Object	Knobs	Abbr	Unit	Values
Application	State size	*State*	MB	1, **10**, 15, 30
	Computing intensity	*CPI*	round	0(low), **2000**(medium), 5000(high)
	Topology length	*TL*	# of operators	**2**, 10
Checkpoint	Checkpoint interval	*CI*	second	NC (disabled), 1 **30**, 45, 60
	Checkpoint Synchronicity	*CS*	-	sync, **async**
	Barrier alignment	*BA*	-	**true**, false

Table 5. Workload suites with distinct purposes.

Workload Suite	Name	Description	Cost
1	WC	Effects of CI on NL and CPU for applications with different $State$	Overhead
2	PI	Effects of CS on NL and CPU for applications with different CPI	
3	WC	Effects of BA on NL and CPU when processing streams with different $Skew$	
4	DT	Effects of TL on RL	Recovery efficiency
5	WC	Effects of CI on RL	

4 Experiments

We implement the evaluation framework to compare the fault tolerance performance of Flink and Storm. We perform our experiments on a 5-node cluster where 1 node is equipped with 24 Intel Xeon E5-2620 CPUs and 31 GB of RAM, and the others with 8 Intel Xeon E5606 CPUs and 94 GB of RAM. The nodes are inter-connected via Gigabit Ethernet and run a CentOS Linux operating system with kernel version 6.5.0. We conduct five sets of experiments to understand the design principles of fault tolerance for each system. We roughly simulate failures by killing multiple worker processes randomly.

Flink. As shown in Fig. 5(a), three operators *src*, *opt* and *snk* together compose a topology, and are partitioned into different slots. *JobManager* is the controller process, and *TaskManager* is the worker process. *src* receives periodic checkpointing requests from *CheckpointCoordinator*, and injects barriers into data streams. *opt* with multiple input streams doesn't make checkpoints until it receives barriers with the same ID from all its input streams. When one barrier arrives, *opt* suspends the corresponding input stream and buffers the follow-up tuples into the input queue. Such a step is called *barrier alignment*. It can be disabled, but precise recovery will not be guaranteed. Once all the barriers with the same version ID arrive, *opt* can either block the normal processing to make checkpoints synchronously, or apply the "copy-on-write" technique to make checkpoints asynchronously. When a failure occurs to *TaskManager* (i.e., all the operators it manages fail as well), as shown in Fig. 5(b), operators that communicate with the failed ones receive no responses, and then inform *JobManager*. *JobManager* marks the job as `Failing` and broadcasts a *Canceling* message to each alive *TaskMangager*. Once received, *TaskManager* forcibly terminates all the operators it manages and sends back a `Canceled` message. *JobManager* will never receive a `Canceled` message from the failed *TaskManager*, and then marks the job as *Restarting* when the threshold of waiting time is reached. The whole

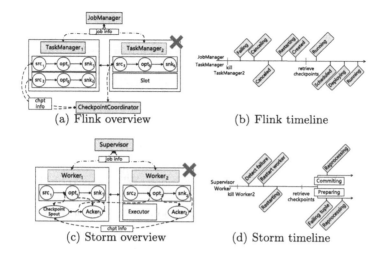

Fig. 5. Fault tolerance routines of Flink and Storm.

topology will be reset and restore `Running` status. Accordingly, all the operators redeployed retrieve their own last checkpoints to rollback the state. Once *src* finishes the rollback, it begins to fetch the tuples that were processed but not reflected into the latest checkpoint.

Storm. We use the same topology to discuss Storm, which is inspired by Flink but has some differences. As Fig. 5(c) shows, *Supervisor* is the controller process, *Worker* is the worker process and *Acker* is responsible for message processing guarantee. *CheckpointSpout* is one kind of *src* but only injects periodic checkpointing messages (i.e., the role of barrier in Flink). When fault tolerance is enabled, Storm will acknowledge all tuples that arrive during a checkpoint interval. We call it *batch-acking*. Storm completes a checkpointing procedure in two phases. In *preparing* phase, each operator receives a preparing message, writes a temporary checkpoint meta data into Redis[5] and then acknowledges *Acker*. Once receiving all the acknowledgments from each operator, the *committing* phase is triggered, so *CheckpointSpout* sends a committing message to inform each operator to write down real checkpoints to Redis synchronously. After that, each operator deletes the previous checkpoint, and performs batch-acking. When a failure occurs to *Worker*, as shown in Fig. 5(d), *Supervisor* always monitors the heartbeats of *Worker*. Unlike Flink, only operators that were managed by the failed *Worker* will be reset. If failure happens in preparing phase, the redeployed operators will rollback to the last checkpoint and actively fail the tuples that were processed from that checkpoint to the failure time; if failure happens in committing phase, since the up-to-date state of Storm is already stored in Redis, the redeployed operators directly continue the normal processing after fetching the corresponding checkpoints. Note, *src* will receive two kinds of `Failing` messages

---

[5] https://redis.io//.

if failure happens in the preparing phase, namely the actively-failed tuples and time-out tuples which are not acknowledged in time by *Acker* due to failure. Tuple replaying and state rollback in Storm execute in parallel, thus it can not provide precise recovery.

4.1   Experimental Results

Workload Suite 1: Since Storm can't function properly with highly frequent checkpointing and large state, we don't run it with 1s-*CI* and 30 MB-*State*. As shown in Fig. 6, for Flink, more frequent checkpointing means more interference on normal processing and more thread scheduling. When checkpointing executes synchronously with normal processing, larger *State* incurs longer pause of normal processing to make and transmit checkpoints. Hence, both *NL* and *CPU* are proportional to *State*, but inversely proportional to *CI*. For Storm, under a certain *CI*, *NL* and *CPU* have a linear relational with *State*. We can conclude that: (1) larger *CI* and *State* usually incur higher *NL* and *CPU*; (2) even the barrier of Flink is aligned which incurs more waiting time, performance of Storm has greater degradation when fault tolerance is enabled, compared with Flink.

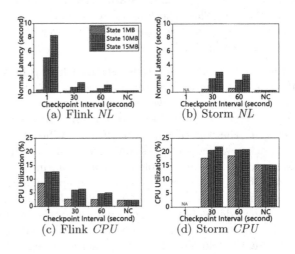

Fig. 6. The effects of *State* and *CI* on *NL* and *CPU*.

Workload Suite 2: Since checkpointing by default executes synchronously with normal processing, and that checkpointing messages are not aligned in Storm, we only evaluate Flink here. As shown in Fig. 7(a)–7(c), if checkpointing executes asynchronously, new incoming tuples will be processed in time; otherwise, they will be buffered in input queues of each operator until checkpointing is finished. Hence, asynchronous checkpointing can optimize the increase of *NL*.

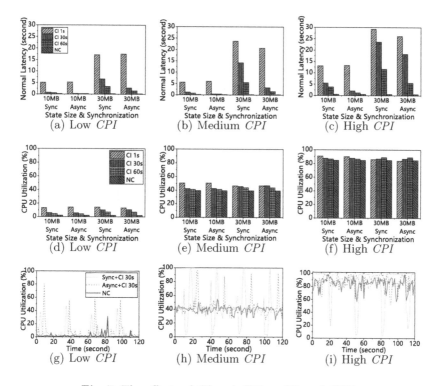

Fig. 7. The effects of *CS* and *CPI* on *NL* and *CPU*.

Moreover, we evaluate *CPU* under different *CPI*. As the total computation amount is constant, the average *CPU* of asynchronous checkpointing is approximate to that of synchronous checkpointing, as shown in Fig. 7(d)–7(f). For further analysis, we evaluate *CPU* trend over time. As illustrated in Fig. 7(g)–7(i), with the increase of *CPI*, *CPU* of synchronous checkpointing changes more violently. Once checkpointing is trigger, each operator suspends its normal processing, which leads to an obvious trough of *CPU*. When checkpointing is finished, the buffered new incoming tuples are first processed, which leads to a peak. In Fig. 7(i), there is no peak but a longer continuously-high period in that *CPU* is already extremely high due to heavy *CPI*. We conclude that asynchronous checkpointing gains lower runtime overhead, but this predominance is weakened under heavy computation amount and highly-frequent checkpointing.

Workload Suite 3: As shown in Fig. 8, with uniform distribution, effects on *NL* have little difference whether barriers are aligned. However, when input streams are highly-skewed, arrival time of barriers on different streams differs sharply with each other, which leads to longer blocking of the stream on which the barrier arrives first, and accordingly higher *NL*. Figure 9 demonstrates *CPU* trend over time under different *Skew*. We also compare high-load nodes with low-load nodes. As Fig. 9(a) and 9(b) demonstrate, when *Skew* is low, there is little difference on CPU whether barriers are aligned or not. But with severe skewness, temporary blocking of some stream causes massive tuples buffered, which leads to an obvious period of peak usage of *CPU*, as shown in Fig. 9(c) and 9(d). We conclude that aligning barriers incurs higher normal latency and unstable CPU status when input streams are of highly-skewed distribution.

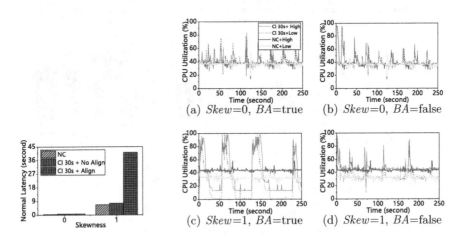

(a) *Skew*=0, *BA*=true   (b) *Skew*=0, *BA*=false

(c) *Skew*=1, *BA*=true   (d) *Skew*=1, *BA*=false

Fig. 8. The effects of *Skew* and *BA* on *NL* in Flink.

Fig. 9. The effects of *Skew* and *BA* on *NL* and *CPU* in Flink.

Workload Suite 4: *JobManager* decides the failure of a failed *TaskManager*, if it receives no responses from *TaskManager* when the threshold of waiting time is reached. As shown in Fig. 10, longer topology lightly increases the rollback latency, but is bound to the timeout threshold of failure detection. We omit the evaluation of Storm for this workload suite in that we observe that the recovery latency is dominated by the replay latency.

Workload Suite 5: Input rate for Storm is adjusted to 500 tuples/s because its mediocre performance. Figure 11 presents the fine-version recovery latency of Flink and Storm. We observe that the rollback latency of Flink is always bound to 45 s, having nothing to do with *State* and *CI*. After reviewing system logs, we find that the default time-out threshold of failure detection is 45 s. However, as Fig. 11(b) and 11(d) show, the replay latency of Flink has a linear relationship with *CI*, but is not affected by *State*; while *State* has greater influence on the volume of replayed tuples than *CI*. We analyze logs and observe that the replay phase begins before all the operators have finished the rollback phase. Once the source operator has finished its rollback, it begins to fetch tuples from *DB*. The bigger *State* implies more time downstream operators spend on rollback. New incoming tuples are buffered before downstream operators have finished the rollback, which may cause backpressure and consequently lead to higher replay latency. For Storm, *RL* is proportional to *CI* as shown in Fig. 11(d), but almost not affected by *State*. We figure out that *RL* is mainly affected by batch-acking and tuple replaying. When *CI* is relatively large, the impact of batch-acking outweighs that of tuple replaying. Hence, when failure happens in preparing phase, *RL* is higher than that at committing phase. While for the smaller *CI*, we draw an opposite conclusion.

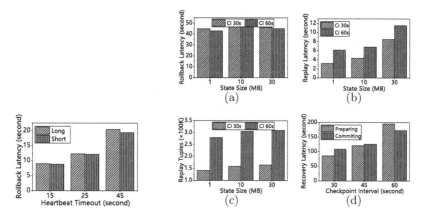

Fig. 10. The effects of *TL* on rollback latency in Flink.

Fig. 11. The effects of *State* and *CI* on fine-version *RL*.

Figure 12 shows the coarse-version recovery latency of Flink and Storm. The first dotted arrow marks the moment when failure occurs, and the second one marks the moment when the system restores the steady throughput. For Flink, after failure is detected, source operators of Flink stop fetching tuples from data broker, which results in a temporary zero throughput. After source operators finish the rollback phase, tuples that were emitted from the latest checkpoint to the failure point are re-fetched, leading to wave crests. For Storm, source operators keep emitting tuples downstream even when failure happens. The wave crests imply the replaying of tuples which are actively failed by downstream operators. We conclude that (1) Flink recovers much more efficiently than Storm.

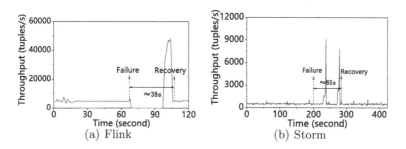

Fig. 12. The coarse-version *RL* of Flink and Storm.

Even all the operators are forced to be redeployed in Flink, Flink gains far less recovery latency than Storm; (2) Checkpoint interval has great effects on recovery latency, as larger interval indicates more tuples to be replayed.

Discussion: Fault tolerance indeed leads to high performance degradation of system. A moderate checkpoint frequency (e.g., 30 s) can incur x4 - x12 severe latency in Flink and Storm. Asynchronous checkpointing technique can mitigate it, but its effect is diminished when the workload is computation-intensive. But if high burst of streams happens to those platforms, checkpointing will occupy the runtime processing all the time. Hence, it is essential to design an adaptive checkpointing technique to adjust checkpoint interval according to real-time workloads. Moreover, the recovery procedure can be dominated by tuple relaying. Even the whole system is reset, retrieving the checkpoints and rebuilding the state are not time-consuming. Until now, the research focuses more on the content to checkpoint instead of the fatal problem in source replaying, and then parallel recovery is necessary in future.

5   Related Work

Linear Road Benchmark [2] is the first benchmark dedicated to DSMSs. It simulates a highway toll system. Lu et al. raise StreamBench [14] to evaluate Storm and Spark Streaming. Apart from performance measurements, StreamBench also evaluates the distributed characteristics of system, such as fault tolerance ability and durability. StreamBench gathers two seed data sets from web log processing and network traffic monitoring, and leverages a message system to inject data into DSPSs on the fly. Based on data type, computation complexity and operator state, StreamBench selects 7 programs and defines 4 synthetic workload suites. However, for the evaluation of fault tolerance ability, StreamBench merely compares the throughput and latency after failures with those before failures. Yahoo! Storm team [6] proposes a open-source streaming benchmark (YSB) which simulates an advertisement analytics pipeline. It uses Kafka and Redis for data fetching and storage respectively. Three DSPSs, namely Flink, Storm and Spark Streaming, are compared in terms of 99th percentile latency and throughput, with checkpointing off by default. Later, Grier [9] extends YSB to measure the latency and maximum throughput of Flink and Storm. Wang [21] also demonstrates a stream benchmark tool called StreamBench to evaluate the event-time latency and throughput of Storm, Flink and Spark Streaming. To distinguish from [14], we rename it as StreamBench'. StreamBench' defines three kinds of workloads to evaluate three representative operations in stream processing, namely aggregation, joining and iterating. Similarly, it utilizes a message system to simulate the on-the-fly data generation, and control the skew distribution.

6   Conclusion

We design an evaluation framework to empirically investigate the fault tolerance performance of DSPSs, which is an urgent requirement from cloud-based/cluster-based applications as the persistent increasing of stream data and strict service quality demands. Experimental results reveal a moderate checkpointing frequency can incur x4 - x12 performance degradation in Flink and Storm. And even Flink forces all the operators to rollback during recovery, it gains x2 recovery efficiency than Storm. These performance gap can be explained by the fault tolerance routine we tease apart. And we conclude that parallel sources recovery and adaptive checkpointing are necessary for improving system performance. Though we have some interesting observations in this work, there are still some points to be covered in the future. First, our work is merely appropriate for DSPSs with continuous-operator model and takes no account of fault tolerance approaches with active and hybrid scheme. The challenge is that SPSs adopting these two fault tolerance schemes either drop behind or with no open-sourced prototypes. Second, all the evaluations in this paper are conducted under stable conditions when DSPSs ingest stable inputs. However, streaming data in real-world is often highly dynamic, and its impact on fault tolerance performance need to be investigated as well. Third, we will involve more complex computation, such as machine learning algorithms, to the framework. Last, a universal measurement of recovery accuracy has to be settled since more stream applications emphasize precise results rather than traditional approximate processing.

Acknowledgement. The work is supported by National Key Research and Development Plan Project (No.2018YFB1003402) and National Science Foundation of China (NSFC) (No.61672233,61802273). Ke Shu is supported by PingCAP.

References

1. Abadi, D.J., Carney, D., Zdonik, S.B., et al.: Aurora: a new model and architecture for data stream management. VLDBJ **12**(2), 120–139 (2003)
2. Arasu, A., Cherniack, M., Tibbetts, R., et al.: Linear road: a stream data management benchmark. In: Proceedings of the 30th VLDB International Conference on Very Large Data Bases, pp. 480–491 (2004)
3. Balazinska, M., Balakrishnan, H., Madden, S., Stonebraker, M.: Fault-tolerance in the borealis distributed stream processing system. In: Proceedings of the 2005 ACM SIGMOD International Conference on Management of Data, pp. 13–24. ACM (2005)
4. Bordin, M.: A Benchmark Suite for Distributed Stream Processing Systems. Ph.D. thesis, Universidade Federal do Rio Grande Do Su (2017)
5. Carbone, P., Katsifodimos, A., Tzoumas, K., et al.: Apache flink^{TM}: stream and batch processing in a single engine. IEEE Data Eng. Bull. **38**(4), 28–38 (2015)
6. Chintapalli, S., Dagit, D., Poulosky, P., et al.: Benchmarking streaming computation engines: storm, flink and spark streaming. In: Proceedings of the 2016 IEEE International Parallel and Distributed Processing Symposium Workshops, pp. 1789–1792 (2016)
7. Fernandez, R.C., Migliavacca, M., Kalyvianaki, E., Pietzuch, P.R.: Integrating scale out and fault tolerance in stream processing using operator state management. In: Proceedings of the 2013 ACM SIGMOD International Conference on Management of Data, pp. 725–736. ACM (2013)

8. Gill, P., Jain, N., Nagappan, N.: Understanding network failures in data centers: measurement, analysis, and implications. In: Proceedings of the 2011 ACM SIG-COMM Conference on Applications, Technologies, Architectures, and Protocols for Computer Communications, pp. 350–361. ACM (2011)

9. Grier, J.: Extending the yahoo! streaming benchmark (2016). https://www.ververica.com/blog/extending-the-yahoo-streaming-benchmark

10. Heinze, T., Zia, M., Fetzer, C., et al.: An adaptive replication scheme for elastic data stream processing systems. In: Proceedings of the 9th ACM DEBS International Conference on Distributed Event-Based Systems, pp. 150–161. ACM (2015)

11. Huang, Q., Lee, P.P.C.: Toward high-performance distributed stream processing via approximate fault tolerance. PVLDB **10**(3), 73–84 (2016)

12. Hwang, J., Çetintemel, U., Zdonik, S.B.: Fast and highly-available stream processing over wide area networks. In: Proceedings of the 24th IEEE ICDE International Conference on Data Engineering, pp. 804–813. IEEE (2008)

13. Kwon, Y., Balazinska, M., Greenberg, A.G.: Fault-tolerant stream processing using a distributed, replicated file system. PVLDB **1**(1), 574–585 (2008)

14. Lu, R., Wu, G., Xie, B., Hu, J.: Streambench: towards benchmarking modern distributed stream computing frameworks. In: Proceedings of the 7th IEEE/ACM International Conference on Utility and Cloud Computing, pp. 69–78. IEEE/ACM (2014)

15. Martin, A., Smaneoto, T., Fetzer, C., et al.: User-constraint and self-adaptive fault tolerance for event stream processing systems. In: Proceedings of the 45th Annual IEEE/IFIP DSN International Conference on Dependable Systems and Networks, pp. 462–473. IEEE/IFIP (2015)

16. Sebepou, Z., Magoutis, K.: CEC: continuous eventual checkpointing for data stream processing operators. In: Proceedings of the 2011 IEEE/IFIP DSN International Conference on Dependable Systems and Networks, pp. 145–156. IEEE/IFIP (2011)

17. Shah, M.A., Hellerstein, J.M., Brewer, E.A.: Highly-available, fault-tolerant, parallel dataflows. In: Proceedings of the 2004 ACM SIGMOD International Conference on Management of Data, pp. 827–838. ACM (2004)

18. Shukla, A., Chaturvedi, S., Simmhan, Y.L.: RIoTbench: an IoT benchmark for distributed stream processing systems. CCPE **29**(21), e4257 (2017)

19. Su, L., Zhou, Y.: Passive and partially active fault tolerance for massively parallel stream processing engines. TKDE **31**(1), 32–45 (2019)

20. Toshniwal, A., Taneja, S., Ryaboy, D.V., et al.: Storm@Twitter. In: Proceedings of the 2014 ACM SIGMOD International Conference on Management of Data, pp. 147–156. ACM (2014)

21. Wang, Y.: Stream Processing Systems Benchmark: StreamBench. Master's thesis, Aalto University (2016)

22. Zaharia, M., Das, T., Stoica, I., et al.: Discretized streams: fault-tolerant streaming computation at scale. In: Proceedings of the 24th ACM SIGOPS Symposium on Operating Systems Principles, pp. 423–438. ACM (2013)

Predicting Human Mobility with Self-attention and Feature Interaction

Jingang Jiang, Shuo Tao, Defu Lian$^{(\boxtimes)}$, Zhenya Huang, and Enhong Chen

Institute of Smart City Research (Wuhu) and School of Data Science,
University of Science and Technology of China, Hefei, China
{liandefu,cheneh}@ustc.edu.cn,
{jjg1210,taoshuo,huangzhy}@mail.ustc.edu.cn

Abstract. Mobility prediction plays an important role in a wide range of location-based applications and services. However, two important challenges are not well addressed in existing literature: 1) explicit high-order interactions of spatio-temporal features are not systemically modeled; 2) most existing algorithms place attention mechanisms on top of recurrent network, so they can not allow for full parallelism and are inferior to self-attention for capturing long-range dependence. To this end, we propose MoveNet, a self-attention based sequential model, to predict each user's next destination based on her most recent visits and historical trajectory. MoveNet first introduces a cross based learning framework for modeling feature interactions. With self-attention on both the most recent visits and historical trajectory, MoveNet can use an attention mechanism to capture user's long-term regularity in a more efficient and effective way. We evaluate MoveNet with three real-world mobility datasets, and show that MoveNet outperforms the state-of-the-art mobility predictor by around 10% in terms of accuracy, and simultaneously achieves faster convergence and over 4x training speedup.

Keywords: Human mobility · Self-attention · Feature interaction

1 Introduction

With the development of location-acquisition techniques and the prevalence of smart devices, human daily routines are much easier to digitize and share with friends in social network websites. Mobility understanding and prediction are of vital importance in a wide range of applications and services, ranging from urban planning [10], traffic forecasting [12] and epidemic control [11] to location-based advertisements and recommendation [30].

The key in mobility prediction is how to capture useful mobility patterns from historical traces. Previous work about mobility prediction is mainly based on either Markov models or recurrent models. Markov models predict next locations conditioning on a few recent visits, and was successfully applied for location

© Springer Nature Switzerland AG 2020
X. Wang et al. (Eds.): APWeb-WAIM 2020, LNCS 12318, pp. 117–131, 2020.
https://doi.org/10.1007/978-3-030-60290-1_9

prediction in GPS trajectories [1], cell tower traces [20] and check-in traces [7,13]. The finding in these work is that pattern frequency determines the order of Markov models, so they are strongly correlated with pattern-based methods [18]. In practice, whatever type of dataset is available, Markov models with Kneser-Ney smoothing [3] or hierarchical Pitman-Yor Process [22] models are used, because they integrate different orders of models. Regarding cell tower traces, 93% human movements can be predicted based on sequential patterns [20], but for social check-ins, mobility predictability is much lower [15]. This is because users often check in unseen locations, while Markov models fail to predict in this case. Leveraging sequential recommendation techniques, Factorizing Personalized Markov Chain (FPMC) [4] and Personalized Ranking Metric Embedding (PRME) [6] are adapted to learn location transitions with distributional representation. Although they can deal with the prediction of unseen locations, these methods sometimes perform worse than Markov models, due to not well capturing sequential patterns. One of underlying reasons may lie in the BPR loss, which does not perform as well as expected in recommendation tasks [14].

The success of recurrent neural networks (RNN) in language modeling motivates researchers to apply RNN-like models for mobility prediction. The pioneer work in [24] separately models short-term sequential contexts and long-term sequential contexts, by replacing (factorizing) Markov models with RNN models and performing optimization with respect to the sampled softmax functions. Spatio-temporal statistics between consecutive visits are also put into the gate functions to control information flow [28]. To further model long-range dependence in long-term sequential contexts, attention mechanisms are applied on top of RNNs [5].

Among these existing works, two important challenges are not well addressed. First, spatio-temporal features generally include location id and time id, and lack consideration for the influence of explicit high-order interaction between features. This may help to distinguish mobility modeling from sequential recommendation and may lead to the improvements of mobility prediction. Second, recurrent networks are time-consuming to train particularly for long sequences and can not be comparable to self-attention mechanisms for capturing long-range dependence according to [23].

To this end, we propose MoveNet, a self-attention based sequential model, to predict movements based on both the most recent visits and the whole historical trajectory. MoveNet first embeds spatial-temporal information of check-ins, including user, time and location, and then models high-order interactions of spatial-temporal feature in the most recent visits based on a cross-based learning framework [16]. Following that, we apply self-attention to the embedding representations of the most recent visits to capture short-term preference and to the embedding of the whole historical trajectory to capture long-term regularity. Long-term regularity in the current context is then extracted by an attention mechanism, by considering representation of the most recent visit from self attention as query, and representations of the historical trajectory as memory. In order to promote efficiency, only the last k representations in the historical trajectory are used for attention, but this does not lead to large performance degradation.

The contributions can be summarized as follows:

- We propose a self-attention based sequential model for predicting user movements, which promotes efficiency and effectiveness of processing lengthy historical trajectories by allowing for full parallelism and capability of modeling long-range dependence.
- We model high-order interactions of spatio-temporal features based on a cross-based learning framework, so that user-location, location-time, user-time interactions can be naturally incorporated. This framework is very general, so it is possible to integrate more useful features of locations and contexts.
- We conduct extensive experiments by evaluating MoveNet on three real-world check-in datasets. The results show that MoveNet not only can outperform the SOTA predictor by about 10%, but is also faster than the SOTA predictor in terms of empirical convergence and running time cost. Moreover, the effect of self-attention and high-order interaction modeling has been verified.

2   Related Works

In computer science, mobility can be predicted based on Markov models, machine learning models, sequence pattern mining, and recurrent networks.

Ashbrook and Starner applied second-order Markov model to predict future movement after automatically clustering the GPS trajectories into meaningful location sequences[1]. Song et al. reported empirical evaluation results of location predictors on WiFi mobility data, and observed that second-order Markov model performed best [21]. Chen et al. investigated variable-order Markov model for next location prediction [2]. Lian et al. utilized Markov models with Kneser-Ney smoothing to predict next check-in location [13] and Gao et al. applied Pitman-Yor process to seamlessly integrate different orders of Markov models [8]. To model long-term dependence between locations, Mathew et al. trained a Hidden Markov Model for each user [17]. Markov models are closely correlated with frequent sequential pattern mining, since transitions with large probability may correspond to frequent sequential patterns. Therefore, several sequential pattern mining based methods [18,27] are proposed, which first extract frequent patterns and predict next location based pattern matching. Treating next location as classes, mobility prediction can be cast into multi-class classification problem [19]. Input features are usually sparse, so such models also suffer from low prediction accuracy of unseen locations.

To better deal with the prediction of unseen locations, personalized transition probability are factorized based on pairwise interaction tensor factorization [4,29] or metric embedding [6] so that locations are represented by distributional representation. To capture long-range dependence between visits, recurrent networks such as LSTM or GRU are used to model location sequences [24]. The problem of gradient vanish in recurrent networks restricts the capability of capture long-term dynamics. Therefore, this work splits historical trajectories into long-term contexts and short-term contexts, and use RNN for short-term contexts and GRU for long-term contexts. To further address the gradient vanish problem, attention mechanisms are usually applied on top of LSTM when modeling long-term context [5]. In order to capture the periodicity in the long-term trajectory pattern, Gao et al. proposed a variational attention mechanism [9]. achieving higher accuracy of mobility prediction.

3   Preliminary

In this paper, we study the mobility prediction problem in the sparse check-in datasets. In the check-in dataset, a user's check-in sequence is $T^u = q_1 \rightarrow q_2 \rightarrow \cdots \rightarrow q_n$, where $q_i = (u, t_i, l_i)$ denotes a check-in record, indicating a user u checked in a location l_i at time t_i. Note that the check-in sequence is subject to chronological order. That is, for any two check-in two records q_i and q_j with $i < j$, we have $t_i < t_j$. Since users selectively issue check-ins when he visited/stayed at some locations due to privacy concerns, the time intervals between consecutive check-ins are usually not even. Therefore, we split each user's check-in sequence into multiple sessions, such that the time interval between consecutive sessions are larger than a given threshold Δt. In a formal way, $\tilde{T}^u = S_1^u \rightarrow S_2^u \rightarrow \cdots \rightarrow S_m^u$, where m is the number of sessions and $S_i^u = q_{i_1} \rightarrow \cdots \rightarrow q_{i_{k_i}}$ of length k_i denotes the i-th session, being a sub-sequence of T^u. The problem of mobility prediction is defined as follows:

Definition 1 (Mobility Prediction). *Given the most recent incomplete session $S_m^u = q_{m_1} \rightarrow q_{m_2} \rightarrow \cdots \rightarrow q_{m_j}$ and the historical sessions $S_1^u \rightarrow S_2^u \rightarrow \cdots \rightarrow S_{m-1}^u$ of a user u, predict the next location $l_{m_{j+1}}$ at which the user will check in.*

Note that such a definition can be applied for mobility prediction with continuously-recorded trajectories, like GPS trajectories. This is because mobility prediction is usually conducted on sequence of stay points[1] while time intervals between consecutive stay of points are also not even.

4   MoveNet

The whole framework of MoveNet is shown in Fig. 1, where we model historical sessions and the most recent session separately.

The goal of modeling historical sessions is to capture long-term regularity. Consequently, the historical sessions are concatenated as the whole trajectory and then fed into a spatial-temporal embedding module. After being concatenated with user embedding, they are further fed into a self-attention module, yielding a sequence of check-in representations with long-range dependence encoded. To improve efficiency, we only use the representations for the last k check-ins as memory slots for subsequent attention use. This is also motivated

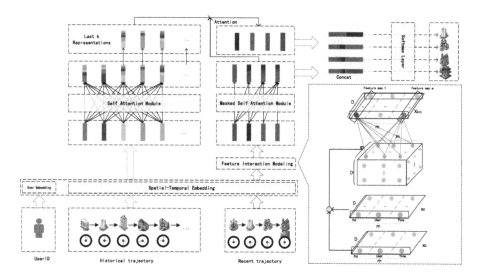

Fig. 1. Framework of MoveNet

by the observation that using the representations of the whole historical trajectory only leads to a very small improvement.

The objective of modeling the trajectory in the most recent session is to capture short-term user preference. As such, the trajectory in the most recent session is first embedded, and then fed together with user embedding into the feature interaction modeling module, in order to capture high-order interaction of spatial-temporal features. Note that the feature interaction modeling module is not applied in the former part, because it is more time-consuming than simple operators and attention mechanism may be a better practice for capturing long-term regularity. The most recent sequence of check-in representation is then fed into the masked self-attention module to capture sequential dependence. Here, the mask is used out of causality concerns, i.e., considering the first j items to predict the $(j+1)$-th check-in location. Following that, each check-in representation in the most recent trajectory attends over k memory slots obtained from modeling historical sessions. Being concatenated with the attended representations, each check-in representation is then used in the softmax layer for multi-class classification.

4.1 Spatial-Temporal Embedding

For check-in locations, we denote by $L \in \mathbb{R}^{N \times d}$ the location embedding matrix. For check-in time, we first convert it to a tuple (hour of day, weekend or not) and denote by $\mathbf{T} \in \mathbb{R}^{48 \times d}$ the time embedding matrix. For each user, we do not have her any side information, so each user is embedded with the embedding matrix $U \in \mathbb{R}^{M \times d}$. Note that the same dimension of embedding matrices is required in the feature interaction modeling module. Since each check-in location is attached with a GPS position, it is also possible to represent each GPS position with a vector, such that a metric value between any two vectors can approximate their sphere distance. However, we do not observe any significant improvements and do not take them into account. Moreover, we will use self-attention for capturing long-range dependence, and usually incorporate positional embedding for encoding relative order information. However, we do also not observe any significant improvements and thus not take them into account.

4.2   Self-attention Module

In the SOTA mobility predictor [5], RNNs like LSTM and GRU are used to process input sequences. However, the capacity of learning long-range dependencies is limited, and its sequential processing style makes it less efficient and less parallelizable. With the great success of Transformer in machine translation, self-attention has been applied to various sequential processing tasks, due to the advantages of capturing long-range dependence and fully parallelizable.

The basis of self-attention is the scaled dot-product attention, which is defined by [23] as follows:

$$\text{Attention}(\boldsymbol{Q}, \boldsymbol{K}, \boldsymbol{V}) = \text{softmax}\left(\frac{\boldsymbol{Q}\boldsymbol{K}^{\top}}{\sqrt{d}}\right)\boldsymbol{V} \tag{1}$$

where $\boldsymbol{Q}$, $\boldsymbol{K}$, $\boldsymbol{V}$ represent queries, keys and values, respectively. The attention layer computes a weighted sum of values in $\boldsymbol{V}$, where the weight reflects the similarity of each query to keys. $\sqrt{d}$ is a scale factor to avoid overly large values of inner product.

Assume the self-attention module takes $\boldsymbol{X} \in \mathbb{R}^{n \times d}$, a sequence of n representations as input, which is obtained from either direct concatenation or the feature interaction modeling module, and convert it into the query, key, value matrices via linear projections. In particular, the output of the self-attention module is calculated by

$$\boldsymbol{Y} = \text{SA}(\boldsymbol{X}) = \text{Attention}\left(\boldsymbol{X}\boldsymbol{W}^{Q}, \boldsymbol{X}\boldsymbol{W}^{K}, \boldsymbol{X}\boldsymbol{W}^{V}\right) \tag{2}$$

where $\boldsymbol{W}^{Q}, \boldsymbol{W}^{K}, \boldsymbol{W}^{V} \in \mathbb{R}^{d \times d}$ are projection matrices. Unlike self-attention in the Transformer, we don't use multi-head attention, since we do not observe benefit of using more than one head.

Following the Transformer, we feed the output of self-attention into a feed-forward network (FFN) to encode a non-linearity transformation following weighted summation. When applied on $\boldsymbol{Y}_j$, the j-th row of $\boldsymbol{Y}$, FFN produces the following output:

$$\boldsymbol{Z}_j = \text{FFN}(\boldsymbol{Y}_j) = \text{ReLU}(\boldsymbol{Y}_i\boldsymbol{W}^{(1)} + \boldsymbol{b}^{(1)})\boldsymbol{W}^{(2)} + \boldsymbol{b}^{(2)}, \tag{3}$$

where $\boldsymbol{W}^{(1)} \in \mathbb{R}^{d \times 4d}$, $\boldsymbol{W}^{(2)} \in \mathbb{R}^{4d \times d}$, $\boldsymbol{b}^{(1)} \in \mathbb{R}^{4d}$, $\boldsymbol{b}^{(2)} \in \mathbb{R}^{d}$. Here each representation is first transformed into a 4-times larger space and is then transformed back after applying the ReLU activation. Note that the linear transformations are the same at different positions.

Causality. When the self-attention module is employed in modeling the most recent session, causality should be imposed, such that future check-ins can not be used for computing representation of the current one. However, this is easy to implement by incorporating mask into self-attention of sequence.

Stacking. Through the transformation of self-attention and feed-forward network, Z_i aggregates representation of all sequentially-dependent check-ins. It might be useful to learn more complex dependence by applying multiple self-attention blocks, each of which consists of self-attention and feed-forward network. Note that parameters in feed-forward network are varied from block to block. Moreover, in order to stabilize and speed up the model training, we perform the following operations

$$f(x) = \text{LayerNorm}(x + \text{Dropout}(\text{Sublayer}(x))) \tag{4}$$

where $\text{Sublayer}(x)$ denotes self-attention or feed-forward network and $\text{LayerNorm}(x)$ denotes layer normalization.

4.3 Feature Interaction Modeling

In the STOA mobility predictor [5], embedding vectors are directly concatenated, without considering high-order interaction of these vectors. This may greatly affect the accuracy of mobility prediction. According to our empirical observations, as shown in Fig. 2, feeding user embedding together with spatial-temporal embedding into the self-attention module performs better than concatenating it with the outputs of the self-attention module. Therefore, the feature interaction modeling module takes user embedding, location embedding and time embedding as input, and should take both second-order and third-order interactions into account. Motivated by the cross-based learning framework [16], we transform the feature matrix X^0, which stacks three embedding vectors by row, into X^1 and X^2 of the same shape through the following equations:

$$X^1_{h,*} = \sum_{i=1}^{3} \sum_{j=1}^{3} W^{h,1}_{ij} \left(X^0_{i,*} \circ X^0_{j,*} \right),$$

$$X^2_{h,*} = \sum_{i=1}^{3} \sum_{j=1}^{3} W^{h,2}_{ij} \left(X^0_{i,*} \circ X^1_{j,*} \right), \tag{5}$$

where $X^1_{h,*}$ denotes the h-th row of X^1, $W^{h,1}, W^{h,2} \in \mathbb{R}^{3\times3}$ denote the parameter matrices of the second-order and third-order interactions respectively. $\circ$ represents the Hadamard product, i.e., element-wise multiplication between two vectors. Here, X^1 captures second-order interaction between any two of three embedding vectors, and X^2 captures third-order interactions among three embedding vectors.

As shown in Fig. 1, the calculation of X^a, $a = \{1, 2\}$ can be achieved by two steps. First, introduce a 3-order tensor $O^a \in \mathbb{R}^{3 \times 3 \times d}$, which consists of the outer products of $X^{a-1}_{*,f}$ and $X^0_{*,f}$ for each dimension f, s.t. $1 \leq f \leq d$. By regarding O^a as an image of size 3×3, X^a is then obtained by applying convolution on the image with $W^{h,a}$ as a filter.

4.4   Attention and Predict

In this section, we discuss how to aggregate short-term preference with long-term regularity and how to train the parameters. Motivated by [5], we will apply use the attention mechanism for this task, by considering the check-in representation of the recent trajectory as query, and the check-in representations of the historical trajectory as memory slots. It is worth mentioning that we use only the last k historical representations. Denoting by $Z_j^{(q)}$ the representation of the last check-in q_j of the most recent trajectory, and by $Z_i^{(v)}$ the representation of the i-th check-in in the historical trajectory.

$$V_j = \sum_i \frac{\exp\left(\langle Z_j^{(q)}, Z_i^{(v)} \rangle\right)}{\sum_{i'} \exp\left(\langle Z_j^{(q)}, Z_{i'}^{(v)} \rangle\right)} Z_i^{(v)} \tag{6}$$

where $\langle x, y \rangle$ denotes dot product between vector x and y. V_j is then concatenated with $Z_j^{(q)}$, and passed it into a fully connected network for prediction. We then use the cross-entropy loss for parameter optimization.

5   Experiments

We will evaluate the proposed algorithm with three check-in datasets, reporting results of the comparison with competing baselines, ablation study and sensitivity analysis.

5.1   Datasets

The three datasets are Foursquare check-in datasets in different cities or at different periods. Table 1 summarizes dataset statistics. Note that the NYC-1 dataset [5] spans from Feb. 2010 to Jan. 2011, while both the NYC-2 dataset and the TKY dataset [25] span from Apr. 2012 to Feb. 2013. These data are the check-in information actively shared by users on the website, including user ID, timestamp, GPS location and poi ID.

Following [5], we split the trajectory into multiple sessions by setting time interval $\Delta t = 72$ hours and then filter out sessions with less than 5 records and users with less than 5 sessions. We then use the first 80% sessions as the training set and the left 20% sessions as the testing set.

Table 1. Dataset statistics

	City	Users	Check-ins	POIs
NYC-1	New York	886	82,575	10,497
NYC-2	New York	935	118,600	13,962
TKY	Tokyo	2,108	323,987	21,395

5.2   Settings

Table 2 gives the default setting of hyperparameters, some of them, such as learning rate, may be fine-tuned to achieve a better accuracy of mobility prediction. Moreover, we use last 10 check-in representations in the historical trajectory as memory slots for attention use. The reason for $k = 10$ is that the experiment shows that when k is around 10, the result is better.

Table 2. The default settings of hyperparameters

Parameter	Value	Parameter	Value
Learning rate	1e−4	location emb. dim	200
Gradient clip	5.0	time emb. dim	200
Decay of lr	0.1	user emb. dim	200
L2 penalty	1e−5	hidden size	600
#block	2	#head	1

5.3   Baselines

We compared the proposed algorithm with the following baselines:

- **Markov Model**, the first-order Markov model, the first algorithm was used in mobility prediction [1].
- **RNN**, a GRU model, is applied on the most recent check-in trajectories, with user, time and location as input at each time step.
- **DeepMove** [5], is the state-of-the-art mobility predictor. It only embeds location and time, and applies GRU for modeling the most recent trajectory, and uses the attention mechanism to capture long-term regularity. The representations from attention and RNN are then concatenated with user embedding to predict the next location.
- **RNN+SA$_{tl}$** [26], first applies GRU on the most recent sequence of location and time, and then uses the self-attention module to capture long-range dependence. The subscript (tl) indicates only time and location included. User embedding is concatenated with each output of self-attention.

- **SA_utl**, a variant of MoveNet, which only model the most recent trajectory without feature interaction. The subscript indicates user, time and location included.
- **FI+SA_utl**, a variant of MoveNet, which only model the most recent trajectory but feature interaction included.

5.4 Comparison with Baselines

Table 3. The comparison results with baselines

	NYC-1			NYC-2			TKY		
	Acc@1	Acc@5	Acc@10	Acc@1	Acc@5	Acc@10	Acc@1	Acc@5	Acc@10
Markov	0.0820	0.1190	0.1212	0.1304	0.1976	0.2019	0.1255	0.1860	0.1900
RNN	0.1453	0.2995	0.3466	0.1883	0.3728	0.4260	0.1259	0.2572	0.3067
DeepMove	0.1322	0.2911	0.3419	0.1763	0.3702	0.4302	0.1451	0.2965	0.3547
RNN+SA_tl	0.1446	0.3041	0.3495	0.1887	0.3902	0.4456	0.1158	0.2433	0.2915
SA_utl (ours)	0.1507	0.3213	0.3701	0.1966	0.4008	0.4574	0.1335	0.2683	0.3205
FI+SA_utl (ours)	0.1491	0.3303	**0.3865**	**0.1976**	0.4196	0.4856	0.1326	0.2711	0.3237
MoveNet (ours)	**0.1534**	**0.3318**	0.3843	0.1972	**0.4227**	**0.4888**	**0.1474**	**0.3100**	**0.3683**

We report the accuracy of the mobility predictor in terms of Acc@1, Acc@5 and Acc@10, and show the results in Table 3. Acc@k means whether the top k items in the predicted result have the correct item. From this table, we have the following observations.

First, the proposed MoveNet outperforms the state-of-the-art predictor, i.e., DeepMove, by 9.82%, 10.91% and 9.95% on average in terms of Acc@1, Acc@5 and Acc@10. The Markov model is the worst of all, indicating the power of neural network sequential models.

Second, self-attention (SA_utl) is better than RNN, the relative improvements are 4.72%, 6.37% and 6.22% on average in terms of Acc@1, Acc@5 and Acc@10. Placing self-attention on top of RNN can improve the accuracy of mobility predictor, but does not perform as well as the self-attention model.

Third, incorporating feature interaction modeling can lead to 2.85% and 3.87% improvements on average in terms of Acc@5 and Acc@10 by comparing FI+SA_utl with SA_utl. The self-attention model with feature interaction modeling even performs comparatively to MoveNet.

Finally, modeling long-term regularity can be beneficial, by comparing MoveNet with FI+SA_utl in the TKY dataset. However, improvements in the other two datasets are marginal.

5.5 How to Use User Embedding

In order to understand how to better incorporate user embedding, we evaluate two GRU models with the most recent trajectory in the NYC-2 dataset. The first GRU model ($U+GRU_{tl}$) takes location and time as input at each step, and concatenate the output of GRU at each step with user embedding for prediction. The second GRU model (GRU_{utl}) takes user, time and location as input, and directly uses the output of GRU for prediction. We then report the Acc@1 and Acc@5 of these two GRUs with user embedding size varied. We can observe that GRU_{utl} is much better than $U+GRU_{tl}$. However, with the growing size of user embedding, the margin between them first increases and then decrease. Overall, we always suggest the second way to incorporate user embedding.

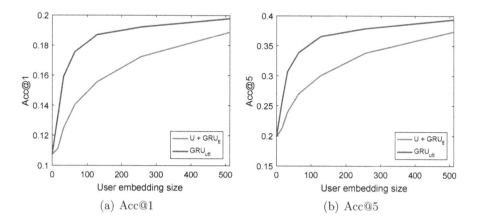

(a) Acc@1   (b) Acc@5

Fig. 2. Accuracy comparison with check-in features

5.6   When Long-Term Regularity Takes Effect

We observe the long-term regularity is only useful in the TKY dataset. To understand when long-term regularity can take effect, we compare the predictability of mobility behavior [20] in these datasets and plot the distribution of predictability over popularity in Fig. 3. We can observe that in the TKY dataset much more users are highly-predictable (>0.71). Predicting mobility for these users is more dependent on the long-term regularity. Also, the statistics show trajectory length in the TKY dataset is around 20% longer than that in the NYC-2 dataset. Therefore, the long-term regularity plays more important role in the TKY dataset.

5.7   Sensitivity Analysis

In natural language processing, the number of blocks and heads in the self-attention module is set to 6 and 8, respectively [23]. These settings may not the best choice for mobility predictor. To this end, we vary the number of blocks from 1 to 3 and the number of heads from 1 to 6 and report the results of evaluation in Table 4. We can make the following observations. First, 2 blocks are better

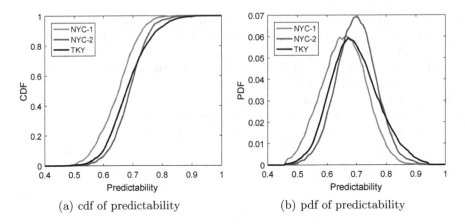

Fig. 3. Predictability of mobility behavior in the three datasets

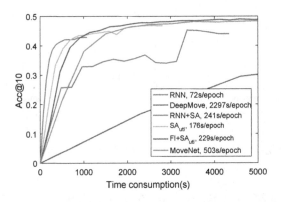

Fig. 4. Training efficiency comparison with baselines

in the NYC datasets, while in the TKY dataset the accuracy is dramatically degraded with the increasing number of blocks. Second, 1 head is better in the NYC datasets, and an increasing number of heads leads to accuracy degradation. However, in the TKY dataset, the better number of heads is 3. In other words, these two parameters should be fine-tuned from task to task, from dataset to dataset.

Table 4. Acc@5 w.r.t the number of heads (#H) and blocks (#B).

#B	NYC-1	NYC-2	TKY	#H	NYC-1	NYC-2	TKY
1	0.3166	0.3889	0.2785	1	0.3213	0.4008	0.2683
2	0.3213	0.4008	0.2683	3	0.3060	0.3880	0.2787
3	0.3215	0.4001	0.0877	6	0.3019	0.3882	0.2779

5.8   Training Efficiency Comparison

Comparing MoveNet with DeepMove, we replace RNN with self-attention, so training efficiency can be significantly promoted due to the capacity of parallel computing. Therefore, we record time cost of training in each epoch and show the results in Fig. 4. We can observe that MoveNet is not only 4x faster in each epoch of training, but also converges faster than DeepMove. And we use the same training strategy as DeepMove, when the accuracy of two consecutive epochs is no longer improved, we will use a smaller learning rate to train from the previous best model and stop training when the learning rate is small enough.

6   Conclusion

In this paper, we proposed MoveNet, a new mobility predictor, based on self-attention and feature interaction modeling. MoveNet is not only faster than the SOTA predictor in terms of empirical convergence and running time cost, but also outperform the competing baselines for mobility prediction according to evaluation with three real-world datasets.

Acknowledgments. This paper is partially supported by Municipal Program on Science and Technology Research Project of Wuhu City (No. 2019yf05) and the Fundamental Research Funds for the Central Universities.

References

1. Ashbrook, D., Starner, T.: Learning significant locations and predicting user movement with GPS. In: Proceedings of ISWC 2002, pp. 101–108. IEEE (2002)
2. Chen, M., Liu, Y., Yu, X.: NLPMM: a next location predictor with Markov modeling. In: Tseng, V.S., Ho, T.B., Zhou, Z.-H., Chen, A.L.P., Kao, H.-Y. (eds.) PAKDD 2014. LNCS (LNAI), vol. 8444, pp. 186–197. Springer, Cham (2014). https://doi.org/10.1007/978-3-319-06605-9_16
3. Chen, S.F., Goodman, J.: An empirical study of smoothing techniques for language modeling. In: Proceedings of ACL 1996, pp. 310–318. ACL (1996)
4. Cheng, C., Yang, H., Lyu, M.R., King, I.: Where you like to go next: successive point-of-interest recommendation. In: Proceedings of IJCAI 2013, pp. 2605–2611. AAAI Press (2013)
5. Feng, J., et al.: Deepmove: predicting human mobility with attentional recurrent networks. In: Proceedings of the 2018 World Wide Web Conference, pp. 1459–1468. International World Wide Web Conferences Steering Committee (2018)
6. Feng, S., Li, X., Zeng, Y., Cong, G., Chee, Y.M., Yuan, Q.: Personalized ranking metric embedding for next new poi recommendation. In: Proceedings of IJCAI 2015, pp. 2069–2075. AAAI Press (2015)
7. Gao, H., Tang, J., Liu, H.: Exploring social-historical ties on location-based social networks. In: Proceedings of ICWSM 2012 (2012)
8. Gao, H., Tang, J., Liu, H.: Mobile location prediction in spatio-temporal context. In: Proceedings of the Mobile Data Challenge at the 10th International Conference on Pervasive Computing (2012)

9. Gao, Q., Zhou, F., Trajcevski, G., Zhang, K., Zhong, T., Zhang, F.: Predicting human mobility via variational attention. In: The World Wide Web Conference, pp. 2750–2756. ACM (2019)
10. Horner, M., O'Kelly, M.: Embedding economies of scale concepts for hub network design. J. Transp. Geogr. **9**(4), 255–265 (2001)
11. Hufnagel, L., Brockmann, D., Geisel, T.: Forecast and control of epidemics in a globalized world. Proc. Natl. Acad. Sci. U. S. A. **101**(42), 15124–15129 (2004)
12. Kitamura, R., Chen, C., Pendyala, R., Narayanan, R.: Micro-simulation of daily activity-travel patterns for travel demand forecasting. Transportation **27**(1), 25–51 (2000)
13. Lian, D., Xie, X., Zheng, V.W., Yuan, N.J., Zhang, F., Chen, E.: CEPR: a collaborative exploration and periodically returning model for location prediction. ACM Trans. Intell. Syst. Technol. **6**(1), 1–27 (2015)
14. Lian, D., Zhao, C., Xie, X., Sun, G., Chen, E., Rui, Y.: GEOMF: joint geographical modeling and matrix factorization for point-of-interest recommendation. In: Proceedings of KDD 2014, pp. 831–840. ACM (2014)
15. Lian, D., Zhu, Y., Xie, X., Chen, E.: Analyzing location predictability on location-based social networks. In: Tseng, V.S., Ho, T.B., Zhou, Z.-H., Chen, A.L.P., Kao, H.-Y. (eds.) PAKDD 2014. LNCS (LNAI), vol. 8443, pp. 102–113. Springer, Cham (2014). https://doi.org/10.1007/978-3-319-06608-0_9
16. Lian, J., Zhou, X., Zhang, F., Chen, Z., Xie, X., Sun, G.: xDeepFM: combining explicit and implicit feature interactions for recommender systems. In: Proceedings of KDD 2018, pp. 1754–1763. ACM (2018)
17. Mathew, W., Raposo, R., Martins, B.: Predicting future locations with hidden Markov models. In: Proceedings of the 2012 ACM Conference on Ubiquitous Computing, pp. 911–918. ACM (2012)
18. Monreale, A., Pinelli, F., Trasarti, R., Giannotti, F.: Wherenext: a location predictor on trajectory pattern mining. In: Proceedings of KDD 2009, pp. 637–646. ACM (2009)
19. Noulas, A., Scellato, S., Lathia, N., Mascolo, C.: Mining user mobility features for next place prediction in location-based services. In: Proceedings of ICDM 2012, pp. 1038–1043. IEEE (2012)
20. Song, C., Qu, Z., Blumm, N., Barabási, A.: Limits of predictability in human mobility. Science **327**(5968), 1018–1021 (2010)
21. Song, L., Kotz, D., Jain, R., He, X.: Evaluating location predictors with extensive Wi-Fi mobility data. In: Proceedings of INFOCOM 2004, vol. 2, pp. 1414–1424. IEEE (2004)
22. Teh, Y.W.: A hierarchical Bayesian language model based on Pitman-Yor processes. In: Proceedings of ACL 2006, pp. 985–992. ACL (2006)
23. Vaswani, A., et al.: Attention is all you need. In: Advances in Neural Information Processing Systems, pp. 5998–6008 (2017)
24. Yang, C., Sun, M., Zhao, W.X., Liu, Z., Chang, E.Y.: A neural network approach to jointly modeling social networks and mobile trajectories. ACM Trans. Inf. Syst. (TOIS) **35**(4), 36 (2017)
25. Yang, D., Zhang, D., Zheng, V.W., Yu, Z.: Modeling user activity preference by leveraging user spatial temporal characteristics in LBSNs. IEEE Trans. Syst. Man Cybern.: Syst. **45**(1), 129–142 (2014)
26. Zeng, J., He, X., Tang, H., Wen, J.: A next location predicting approach based on a recurrent neural network and self-attention. In: Wang, X., Gao, H., Iqbal, M., Min, G. (eds.) CollaborateCom 2019. LNICST, vol. 292, pp. 309–322. Springer, Cham (2019). https://doi.org/10.1007/978-3-030-30146-0_21

27. Zhang, C., Han, J., Shou, L., Lu, J., La Porta, T.: Splitter: mining fine-grained sequential patterns in semantic trajectories. Proc. VLDB Endow. **7**(9), 769–780 (2014)
28. Zhao, P., et al.: Where to go next: a spatio-temporal gated network for next poi recommendation. In: Proceedings of the AAAI Conference on Artificial Intelligence, vol. 33, 5877–5884 (2019)
29. Zhao, S., Zhao, T., Yang, H., Lyu, M.R., King, I.: Stellar: spatial-temporal latent ranking for successive point-of-interest recommendation. In: Proceedings of AAAI 2016 (2016)
30. Zheng, V., Zheng, Y., Xie, X., Yang, Q.: Towards mobile intelligence: learning from GPS history data for collaborative recommendation. Artif. Intell. **184**, 17–37 (2012)

Predicting Adverse Drug-Drug Interactions via Semi-supervised Variational Autoencoders

Meihao Hou[1,2], Fan Yang[3,4], Lizhen Cui[1,2(✉)] [iD], and Wei Guo[1,2]

[1] School of Software, Shandong University, Jinan, China
hmhhhg@163.com
[2] Joint SDU-NTU Centre for Artificial Intelligence Research(C-FAIR),
Shandong University, Jinan, China
{clz,guowei}@sdu.edu.cn
[3] School of Public Health, Cheeloo College of Medicine, Shandong University,
Jinan, Shandong, China
fanyang983@gmail.com
[4] Institute for Medical Dataology, Shandong University, Jinan, Shandong, China

Abstract. Adverse Drug-Drug Interactions (DDIs) are a very important risk factor in the medical process, which may lead to readmission or death. Although a part of DDIs can be obtained through *in vitro* or *in vivo* experiments in the drug development stage, a large number of new DDIs still appear after the market, more and more researchers begin to pay attention to the research related to drug molecules, such as drug discovery, drug target prediction, DDIs prediction, etc. In recent years, many computational methods for predicting DDIs have been proposed. However, most of them only used labeled data and neglect a lot of information hidden in unlabeled data. Moreover, they always focus on binary prediction instead of multiclass prediction, although the exact DDI type is very helpful for our reasonable choice of medication. In this paper, a Semi-Surpervised Variational Autoencoders (SPRAT) method for predicting DDIs is proposed, which is composed of a neural network classifier and a Variational autoencoders (VAE). Classifier is the core components, VAE plays a role of calibration. In the end, the predicted label is a multi-hot vector which indicates specific DDI types between drug pairs. Finally, the experiments on real world dataset demonstrate the effectiveness of the proposed method in this paper.

Keywords: Drug-drug interaction · Semi-surpervised learning · Variational autoencoders · Prediction

1 Introduction

Drug-Drug interactions usually occur when patients take the combination drugs, because a drug can affect the activity of another drug in the body [9], which is likely to cause serious incidence rate and mortality [11]. Although some adverse

© Springer Nature Switzerland AG 2020
X. Wang et al. (Eds.): APWeb-WAIM 2020, LNCS 12318, pp. 132–140, 2020.
https://doi.org/10.1007/978-3-030-60290-1_10

DDIs have been screened out by *in vivo* and *in vitro* experiments during the drug development stage, many new DDIs have been found accidentally after the drug was put on the market [8]. With the abundance of drug-related molecular data and adverse event reporting data, such as Drugbank and FDA Adverse Event Reporting System (FAERS), a large number of researchers have focused their attention on the study of adverse DDIs.

Although there are many computational methods to predict potential DDIs, such as similarity based [5,7,14], classification based [3,10] and network-based [15,16], there are still some problems that are not highlighted.The first problem is that many works regard DDI prediction as binary prediction rather than multiclass prediction.However, it is very important to predict the specific types of DDI for patient's medication [13]. Another problem is that most of the previous methods are supervised learning, which depends on adequate labeled data. Many existing databases contain a lot of known DDI, but compared with the whole search space, it is still insufficient. Therefore, the supervised method will be affected by over fitting, which will reduce the prediction accuracy. Similarly, when unsupervised learning is used, the model will be a two-step rather than an end-to-end learning model, which will also greatly affect the prediction performance.

In order to overcome the above two problems, this paper focuses on the prediction of specific adverse drug reactions, and makes better use of data resources to improve the prediction performance. Therefore, we develope a Semi-Surpervised Variational Autoencoders (SPRAT) method, which actually can be seen as an ensemble model composed of a deep network classifier and a Variational Autoencoders (VAE). Discrimination classifier is the core module, which is calibrated by VAE. When the input is unlabeled data, the optimization of VAE reconstruction error is helpful to get a better classifier, so as to get more accurate ADRs prediction results. Finally, the experimental results using real datasets demonstrate our SPRAT can get a better ADRs predictive performance than other baseline methods.

2   Preliminaries

In order to describe the proposed method, in this section, some notations will be briefly defined, and introduce a main construction of the model: variational autoencodesr.

Definition 1. *Set of Labeled Drug Pairs and Set of Unlabeled Drug pairs*

In order to make better use of the information in the data set, we use the known DDI as the tag data, and the other DDI as the unmarked data. Therefore, set D_L is the set of labeled drug pairs and D_U is the set of unlabeled drug pairs.

Definition 2. *DDI Data*

The DDI data includes n drugs, w pairs of drug interaction and v types of adverse drug reactions. We denote $D = \{d_1, d_2, ..., d_n\}$ as the set of drugs, $I = \{i_1, i_2, .., i_w\}$ as known DDI drug pairs and $R = \{r_1, r_2, ..., r_v\}$ as all types of adverse drug reaction between drug pairs. Therefore, we can denote labeled data D_L described in the last section as $D_L = \{(d_p, r, d_q)|d_p, d_q \in D, 0 < p, q < n, r \subset R\}$.

Definition 3. *Drug Side Effects*

Each drug has its own side effects, except for adverse drug-drug interactions. Define all side effects exist in our DDI data as S, $S = \{s_1, s_2, ..., s_k\}$. Then, we denote $s(s \subset S)$ as owned side effects of one drug.

Variational Autoencoders

VAE is a series of models in which the input data is transformed into a coding vector, and each dimension represents some learning attributes about the data and decoder network, and then obtains these values and attempts to reconstruct the original input. It is worth noting that original autoencoders output a single value for each encoding dimension in latent representation, whereas a variational autoencoder provides a probability distribution for each latent attribute. So that it can serve as a generative model as G̲enerative A̲dversarial N̲etworks (GAN) do.

3   Method

3.1   Overview of Our Method

The proposed method consists of three parts, as shown in Fig. 1: classifier, encoder and decoder. Moreover, the encoder and the decoder together form a VAE. In brief, classifier can be seen core component in our model with VAE as a calibrator to improve performance of the classifier. Specifically, the VAE encode its input into latent representation z, if we join a label y into z, then decoder strive to reconstruct the input based on z and y. As in conditional VAE, a more accurate y can be more informative and helpful for the reconstruction process. Similarly the predicted label y' of our classifier will do so as to. In this way, the classifier will be benefited when the input is unlabeled data, while we optimizing the reconstruction loss of VAE, which is exactly what we want.

Adverse Drug-Drug Interaction Prediction Task The task is to predict unknown new adverse reactions between drug pairs. The following part will specifically introduce the model architecture centered on our prediction task. First, we gain labeled data (x, y) from D_L and unlabeled data x from D_U. Then, we input the concatenated feature vector representation $[x_i, x_j]$ of the drug pairs (d_i, d_j) to classifier and encoder, whether it is labeled or unlabeled. In the next step, the training of the model will be divided into two situations. The first is that the data is labeled, we directly incorporate the label y to latent variable z. In that case, both classifier loss and VAE loss need to be optimized. The other is the data is unlabeled, the predicted label y' from classifier is added to latent representation z and we just require to reduce the loss of VAE. At last, the overall loss of the model is the sum of the two parts, a multiple hot-label y' representing adverse drug reactions is obtained.

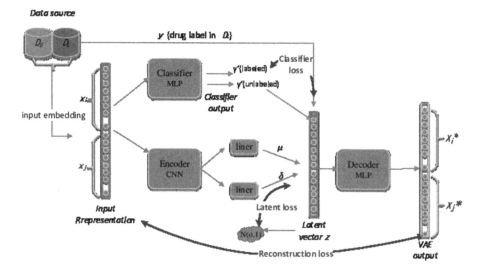

Fig. 1. The overview of our SPRAT model for DDIs prediction

3.2   Conditional VAE Model

Conditional variational autoencoders (CAVE) refer to adding label y to the model to aid in the generative module. CVAE involves a series of models instead of one, depending on how the label y is added. For this model we have two cases to consider, in the first case y is given directly, in the other y can be calculated by a discriminative model. Accurately, our method is based on the second situation exactly for this knowledge can help us form a better classifier and predict the labels of unseen data.

In the first case, the variational lower bound is similar to Eq. (1). In the second case, assume $q(y|x)$ represents the predicted layel via discriminative network. Therefore, the variational lower bound is shown in the following Eq. (2).

$$\log(p(x,y)) \geq E_{q(z|x,y)} \log(p(x|y,z)) - \mathrm{KL}(q(z|x,y)||p(z)) + \log p(y)$$
$$= -\mathcal{L}(x) \tag{1}$$

$$\log p(x) \geqslant E_{q(y,z|x)}[\log p(x|y,z) + \log p(y) + \log p(z) - \log(y,z|x)]$$
$$= \sum_y q(y|x)(-\mathcal{L}(x,y)) + \mathcal{H}(q(y|x)) \tag{2}$$
$$= -\mathcal{U}(x)$$

Loss Function
The training process for the model is described in detail below.

Goal Since the model is composed of a classifier network and a VAE, and the data can be divided into labeled and unlabeled, our training object is to optimize the following three losses:

$$\mathcal{J} = \mathcal{L}(x)_{(x,y)\subset D_L} + \mathcal{U}(x)_{(x)\subset D_U} + \mathrm{Classifier\_loss}_{(x,y)\subset D_L} \tag{3}$$

The input mentioned above for our classifier and encoder is the feature vector of (d_i, d_j). Next, there are two situations. The first is when input comes from D_L, y is an exact vector given by classifier. Thus, the optimization of VAE is just concatenating y to the latent variable z on the original basis. The specific calculation formula of loss during training is shown in Eq. (4).

$$\mathcal{L}(x)_{(x,y) \subset D_L} = \min\{\mathcal{D}(x*, x)^2 + \mathrm{KL}(q(z|x,y)\|p(z))\} \tag{4}$$

$\mathcal{D}(x*, x)^2$ represents reconstruction loss which can be obtained directly with machine learning tools. Moreover, $q(z|x, y)$ generally selects normal gaussian distribution and $p(z)$ is unit gaussian distribution. Finally, formula to be optimized is shown in Eq. (5)

$$\mathrm{KL}(q(z|x, y)\|p(z)) = \mathrm{KL}(N(\mu, \delta^2)\|N(0, 1)) = \frac{1}{2}(\mu^2 + \delta^2 - \log \delta^2 - 1) \tag{5}$$

Another situation is, y is output by classifier when input comes form D_U. We assume that the predicted label y' is added to only affect the mean of the distribution without affecting the variance. As a result, the loss function of this situation can be expressed as Eq. (6)

$$\mathcal{U}(x)_{(x) \subset D_U} = \mathcal{D}(x*, x)^2 + \frac{1}{2}((\mu - \mu^Y)^2 + \delta^2 - \log \delta^2 - 1) \tag{6}$$

4 Experiments

This section briefly describes the datasets and experimental settings used. At the end, the experimental results on these datasets are explained.

4.1 Datasets

DDI Data
The FDA Adverse Event Reporting System (FAERS) is a database designed to support FDA post-marketing surveillance programs for pharmaceuticals and therapeutic biologics, including all adverse event information and medication error information collected by FDA. As a sub-database extracted from the FAERS, TWOSIDES [14] contains all types of adverse reactions between reported and confirmed drug pairs.

Drug Feature Information
Like TWOSIDES, OFFSIDES [14] is also a sub-database extracted from FAERS, which includes the drug side effects information about drugs. According to [1], it can be used as a phenotypic feature information to improve our performance

of prediction. In addition, the drug structure fingerprint can be received from PubChem [6], where the drug is represented as an 881 dimensional binary vector, and each bit represents whether there is a chemical substructure.

As described in the previous datasets, we eventually have 635 drugs, 63,055 distinct drug pairs and each drug own a 5,394-dimensional binary feature vector (4,513 side effect types and 881-dimensional fingerprint). We construct a DDI matrix used to query whether a group of drug pairs is labeled data, where 1 indicating that the two drugs interact and 0 means that the two drugs do not interact as far as we know, by the way, the diagonal elements are all set to 0.

4.2 Evaluations

In order to optimize the prediction results, cross validation is designed as an effective method to estimate the generalization error. First, we randomly assigned 10% of the drugs and all DDIs associated with these drugs to be tested. The remaining 90% were then divided into K groups (generally equal). Each group is verified once, and the rest k-1 subset is used as training set. Therefore, under the condition of k-CV, the average value of classification accuracy of the final verification set of K model is used as the performance index of the classifier. To increase the randomness, repeat the K-CV process 50 times. In addition, because of the imbalance of DDIs data, that is, the known positive samples are much smaller than the unknown samples, so the area under the precise recall curve (AUPR) [2] should be used as a measure of model performance.

4.3 Experimental Setup

We construct a DDI matrix used to query whether a group of drug pairs is labeled data, where 1 indicating that the two drugs interact and 0 means that the two drugs do not interact as far as we know, by the way, the diagonal elements are all set to 0. From a macro point of view, our SPRAT method is composed of a classifier and a VAE. From a macro point of view, our SPRAT method is composed of a classifier and a VAE. But in more detail, it contains three components across which the classifier and the decoder of VAE is realized with general deep network, the decoder of VAE is implemented by CNN.

The proposed method is compared with other methods which are completely different but perform well in DDIs prediction: Concatenated drug features, Dyadic prediction [4] and LoNAGE graph embedding [12].

4.4 Experimental Results

Experiment I: *Binary prediction*
First of all, in order to verify the advantages of the proposed model in ADRs prediction, the comparative method is applied to binary prediction, that is, only to find out whether two drugs interact, rather than to predict specific drug types. Table 1 shows the results w.r.t AUROC score and AUPR score. From the results we can

draw a conclusion our method performs better than other alternative approaches. Simultaneously, we find that deep learning based approaches (LoNAGE and our model) perform much better that general machine learning methods because of its powerful non-linear learning ability. Furthermore, AUROC score improves while AUPR score reduces when the K value of Cross-validation is increased.

Table 1. Comparison with Three State-of-the-Art Approaches by 50 Runs of 5-CV and 10-CV

Evaluation	Method	AUROC	AUPR
5-CV	Concatenated drug features	0.793	0.456
	Dyadic prediction	0.705	0.375
	LoNAGE graph embedding	0.857	0.482
	SPRAT(our model)	0.876	0.513
10-CV	Concatenated drug features	0.798	0.429
	Dyadic prediction	0.739	0.331
	LoNAGE graph embedding	0.883	0.447
	SPRAT(our model)	0.893	0.486

Experiment II: *Multi-class prediction*

Most importantly, we need to prove the effectiveness of our method in multiple ADRs prediction. In the LoNAGE method, latent representations output by encoder are input into a SVM for prediction label y. As shown in Fig. 2, compared with binary prediction, the multi-class prediction performance of all methods is reduced, which reveals that comprehensive prediction is more difficult than binary prediction. Despite this, our approach is still better than others in terms of both AUROC and AUPR.

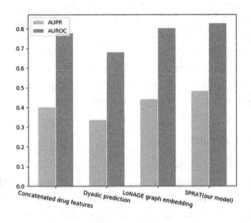

Fig. 2. The results of multi-class ADRs prediction under 5-CV.

5   Conclusion

This paper proposes a new method to predict the adverse reactions between drug combinations. In order to improve the prediction efficiency, this method uses the variational autoencoder to integrate the discriminant classifier. The greatest advantage of this model is that it is a semi-supervised learning method which can make full use of the effective information hiddened in unlabeled data. In order to verify the effectiveness of this method, experiments are carried out on a large real world dataset (Twosides) and compared with several representative methods. Finally, the experiments results demonstrate that SPRAT performs better than the other three state-of-the-art approaches. The direction of future work is to combine our method with the graph and add more drug-related data to improve the prediction accuracy of specific ADRs types.

Acknowledgements. This work is partially supported by the NSFC No. 91846205; the National Key R&D Program No. 2017YFB1400100; the Innovation Method Fund of China No. 2018IM020200; the Shandong Key R&D Program No. 2018YFJH0506, 2019JZZY011007.

References

1. Campillos, M., Kuhn, M., Gavin, A.C., Jensen, L.J., Bork, P.: Drug target identification using side-effect similarity. Science **321**(5886), 263–266 (2008)
2. Davis, J., Goadrich, M.: The relationship between precision-recall and ROC curves, pp. 233–240 (2006)
3. Jamal, S., Goyal, S., Shanker, A., Grover, A.: Predicting neurological adverse drug reactions based on biological, chemical and phenotypic properties of drugs using machine learning models. Sci. Rep. **7**(1), 872–872 (2017)
4. Jin, B., Yang, H., Xiao, C., Zhang, P., Wei, X., Wang, F.: Multitask dyadic prediction and its application in prediction of adverse drug-drug interaction, pp. 1367–1373 (2017)
5. Kastrin, A., Ferk, P., Leskosek, B.: Predicting potential drug-drug interactions on topological and semantic similarity features using statistical learning. PLOS ONE **13**(5), e0196865 (2018)
6. Kim, S., et al.: PubChem substance and compound databases. Nucleic Acids Res. **44**, 1202–1213 (2016)
7. Li, P., et al.: Large-scale exploration and analysis of drug combinations. Bioinformatics **31**(12), 2007–2016 (2015)
8. Percha, B., Altman, R.B.: Informatics confronts drug-drug interactions. Trends Pharmacol. Sci. **34**(3), 178–184 (2013)
9. Qato, D.M., Wilder, J., Schumm, L.P., Gillet, V., Alexander, G.C.: Changes in prescription and over-the-counter medication and dietary supplement use among older adults in the united states, 2005 vs 2011. JAMA Intern. Med. **176**(4), 473–482 (2016)
10. Shi, J., Li, J., Gao, K., Lei, P., Yiu, S.: Predicting combinative drug pairs towards realistic screening via integrating heterogeneous features. BMC Bioinformatics **18**(12), 409 (2017)

11. Tatonetti, N.P., Ye, P.P., Daneshjou, R., Altman, R.B.: Data-driven prediction of drug effects and interactions. Sci. Transl. Med. **4**(125), 125ra31 (2012)
12. Tran, P.V.: Learning to make predictions on graphs with autoencoders, pp. 237–245 (2018)
13. Vilar, S., Friedman, C., Hripcsak, G.: Detection of drug-drug interactions through data mining studies using clinical sources, scientific literature and social media. Brief. Bioinform. **19**(5), 863–877 (2018)
14. Zhang, P., Wang, F., Hu, J., Sorrentino, R.: Label propagation prediction of drug-drug interactions based on clinical side effects. Sci. Rep. **5**(1), 12339–12339 (2015)
15. Zhang, W., Chen, Y., Liu, F., Luo, F., Tian, G., Li, X.: Predicting potential drug-drug interactions by integrating chemical, biological, phenotypic and network data. BMC Bioinformatics **18**(1), 18 (2017)
16. Zitnik, M., Agrawal, M., Leskovec, J.: Modeling polypharmacy side effects with graph convolutional networks. Bioinformatics **34**(13), 457–466 (2018)

Smarter Smart Contracts: Efficient Consent Management in Health Data Sharing

Mira Shah[✉], Chao Li, Ming Sheng, Yong Zhang, and Chunxiao Xing

Research Institute of Information Technology, Beijing National Research Center
for Information Science and Technology, Department of Computer Science
and Technology, Institute of Internet Industry,
Tsinghua University, Beijing 100084, China
mira.vijay.shah@gmail.com,
{li-chao,shengming,zhangyong05,xingcx}@tsinghua.edu.cn

Abstract. The healthcare industry faces serious problems in data fragmentation and insufficient data sharing between patients, healthcare service providers and medical researchers. At the same time, patients' privacy must be protected, and patients should have authority over who can access their data. Researchers have proposed blockchain-based solutions to health data sharing, using blockchain for consent management. However, the implementation of the smart contracts that underpin these solutions has not been studied in detail. In this paper, we develop a blockchain-based framework for consent management in interorganizational health data sharing. We study the design of smart contracts that support the operation of our framework and evaluate its efficiency based on the execution costs on Ethereum. Our design improves on those previously proposed, lowering the computational costs of the framework significantly. This allows the framework to operate at scale and is more feasible for widespread adoption. Additionally, we introduce a novel contract that supports searching for patients in the framework that match certain criteria. This feature would be useful to medical researchers looking to obtain patient data.

Keywords: Blockchain · Smart contracts · Consent management · Health data

1 Introduction

The novel coronavirus COVID-19 has infected more than 5 millions people in more than 100 countries. However, the panic induced by the rapid spread of the disease has disrupted society more than the disease itself. The current situation shows that the rapid dissemination of accurate and trustworthy information is crucial in combating such threats to public health [1]. A system for sharing and disseminating medical information, where patients can share updates on their

ⓒ Springer Nature Switzerland AG 2020
X. Wang et al. (Eds.): APWeb-WAIM 2020, LNCS 12318, pp. 141–155, 2020.
https://doi.org/10.1007/978-3-030-60290-1_11

health status with doctors for remote monitoring, or even with the public, is thus urgently needed. To ensure viewers that medical data is trustworthy, this system should ensure that the origin of the data can be traced, such that it can be verified.

Such a system would also address the well known problem of medical data fragmentation. Patients' medical histories are stored across the healthcare organizations they have visited over their lives, and both doctors and patients are unable to access complete medical histories [26]. This may lower the quality of medical care patients received as doctors have less information on which to base their diagnoses and treatments. Additionally, a system to facilitate medical data sharing must prioritize patients' rights due to the sensitive nature of medical data [5]. This should empower patients to control who can access their data, and what parts of their data they can access, restoring ownership over medical data to the patients themselves.

Furthermore, patients lack the motivation to share their data with medical researchers as they do not receive immediate benefits. Therefore, a system that directly rewards patients for sharing their data with medical researchers would facilitate the creation of an ecosystem where patients are incentivised to share their data, and the community as a whole benefits from improved research outcomes.

A blockchain-based system could potentially meet these requirements. A blockchain, or distributed ledger, is an immutable, append-only chain of records that are stored in multiple nodes in a network. Using public-key cryptography, a consistent record of transactions is maintained in multiple machines in the absence of a trusted third party. Since a copy of the ledger is stored in every machine, the records are available to all members, providing for auditability and accountability. Using a consensus algorithm, records are added to the blockchain by through a process known as mining. In Bitcoin's Proof of Work consensus protocol, miners compete to extend the blockchain by solving a computationally intensive puzzle; the successful mining node appends a block (or group of transactions) to the chain and is rewarded for its effort with some Bitcoins. This new block is propagated to the other nodes, ensuring that a consistent record of transactions exists across all nodes in the Bitcoin network. The mining activities in a blockchain open the possibility of incentivising and rewarding certain behaviours [6].

To address the challenges to data sharing outlined above, we have previously proposed CrowdMed [16], a blockchain-based approach to managing patient consent and sharing medical data. It can be integrated into existing data management infrastructure, facilitating easy adoption [8]. CrowdMed is supported by the Ethereum network, as its support for smart contracts and mining activities meet our design requirements. Smart contracts can be understood as programs that are executed in a distributed manner on a blockchain network that enable different transactions to occur. The design and implementation of smart contracts in health data sharing systems has not been explored and evaluated in previous studies. In this paper, we study the design of the smart contracts to support the large-scale adoption of our proposed framework. As the number of users and network density increases, computation costs to execute these smart contracts may rise to a point where the framework can no longer operate. Through simulation and experimentation, we demonstrate that our smart contract designs improve on those previously proposed. Our design has lower computational costs, and scales sustainably as the network grows. We also introduce a novel contract that supports searching of patient data, allowing medical researchers to discover patients who own useful data for their needs. We summarize the contributions of this paper as follows:

- We implement a smart contract structure that has been previously proposed [6], and another that we have designed. We also implement an additional improvement to these two structures, thus implementing and evaluating a total of four smart contract systems. We show that our smart contract structure and proposed improvements exhibit better performance than those previously proposed.
- We deploy the smart contracts to an Ethereum test network and conduct extensive simulations to evaluate the smart contracts and demonstrate the benefits of our proposed improvements. To the best of our knowledge, this is the first in-depth study in the development of smart contracts for health data sharing where contracts were evaluated in isolation.
- We develop a smart contract to support querying patient data, and assess the practicability of our design. This is a novel feature in health data sharing systems.

The paper is organized as follows. In Sect. 2, we discuss related work. In Sect. 3, we introduce the Ethereum network and the function of smart contracts. In Sect. 4, we describe the design of the framework. In Sect. 5, we elaborate on the smart contract designs evaluated. In Sect. 6, we describe the experiments used for evaluating our designs. In Sect. 7, we discuss the limitations and implications of our research. Finally, we conclude the paper and discuss the future direction of this research in Sect. 8.

2   Related Work

2.1   Blockchain in Medical Data Sharing

Kumar et al. [13] give an overview of the potential applications of blockchain in healthcare, including for data sharing, data access control and maintaining medical history. The authors highlight the use of smart contracts to realize blockchain applications in healthcare, and raise the concern of scalability in developing such applications. We directly address this concern, studying the scalability of smart contracts developed for medical data sharing. Several blockchain-based systems for securely sharing and transferring medical data have been proposed, such as [2,17], and [6]. As in our research, smart contracts are the key innovation that enables this. However, the authors of [2] do not describe the design of the smart contracts specifically in depth. The authors of [17] provide a brief description of the smart contracts implemented in their system while [6] provides a detailed description of the structure and function of their proposed smart contracts. However, neither paper implements and conducts simulations on the smart contracts in isolation. In our paper, we evaluate the smart contract designs proposed and compare it with our novel design. Moreover, the ability to search patients' data on the blockchain is not explored in our literature review.

2.2 Blockchain Technologies

The success of Bitcoin prompted interest in studying other applications of blockchain. This is realised in the Ethereum network, which introduces smart contracts in blockchain networks. Harris [12] discusses the development of smart contracts and how common bugs can be avoided. These papers inform our development of smart contracts for our framework.

Data provenance is closely related to the function of the blockchain in our framework. An et al. [3] explore smart contracts for data trading while Neisse et al. [14] propose smart contracts for data provenance tracking. While applied in a different domain, the ideas presented by these authors, specifically in the evaluation of smart contract motivate our experimentation and design considerations. Focusing on whole systems rather than smart contracts, Ruan et al. [15] propose LineageChain, a blockchain system for data provenance tracking. The authors of [21] develop an access control system in blockchain; the system includes a search mechanism of blockchain data. We propose a similar system that is specifically designed for medical data sharing.

Search mechanism on blockchains is a key part of our research. The authors of [10] explore how encrypted data stored on a blockchain can be searched securely using smart contracts. Chen et al. [7] propose a searchable encryption scheme for electronic health record sharing. The ideas presented in these papers inform the design of the search contract proposed in our research, allowing us to integrate patient data search in health data sharing systems, a novel feature that has not been previously explored.

3 Smart Contract Preliminaries

In this section, we give an overview of Ethereum and smart contracts.

Ethereum was developed as a generalized application of blockchain, on which any transaction-based state machine can be built. This was achieved through the introduction of smart contracts. Smart contracts are code that is stored on the blockchain; smart contracts contain both data and functions that operate on the data. Smart contracts thus define transaction-based state machines, where the state is stored in the contract and can be altered by executing functions. Users execute the functions in a smart contract by sending transactions to them. Transactions sent to the blockchain are logged, providing auditability.

Ethereum contracts are coded using Solidity, a Turing-complete programming language. To prevent network abuse and ensure that all transactions eventually end, computation in Ethereum is bound by *gas*. Gas is the cost of computation in Ethereum; users pay miners a certain amount of gas for every transaction they send to a contract. Every transaction specifies a gas limit. If the computation associated with the transaction exceeds this limit, the transaction will not be mined and added to the blockchain. It is thus in a developer's interest to ensure that the computation costs associated with their smart contracts are not too high, and do not grow exponentially large as the number of users (and amount of data stored) increases. We thus evaluate our smart contracts on gas consumption and scalability.

4 Framework Design

In this section, we briefly describe the users of CrowdMed and the functionality of the framework, focusing on the functions that interact with the blockchain component. These inform the design of the smart contracts in Sect. 5, as well as the experiments run to evaluate the contracts in Sect. 6.

The users of CrowdMed are grouped into three types: patients, data creators and data viewers. Patients are the subjects of the medical data and regarded as the central authority over the data. They are the only users who can determine who may access their data. Data creators (primarily medical providers) are responsible for creating medical data records; every record created can be traced to this user and are thus responsible for its accuracy. In this paper, we shall treat medical providers as the only data creators. In the future, the framework can be easily extended for patients to be data creators as well, enabling them to share data such as readings from wearable monitoring devices. Lastly, data viewers are those who request to view patients' data. These are primarily also doctors (who may be requesting historical data) and medical researchers.

The key innovation of CrowdMed lies in its use of blockchain to maintain a record of actions performed on medical data, providing for auditability and accountability. In this paper, we focus on the data stored in the blockchain, and functions that users interact with. Actions such as creating medical data, sharing data and viewing data are executed by sending transactions to functions in smart contracts, thus creating an immutable log that can be traced and verified.

The key functions carried out on the blockchain are:

1. Data creation - *DC()*. This is executed by a data creator or doctor, who stores a pointer (to the data on his own database) as an entry in the patient's medical records. In this prototype, we treat this pointer as a query string that can be executed on the doctor's SQL database. A requesting party can thus obtain this query string, and execute it on the creator's database to obtain the patient's medical records.
2. Viewer authorisation - *VA()*. This is executed by the patient, and details the data that a viewer can access. In this prototype, we treat this as a compound query string corresponding to the medical records that the patient permits

the viewer to access. This function involves storing a query string that is associated with a specific viewer in the patient's permission settings.

3. Data transfers - *DT()*. This is executed by a viewer who requests a patient's data. The contract returns the query string corresponding to the medical records that the viewer is permitted to access.

The smart contracts we propose are evaluated against each other in terms of the computational costs associated with performing the above functions, and how it scales with load. Additionally, patients maintain a special permissions setting for medical researchers. Researchers can use a separate search contract to search for patients who match their criteria. They can then request data from patients according to the patient's permissions settings, in exchange for a fee. This fee is determined according to the amount and detail of the data shared, and can be issued in the form of tokens that can be exchanged for real-world benefits as determined by the government. In this way, patients are incentivised to share their medical data for research, and medical researchers can obtain real medical data directly from patients.

5 Smart Contract Design

In this section, we provide a detailed description of the smart contracts implemented. Sections 5.1–5.2 describe two different smart contract structures that support the key functions described in Sect. 4, and are compared in our experiments. Section 5.3 describes an improvement that can be applied to either structure. Lastly, Sect. 5.4 describes the smart contract that supports the patient search feature.

5.1   Patient-Provider Relationship-Centric Contract Structure

To structure the data stored on the blockchain, the Patient-Provider Relationship (PPR)-centric contract structure utilises three types of contracts as proposed in [6]. The data stored in each contract and relationships between the contracts are illustrated in Fig. 1.

The Registrar Contract (RC) stores a mapping of a user's unique identifier to their Ethereum address and Summary Contract (SC). This contract is used to link user's real-world identities to their digital identities. The unique identifier would be a hash of some real-world identifier, such as a government issued identification number.

A patient's SC contains information on recovering the patient's medical history and handles most of the key functions of the blockchain. It stores a list of PPR contracts, along with a status object that notifies users of changes to their PPRs. The creation of medical records, viewer authorisation and data requests are directed to the SC, which then updates the relevant PPR contract accordingly.

A PPR contract between a patient and a provider stores information on the patient's medical records that were created by the medical service provider, and

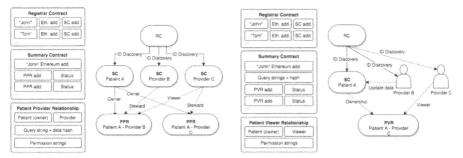

(a) PPR-centric contract structure   (b) PVR-centric contract structure

Fig. 1. Smart contract structures

is thus managed by the provider. Medical records are stored in the contract in the form of database query strings that are executed on the provider's database in order to recover the records themselves. To ensure data integrity, a hash of the data is also stored in the contract for cross-checking. Permission details are also stored in the PPR contract. This is stored in the form of query strings that correspond to a subset of the medical records stored in the PPR. The construction of these query strings are out of the scope of this paper.

In the Patient-Viewer Relationship (PVR)-centric contract structure, we use three types of contracts as illustrated in Fig. 2. The RC is identical to that is used in the PPR-centric contract structure.

In this structure, a patient's SC itself contains the patient's medical records, as well as handles the key functions of the blockchain. The patient's medical records are stored as a list of database query strings, along with the hash of the data. The SC also stores a list of PVR contracts, along with a status object that notifies users of changes to the PVRs. Creation of medical records is directed to and handled by the SC, while viewer authorisation and data requests are directed to the SC, which then updates the relevant PVR contract accordingly.

A PVR contract exists between a patient and a viewer, and handles the permission details of the viewer. The contract stores query strings that correspond to a subset of the medical records stored in the SC, and these query strings can only be updated by the patient. When a viewer requests a patient's data, the viewer sends a transaction to the SC. Using the sender's identification details, the SC finds the appropriate PVR contract, and returns the query strings stored in the PVR to the viewer.

We propose this contract structure as it allows for more efficient retrieval of medical records as they are stored in one contract, rather than across multiple contracts. In the situation where a patient interacts with many providers, iterating over the various PPR contracts to obtain the patient's complete medical history raises computation costs in the blockchain significantly. Updating a viewer's authorisation details also requires updating several PPR contracts. Hence, we hypothesise that the PVR-centric contract structure is more scalable as the number of patient-provider relationships increases. As one of the main benefits of adopting this framework is giving patients the freedom to visit different doctors, this is a major advantage of the PVR-centric contract structure.

5.2 Group-Based Access Rights

We hypothesise that a user is likely to define access groups for groups of viewers, rather than unique permissions for individual users. For example, a patient is likely to authorise all the doctors and healthcare providers they interact with to their complete medical history with the full amount of detail, and all medical researchers to a subset of their medical data. Thus, we propose group-based access rights to improve the efficiency of our smart contracts. The patient defines several groups of viewers, such as "clinics" and "researchers", and specifies access rights for these groups. Then, when a new viewer requests access to the patient's data, they can simply assign them to the appropriate group.

This modification to the smart contracts improves the efficiency of storing and updating access rights. Firstly, instead of storing multiple duplicates of complicated query strings for each viewer, we only need to store the query string once per group, and simply map viewers to groups. Secondly, updating the query strings for a viewer (e.g. when a new medical record is created) is significantly more efficient as only one query string must be updated, rather than multiple duplicates. The access rights are thus easier to maintain. Our framework does not place a limit on the number of groups a patient can create. The patient thus still has the freedom to create highly specific access rights for individual viewers if they wish.

5.3 Search Contract

In implementing the search function of our framework, we adapt ideas proposed in [10]. The search contract maintains a mapping of keywords to patients, returning a list of patients that match input keywords. These keywords can be updated by patients and doctors. For example, patients can expose their personal information such as age and gender to searchers by appending the keyword 'gender: male' to their keyword list. Meanwhile, doctors can append keywords such as 'diabetes' or other terms describing diagnoses and prescriptions to the patient's keyword list. To protect patients' privacy, these keywords are hashed before being stored in the search contract. When executing a query, the query term is also hashed. Upon obtaining the list of patients' addresses, the searcher can request access to a patient's data using the functions provided by the smart contracts described above.

To limit computational work for an action that should incur as little cost as possible, keyword searches are executed on single query terms. The client then handles the ranking of returned patients according to how well they match the query terms.

6   Experiments

In this section, we describe the experiments conducted to evaluate the smart contracts described in Sect. 5, and present the results of the experiments. We ran two different experiments. The first was to evaluate the smart contract structures based on gas consumption. From this, we chose the most optimal structure and conducted further performance evaluation, measuring transaction throughput and latency.

6.1   Experiment Design

For our first experiment, we evaluated our smart contracts by executing a sequence of transactions on a simulated Ethereum network, logging the gas consumption of each transaction. The simulated network uses ganache-cli v6.5.0. Smart contracts were written in Solidity v0.5.13 and compiled using solc v0.5.10. For the second experiment, we executed the same sequence of transactions on a locally hosted Ethereum network, measuring transaction throughput and latency. The network was built using geth v1.9.12.

Data. For our experiments, we obtain electronic medical records from the MIMIC-III critical care database[1]. Our smart contracts store query strings and data hashes that correspond to medical records created from patient visits. Thus, we first generate query strings that obtain full medical records that correspond to a single patient visit to a hospital in the database. The relevant table for this is the EVENTS table, and we join this with the remaining tables in the database to generate a complete medical record. We then obtain the SHA-256 hash of the medical record. These query string and data hash pairs are then randomly drawn to simulate the event where a patient visits a medical provider.

Procedure. Our test network in both experiments consists of 511 nodes, corresponding to 1 registration authority, 10 medical providers and 500 patients. We first register the doctors and patients on the network. Then, for each doctor, we execute the following operations and log the gas consumption:

1. For every doctor after the first, authorise the doctor to each patient's complete medical history.
2. Transfer each patient's complete medical history to the doctor.
3. Create 10 medical records for each patient.

This simulates the real-life scenario where patients change doctors over time. For simplicity, we assume that the patient authorises every doctor to their complete medical history.

For the second experiment, we varied the number of mining nodes and measured transaction throughput and latency.

---

[1] https://mimic.physionet.org/.

6.2 Results

The total number of transactions, gas cost and storage requirements of each of our contract structures is summarised in Table 1. The PVR-centric structures have lower gas costs, but this is traded off in larger storage requirements. However, the storage requirements of all contract structures implemented are relatively small. We discuss the results further below, in terms of the key functions executed on the blockchain. The four contract structures are compared in detail, followed by a brief assessment of the search contract.

Table 1. Summary of results

	Number of transactions	Total gas cost	Storage requirements
PPR-centric	64510	17,175 million	22.5 MB
PPR-centric, group-based access	69510	17,860 million	22.8 MB
PVR-centric	64010	15,147 million	27.8 MB
PVR-centric, group-based access	64510	14,343 million	27.5 MB

Gas consumption of creating medical records for patients is approximately constant with the number of medical records added, and implementing group-based access does not affect this trend. In both implementations of the PPR-centric structure, the gas cost of a single data creation operation fluctuates around an average of 249,000 while in the PVR-centric structures, the average gas cost is slightly lower at 243,000. This is likely because in the PVR-centric structure, data is stored directly in the summary contract, eliminating the need for an internal contract call.

Figure 2a shows the gas consumption of granting authorisation to a viewer, against the number of doctors the patient has previously seen. We can see that our hypotheses in Sects. 5.2 and 5.3 are verified. As the number of relationships increases, the gas consumption of authorising a viewer increases linearly in the PPR-centric contract structure. On the other hand, this remains constant in the PVR-centric contract structure. Additionally, implementing group-based access lowers gas consumption significantly, as the data being stored in the contract is simpler.

Figure 2b shows the gas consumption of transferring data to a viewer, against the number of doctors a patient has previously seen. Similar to viewer authorisation, the gas consumption of transferring medical data increases linearly in the PPR-centric contract structure, and remains constant in the PVR-centric contract structure. Group-based access raises gas consumption in the PPR-centric structure slightly, but does not have an effect in the PVR-centric structure.

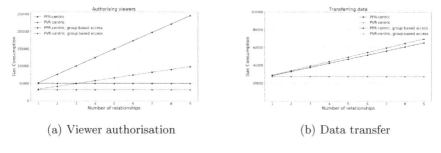

(a) Viewer authorisation   (b) Data transfer

Fig. 2. Gas consumption evaluation

Note that the data for the PVR-centric structure is identical with or without group-based access, thus the plots overlap completely.

Lastly, we assess the efficiency of the search contract. Updating the keyword list of a patient incurs an average gas cost of 63,000 per keyword, and a query incurs an average cost of 25,000. Since the minimum gas cost of a transaction is 21,000, we can see that our search contract operates efficiently, incurring relatively little gas to update keywords and execute queries.

From our results, we can see that the improvements proposed in Sects. 5.2 and 5.3 do indeed lower the gas consumption and thus computational complexity of executing the key functions of our framework. Most significantly, the improvements allow our framework to scale sustainably as the network becomes more dense and patients interact with more medical providers. In both viewer authorisation and data transfer, the PVR-centric structure improves performance from $O(n)$ in the PPR-centric structure to $O(1)$. We thus select the PVR-centric structure with group-based access as the optimum smart contract design and further evaluate its performance.

From Fig. 3a, it can be seen that transaction latency increases as the network size increases. The average transaction latency increases from about 2 s with 1 node, to just over 4 s with 8 nodes. However, the latency for registration transactions is significantly higher than the average. As registration transactions are one-time actions, they are not as significant as the EMR creation, viewer authorisation and data retrieval transactions (the key transactions). When considering the average latency of key transactions, latency is more acceptable, increasing from less than 1 s with one node, to about 3 s with 8 nodes.

Figure 3b shows that transaction throughput falls as the network size increases. This is expected as transaction latency increases with network size; as transactions take longer to be confirmed, the number of transactions confirmed per second falls. Average throughput falls from about 350 transactions per second with 1 node, to just over 50 with 8 nodes. Again, throughput for registration transactions is significantly lower than average. When only key transactions are considered, throughput is about 425 transactions per second with 1 node, to about 50 with 8 nodes.

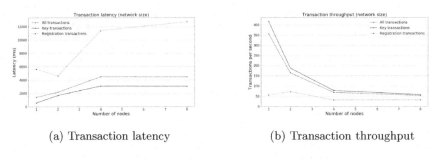

(a) Transaction latency   (b) Transaction throughput

Fig. 3. Performance with increasing network size

The significantly higher latency and lower throughput associated with registration transactions is due to the higher gas costs they incur. The number of transactions that can be included in a block is limited by the total gas of transactions in that block. Fewer registration transactions can be mined per block, resulting in higher latency and lower throughput. The importance of keeping gas consumption low in smart contract design can thus be seen in the performance impact of high-gas transactions.

7   Discussion

In this section, we first analyze the results of our findings. Next, we discuss some of the limitations of our research.

As shown in the previous section, as the network size increases, the performance of the blockchain worsens. More time is needed to achieve consensus, raising transaction latency and lowering throughput. This has adverse impact on the system as a whole. Patients must wait longer for their transactions to be confirmed, making it harder for them to track the activity relating to their data accurately. Nevertheless, CrowdMed can continue to operate reliably even if latency and throughput are sub-optimal, although the user experience would be significantly worse. The low performance of CrowdMed can be mitigated by using a consortium blockchain, where nodes have to be approved before they can join the network. In this way, the number of nodes in the blockchain can be restricted to ensure acceptable performance.

The smart contracts studied in this paper support the realization of a blockchain-based framework to enable medical data sharing. The smart contract structure we designed, together with the introduction of group-based access ensure the scalability of the framework as the number of users grows. The observation that gas costs of key functions do not grow rapidly as patients interact with more medical providers is crucial to goals of our framework. By empowering patients in medical data sharing, we enable patients to freely visit providers of their choice. As data can be shared over the Internet, patients can also obtain medical advice remotely from online service providers, which would be beneficial in the current COVID-19 outbreak. In this landscape, patients may interact with many more healthcare providers than they currently do. They may freely seek second, third or even fourth opinions on medical diagnoses and prescribed treatment plans, empowering the patient. This will democratize the healthcare industry as patients have greater bargaining power.

The inclusion of a mechanism for medical researchers to search for patients also enhances the usefulness of our framework. Researchers can search for highly specific patient data, building medical datasets that contain a wealth of useful data to mine for insights. For example, a research study on patients with diabetes can search for and obtain medical records from patients with diabetes. Assuming the global adoption of CrowdMed, the data collected can span patients from different countries, age groups and background, creating a comprehensive dataset from which new insights can be gained. Using today's traditional technologies and data collection methods, it is very difficult and costly for medical researchers to amass such a collection of data. Moreover, medical research organizations, particularly smaller institutions that do not have the backing of larger organizations, will no longer be hampered by the difficulty of obtaining sensitive, real-world medical data.

Several areas of the implementation of our framework are not explored in this paper. Firstly, the construction of query strings (particularly of those that describe access rights) is not addressed. The constructed query string should allow access to the desired subset of medical records, which could be realized by borrowing techniques from the rich body of studies about string similarity search and join [18–20,22–25]. Additionally, the patient should be able to select fields that a viewer can access. This may potentially complicate the construction of query strings. However, this would be handled by the application, rather than by the blockchain. Thus, we did not consider this in our development of smart contracts. Secondly, how the query strings will be executed on providers' databases is not addressed. We envision that a URL endpoint would handle this, and that minimal additional information would need to be encoded in the smart contracts. Lastly, the limitations of blockchain technologies remain a potential obstacle to our framework. As blockchain technologies are constantly being refined and improved, we hope that blockchain systems and networks can overcome the throughput and latency issues currently faced, such as those is processing streaming data [4,9,11]. In emergency situations, medical data is often urgently required. The real-life applicability of our framework thus rests on the continuous improvement of the Ethereum network and blockchain in general.

8   Conclusion and Future Work

Our proposed framework empowers patients with authority over their medical data, and encourages greater medical data sharing. The smart contracts developed in this paper execute the key functions of the framework efficiently. As shown in our experiments, our best design scales linearly with network density, and improves significantly on previous work in this area. Moreover, the inclusion of the search contract greatly increases the usefulness of our framework. We hope that smart contract developers can adapt our contracts for applications in other domains, particularly in the Internet of Things where data access management is a key concern.

In the future, we intend to create a complete, working prototype of the framework to address the limitations of this study described in Sect. 7. In developing the framework, ensuring that the application is secure and protects patients' privacy is our main priority, as well as ensuring the design is intuitive and useful. Finally, data harmonisation remains an obstacle in integrating data from heterogeneous sources, particularly in medical data where a universal set of data standards does not exist. We intend to explore this topic more, and integrate existing processes into our framework to fully realise a future in which patients have full ownership over their medical data, and medical data can be easily shared and mined for valuable insights.

Acknowledgements. This work was supported by National Key R&D Program of China (2018YFB1402701, 2018YFB1404401), NSFC (91646202).

References

1. COVID-19: fighting panic with information. Lancet **395**(10224), 537 (2020)
2. Amofa, S., et al.: A blockchain-based architecture framework for secure sharing of personal health data. In: Healthcom, pp. 1–6 (2018)
3. An, B., Xiao, M., Liu, A., Gao, G., Zhao, H.: Truthful crowdsensed data trading based on reverse auction and blockchain. In: Li, G., Yang, J., Gama, J., Natwichai, J., Tong, Y. (eds.) DASFAA 2019. LNCS, vol. 11446, pp. 292–309. Springer, Cham (2019). https://doi.org/10.1007/978-3-030-18576-3_18
4. Ao, X., Shi, H., Wang, J., Zuo, L., Li, H., He, Q.: Large-scale frequent episode mining from complex event sequences with hierarchies. ACM TIST **10**(4), 36:1–36:26 (2019)
5. Asghar, M.R., Lee, T., Baig, M.M., Ullah, E., Russello, G., Dobbie, G.: A review of privacy and consent management in healthcare: a focus on emerging data sources. In: e-Science, pp. 518–522 (2017)
6. Azaria, A., Ekblaw, A., Vieira, T., Lippman, A.: MedRec: using blockchain for medical data access and permission management. In: OBD, pp. 25–30 (2016)
7. Chen, L., Lee, W., Chang, C., Choo, K.R., Zhang, N.: Blockchain based searchable encryption for electronic health record sharing. Future Gener. Comput. Syst. **95**, 420–429 (2019)
8. Cohen, S., Zohar, A.: Database perspectives on blockchains. CoRR abs/1803.06015 (2018)
9. Das, A., Wang, J., Gandhi, S.M., Lee, J., Wang, W., Zaniolo, C.: Learn smart with less: building better online decision trees with fewer training examples. In: IJCAI, pp. 2209–2215 (2019)
10. Do, H.G., Ng, W.K.: Blockchain-based system for secure data storage with private keyword search. In: SERVICES, pp. 90–93 (2017)
11. Gu, J., Wang, J., Zaniolo, C.: Ranking support for matched patterns over complex event streams: the CEPR system. In: ICDE, pp. 1354–1357 (2016)
12. Harris, C.G.: The risks and challenges of implementing ethereum smart contracts. In: ICBC, pp. 104–107 (2019)

13. Kumar, T., Ramani, V., Ahmad, I., Braeken, A., Harjula, E., Ylianttila, M.: Blockchain utilization in healthcare: key requirements and challenges. In: Healthcom, pp. 1–7 (2018)
14. Neisse, R., Steri, G., Fovino, I.N.: A blockchain-based approach for data accountability and provenance tracking. In: ARES, pp. 14:1–14:10 (2017)
15. Ruan, P., Chen, G., Dinh, A., Lin, Q., Ooi, B.C., Zhang, M.: Fine-grained, secure and efficient data provenance for blockchain. PVLDB **12**(9), 975–988 (2019)
16. Shah, M., Li, C., Sheng, M., Zhang, Y., Xing, C.: CrowdMed: a blockchain-based approach to consent management for health data sharing. In: Chen, H., Zeng, D., Yan, X., Xing, C. (eds.) ICSH 2019. LNCS, vol. 11924, pp. 345–356. Springer, Cham (2019). https://doi.org/10.1007/978-3-030-34482-5_31
17. Theodouli, A., Arakliotis, S., Moschou, K., Votis, K., Tzovaras, D.: On the design of a blockchain-based system to facilitate healthcare data sharing. In: TrustCom/BigDataSE, pp. 1374–1379 (2018)
18. Tian, B., Zhang, Y., Wang, J., Xing, C.: Hierarchical inter-attention network for document classification with multi-task learning. In: IJCAI, pp. 3569–3575 (2019)
19. Wang, J., Lin, C., Li, M., Zaniolo, C.: An efficient sliding window approach for approximate entity extraction with synonyms. In: EDBT, pp. 109–120 (2019)
20. Wang, J., Lin, C., Zaniolo, C.: MF-Join: efficient fuzzy string similarity join with multi-level filtering. In: ICDE, pp. 386–397 (2019)
21. Wang, S., Zhang, Y., Zhang, Y.: A blockchain-based framework for data sharing with fine-grained access control in decentralized storage systems. IEEE Access **6**, 38437–38450 (2018)
22. Wu, J., Zhang, Y., Wang, J., Lin, C., Fu, Y., Xing, C.: Scalable metric similarity join using MapReduce. In: ICDE, pp. 1662–1665 (2019)
23. Yang, J., Zhang, Y., Zhou, X., Wang, J., Hu, H., Xing, C.: A hierarchical framework for top-k location-aware error-tolerant keyword search. In: ICDE, pp. 986–997 (2019)
24. Zhang, Y., Li, X., Wang, J., Zhang, Y., Xing, C., Yuan, X.: An efficient framework for exact set similarity search using tree structure indexes. In: ICDE, pp. 759–770 (2017)
25. Zhang, Y., Wu, J., Wang, J., Xing, C.: A transformation-based framework for KNN set similarity search. IEEE Trans. Knowl. Data Eng. **32**(3), 409–423 (2020)
26. Zhao, K., et al.: Modeling patient visit using electronic medical records for cost profile estimation. In: Pei, J., Manolopoulos, Y., Sadiq, S., Li, J. (eds.) DASFAA 2018. LNCS, vol. 10828, pp. 20–36. Springer, Cham (2018). https://doi.org/10.1007/978-3-319-91458-9_2

Joint Learning-Based Anomaly Detection on KPI Data

Yongqin Huang, Yijie Wang$^{(\boxtimes)}$, and Li Cheng

Science and Technology on Parallel and Distributed Processing Laboratory,
College of Computer, National University of Defense Technology, Changsha, China
huangyqin@163.com, {wangyijie,chengli09}@nudt.edu.cn

Abstract. Unsupervised anomaly detection on KPI (Key Performance Indicator) is an important research problem that has broad industrial applications. The dynamic change and infinity of KPI data make it a challenging problem to estimate the outlierness of KPI data. Existing methods detect anomalies only from a single perspective, which fails to capture the dynamic change of KPI data, leading to unsatisfying performance. In this paper, we propose a Joint Learning-based Anomaly Detection algorithm (JLAD) which integrates a bias-based model and a similarity-based model from two perspectives at the same time. Specifically, the similarity-based model motivates a data driven abnormal ratio setting which automatically obtains abnormal ratio for bias-based model to avoid manual setting. In turn, based on the bias-based model, we develop an automatic anomaly templates adding method that adds anomaly templates for similarity-based model to timely improve the prior knowledge. Experiments on 13 public KPI datasets empirically confirm the superiority of our algorithm with a F1-Score improvement up to 20.5% on average.

Keywords: KPI anomaly detection · Joint learning · Data-driven threshold setting · Automatic template adding

1 Introduction

Unsupervised Anomaly detection on KPI (Key Performance Indicator) data is a very hot issue and has many applications, such as Internet, business, etc. Once the related systems fail, it will cause losses to individuals and companies. For example, in order to reduce or avoid losses, many large Internet companies monitor the related KPI (e.g. response time) to find and resolve faults that is abnormal in KPI in time [1].

Supported by the National Key Research and Development Program of China (Grant No. 2016YFB1000101), the National Natural Science Foundation of China (Grant No. 61379052), the Science Foundation of Ministry of Education of China (Grant No. 2018A02002), the Natural Science Foundation for Distinguished Young Scholars of Hunan Province (Grant No. 14JJ1026).

X. Wang et al. (Eds.): APWeb-WAIM 2020, LNCS 12318, pp. 156–163, 2020.
https://doi.org/10.1007/978-3-030-60290-1_12

KPI data is typical time series data, which has the characteristics of dynamic change and infinity. Firstly, the characteristic of dynamic change over time makes it difficult to capture the anomaly from the perspective of abnormal data. Even domain experts may not be able to give complete prior knowledge (e.g. types of anomaly) [2], leading to missing some potential and meaningful anomalies. Secondly, with the uninterrupted operation of the system, the amount of KPI will be larger and larger, which will make obtaining labeled data a problem. Therefore, a rich body of literature about detecting KPI anomalies [3–13], as bias-based algorithms discussed in Sect. 2.1, is unsupervised and generally from the perspective of normal data. While this kind of algorithms, such as EWMA [3], require manually setting abnormal ratio in the process of converting anomaly scores into labels.

Therefore, we propose a joint learning-based anomaly detection algorithm (JLAD), which is unsupervised and from two perspectives on stream data. The main contributions of this paper are summarized as follows.

- We build two models from two perspectives to eliminate the impact of single perspective. The two models are *Bias-ADisc* (Bias-based Anomaly Discrimination) Model and *Similarity-ACap* (Similarity-based Anomaly Capturing) Model.
- We design a data-driven abnormal ratio setting method for the Bias-ADisc model to avoid the influence of human factors.
- We also develop an automatic anomaly template adding method for the Similarity-ACap model to achieve the purpose of dynamic update and improvement of anomaly templates on stream data.

2   Related Work

2.1   Bias-Based Algorithms

The main idea of the bias-based algorithms is using bias between the real data and the reconstructed or predicted data as anomaly score.

Prediction-Based Algorithms. MA (Moving Average) and its variant algorithms EWMA (Exponentially Weighted Moving Average) etc., calculate the average value of historical data of a certain length as the predicted value.

Decomposition-Based Algorithms. STL (Seasonal and Trend decomposition using Loess) [4] adopts LOESS (Locally Weighted Scatterplot Smoothing) [16] to estimate the seasonal components. It decomposes trend, seasonal and residuals, and then uses residuals as anomaly scores.

Neural Network-Based Algorithms. Donut, based on deep generative model-VAE(Variational Auto-Encoder), adopts modified ELBO and missing data injection, and MCMC imputation to reconstruct data [5]. And IF establishes an Independent-Frame based-on VAE to reconstruct data [6].

Integrated-Based Algorithms. IForest [8] classifies data through multiple independent trees, assigns different anomaly scores to the data at different leaf nodes, and integrates the results of multiple trees into the final anomaly scores; Also, a simple integration of multiple algorithms based on prediction and decomposition, use majority vote [17] or normalization [18] to detect anomalies.

Statistical Analysis-Based Algorithms. This kind of algorithm needs to calculate statistic and critical value. And then loop the specified number of times that theoretically equals to the number of true anomalies to compare the two values. If the statistic value is greater than the critical value, there is an anomaly. ESD (Extreme Studentized Deviate test), S-ESD (Seasonal ESD) and S-H-ESD (Seasonal Hybrid ESD) are based on the residual term of STL.

The above algorithms all need to specify the number or ratio of anomalies in real application scenarios, which may be affected by human subjective factors.

2.2 Similarity-Based Algorithms

In similarity-based algorithms, the distance-based method generally are used. Pei et al. develop Label-Less to label KPI, which is based on DTW [14,15]. Label-Less is a semi-automated labeling tool for anomaly detection, which needs anomaly templates that need given in advance and may be incomplete. And, they found the performance of DTW has certain advantages over SBD [19] and ED [2]. So we also adopt DTW in our method. Unlike Pei's work, we implement automatic template adding, without adding manually.

3   The Proposed Method

JLAD is mainly composed of two models. The first model adopts the bias-based algorithm that can detect unknown types of anomalies from the perspective of normal data; the second model uses the similarity-based algorithm that can detect known types of anomalies from the perspective of abnormal data. Define the data to be detected as D, where $D = <d_1, \ldots, d_t, \ldots, d_{|D|}>$.

3.1 Bias-ADisc Model

The Bias-ADisc model predicts the data in D, and then calculates its deviation from the real data as anomaly scores. EWMA is used to predict data, because the moving average of EWMA can well reflect the change trend of KPI. The predicted value v_t is obtained by weighted average of the predicted value v_{t-1} and the real value d_t, as shown in Eq. (1). The smaller the β is, the lower influence the older data has, and the larger influence the more recent data has. And the anomaly score equals to the absolute value of difference between v_t and d_t. Meanwhile, EWMA only needs to load d_t and v_{t-1} when calculating v_t, so it takes very little memory. With a abnormal ratio, the labels of D can be gotten.

$$v_t = \begin{cases} d_t & t = 1 \\ \beta * v_{t-1} + (1 - \beta) * d_t & t > 1 \end{cases} \tag{1}$$

3.2 Similarity-ACap Model

The Similarity-ACap model uses distance as similarity metrics, which is divided into three steps.

In order to improve time efficiency, adopt KNN (K-Nearest Neighbours) to pre-process D to get a set of anomalies P [2]. Convenient for KNN and inspired by ensemble learning [20,21], use first-order difference [20], MA, WMA, EWMA and Holt-winters [11] to convert KPI from one-dimensional to five-dimensional.

Firstly, acquire candidate segments. For the two adjacent point, p_i and p_j in P ($i < j$ and $i, j \in [0, |D| - 1]$) , if $j - i \leq a$ (default $a = 10$), p_j will be added to the segment where p_i is located; otherwise, p_i will be the tail of this segment and p_j will be the head of a new segment; on this basis, the obtained segments are expanded m and n (default $m = 5, n = 5$) points respectively forward and backward in D to obtain candidate segments which make up C.

Secondly, screen anomaly segments. (1) Select a template $T_i (i \in [0, |T| - 1])$ from T in turn; (2) Calculate the similarity distances between each candidate segment $C_j (j \in [0, |C| - 1])$ and T_i by DTW to obtain $|C|$ similarity distances; (3) Select q (default $q = |C| * 0.1$)segments with the smallest similarity-distance as the anomaly segments similar to the ith template; (4) Delete the q segments from C, and then update $|C|$. Repeat the above process until each template in T is compared or $|C| = 0$. And then, if the *range* (equal to the maximum minus the minimum) of the segment is less than a ratio v of the *range* of D, discard it.

Thirdly, locate anomaly. We divide the anomaly templates into two categories. **Single anomaly:** In a segment, only a few points suddenly deviate from the normal fluctuation range, as shown in Fig. 1(a) and 1(b). **Continuous anomaly**: In a segment, there is a continuous period of time that the data deviates from the normal range, as shown in Fig. 1(d). If the type of anomaly is **Single anomaly**, S-H-ESD is used. Otherwise, use first-order difference to judge the mutation point, which represents a anomaly.

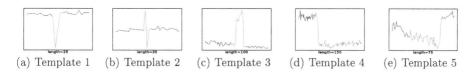

(a) Template 1   (b) Template 2   (c) Template 3   (d) Template 4   (e) Template 5

Fig. 1. Partial anomaly templates. Red part: abnormal data; Blue part: normal data. (Color figure online)

3.3 Joint Learning

This section achieves anomaly detection by joining two models and strengthening cooperation between the two models. It consists of three parts.

Firstly, set abnormal ratio. The Similarity-ACap model is used to provide the abnormal ratio. Suppose the number of anomalies detected by the Similarity-ACap model is n, and the number of anomalies that should be detected by the Bias-ADisc model is $f(n)$, calculated from Eq. (2). Then the abnormal ratio equals to $f(n)/|D| * 100\%$, and we will select anomalies according to this ratio. The existence of continuous anomalies depends on whether the anomaly is obtained from a template with continuous anomalies. For the Bias-ADisc model, the term $+2$ is because the model can detect unknown types of anomalies to avoid missing anomalies; Processing with a limit of 10 and dividing by 3 are to avoid excessive false alarms, due to the bad detection ability for data that has always shown a stable abnormal state.

$$f(n) = \begin{cases} 2 & n = 0 \\ n + 2 & n > 0 \text{ and no continous anomalies} \\ n + 2 & 0 < n \leq 10 \text{ and existing continous anomalies} \\ \lfloor n/3 \rfloor + 2 & n > 10 \text{ and existing continous anomalies} \end{cases} \qquad (2)$$

Secondly, add anomaly templates. (1) Select anomaly only detected by the Bias-ADisc model. Generate segments for these abnormal points according to the candidate segment acquiring method in Sect. 3.2. If the range of the segment is greater than the ratio v of the range of all historical data, mark this segment as a potential template, and mark the point with the highest anomaly score as p_a. (2) Calculate the difference between p_a and each point around it. If both the front and back sides have consistent positive and negative signs, it is considered as single anomaly locating method, as shown in Fig. 1(a). If one side has positive/negative sign, and another has mixed sign and stays in a small range, it is considered as a continuous anomaly method, as shown in Fig. 1(d).

Thirdly, combine the results of the two models. The union method is adopted.

4   Experiments

Because it is stream-oriented anomaly detection, the following assumptions are given: if the length of the data that arrives in each unit time is less than 1000, combine historical data with the current data to make up 1000 as D, otherwise use the newly arrived data as D, so the length of D satisfies $|D| \geq 1000$.

4.1   Experiment Results

There are 13 public desensitization KPI datasets, which are from the well-known Internet companies (e.g. Baidu, Tencent, and Alibaba). According to the strategy shown in Fig. 2, set Advanced and Delay to 1. If the algorithm detects an anomaly in the seg 1 area, that is, the label "1" appears, it is considered that the anomalies in the seg 2 area is correctly detected. The red part of the predicted label in the figure will be modified, and the detection results other than seg 2

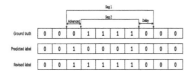

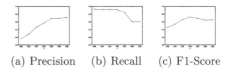

(a) Precision   (b) Recall   (c) F1-Score

Fig. 2. Illustration of the modified strategy. (Color figure online)

Fig. 3. Effect of parameter v on performance

are not processed. The modified result is shown in the revised label. Then precision, recall, and f1-score are computed. The information of the datasets and the results of JLAD and the comparison algorithms are shown in Table 1. IF (IForest), Donut, Z-Score, MA and HW(Holt-Winters) are selected as comparison algorithms, with the abnormal ratio 0.5%. As can be seen from the Table 1, JLAD has a high recall, and this is more in line with actual needs. Using F1-score as the performance metrics, in 13 datasets, JLAD's average performance is better than the comparison algorithm, and on 9 datasets, JLAD is preferred to all comparison algorithms. Totally, there is a performance improvement from 8% to 59%, with an average of 20.5%.

Table 1. Information of datasets and Result of JLAD and comparison algorithms

			JLAD			IF	Donut	Z-score	MA	HW
Data	#N	#o	r	Precision	Recall	F1-score	F1-score			
kpi-0	115686	10218	8.83%	0.8616	0.9898	**0.9213**	0.9149	0.8671	0.8457	0.9003	0.8929
kpi-1	116196	7216	6.21%	0.8402	0.9731	0.9018	0.9543	**0.9629**	0.9564	0.9572	0.9255
kpi-2	115948	9522	8.21%	0.8739	0.9982	0.932	0.9728	**0.9896**	0.9780	0.9775	0.9551
kpi-3	90209	546	0.61%	0.6769	0.7253	0.7003	0.676	0.5603	0.4539	**0.7664**	0.3728
kpi-4	132882	1014	0.76%	0.7841	0.9744	**0.869**	0.688	0.7402	0.6748	0.8043	0.2561
kpi-5	132901	331	0.25%	0.754	1	**0.8597**	0.5473	0.6775	0.4598	0.6077	0.1765
kpi-6	116488	406	0.35%	0.8185	1	**0.9002**	0.6465	0.7223	0.5815	0.6755	0.2540
kpi-7	132289	3008	2.27%	0.9318	1	**0.9647**	0.9075	0.9600	0.9330	0.9238	0.8339
kpi-8	124113	361	0.29%	0.7597	0.9723	**0.853**	0.623	0.5379	0.5754	0.6617	0.2105
kpi-9	132893	463	0.35%	0.8434	1	**0.915**	0.5776	0.7436	0.7097	0.6667	0.1737
kpi-10	132847	993	0.75%	0.7477	0.9698	**0.8444**	0.7723	0.5803	0.6783	0.8027	0.4853
kpi-11	116112	7579	6.53%	0.9394	0.9918	0.9649	0.7411	0.9688	**0.9747**	0.9644	0.9146
kpi-12	132302	2994	2.26%	0.9333	1	**0.9655**	0.9058	0.9571	0.9344	0.9231	0.8345
Avg				0.828	0.9688	**0.8917**	0.7811	0.7889	0.7504	0.8178	0.5604
Imp							14.16%	13.03%	18.83%	9.04%	59.12%

4.2   Discussion About Pre-process and Parameter-v

Performance of KNN in Pre-process: In Sect. 3.2, KNN is adopted to improve time efficiency. Here IForest, OCSVM(One-Class SVM) [12], LOF(Local Outlier Factor) [13], and method without pre-process for comparison are used. For KNN, IForest, OCSVM and LOF, the same features and abnormal ratio with

10% are set. KNN has the best performance in all aspects, especially compared to the method without pre-process, as shown in the Table 2. Attributes *Time* is the average time required to process 1000 points.

Table 2. Comparison of average performance metrics between KNN and other ways.

	Time(s)	Precision	Recall	F1-score
KNN	**0.7176**	**0.8616**	**0.9898**	**0.9213**
IForest	1.349	0.7662	0.9589	0.8518
OCSVM	0.8131	0.8532	0.9814	0.9128
LOF	0.983	0.8443	0.9869	0.9100
No Pre-process	1.805	0.7206	0.9744	0.8285

Parameter-v: Parameter v further rejects segments similar to anomaly templates but fluctuation in the normal range. By balancing precision, recall and f1-score, the detection effect is best when $v = 0.2$, as shown in Fig. 3.

5 Conclusion

In this paper, the unsupervised algorithm-JLAD on stream data is proposed. JLAD models both from the perspective of normal and abnormal data at the same time, which makes up for the shortcomings of a single perspective, and enhances the cooperation between the two models by data-driven abnormal ratio setting and automatical templates adding, which reduces or eliminates the influence of human factors. The performance of JLAD exceeds the performance of existing anomaly detection algorithms on 13 public KPI datasets. And it has 8% to 59% performance improvement than other algorithms. In the future, domain knowledge can be added to enable the algorithm to better detect anomalies that are of interest to domain experts.

References

1. Chen, Y., Mahajan, R., Sridharan, B.: A provider-side view of web search response time. In: ACM International Conference on Applications, Technologies, Architectures, and Protocols for Computer Communication, pp. 243–254. ACM (2013)
2. Zhao, N., Zhu, J., Liu, R.: Label-Less: a semi-automatic labelling tool for KPI anomalies. In: IEEE International Conference on Computer Communications, pp. 1882–1890. IEEE (2019)
3. Lucas, J.M., Saccucci, M.S.: Exponentially weighted moving average control schemes: properties and enhancements. Technometrics **32**(1), 1–12 (1990)
4. Cleveland, R.B., Cleveland, W.S., McRae, J.E.: STL: a seasonal-trend decomposition procedure based on loess. J. Off. Stat. **6**(1), 3–73 (1990)

5. Xu, H., Chen, W., Zhao, N.: Unsupervised anomaly detection via variational auto-encoder for seasonal KPIs in web applications. In: Proceedings of the 2018 World Wide Web Conference, pp. 187–196. ACM (2018)
6. Kieu, T., Yang, B., Guo, C.: Outlier detection for time series with recurrent autoencoder ensembles. In: 28th International Joint Conference on Artificial Intelligence, pp. 2725–2732. ACM (2019)
7. Xu, H., Wang, Y., Wu, Z., Wang, Y.J: Embedding-based complex feature value coupling learning for detecting outliers in non-IID categorical data. In: Proceedings of the AAAI Conference on Artificial Intelligence, pp. 5541–5548. AAAI Press (2019)
8. Liu, F.T., Ting, K.M., Zhou, Z.H.: Isolation forest. In: Proceedings of the 2008 8th IEEE International Conference on Data Mining, pp. 413–422. IEEE (2008)
9. Xu, H., Wang, Y., Wang, Y., Wu, Z.: MIX: a joint learning framework for detecting both clustered and scattered outliers in mixed-type data. In: 2019 IEEE International Conference on Data Mining (ICDM), pp. 1408–1413. IEEE (2019)
10. Hochenbaum, J., Vallis, O.S., Kejariwal, A.: Automatic anomaly detection in the cloud via statistical learning. arXiv preprint arXiv:1704.07706 (2017)
11. Yan, H., Flavel, A., Ge, Z.: Argus: end-to-end service anomaly detection and localization from an ISP's point of view. In: IEEE International Conference on Computer Communications, pp. 2756–2760. IEEE (2012)
12. Amer, M., Goldstein, M., Abdennadher, S.: Enhancing one-class support vector machines for unsupervised anomaly detection. In: Proceedings of the ACM SIGKDD Workshop on Outlier Detection and Description, pp. 8–15. ACM (2013)
13. Breunig, M.M., Kriegel, H.P., Ng, R.T.: LOF: identifying density-based local outliers. In: International Conference on Management of Data, pp. 93–104. ACM (2000)
14. Berndt, D.J., Clifford, J.: Using dynamic time warping to find patterns in time series. In: Proceedings of the 3rd International Conference on Knowledge Discovery and Data Mining, pp. 359–370. AAAI Press (1994)
15. Rakthanmanon, T., Campana, B., Mueen, A.: Searching and mining trillions of time series subsequences under dynamic time warping. In: Proceedings of the 18th ACM SIGKDD International Conference on Knowledge Discovery and Data Mining, pp. 262–270. ACM (2012)
16. Cleveland, W.S.: Robust locally weighted regression and smoothing scatterplots. J. Am. Stat. Assoc. **74**, 829–836 (1979)
17. Fontugne, R., Borgnat, P., Abry, P.: MAWILab: Combining diverse anomaly detectors for automated anomaly labeling and performance benchmarking. In: Proceedings of the 6th International Conference, pp. 1–12. ACM (2010)
18. Shanbhag, S., Wolf, T.: Accurate anomaly detection through parallelism. IEEE Netw. **23**(1), 22–28 (2009)
19. Paparrizos, J., Gravano, L.: k-Shape: efficient and accurate clustering of time series. In: Proceedings of the 2015 ACM SIGMOD International Conference on Management of Data, pp. 1855–1870. ACM (2015)
20. Liu, D., Zhao, Y., Xu, H.: Opprentice: towards practical and automatic anomaly detection through machine learning. In: Proceedings of the 2015 Internet Measurement Conference, pp. 211–224. ACM (2015)
21. Laptev, N., Amizadeh, S., Flint, I.: Generic and scalable framework for automated time-series anomaly detection. In: Proceedings of the 21th ACM SIGKDD International Conference on Knowledge Discovery and Data Mining, pp. 1939–1947. ACM (2015)

Parallel Variable-Length Motif Discovery in Time Series Using Subsequences Correlation

Chuitian Rong[1,2(✉)], Lili Chen[1], Chunbin Lin[3], and Chao Yuan[1]

[1] School of Computer Science and Technology, Tiangong University, Tianjin, China
{chuitian,yuanchao}@tiangong.edu.cn
[2] Tianjin Key Laboratory of Autonomous Intelligence Technology and Systems, Tianjin, China
[3] Amazon AWS, Seattle, USA
lichunbi@amazon.com

Abstract. The repeated patterns in a long time series are called as time series motifs. As the motifs can reveal much useful information, time series motif discovery has been received extensive attentions in recent years. Time series motif discovery is an important operation for time series analysis in many fields, such as financial data analysis, medical and health monitoring. Although many algorithms have been proposed for motifs discovery, most of existing works are running on single node and focusing on finding fixed-length motifs. They cannot process very long time series efficiently. However, the length of motifs cannot be predicted previously, and the Euclidean distance has many drawbacks as the similarity measure. In this work, we propose a parallel algorithm based on subsequences correlation called as PMDSC (Parallel Motif Discovery based on Subsequences Correlation), which can be applied to find time series motifs with variable lengths. We have conducted extensive experiments on public data sets, the results demonstrate that our method can efficiently find variable-length motifs in long time series.

Keywords: Time series · Motif discovery · Parallel · Spark

1 Introduction

Time series Motif Discovery is a task to discover repeated and similar (correlated) patterns in time series. In recent years, time series motif discovery has been received extensive attentions. It has been applied in many time series data mining and analysis tasks, such as data classification, clustering, activity recognition and outlier detection.

In the past decade, a large number of motif discovery algorithms have been proposed. Most existing algorithms aim to find fixed-length motifs. While, the length of motifs cannot be predicted previously in most cases. So, some interesting motifs with different lengths will be lost. Mostly, finding variable-length

X. Wang et al. (Eds.): APWeb-WAIM 2020, LNCS 12318, pp. 164–175, 2020.
https://doi.org/10.1007/978-3-030-60290-1_13

motifs in the time series can reveal more latent patterns than fixed-length motifs. So, there are some works such as [3,4] have tried to discover the variable-length motifs. The biggest challenge of variable-length motifs discovery is the massive computations. The complexity of variable-length motif discovery is 10 times higher than the fixed-length motif discovery in [17]. For example, if the lengths of motifs are ranging from 300 to 10300, the brute-force algorithm will take 5×10^{18} Euclidean distance calls [3]. In fact, many industrial applications generate very large time series. While, most algorithms use a single compute node to analyze large-scale time series. So, that is difficult to complete the analysis in a feasible time. Therefore, in recent years, distributed and parallel computing platforms are widely used in the data mining and analysis of large-scale time series.

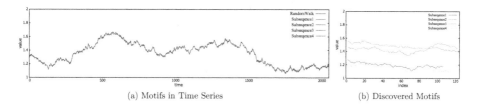

(a) Motifs in Time Series   (b) Discovered Motifs

Fig. 1. Variable-length motifs discovered by PMDSC algorithm on random walk dataset

In addition, there are some other limitations in these motif discovery algorithms. For example, the algorithms apply Euclidean distance as the similarity and require the two compared subsequences with the same length, which is not suitable in most applications. So, we propose a variable-length motif discovery algorithm using Pearson Correlation Coefficient as the similarity measure. The Pearson Correlation Coefficient is a commonly used similarity measure for time series data mining due to its multiple beneficial mathematical properties, such as it is invariant to scale and offset. The Pearson Correlation Coefficient can reveal the true similarity of two time series. Therefore, we argue that the Pearson Correlation Coefficient is a good similar measure in time series motif discovery. In Fig. 1, we showed one of the results found by our proposed algorithm.

In order to solve the existing drawbacks and improve the efficiency of motif discovery in long time series, we introduced a parallel motif discovery algorithm on Spark platform. This algorithm applies the Pearson Correlation Coefficient as the similarity measure to find variable-length motifs in large-scale time series.

In short, the main works of this paper are:

1. We propose a parallel algorithm for variable-length motifs discovery based on subsequences correlation using Spark.
2. In order to compute the correlation efficiently, we proposed a parallel FFT algorithm using Spark.
3. In order to improve the concurrency of parallel jobs, we proposed a time series segmentation method and dot product matrix partition method.

4. We demonstrate the efficiency and scalability of the proposed algorithm using extensive experiments.

The rest of the paper is organized as follows. Section 2 discusses Related Works of motif discovery. In Sect. 3, we introduce the problem definition and background concepts used in this paper. In Sect. 4, we introduce our proposed parallel PMDSC algorithm. The experimental results are shown in Sect. 5 and the conclusions are given in Sect. 6.

2   Related Works

Time series motif discovery approach was proposed in 2002 [7]. Then, time series motif discovery has received extensive attentions and many motif discovery algorithms have been proposed. These methods discover the motif as the most similar subsequences using some similar measures. Time series motif discovery is a basic operation in time series data analysis, so a large amount of motif discovery research works have been proposed in recent years.

The existing algorithms for time series motif discovery are mainly divided into two strategies: fixed-length and variable-length. The fixed-length algorithms proposed in [15] are based on SAX (Symbolic Aggregate approXimation) [6], which was applied to represent the time series with symbols. These methods mainly focus on fixed-length motif discovery. [10] proposed a MK algorithm to find the most similar pair subsequences as motifs, which is adopted a pruning method to speed up the Brute Force Algorithm. In [5], authors introduced a Quick-Motif algorithm, whose calculation speed is increased by 3 orders of magnitude compared with the traditional fixed-length motif discovery algorithm in [10]. Several recent works focus on fixed-length motif discovery, [16] introduces an algorithm named STAMP combined with MASS algorithm[1] to find exact motifs for a given length. An algorithm named STOMP was proposed in [17], which reduced the time complexity of STAMP from $O(n^2 \log n)$ to $O(n^2)$.

As variable-length motifs can reveal much more interesting latent patterns than fix-length do, many research works have focused on variable-length motif discovery in recent years. In 2011, the VLMD algorithm [11] was proposed by calling fixed-length motif discovery algorithm to find K pair-motifs with variable-length. In [9], the authors proposed an algorithm using Euclidean distance as the similarity measure for Z-Normalized segments. It applied a lower-bound to reduce the computing time of variable-length motifs discovery. In [14], the authors proposed a novel method, which incorporated the grammar induction to find approximate motifs with variable-length. Its running time is faster than other algorithms. However, the idea of this algorithm is based on grammar induction, so this method may be limited in some applications. [2] proposed a method based on discretization and the subsequences do not overlap with their adjacents, which may lead to loss some real results. [3] introduced an algorithm named HIME based on SAX and Induction Graph to find variable-length motifs. This

---

[1] https://www.cs.unm.edu/~mueen/FastestSimilaritySearch.html.

approach can find exact motifs in an acceptable time. However, this method is difficult to implement.

In summary, the existing motif discovery algorithms mostly find fixed-length motifs and mainly using Euclidean distance as a measure of similarity. As illustrated above, these algorithms have many limitations. In this paper, we propose an efficient parallel time series motif discovery method on Spark. Our approach is using subsequences correlation, combined with parallel FFT algorithm and time series segmentation method, can efficiently find motifs with variable-length.

Table 1. Symbols and Definitions

Symbol	Definition
T	Time Series T
$|T|$	The length of time series T
L	The length of motif
L_{min}	The smallest length of motif
len	The length of the subsequence in each segment
$Corre(T', T'')$	Correlation coefficient between subsequences T' and T''
$W(n)$	Butterfly coefficient of FFT
$X(k)$	The result of FFT
I	The index of a data point in the time series
P	The segment index during time series segmentation
$\mathcal{Z}$	The Dot-Product Matrix of two time series subsequences
$\mathcal{Z}'$	A number of consecutive columns(one block) in $\mathcal{Z}$

3   Problem Definition and Background

In this section, we present the problem definitions and introduce the background concepts used in this paper. The symbols used in this paper are listed in Table 1.

Definition 1 *(Time Series). A Time Series T is a sequence of real numbers observed in the same time interval. $T = [t_1, t_2, \ldots, t_n]$, where n is the length of time series T.*

Definition 2 *(Subsequence). A Subsequence with the length of m in time series T is a set of continuous points $T[j : j + m] = [t_j, t_{j+1}, \ldots, t_{j+m-1}]$ starting at position j.*

Definition 3 *(K-Frequent Motif). Given a time series T and a minimum length L_{min} of motif, K-frequent motif of T is defined as a set of subsequences that have at least K matches and denoted as ϕ, $|\phi| \geq K$. $\phi = \{T'' | \forall T' \subset T, \exists T'' \subset T \wedge Corre(T', T'') \geq \theta\}$. T' and T'' are subsequences of the time series T with $|T'| \geq L_{min}$ and $|T''| \geq L_{min}$. $Corre(T', T'')$ is the correlation coefficient between T' and T'', θ is a similarity threshold of the correlation given by user.*

Definition 4 *(Pearson Correlation Coefficient). Pearson Correlation Coefficient is a measure of the correlation between two variables. It can reflect the degree of similarity between two subsequences. For two subsequences T' and T'', the Pearson Correlation Coefficient can be computed as following.*

$$Corre(T', T'') = \frac{(E[(T' - E(T'))(T'' - E(T''))])}{(\sigma_{T'} \sigma_{T''})} \tag{1}$$

The above calculation formula of the Pearson Correlation Coefficient can also be defined as Formula 2, where T' and T'' are the subsequences of T, $u_{T'}$, $\mu_{T''}$ and $\sigma_{T'}$, $\sigma_{T''}$ are the mean and Standard deviation of T' and T'' respectively, and the $\sum T'T''$ can be calculated from the dot product between the subsequences.

$$Corre(T', T'') = \frac{(\sum T'T'' - m\mu_{T'}\mu_{T''})}{(m\sigma_{T'}\sigma_{T''})} \tag{2}$$

FFT (*Fast Fourier Transform*) is an efficient algorithm to compute the DFT (*Discrete Fourier Transform*) of a sequence. In many applications, we are interested in finding motifs or the similar shapes. Before computing the correlation coefficient, we normalized two subsequences by *Z-Normalization*. After *Z-Normalization*, FFT can be used to compute the cross products of arbitrary subsequences of two sequences. By doing this, the computational time complexity of $\sum T'T''$ in Formula 2 can be reduced to $O(n \log n)$. In order to improve the efficiency of motif discovery, we implemented a parallel FFT on Spark. In order to avoid redundant computations, we computed the dot products of all time series subsequences previously using parallel FFT and organized them as a Dot-Product-Matrix $\mathcal{Z}$.

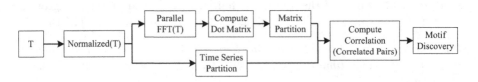

Fig. 2. The Framework of PMDSC Algorithm

Algorithm 1: Segmentation(T, P_{max}, len, L_{min})

Input : T: the normalized time series
           P_{max}: the number of partitions
           len: the length in each partition
           L_{min}: the minimum length of subsegments
1 **foreach** $T(i) \in T$ **do**
2    $newValue \leftarrow < i, T(i) >$;
3   **for** $P = 0 \rightarrow P_{max}$ **do**
4   **if** $key \geq P * (len - L_{min}) \&\& key \leq (P+1) * len - P * L_{min}$ **then**
5          $midresult \leftarrow \langle P, newValue \rangle$;

6 $partitions \leftarrow midresult.partitionBy(\_.1)$;
7 $segments \leftarrow partitions.gorupByKey(\_.\_.1)$;

---

4 Parallel Variable-Length Motifs Discovery

In this section, we present the implementation details of the parallel motif discovery using subsequences correlation using Spark. Our approach is based on new parallel FFT and data segmentation techniques. Figure 2 shows the framework of our motif discovery algorithm. In following, we first introduce the time series segmentation method. Then, we describe the Dot-Product-Matrix computation and partition method. Finally, we describe the details of motif discovery.

4.1 Time Series Segmentation

In order to make better utilize the properties of RDD (Resilient Distributed DataSet), we introduced a partition approach that divides time series into multiple segments (subsequences) with equal length len. To assure the exact of results, we keep an overlap between the adjacent segments with the length of L_{min}. For each segment, we can get the range of indices for its data points by using Formulas 3 and 4, in which I_{min} and I_{max} are the minimum and maximum data points indices in S_P, respectively. Also, we can get the number of segments P_{max} for a time series based on the len and L_{min} using Formula 5. The Algorithm 1 describes its implementation using Spark.

$$I_{min} \geq P * (len - L_{min}) \tag{3}$$

$$I_{max} \leq (P+1) * len - P * L_{min} \tag{4}$$

$$P_{max} = \frac{n - L_{min}}{len - L_{min}} + 1 \tag{5}$$

In Spark, we use the *map*, *partitionBy* and *groupByKey* operators to complete the time series segmentation task as presented in Algorithm 1. As presented in Algorithm 1, the *map* operator is used to transform the time series data points into $\langle key, value \rangle$ pairs (Lines 1–2). Here, the *value* is the data point $T(i)$ and the *key* is the index i of the data point. For each data point, we assign its partition number P as its new key according to Formulas 3 and 4 and transform it

---

Algorithm 2: $\mathcal{Z}$–ComputationAndPartition$(T, P_{max}, len_1, len_2)$

Input : T: the normalized time series
P_{max}: the partition number of time series
len_1, len_2: the length of two subsequences
Output: $\mathcal{Z}'$: the blocks of dot product matrix

1 $N \leftarrow T.length$;
2 **for** $i = 0 \rightarrow N$ **do**
3     $T_i \leftarrow T.takeRight(m - i)$;
4   **for** $j = 0 \rightarrow 2*N$ **do**
5        $T \leftarrow Array[T, 0]$;
6        $T_i \leftarrow Array[T_i, 0]$;
7     $T \leftarrow FFT(T), T_I \leftarrow FFT(T_i)$;
8     $\mathcal{Z} \leftarrow T * T_I$;

9 **for** $P_1 = 0 \rightarrow P_{max}$ **do**
10   **for** $P_2 = 0 \rightarrow P_{max}$ **do**
11   **if** $P_1! = P_{max} \&\& P_2! = P_{max}$ **then**
12          $v = N + (P_2 - P_1 + 1) * L_{min}$;
13          $v_1 = (v + (P_1 - 1) * len_1 - P_2 * len_2)$;
14          $v_2 = (v + P_1 * len_1 - (P_2 - 1) * len_2)$;
15   **for** $j = v_1 \rightarrow v_2$ **do**
16             $\mathcal{Z}' \leftarrow iFFT(\mathcal{Z}(j))$;
17          $\mathcal{Z}' \leftarrow <(P_1, P_2), \mathcal{Z}'>$

---

into $\langle P, (i, T(i)) \rangle$ (Lines 3–5). Then, the *partitionBy* operator is used to partition the new key/value pairs into multiple partitions according to the partition number (Line 6). Finally, the *groupByKey* operator is used to aggregate the new key/value pairs in multiple groups with the same order as in the original time series (Line 7). By doing this, the segmentation is completed.

Each time series is processed in the similar way. After that, in order to pair all possible subsequences. First, we use the *map* operator to assign a new key to the divided subsequences according to the maximum partition number P_{max} of each time series. Then, we joined the subsequences from different two time series using the *join* operator. This step generates records in the form $\langle (P_1, P_2), (Iterable[T'], Iterable[T'']) \rangle$, where P_1 and P_2 are the indices of two subsequences.

4.2 Dot-Product-Matrix Computation and Partition

Variable-length motifs discovery can reveal much more interesting latent patterns than fix-length motifs discovery. However, it is a very expensive in time cost. As the motif discovery is a pairwise operation to compute the correlations of all possible subsequences, there are many redundant computations [8]. In order to avoid redundant computations, we compute the correlations previously using parallel FFT and store the results in the Dot-Product-Matrix $\mathcal{Z}$. In fact, the matrix partition is implemented during its computation and stored in multiple distributed blocks, as shown in Algorithm 2.

The Dot-Product-Matrix $\mathcal{Z}$ stores the shift-cross products of all possible subsequences from tow time series. For parallel processing, the naive way to use the $\mathcal{Z}$ is to send it to all worker nodes. In fact, just a little of columns in $\mathcal{Z}$ is used to compute the correlations of each pair subsequences. In order to avoid unnecessary data transfer and improve the efficiency, we proposed a partition technique for $\mathcal{Z}$. For each pair of subsequences, we can get the corresponding blocks in $\mathcal{Z}$ according to their partition numbers. Without losing generality, we assuming the partition number P_1 and P_2 of two subsequences T' and T'' with lengths len_1 and len_2. The necessary corresponding part $\mathcal{Z}' \in \mathcal{Z}$ for computing $\mathrm{Corre}(T'', T')$ is from $\mathcal{Z}[*][|T| + (P_2 - P_1 + 1) * L_{min} + P_1 * len_1 - (P_2 + 1) * len_2]$ to $\mathcal{Z}[*][|T| + (P_2 - P_1 - 1) * L_{min} + (P_1 + 1) * len_1 - P_2 * len_2]$.

In Algorithm 2, the first part is to compute the $\mathcal{Z}$ (lines 1–8). It gets all subsequences of T (lines 2–3)and extend their length to the twice of length T (lines 4–6). Then, each subsequence T_i of T and itself will be transformed using FFT (line 7) and get their cross products (line 8). Finally, a part of the Dot-Product-Matrix is retrieved by doing inverse Fourier transform (line 9). This algorithm returns a two-dimensional array, which contains the sum of the products of the elements in T and T_i for different shifts of T. The $FFT()$ (line 7) ensures that this process can be done in $O(n \log n)$ time. The FFT is a parallel implementation [13]. The parallel FFT algorithm is implemented as the following four steps.

1. Get the original index for each element in time series.
2. Compute the binary code $\mathcal{B}(\mathcal{I})$ for each element according to its original index and the length of time series.
3. Compute the butterfly coefficient using Formula 6 based on the values of bits in $\mathcal{B}(\mathcal{I})$.
4. Compute the final result for each element using Formula 7.

$$W(n) = \prod W_{2^j}^k * (-1)^t, k \in [0, 2^{j-1}) \quad t = \begin{cases} 0 & n = k \\ 1 & n = k + 2^{j-1} \end{cases} \tag{6}$$

$$X(n) = \sum_{i=0}^{n-1} x(i) * W(n) \tag{7}$$

The last part of Algorithm 2 (lines 9–16) shows the details of the matrix $\mathcal{Z}$ partition. When computing the $\mathcal{Z}$, we assign a key to the elements belongs to the same block according to the partition number of the two subsequences. The $\mathcal{Z}$ is organized and stored in the form of key/value pairs. By doing this, we completed the matrix partition task. When performing motif discovery and computing the correlations of each pair of subsequences, the subsequence pair along with the corresponding block of $\mathcal{Z}' \in \mathcal{Z}$ will be grouped together and shuffled to the same worker node according to their assigned key in Algorithm 3.

Algorithm 3: CorrelationComputation($list, L_{min}, \mathcal{Z}', \theta$)

Input : $list$: $\langle (Segment_{T'}, Segment_{T''}) \rangle$
L_{min} : the minimum length of motif
$\mathcal{Z}'$: the corresponding block in $\mathcal{Z}$
θ : the threshold of correlation
Output: $result$: the motifs with correlation $\geq \theta$

1 $n \leftarrow list.\_1.length$, $m \leftarrow list.\_2.length$;
2 $m_{len} = L_{min}$;
3 **for** $i = 0 \rightarrow m$ **do**
4   **for** $j = 0 \rightarrow n$ **do**
5          $maxLength \leftarrow \min(m - i + 1, n - j + 1)$;
6          $len \leftarrow L_{min}$;
7   **while** $len < maxLength$ **do**
8              $\sum T'T'' \leftarrow \mathcal{Z}'$;
9   /* $S_i \in Segment_{T'}, S_j \in Segment_{T''}$ */
10              $mean \leftarrow getMean(S_i, S_j)$;
11              $stdv \leftarrow getStdv(S_i, S_j)$;
12              $C \leftarrow \frac{\sum T'T'' - len * mean}{len * stdv}$;
13   **if** $C > \theta \&\& m_{len} \geq len$ **then**
14                  $m_i = i, m_j = j$;
15                  $m_{len} = len$;
16                  $result \leftarrow (m_i, m_j, m_{len}, C)$;
17              $len \leftarrow len + +$;

18 /*filter out the covered subsequence pairs*/
19 $result \leftarrow result.maxBy(m_{len})$;

4.3 K-Frequent Motif Discovery

In this part, we introduce the algorithms for discovering K-Frequent motifs, as shown in Algorithm 3. Algorithm 3 is used to compute the correlation of all possible subsequence pairs and filter out the covered subsequence pairs to get the longest ones.

In Algorithm 3, the input $list$ contains two segments, $Segment_{T'}$ and $Segment_{T''}$, generated by using segmentation method 1 on two time series. In order to get variable-length motifs, we should compute the correlations of all possible subsequences contained in these two segments (Lines 3–11). According to the Dot-Matrix-Partition method, only a little block of $\mathcal{Z}' \in \mathcal{Z}$ is needed for each pair of segments to compute the correlations of contained subsequences (Line 8). For each pair of subsequences (S_i, S_j), in which $S_i \in Segment_{T'}$ and $S_j \in Segment_{T''}$, the mean and standard deviation of data points contained by S_i and S_j should be computed (Lines 9–10). After that, we can use Formula 2 to compute the correlation coefficient of two subsequences (Line 11). Then, we will apply the filtering method to select the required subsequence pairs (Lines 12–15). It's to be noted that, some found short subsequence pairs can be covered by the longer ones. So, it is necessary to remove the covered subsequence pairs. At the last step, we filter out the short ones and keep the long ones (Line 17). Finally, Algorithm 3 returns the longest subsequences pair contained in each segments pair.

After that, we use *groupByKey* operator to aggregate the motifs with the same key, and we can get a series motifs of the form $\langle Pid_1, Iterable(Pid_2, len, Correlation)\rangle$. So, we can find the motifs whose frequency is more than K easily.

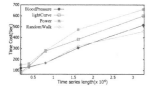 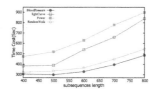 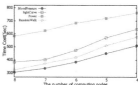

Fig. 3. Time series length.   **Fig. 4.** Partition segment length.   **Fig. 5.** Computing nodes number

5 Experiments

We have implemented our proposed algorithm using the Scala programming language on Spark. Our experiments are conducted on Spark-2.1.0 cluster, in which there is one master node and 8 worker nodes. Each node in the cluster are equipped with Linux CentOS 6.2, 4 cores, 6 GB of memory and 500 GB of disk storage. In this section, we evaluated the experimental results with the variations of different parameters, including the segment length of motif, the length of time series and the threshold θ. We also testified the scalability by changing the number of computing nodes. All the experiments are tested on public datasets that are downloaded from the web site[2]. There are four datasets used in our experiments, including *Blood Pressure* [1], *Light Curve* [12], *Power* [8] and *Random Walk*.

5.1 Effect of Time Series Length

In this experiment, we verify the efficiency of PMDSC by changing the length of time series from 2000 to 32,768. In this experiment, we set the minimum motif length $L_{min} = 100$, the correlation threshold $\theta = 0.9$ and the partitioned segment length $len = 400$. The experimental results are shown in Fig. 3.

From the Fig. 3, we can observe that the time cost is increasing near linearly on the four different data sets as the length of time series increasing. Compared with the time costs on these four data sets, we find that the time cost on the *Power* data is the most. It is because the *Power* dataset has large spikes that cause increased time to compute the correlation in each partition. The time costs on the two datasets *Blood Pressure* and *Random Walk* is smaller and near the same. The reason is that after normalization, the spikes and changing frequencies of the two datasets are like to each other.

---

[2] https://files.secureserver.net/0fzoieonFsQcsM.

5.2   Effect of the Segment Length

In this test, we test the time costs by changing the segment length *len* from 400 to 800 with the interval 100. In this experiment, we set the time series length to 16,384, the correlation threshold $\theta = 0.9$ and $L_{min} = 100$. Figure 4 shows the effects of segment length variations on time costs.

From Fig. 4, we can find that the time costs are increasing on four different datasets as the segment length increasing. The reason is that increasing the segment length will bring more subsequence pairs to be processed in each segment. We can also find that the time costs increasing trend is different on four data sets. When the segment length is more than 500, the time costs increase mostly on *Power* data set followed by *Light Curve* data set. It is caused by the large variations of data values contained in the two time series. While, the distribution of data point values in other two data sets are relatively stable. So, the time costs changing on *Blood Pressure* and *Random Walk* is relatively smaller.

5.3   Effect of the Number of Computing Nodes

In this part, we test the scalability of our proposed method by changing the number of computing nodes in the cluster. In this experiment, we set the length of time series to 16,384, the segment length $len = 400$ and the correlation threshold $\theta = 0.9$. The experimental results are shown in Fig. 5. In Fig. 5, the time costs on four data sets are decreasing when the computing nodes number is increased from 4 to 8. The more computing nodes in the cluster means more computing power and higher parallel concurrency.

6   Conclusion

Time series motif is the repetitive similar patterns in time series. In this paper, we introduce a parallel algorithm to discover the time series motifs with variable-length. This algorithm can process large-scale time series in an acceptable time. Experimental results demonstrate that our algorithm can efficiently and precisely find motifs in large-scale time series. In the future, we will improve our method to find motifs from multivariate time series.

Acknowledgment. This work was supported by the project of Natural Science Foundation of China (No. 61402329, No. 61972456), the Natural Science Foundation of Tianjin (No. 19JCYBJC15400) and Natural Science Foundation of Tianjin-Science and Technology Correspondent Project (No. 18JCTPJC63300).

References

1. Bugenhagen, S.M., Cowley Jr., A.W., Beard, D.A.: Identifying physiological origins of baroreflex dysfunction in salt-sensitive hypertension in the Dahl SS rat. Physiol. Genomics **42**, 23–41 (2010)

2. Castro, N., Azevedo, P.J.: Multiresolution motif discovery in time series. In: SIAM, pp. 665–676 (2010)
3. Gao, Y., Lin, J.: Efficient discovery of variable-length time series motifs with large length range in million scale time series. CoRR abs/1802.04883 (2018)
4. Gao, Y., Lin, J., Rangwala, H.: Iterative grammar-based framework for discovering variable-length time series motifs. In: ICMLA, pp. 7–12 (2016)
5. Li, Y., U, L.H., Yiu, M.L., Gong, Z.: Quick-motif: an efficient and scalable framework for exact motif discovery. In: ICDE. pp. 579–590 (2015)
6. Lin, J., Keogh, E., Li, W., Lonardi, S.: Experiencing SAX: a novel symbolic representation of time series. Data Min. Knowl. Discov. **15**, 107–144 (2007). https://doi.org/10.1007/s10618-007-0064-z
7. Lin, J., Keogh, E., Lonardi, S., Patel, P.: Finding motifs in time series. In: Proceedings of 2nd Workshop on Temporal Data Mining at KDD, pp. 53–68 (2002)
8. Mueen, A., Hamooni, H., Estrada, T.: Time series join on subsequence correlation. In: ICDM, pp. 450–459 (2014)
9. Mueen, A.: Enumeration of time series motifs of all lengths. In: ICDM, pp. 547–556 (2013)
10. Mueen, A., Keogh, E.J., Zhu, Q., Cash, S., Westover, M.B.: Exact discovery of time series motifs. In: SIAM, pp. 473–484 (2009)
11. Nunthanid, P., Niennattrakul, V., Ratanamahatana, C.A.: Discovery of variable length time series motif. In: EEE, pp. 472–475 (2011)
12. Rebbapragada, U., Protopapas, P., Brodley, C.E., Alcock, C.: Finding anomalous periodic time series. Mach. Learn. **74**, 281–313 (2009). https://doi.org/10.1007/s10994-008-5093-3
13. Rong, C., Chen, L., Silva, Y.N.: Parallel time series join using spark. Concurr. Comput. Pract. Exp. **32**(9), e5622 (2020)
14. Senin, P., et al.: GrammarViz 2.0: a tool for grammar-based pattern discovery in time series. In: Calders, T., Esposito, F., Hüllermeier, E., Meo, R. (eds.) ECML PKDD. LNCS, vol. 8726, pp. 468–472. Springer, Heidelberg (2014). https://doi.org/10.1007/978-3-662-44845-8_37
15. Tanaka, Y., Iwamoto, K., Uehara, K.: Discovery of time-series motif from multi-dimensional data based on MDL principle. Mach. Learn. **58**, 269–300 (2005). https://doi.org/10.1007/s10994-005-5829-2
16. Yeh, C.C.M., Yan, Z., Ulanova, L., Begum, N., Keogh, E.: Matrix profile I: all pairs similarity joins for time series: a unifying view that includes motifs, discords and shapelets. In: ICDM, pp. 1317–1322 (2016)
17. Zhu, Y., Zimmerman, Z., Senobari, N.S., et al.: Matrix profile II: exploiting a novel algorithm and gpus to break the one hundred million barrier for time series motifs and joins. In: ICDM, pp. 739–748 (2016)

Learning Ability Community for Personalized Knowledge Tracing

Juntao Zhang(iD), Biao Li, Wei Song(iD), Nanzhou Lin, Xiandi Yang$^{(\boxtimes)}$, and Zhiyong Peng

School of Computer Science, Wuhan University, Wuhan, Hubei, China
{juntaozhang,biao.li,songwei,linnzh,xiandiy,peng}@whu.edu.cn

Abstract. Knowledge tracing is an essential task that estimates students' knowledge state as they engage in the online learning platform. Several models have been proposed to predict the state of students' learning process to improve their learning efficiencies, such as Bayesian Knowledge Tracing, Deep Knowledge Tracing, and Dynamic Key-Value Memory Networks. However, these models fail to fully consider the influence of students' current knowledge state on knowledge growth, and ignore the current knowledge state of students is affected by forgetting mechanisms. Moreover, these models are a unified model that does not consider the use of group learning behavior to guide individual learning. To tackle these problems, in this paper, we first propose a model named Knowledge Tracking based on Learning and Memory Process (LMKT) to solve the effect of students' current knowledge state on knowledge growth and forgetting mechanisms. Then we propose the definition of learning capacity community and personalized knowledge tracking. Finally, we present a novel method called Learning Ability Community for Personalized Knowledge Tracing (LACPKT), which models students' learning process according to group dynamics theory. Experimental results on public data sets show that the LMKT model and LACPKT model are effective. Besides, the LACPKT model can trace students' knowledge state in a personalized way.

Keywords: Personalized Knowledge Tracing · Learning ability community · Knowledge growth · Knowledge state

1 Introduction

With the development of Intelligent Tutoring Systems (ITS) [1] and Massive Open Online Courses (MOOCs) [15], a large number of students are willing to learn new courses or acquire knowledge that they are interested in through the online learning platform. When students have completed some exercises or courses, the online learning platform can obtain the knowledge state they mastered according to their learning records. For example, when a student tries to solve the exercise "$x^2 - 2x + 1 = 0$", the online learning system can estimate

© Springer Nature Switzerland AG 2020
X. Wang et al. (Eds.): APWeb-WAIM 2020, LNCS 12318, pp. 176–192, 2020.
https://doi.org/10.1007/978-3-030-60290-1_14

the probability that the student will answer this exercise correctly according to the student whether had mastered arithmetic operations and quadratic equation with one unknown. In online learning platform, the task of knowledge tracing is to model the learning process of students to trace their future knowledge state based on their historical performance on exercises and the underlying knowledge concepts they had mastered. Knowledge tracing can be formalized as: given observations of interactions $X = \{x_1, ..., x_t\}$ taken by a student on a past exercise task, predict the probability that the student answers the next interaction x_{t+1} correctly. In the knowledge tracing, interactions take the form of a tuple of $x_t = (q_t, r_t)$ that combines a tag for the exercise being answered q_t with whether or not the exercise was answered correctly r_t [18]. Therefore, knowledge tracing technology can help teachers to teach according to their aptitude and give students personalized guidance and can help students to strengthen training on unfamiliar or less familiar knowledge concepts, which is very meaningful in the teaching process.

Knowledge tracing is inherently difficult as the complexity of the human brain learning process and the diversity of knowledge. Several models have been proposed to model the knowledge state of students in a concept specific manner, such as Bayesian Knowledge Tracing (BKT) [2,5], Deep Knowledge Tracing (DKT) [18], Dynamic Key-Value Memory Networks (DKVMN) [24]. BKT divides students' knowledge states into different concept states and assumes the concept state as a binary latent variable, *known* or *unknown*, and uses the Hidden Markov Model to update the posterior distribution of the binary concept state. Although BKT can express each knowledge concept state for each student, it requires students to define knowledge concepts in advance. Moreover, BKT assumes that once students have mastered the knowledge, they will never forget it, which limits its ability to capture the complicated relationship between different knowledge concepts and model long-term dependencies in an exercise sequence.

In recent years, inspired by the successful application of deep learning [12], the deep learning model is beginning to be used to solve the knowledge tracing problem. DKT is the first deep knowledge tracing model, which exploits Recurrent Neural Networks (RNNs) to the problem of predicting students to exercise based on students' previous learning sequences. Because of the RNNs has hidden layers with a large number of neurons, it can comprehensively express the relationships between different concepts to improve the accuracy of prediction. However, DKT summarizes a student's knowledge state of all concepts in one hidden state, which makes it difficult to trace how much a student has mastered a certain concept and pinpoint which concepts a student is good at or unfamiliar with [11]. To address this deficiency, Zhang et al. proposed the DKVMN model based on Memory Augmented Neural Networks (MANNs) [19,21], which can discover the correlation between input exercises and underlying concepts and reveal the evolving knowledge state of students through using a key-value memory. However, there are still some knowledge tracking problems that need to be addressed, as follows:

- The knowledge growth of DKVMN is calculated by multiplying students'
  exercises $x_t = (q_t, r_t)$ with a trained embedded matrix, which means that
  knowledge growth is only related to the absolute growth of this exercise.
  According to human cognitive processes, students' knowledge growth is
  related to their current knowledge states [3], so the calculation method of
  knowledge growth has limitations.
- The reading process of the DKVMN model ignores the effect of forgetting
  mechanism on students' knowledge state. According to the research that forgetting occurs along an exponential curve [7], forgetting means that a student's knowledge decreases over time, we believe that the knowledge state of
  students is affected by the forgetting mechanism.
- Existing knowledge tracing models assume that all students have the same
  learning ability without considering their inherent differences, and then construct a unified model to predict the probability that students answer the
  exercise correctly at the next moment, which lacking personalized ability.

To solve the above problems, inspired by the literature [17,20], we propose a
novel method called Learning Ability Community for Personalized Knowledge
Tracing (LACPKT) based on the learning ability community and learning and
memory process. The main contributions of our paper are summarized as follows:

- We present a knowledge tracing model called Knowledge Tracking based on
  Learning and Memory Process (LMKT), which solves the impact of the current knowledge state of students on knowledge growth and consider the effect
  of forgetting mechanisms on the current knowledge state of students.
- We first define the learning ability degree and learning ability community and
  propose the definition of personalized knowledge tracking according to group
  dynamics theory.
- We propose a novel method called Learning Ability Community for Personalized Knowledge Tracing (LACPKT), which models the learning process of
  students in a personalized way.
- We conduct experiments on four public datasets to verify the effectiveness of
  the LMKT model and LACPKT model.

2   Related Work

There are many kinds of research to estimate the knowledge state of students.
Bayesian Knowledge Tracing (BKT) [5] is the most popular knowledge tracing
model based on machine learning, which is also a highly constrained and structured model. BKT models every knowledge concept for every student, and each
knowledge concept only changes from the unmastered state to the mastery state.
Some variants of BKT have also raised. For example, Yudelson et al. [23] proposed
an individualized Bayesian knowledge tracing models. Baker et al. [2] presented a
more accurate student state model by estimating the $P(G)$ and $P(S)$ contexts in
BKT. Pardos et al. [16] added the item difficulty of item response theory (IRT) [10]

to the BKT to increase the diversity of questions. Other information or technologies [6,8,9] have also been introduced into the Bayesian network framework.

Deep Knowledge Tracing (DKT) [18] applied the vanilla Recurrent Neural Networks (RNNs) to trace knowledge concept state, reports substantial improvements in prediction performance. DKT uses the RNNs with a hidden layer map an input sequence of vectors $X = \{x_1, x_2, ..., x_t\}$ to an output sequence of vectors $Y = \{y_1, y_2, ..., y_t\}$ to model student learning and predict student's state of all knowledge concepts. Zhang et al. [25] improved the DKT Model by incorporating more problem-level features and then proposed an adaptive DKT model structure that converts the dimensional input into a low dimensional feature vector that can effectively improve accuracy. Cheung et al. [4] proposed an automatic and intelligent approach to integrating the heterogeneous features into the DKT model that can capture students behaviors in the exercises. Nagatani et al. [14] extended the DKT model behavior to consider forgetting by incorporating multiple types of information related to forgetting, which improves the predictive performance. Memory Augmented Neural Networks (MANNs) have made progress in many areas, such as question answering [21] and one-shot learning [19]. MANNs consists of two operations, reading and writing that are achieved through additional attention mechanisms. Because of the recurrence introduced in the read and write operations, MANNs is a special variant structure of RNNs, it uses an external memory matrix that stores the knowledge state of a student. Zhang et al. put forward a Dynamic Key-Value Memory Networks (DKVMN) [24] that uses the concepts of Memory Augmented Neural Networks (MANNs) to reveal the evolving knowledge state of students and learn the relationships between concepts. DKVMN with one static *key* matrix that stores the concept representations and one dynamic *value* matrix that stores and updates the students understanding concept state of each concept, thus it has more capacity to handle knowledge tracking problems.

3 The Proposed Model

In this section, we first give the formalization of definitions and then introduce Knowledge Tracking based on Learning and Memory Process. Finally, we propose a novel method named Learning Ability Community for Personalized Knowledge Tracing to model the learning process of students. In description below, we assume a student's exercise sequence $X = \{x_1, x_2, ..., x_t\}$ contains N latent knowledge concepts $C = \{c_1, c_2, ..., c_N\}$, where $x_t = (q_t, r_t)$ is a tuple containing the question q_t and the correctness of the students answer r_t, and all exercise sequences of M students $U = \{u_1, u_2, ..., u_M\}$ are $\boldsymbol{X} = \{X^1, X^2, ..., X^M\}$. The details are elaborated in the following three subsections.

3.1 Definition Formulation

Learning ability represents the internal quality of an individual that can cause lasting changes in behavior or thinking, which can be formed and developed through certain learning practices. In the knowledge tracing problem, because of the cognitive level of each student is different, the result of each student's exercise sequence reflect their learning ability. We introduce the definition of learning ability degree δ according to the exercise sequence of students.

Definition 1. *Learning Ability Degree.* *We assume that the exercise of student u_i is $x_t = (q_t, r_t)$ contains knowledge concept c_j, the learning ability degree of student u_i is $\delta_{u_i}^{c_j} = s_{max}^{c_j}/s_{length}^{c_j}$ that represents the learning ability of student u_i to learn the knowledge concept c_j in question q_t.*

Where a big $\delta_{u_i}^{c_j} \in [1, s_{max}^{c_j}]$ indicates that the student u_i has a strong ability to learn this question q_t, $s_{length}^{c_j}$ represents the number of times that the student u_i repeatedly learns the knowledge concept c_j, $s_{max}^{c_j}$ represents the maximum number of times that a student repeatedly learns the knowledge concept c_j. Because of the exercise sequence of student u_i is $X_i = \{x_1^i, ..., x_t^i\}$ contains knowledge concepts $\{c_1, ..., c_j\}$, the learning ability degree sequence of student u_i is $\delta_{u_i} = \{\delta_{u_i}^{c_1}, \delta_{u_i}^{c_2}, ..., \delta_{u_i}^{c_j}\}$. Therefore, according to the learning ability degree sequence of all students, we definite the Learning Ability Community is as follows:

Definition 2. *Learning Ability Community.* *We Suppose that the learning ability sequence of student u_i and student u_j are $\delta_{u_i} = \{\delta_{u_i}^{c_1}, \delta_{u_i}^{c_2}, ..., \delta_{u_i}^{c_j}\}$ and $\delta_{u_j} = \{\delta_{u_j}^{c_1}, \delta_{u_j}^{c_2}, ..., \delta_{u_j}^{c_j}\}$, if $|\delta_{u_i} - \delta_{u_j}| \leq \varepsilon$, we believe that student u_i and student u_j have similar learning abilities. In other words, they belong to the same learning ability community.*

According to the exercise sequence of students and the definition of learning ability community, we use an unsupervised deep clustering algorithm to minimize ε to divide students into their range of learning ability through continuous iteration and acquire multiple different learning ability communities. In a learning ability community k, we input all exercise sequences into a basic knowledge tracing model for training and get a corresponding optimization model by adjusting the parameters of the basic model. Because all students have similar learning abilities in the learning ability community k, we can use group learning characteristics to guide individual learning. Therefore, we give the definition of the Personalized Knowledge Tracing is as follows:

Definition 3. *Personalized Knowledge Tracing.* *We Suppose that m students had already learned the exercise sequences $X = \{x_1, x_2, ..., x_T\}$ contain knowledge concepts $\{c_1, c_2, ..., c_j\}$ in the learning ability community k, if a student u_{m+i} wants to learn this exercise sequences, we are able to trace the personalized knowledge state of student u_{m+i} according to the knowledge state of m students. In other words, we can predict the probability that student u_{m+i} correctly answer this exercise sequence, which is called Personalized Knowledge Tracing.*

3.2 Knowledge Tracking Based on Learning and Memory Process

Despite being more powerful than DKT and BKT in storing and updating the exercise sequence of students, DKVMN still has deficiencies when solved the knowledge tracing problem. To solve the problem, we propose the model: Knowledge Tracking based on Learning and Memory Process (LMKT), its framework is shown in Fig. 1. We assume the *key* matrix $\mathbf{M}^k$ (of size $N \times d_k$) is a static matrix that stores the concept representations and the *value* matrix $\mathbf{M}^v_t$ (of size $N \times d_v$) is a dynamic value matrix that stores the student's mastery levels of each concept, meanwhile $\mathbf{M}^v_t$ updates over time. The task of knowledge tracing is completed by three mechanisms of LMKT: *attention, reading* and *writing*.

Attention. For the input exercise q_t of a student u_i, we utilize the attention mechanism to determine which concepts are relevant to it. Thus, we multiply q_t by embedding matrix $\mathbf{A}$ to get an embedding vector $\boldsymbol{k}_t$. Relevance probability of q_t belongs to every concept in $\mathbf{M}^k$ is computed by comparing the question to each *key* matrix slot $\mathbf{M}^k(i)$, which is defined as attention weight vector $\boldsymbol{w}_t$. $\boldsymbol{w}_t$ represents the weight of each student's attention between exercise and each concept and will be applied to read and write processes.

$$\boldsymbol{w}_t(i) = Softmax(\boldsymbol{k}_t^T \mathbf{M}^k(i)), \tag{1}$$

where $Softmax(x) = e^x / \sum_y (e^y)$.

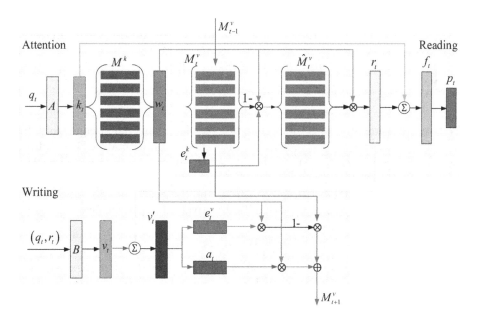

Fig. 1. The framework of Knowledge Tracking based on learning and memory process

Reading. When an exercise q_t comes, the *value* matrix $\mathbf{M}_t^v$ of students' current knowledge state cannot remain unchanged, because of the influence of human forgetting mechanism. Therefore, we assume the *forgetting* vector $\mathbf{e}_t^k$ represents the forgetting of current knowledge state during the reading process, and students' current knowledge state $\mathbf{M}_t^v(i)$ will be updated as $\hat{\mathbf{M}}_t^v(i)$.

$$\mathbf{e}_t^k = Sigmoid(\mathbf{E}_k^T \mathbf{M}_t^v + \boldsymbol{b}_k), \tag{2}$$

$$\hat{\mathbf{M}}_t^v(i) = \mathbf{M}_t^v(i)[1 - \boldsymbol{w}_t(i)\mathbf{e}_t^k], \tag{3}$$

where $\mathbf{E}_k^T$ is a transformation matrix, the elements of $\mathbf{e}_t^k$ lie in the range $(0, 1)$. Then, according to the attention weight $\boldsymbol{w}_t$, we can calculate the read content $\boldsymbol{r}_t$ that stands for a summary of the student's mastery level of this exercise through the *value* matrix $\hat{\mathbf{M}}_t^v(i)$.

$$\boldsymbol{r}_t = \sum_i^N \boldsymbol{w}_t(i)\hat{\mathbf{M}}_t^v(i). \tag{4}$$

next, we concatenate the read content $\boldsymbol{r}_t$ and the input exercise embedding $\boldsymbol{k}_t$ and then pass through a multilayer perceptron with the Tanh activation function to get a summary of knowledge state vector $\boldsymbol{f}_t$, which contains the student's mastery level and the difficulty of exercise q_t.

$$\boldsymbol{f}_t = Tanh(\boldsymbol{W}_1^T[\boldsymbol{r}_t, \boldsymbol{k}_t] + \boldsymbol{b}_1). \tag{5}$$

finally, after $\boldsymbol{f}_t$ pass through the sigmoid activation function, we can get the predicted scalar $\boldsymbol{p}_t$ that represents the probability of answering the exercise q_t correctly.

$$\boldsymbol{p}_t = Sigmoid(\boldsymbol{W}_2^T \boldsymbol{f}_t + \boldsymbol{b}_2), \tag{6}$$

where $\boldsymbol{W}_1^T, \boldsymbol{W}_2^T$ stand for the weight and $\boldsymbol{b}_1, \boldsymbol{b}_2$ stand for the bias.

Writing. Writing process is the update process of students' knowledge state. In DKVMN model, The (q_t, r_t) embedded with an embedding matrix $\mathbf{B}$ to obtain the *knowledge growth* $\boldsymbol{v}_t$ of the students after working on this exercise [24], which is insufficient to express the actual gains in the learning process. However, concatenate the original *knowledge growth* $\boldsymbol{v}_t$ and the read content $\boldsymbol{r}_t$ and pass it through a fully connected layer with a Tanh activation to get the new *knowledge growth* $\boldsymbol{v}_t'$.

$$\boldsymbol{v}_t' = Tanh(\boldsymbol{W}_3^T[\boldsymbol{v}_t, \boldsymbol{r}_t] + \boldsymbol{b}_3). \tag{7}$$

before writing the student's *knowledge growth* into the *value* matrix $\mathbf{M}_t^v$, we should consider the forgetting according to human learning and cognitive processes. We assume that the *forgetting* vector $\mathbf{e}_t^v$ that is computed from $\boldsymbol{v}_t'$.

$$\mathbf{e}_t^v = Sigmoid(\mathbf{E}_v^T \boldsymbol{v}_t' + \boldsymbol{b}_v), \tag{8}$$

where $\mathbf{E}_v^T$ is a transformation matrix, the elements of $\mathbf{e}_t^v$ lie in the range (0,1). After the *forgetting* vector $\mathbf{e}_t^v$, the memory vectors component $\mathbf{M}_{t-1}^v(i)$ from the previous timestamp are modified as follows:

$$\widetilde{\mathbf{M}}_t^v(i) = \mathbf{M}_{t-1}^v(i)[1 - \boldsymbol{w}_t(i)\mathbf{e}_t^v], \tag{9}$$

where $\boldsymbol{w}_t(i)$ is the same as in the reading process. After forgetting, the *add* vector $\boldsymbol{a}_t$ is the actual gains of the new *knowledge growth* $\boldsymbol{v}_t'$, which is calculated as follows:

$$\boldsymbol{a}_t = Tanh(\boldsymbol{W}_a^T \boldsymbol{v}_t' + \boldsymbol{b}_a), \tag{10}$$

where $\boldsymbol{W}_a^T$ is a transformation matrix. Finally, the *value* matrix is updated at each time t based on $\widetilde{\mathbf{M}}_t^v(i)$ and $\boldsymbol{a}_t$.

$$\mathbf{M}_t^v(i) = \widetilde{\mathbf{M}}_t^v(i) + \boldsymbol{w}_t(i)\boldsymbol{a}_t. \tag{11}$$

Training. All parameters of the LMKT model, such as the embedding matrices $\mathbf{A}$ and $\mathbf{B}$ as well as other weight parameters, are trained by minimizing a standard cross entropy loss between the prediction label p_t and the ground-truth label r_t.

$$\mathcal{L} = -\sum_t (r_t \log p_t + (1 - r_t) \log (1 - p_t)) \tag{12}$$

3.3 Learning Ability Community for Personalized Knowledge Tracing

In this subsection, we introduce Learning Ability Community for Personalized Knowledge Tracing (LACPKT) based on the previous two subsections. The framework of LACPKT is shown in Fig. 2, the process of the LACPKT is as follows:

Firstly, we input the exercise sequences of all students into the LMKT model for training and get a basic $LMKT_0$ model suitable for all students.

Secondly, According to Definition 1, we process each student's exercise sequence to obtain their learning ability degree sequence $\{\delta_1, \delta_1, ..., \delta_L\}$.

Thirdly, we input the learning ability degree sequence of all students into the deep clustering network (DCN) [22], which joints dimensionality reduction and K-means clustering approach in which DR is accomplished via learning a deep neural network. According to the Definition 2, we assume that we obtain k learning ability communities (LAC) as follows:

$$\{LAC_1, LAC_2, ..., LAC_k\} \Leftarrow \{(\delta_1, \delta_1, ..., \delta_L), DCN\}. \tag{13}$$

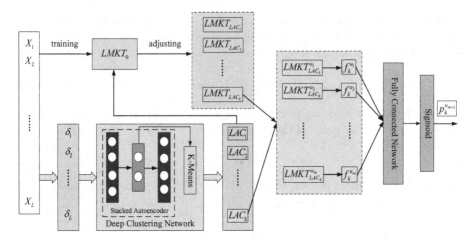

Fig. 2. The framework of learning ability community for Personalized Knowledge Tracing

Then, we input the exercise sequences of k learning ability communities into the basic $LMKT_0$ model for training, and acquire k optimized LMKT models by adjusting the parameters of the basic model, as shown in Eq. (14). In any learning ability community, we can trace the personalized knowledge state of each student.

$$\{LMKT_{LAC_1}, ..., LMKT_{LAC_k}\} \Leftarrow \{(LAC_1, ..., LAC_k), LMKT_0\}. \qquad (14)$$

Next, according to the Definition 3, if there are m students had already learned the exercise sequence $X = \{x_1, x_2, ..., x_t\}$ involves knowledge concepts $\{c_1, c_2, ..., c_j\}$ in the learning ability community k, we are able to construct m personalized knowledge models for these m students, and obtain these m students' current knowledge state $\{f_k^{u_1}, f_k^{u_2}, ..., f_k^{u_m}\}$, as shown in Eq. (15) and Eq. (16).

$$\{LMKT_{LAC_k^{u_1}}, ..., LMKT_{LAC_k^{u_m}}\} \Leftarrow \{(u_1, ..., u_m), LMKT_{LAC_k}\}, \qquad (15)$$

$$\{f_k^{u_1}, f_k^{u_2}, ..., f_k^{u_m}\} \Leftarrow \{LMKT_{LAC_k^{u_1}}, ..., LMKT_{LAC_k^{u_m}}\}. \qquad (16)$$

Finally, when student u_{m+1} wants to learn the exercise sequence $X = \{x_1, ..., x_t\}$, we concatenate these m students' current knowledge state $\{f_k^{u_1}, f_k^{u_2}, ..., f_k^{u_m}\}$ and then pass it through a fully connected network with the Sigmoid activation function to predict the probability $p_k^{u_{m+1}}$ that student u_{m+1} will correctly answer this exercise sequence.

$$p_k^{u_{m+1}} = Sigmoid(W_k^T[f_k^{u_1}, f_k^{u_2}, ..., f_k^{u_m}] + b_k), \qquad (17)$$

where $\boldsymbol{W}_k^T$ and $\boldsymbol{b}_k$ stand for the weight and bias of student u_{m+1}. The optimized objective function is the standard cross entropy loss between the prediction label $p_k^{u_{m+1}}$ and the ground-truth label r_t.

$$L_k^{u_{m+1}} = -\sum_t \left(r_t \log p_k^{u_{m+1}} + (1 - r_t) \log \left(1 - p_k^{u_{m+1}}\right)\right). \tag{18}$$

4 Experiments

In this section, we first evaluate the performance of our LMKT model against the state-of-the-art knowledge tracing models on four experimental datasets. Then, we verify the validity of our LACPKT model and analyze the effectiveness of Personalized knowledge tracing.

4.1 Experiment Settings

Datasets. We use four public datasets from the literature [18,24]: Synthetic-5[1], ASSISTments2009[2], ASSISTments2015[3], and Statics2011[4], where Synthetic-5 is one synthetic dataset, the other three are the real-world datasets obtained from online learning platforms. The statistics of four datasets are shown in Table 1.

Implementation Details. First, we encoded the experimental datasets with one-hot encoding, and the length of the encoding depends on the number of different questions. In the synthetic-5 dataset, 50% of exercise sequences were used as a training dataset, but in the other three dataets, 70% of exercise sequences were used as a training dataset. A total 20% of the training dataset was split to form a validation dataset that was used to find the optimal model architecture and hyperparameters, hyperparameters were tuned using the five-fold cross-validation. Then, we constructed the deep clustering network consist of four hidden layers to cluster learning ability community, of which the number of neurons in the four hidden layers is 1000,800,500,100, in addition to every layer is pre-trained for 100 epochs and the entire deep network is further finetuned for 50 epochs. Next, in all experiments of our model, we trained with Adam optimizer and repeated the training five times to obtain the average test results. Finally, about evaluation indicators, we choose the $AUC \in [0,1]$, which is the area under the Receiver Operating Characteristic (ROC) curve, to measure the performance of all models.

---

[1] https://github.com/chrispiech/DeepKnowledgeTracing/tree/master/data/synthetic.
[2] https://sites.google.com/site/assistmentsdata/home/assistment-2009-2010-data/skill-builder-data-2009-2010.
[3] https://sites.google.com/site/assistmentsdata/home/2015-assistments-skill-builder-data.
[4] Statics2011:https://pslcdatashop.web.cmu.edu/DatasetInfo?datasetId=507.

Table 1. The statistics of four datasets.

Datasets	Students	Questions	Exercises
Synthetic-5	4000	50	200,000
ASSISTments2009	4,151	110	325,637
ASSISTments2015	19,840	100	683,801
Statics2011	333	1223	189,297

4.2 Results and Analysis

LMKT Model Performance Evaluation. We evaluate our LMKT model against the other three knowledge tracing models: BKT, DKT and DKVMN. The test AUC results are shown in Table 2.

Table 2. The AUC results of the four models on four datasets.

Datasets	Test AUC (%)			
	BKT	DKT	DKVMN	LMKT
Synthetic-5	62	80.34	82.76	**82.95**
ASSISTments2009	63	80.53	81.52	**81.77**
ASSISTments2015	64	72.52	72.73	**72.94**
Statics2011	73	80.20	82.33	**82.76**

Since the performance of the BKT model and the DKT model is lower than the DKVMN model, the AUC results of these two models refer to the optimal results in [24]. For the DKVMN model, we set the parameters of it to be consistent with those in the original literature, then trained five times on four datasets to obtain the final average test results. In our LMKT model, we adjusted the model parameters to find the best model structure and obtain the best results according to the change of our model structure. It can be seen that our model outperformed the other models over all the four datasets. Although the performance of our model is improved by 0.25% to 0.5% compared to the DKVMN model, it proved the effectiveness of dealing with knowledge tracking problems based on human learning and memory processes. Besides, the state dimensions and memory size of the LMKT model are 10 or 20, it can get better results. However, the state dimensions and memory size of the DKVMN model are 50 or 100, which leads to problems such as more model parameters and longer training time. As shown in Fig. 3, the performance of the LMKT model is better than the DKVMN model, especially the LMKT model can reach the optimal structure of the model in fewer iterations. However, In the Statics2011 dataset, although the performance of the LMKT model and the DKVMN model are similar, the gap exists between the training AUC and the validation AUC of the DKVMN model is larger than the LMKT model, so the over-fitting problem of the LMKT model is smaller than the DKVMN model.

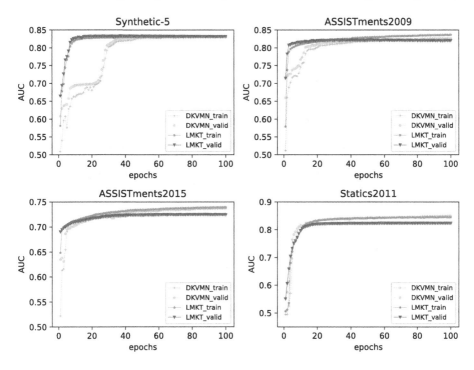

Fig. 3. Training AUC and validation AUC of DKVMN and LMKT on four datasets

Learning Ability Community Analysis. By analyzing the exercise sequences of the four experimental datasets, we divide each student into different learning ability communities thought the deep clustering network. According to Definitions 1 and 2, we knew that δ determines the difference in learning ability among students and then normalized the learning ability degree is between 0 and 1. However, we set up clusters of deep clustering networks to determine the number of learning ability communities and divide students into the learning ability communities to which they belong. We set the ASSISTments2015 dataset contains six different learning ability communities and the other three datasets contain five different learning ability communities, and visualize each dataset through t-SNE [13]. Figure 4 shows the results of the visualization of the learning ability community, where each color represents a learning ability community. In the Synthetic-5 dataset, because it is obtained by artificially simulating the student's answering process, the effect of dividing the learning ability community shows discrete characteristics. In ASSISTments2009 and ASSISTments2015 dataset, because of the exercise sequences are shorter in the datasets or the exercise questions are repeated multiple times in the same exercise sequence, some data is far from the center of the learning ability community. Moreover, the dataset ASSISTments2015 contains 19,840 students, so the number of learning ability communities set is not enough to meet the actual situation, so it has the problem of overlapping learning ability communities. In the Statics2011 dataset, since it contains only 333 students, the overall clustering effect is sparse.

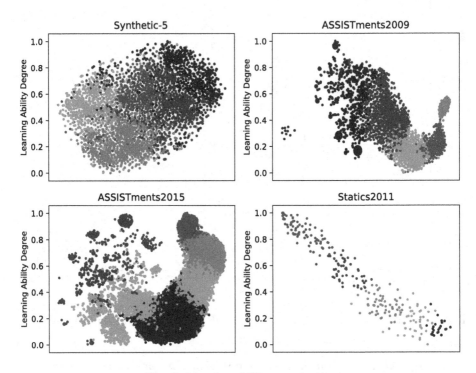

Fig. 4. Learning ability community

Personalized Knowledge Tracing. Because the dataset ASSISTments2015 is an updated version of the data set ASSISTments2009, and the data set Statics2011 has only 333 student exercise sequences, we chose the datasets Synthetic-5 and ASSISTments2015 for experimental verification of personalized knowledge tracing. Through the analysis of the dataset and the learning ability community, we set the number of learning ability communities of the datasets Synthetic-5 and ASSISTments2015 to 4 and 6. To ensure the sufficiency and reliability of personalized knowledge tracing experiment, we input different learning ability communities to DKVMN called the LAC_DKVMN model and compare it with LACPKT. According to Definition 3, we conducted experiments to validate the validity of the LACPKT model, the experimental results are shown in Fig. 5.

According to Fig. 5(a) and (b), we found that the personalized knowledge tracking capability of the LACPKT model is better than the LAC_DKVMN model in all learning capability communities of the two datasets. In dataset Synthetic-5, the AUC results of the LACPKT model in the four learning ability communities are 83.96%, 84.98%, 82.56%, 81.67%, respectively. In dataset

ASSISTments2015, the AUC results of the LACPKT model in the six learning ability communities are 76.25%, 70.34%, 73.23%, 71.87%, 70.68%, 72.72%, respectively. From the experimental results, when the LACPKT model tracks the knowledge status of students in different learning ability communities, its performance is shown to be different. The reason is that students learn different exercise sequence length and problems in different learning ability communities, so the performance of the LACPKT model is different in different learning ability communities. Figure 5(c) and (d) show the changing state of AUC of the LACPKT model in the validation dataset. In dataset Synthetic-5, because it is an artificial simulation dataset, the length and questions of each student's exercise sequence are the same, the test results and the verification results of the LACPKT model remain the same. However, in ASSISTments2015 dataset, because each student's exercise sequence length and questions are different, the performance of the LACPKT model in different learning communities is different. For different learning ability communities, the LACPKT model can model students' learning processes according to different learning abilities, and track students' personalized knowledge status based on the effect of group learning behavior on individuals. Therefore, the experimental results proved the effectiveness of dividing the learning ability community and the effectiveness of the LACPKT model in tracing students' personalized knowledge state.

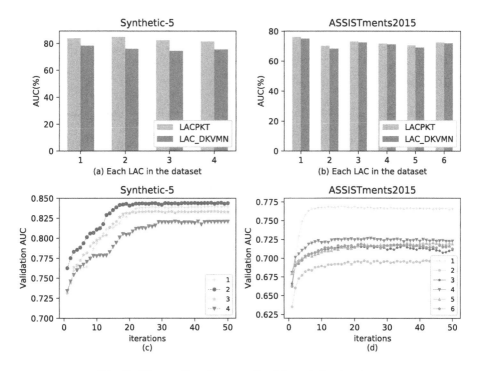

Fig. 5. The results of personalized knowledge tracing.

5   Conclusions and Future Work

In this paper, we propose a novel method that is called Learning Ability Community for Personalized Knowledge Tracing (LACPKT) to model the learning process of students and trace the knowledge state of students. The LACPKT model consists of two aspects, on the one hand, we propose the definition of learning ability community, which utilizes the effect of group learning on individuals to trace the personalized knowledge state of students; On the other hand, we propose a Knowledge Tracking based on Learning and Memory Process model that considers the relationship between the current knowledge state and knowledge growth and forgetting mechanisms. Finally, we demonstrate the effectiveness of the LACPKT model in tracing students' personalized knowledge on public datasets. For future work, we will integrate the content information of the problem to optimize the learning ability community and optimize the network structure to improve the prediction ability.

Acknowledgements. This work is supported by the key projects of the national natural science foundation of China (No. U1811263), the major technical innovation project of Hubei Province (No. 2019AAA072), the National Natural Science Foundation of China (No. 61572378), the Science and technology project of State Grid Corporation of China (No. 5700-202072180A-0-0-00), the Teaching Research Project of Wuhan University (No. 2018JG052), the Natural Science Foundation of Hubei Province (No. 2017CFB420). We also thank anonymous reviewers for their helpful reports.

References

1. Antunes, C.: Acquiring background knowledge for intelligent tutoring systems. In: Educational Data Mining 2008 (2008)
2. Baker, R.S.J., Corbett, A.T., Aleven, V.: More accurate student modeling through contextual estimation of slip and guess probabilities in Bayesian knowledge tracing. In: Woolf, B.P., Aïmeur, E., Nkambou, R., Lajoie, S. (eds.) ITS 2008. LNCS, vol. 5091, pp. 406–415. Springer, Heidelberg (2008). https://doi.org/10.1007/978-3-540-69132-7_44
3. Brod, G., Werkle-Bergner, M., Shing, Y.L.: The influence of prior knowledge on memory: a developmental cognitive neuroscience perspective. Front. Behav. Neurosci. **7**, 139 (2013)
4. Cheung, L.P., Yang, H.: Heterogeneous features integration in deep knowledge tracing. In: Liu, D., Xie, S., Li, Y., Zhao, D., El-Alfy, E.S. (eds.) ICONIP 2017. LNCS, pp. 653–662. Springer, Cham (2017). https://doi.org/10.1007/978-3-319-70096-0_67
5. Corbett, A.T., Anderson, J.R.: Knowledge tracing: modeling the acquisition of procedural knowledge. User Model. User-Adapt. Interact. **4**(4), 253–278 (1994)
6. David, Y.B., Segal, A., Gal, Y.K.: Sequencing educational content in classrooms using Bayesian knowledge tracing. In: Proceedings of the Sixth International Conference on Learning Analytics & Knowledge, pp. 354–363. ACM (2016)

7. Ebbinghaus, H.: Memory: a contribution to experimental psychology. Ann. Neurosci. **20**(4), 155 (2013)
8. Feng, J., Zhang, B., Li, Y., Xu, Q.: bayesian diagnosis tracing: application of procedural misconceptions in knowledge tracing. In: Isotani, S., Millán, E., Ogan, A., Hastings, P., McLaren, B., Luckin, R. (eds.) AIED 2019. LNCS (LNAI), vol. 11626, pp. 84–88. Springer, Cham (2019). https://doi.org/10.1007/978-3-030-23207-8_16
9. Hawkins, W.J., Heffernan, N.T., Baker, R.S.J.D.: Learning Bayesian knowledge tracing parameters with a knowledge heuristic and empirical probabilities. In: Trausan-Matu, S., Boyer, K.E., Crosby, M., Panourgia, K. (eds.) ITS 2014. LNCS, vol. 8474, pp. 150–155. Springer, Cham (2014). https://doi.org/10.1007/978-3-319-07221-0_18
10. Johns, J., Mahadevan, S., Woolf, B.: Estimating student proficiency using an item response theory model. In: Ikeda, M., Ashley, K.D., Chan, T.-W. (eds.) ITS 2006. LNCS, vol. 4053, pp. 473–480. Springer, Heidelberg (2006). https://doi.org/10.1007/11774303_47
11. Khajah, M., Lindsey, R.V., Mozer, M.: How deep is knowledge tracing? In: Proceedings of the 9th International Conference on Educational Data Mining, EDM 2016, Raleigh, North Carolina, USA, 29 June–2 July 2016 (2016)
12. LeCun, Y., Bengio, Y., Hinton, G.: Deep learning. Nature **521**(7553), 436–444 (2015)
13. van der Maaten, L., Hinton, G.: Visualizing data using t-SNE. J. Mach. Learn. Res. **9**(Nov), 2579–2605 (2008)
14. Nagatani, K., Zhang, Q., Sato, M., Chen, Y.Y., Chen, F., Ohkuma, T.: Augmenting knowledge tracing by considering forgetting behavior. In: The World Wide Web Conference, pp. 3101–3107. ACM (2019)
15. Pappano, L.: The year of the MOOC. N. Y. Times **2**(12), 2012 (2012)
16. Pardos, Z.A., Heffernan, N.T.: KT-IDEM: introducing item difficulty to the knowledge tracing model. In: Konstan, J.A., Conejo, R., Marzo, J.L., Oliver, N. (eds.) UMAP 2011. LNCS, vol. 6787, pp. 243–254. Springer, Heidelberg (2011). https://doi.org/10.1007/978-3-642-22362-4_21
17. Pardos, Z.A., Trivedi, S., Heffernan, N.T., Sárközy, G.N.: Clustered knowledge tracing. In: Cerri, S.A., Clancey, W.J., Papadourakis, G., Panourgia, K. (eds.) ITS 2012. LNCS, vol. 7315, pp. 405–410. Springer, Heidelberg (2012). https://doi.org/10.1007/978-3-642-30950-2_52
18. Piech, C., et al.: Deep knowledge tracing. In: Advances in Neural Information Processing Systems 28: Annual Conference on Neural Information Processing Systems 2015, 7–12 December 2015, Montreal, Quebec, Canada, pp. 505–513 (2015)
19. Santoro, A., Bartunov, S., Botvinick, M., Wierstra, D., Lillicrap, T.: Meta-learning with memory-augmented neural networks. In: International Conference on Machine Learning, pp. 1842–1850 (2016)
20. Trivedi, S., Pardos, Z.A., Heffernan, N.T.: Clustering students to generate an ensemble to improve standard test score predictions. In: Biswas, G., Bull, S., Kay, J., Mitrovic, A. (eds.) AIED 2011. LNCS (LNAI), vol. 6738, pp. 377–384. Springer, Heidelberg (2011). https://doi.org/10.1007/978-3-642-21869-9_49
21. Weston, J., Chopra, S., Bordes, A.: Memory networks. In: 3rd International Conference on Learning Representations, ICLR 2015, San Diego, CA, USA, 7–9 May 2015, Conference Track Proceedings (2015)
22. Yang, B., Fu, X., Sidiropoulos, N.D., Hong, M.: Towards k-means-friendly spaces: simultaneous deep learning and clustering. In: Proceedings of the 34th International Conference on Machine Learning, vol. 70, pp. 3861–3870 (2017)

23. Yudelson, M.V., Koedinger, K.R., Gordon, G.J.: Individualized Bayesian knowledge tracing models. In: Lane, H.C., Yacef, K., Mostow, J., Pavlik, P. (eds.) AIED 2013. LNCS (LNAI), vol. 7926, pp. 171–180. Springer, Heidelberg (2013). https://doi.org/10.1007/978-3-642-39112-5_18
24. Zhang, J., Shi, X., King, I., Yeung, D.Y.: Dynamic key-value memory networks for knowledge tracing. In: Proceedings of the 26th International Conference on World Wide Web, pp. 765–774. International World Wide Web Conferences Steering Committee (2017)
25. Zhang, L., Xiong, X., Zhao, S., Botelho, A., Heffernan, N.T.: Incorporating rich features into deep knowledge tracing. In: Proceedings of the Fourth (2017) ACM Conference on Learning@ Scale, pp. 169–172. ACM (2017)

LOCATE: Locally Anomalous Behavior Change Detection in Behavior Information Sequence

Dingshan Cui[1], Lei Duan[1(✉)], Xinao Wang[1], Jyrki Nummenmaa[2], Ruiqi Qin[1], and Shan Xiao[1]

[1] School of Computer Science, Sichuan University, Chengdu, China
cuidingshans@163.com, leiduan@scu.edu.cn, xiaoshan_1012@163.com,
richforgood@163.com, scdxwxa@gmail.com
[2] Faculty of Information Technology and Communication Sciences, Tampere University, Tampere, Finland
jyrki.nummenmaa@tuni.fi

Abstract. With the availability of diverse data reflecting people's behavior, behavior analysis has been studied extensively. Detecting anom-alies can improve the monitoring and understanding of the objects' (e.g., people's) behavior. This work considers the situation where objects behave significantly differently from their previous (past) similar objects. We call this locally anomalous behavior change. Locally anomalous behavior change detection is relevant to various practical applications, e.g., detecting elderly people with abnormal behavior. In this paper, making use of objects, behavior and their associated attributes as well as the relations between them, we propose a behavior information sequence (BIS) constructed from behavior data, and design a novel graph information propagation autoencoder framework called LOCATE (locally anomalous behavior change detection), to detect the anomalies involving the locally anomalous behavior change in the BIS. Two real-world datasets were used to assess the performance of LOCATE. Experimental results demonstrated that LOCATE is effective in detecting locally anomalous behavior change.

Keywords: Behavior analysis · Anomaly detection · Network embedding

1 Introduction

People's behavior data is widely used in various applications areas, such as point-of-interest prediction [10], product recommendation [8] and change detection [11]. Detecting anomalies from behavior data can unveil interesting/fraudulent

This work was supported in part by National Natural Science Foundation of China (61972268, 61572332).

© Springer Nature Switzerland AG 2020
X. Wang et al. (Eds.): APWeb-WAIM 2020, LNCS 12318, pp. 193–208, 2020.
https://doi.org/10.1007/978-3-030-60290-1_15

behavior and identify crowd activities or emergencies. In this work, we consider detecting locally anomalous behavior change from behavior data.

Take the care of the elderly for example. In some European countries, the care-taking of the elderly has posed a significant challenge, due to some factors such as the increased physical distances, demanding work life and other duties of care-givers. Typically, worrying changes in health and well-being are indicated by a change in an elderly's regular behavior. While the elderly often wear and use intelligent devices that help in collecting data to find indications of their changed behavior, the better ways to utilize those collected data to identify changed behavior, which can be considered as anomalies, are still under investigation.

Some research has detected specific anomalous changes, e.g., abrupt changes [13], changes to community [9], change in neighbors [12], and the sudden appearance of a large dense subgraph in networks [6]. It seems that we can find anomalies through detecting abrupt changes in behavior. However, there are some normal changes, such as preparing for a festive season and new activities being introduced in a nursing home.

Example 1. Figure 1 shows one scenario with the elderly people's activities in two weeks in a nursing home around Thanksgiving Day. Consider the distinct elderly persons A, B, C and D. In daily life, A, B, C and D always exercised together and sometimes they read books separately. On Thanksgiving Day, A, B and C ate turkey prepared by the nursing home. The next day, A, B and C watched movie. Compared with behavior in daily life, their behavior changes a lot. Abrupt change detection will identify A, B and C as anomalous, although their changes are normal changes. However, instead of going with A, B and C together, D read a book alone on Thanksgiving Day. Here, D should be identified as anomalous. This situation is what we call locally anomalous behavior change.

Fig. 1. A scenario in a nursing home around Thanksgiving Day.

From Example 1, we can see that an object has a local neighbourhood group (e.g., friends, coworkers, followers), in which every object has similar behavior with the object. We focus on detecting changes that imply anomalous behavior within a local neighbourhood group. In a neighborhood group, such behavior changes can be sorted into two types: (1) individual changing behavior; (2)

the neighbourhood group locally changing behavior in a way that the individual does not follow, like Example 1 shows. The target of our work is detecting locally anomalous behavior change.

Detecting locally anomalous behavior change is a challenging problem for the following reasons. First, behavior is time-varying. Because with the influence of external conditions or internal demands, behavior can be capricious and vary from week to week or from month to month. For example, people's behavior will change on the coming of Thanksgiving Day. Thus, detection approaches should consider the temporal factors. Second, objects and behavior are inherently associated with a rich set of attributes, for example, age and gender of people, time, location and type of behavior. These attributes need to be considered during locally anomalous behavior change detection.

Coping with the above challenges, we make the following contributions: (1) proposing a novel structure, named behavior information sequence (BIS) to model objects, behavior and associated attributes as well as the relations between them at different times; (2) proposing a novel graph information propagation autoencoder framework, called LOCATE (locally anomalous behavior change detection), to learn vector representations of vertices from the constructed BIS and detect locally anomalous behavior change; (3) conducting extensive experiments on real-world datasets to demonstrate the effectiveness of LOCATE on detecting locally anomalous behavior change.

The rest of this paper is organized as follows. Section 2 formulates the problem of locally anomalous behavior change detection. Section 3 surveys related work. Section 4 introduces the design of LOCATE. Section 5 empirically evaluates LOCATE on real-world datasets. Finally, Sect. 6 concludes this paper.

2   Problem Definition

In this section, we introduce definitions, notations and problem formulation for locally anomalous behavior change detection.

A **behavior network** is a directed graph, which models the relations between objects (e.g., people) and behavior over a period $[t^+, t^-)$, as well as their corresponding attributes, denoted by $\mathcal{G}(t^+, t^-) = (\mathcal{V}, \mathcal{E}, \mathcal{X}, t^+, t^-)$. $\mathcal{V} = \{v_1, v_2, ..., v_m\}$ denotes the set of nodes. $\mathcal{E}$ denotes the set of edges. $\mathcal{X} = \{\mathbf{x}_1, \mathbf{x}_2, ... \mathbf{x}_m\}$ refers to the set of node attributes, where $\mathbf{x}_i{}^1$ denotes the attribute information for node v_i. t^+ denotes the starting time point of the period and t^- denotes the ending time point of the period. A behavior network $\mathcal{G}$ is also associated with a node type mapping function $\phi : \mathcal{V} \rightarrow \mathcal{A}$ and an edge type mapping function $\psi : \mathcal{E} \rightarrow \mathcal{R}$. $\mathcal{A}$ and $\mathcal{R}$ denote the sets of node types and edge types, respectively, where $|\mathcal{A}| > 1$ or $|\mathcal{R}| > 1$.

---

[1] Attribute information describes the attributes associated with the node i, and attribute information associated with different types of nodes has different dimensions.

Obviously, a behavior network is an attributed heterogeneous network [21]. A behavior network includes two types of nodes: objects (o) and behavior (b), and each node has its corresponding attributes.

Observation 1. *Periodicity naturally exists in behavior, i.e., the behavior approximately follows the same routines over regular time intervals. For example, a student always attends "Data Structure" course every Monday morning and goes to the English Corner every Friday evening.*

Considering this periodicity of behavior, we construct one behavior network per period $[t^+, t^-)$. A **behavior information sequence** Q is a list of behavior networks, ordered by their starting time points, of the form $Q =< \mathcal{G}_1(t_1^+, t_1^-), \mathcal{G}_2(t_2^+, t_2^-), ..., \mathcal{G}_n(t_n^+, t_n^-) >$, where $0 \le t_i^+ \le t_j^+$, $t_i^- \le t_{i+1}^+$ ($1 \le i < j \le n$). The time of all behavior networks adds up to the whole time $t_n^- - t_1^+$. The set of starting time point of each element denoted by $Q.s = \{t_1^+, t_2^+, ..., t_n^+\}$. Similarly, the set of ending time point of elements denoted by $Q.e = \{t_1^-, t_2^-, ..., t_n^-\}$. Note that the length of time of each behavior network can be different.

Let T_{rec} denote the recent time window, representing one recent period that we are interested in. Let T_{ref} denote the reference (past) time window, representing one or more continuous reference (past) periods before T_{rec}. The two time windows both are input parameters given by the user in the form of $T = [t^+, t^-)$, where the t^+ is chosen from $Q.s$ and t^- is chosen from $Q.e$.

Example 2. Taking the behavior information sequence Q in Fig. 2 for instance, Q consists of seven behavior networks. The reference time window $T_{ref} = [t_3, t_6)$ and the recent time window $T_{rec} = [t_6, t_7)$ are given by users as input parameters.

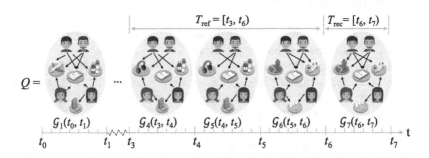

Fig. 2. An example of the behavior information sequence Q.

Given the behavior information sequence Q, the recent time window T_{rec} and the reference time window T_{ref}, the goal of locally anomalous behavior change detection problem is to detect the objects (e.g., people) that are significantly different in the given recent time window T_{rec}, with respect to the previous similar objects in T_{ref}.

3 Related Work

In this section, we briefly review related work from two areas : (1) anomaly detection in network, (2) network embedding.

3.1 Anomaly Detection in Network

Anomaly detection has been studied extensively in the context of static networks [2], including attributed networks [3] and heterogeneous networks [15]. For describing objects and relationships with temporal factors, anomaly detection over streaming networks has received an increasing amount of attention in the past decades, which can be divided into three categories: anomalous edge detection, online network anomaly detection, and change detection.

Anomalous edge detection aims to identify unusual bridging edges. For instance, CAD [17] introduces a commute time distance model to detect edges that cause anomalous changes in network structure. Recently developed methods [16,22] detect anomalous edges based on historical evidence and vertices' neighborhood. These methods focus on the anomalous edges, missing the anomalous nodes with complex structural changes.

Online network anomaly detection focuses on structure anomalies with respect to all nodes or community members. Recently invented methods [1,20] identify the structure anomalies in real-time. For instance, Aggarwal et al. [1] first propose the real-time and dynamic method for structural anomaly detection in graph streams leveraging structural reservoir sampling. They only consider deviation from most of the nodes or communities at a certain time, but they cannot consider comparing the difference between the recent data and historical data.

Change detection focuses on anomalous change. StreamSpot [13] introduced a representation of heterogeneous networks based on their relative frequency of local substructures and then leveraged a centroid-based clustering method to flag the anomalous heterogeneous networks which have not been observed so far. Furthermore, recent work starts to consider more specific anomalous change, e.g., the sudden appearance of a large dense subnetwork [6], changes to community [9], change in neighbors [12]. ECOutlier [9] first needs communities given by users, which roughly divide the nodes into several huge groups, and then it identifies the anomalous changes with respect to community change trends by community-match based methods. IcLEOD [12] maintains the information about changes in neighbors of adjacent snapshots, represented by scores and then rank the score to identify the node with anomalous change in its Corenet, which contains two-step neighbors, but it is applicable only for homogeneous graphs without attributes and cannot consider high-order node proximity.

Generally, existing approaches are not, at least directly, applicable to our motivating scenario as they do not exhibit all of the desired properties simultaneously: handling rich attribute information of behavior and objects, heterogeneous networks, and streaming nature for locally anomalous behavior change.

3.2 Network Embedding

Network embedding automatically learns the latent feature vectors to embed the whole network, which preserves certain information among nodes.

Inspired by word embedding, which preserves the neighborhood structure extracted from words in each sentence, DeepWalk [14] and Node2Vector [7] learn low-dimension node representation by maximizing the likelihood of preserving graph neighborhoods of nodes. Yu et al. [20] proposed NetWalk, a dynamic graph embedding based on the random walk and reservoir-based sampling for anomaly detection. However, they only focus on the preservation of structural similarity. Some models are proposed to learn the representation of a heterogeneous graph, considering the different types of nodes carrying different information. Metapath2vec [4] yields various sequences of nodes through meta-path based random walk, and feed the sequences into the Skip-Gram model to obtain the representation of nodes. The work of Dominant [3] can preserve structural factors and attribute factors. We cannot use Dominant and Metapath2vec, since they do not consider the multiple heterogeneous factors and attribute factors simultaneously.

4 Design of LOCATE

In this section, we present the details of LOCATE. The overview of LOCATE is illustrated in Fig. 3. It has two components: (1) network representation learning, (2) anomaly detection based on the latent representations. The core idea behind LOCATE is to build a model describing the object behavior using structure, attribute and temporal factors in the first component. Then the model can be further used to measure the locally anomalous behavior change. LOCATE starts with building a behavior information sequence from the original data.

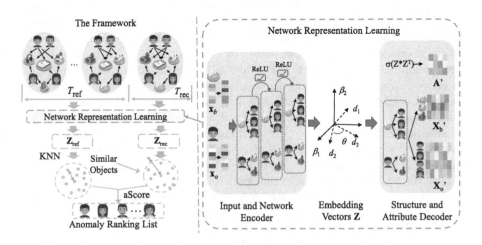

Fig. 3. The framework of LOCATE.

4.1 Behavior Information Sequence Construction

We will introduce how to construct a behavior information sequence taking the scenario of campus as an example. First, we construct a behavior information sequence by aggregating student behavior records, student information and location information (location profiles). A behavior network consists of object (student) nodes and behavior nodes, with their corresponding attributes.

As mentioned in Sect. 2, the behavior has periodicity. Considering the class schedule, without loss of generality, we set the length of the period of each behavior network as 7 days. Note that the 7-day periods are not restrictive - our approach is fully general and a 7-day period is not restricted to start from Monday 00:00 but can start from any time, for example, from Sunday 1:00 a.m. Then we divide a period into 28 time slots, considering 4 time slots per day. Then we can encode a timestamp t to a certain time slot id.

The construction of the behavior information sequence contains three steps. (1) Split all student behavior records into 7-day periods. (2) Build the behavior network. In this step, for every behavior network, we aggregate the student behavior with the same time slot id, the same type of behavior, the same location and the same cost (the cost has been discretized) into one behavior node. And we abstract and normalize the attributes of students and behavior from original data and then regard them as node attributes. (3) Associate all behavior networks built in the previous step into a behavior information sequence. Specifically, each node locating in one behavior network is associated with its counterparts with edges.

Then we adopt the concept of meta-path [18] to formulate semantic relationships among nodes in a behavior network. A meta-path ρ is defined on the behavior network in the form of $A_1 \xrightarrow{R_1} A_2 \xrightarrow{R_2} \cdots \xrightarrow{R_l} A_{l+1}$ (abbreviated as $A_1 A_2 \cdots A_{l+1}$). For example, the meta-path $S \xrightarrow{participate} B \xrightarrow{participate^{-1}} S$ (denoted by SBS) means that two students can be connected through the path where they both have a behavior with the same time slot id, the same location and so on. Given meta-path ρ and a path $p = (a_1, a_2, ..., a_l)$, if for $\forall i, \phi(a_i) = A_i, \psi(r_i) = R_i$, we say that p follows ρ. Further, paths $p_{i \rightsquigarrow j}$ between node v_i and v_j are called path instances of ρ, denoted as $p_{i \rightsquigarrow j} \in \rho$.

4.2 Network Representation Learning

In order to detect locally anomalous behavior change in a BIS, our method needs a scalable time-aware representation learning method to encode the information of the BIS. The network representation learning method we use consists of two modules: (1) input and network encoder, (2) structure and attribute decoder.

For preserving topology structure and node attribute information, inspired by [3], we use deep autoencoder architecture, which is an unsupervised learning framework with multiple layers of encoding and decoding functions. Deep autoencoder applies encoder to map the data into a latent low dimensional feature space and then recover the original data based on the latent representation through decoder. The objective of deep autoencoder can be described as minimizing the reconstruction errors, including network topology structure and node attribute information reconstruction errors.

Besides, the behavior information sequence is a temporal sequence. To model the temporal factors of a behavior network, we define a time decay weight for k-th behavior network $\mathcal{G}_k(t_k^+, t_k^-)$, defined by $D(k) = 2^{-\lambda(T_{max}-k)}$, where T_{max} denotes the index of the latest behavior network $\mathcal{G}_{T_{max}}$ in time window T, and λ is the decay factor, which controls the impacts of time decay. The half-life of the behavior information sequence is $1/\lambda$. $\mathcal{K}_{ij}^\rho$ denotes the set of the index of behavior network where the node v_i and v_j can be connected though meta-path ρ, defined by $\mathcal{K}_{ij}^\rho = \{k, p_{i \rightsquigarrow j} \in \rho | \mathcal{G}_k(t_k^+, t_k^-)\}$.

Input and Network Encoder. To encode a behavior information sequence, we face the following challenges: network sparsity, complex higher-order relationships and heterogeneous information (i.e., different types of nodes). We proposed a new network encoding algorithm, which learns latent representations through multi-layer neighbor information propagation along meta-path.

We take the node attributes $\mathcal{X}$ as the input of the encoder. First, we need to project the node attributes with different dimensions to a common space for utilizing various types of nodes uniformly. For this end, we use linear transformation to get a new latent representation ($\mathbf{h}_i \in \mathbb{R}^d$), defined by:

$$\mathbf{h}_i = \mathbf{W}_1^{\phi(i)}\mathbf{x}_i + \mathbf{b}^{\phi(i)},$$

where $\mathbf{x}_i$ denotes the attribute vector of the node v_i, $\phi(i)$ denotes the type of the node v_i, $\mathbf{W}_1^{\phi(i)} \in \mathbb{R}^{d \times k(i)}$ and $\mathbf{b}^{\phi(i)} \in \mathbb{R}^d$ denote the weight matrix and bias vector based on the type $\phi(i)$, $k(i)$ is the dimension of the node attribute vector of v_i, and d is the dimension of the latent representations.

We now describe the first information propagation layer. Given a node v_i and a meta-path ρ, the meta-path based neighbors are defined as the set of neighbors under the given meta-path ρ for the node v_i, denoted by $\mathcal{N}_i^\rho$. We sample $\mathcal{N}_i^\rho$ from the meta-path based neighbors in each epoch of training procedure. Due to the different effect of the meta-path based neighbors, we introduce an attention mechanism to control what information is propagated from different meta-path based neighbors. For node v_i and its meta-path ρ based neighbors $\mathcal{N}_i^\rho$, we define an attention score e_{ij} and apply the softmax function to normalize the attention score as follow:

$$e_{ij} = (\mathbf{c}^\rho)^{\mathrm{T}} tanh(d_{ij}\mathbf{W}^\rho\mathbf{h}_j + \mathbf{b}^\rho),$$

$$\alpha_{ij} = \frac{exp(e_{ij})}{\sum_{k \in \mathcal{N}_i^\rho} exp(e_{ik})},$$

where the context vector $\mathbf{c}^\rho \in \mathbb{R}^d$, the weight matrix $\mathbf{W}^\rho \in \mathbb{R}^{d \times d}$ and the bias vector $\mathbf{b}^\rho \in \mathbb{R}^d$ are parameters based on the meta-path ρ, and d_{ij} controls the weight of edge, calculated by $d_{ij} = \sum_{k \in \mathcal{K}_{ij}} D(k)$. To characterize the connectivity structure base on meta-path ρ of $\mathbf{h}_i$, we calculate aggregating features of its meta-path based neighbors $\mathcal{N}_i^\rho$:

$$\mathbf{h}_{\mathcal{N}_i}^\rho = \sum_{j \in \mathcal{N}_i^\rho} \alpha_{ij} \mathbf{h}_j.$$

Next, we fuse the latent representation of a node and its neighbors based on meta-path to represent fusing latent representation $\mathbf{h}_i^{(l)}$, which is the output of first layer of information propagation:

$$\mathbf{h}_i^{(1)} = f(\mathbf{h}_{\mathcal{N}_i}^\rho, \mathbf{h}_i)$$
$$= ReLU(\mathbf{h}_{\mathcal{N}_i}^\rho + \mathbf{h}_i).$$

So far, we obtain first-order representations of all nodes through the first layer of information propagation. For capturing the higher-order connectivity information, we further recursively feed the output of the current layer into the next hidden layer, to update the representation of nodes:

$$\mathbf{h}_i^{(l)} = f(\mathbf{h}_{\mathcal{N}_i}^{\rho\,(l-1)}, \mathbf{h}_i^{(l-1)}).$$

As a result, the information from higher-order neighbors based on the meta-path can be aggregated into a node. Thus, nodes that share the higher-order connectivity tend to have similar latent representations. After applying multi-layer propagation, the input behavior information sequence can be encoded into the latent representations $\mathbf{Z}$, which can capture the high non-linearity in the topological network structure and node attributes.

Structure and Attribute Decoder. Now, we discuss how to reconstruct the original network structure and node attributes with the latent representations $\mathbf{Z}$, which is obtained from the encoder.

For reconstructing the node attribute information, we leverage another information propagation layer and a linear transformation to approximate the original node attributes. The reconstructed node attribute $\tilde{\mathbf{x}}_i$, defined as follows:

$$\tilde{\mathbf{z}}_i = f(\mathbf{z}_{\mathcal{N}_i}^\rho, \mathbf{z}_i),$$
$$\tilde{\mathbf{x}}_i = \mathbf{W}_2^{\phi(i)} \tilde{\mathbf{z}}_i + \mathbf{b}_2^{\phi(i)},$$

where $\mathbf{z}_i$ denotes the latent representation of node v_i and $\mathbf{z}_{\mathcal{N}_i}^\rho$ denotes the aggregating features of node v_i meta-path based neighbors generated from the previous encoding module. And $\mathbf{W}_2^{\phi(i)} \in \mathbb{R}^{k(i) \times d}$ and $\mathbf{b}_2^{\phi(i)} \in \mathbb{R}^k(i)$ denote the weight matrix and bias vector based on the node type $\phi(i)$.

We reconstruct the structure information as follows:

$$\tilde{\mathbf{A}} = sigmoid(\mathbf{Z}\mathbf{Z}^T).$$

Optimization. To optimize the network representation learning model, the object function can be formulated as:

$$\mathcal{L}_A = \sqrt{\sum_{\mathbf{x}_i \in \mathcal{X}} (\tilde{\mathbf{x}}_i - \mathbf{x}_i)^2}, \quad \mathcal{L}_S = \sqrt{\sum_{(i,j) \in \mathcal{E}_Q} d_{ij} \left(\tilde{\mathbf{A}}_{ij} - \mathbf{A}_{ij} \right)^2},$$
$$\mathcal{L} = \eta(\mathcal{L}_A) + (1 - \eta)\mathcal{L}_S + \gamma \|\Theta\|_2^2,$$

where $\Theta = \{\mathbf{W}_1^{\phi(i)}, \mathbf{W}_2^{\phi(i)}, \forall l \in R, \mathbf{W}_\rho^{(l)}, \mathbf{b}_\rho^{(l)}\}$ is the model parameter set, η is an important controlling parameter which balances the impacts of structure reconstruction and node attribute reconstruction, and γ is the parameter of L_2 regularization to prevent overfitting. $A(i,j) = 1$, if the edge (i,j) are active in the input subsequence Q, otherwise $A(i,j) = 0$. We optimize LOCATE using AdaGrad optimization [5].

4.3   Anomaly Detection Based on the Latent Representations

Once we have trained the model and obtained different representations for objects in the recent time window and the reference time window, we can perform locally anomalous behavior change detection by simple computations on vectors.

Given an object o, we first find its k previous similar objects $\mathcal{S}_o$ in the reference time window T_{ref} using k-nearest neighbors algorithm based on node vectors, and then compute the similarity scores of the object o with respect to $\mathcal{S}_o$ in T_{rec} and T_{ref}. Given $\mathcal{S}_o$, object representations obtained in a time window T, the similarity score, denoted by $sScore((o,T), \mathcal{S}_o)$, is defined by:

$$sScore((o,T), \mathcal{S}_o) = \|\mathbf{c}^T - f^T(o)\|_2,$$

where $f^T(o)$ is the learned representation for o in T and $\mathbf{c}$ is the center of $\mathcal{S}_o$. After getting the similarity scores in T_{rec} and T_{ref}. Then we can compare it in T_{rec} and T_{ref} by the anomalous score. Given $\mathcal{S}_o$, two time windows T_{rec}, T_{ref}, the anomalous score of the object o in T_{rec}, is defined by:

$$aScore(o, (T_{rec}, T_{ref})) = |sScore((o, T_{rec}), \mathcal{S}_o) - sScore((o, T_{ref}), \mathcal{S}_o)|.$$

The anomalous score will be greater when the object behaves significantly differently from previous (past) similar objects in the recent time window.

5   Empirical Evaluation

In this section, we report an empirical study on real-world datasets to verify the performance of LOCATE in detecting locally anomalous behavior changes. We first describe the datasets and the experimental setting, compare LOCATE with the other baseline methods, and then study the impacts of different parameters.

5.1   Dataset

We use two real-world datasets for the evaluation of the proposed LOCATE:

- **Campus Card Dataset.** We collected the behavior data of 2,449 students on three campuses of Sichuan University (one of the universities with the largest number of students). The data contains (1) consumption records for students spending in canteens, convenience stores, bathhouses, etc. provided by the campus logistic department and (2) access control records for students entering or leaving teaching buildings, stadiums, dormitory buildings, etc. provided by the campus security office. In total, we got 129,820 records and profiles of 2,449 students (age, major, etc.), which are available for download[2].
- **Foursquare Dataset** [19]. The dataset contains the user profile (id, gender, etc.) and check-ins shared by users. We filtered out the noise and invalid check-ins, and then selected 9,930 active users (defined as users who have performed at least 10 check-ins) in New York City. In total, we got 22,471 check-in records and profiles of 9,930 users.

We used the above two datasets to construct the student behavior information sequence (student BIS) and the Foursquare behavior information sequence (Foursquare BIS). The period length for each behavior network was set to one week. And the length of behavior information sequence was 6 and 11 respectively for the Campus Card dataset and Foursquare dataset. Due to the challenges in collecting data with the ground truth of locally anomalous behavior change in the above datasets, we need to inject anomalies for our empirical evaluation. We refer to an anomaly injection method [12] to generate a set of locally anomalous behavior changes. Specially, we randomly chose a couple of objects. And if the objects are far apart from common acquaintances few enough in the last element of the student BIS and Foursquare BIS, we swap them. The details of the two BISs are shown in Table 1.

Table 1. Characteristics of the two behavior information sequences

	Student BIS	Foursquare BIS
Objects	2,449	9,930
Behavior	4,958	5,576
Edges	129,820	22,471
Networks	6	11
Outliers	100	300
Time Span	2018/03/01-2018/04/12	2012/10/13-2012/12/29

---

[2] https://github.com/lucyding/LOCATE-Datesets.

5.2 Experimental Setting

We implemented LOCATE in Pytorch and conducted experiments on Linux with 2.30 GHz Intel Xeon Processors, NVIDIA GeForce RTX 2080 Ti, and 256 GB main memory. The metric applied to measure the performance of all methods, is AUC (the area under the ROC curve), which is widely used evaluation metric in the anomaly detection methods [3,20]. It represents the probability that a randomly chosen abnormal node is ranked higher than a normal node.

Baseline Methods. We compared LOCATE with the following two categories of methods, including the anomalous change detection method IcLEOD and the state-of-the-art network-embeddings-based anomaly detection methods Dominant and NetWalk.

- **IcLEOD** [12]. IcLEOD focuses on the changes in neighbors. It detects the objects with anomalous evolutionary behavior only with respect to their local neighborhood based on counting object's changed neighbors. It stores the neighborhood subgraph for each object and then compares the subgraph at different snapshots to qualify how outlying an object is.
- **Dominant** [3]. The state-of-the-art attribute network embedding method for anomaly detection. Dominant proposes an attributed network autoencoder framework inspired by the graph convolutional network (GCN) which considers the high-order node proximity when learning the latent representations.
- **NetWalk** [20]. The state-of-the-art dynamic network embedding method for anomaly detection. NetWalk first obtains node latent representations through random walk incrementally and then detects anomaly using clustering techniques based on the node latent representations.

Parameter Settings. For all experiments on different datasets, the weight decay for regularization was fixed to $5e-7$. The learning rate was fixed to 0.005 and training epochs to 1000 to evaluate the performance. The parameters involved in LOCATE include the latent representation dimension d, number of information propagation layers l, time decay factor λ and balance factor η. The default parameters used for the Campus Card dataset were $d = 64$, $l = 4$, $\lambda = 3$ and $\eta = 0.5$, and parameters for Foursquare dataset were $d = 64$, $l = 3$, $\lambda = 4$ and $\eta = 0.75$. The meta-paths for information propagation used in the experiment included *Student $\rightarrow$ Behavior* and *Behavior $\rightarrow$ Student*. For the baseline algorithms, the settings described in the corresponding paper are retained.

5.3 Performance Comparison

In the experiments, we evaluated the performance of LOCATE by comparing it with the baselines. We presented the experimental results in terms of AUC on two real-world datasets.

For the two datasets, the recent time window was set to the last behavior network of the corresponding BIS. Then we changed the sizes of the reference time window to conduct the experiments. As all the baseline methods are designed for homogeneous network, we considered the objects that participate the same behavior as neighbors to construct corresponding networks. For the IcLEOD, we regard its Outlying Score as anomalous score. For the last two network-embeddings-based anomaly detection baselines NetWalk and Dominant, we used the same anomalous score computation method of LOCATE based on the learned representations. We got the results in terms of AUC based on the anomalous score of all methods.

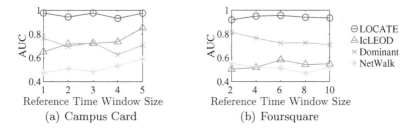

Fig. 4. AUC results on two real-world datasets w.r.t. reference time window size.

The results of the performance comparison are reported in Fig. 4. We can observe that (1) when the size of the reference time window varies, LOCATE always performs better than other baselines by a large margin in locally anomalous behavior change detection; (2) the results of IcLEOD for two data are very different, which may be due to the reason that the simple count-based operations of IcLEOD cannot handle sparse data (the networks in student BIS is nearly 90 times denser than the networks in Foursquare BIS); (3) considering the embedding based methods, LOCATE and Dominant perform better than NetWalk. Note that, both LOCATE and Dominant consider the attribute factors. In general, the results verified the effectiveness of LOCATE for detecting locally anomalous behavior changes.

5.4 Sensitivity Analysis

Then, we investigated the impact of the parameters on LOCATE. Due to space limitations, we only report the results for Campus Card dataset. To ensure the accuracy of the results, we performed 10 experiments and reported the average AUC for each parameter setting.

The performance variance results on the Campus Card dataset are reported in Fig. 5. In Fig. 5(a), we can see that when $d = 64$, we achieved considerably better performance than that with other values. Figure 5(b) shows it is evident that AUC initially improves with l and the best effect is achieved when $l = 4$. It indicates that LOCATE learns meaningful representations by the information propagation between objects and behavior. Figure 5(c) has a rising trend at first and then a falling trend, and the optimal result is obtained when $\lambda = 3$. We can observe that the effect of the model is very poor at $\lambda = 1$, indicating that the idea of decaying the influences of behavior in different periods adopted by LOCATE is reasonable and effective. Figure 5(d) shows the effects of η, we observe that the best result appears at $\eta = 0.5$. This phenomenon tells us that both attribute and structure have rich information to detect locally anomalous behavior changes. However, finding the balance between them according to the characteristics of the dataset can produce more favorable performance.

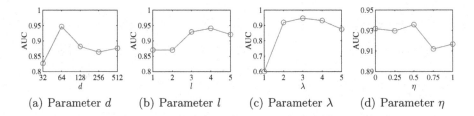

(a) Parameter d (b) Parameter l (c) Parameter λ (d) Parameter η

Fig. 5. AUC results w.r.t. parameters.

5.5   Case Study

We analysed objects with interesting locally anomalous behavior change detected by LOCATE on the two real-world datasets, intuitively demonstrating the effectiveness of LOCATE.

Case study in Campus Card dataset: a student who lost her campus card, index 1782. By querying the campus card usage records, we found that the student's campus card had been lost, because this card has a consumption record in a never-visited dormitory. Specifically, the student who lost the campus card did make changes in her behavior, but this did not affect other similar students performing their usual behavior, which resulted in locally anomalous behavior change. This case indicates that LOCATE can identify an individual whose behavior changes deviate from neighbourhood group and label it as an outlier.

Case study in Foursquare dataset: a business elite who was still working at Christmas, index 171074. We think that the main reason why this user was detected as an outlier is that the usual habit of flying was still maintained at Christmas. In contrast, users who had similar flying habit in the reference time window (index 200642, 132999, etc.) do not have flying behavior anymore near Christmas. We think that another reason is that Christmas has a relatively larger impact on long-distance travel behavior than dining, playing or other behavior. Our algorithm correctly labeled the user as an outlier whose individual behavior does not follow the neighbourhood group's locally changing behavior.

6   Conclusion

In this paper, we studied the problem of locally anomalous behavior change detection. We proposed a structure, named behavior information sequence, constructed from timestamped behavior or usage data, and presented a framework LOCATE. We first learn the latent representation of all nodes in reference and recent time windows by reconstructing the original behavior information sequence. The learned latent representations are then employed to detect locally anomalous behavior changes. Our experiments on real-world datasets verified that our proposed LOCATE is effective.

In the future, we intent to learn the controlling parameter which balances the impacts of structure and node attribute reconstruction by a tuning mechanism.

References

1. Aggarwal, C.C., Zhao, Y., Yu, P.S.: Outlier detection in graph streams. In: ICDE, pp. 399–409 (2011)
2. Akoglu, L., Tong, H., Koutra, D.: Graph based anomaly detection and description: a survey. Data Min. Knowl. Disc. **29**(3), 626–688 (2015). https://doi.org/10.1007/s10618-014-0365-y
3. Ding, K., Li, J., Bhanushali, R., Liu, H.: Deep anomaly detection on attributed networks. In: SDM, pp. 594–602 (2019)
4. Dong, Y., Chawla, N.V., Swami, A.: Metapath2vec: scalable representation learning for heterogeneous networks. In: KDD, pp. 135–144 (2017)
5. Duchi, J.C., Hazan, E., Singer, Y.: Adaptive subgradient methods for online learning and stochastic optimization. J. Mach. Learn. Res. **12**, 2121–2159 (2011)
6. Eswaran, D., Faloutsos, C., Guha, S., Mishra, N.: Spotlight: detecting anomalies in streaming graphs. In: KDD, pp. 1378–1386 (2018)
7. Grover, A., Leskovec, J.: Node2Vec: scalable feature learning for networks. In: KDD, pp. 855–864 (2016)
8. Guo, G., Ouyang, S., He, X., Yuan, F., Liu, X.: Dynamic item block and prediction enhancing block for sequential recommendation. In: IJCAI, pp. 1373–1379 (2019)
9. Gupta, M., Gao, J., Sun, Y., Han, J.: Integrating community matching and outlier detection for mining evolutionary community outliers. In: KDD, pp. 859–867 (2012)
10. Hang, M., Pytlarz, I., Neville, J.: Exploring student check-in behavior for improved point-of-interest prediction. In: KDD, pp. 321–330 (2018)
11. Hariri, N., Mobasher, B., Burke, R.: Adapting to user preference changes in interactive recommendation. In: IJCAI, pp. 4268–4274 (2015)
12. Ji, T., Yang, D., Gao, J.: Incremental local evolutionary outlier detection for dynamic social networks. In: KDD, pp. 1–15 (2013)
13. Manzoor, E., Milajerdi, S.M., Akoglu, L.: Fast memory-efficient anomaly detection in streaming heterogeneous graphs. In: KDD, pp. 1035–1044 (2016)
14. Perozzi, B., Al-Rfou, R., Skiena, S.: DeepWalk: online learning of social representations. In: KDD, pp. 701–710 (2014)
15. Ranjbar, V., Salehi, M., Jandaghi, P., Jalili, M.: QANet: tensor decomposition approach for query-based anomaly detection in heterogeneous information networks. IEEE Trans. Knowl. Data Eng. **31**(11), 2178–2189 (2019)

16. Ranshous, S., Harenberg, S., Sharma, K., Samatova, N.F.: A scalable approach for outlier detection in edge streams using sketch-based approximations. In: SDM, pp. 189–197 (2016)
17. Sricharan, K., Das, K.: Localizing anomalous changes in time-evolving graphs. In: SIGMOD, pp. 13470–1358 (2014)
18. Sun, Y., Han, J., Yan, X., Yu, P.S., Wu, T.: PathSim: meta path-based top-k similarity search in heterogeneous information networks. Proc. VLDB Endow. **4**(11), 992–1003 (2011)
19. Yang, D., Qu, B., Cudré-Mauroux, P.: Privacy-preserving social media data publishing for personalized ranking-based recommendation. IEEE Trans. Knowl. Data Eng. **31**(3), 507–520 (2019)
20. Yu, W., Cheng, W., Aggarwal, C.C., Zhang, K., Chen, H., Wang, W.: NetWalk: a flexible deep embedding approach for anomaly detection in dynamic networks. In: KDD, pp. 2672–2681 (2018)
21. Zhang, Y., et al.: Your style your identity: leveraging writing and photography styles for drug trafficker identification in darknet markets over attributed heterogeneous information network. In: WWW, pp. 3448–3454 (2019)
22. Zheng, L., Li, Z., Li, J., Li, Z., Gao, J.: AddGraph: anomaly detection in dynamic graph using attention-based temporal GCN. In: IJCAI, pp. 4419–4425 (2019)

Hyperthyroidism Progress Prediction with Enhanced LSTM

Haiqin Lu[1], Mei Wang[1], Weiliang Zhao[1(✉)], Tingwei Su[2], and Jian Yang[3]

[1] Donghua University, Shanghai, China
18360019168@163.com, wangmei@dhu.edu.cn, weiliang.zhao@mq.edu.au
[2] Ruijin Hospital, School of Medicine Shanghai Jiao Tong University,
Shanghai, China
stw11102@rjh.com.cn
[3] Macquarie University, Sydney, Australia
jian.yang@mq.edu.au

Abstract. In this work, we propose a method to predict the progress of the hyperthyroidism disease based on the sequence of the patient's blood test data in the early stage. Long-Short-Term-Memory (LSTM) network is employed to process the sequence information in the tests. We design an adaptive loss function for the LSTM learning. We set bigger weights to the blood test data samples which are nearby the range boundaries when judging the hyperthyroidism. We have carried out a set of experiments against a real world dataset from a hospital in Shanghai, China. The experimental results show that our method outperforms the traditional LSTM significantly.

Keywords: Hyperthyroidism · Progress prediction · LSTM · Adaptive loss function

1 Introduction

Health care is always a major public concern around the World. According to the Global Health and Aging report presented by the World Health Organization (WHO), the leading cause of deaths has changed from infections to chronic non-communicable diseases [8]. How to make a timely treatment decision to prevent the fast developments of chronic diseases are becoming increasingly important. Normally there are quite a lot of medical data for individual patients of these chronic diseases. Based on these big data, artificial intelligence techniques have been increasingly applied to the prediction, prevention, diagnosis and prognosis of diseases and have shown the capability to help better decision-making. For example, the study in [7] shows that a developed AI system outperforms expert radiologists in accurately interpreting mammograms from screening programmes.

Thyroid disease is one of the most common diseases all over the world. For the thyroid disease, the ratio of patients with hyperthyroidism (overactive thyroid) is more than 30%–50%. As a kind of endocrine and chronic disease with

X. Wang et al. (Eds.): APWeb-WAIM 2020, LNCS 12318, pp. 209–217, 2020.
https://doi.org/10.1007/978-3-030-60290-1_16

a high incidence, hyperthyroidism often affects the whole body of a patient and leads to a number of complicated health issues as heart problems, eye problems etc. [3]. Some recent work reports the increased risk of cancers for patients with hyperthyroidism [6]. The judgement of the disease stages of the hyperthyroidism is important in the treatment decision and the screening processes of related diseases. It is highly desirable to have a solution to evaluate the current situation of a patient and predict his/her disease development based on the medical examination data and related information. This evaluation and prediction will be used as the foundation for treatments such as the medication strategy, unconventional inspection, or other early active interventions.

Quite a few efforts have been made for predicting the progression of the hyperthyroidism and other thyroid related diseases. Measurement scores were proposed to predict the development of the thyroid disease or the risk of recurrence [1,9,10]. Most of these methods are based on simple statistical analysis. It is often difficult to draw insights from various examination data due to its complex and heterogeneous nature. In recent years, machine learning techniques have advanced rapidly and have been used in the research of medical informatics. In [11], an artificial neural network is proposed to predict the progression of thyroid-associated ophthalmopathy (TAO) at the first clinical examination. In [12], a multivariate regression analysis is employed to predict the risk from subclinical hyperthyroidism to overt hypothyroidism. The literatures [13–15] have demonstrated that the temporal features in the historical data are very important in the prediction for future diseases.

In this paper, We propose a method to predict the progress of hyperthyroidism based on the blood test data of a patient in the early stage. The contributions of this work are summarized as follows:

– We propose an Enhanced LSTM approach to predict the progress of hyperthyroidism based on the sequence of patient's blood test data.
– We design an adaptive loss function with more weights assigned to the patients with more uncertainty when evaluating the progress of hyperthyroidism, whose blood test data are nearby range boundaries.
– We have carried out a set of experiments against a real world dataset from a hospital in Shanghai, China. The experimental results show that our method outperforms the traditional LSTM significantly.

The rest of the paper is organized as follows. Section 2 presents the proposed prediction method. Section 3 provides the experimental results and discussion. Section 4 concludes this paper.

2 The Proposed Method

In this work, we propose an enhanced LSTM model to predict the hyperthyroidism development at the future time point t according to patient's examination data in the first k months. We first present the proposed LSTM based prediction method, and then provide the details of the loss function.

Table 1. The reference ranges for different measurements of hyperthyroidism

	Low	Normal	high
FT3/(pmol/L)	0.5 ~ 2.62	2.63 ~ 5.70	5.71 ~ 46.08
FT4/(pmol/L)	5.15 ~ 9.00	9.01 ~ 19.04	19.05 ~ 77.22
TSH/(ìIU/mL)	0.0 ~ 0.35	0.3529 ~ 4.9355	4.9442 ~ 100.0
TRAb/(U/L)	-	0.1 ~ 1.75	1.76 ~ 395.3

2.1 LSTM Based Prediction

The stage of hyperthyroidism progress is related with four key tests as free triiodothyronine (FT3), free thyroxine (FT4), thyrotropin (TSH), and thyroid receptor antibody (TRAb) [5]. Patients with different genders and ages normally demonstrate different trends in the hyperthyroidism development. The four key tests, gender, and age are the six properties to be considered in this work. The features for each patient are denoted with a two-dimensional vector $X = \{X_0, X_1, \ldots, X_{T-1}\}$, where T is the number of blood test records of the patient in the first k months. Each component X_i represents the patient's ith test result, as a 6-dimensional tuple, $X_i = \{Sex, Age, FT3, FT4, TSH, TRAb\}$. The whole patient's feature data is denoted as $\mathbb{X}$.

We define a one-dimensional vector Y with four components, $Y = \{Y_1, Y_2, Y_3, Y_4\}$, to hold the labels of the 4 test values in the future time t. If the value of the measurement is in the normal reference range, then the label of the corresponding measurement is 1; if the level is abnormally low, the label is set to be 0; otherwise if it is abnormally high, the label is set to be 2. The stage of the hyperthyroidism development is represented with these labels. For example, if the TRAb level is abnormally high ($Y_3 = 2$) but the FT3, FT4 and TSH are normal ($Y_1 = 1; Y_2 = 1; Y_3 = 1$) for a given patient, the stage would be biochemical remission. The true value of the measurement is denoted with an one-dimensional vector O, which contains four components, $O = \{O_1, O_2, O_3, O_4\}$, where each component represents the true value of the corresponding measurement. In the proposed method, the values of the measurements are predicted first, and then the labels are generated by comparing the values with the boundaries of reference ranges. The boundaries of reference ranges for four measurements are illustrated in Table 1.

It is easy to see that X can be regarded as a time series. Since LSTM can capture long-term dependencies and nonlinear dynamics along the timing [4], we exploit the LSTM for the prediction.

The LSTM network is made up of three layers: input layer (*Input_layer*), LSTM hidden layer (*LSTM_layer*), and output layer (*Output_layer*). First, X is transformed from the input feature space into the hidden layer feature space (cell_num dimensions) with the input layer weight parameters and the deviation parameters. The output obtained after the input layer is denoted as I. Then, I enters the LSTM hidden layer to perform LSTM cycle. After LSTM cell calculation, an output h_t and cell state C_t are generated, then h_t and C_t are added to

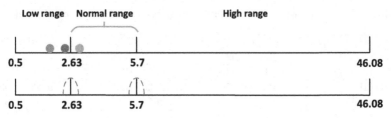

Fig. 1. Labels at different ranges

the calculation of the next time LSTM cells based on the weights and deviations within the LSTM cells. The network continuously updates h_t and C_t during T cycles. The output obtained after the LSTM hidden layer is denoted H, where $H = \{h_0, h_1, ..., h_{T-1}\}$ contains the output at all time points. We put the output of the last moment h_{T-1} into the output layer, and transform it from the hidden layer feature space to the target feature space (4 dimensions) under the control of the output layer weight and the deviation. The final output O' is obtained. The label vector $Y' = [Y1', Y2', Y3', Y4']$ is built up by evaluating which range the O' falls in (all ranges are listed in Table 1).

The parameters (weights and deviations) of the input layer, the LSTM hidden layer, and the output layer are shared for every sample and every loop in the iteration. This parameter sharing mechanism greatly reduces the number of parameters and simplifies the learning process.

2.2   Loss Function

For the parameter learning, the model minimizes the distance between the predicted values and the target values as follows:

$$J(\Theta) = \frac{1}{N} \sum_{i=1}^{N} L(O_i, O_i'). \tag{1}$$

where Θ denotes the model parameter space, N is the number of data samples, L is the loss function, which is mostly often used as the squared error or the absolute value error.

The above equation is rewritten as:

$$J(\Theta) = \sum_{i=1}^{N} \frac{1}{N} L(O_i, O_i') = \sum_{i=1}^{N} w_i L(O_i, O_i') \tag{2}$$

where each w_i is equal to $\frac{1}{N}$, which means that each sample has the same weight for the loss. However, it is reasonable that the samples which are uncertain when judging the hyperthyroidism disease should obtain more importance in the parameter estimation. Figure 1 shows that, for a target value O_i, there exists the estimated value O_i' with a small distance between O_i and O_i' but they are in different ranges; there exists the estimated value O_i'' with a quite big distance between O_i and O_i' but they are in the same range. Obviously in this situation $L(O_i, O_i')$ is smaller than $L(O_i, O_i'')$, the model will learn the parameter that converges to the O_i'. Clearly, it will give the wrong estimation of the normal, abnormal label. The samples near the range boundary should obtain more weights in parameter estimation to improve the discriminative power of the model.

Inspired by this idea, we design an adaptive piece wise error loss function. At first, for each measurement of {FT3, FT4, TSH, TRAb}, we define the boundary neighborhood as follows:

$$NN = \{x \mid |x - lb| \leq \delta_l \cup |x - rb| \leq \delta_r\} \tag{3}$$

where x is the value of the measurement. lb and rb are the left boundary and right boundary of the reference range for the given test. δ_l and δ_r are the left radius and right radius of the neighborhoods. For example, for test FT3, lb and rb are to be 2.63 and 5.7 respectively according to Table 1.

Then the adaptive loss is defined as:

$$J'(\Theta) = \sum_{i=1}^{N} w_i L(O_i, O_i') \tag{4}$$

$$w_i = \frac{\alpha_i}{\sum_{i=1}^{N} \alpha_i} \tag{5}$$

$$where\ \alpha_i = \begin{cases} A, & if\ O_i \in NN\ \ or\ \ O_i' \in NN \\ 1. & else \end{cases} \tag{6}$$

where A is the weight larger than 1. In the proposed loss function, the sample that falls within the boundary neighborhood will be assigned a larger weight, which is more effective for the model to focus on learning in the uncertain area.

3   Experiments

3.1   Experimental Setup

Dataset. We run experiments against a large real-world clinic hyperthyroidism dataset. The patients who satisfy the following two conditions are selected to the dataset. The first condition is that the first three diagnoses are about the hyperthyroidism and at least one of the of TRAb levels in the first three test results is abnormally high. This condition is used to filter out the pseudo-hyperthyroidism. The second condition is that the time periods of records are more than 2 years because our method is designed for a future prediction. There are 2,460 patients in the final dataset.

In the dataset, patients have different numbers of measurement records. According to the statistics of the records, we found that almost half of the patients have about 7 records in the first six months. So we fix the number of the examination results at the 6 month to be 7. For the patients whose records were less than 7 times, we filled missing ones with the test results closest in time.

After preprocessing the dataset, we divided the whole dataset into a training set and a test set. The training set consists of 1960 patients and the remaining 500 patients are in the test set.

Table 2. The overall performance of the proposed method and the traditional LSTM-based prediction

The Performance of The Proposed method		Precision	Recall	F_1	Support	Accuracy
FT3	low	0.53 ± 0.02	0.79 ± 0.04	0.63 ± 0.00	8	$94.12\% \pm 0.40\%$
	normal	0.97 ± 0.00	0.96 ± 0.00	0.96 ± 0.00	412	
	high	0.84 ± 0.01	0.86 ± 0.01	0.86 ± 0.00	73	
FT4	low	0.88 ± 0.01	0.77 ± 0.03	0.82 ± 0.02	20	$96.23\% \pm 0.34\%$
	normal	0.97 ± 0.01	0.96 ± 0.00	0.96 ± 0.01	434	
	high	0.90 ± 0.01	0.80 ± 0.02	0.84 ± 0.01	41	
TSH	low	0.94 ± 0.01	0.82 ± 0.02	0.88 ± 0.01	147	$91.56\% \pm 0.61\%$
	normal	0.92 ± 0.01	0.95 ± 0.01	0.94 ± 0.01	308	
	high	0.78 ± 0.02	0.98 ± 0.04	0.87 ± 0.03	31	
TRAb	normal	0.93 ± 0.01	0.89 ± 0.01	0.91 ± 01	226	$90.50\% \pm 0.71\%$
	high	0.88 ± 0.01	0.92 ± 0.01	0.90 ± 0.01	195	
The Performance of The Traditional LSTM Prediction		Precision	Recall	F_1	Support	Accuracy
FT3	low	0.43 ± 0.06	0.4 ± 0.1	0.41 ± 0.1	8	$92.30\% \pm 0.5\%$
	normal	0.94 ± 0.01	0.98 ± 0.01	0.96 ± 0.01	412	
	high	0.87 ± 0.03	0.66 ± 0.04	0.75 ± 0.03	73	
FT4	low	0.71 ± 0.05	0.44 ± 0.12	0.54 ± 0.10	20	$95.38\% \pm 0.61\%$
	normal	0.96 ± 0.01	0.99 ± 0.01	0.98 ± 0.01	434	
	high	1.00 ± 0.00	0.79 ± 0.05	0.89 ± 0.03	41	
TSH	low	0.93 ± 0.02	0.27 ± 0.07	0.42 ± 0.08	147	$74.94\% \pm 1.56\%$
	normal	0.72 ± 0.01	0.99 ± 0.00	0.83 ± 0.01	308	
	high	0.98 ± 0.03	0.56 ± 0.08	0.71 ± 0.06	31	
TRAb	normal	0.83 ± 0.06	0.95 ± 0.03	0.88 ± 0.03	226	$88.29\% \pm 3.25\%$
	high	0.95 ± 0.03	0.82 ± 0.09	0.88 ± 0.04	195	

Parameter Setting. In the LSTM network training, we use the Truncated Normal Distribution to initialize the weights of the input and the output layers.

The hidden layer is expanded to 2 layers, each layer contains 128 LSTM cell units. The learning rate is set to be $1e-3$ and the number of iterations is set to be 1000. We employ the dropout method to reduce over-fitting and apply the Adam-Optimizer in training. The training set is further divided into 10 batches for the mini-batch training. Each experiment runs for 10 times and each data given in the experimental results is the average of the 10 runs. The proposed method take the 0-Score normalization in a sample-by-sample way. Specifically, given the feature matrix X of a patient, we calculate the statistical data *mean* and *variance* based on each measurement dimension of the patient, then we normalize X. The loss function is the adaptive loss based on the absolute error.

The adjustable parameters in the loss function include: (1) A, the weight of the samples in neighborhood contributed to the loss. (2) δ_l and δ_r, the radius of the neighborhood for the left boundary and the right boundary. These parameters are determined according to their performances on the validation set. In the experiments, A is set to be 2. Note that the size of the neighborhood are set according to the range of different tests. The values are set as follows: FT3: $|x - 2.63| \le 3$ & $|x - 5.70| \le 3$; FT4: $|x - 9.01| \le 1$ & $|x - 19.04| \le 1$; TSH: $|x - 0.3529| \le 3$ & $|x - 4.9355| \le 3$; TRAb: $|x - 1.75| \le 5$.

Evaluation Metrics. As described in Sect. 2.1, after predicting, the label vector $Y' = [Y1', Y2', Y3', Y4']$ is generated for four hyperthyroidism measurements. Each Yi' is treated as a classification label. Therefore, we use Recall, Precision, F_1 and Accuracy to measure the effectiveness of the proposed method. For a given measurement in [FT3, FT4, TSH, TRAb], assume it has p different labels. Given one label l, let TP models the positive samples in the test set and the predictions are correct. TN represents the negative samples and the predictions are correct. FN represents the positive samples and the predictions are negative. FP represents the negative samples and the predictions are positive. The Recall, Precision, F_1 and Accuracy are defined as follows [2]:

$$Recall = \frac{|TP|}{|TP|+|FP|}, \quad Precision = \frac{|TP|}{|TP|+|FN|}, \quad F_1 = \frac{2*Recall*Precision}{Recall+Precision},$$
$$Accuracy = \frac{|TP|+|TN|}{|TP|+|FP|+|FN|+|TN|}.$$

3.2 Experimental Results

We compare our prediction method with the traditional LSTM-based method. The performance for each range of all the four measurements are provided in Table 2. The number of samples in each range are provided in the table as column "support". Table 2 shows that the average accuracy of the proposed method has achieved 93.1%, which is improved by 5% compared to the traditional LSTM method. Especially, for measurements TSH, the accuracy has been improved from 75% to 91.5%. The precision, recall, and F_1 of each measure are all better than that of the traditional method. Compared with $FT3$ and $FT4$, the normal ranges of TSH and TRAb are smaller than the abnormal range as shown in Table 1. The prediction results are more likely to be disturbed by the samples with a large uncertainty.

In the proposed method, we assign bigger weights to the samples nearby range boundaries to deal with the uncertainty problem effectively. The accuracy of TSH and TRAb has been improved significantly. Since the parameters are randomly initialized in the LSTM training process, we provide the average range ($\pm$) of the results over the 10 runs. It is clear that the variation is not changed so much for our method, which means our method can provide a stable prediction.

4 Conclusions

This work proposes a hyperthyroidism progress prediction method with Enhanced LSTM. An adaptive loss function has been designed for the LSTM learning. Experimental results show that our method is effective and outperforms the traditional LSTM method. Since there are multiple measurements to be predicted, different parameter settings may have different impacts on these measurements. How to find the optimal setting for each measurement will be considered in the future work. We will also consider more features to the proposed method for the hyperthyroidism progress prediction.

This work was supported by the National Key RD Program of China under Grant 2019YFE0190500.

References

1. Strieder, T.G.A., et al.: Prediction of progression to overt hypothyroidism or hyperthyroidism in female relatives of patients with autoimmune thyroid disease using the thyroid events amsterdam (THEA) score. Arch. Intern. Med. **168**(15), 1657 (2008)
2. Wu, C.C., Yeh, W.C., et al.: Prediction of fatty liver disease using machine learning algorithms. Comput. Methods Programs Biomed. **170**, 23–29 (2018)
3. Wang, Y., Zhao, F., et al.: Role of selenium intake for risk and development of hyperthyroidism. J. Clin. Endocrinol. Metab. **104**, 568–580 (2019)
4. Sarraf, S.: French word recognition through a quick survey on recurrent neural networks using long-short term memory RNN-LSTM. Am. Sci. Res. J. Eng. Technol. Sci. **39**(1), 250–267 (2018)
5. Iyidir, O.T., et al.: Evaluation of ambulatory arterial stiffness index in hyperthyroidism. Turk. J. Med. Sci. **47**, 1751–1756 (2017)
6. Chen, Y.K., Lin, C.L., et al.: Cancer risk in patients with Graves' disease: a nationwide cohort study. Thyroid **23**(7), 879–884 (2013)
7. Mckinney, S.M., et al.: International evaluation of an AI system for breast cancer screening. Nature **577**, 89–94 (2020)
8. World Health Organization, Global Health and Aging. https://www.who.int/ageing/publications/global_health.pdf
9. Vos, X.G., Endert, E., et al.: Predicting the risk of recurrence before the start of antithyroid drug therapy in patients with Graves' hyperthyroidism. J. Clin. Endocrinol. Metab. **101**, 1381–1389 (2016)
10. Wiersinga, W., et al.: Predictive score for the development or progression of Graves' orbitopathy in patients with newly diagnosed Graves' hyperthyroidism. Eur. J. Endocrinol. **178**, 635–643 (2018)

11. Salvi, M., et al.: Prediction of the progression of thyroid-associated ophthalmopathy at first ophthalmologic examination: use of a neural network. Thyroid **12**(3), 233–6 (2002)
12. Stephanie, L.L., et al.: What is the typical disease progression of hyperthyroidism? Medscape Monday, 24 February 2020
13. Choi, E., Bahadori, M.T., et al.: GRAM: graph-based attention model for healthcare representation learning. In: Proceedings of the 23rd ACM SIGKDD 2017, pp. 787–795 (2017)
14. Ma, F.L., You, Q.Z., et al.: KAME: knowledge-based attention model for diagnosis prediction in healthcare. In: CIKM 2018, pp. 743–752 (2018)
15. Ma, F.L., Chitta, R., et al.: Dipole: diagnosis prediction in healthcare via attention-based bidirectional recurrent neural networks. In: Proceedings of the 23rd ACM SIGKDD 2017, pp. 1903–1911 (2017)

Text Analysis and Mining

DeepStyle: User Style Embedding for Authorship Attribution of Short Texts

Zhiqiang Hu[1], Roy Ka-Wei Lee[2(✉)], Lei Wang[3], Ee-peng Lim[3], and Bo Dai[1]

[1] University of Electronic Science and Technology of China, Chengdu, China
zhiqianghu@std.uestc.edu.cn, daibo@uestc.edu.cn
[2] University of Saskatchewan, Saskatoon, Canada
roylee@cs.usask.ca
[3] Singapore Management University, Singapore, Singapore
lei.wang.2019@phdcs.smu.edu.sg, eplim@smu.edu.sg

Abstract. Authorship attribution (AA), which is the task of finding the owner of a given text, is an important and widely studied research topic with many applications. Recent works have shown that deep learning methods could achieve significant accuracy improvement for the AA task. Nevertheless, most of these proposed methods represent user posts using a single type of features (e.g., word bi-grams) and adopt a text classification approach to address the task. Furthermore, these methods offer very limited explainability of the AA results. In this paper, we address these limitations by proposing DeepStyle, a novel embedding-based framework that learns the representations of users' salient writing styles. We conduct extensive experiments on two real-world datasets from Twitter and Weibo. Our experiment results show that DeepStyle outperforms the state-of-the-art baselines on the AA task.

Keywords: Authorship attribution · Style embedding · Triplet loss

1 Introduction

Motivation. Authorship attribution (AA), the task of finding the owner of a given text, plays a vital role in many applications. Particularly in the context of social media, AA is crucial in tackling the growing problem of online falsehood, vicious sock-puppets, and evidence gathering in forensic investigations. Although the AA task has been widely studied and many features have been explored [6,7,12–14,17], the traditional document-based methods did not perform well on the social media posts as they tend to be shorter and less former [6,15].

To overcome the short-text challenge, several previous AA works have aggregated multiple social media posts of the same user into a single long document before training a classifier to predict the author labels using the long document

Electronic supplementary material The online version of this chapter (https://doi.org/10.1007/978-3-030-60290-1_17) contains supplementary material, which is available to authorized users.

X. Wang et al. (Eds.): APWeb-WAIM 2020, LNCS 12318, pp. 221–229, 2020.
https://doi.org/10.1007/978-3-030-60290-1_17

features, [4,7]. Such an approach is, however, not effective in handling AA for individual query or a single social media post, which is necessary for some applications, e.g., detecting if two social media posts sharing a rumor originate from the same person. In a recent study, [15] used n-grams of individual Twitter posts to train a Convolutional Neural Network (CNN) model for AA. While CNN and other deep learning models can achieve improved accuracy for the AA task, they still have several limitations. Firstly, the existing models only utilized single input feature types (e.g., bi-gram) to represent the post. Such approaches neglect the rich types of features which had been explored in previous studies to overcome data sparsity in representing the user's writing styles from short text [13]. Secondly, the deep learning approach usually offers limited explainability on how some factors contribute to good (or bad) AA results as the models themselves are black boxes.

Research Objectives. In this paper, we address the limitations in existing methods and propose DeepStyle[1], an embedding-based framework specifically designed to learn the user style representations using deep learning. The key idea behind DeepStyle is to extract salient features from the users' social media posts. At the high level, our proposed DeepStyle is divided into two parts. The first part learns a multi-view representation of a user's posts using deep neural networks over different types of features. Unlike existing deep learning AA methods which use Cross-Entropy loss as objective function, we adopt Triplet loss [3] to learn the post embeddings such that posts that belong to the same user should be close to one another in the post embedding space, while posts from different users will be pushed further away from one another. The second part involves the use of an aggregation function to combine the post embeddings of a single user into the user's style embedding. The underlying intuition is that the style embeddings of different users should be far apart from one another in the embedding space, thereby distinguishing the users' writing styles. Finally, the learned user style embeddings are used to perform the AA task.

There are benefits to learning user style embeddings. Firstly, the user style embedding allows us to perform AA in both unsupervised (i.e., finding the most similar user in the embedding space for a given query post) and supervised (i.e., as input to a classifier) settings. Secondly, the visualization of user style embedding enables us to gain an understanding of the feature differences and relationships between user writing styles. Lastly, beyond AA, the user style embedding can also be used for other forensic investigations such as clone [18] or sock-puppet account detection [2] by finding the nearest neighbors in the embedding space, i.e., user accounts who share most similar writing style.

Contributions. Our main contributions in this work consist of the following.

- We propose a novel embedding-based framework called DeepStyle, which utilizes multi-view representations of a user's post and Triplet loss objective functions to learn users' writing style for AA.

---

[1] Code implementation: https://gitlab.com/bottle_shop/style/deepstyle.

- Using DeepStyle, we manage to learn the latent representation of users' writing style. To the best of our knowledge, this is the first work that embeds user's writing style for AA.
- We conduct extensive experiments on two real-world datasets from Twitter and Weibo. The experiment results show that DeepStyle consistently outperforms state-of-the-art methods regardless of the text's languages.

2   Related Works

Authorship attribution (AA) is a widely studied research topic. Traditionally, feature engineering approaches were used to derive textual-related features from long documents such as emails and news articles. Subsequently, these derived features are used to train a classifier to identify an input document's owner [5,16]. Commonly used features in AA includes character n-grams [6,7,12,14], lexical features, syntactical features, and document topics [13,17]. There are also recent studies that explore various deep learning approaches for AA.

In recent years, the AA task has been studied in the social media context. A comprehensive survey [9] provides an overview of AA methods for social media content. The short social media content poses some challenges to the traditional AA methods, [6,15]. To overcome the short text challenge, the existing methods aggregate multiple social media posts of a user into a single document and before applying the AA methods, [4,7]. Such an approach cannot adequately handle queries at the single social media post level. Shrestha et al. [15] attempted to overcome this challenge by performing AA using a CNN model with character n-gram features. The n-gram CNN model considers each short text post of a user as input to train a CNN model for AA. In similar studies, Ruder et al. [10] investigated the use of CNN with various types of word and character level features for AA, while Boenningoff et al. [1] proposed a hybrid CNN-LSTM on word level features to perform AA. Although these works achieved reasonably good accuracy for AA in social media, they had utilized single input feature types to represent the users' posts used in training the deep neural network classifier and offer limited explainability. In this work, we address the limitations of the state-of-the-art by proposing DeepStyle, an embedding-based framework that learns the user style embedding representations using multiple types of features derived from posts to perform AA.

3   Proposed Model

3.1   Authorship Attribution Problem

Let U be a set of users in a social media platform, $U = \{u_1, u_2, ..., u_N\}$, where N is the total number of users in the platform. Each user u has a set of posts, $P_u = \{p_{u,1}, p_{u,1}, ..., p_{u,M_u}\}$, where M_u is the number of posts belong to user u. Given U, P_u, and a query post q, we aim to predict the most likely author of q.

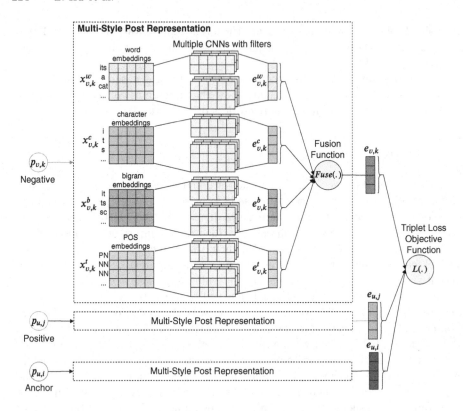

Fig. 1. Post embedding module of the DeepStyle framework

Traditionally, a classifier will be trained using the known posts of all users to predict the most plausible author of q. In this paper, we adopt a different approach by first learning post embeddings of a user u with M_u posts. The symbol $e_{u,i}$ denotes the post representation of post $p_{u,i}$. The learned post embeddings $E_u = \{e_{u,1}, \cdots, e_{u,M_u}\}$ will then be aggregated to form the user style embedding s_u. Finally, we compute for each user u the cosine similarity between the query post embedding e^q and s_u, denoted by $cos(e^q, s_u)$. Our model predicts the top similar user to be most plausible author of query post q. In the following, we elaborate both the *post embedding* and *user style aggregation* modules.

3.2 Post Embedding Module

Figure 1 illustrates the overall architecture of the post embedding module in our DeepStyle framework. The module learns the post embedding representations using triplet loss. Each triplet is formed by first randomly sampling an anchor post $p_{u,i}$ and a positive post $p_{u,j}$ that belongs to the same user u. We also randomly sample a negative post $p_{v,k}$, which is a post belonging to another user v. With a set of triplets of posts, we learn the post embeddings using *Multi-Style Post Representation*. In this *Multi-Style Post Representation* scheme, we first perform data pre-possessing to extract different types of feature embeddings (e.g., word, character, bigram, POS tags) for each post among the triplets. These feature embeddings will be used as input for a set of Convolution Neural Networks (CNNs) to process and output latent representations of the individual features. Subsequently, a fusion function is used to combine the latent representations and output a post embedding. Finally the three post embeddings, $e_{u,i}$, $e_{u,j}$, and $e_{v,k}$, will be optimized using the triplet loss objective function.

Feature Embeddings Extraction. Previous studies have extensively explored the different types of features, such as words, characters, n-grams, syntactic, and semantic information for AA, [4,13,16]. We leverage on the insights from previous studies to extract the following types of feature embeddings to represent a post $p_{u,i}$, $p_{u,j}$ or $p_{v,k}$. For simplicity, we use $p_{v,k}$ as an example.

For the four types of input embeddings $\{x_{v,k}^w, x_{v,k}^c, x_{v,k}^b, x_{v,k}^t\}$, we obtain four types of output latent representations through multi-level CNN layer , i.e., word latent representation $e_{v,k}^w$, character latent representation $e_{v,k}^c$, bi-gram latent representation $e_{v,k}^b$, and POS tag latent representation $e_{v,k}^t$.

Post Features Fusion Function. After learning the latent representations of the various types of feature embeddings, we use a fusion function to combine the various latent representations of a post:

$$e_{v,k} = Fuse(e_{v,k}^w, e_{v,k}^c, e_{v,k}^b, e_{v,k}^t) \tag{1}$$

where $Fuse(\cdot)$ is a typical fusion kernel, and $e_{v,k}$ has the same dimension as the input latent representations. In our proposed framework, we explore five different implementations the of $Fuse(\cdot)$: *Mean, Max, Multilayer perceptron (MLP), Attention* [19], and *Capsule* [11].

3.3   User Style Aggregation Module

A user publishes multiple posts on social media platforms. Each post contains some information that defines the user's writing style, which ultimately would help in authorship attribution. There are multiple ways to combine the post embeddings of a user v to form the final user style embedding representation, S_v. In this paper, we introduce three types of aggregators for learning the post embedding of a user: *Mean, Max*, and *Capsule* [11].

Using the above three aggregators, we aggregated the users' post embeddings to form the user style embeddings, $S = \{s_1, s_2, ..., s_N\}$. The user style embeddings will be used to perform AA. We will further evaluate the three aggregation methods in our experiments.

4   Experimental Evaluation

4.1   Experiment Setup

Datasets. We conducted our experiments on two publicly available datasets, namely Weibo[2] and Twitter [14]. The Twitter dataset is widely used in AA

---

[2] https://hub.hku.hk/cris/dataset/dataset107483.

Table 1. P@k of various baselines and DeepStyle on Twitter and Weibo datasets. We vary $k = [1, 10, 50, 100]$. The improvement of DeepStyle over the best baselines (i.e., CNN-1) is significant at 0.01 level using paired t-test.

Method	Twitter				Weibo			
	P@1	P@10	P@50	P@100	P@1	P@10	P@50	P@100
ToS [13]	9.8	20.4	32.2	43.0	12.1	25.9	38.6	48.3
CNN-1 [10, 15]	18.7	30.7	43.1	49.9	22.0	35.2	48.4	55.9
CNN-2 [15]	20.1	33.7	47.6	55.3	17.5	29.7	41.3	17.5
CNN-W [10, 15]	16.4	27.1	37.6	44.0	21.0	36.5	48.6	54.8
LSTM-1	15.3	25.6	35.9	42.0	19.0	33.6	48.1	55.5
LSTM-2 [15]	15.5	28.0	40.9	48.6	15.8	31.5	43.5	49.8
LSTM-W	11.7	23.7	41.2	48.1	18.7	34.1	48.0	55.2
DeepStyle	**21.4**	**37.1**	**51.5**	**59.2**	**23.9**	**38.1**	**51.6**	**58.9**

research [14, 15], while the Weibo dataset, which consists of short Chinese texts, demonstrates the language-agnostic nature of our model. The Twitter dataset contains tweets from 7,026 users, while the Weibo dataset contains posts from 9,819 users. In both datasets, each user has about 1000 posts.

Baselines. For evaluation, we compare our proposed DeepStyle model with the following state-of-the-art baselines:

– **ToS**: Based on [13]'s work, ToS method derives content and style-based features from the users' posts to train a Logistic Regression classifier.
– **CNN**: Following the studies in [10, 15], we train a CNN model each on character features (called CNN-1), bigram features (called CNN-2), and word features (called CNN-W).
– **LSTM**: Long-Short Term Memory (LSTM) model has also been implemented as a baseline in previous study [15] and the model has been successfully used for text classification [8]. We train an LSTM at the character level (LSTM-1), bigram level (LSTM-2), and word (LSTM-W) level.

All the parameters of baselines are empirically set to yield optimal results.

4.2   Experiment Results

Table 1 shows the experiment results on Twitter and Weibo datasets. In this experiment, we use 100 posts from each user for training and test on 20 posts from each user. All users on Twitter and Weibo are used in this experiment. Note that the DeepStyle model in this experiment is configured with *Capsule* as the feature fusion function to combine the various latent representations of a post and we select *Mean* as the aggregator to combine the users' post embeddings into final user style embeddings. The same DeepStyle setting is used for the results reported in Tables 2 and 3. From the results, we observe that DeepStyle

Table 2. P@1 for DeepStyle and baselines on varying number of users in Twitter and Weibo.

Method	#Twitter Users					#Weibo Users				
	50	100	500	5000	All	50	100	500	5000	All
ToS [13]	48.3	31.2	22.0	15.7	9.8	50.5	39.5	22.2	16.0	12.1
CNN-1 [10,15]	60.9	47.1	35.6	23.1	18.7	61.3	52.6	38.8	25.1	22.0
CNN-2 [15]	59.3	46.7	36.5	24.6	20.1	47.6	42.4	30.4	18.7	17.5
CNN-W [10,15]	50.0	37.1	28.4	17.7	16.4	56.8	48.3	36.2	23.8	21.0
LSTM-1	40.3	29.6	27.3	16.1	15.3	37.5	32.5	30.9	20.1	19.0
LSTM-2 [15]	45.1	34.5	25.2	16.5	15.5	28.1	26.4	19.6	16.8	15.8
LSTM-W	35.0	22.8	19.3	12.0	11.7	35.0	33.4	28.8	19.8	18.7
DeepStyle	**64.8**	**51.2**	**37.9**	**25.5**	**21.4**	**65.2**	**56.6**	**42.8**	**27.9**	**23.9**

Table 3. P@1 for DeepStyle and baselines on varying number of posts for 50 Twitter and Weibo users.

Method	Twitter#posts				Weibo#posts			
	500	200	100	50	500	200	100	50
ToS [13]	47.4	45.1	40.5	36.2	49.2	44.9	40.8	34.7
CNN-1 [10,15]	59.6	56.0	51.7	49.3	60.5	56.7	52.2	49.1
CNN-2 [15]	61.7	54.1	48.4	44.4	59.4	56.3	51.8	47.5
CNN-W [10,15]	52.1	48.0	43.3	40.2	58.0	53.1	47.9	44.2
LSTM-1	55.7	49.5	39.8	32.9	54.7	48.7	37.6	32.0
LSTM-2 [15]	53.2	39.4	34.2	30.4	51.0	42.4	35.5	31.4
LSTM-W	47.6	41.5	35.2	30.5	52.8	41.9	36.1	31.2
DeepStyle	**62.8**	**58.7**	**56.3**	**50.9**	**62.5**	**58.2**	**56.1**	**51.1**

outperforms the state-of-the-art baselines for different k values using the $P@k$ measure. The improvements of DeepStyle over the best baselines (i.e., CNN-1 and CNN-2) are significant at 0.01 level using paired t-test. Similar to the previous study [15], we observe that the CNN models out perform the LSTM models in both datasets. More interestingly, CNN-2 performs better than CNN-1 for the Twitter dataset, while CNN-1 outperforms CNN-2 for the Weibo dataset. This observation could be attributed to the difference in languages; Chinese characters may encode more semantics or definitive user styles. Hence, the Chinese character unigrams can yield better results. DeepStyle, which utilizes multi-style post representations, outperforms all state-of-the-art baselines in both English (i.e., Twitter) and Chinese (i.e., Weibo) datasets.

Varying Number of Users and Posts. Similar to previous studies [14,15], we also want to explore how DeepStyle performs when the AA problem becomes more difficult, i.e., when the number of users increases or when the number of tweets per author is reduced. Table 2 shows the $P@1$ of DeepStyle and various baselines varying the number of users in Twitter and Weibo from 50 to all users. For this experiment, we use 100 posts from each user for training and test on 20 posts from each user. We note that although the precision decreases with the increasing number of users, DeepStyle is able to outperform state-of-the-art baselines consistently. Even in the worse case of all users, i.e., over 7,000 and 9,000 Twitter and Weibo users respectively, DeepStyle is still able to outperform the best baselines and the improvements over the best baselines are significant at 0.01 level using paired t-test.

Besides varying the number of users, we also conducted experiments to evaluate the models' performance with different amounts of training data. Table 3 shows the results of the models trained with a different number of posts per user for 50 randomly selected Twitter and Weibo users. We observe the $P@1$ of various models drops as we reduce the number of posts. However, DeepStyle still consistently outperforms the baselines even with reduced training data.

5 Conclusion

In this paper, we proposed a novel embedding-based framework call DeepStyle, which utilized multiple feature types to learns the embedding representation of the user's writing style for authorship attribution (AA). We evaluated Deep-Style using publicly available real-world datasets, and our extensive experiments have shown that DeepStyle is language-agnostic and outperforms the baselines in different experimental settings. For future works, we will like to consider the evolution of the user's writing style by modeling the time-series aspect of the user's posts and consider other better forms of visualizations to explain the user's writing style.

References

1. Boenninghoff, B., Hessler, S., Kolossa, D., Nickel, R.: Explainable authorship verification in social media via attention-based similarity learning. In: 2019 IEEE International Conference on Big Data (Big Data). IEEE (2019)
2. Bu, Z., Xia, Z., Wang, J.: A sock puppet detection algorithm on virtual spaces. Knowl.-Based Syst. **37**, 366–377 (2013)
3. Cheng, D., Gong, Y., Zhou, S., Wang, J., Zheng, N.: Person re-identification by multi-channel parts-based CNN with improved triplet loss function. In: IEEE CVPR (2016)
4. Ding, S.H., Fung, B.C., Iqbal, F., Cheung, W.K.: Learning stylometric representations for authorship analysis. IEEE Trans. Cybern. **49**(1), 107–121 (2017)
5. Koppel, M., Schler, J., Argamon, S.: Computational methods in authorship attribution. J. Am. Soc. Inform. Sci. Technol. **60**(1), 9–26 (2009)
6. Koppel, M., Winter, Y.: Determining if two documents are written by the same author. J. Assoc. Inform. Sci. Technol. **65**(1), 178–187 (2014)
7. Layton, R., Watters, P., Dazeley, R.: Authorship attribution for twitter in 140 characters or less. In: IEEE Cybercrime and Trustworthy Computing Workshop (2010)

8. Liu, P., Qiu, X., Huang, X.: Recurrent neural network for text classification with multi-task learning. In: IJCAI (2016)
9. Rocha, A., et al.: Authorship attribution for social media forensics. IEEE Trans. Inf. Forensics Secur. **12**(1), 5–33 (2016)
10. Ruder, S., Ghaffari, P., Breslin, J.G.: Character-level and multi-channel convolutional neural networks for large-scale authorship attribution. Insight Centre for Data Analytics. National University of Ireland Galway, Technical Report (2016)
11. Sabour, S., Frosst, N., Hinton, G.E.: Dynamic routing between capsules. In: NIPS (2017)
12. Sapkota, U., Bethard, S., Montes, M., Solorio, T.: Not all character N-grams are created equal: a study in authorship attribution. In: NAACL (2015)
13. Sari, Y., Stevenson, M., Vlachos, A.: Topic or style? Exploring the most useful features for authorship attribution. In: COLING (2018)
14. Schwartz, R., Tsur, O., Rappoport, A., Koppel, M.: Authorship attribution of micro-messages. In: EMNLP (2013)
15. Shrestha, P., Sierra, S., Gonzalez, F., Montes, M., Rosso, P., Solorio, T.: Convolutional neural networks for authorship attribution of short texts. In: EACL (2017)
16. Stamatatos, E.: A survey of modern authorship attribution methods. J. Am. Soc. Inform. Sci. Technol. **60**(3), 538–556 (2009)
17. Sundararajan, K., Woodard, D.: What represents "style" in authorship attribution? In: COLING (2018)
18. Xiao, C., Freeman, D.M., Hwa, T.: Detecting clusters of fake accounts in online social networks. In: ACM Workshop on Artificial Intelligence and Security (2015)
19. Yang, Z., Yang, D., Dyer, C., He, X., Smola, A.J., Hovy, E.H.: Hierarchical attention networks for document classification. In: NAACL: HLT (2016)

Densely-Connected Transformer with Co-attentive Information for Matching Text Sequences

Minxu Zhang[1(✉)], Yingxia Shao[3], Kai Lei[1], Yuesheng Zhu[1], and Bin Cui[2]

[1] School of Electronic and Computer Engineering, Peking University and Peking University Shenzhen Graduate School, Shenzhen, China
zmxdream@pku.edu.cn, {leik,zhuys}@pkusz.edu.cn
[2] Department of Computer Science and National Engineering Laboratory for Big Data Analysis and Applications, Peking University, Beijing, China
bin.cui@pku.edu.cn
[3] Beijing Key Lab of Intelligent Telecommunications Software and Multimedia, BUPT, Beijing, China
shaoyx@bupt.edu.cn

Abstract. Sentence matching, which aims to capture the semantic relationship between two sequences, is a crucial problem in NLP research. It plays a vital role in various natural language tasks such as question answering, natural language inference and paraphrase identification. The state-of-the-art works utilize the interactive information of sentence pairs through adopting the general Compare-Aggregate framework and achieve promising results. In this study, we propose Densely connected Transformer to perform multiple matching processes with co-attentive information to enhance the interaction of sentence pairs in each matching process. Specifically, our model consists of multiple stacked matching blocks. Inside each block, we first employ a transformer encoder to obtain refined representations for two sequences, then we leverage multi-way co-attention mechanism or multi-head co-attention mechanism to perform word-level comparison between the two sequences, the original representations and aligned representations are fused to form the alignment information of this matching layer. We evaluate our proposed model on five well-studied sentence matching datasets and achieve highly competitive performance.

Keywords: Sentence matching · Transformer · Co-attention

1 Introduction

Sentence matching is a long standing core research problem in natural language processing. In this task, a model takes two sequences as input and identify the relationship between them. A wide range of natural language applications, including natural language inference [2,13], paraphrase identification [34] and

X. Wang et al. (Eds.): APWeb-WAIM 2020, LNCS 12318, pp. 230–244, 2020.
https://doi.org/10.1007/978-3-030-60290-1_18

answer selection [36] would benefit from the technical innovations in this task. Despite that sentence matching has been A question-answer example from Wik-iQA dataset [36] is illustrated in Table 1. The question is what countries are in Central America, a negative answer gives the borders of Central America. Although sentence matching has been extensively studied in many literature [17,18], this task still remains a challenge since it requires to effectively capture the complex relationship between two text sequences.

Table 1. An example question and candidate answers

Question	What countries are in Central America?
Positive answer	Central America consists of seven countries: Belize, Costa Rica, El Salvador, Guatemala, Honduras, Nicaragua, and Panama
Negative answer	It is bordered by Mexico to the north, the Caribbean Sea to the east, the North Pacific Ocean to the west, and Colombia to the south-east

Inspired by the success of deep learning models in various natural language processing tasks [4,9–11,14,29], much efforts have been devoted to designing deep learning architectures for solving the sentence matching task. In previous works, three types of general deep learning frameworks are proposed for matching sentence pairs: Siamese network [8], attention-based model [37] and Compare-Aggregate framework [1,21,33]. Siamese network builds the representations for question and answer separately and then matches them. This type of structure cannot achieve state-of-the-art performance because of the absence of interaction between sentence pairs. To tackle the problem, attention mechanism is introduced to take interaction information into consideration, it allows sentence pairs to better focus on the relevant parts of each other, thus obtaining better representations that are less distracted by non-useful information. Previous attention-based approaches usually represent questions by a feature vector and use it to attend to answers. These approaches work at sentence level and lack of word-level interaction. Compared to attention-based models, the Compare-Aggregate framework focuses more on interaction, this kind of framework often performs word-level matching and acquires significant improvement on performance.

However, we work out two limitations of existing Compare-Aggregate frameworks as follows: Firstly, many previous studies proposed to leverage stacked models with multiple matching processes to gradually refine predictions, most of these models use bidirectional LSTM to encode the contextual information, thus the computation efficiency is low. Secondly, most of them perform word-level matching utilizing a single attention function which is definitely insufficient to model the complex semantic relation between sentence pairs.

In this paper, we leverage Densely-connected Transformer to solve the above limitations. Our work outlines the general framework with multiple matching processes. In each matching process, a transformer layer is firstly used to obtain refined representations for two text sequences separately and multi-head co-attention mechanism or multiway co-attention mechanism is then adopted to further enhance the interaction between sentence pairs, attentive representations and original representations are finally fused to form the alignment information of this matching process. The feature representations from the final matching layer are passed to a MeanMax pooling layer which converts feature vectors to a fixed dimension vector. The output of pooling layer for two text sequences are first concatenated and passed through a multi-layer feed-forward neural network to predict the label for sentence pairs.

The overall contributions of our paper can be summarized as follows:

- We propose a stacked model with multiple matching processes which repeatedly refine representations of text sequences using transformer layer.
- We employ multi-head co-attention mechanism or multi-way co-attention mechanism in each matching process to take interaction information from multiple perspectives into consideration.
- Extensive experiments are conducted to show the superiority of our proposed model which outperforms many other neural architectures and achieves competitive performance on five real-world datasets.

2   Related Work

Recently, deep learning methods are the most popular choices in sentence matching. In previous works, CNN or RNN are used to encode text sequences separately, then a similarity function is adopted for sentence matching [8]. Because of the absence of interaction between sentence pairs, attention mechanism is introduced to focus on only the most relevant information for prediction. Previous attention-based methods work in sentence level but lack word level interaction. To further enhance the interaction between sentence pairs, Compare-Aggregate framework [33] was proposed to perform word-level matching. This kind of frameworks enables word-level interaction and achieves very promising results.

In order to boost model performance, a large amount of studies focus on the enhancement of interaction between sentence pairs. CSRAN [26] leverages CAFE components and stacked recurrent encoders to repeatedly refine representations for sentence pairs and performs matching across representation hierarchies.

In addition to the development of architectures, some works [20] proposed to leverage external knowledge from knowledge graph to learn the knowledge-based representations of the input text, together with the context-based representations, as input features to the Siamese networks. The extensive experiments demonstrate the effectiveness of background knowledge in answer selection task. Multi-task learning has been shown to be useful in various NLP tasks and the key intuitive is to leverage the information from other related tasks to improve generalization. Inspired by that, MTL [7] proposed to tackle answer selection and knowledge base question answering simultaneously and boost the performance of both tasks. In this paper, we also proposes a deep architecture based on the Compare-Aggregate framework, which focuses more on the interaction of sentence pairs.

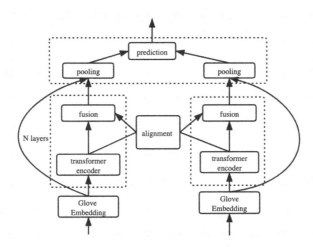

Fig. 1. The architecture of densely connected transformer

3   Our Approach

In this section, we describe the architecture of our proposed model for sentence matching. The overall architecture is illustrated in Fig. 1. It consists of the following three components:

1) *Input Embedding.* We use pre-trained word embedding as the input representation for each token in input text sequences and then use a position-wise feed-forward neural network to obtain the contextual representation.
2) *Matching Layer.* This component consists of N same-structure sub-layers. Each sub-layer contains a transformer encoder, an alignment module and a fusion module. We use transformer encoder to refine representations for text sequences and alignment module to perform matching. Inside the alignment module, we investigate the usage of two alignment strategies: multi-way co-attention mechanism and multi-head co-attention mechanism, to perform word-level matching and obtain matching information. Aligned representation and original representation are fused in fusion module to form the matching result of matching layer.
3) *Pooling and Prediction Layer.* The pooling layer converts vector sequences to a fixed dimensional feature vector. The prediction layer takes feature representations from the pooling layer as input and make a prediction using multi-layer feed-forward neural networks.

3.1   Input Embedding

Our model accepts two text sequences $A = \{a_1, a_2, ..., a_{l_A}\}$ and $B = \{b_1, b_2, ...,$ $b_{l_B}\}$. Both sequences are passed through a word embedding layer(shared between two text sequences) which is parameterized by $W_e \in R^{d \times |V|}$ and returns two sequences of d dimensional vectors $E^A \in R^{d \times l_A}$ and $E^B \in R^{d \times l_B}$. $|V|$ denotes the set of all words in the vocabulary. d is the dimension of word embedding. We initialize this layer with pre-trained word embeddings and fix it during training phase.

The outputs of the word embedding layer are then passed through a position-wise feed-forward neural network which has fewer trainable parameters to project sentence pairs to sequences of h dimensional vectors $H^A \in R^{h \times l_A}$ and $H^B \in R^{h \times l_B}$, as follows:

$$H^A = \sigma(W^s E^A + b^s) \odot \tanh(W^t E^A + b^t),$$
$$H^B = \sigma(W^s E^B + b^s) \odot \tanh(W^t E^B + b^t).$$

$$(1)$$

This component consists of N stacked same-structure sub-layers. Inside each sub-layer, a transformer encoder first computes refined representations for sentence pairs separately, the outputs of the transformer encoder are then fed into the alignment module to obtain attentive representations for two sequences respectively, attentive representations and origin representations are fused in the fusion module. The details about the three modules including co-attention mechanism used in the alignment module and dense connection are introduced as follows:

Transformer Encoder. The inputs of transformer encoder are the representations $H^a = \{h_1{}^a, h_2{}^a, ..., h_{l_a}^a\}$ and $H^b = \{h_1{}^b, h_2{}^b, ..., h_{l_b}^b\}$ for text sequences which are the concatenation of outputs of word embedding layer and all the previous sub-layers. We leverage transformer encoder [31] to obtain refined representation for two text sequences separately. Transformer is a recently proposed neural architecture which based solely on attention mechanisms, it achieves remarkable performance on neural machine translation task while being more parallelizable and requiring significantly less time to train. Due to the high computation efficiency of transformer, we use it to compute contextual representations of the text sequences. The output of the transformer encoder are represented as $\widetilde{H^a}$ and $\widetilde{H^b}$:

$$\widetilde{H^a} = TE(H^a),$$
$$\widetilde{H^b} = TE(H^b).$$

$$(2)$$

where TE represents transformer encoder.

Alignment Module. The inputs of the alignment module are the outputs of transformer encoder. In this module, we perform matching between sentence pairs to obtain alignment information. Previous studies usually perform a single attention function in this module which is insufficient to capture the complex semantic relationship between sentence pairs. In this module, we investigate the usage of two alignment strategies.

Multiway Co-attention. Inspired by the MwAN [21], we propose to use multi-way co-attention mechanism to perform matching. Different from original MwAN whose attention mechanism is one-directional, our proposed model considers both sides of question and answer by adopting general co-attention framework. Specifically, we employ four attention functions: the most commonly used Dot-Product Attention and three functions from the original MwAN, namely Dot Attention, Minus Attention and Concat Attention.

The matching process is divided into two steps. Firstly, we compute similarity matrix E for sentence pairs $\widetilde{H^a}$ and $\widetilde{H^b}$, where $e_{ij} \in E$ denotes the similarity of $\widetilde{h_i}^a$ and $\widetilde{h_j}^b$. Secondly, we obtain soft-aligned co-attentive representations for $\widetilde{h_i}^a$ and $\widetilde{h_j}^b$, denoted as $\hat{h_i}^a$ and $\hat{h_j}^b$. The four attention functions we employed are presented as follows:

(1) *Dot-Product Attention*

$$e_{ij} = \widetilde{h_i}^a \cdot \widetilde{h_j}^b, \tag{3}$$

(2) *Dot Attention*

$$e_{ij} = v_d{}^T \tanh(W_d(\widetilde{h_i}^a \odot \widetilde{h_j}^b)), \tag{4}$$

(3) *Minus Attention*

$$e_{ij} = v_m{}^T \tanh(W_m(\widetilde{h_i}^a - \widetilde{h_j}^b)), \tag{5}$$

(4) *Concat Attention*

$$e_{ij} = v_c{}^T \tanh(W_c{}^1 \widetilde{h_i}^a + W_c{}^2 \widetilde{h_j}^b). \tag{6}$$

The co-attentive representations of each attention function are then obtained as follows:

$$\hat{h_i}^a = \sum_{j=1}^{l_b} e_{ij} \widetilde{h_j}^b,$$
$$\hat{h_j}^b = \sum_{i=1}^{l_a} e_{ji} \widetilde{h_i}^a. \tag{7}$$

Given attentive representation of each attention function, we match original representation with its corresponding co-attentive representation for each word in sentence pairs. To be specific, a comparison function is used to match each pair of $\widetilde{h_i}^a$(the word representation of the ith word in $\widetilde{H^a}$) and $\hat{h_i}^a$(an attention-weighted sum of the column vectors of $\widetilde{H^b}$) into a vector t_i^a to represent the comparison result, then we add a gate to determine the importance of the new vector, and analogously for t_j^b. In our experiments, we consider the following definition of comparison function:

$$t_i^a = f(\widetilde{h_i}^a, \hat{h_i}^a) = \widetilde{h_i}^a \odot \hat{h_i}^a,$$
$$g = \sigma(W_g t_i^a),$$
$$t_i{}^a = g t_i^a. \tag{8}$$

For each attention function, the results are sequences of vectors for sentence pairs, denoted as $T_j^a = \{t_1^a, t_2^a, ..., t_{l_a}^a\}_j$ and $T_j^b = \{t_1^b, t_2^b, ..., t_{l_b}^b\}_j$, where $j = \{dp, d, m, c\}$ represents the four attention functions. We combine comparison results from four attention functions using the following attention mechanism:

$$s_j = v^T(W^1\{t_i^a\}_j + W^2 v^2)(j = dp, d, m, c), \tag{9}$$

$$a_j = \frac{exp(s_j)}{\Sigma_{k=(dp,d,m,c)} exp(s_k)}, \tag{10}$$

$$t_i^a = \Sigma_{j=(dp,d,m,c)} a_j \{t_i^a\}_j. \tag{11}$$

where W^1, W^2, v and v^2 are trainable parameters.

Multi-head Co-attention. Motivated by the success of multi-head self attention in neural machine translation task, we leverage multi-head co-attention mechanism to perform matching. Following is the general single head co-attention mechanism

$$E_i = f(\widetilde{H_i^A} W_i^A, \widetilde{H_i^B} W_i^B),$$
$$\hat{H}_i^A = softmax(E_i)\widetilde{H_i^B} W_i^B, \tag{12}$$
$$\hat{H}_i^B = softmax(E_i^T)\widetilde{H_i^A} W_i^A,$$

where f is the scaled dot-product attention, i represents the i-th head. The multi-head co-attentive representations are then obtained as follows:

$$\hat{H}^A = Concate(\hat{H}_1^A, \hat{H}_2^A, ...\hat{H}_n^A)W^A,$$
$$\hat{H}^B = Concate(\hat{H}_1^B, \hat{H}_2^B, ...\hat{H}_n^B)W^B. \tag{13}$$

Fusion Module. In the Fusion module, we compare original representations and attentive representations as follows:

$$\widetilde{h_i} = M([h_i; \hat{h}_i; h_i - \hat{h}_i; h_i \odot \hat{h}_i]). \tag{14}$$

where h_i represents the original representation of i-th word of the text sequence and $\overrightarrow{h_i}$ is the attentive representation of it. M is a multi-layer feed-forward neural network.

Dense Connection. Our model consists of stacked matching sub-layers and is difficult to train. Previous works usually adopt residual connections [12] or highway layers which introduces skip connections to help feature propagation from shallower layers to deeper layers via shortcuts. DCT adopts dense connections to connect all matching layers. Specifically, for a sequence of length l, the input of the n-th matching layer $x^n = (x_1^{(n)}, x_2^{(n)}, ...x_l^{(n)})$ is the concatenation of the output of embedding layer and output of all previous matching layers:

$$x^n = [x^1; x^2; ...x^{n-1}]. \tag{15}$$

where [;] denotes the concatenation operation.

3.2   Pooling and Prediction Layer

Inputs of the pooling layer are the output of the final matching layer, we employ the MeanMax pooling function to convert text sequences to fixed dimensional vectors. Specifically, we concatenate the result of max pooling and average pooling:

$$V_{a'} = MeanMax(V_a),$$
$$V_{b'} = MeanMax(V_b). \tag{16}$$

The feature vectors obtained from pooling layer are the final representations for two text sequences $V_{a'}$ and $V_{b'}$ which are concatenated and fed into a multi-layer perceptron (MLP) classifier for the probability of each label as follows:

$$\hat{y} = M[V_{a'}; V_{b'}; V_{a'} - V_{b'}; V_{a'} \odot V_{b'}]. \tag{17}$$

where M is a multi-layer feed-forward neural network, $\hat{y} \in R^C$ represents the final prediction score where C is the number of classes.

4   Experiments and Results

4.1   Datasets

To demonstrate the effectiveness of our proposed model, we conduct experiments on five well-studied benchmark datasets. In this subsection, we briefly introduce datasets used in our experiments and their corresponding evaluation metrics. The statistics of all datasets are given in Table 2.

Table 2. Summary statistics of used datasets.

Dataset	Task	#Pairs
SNLI	Natural Language Inference	570K
Scitail	Entailment Classification	27K
WikiQA	Answer Selection	29.3K
YahooQA	Answer Selection	316.4K
InsuranceQA	Answer Selection	2337.1K

SNLI [2] (Stanford Natural Language Inference) is a well-studied benchmark dataset for natural language inference. This task takes two asymmetrical sequences as input and determines if two sequences entail, contradict or are neutral to each other. The original dataset contains 570k sentence pairs, each labeled with one of the following relationships: "entailment", "contradiction", "neutral" and "-", where "-" indicates a lack of human annotation and we discarded sentence pairs with this kind of label following previous studies [2]. We adopt accuracy as the evaluation metric for this dataset.

SciTail [13] (Science Entailment) is an entailment classification dataset constructed from science questions and answers. Sentence pairs in this dataset are labeled with either "neutral" or "entailment". We use the data split as in the original paper which contains 27k sentence pairs and accuracy is used as the evaluation metric for this dataset.

WikiQA [36] is a recently proposed popular benchmark dataset for open-domain question-answering. WikiQA is constructed from real queries of Bing and Wikipedia search logs. For each question, the authors selected Wikipedia pages and used sentences in the summary paragraph as candidates, which are then annotated on a crowdsourcing platform. We remove all questions with no correct candidate answers. In total, the excluded WikiQA has 873 training questions, 126 development questions and 243 test questions and 8627/1130/2351 question-answer pairs for train/dev/test split. We adopt Mean average precision (MAP) and mean reciprocal rank (MRR) as the evaluation metrics for this dataset.

YahooQA is an open-domain community-based dataset containing 142627 QA pairs collected from the CQA platform Yahoo Answers. We use the pre-processing splits provided by the work [24] which is obtained by filtering out questions and answers whose length is out of 5–50 and generating 4 negative samples for each question by sampling from top 1000 hits obtained using Lucene search.

InsuranceQA [8] is a large-scale non-factoid QA dataset from the insurance domain. The dataset is already split into a training set, a validation set and two test sets. For each question in the development and test sets, the InsuranceQA includes an answer pool of 500 candidate answers, which include ground-truth answers and randomly selected negative answers. The average length of questions and answers in tokens are 7 and 95 respectively, such differences impose additional challenges for the answer selection task.

4.2   Implementation Details

In this subsection, we introduce the implementation details for our proposed model. We use Adam optimizer for all datasets with learning rate tuned amongst $\{10^{-3}, 2 \times 10^{-3}, 3 \times 10^{-3}\}$. The number of stacked matching layers is tuned from 2 to 5. Word embeddings are initialized with 840B-300d GloVe word vectors [16] and are not updated during training. Embeddings of out-of-vocabulary words are initialized to zeros. The head number for transformer encoder and multi-head co-attention is tuned from 4 to 8. The training batch size is tuned from 64 to 512. We denote models using multi-way co-attention and multi-head co-attention in matching layer as DCT(multiway) and DCT(multihead) respectively.

4.3   Results on Answer Selection

For the answer selection task, we conduct experiments on following three datasets: WikiQA, YahooQA and InsuranceQA.

The key competitors of WikiQA dataset are the Dynamic Clip Attention model [1], the Compare-Aggregate model [33], BiMPM [34], IWAN [32] and

Table 3. Results on WikiQA test set.

Model	MAP	MRR
BiMPM [34]	0.718	0.731
IWAN [19]	0.733	0.750
Compare-Aggregate [33]	0.743	0.755
RE2 [35]	0.745	0.762
Dynamic clip attention [1]	<u>0.754</u>	<u>0.764</u>
DCT (multiway)	**0.757**	**0.773**
DCT (multihead)	0.750	0.759

RE2 [35]. The experimental results on WikiQA dataset are presented in Table 3. For WikiQA dataset, the learning rate of optimization is set to 10^{-3}. Batchsize is set to 64 during training. The length of question and answer are 25 and 60 respectively. The number of matching layers for the results is 3. Some of the previous methods are trained by the pairwise ranking loss or listwise ranking loss, we train our model using pointwise objective function. Our proposed model achieves highly competitive results compared with the state-of-the-art reported on this dataset where DCT (multiway) obtains the best MAP and MRR score, outperforming strong baselines such as Dynamic clip attention model [1] by +0.9% in terms of MRR. Secondly, the performance of DCT (multiway) is better than DCT(multihead), the latter is also highly competitive.

Table 4. Results on YahooQA test set

Model	P@1	MRR
HD-LSTM [24]	0.5569	0.7347
CTRN [27]	0.601	0.755
KAN [6]	0.744	0.840
HyperQA [28]	0.683	0.801
MTL [7]	<u>0.833</u>	<u>0.909</u>
DCT (multiway)	**0.855**	**0.936**
DCT (multihead)	0.851	0.935

Table 5. Results on Insurance test set.

Model	Test1	Test2
MAN [30]	<u>0.705</u>	<u>0.669</u>
IARNN-Gate [32]	0.701	0.628
IARNN-Occam [32]	0.689	0.651
Improve Representation [22]	0.690	0.648
CNN with GESD [5]	0.653	0.610
DCT (multiway)	**0.730**	**0.694**
DCT (multihead)	0.718	0.685

For YahooQA dataset, we compare against a large number of competitive baselines: HD-LSTM [24], CTRN [27], HyperQA [28], KAN [6] and the state-of-the-art Multi-Task Learning with Multi-View Attention for AS and KBQA [7]. The results are listed in Table 4. Pointwise loss function is adopted for training with no regularization. Batchsize is set to 64 during training. We set the length of question and answer in tokens to 30 and 60 respectively. Questions and answers are truncated or padded to the preset values for batch training. We observe that our proposed model achieves the best performance on this dataset. Notably, we outperform existing state-of-the-art model MTL [7] by +2.2% in terms of P@1 and +2.7% in terms of MRR.

For InsuranceQA dataset, we compare our model with the CNN with GESD [5], IARNN-Gate [32], IARNN-Occam [32], Improved representation learning [22] and the multihop attention networks [30]. Table 5 describe the experimental results. In our experiment, we set batchsize to 64, length of question and answer to 20 and 120 respectively. Our proposed model achieves very promising performance on the Insurance dataset compared with previous studies. Notably, we outperform MAN [30] by +2.5% in terms of top-1 accuracy both on test1 dataset and test2 dataset. The performance of DCT(multihead) falls short of DCT(multiway), but still remains competitive on this dataset.

4.4 Results on Natural Language Inference

In this task, we compare against a large number of competitive baselines: DecompAtt [15], BiMPM [34], ESIM [3], MwAN [21] , CAFE [25], on SNLI dataset. Table 6 reports the experimental results on the SNLI dataset. Batchsize is set to 64 during training. Accuracy is used as the evaluation metric for this dataset. We observe that our proposed model achieves competitive performance compared with state-of-the-art models (e.g... MwAN [21] and CAFE [25]) on this dataset.

Table 6. Results on SNLI test set

Model	Acc(%)
DecompAtt [15]	86.8
BiMPM [34]	86.9
ESIM [3]	88.0
MwAN [21]	88.3
CAFE [25]	**88.5**
DCT (multiway)	88.3
DCT (multihead)	88.1

Table 7. Results on SciTail test set.

Model	Acc(%)
ESIM [3]	70.6
DecompAtt [15]	72.3
DGEM [13]	77.3
HCRN [23]	80.0
CAFE [25]	83.3
DCT (multiway)	85.3
DCT (multihead)	**85.4**

4.5 Results on Entailment Classification

For the sentence entailment classification task, we compare against multiple state-of-the-art models. Specifically, we compare our model with the ESIM [3], DecompAtt [15], DGEM [13], HCRN [23] and CAFE [25]. Our results on SciTail dataset is summarized in Table 7. In the experiment, we set batchsize to 128.

Firstly, our model achieves the best performance compared with previous works reported on this dataset, outperforms CAFE [25] by 2.1% in terms of accuracy. Secondly, two alignment strategies show approximately equal performance on this dataset.

Table 8. Ablation Study on WikiQA dev dataset.

Model	MAP	MRR
DCT (multiway)	0.753	0.762
(1) dot-product attention	0.743	0.751
(2) w/o dense connection	0.731	0.738
(3) w/o stacked matching layers	0.733	0.740

4.6   Ablation Study

We conduct an extensive ablation study to explore the relative effectiveness of the key components in our proposed model. Table 8 reports the results on the development set of the WikiQA dataset. We adopt DCT(multiway) as the original model and the number of matching layers for the experiment is set to 3. There are three ablation settings as follows: (1) "dot-product attention": we perform matching using single dot-product attention function; (2) "w/o dense connection": we use feature representations only from the previous matching layer aiming to showcase that matching information from all matching layers plays a crucial role in model performance; (3) "w/o stacked matching layers": we remove stacked matching layers.

From our ablation study results, we conclude the following observations: Firstly, using a single attention function leads to significant performance degradation. For example, for model (1), which performs matching only using dot-product attention, MRR on the dev set drops from 0.762 to 0.751. Secondly, the model performance decreases a lot without aggregating matching information from all matching layers to make a prediction. A reasonable explanation is that feature representations from all matching layers form a feature hierarchy. Combining these representations can strengthen the propagation of lower-level features, thus can help deep model training. The last observation is that removing stacked matching layers significantly decreases the model performance, MRR drops approximately 2%.

4.7   Parameter Sensitivity

Our model is motivated by the intuition that enhancing the interaction between text sequences can boost the model performance. To this end, we perform multiple matching processes and adopt multi-head co-attention mechanism or multiway co-attention mechanism within each matching process, the results from ablation study have shown the effectiveness of the key components of our model. The number of matching layers is the key factor that can significantly affect the model performance. To explore the influence of the number of matching layers on the overall performance of model, we evaluate model DCT(multiway) with different number of matching layers on the development set of WikiQA dataset and adopt MRR score as the evaluation metric. We report the average score of 5 runs. The results are illustrated in Fig. 2. We can observe that with the number of matching layers increasing from 1 to 3, the performance of DCT(multiway) increases. However, with the incremental increase in the number of matching layers, the performance declines significantly.

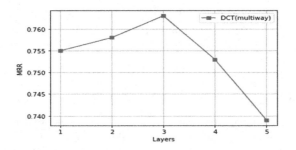

Fig. 2. Effect of number of matching layers.

5   Conclusion

In this paper, we propose Densely connected Transformer with co-attention information for sentence matching. It performs multiple matching processes utilizing stacked matching layers, inside each layer, it first refines representations for text sequences using transformer encoder and then performs matching leveraging the multiway co-attention mechanism or multi-head co-attention mechanism, which can effectively enhance the interaction between text sequences. Our proposed model achieves highly competitive performance on five well-studied benchmark datasets.

Acknowledgements. This work is supported by the National Natural Science Foundation of China (NSFC) (No. 61832001, 61702015, 61702016, U1936104,), National Key R&D Program of China (No. 2018YFB1004403), PKU-Baidu Fund 2019BD006.

References

1. Bian, W., Li, S., Yang, Z., Chen, G., Lin, Z.: A compare-aggregate model with dynamic-clip attention for answer selection. In: Proceedings of the 2017 ACM on Conference on Information and Knowledge Management, pp. 1987–1990. ACM (2017)

2. Bowman, S.R., Angeli, G., Potts, C., Manning, C.D.: A large annotated corpus for learning natural language inference. arXiv preprint arXiv:1508.05326 (2015)

3. Chen, Q., Zhu, X., Ling, Z., Wei, S., Jiang, H., Inkpen, D.: Enhanced lstm for natural language inference. arXiv preprint arXiv:1609.06038 (2016)

4. Chen, X., et al.: Sentiment classification using negative and intensive sentiment supplement information. Data Sci. Eng. **4**(2), 109–118 (2019)

5. Collobert, R., Weston, J., Bottou, L., Karlen, M., Kavukcuoglu, K., Kuksa, P.: Natural language processing (almost) from scratch. J. Mach. Learn. Res. **12**, 2493–2537 (2011)

6. Deng, Y., et al.: Knowledge as a bridge: improving cross-domain answer selection with external knowledge. In: Proceedings of the 27th International Conference on Computational Linguistics, pp. 3295–3305 (2018)

7. Deng, Y., et al.: Multi-task learning with multi-view attention for answer selection and knowledge base question answering. In: Proceedings of the AAAI Conference on Artificial Intelligence, vol. 33, pp. 6318–6325 (2019)

8. Feng, M., Xiang, B., Glass, M.R., Wang, L., Zhou, B.: Applying deep learning to answer selection: a study and an open task. In: 2015 IEEE Workshop on Automatic Speech Recognition and Understanding (ASRU), pp. 813–820. IEEE (2015)

9. Guo, L., Hua, L., Jia, R., Zhao, B., Wang, X., Cui, B.: Buying or browsing? Predicting real-time purchasing intent using attention-based deep network with multiple behavior. In: Proceedings of the 25th ACM SIGKDD International Conference on Knowledge Discovery & Data Mining, pp. 1984–1992 (2019)

10. Guo, L., Zhang, D., Wang, L., Wang, H., Cui, B.: CRAN: a hybrid CNN-RNN attention-based model for text classification. In: Trujillo, J., et al. (eds.) International Conference on Conceptual Modeling. LNCS, vol. 11157, pp. 571–585. Springer, Cham (2018). https://doi.org/10.1007/978-3-030-00847-5_42

11. Habimana, O., Li, Y., Li, R., Gu, X., Yu, G.: Sentiment analysis using deep learning approaches: an overview. Sci. China Inf. Sci. **63**(1), 1–36 (2020)

12. He, K., Zhang, X., Ren, S., Sun, J.: Deep residual learning for image recognition. In: Proceedings of the IEEE Conference on Computer Vision and Pattern Recognition, pp. 770–778 (2016)

13. Khot, T., Sabharwal, A., Clark, P.: SciTaiL: a textual entailment dataset from science question answering. In: Thirty-Second AAAI Conference on Artificial Intelligence (2018)

14. Liu, X., Pan, S., Zhang, Q., Jiang, Y.G., Huang, X.: Reformulating natural language queries using sequence-to-sequence models. Sci. China Inf. Sci. **12**, 24 (2019)

15. Parikh, A.P., Täckström, O., Das, D., Uszkoreit, J.: A decomposable attention model for natural language inference. arXiv preprint arXiv:1606.01933 (2016)

16. Pennington, J., Socher, R., Manning, C.: Glove: global vectors for word representation. In: Proceedings of the 2014 Conference on Empirical Methods in Natural Language Processing (EMNLP), pp. 1532–1543 (2014)

17. Santos, C., Tan, M., Xiang, B., Zhou, B.: Attentive pooling networks. arXiv preprint arXiv:1602.03609 (2016)

18. Severyn, A., Moschitti, A.: Learning to rank short text pairs with convolutional deep neural networks. In: Proceedings of the 38th International ACM SIGIR Conference on Research and Development in Information Retrieval, pp. 373–382. ACM (2015)

19. Shen, G., Yang, Y., Deng, Z.H.: Inter-weighted alignment network for sentence pair modeling. In: Proceedings of the 2017 Conference on Empirical Methods in Natural Language Processing, pp. 1179–1189 (2017)

20. Shen, Y., et al.: Knowledge-aware attentive neural network for ranking question answer pairs. In: The 41st International ACM SIGIR Conference on Research & Development in Information Retrieval, pp. 901–904 (2018)

21. Tan, C., Wei, F., Wang, W., Lv, W., Zhou, M.: Multiway attention networks for modeling sentence pairs. In: IJCAI, pp. 4411–4417 (2018)

22. Tan, M., Dos Santos, C., Xiang, B., Zhou, B.: Improved representation learning for question answer matching. In: Proceedings of the 54th Annual Meeting of the Association for Computational Linguistics, vol. 1, Long Papers, pp. 464–473 (2016)

23. Tay, Y., Luu, A.T., Hui, S.C.: Hermitian co-attention networks for text matching in asymmetrical domains. In: IJCAI, pp. 4425–4431 (2018)

24. Tay, Y., Phan, M.C., Tuan, L.A., Hui, S.C.: Learning to rank question answer pairs with holographic dual lstm architecture. In: Proceedings of the 40th International ACM SIGIR Conference on Research and Development in Information Retrieval, pp. 695–704. ACM (2017)

25. Tay, Y., Tuan, L.A., Hui, S.C.: Compare, compress and propagate: enhancing neural architectures with alignment factorization for natural language inference. arXiv preprint arXiv:1801.00102 (2017)

26. Tay, Y., Tuan, L.A., Hui, S.C.: Co-stack residual affinity networks with multi-level attention refinement for matching text sequences. arXiv preprint arXiv:1810.02938 (2018)

27. Tay, Y., Tuan, L.A., Hui, S.C.: Cross temporal recurrent networks for ranking question answer pairs. In: Thirty-Second AAAI Conference on Artificial Intelligence (2018)

28. Tay, Y., Tuan, L.A., Hui, S.C.: Hyperbolic representation learning for fast and efficient neural question answering. In: Proceedings of the Eleventh ACM International Conference on Web Search and Data Mining, pp. 583–591. ACM (2018)

29. Tong, P., Zhang, Q., Yao, J.: Leveraging domain context for question answering over knowledge graph. Data Sci. Eng. 4(4), 323–335 (2019)

30. Tran, N.K., Niedereée, C.: Multihop attention networks for question answer matching. In: The 41st International ACM SIGIR Conference on Research & Development in Information Retrieval, pp. 325–334. ACM (2018)

31. Vaswani, A., et al.: Attention is all you need. In: Advances in Neural Information Processing Systems, pp. 5998–6008 (2017)

32. Wang, B., Liu, K., Zhao, J.: Inner attention based recurrent neural networks for answer selection. In: Proceedings of the 54th Annual Meeting of the Association for Computational Linguistics, Long Papers, vol. 1, pp. 1288–1297 (2016)

33. Wang, S., Jiang, J.: A compare-aggregate model for matching text sequences. arXiv preprint arXiv:1611.01747 (2016)

34. Wang, Z., Hamza, W., Florian, R.: Bilateral multi-perspective matching for natural language sentences. arXiv preprint arXiv:1702.03814 (2017)

35. Yang, R., Zhang, J., Gao, X., Ji, F., Chen, H.: Simple and effective text matching with richer alignment features. arXiv preprint arXiv:1908.00300 (2019)

36. Yang, Y., Yih, W., Meek, C.: Wikiqa: a challenge dataset for open-domain question answering. In: Proceedings of the 2015 Conference on Empirical Methods in Natural Language Processing, pp. 2013–2018 (2015)

37. Yin, W., Schütze, H., Xiang, B., Zhou, B.: Abcnn: attention-based convolutional neural network for modeling sentence pairs. Trans. Assoc. Comput. Linguist. 4, 259–272 (2016)

WEKE: Learning Word Embeddings for Keyphrase Extraction

Yuxiang Zhang[1(✉)], Huan Liu[1], Bei Shi[2], Xiaoli Li[3], and Suge Wang[4]

[1] School of Computer Science and Technology, Civil Aviation University of China,
Tianjin, China
yxzhang@cauc.edu.cn, hliu_h@outlook.com
[2] Tencent AI Lab, Shenzhen, China
beishi@tencent.com
[3] Institute for Infocomm Research, A*STAR, Singapore, Singapore
xlli@i2r.a-star.edu.sg
[4] School of Computer and Information Technology,
Shanxi University, Taiyuan, China
wsg@sxu.edu.cn

Abstract. Traditional supervised keyphrase extraction models depend on the *features* of labeled keyphrases while prevailing unsupervised models mainly rely on *global structure* of the word graph, with nodes representing candidate words and edges/links capturing the co-occurrence between words. However, the *local context information* of the word graph can not be exploited in existing unsupervised graph-based keyphrase extraction methods and *integrating different types of information into a unified model* is relatively unexplored. In this paper, we propose a new word embedding model specially for keyphrase extraction task, which can capture local context information and incorporate them with other types of crucial information into the low-dimensional word vector to help better extract keyphrases. Experimental results show that our method consistently outperforms 7 state-of-the-art unsupervised methods on three real datasets in Computer Science area for keyphrase extraction.

Keywords: Word embedding · Graph-based keyphrase extraction model

1 Introduction

Automatic keyphrase extraction aims to extract a set of representative phrases related to the main *topics* discussed in a document [8]. Since keyphrases can provide a high-level topic description of a document, they are very useful for a wide range of natural language processing (NLP) tasks, such as text summarization [25], information retrieval [21] and question answering [19]. Nevertheless, the performance of existing methods is still far from being satisfactory, as it is very challenging, if not impossible, to determine if a set of phrases accurately captures the main topics presented in a given document.

© Springer Nature Switzerland AG 2020
X. Wang et al. (Eds.): APWeb-WAIM 2020, LNCS 12318, pp. 245–260, 2020.
https://doi.org/10.1007/978-3-030-60290-1_19

Existing methods for keyphrase extraction can be broadly divided into supervised or unsupervised methods. Specifically, the supervised methods treat the keyphrase extraction as a binary classification task, in which a classifier is trained on the *features of labeled keyphrases* to determine whether a candidate phrase is a keyphrase [5]. In unsupervised methods, on the other hand, various measures, such as *tf-idf* (term frequency-inverse document frequency), graph-based ranking scores (*e.g.*, *degree centrality* and *PageRank score*), are used to score individual candidate words that are later summed up to obtain total scores for phrases [3,4,8,11,21,22].

The PageRank-based models (*i.e.*, random-walk models) are widely used in the unsupervised scenario and considered as the current state of the arts. These models first build a *word graph* in which each node denotes a candidate word and each edge represents a co-occurrence relation between words within a document. Random walk techniques are subsequently used on the word graph to rank words. Since TextRank [11] firstly computed ranking scores of candidate words using PageRank algorithm [13] on the word graph, many TextRank-based extensions have been proposed, aiming at integrating various types of information into modified PageRank models to improve the performance of keyphrase extraction. For example, TopicalPageRank (TPR) [8], CiteTextRank [4] and PositionRank [3] integrate topical information, citation context and position information into the PageRank-based framework, respectively.

Although remarkable efforts have been made on PageRank-based framework for keyphrase extraction, these traditional models cannot utilize the *local context information* of the word graph, which can be considered as the local collocation pattern between words at the semantic level or as the semantic similarity between words. The reason for this is that the PageRank-based ranking model is a way to decide the importance of a node within a given graph, by taking into account *global* structural information recursively computed from the entire graph, rather than relying only on *local* structural information [11]. In addition, this intrinsic nature of PageRank-based models makes it extremely challenging to integrate different types of information into a unified model to achieve better performance on keyphrase extraction. Thus, the existing PageRank-based models leverage *separately* different types of information (*e.g.*, topical and position information) by directly modifying the corresponding transition or reset probability, rather than incorporating various types of information through a unified model.

In this paper, we first design a word graph representation learning technique which can capture *local context information* of the word graph and deeply incorporate this information with some *crucial features* of nodes and links (*e.g.*, topical information of candidate words and co-occurrence information between words) through a unified model. Although many word representation methods, such as Skip-gram [12], PTE [18] and TWE [7], have been proposed, they are mainly designed for general NLP tasks such as text classification and document visualization, rather than for keyphrase extraction. Secondly, we propose a novel random-walk ranking model to leverage the learned word embeddings and *global structure* of the word graph to rank candidate words in the word co-occurrence graph. Finally, we conduct comprehensive experiments over three publicly-available datasets in Computer Science area. Our experimental results show that our approach outperforms 7 state-of-the-art unsupervised methods.

2 Related Work

Our work is mainly related to graph-based approaches which have been proven to be effective in the keyphrase extraction task. Following TextRank [11] which is the first to use PageRank algorithm [13] to rank candidate words, numerous extensions integrate various types of information into PageRank framework in three different ways.

In the word graph, *link-associated information*, which is derived from different background knowledge and used to enhance the accuracies of links/co-occurrences between words, is incorporated into the PageRank model by modifying the *transition probability*. For example, ExpandRank [21] leverages a small number of nearest neighbor documents to compute more accurate co-occurrences. CiteTextRank [4] exploits evidence from the citation contexts to enhance co-occurrences in the weighted word graph considering three types of contexts. Secondly, *node-associated information*, which reflects the importance of candidate words among different aspects, is incorporated into the PageRank model by modifying the *reset probability*. For instance, TopicalPageRank (TPR) [8] first integrates topical information into a biased PageRank model to increase the weight of important topics generated by latent Dirichlet al.location (LDA) [2]. Single-TPR [17] and Salience-Rank [20] only run PageRank model once instead of L times (L is the number of topics used in LDA) as in the TPR. PositionRank [3] integrates position information from all positions of a word's occurrences into a biased PageRank. Finally, both link-associated and word-associated information are *simultaneously* integrated by PageRank optimization models, such as SEAFARER [24] and MIKE [25]. However, these methods do not consider the *local context information* of the word graph.

Although a few recent studies have integrated some background knowledge into PageRank framework using word embedding techniques, the word embeddings used in these studies are learned by the traditional word embedding models such as Skip-gram on Wikipedia [23] or domain-specific corpus [26]. In contrast, the word embedding model proposed in this work is *designed especially for the keyphrase extraction task*, rather than for other general NLP tasks.

3 Proposed Model: WEKE

3.1 Preliminaries

Definition 1 (Keyphrase extraction). Let $D = \{d_1, d_2, ..., d_c\}$ be a set of c text documents. Each document $d_i \in D$ includes a set of candidate words or phrases $W_i = \{w_{i1}, w_{i2}, ..., w_{in_i}\}$. The goal of a keyphrase extraction model is to find a function to map each $w_{ij} \in W_i$ into a score, and then extract a top ranked list of candidates that best represents d_i.

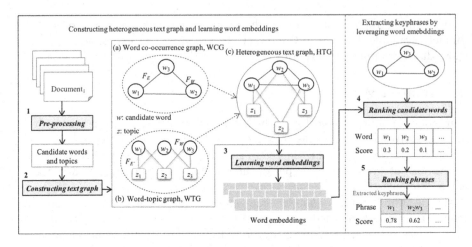

Fig. 1. An overview of the proposed approach.

Algorithms for graph-based keyphrase extraction commonly involve four basic steps: candidate word selection, word graph construction, candidate word ranking and keyphrase extraction [3,4]. In this work, these basic steps are included and extended to leverage the word embeddings for keyphrase extraction. The overview of our proposed method illustrated in Fig. 1 consists of the following five steps:

1. **Text Pre-processing.** This step includes selecting candidate keywords and computing topic distribution that a word occurs in a given topic. Only nouns and adjectives are selected as candidate words because most of keyphrases are noun phrases and they commonly consist of nouns and adjectives [4,8]. In addition, the topic distribution is obtained by LDA model in this work.

2. **Heterogeneous Text Graph Construction.** A heterogeneous text graph is built, which consists of the word-word graph (*i.e.*, traditional word graph) and word-topic graph. The word-topic graph is built according to the generative relation that the word occurs in the given topic.

3. **Word Embedding on Heterogeneous Text Graph.** The heterogeneous text graph embedding model is proposed for learning word embeddings in which some crucial types of information (*e.g.*, local context information and topical information) are preserved. Compared to previous works in which each type of information is exploited separately in PageRank-based methods, our work integrates the different types of information into word embeddings through a heterogeneous text graph embedding model.

4. **Candidate Word Ranking.** A new random-walk-based word ranking model is designed to leverage the both learned word embeddings, which preserve some crucial information for the keyphrase extraction task, and global structural information of the word graph to score candidate words.

5. **Phrase Ranking and Keyphrase Extraction.** Consecutive words, phrases or n-grams are scored by using the sum of scores of individual

words [25]. The top-scoring candidate phrases/words will be output as the final keyphrases.

To summarize, our main contributions lie in the step 3 to step 4, and the core technical contribution of our method is to learn the **W**ord **E**mbeddings for **K**eyphrase **E**xtraction, *i.e.*, WEKE.

3.2 Learning Word Embeddings for Keyphrase Extraction

We firstly construct the heterogeneous text graph, and then jointly learn word embeddings on this heterogeneous text graph for the keyphrase extraction task.

Word Co-occurrence Graph Embedding

Definition 2 (Word co-occurrence graph, WCG). WCG is a word graph, defined as a four-tuple $G = (W, E, F_W, F_E)$, where W is the set of nodes denoting the different candidate words, E is the set of undirected edges representing the co-occurrence relationships between two different words, F_W is the set of node features (*e.g.*, *term frequency* of a candidate word in a corpus) and F_E is the set of edge features (*e.g.*, *co-occurrence frequency* between two words). An example is shown in Fig. 1(a).

The word co-occurrences captured by the word graph have been learned by the existing word embedding models for the general NLP tasks. Besides the word co-occurrences, some crucial *features* of candidate words and co-occurrences between candidate words, which have been proven to be very effective to improve performance of keyphrase extraction, should be preserved. Next, we present the word co-occurrence graph embedding model for keyphrase extraction.

For each candidate word w_i in a word co-occurrence graph G, we can find its neighbor's neighbor set $C(i)$. To learn a vector representation $\mathbf{v}_i^w$ of w_i, which supports the keyphrase extraction, we minimize the following KL-divergence of two probability distributions:

$$\mathcal{L}_c(W) = \sum_{i \in W} \lambda_i \, KL\big(\hat{p}(w_c|w_i) || p(w_c|w_i)\big)$$
$$= \sum_{i \in W} \sum_{w_c \in C(i)} \lambda_i \, \hat{p}(w_c|w_i) \, \log \frac{\hat{p}(w_c|w_i)}{p(w_c|w_i)}. \tag{1}$$

By simplifying the above formula and omitting some constants, the corresponding objective function can be given as:

$$\mathcal{L}_c(W) = - \sum_{i \in W} \sum_{w_c \in C(i)} \lambda_i \, \hat{p}(w_c|w_i) \log p(w_c|w_i), \tag{2}$$

where $\lambda_i \in F_W$ is the importance weighting of w_i contributing to its neighbors, defined as the *term frequency* $\lambda_i = tf(w_i)$ of w_i in the corpus. The empirical distribution $\hat{p}(w_c|w_i)$ is defined as $\hat{p}(w_c|w_i) = \frac{\omega_{ic}}{\sum_{j \in C(i)} \omega_{ij}}$, where ω_{ic} is the importance weighting of edge (w_i, w_c), defined as:

$$\omega_{ic} = \sum_{k=1}^{cf(w_i, w_c)} \frac{1}{d_k(w_i, w_c)}, \tag{3}$$

where $d_k(w_i, w_c)$ is the number of words of k-th co-occurrence between w_i and w_c within a predefined window size, $cf(w_i, w_c)$ is the co-occurrence frequency between w_i and w_c in a given corpus. In this work, the importance weighting of a edge depends on its both co-occurrences and distance between words, rather than only the co-occurrences used in existing works for general NLP tasks.

In order to learn the word embedding from a word co-occurrence graph G, for each edge (w_i, w_j), we define the probability $p(w_c|w_i)$ that w_i generates w_c when compared with how w_i generates other nodes. $p(w_c|w_i)$ is estimated using the following softmax function:

$$p(w_c|w_i) = \frac{\exp(\mathbf{v}_c^{w\top} \cdot \mathbf{v}_i^w)}{\sum_{c' \in W} \exp(\mathbf{v}_{c'}^{w\top} \cdot \mathbf{v}_i^w)}, \tag{4}$$

where $\mathbf{v}_i^w \in \mathbb{R}^d$ and $\mathbf{v}_c^w \in \mathbb{R}^d$ are the d-dimensional embedding of target word w_i and corresponding context w_c, respectively.

Besides the local information of the word graph, the importance weighting of candidate words and two pieces of information related to the co-occurrences between two candidate words are captured in this word graph embedding model.

Word-Topic Graph Embedding. A set of keyphrases for a document should ideally cover the main topics discussed in it. To encode the topical information, we introduce the word-topic graph to capture topics of documents and words.

Definition 3 (Word-topic graph, WTG). Let Z be the set of topics discussed in given corpus. A word-topic graph is a bipartite graph, defined as a three-tuple $G' = (W', E', F_{E'})$, where $W' = W \cup Z$ is the set of nodes consisting of words and topics, $E' = \{(w, z)|w \in W \wedge z \in Z\}$ is the set of edges between words and topics, and $F_{E'}$ is the set of features of edges (*e.g.*, *probability* $Pr(w|z)$ obtained by the LDA model [2]). An example is shown in Fig. 1(b).

To preserve topical influence on each candidate word, the objective is to minimize the following KL-divergence of two probability distributions:

$$\begin{aligned} \mathcal{L}_z(W, Z) &= \sum_{i \in W} \lambda_i^z \, KL\big(\hat{p}(z_j|w_i)||p(z_j|w_i)\big) \\ &= \sum_{i \in W} \sum_{j \in Z} \lambda_i^z \, \hat{p}(z_j|w_i) \log\frac{\hat{p}(z_j|w_i)}{p(z_j|w_i)}. \end{aligned} \tag{5}$$

By simplifying the above formula and omitting some constants, the corresponding objective function can be given as:

$$\mathcal{L}_z(W, Z) = -\sum_{i \in W} \sum_{j \in Z} \lambda_i^z \, \hat{p}(z_j|w_i) \log p(z_j|w_i), \tag{6}$$

where $\lambda_i^z \in F_W$ is an importance weighting of w_i contributing to all the topics, and defined as the *topical specificity* of word w_i, which was proposed in the related works [20]. It describes how informative the specific word w_i is for determining the generating topic, versus a randomly-selected word w_r, given as:

$$\lambda_i^z = \sum_{j \in Z} \hat{p}(z_j | w_i) \log \frac{\hat{p}(z_j | w_i)}{\hat{p}(w_r | z_j)}, \tag{7}$$

where $\hat{p}(z_j | w_i) = Pr(z_j | w_i)$ is the empirical distribution calculated by LDA model, and $\hat{p}(w_r | z_j)$ is the empirical distribution that any randomly selected word w_r is generated by the topic z_j.

To learn the word embedding from a word-topic graph G', for each edge (w_i, z_j), we define the probability $p(z_j | w_i)$ that w_i generates z_j when compared with how w_i generates other topics, which is estimated by the softmax function:

$$p(z_j | w_i) = \frac{\exp(\mathbf{v}_j^{z \top} \cdot \mathbf{v}_i^w)}{\sum_{j' \in Z} \exp(\mathbf{v}_{j'}^{z \top} \cdot \mathbf{v}_i^w)}, \tag{8}$$

where $\mathbf{v}_i^w \in \mathbb{R}^d$ is the embedding of w_i, $\mathbf{v}_j^z \in \mathbb{R}^d$ is the embedding of topic z_j.

The topical closeness between words and topics and importance weighting of words contributing to all topics are captured in this word-topic graph embedding.

Heterogeneous Text Graph Embedding

Definition 4 (Heterogeneous text graph, HTG). A heterogeneous text graph $G'' = (W'', E'', F_{W''}, F_{E''})$ is a combination of word co-occurrence graph G and word-topic graph G' as: (1) $W'' = W'$, and $E'' = E \cup E'$; (2) $F_{W''} = F_W$, and $F_{E''} = F_E \cup F_{E'}$, as shown in Fig. 1(c).

The heterogeneous text graph can simultaneously capture all the information appeared in both the word co-occurrence and the word-topic graph. To learn the embeddings of the heterogeneous text graph, an intuitive approach is to collectively embed the two graphs, which can be achieved by minimizing the following objective function:

$$\mathcal{L} = \mathcal{L}_c(W) + \mathcal{L}_z(W, Z). \tag{9}$$

Similar to PTE [18], Eq. (9) can be optimized in two strategies, depending on how the word-topic graph is used. One is to learn the embeddings with the word co-occurrence graph first, and then fine-tune the embeddings with the word-topic graph. We call this strategy the *pre-training and fine-tuning*. An alternative solution is to learn the embeddings with the word co-occurrence graph and the word-topic graph simultaneously. We call this *joint training*. In our experiments, the first strategy gives better results, and thus we only presented it here.

Algorithm 1. Learning embeddings algorithm

Input: *(1) Heterogeneous text graph G''; (2) Dimension of embeddings d; (3) learning rate η; (4) Number of samples of edges S; (5) Number of negative samples K*
Output: *Embedded vector $\mathbf{v}_i^w$ for each $w_i \in W$*
1: **Initialize:** $\mathbf{v}_i^w, \mathbf{v}_c^w, \forall w \in W; \mathbf{v}_j^z, \forall z \in Z$
2: **for** $iter = 0; \ iter < S; \ iter = iter + 1$ **do**
3:     Sample an edge (w_i, w_c) from G
4:     Update $\mathbf{v}_c^w$ based on Eq. (13) with η
5:     **for** $k = 0; \ k < K_1; \ k = k + 1$ **do**
6:         Sample a negative word $w_{c'}$
7:         Update $\mathbf{v}_{c'}^w$ with η
8:     **end for**
9:     Update $\mathbf{v}_i^w$ based on Eq. (12) with η
10: **end for**
11: **for** $iter = 0; \ iter < S; \ iter = iter + 1$ **do**
12:     Sample an edge (w_i, z_j) from G'
13:     Update $\mathbf{v}_j^z$ based on Eq. (14) with η
14:     **for** $k = 0; \ k < K_2; \ k = k + 1$ **do**
15:         Sample a negative topic $z_{j'}$
16:         Update $\mathbf{v}_{j'}^z$ with η
17:     **end for**
18:     Update $\mathbf{v}_i^w$ based on Eq. (12) with η
19: **end for**
20: **return** Embedded vector $\mathbf{v}_i^w$

Model Optimization. We train our model Eq. (9) using the stochastic gradient descent, which is suitable for large-scale data processing. However, computing the gradients of the conditional probability $p(w_c|w_i)$ in Eq. (4) and $p(z_j|w_i)$ in Eq. (8) require the costly summation over all inner product with every node of the respective graphs. To improve the training efficiency, we adopt the negative sampling approach [12]. The equivalent counterparts of the objective function can be derived, given as follows:

$$\log p(w_c|w_i) \propto \ \log \sigma(\mathbf{v}_c^{w\top} \cdot \mathbf{v}_i^w) + \sum_{i=1}^{K_1} E_{w_{c'} \sim p_{c'}(w)} \log \sigma(-\mathbf{v}_{c'}^{w\top} \cdot \mathbf{v}_i^w), \quad (10)$$

$$\log p(z_j|w_i) \propto \ \log \sigma(\mathbf{v}_j^{z\top} \cdot \mathbf{v}_i^w) + \sum_{i=1}^{K_2} E_{z_{j'} \sim p_{j'}(z)} \log \sigma(-\mathbf{v}_{j'}^{z\top} \cdot \mathbf{v}_i^w), \quad (11)$$

where $\sigma(x) = 1/(1 + exp(-x))$ is the sigmoid function. The K_1 negative words and K_2 negative topics are sampled following the noise distribution $p(w)$ and $p(z)$, respectively. Mikolov et al. [12] have investigated many choices for $p(.)$ and found that the best $p(.)$ is equal to the unigram distribution raised to the $3/4rd$ power. As such, we also use the same setting of $p(.)$ as in work [12].

Thus the gradients of the objective function $\mathcal{L}$ with respect to $\mathbf{v}_i^w$, $\mathbf{v}_c^w$ and $\mathbf{v}_j^z$ can be formulated as follows:

$$\frac{\partial \mathcal{L}}{\partial \mathbf{v}_i^w} = \varphi_i^w \left([1-\sigma(\mathbf{v}_c^{w\top} \cdot \mathbf{v}_i^w)]\mathbf{v}_c^w - \sigma(\mathbf{v}_{c'}^{w\top} \cdot \mathbf{v}_i^w)\mathbf{v}_{c'}^w \right)$$
$$+ \varphi_i^z \left([1-\sigma(\mathbf{v}_j^{z\top} \cdot \mathbf{v}_i^w)]\mathbf{v}_j^z - \sigma(\mathbf{v}_{j'}^{z\top} \cdot \mathbf{v}_i^w)\mathbf{v}_{j'}^z \right), \tag{12}$$

$$\frac{\partial \mathcal{L}}{\partial \mathbf{v}_c^w} = \varphi_i^w \left([1-\sigma(\mathbf{v}_c^{w\top} \cdot \mathbf{v}_i^w)]\mathbf{v}_i^w \right), \tag{13}$$

$$\frac{\partial \mathcal{L}}{\partial \mathbf{v}_j^z} = \varphi_i^z \left([1-\sigma(\mathbf{v}_j^{z\top} \cdot \mathbf{v}_i^w)]\mathbf{v}_i^w \right), \tag{14}$$

where φ_i^w and φ_i^z are defined as $\varphi_i^w = \lambda_i \, \hat{p}(w_c|w_i)$ and $\varphi_i^z = \lambda_i^z \, \hat{p}(z_j|w_i)$, respectively. Due to space limitation, we omit the gradients of $\mathbf{v}_{c'}^w$ and $\mathbf{v}_{j'}^z$.

This detailed learning algorithm using the pre-training and fine-tuning training strategy is given in Algorithm 1. Its time complexity is $O(dK|E|)$, where d is the dimension of embeddings, K is the number of negative samples and $|E|$ is the number of edges.

3.3 Keyphrase Extraction Using Word Embeddings

The PageRank-based methods score the nodes in the word co-occurrence graph G (corresponding to candidate words) using a unified random-walk framework. The PageRank score $R(w_i)$ for a candidate word w_i is computed recursively as:

$$R(w_i) = \lambda \sum_{j:w_j \to w_i} \frac{e(w_j, w_i)}{out(w_j)} R(w_j) + (1-\lambda)r(w_i), \tag{15}$$

where λ is a damping factor, $e(w_j, w_i)$ is a weight of edge (w_j, w_i), $out(w_j) = \sum_{w_k:w_j \to w_k} e(w_j, w_k)$ is a out-degree of word w_j, and $r(w_i)$ is a reset probability. The final PageRank scores will prefer the words with larger value of $r(w_i)$.

In our **M**odified **P**age**R**ank-based ranking model (MPR), the reset probability is defined as $r(w_i) = \frac{\varpi(w_i)}{\sum_w \varpi(w)}$, where $\varpi(w_i)$ is a weight assigned to word w_i, calculated as $\varpi(w_i) = tf\text{-}idf(w_i)$. The weight on the edge (w_j, w_i) is computed as the product of *semantic relationship strength* $srs(w_j, w_i)$ which reflects the degree of semantic similarity between two words, *dice score* $dice(w_j, w_i)$ [6] which measures the probability of two words co-occurring in a phrase, and *CiteTextRank score* $ctr(w_j, w_i)$ [4] which captures some evidence from citation contexts, given as

$$e(w_j, w_i) = \underbrace{\frac{tf(w_j) \cdot tf(w_i)}{\|\mathbf{v}_j^w - \mathbf{v}_i^w\|_2}}_{srs(w_j,w_i)} \cdot \underbrace{\frac{2 \cdot cf(w_j, w_i)}{tf(w_j) + tf(w_i)}}_{dice(w_j,w_i)} \cdot \underbrace{\sum_{t \in T} \sum_{c \in C_t} \mu_t \cdot cossim(c,d) \cdot cf_c(w_j, w_i)}_{ctr(w_j,w_i)}, \tag{16}$$

where $\mathbf{v}_i^w$ is an embedding vector of word w_i, $tf(w_i)$ is a term frequency of word w_i in the corpus, $cossim(c, d)$ is a cosine similarity between the *tf-idf* vectors of any context c of d and given document d [9], $cf_c(w_i, w_j)$ is a co-occurrence frequency between two words in context c, C_t is a set of contexts of type $t \in T$, and μ_t is a weight for contexts of type t that is set to the same as in CiteTextRank [4].

Finally, a phrase p is scored by using the sum of scores of individual words that comprise p, computed by

$$R(p) = \psi_p \sum_{w \in p} R(w), \qquad (17)$$

where $R(w)$, computed using Eq. (15), represents the ranking score of candidate word w, and ψ_p is a weight of p according to the length of phrase p. The top-scoring phrases are output as the final results (the keyphrases for document).

4 Experimental Results

4.1 Experimental Datasets and Settings

Benchmark Datasets. For evaluating the proposed model more comprehensively, three widely-adopted scientific publication datasets were used. Each dataset consists of the research paper titles, abstracts and corresponding author manually labeled keyphrases (gold standard).

- *WWW and KDD datasets* [4]: These two datasets also contain the *citation network information* (cited and citing contexts), and are from two top-tier international conferences: ACM WWW and SIGKDD.
- *KP20k* [10]: Compared with other two datasets, this large dataset includes but is not limited to the specific subfield of computer science, and does not contain the citation network information. Due to the memory limits of implementation, we randomly select 3,000 articles from them.

Some statistics of the three datasets are summarized in Table 1, including number of papers/abstracts (*#Abs.*), average number of keyphrases per paper (*#AKPs*), percentage of missing keyphrases in the abstracts (*MissingKPs*), and number of unigrams (*#unigrams*), bigrams (*#bigrams*), trigrams (*#ttrigrams*) and more than three grams (*#>trigrams*).

For data preprocessing, we first use Python and Natural Language Toolkit (NLTK) [1] package[1] to tokenize the raw text strings, and then assign parts of speech (POS) to each word. Next, we retain only nouns and adjectives by POS filtering. Finally, we employ Porter's stemmer [15][2] to normalize the words. Thus, the candidate words used to construct the word graph are eventually obtained.

---

[1] http://www.nltk.org/.
[2] http://tartarus.org/martin/PorterStemmer/.

Table 1. Statistics of the three benchmark datasets

Dataset	#Abs.	#AKPs	MissingKPs	#unigrams	#bigrams	#trigrams	#>trigrams
WWW	425	4.87	56.39%	680	1036	247	110
KDD	365	4.03	51.12%	363	853	189	66
KP20k	3000	5.27	53.82%	5103	7418	2446	846

Evaluation Metrics. We have employed 4 widely used evaluation metrics for keyphrase extraction, including precision (P), recall (R), F1-score (F1) and Mean Reciprocal Rank (MRR) to evaluate various methods [9]. Note for each metric, the average top-p predictions (*average p*) are examined in evaluation where p refers to the average number of keyphrases for each dataset. For instance, *average* $p = 5$ for WWW and *average* $p = 4$ for KDD. MRR is used to evaluate how the first correct keyphrase for each document is ranked. Specifically, for a document d, MRR is defined as MRR= $\frac{1}{|D|} \sum_{d \in D} \frac{1}{rank_d}$ where D is the set of target documents and $rank_d$ is the rank of the first correct keyphrase from all our extracted keyphrases.

Comparative Methods. We have compared our WEKE with 7 state of the arts, including 4 PageRank-based methods and 3 word embedding models.

Specifically, the 4 PageRank-based methods are: (1) *TextRank* [11], which is the first method to rank candidate words using PageRank, in which $e(w_j, w_i)$ is defined as the co-occurrence frequency of w_j and w_i from the target document only; (2) *Single-TPR* [17], which integrates the full topical information into the reset probability of PageRank, in which $r(w_i)$ is calculated by the cosine similarity between the two vectors that are word-topic probabilities and document-topic probabilities obtained by LDA model; (3) *CiteTextRank* [4], which uses the citation context in addition to the target document to enhance word co-occurrence relations, in which $e(w_j, w_i)$ is defined as $ctr(.,.)$ in Eq. (16); (4) *WordAttraction-Rank* (WAR) [23], which first uses word embeddings pre-trained over Wikipedia to enhance word co-occurrence relations, in which $e(w_j, w_i)$ is computed by a variation of $srs(.,.) \cdot dice(.,.)$ in Eq. (16). In repeated experiments, we use the publicly-available word vectors trained by fastText over Wikipedia [14][3].

In addition, we also compare the word embedding model in our WEKE with 3 representation learning models, which are summarized as follows: (1) *Skip-gram* [12], which is capable of accurately modeling the context (*i.e.*, surrounding words) of the target word within a given corpus, (2) *TWE* [7], which first assigns different topics obtained by LDA model for each target word in the corpus, and then learns different topical word embeddings for each word-topic combination; (3) *STE* [16], which learns different topic-specific word embeddings, in which topic assignments and word embeddings are jointly learned in a unified manner. In our experiments, the word similarity is evaluated using the similarity between the most probable vectors of each word over the assignments of topics.

---

[3] https://github.com/facebookresearch/fastText.

For our **WEKE**, according to different optimization strategies, the different types of word embeddings learned by our WEKE include: 1) WE_c: this is obtained directly by embedding WCG; 2) WE_t: this is obtained by embedding WCG and WTG using the pre-training and fine-tuning training strategy; that is, we learn the embeddings with WCG, and then fine-tune the embeddings with WTG; 3) $WE_{c\oplus t}$: this is obtained by simply concatenating two word embeddings learned separately with WCG and WTG; 4) WE_h: this is obtained by embedding HTG using the joint training strategy.

4.2   Parameters and Influences

Some parameters of WEKE are empirically set as follows: 1) the size of co-occurrence window is set as $window\_size = 3$, which is used to add edges between candidate words /nodes in the word graphs; 2) similar to some of existing studies, the learning rate is set as $\eta_i = \eta_0(1-i/S)$, in which S is the total number of mini-batches or edge samples and $\eta_0 = 0.025$; 3) the number of negative samples is set as $K = 5$; 4) all the word embeddings are finally normalized by setting $\|\mathbf{v}^w\|_2 = 1$; 5) the damping factor λ is set to 0.85, same with many existing PageRank-based methods; 6) the weight ψ_p in Eq. (17) is used to adjust the final ranking score $R(p)$ according to the length of phrase p, and set as follows: $\psi_p = 1$, if $|p| = 1$; $\psi_p = 0.55$ for WWW and 0.62 for KDD, if $|p| = 2$; $\psi_p = 0.3$, if $|p| \geq 3$.

Besides empirical parameters mentioned above, we firstly study how the number of samples S impacts the performance of our method. Figure 2 reports these results on both WWW and KDD. On both datasets, we observe that the performance of our proposed WEKE increases firstly and then slowly decreases as S grows, and its performance converges when S becomes large enough. The up and down trend in WEKE is different from a growing firstly and then converging trend where the local context information is mainly learned as in PTE [18]. The reason for these differences may be that the word embedding of WEKE preserves different proportions of local context information of the word graph and crucial features of candidate words and edges, rather than only the local context information, and these proportions change with the number of samples. The best-performing settings are $S = 0.5$ on WWW and $S = 0.3$ on KDD.

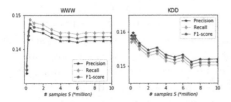

Fig. 2. Influence of # *samples* S

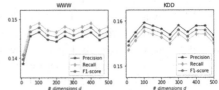

Fig. 3. Influence of # *dimensions* d

To illustrate the influence of the dimensionality of the embeddings, we then test values of parameter d in the range of [10]. According to Fig. 3, WEKE rapidly achieves good performance and then fluctuates on both WWW and KDD datasets, as the dimensionality increases. It achieves good performance *consistently* when the dimensionality setting is around 100 on both datasets. $d = 100$ is the final setting in comparison experiments. It is well known that low-dimensional representation implies low computational cost. Thus, the proposed embedding model is very efficient.

Finally, we study the influence of the number of topics in WEKE. We test values of this parameter $\# topics$ in the range of 1 to 500. We observe that the performance of WEKE increases and then slowly decreases on both WWW and KDD datasets as the number of topics grows. The best-performing setting is $\# topics = 50$ on two datasets, which is finally used in the comparison experiments. Due to space limitation, we omit the corresponding figure.

4.3   Performance Comparison

Performance on both WWW and KDD Datasets. We compare the proposed WEKE with several state-of-the-art methods at *average p* = 5 for WWW and 4 for KDD dataset. Note that the *average p* are very close to the average numbers of keyphrases *AKPs* in given research papers ($AKPs = 4.87$ on WWW and 4.03 on KDD), as shown in Table 1, reflecting the real-world applications. The results of experiments are tabulated in Table 2.

We first focus on the different optimization strategies used in the word embedding learning step of WEKE. As the results show in Rows 9–12 of Table 2, the $WEKE(\text{WE}_t)$ shows the best performance in terms of all performance measures on both WWW and KDD datasets, indicating that the pre-training and fine-tuning training strategy indeed outperforms the other two strategies, including the concatenating and the joint training.

Secondly, we use the same ranking model MPR to compare the proposed word embedding models with other three state-of-the-art embedding models including Skip-gram, TWE-1, and STE. According to Rows 6–12 of Table 2, the worst performance among our WE_t, $\text{WE}_{c\oplus t}$ and WE_h is better than the best performance among TWE-1 and STE on both datasets in which all embedding models preserve the topical information; $\text{WE}_{c\oplus t}$, which has the worst performance among our embedding models, is better than the best method STE on WWW while our worst model WE_c is worse than the best TWE-1 on KDD. These results demonstrate that the proposed word embedding models are more effective than existing embedding models and the topical information preserved in word embeddings on KDD may be more effective than on WWW.

Finally, we compare WEKE(WE$_t$), which achieves the best performance among WEKEs, with TextRank, CiteTextRank, WAR(fastText) and WAR(WE$_t$). The results show WEKE(WE$_t$) outperforms other methods in terms of all performance measures consistently on both WWW and KDD datasets.

Performance on KP20k Dataset. To further verify the effectiveness of our learned word embeddings of WEKE, we conduct additional experiment on *large* KP20k dataset, in which the citation information is removed to highlight the effectiveness of word embeddings. Correspondingly, the weight on the edge (w_j, w_i) in Eq. (16) is replaced by $e(w_j, w_i) = srs(w_j, w_i) \cdot dice(w_j, w_i)$.

Finally, we compare our best WEKE(WE$_t$) with the aforementioned existing methods at *average* $p = 6$. Some parameters, which are different from those used in the first experiment on both WWW and KDD datasets, are refined according to the same experimental analysis as in the first experiment, setting as follows: 1) the number of samples is set to $S = 3$; 2) the dimensionality of word embeddings is $d = 100$; 3) the number of topics is $\#\ topics = 10$; 4) the weight ψ_p in Eq. (17) is set as $\psi_p = 1$, if $|p| = 1$; $\psi_p = 0.5$, if $|p| = 2$; $\psi_p = 0.2$, if $|p| \geq 3$.

The results are presented in Table 3. We found WEKE(WE$_t$) outperforms all the baselines consistently. we also observe that our proposed word embedding model achieves better performance than other state-of-the-art embedding models, including skip-gram, TWE-1 and STE. The main reason is that, compared with these embedding models, our embedding model also integrates some crucial features of candidate words and edges in the word graph.

Table 2. Comparison of WEKE with other methods at *average* $p = 5$ on WWW and 4 on KDD datasets

No.	Method	WWW				KDD			
		P(%)	R(%)	F1(%)	MRR(%)	P(%)	R(%)	F1(%)	MRR(%)
1	TextRank	11.48	11.24	11.36	25.59	12.01	10.94	11.45	24.27
2	Single-TPR	13.10	13.36	13.23	29.62	12.89	12.78	12.83	27.92
3	CiteTextRank	14.00	14.28	14.14	30.39	14.63	14.48	14.55	31.42
4	WAR(fastText)	12.53	12.78	12.66	28.05	12.69	12.58	12.63	26.26
5	WAR(WE$_t$)	13.19	13.46	13.32	31.96	14.29	14.14	14.21	30.23
6	MPR(Skip-gram)	14.02	14.28	14.15	34.60	14.65	14.48	14.56	32.65
7	MPR(TWE-1)	14.09	14.38	14.23	33.68	15.26	15.09	15.17	34.02
8	MPR(STE)	14.20	14.47	14.34	34.47	15.12	14.96	15.04	33.26
9	WEKE(WE$_c$)	14.29	14.52	14.41	35.10	14.93	14.75	14.84	33.01
10	WEKE(WE$_t$)	**14.76**	**15.00**	**14.88**	**35.24**	**15.88**	**15.70**	**15.79**	**35.25**
11	WEKE(WE$_{c \oplus t}$)	14.24	14.47	14.35	34.82	15.47	15.30	15.38	33.45
12	WEKE(WE$_h$)	14.53	14.81	14.67	35.18	15.26	15.09	15.17	33.56

Table 3. Comparison of WEKE with other methods at *average p = 6* on KP20k dataset

Method	KP20k			
	P(%)	R(%)	F1(%)	MRR(%)
TextRank	9.72	11.07	10.35	22.01
Single-TPR	10.57	12.03	11.26	23.39
WAR(fastText)	10.05	11.44	10.70	22.31
MPR(Skip-gram)	11.38	12.96	12.12	25.75
MPR(TWE-1)	11.37	12.95	12.11	25.57
MPR(STE)	10.89	12.39	11.59	24.82
WEKE(WE_t)	**11.67**	**13.29**	**12.43**	**29.61**

5   Conclusions

We studied the problem of extracting keyphrases from scientific papers. A representation learning model with the objective to learn the word embedding is first proposed, which not only deeply integrates some different types of crucial information, including *local* context information of the word graph, vertex (word) features and edge (co-occurrence relation) features, but also has a strong predictive power for the keyphrase extraction task. Secondly, a novel PageRank-based model which ranks the candidate words is proposed to incorporate the embedded information and other commonly used information, especially *global* structural information of the word graph. Our experiments conducted on three datasets show that our method outperforms 7 state-of-the-art methods consistently.

Acknowledgements. This work was partially supported by grants from the National Natural Science Foundation of China (Nos. U1933114, 61573231) and Open Project Foundation of Intelligent Information Processing Key Laboratory of Shanxi Province (No. CICIP2018004).

References

1. Bird, S., Klein, E., Loper, E.: Natural Language Processing with Python: Analyzing Text with the Natural Language Toolkit. O'Reilly Media, Sebastopol (2009)
2. Blei, D.M., Ng, A.Y., Jordan, M.I.: Latent Dirichlet allocation. J. Mach. Learn. Res. **3**, 993–1022 (2003)
3. Florescu, C., Caragea, C.: Positionrank: an unsupervised approach to keyphrase extraction from scholarly documents. In: Proceedings of ACL, pp. 1105–1115 (2017)
4. Gollapalli, S.D., Caragea, C.: Extracting keyphrases from research papers using citation networks. In: Proceedings of AAAI, pp. 1629–1635 (2014)
5. Gollapalli, S.D., Li, X., Yang, P.: Incorporating expert knowledge into keyphrase extraction. In: Proceedings of AAAI, pp. 3180–3187 (2017)
6. Lee, D.R.: Measures of the amount of ecologic association between species. Ecology **26**(3), 297–302 (1945)

7. Liu, Y., Liu, Z., Chua, T.S., Sun, M.: Topical word embeddings. In: Proceedings of AAAI, pp. 2418–2424 (2015)
8. Liu, Z., Huang, W., Zheng, Y., Sun, M.: Automatic keyphrase extraction via topic decomposition. In: Proceedings of EMNLP, pp. 366–376 (2010)
9. Manning, C.D., Raghavan, P., Schütze, H.: Introduction to Information Retrieval. Cambridge University Press, New York (2008)
10. Meng, R., Zhao, S., Han, S., He, D., Brusilovsky, P., Chi, Y.: Deep keyphrase generation. In: Proceedings of ACL, pp. 582–592 (2017)
11. Mihalcea, R., Tarau, P.: Textrank: bringing order into text. In: Proceedings of EMNLP, pp. 404–411 (2004)
12. Mikolov, T., Sutskever, I., Chen, K., Corrado, G., Dean, J.: Distributed representations of words and phrases and their compositionality. In: Proceedings of NIPS, pp. 3111–3119. MIT Press (2013)
13. Page, L., Brin, S., Motwani, R., Winograd, T.: The pagerank citation ranking: Bringing order to the web. Technical report, Stanford InfoLab (1999)
14. Piotr, B., Edouard, G., Armand, J., Tomas, M.: Enriching word vectors with subword information. TACL **5**, 135–146 (2017)
15. Porter, M.F.: An algorithm for suffix stripping. Program Electron. Libr. Inf. Syst. **40**(3), 211–218 (2006)
16. Shi, B., Lam, W., Jameel, S.: Jointly learning word embeddings and latent topics. In: Proceedings of SIGIR, pp. 375–384 (2017)
17. Sterckx, L., Demeester, T., Deleu, J.: Topical word importance for fast keyphrase extraction. In: Proceedings of WWW, pp. 121–122 (2015)
18. Tang, J., Qu, M., Mei, Q.: Pte: predictive text embedding through large-scale heterogeneous text networks. In: Proceedings of SIGKDD, pp. 1165–1174 (2015)
19. Tang, Y., Huang, W., Liu, Q., Zhang, B.: Qalink: enriching text documents with relevant Q&A site contents. In: Proceedings of CIKM, pp. 3159–3168 (2017)
20. Teneva, N., Cheng, W.: Salience rank: efficient keyphrase extraction with topic modeling. In: Proceedings of ACL, pp. 530–535 (2017)
21. Wan, X., Xiao, J.: Single document keyphrase extraction using neighborhood knowledge. In: Proceedings of AAAI, pp. 855–860 (2008)
22. Wang, F., Wang, Z., Wang, S., Li, Z.: Exploiting description knowledge for keyphrase extraction. In: Pham, D.-N., Park, S.-B. (eds.) PRICAI 2014. LNCS (LNAI), vol. 8862, pp. 130–142. Springer, Cham (2014). https://doi.org/10.1007/978-3-319-13560-1_11
23. Wang, R., Liu, W., McDonald, C.: Corpus-independent generic keyphrase extraction using word embedding vectors. In: Proceedings of DL-WSDM, pp. 39–46 (2015)
24. Zhang, W., Feng, W., Wang, J.: Integrating semantic relatedness and words' intrinsic features for keyword extraction. In: Proceedings of IJCAI, pp. 2225–2231 (2013)
25. Zhang, Y., Chang, Y., Liu, X., Gollapalli, S.D., Li, X., Xiao, C.: Mike: keyphrase extraction by integrating multidimensional information. In: Proceedings of CIKM, pp. 1349–1358 (2017)
26. Zhang, Z., Gao, J., Ciravegna, F.: Semre-rank: improving automatic term extraction by incorporating semantic relatedness with personalised pagerank. ACM Trans. Knowl. Discov. Data (TKDD) **12**(5), 57:1–57:41 (2018)

Contribution of Improved Character Embedding and Latent Posting Styles to Authorship Attribution of Short Texts

Wenjing Huang, Rui Su, and Mizuho Iwaihara[(✉)]

Graduate School of Information, Production and Systems, Waseda University, 2-7 Hibikino, Wakamatsu-ku, Kitakyushu-shi, Fukuoka 808-0135, Japan
huangwj_wendy@akane.waseda.jp, surui@toki.waseda.jp,
iwaihara@waseda.jp

Abstract. Text contents generated by social networking platforms tend to be short. The problem of authorship attribution on short texts is to determine the author of a given collection of short posts, which is more challenging than that on long texts. Considering the textual characteristics of sparsity and using informal terms, we propose a method of learning text representations using a mixture of words and character n-grams, as input to the architecture of deep neural networks. In this way we make full use of user mentions and topic mentions in posts. We also focus on the textual implicit characteristics and incorporate ten latent posting styles into the models. Our experimental evaluations on tweets show a significant improvement over baselines. We achieve a best accuracy of 83.6%, which is 7.5% improvement over the state-of-the-art. Further experiments with increasing number of authors also demonstrate the superiority of our models.

Keywords: Authorship attribution · Short texts · Social network platforms · Character n-grams · CNN · LSTM · Latent posting styles

1 Introduction

As online social activities become active, massive short texts are generated over social media platforms. The problem of Authorship Attribution (AA) on short texts has stimulated growing interest along with the explosion of social network traffic [11]. The task of AA is intended to identify the authors of given texts. The AA system can be applied to detect multiple IDs of a unique user, filter spams [6] and avoid identity frauds [11].

The core of solving the AA problem is to capture writing styles of target authors, which is relatively easy to achieve for long texts but restricted by sparse features in short texts. Several classification models implemented on AA, such as SVM [11], CNN [12] and RNN [1], have achieved certain success and showed outstanding performance of word n-grams and character n-grams in discriminating the writing styles of authors. Inspired by this, we propose a method of applying improved character embedding on neural networks, that is, to embed a sequence of character n-grams mixed with special words into neural networks (e.g., CNN, LSTM).

© Springer Nature Switzerland AG 2020
X. Wang et al. (Eds.): APWeb-WAIM 2020, LNCS 12318, pp. 261–269, 2020.
https://doi.org/10.1007/978-3-030-60290-1_20

Twitter stipulated that the length of tweets was no more than 140 characters by 2017, allowing users to express core content in a very short space. Although the restricted length of the tweets is short enough, the actual length of the tweets varies from author to author. Social medias, including Twitter, provide functions that users can mention others (e.g., @Jack) and join topics (e.g., #Titanic). Emoticons are also popular among users. In addition, certain users tend to use URLs, numbers, time and dates more often than others. Apart from the writing styles of the posts, the sentiment tendency expressed by authors in the posts is a concern [6]. Most previous work indicates that authors' expressions are classified as positive, neutral and negative [7]. For example, *"How charming Jack is"*, *"Jack gave the chance of survival to Rose"* and *"I cry for this sad story"* respectively voice the above three categories of sentiment. Another focus of opinion mining is subjective and objective expressions in posts, *"Jack hits my heart"* and *"Jack is dead but love will go on"* respectively represents these two expressions.

In this paper, we capture ten latent posting features from posts: text length, number of @<username>, #<topic>, emoticons, URLs, numeric expressions, time expressions, date expressions, polarity-level and subjectivity-level. Then we integrate these extended latent posting features into the neural network models.

2 Related Work

The large coverage of social networks has led to increasing research efforts on content generated by social media. AA researches have been gradually extended to social media [4]. Word n-grams and character n-grams are widely used in AA methods [5, 6, 11–13], since they can capture syntactic features of texts. Some work is based on word embedding over certain special word n-grams and character n-grams [6, 11]. [12] is based on character embedding with character n-grams. There is no precedent work that is based on character embedding with mixed words and character n-grams. With the development of deep learning methods, CNNs [9, 10, 12, 16] and RNNs [1] have been applied in AA, showing outstanding performance. Especially, the effect of character n-grams applied on the CNN model is remarkable [12]. LSTM, as a variant of RNN, has been successfully applied in text classification [2, 14, 15]. The method of applying character n-grams on LSTMs also performs competitively [12].

Short text classification not only relies on explicit text representations, but implicit text features also contribute. [2, 3, 16] conceptualize texts utilizing external knowledge base to enhance the semantic features of short texts. Features hidden in posts can also be utilized for AA of short texts. Authors' sentiment orientations, text length of posts, number of using user mentions, topic mentions and URLs help characterize authors' writing styles [6]. We also focus on the role of these latent posting features.

3 Methodology

In this section, we describe our proposed CNN and LSTM-based models for AA utilizing improved character embedding and latent posting styles.

3.1   Improved Character Embedding Method

Our proposed model is inspired by N-gram CNN [12] that combines character n-grams and CNN. We propose a method of applying improved character embeddings on neural networks such as CNN and LSTM.

Character n-grams. The character n-gram method has a remarkable performance in previous work on AA of short texts [12]. It has been observed that social networking platforms often emerge with informal terms. The character n-gram method can tolerate misspellings and informal usages of punctuation [13]. For example, the character bigrams of "nooooooo" are represented as "no" and "oo", which restore the form of the term "no". Another example is emoticons composed of punctuations. The character bigrams of emoticons ":-)" and ":-(" are respectively represented as ":-", "-)" and ":-", "-(", although the two emoticons have the same component ":-", the different components "-)" and "-(" hide the key sentiments of the emoticons.

Improved Character Embedding. We observe that users frequently use mentions @<username> and hashtags #<topic> on social networking platforms such as Twitter. Schwartz et al. [11] replace all the forms of mentions @<username> with the same tag, ignoring the information of the user groups followed by the authors. However, our method retains the characteristics of user reference information, since we believe the same users mentioned frequently in posts will help identify authorship. Similarly, topic references are useful features. In our method, we keep all forms @<username> and #<topic> from being split by the character n-grams method. In this way, we obtain sequences of mixed words and character n-grams.

Then we use Word2Vec's Skip-Gram model to pre-train 300-dimension word vectors on the training set which includes mixtures of words and character n-grams. In the character embedding module, we use pre-trained word vectors to represent the mixed sequences of words and character n-grams. The dimension of the embedding matrix is set to 140 on Twitter datasets and sequences with a length shorter than 140 are padded.

Neural Network Models. We apply our improved character embedding method on typical neural networks, namely CNN and LSTM. Our proposed architecture receives a mixed sequence of words and character n-grams as input. Then we use neural network models to automatically extract textual features of the sequence and obtain a compact feature vector representation. Finally, the representation is passed to a fully connected module with softmax function for author identification.

Figure 1a presents the adoption of the CNN model into this architecture. In the convolutional layer, we use three types of filters with different sizes w and n. Then the convolution results representing text features are upstreamed to a pooling layer with a max-pooling function to extract the most important features. Finally, the representation from concatenated pooling outputs is passed to the fully connected layer. Figure 1b adopts a two-layer bi-directional LSTM (Bi-LSTM) model to obtain the feature representation of an input sequence. Then we take the output of the last time step as the input to the fully connected module.

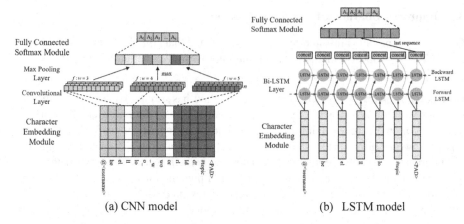

(a) CNN model   (b) LSTM model

Fig. 1. Neural network models with improved character embedding.

3.2 Latent Posting Styles

Most previous work focuses on textual features in AA tasks while very few explore latent features hidden in posts. Authors' sentiment orientation and other posting expressions can help identify authors' writing styles [6]. We divide the text length into 5 levels (L1, L2, L3, L4, L5) ranging from 0 to 140. For the characteristics @ <username>, #<topic>, URLs, numbers, time, dates and emoticons, we respectively use the letters "M", "T", "U", "N", "T'", "D", "E" and their frequency of occurrence to represent them. Each post carries its author's sentiment, which may be positive/neutral/negative, and objective/subjective. We use polarity and subjectivity scores generated by TextBlob [8] for these abstract sentiments. Polarity scores vary from −1.0 to 1.0, where 1.0 is positive. Subjective score describes the degree of subjectivity of a post, which varies from 0 to 1.0. To incorporate sentiment characteristics into posting style vectors, we assign discrete levels P1, P2, P3, P4, P5 to polarity scores, and similarly assign discrete levels S1, S2, S3, S4, S5 to subjectivity scores.

All the latent features of posts are extracted to form a dataset with sequences of feature tags. Then we train a CNN or LSTM model, using posting-style vectors pre-trained by Skip-Gram in the word embedding layer, to generate vector representations of posting styles. Finally, we concatenate these tag representations with the text representations, as input to the fully connected softmax module (see Fig. 2). We set two combinations of (text, CNN) ⊕ (feature tags, CNN) and (text, LSTM) ⊕ (feature tags, LSTM), where each bracket represents (input sequence, neural network model).

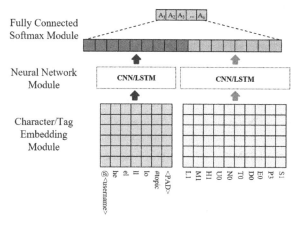

Fig. 2. Proposed model with latent posting styles.

4 Experiments

In the experiments, we use the Twitter dataset from Schwartz et al. [11], which contains about 9000 Twitter users with up to 1000 posts for each user, and approximately 9 million posts in total. We employ 10-fold cross validation on all experiments.

Pre-Processing. Considering textual sparsity, we replace URLs, numbers, dates and time with tags 'U', 'N', 'D', 'T' respectively. Since @ and # may express different meanings in tweets, we distinguish mentions @<username> from occurrences of '@' in email addresses, emoticons ':@' and @ meant as 'at'. We also distinguish hashtags in the forms #<topic> from others.

Baselines. We construct a logistic regression classifier over TF-IDF scores of words as a baseline. We also refer to the experimental results of [12], which applies word-level or character-level word embeddings on CNN and LSTM models, for comparisons.

Our Models. We train CNN and LSTM models over word vectors of mixed words and character n-grams (n = 1, 2, 3) which are pre-trained by Skip-Gram. We further incorporate embeddings of latent posting styles, and evaluate their effectiveness over the above models. All the methods used for our experiments are listed in Table 1.

4.1 Experimental Details

The details of hyperparameters for our experiments are shown in Table 2.

In addition, we add a dropout layer with keep_prob of 0.5 to prevent the models from overfitting. We set the batch_size of 64 to process the data in batches for speeding up the model training process. We set a learning rate of 1e-3 and a learning rate decay of 0.9 to help the model converge while training. Besides, we introduce gradient clipping with the threshold set to 6.0 to solve the problem of gradient explosion. We limit the training epoch to 100 and screen out the best models with the minimum validation error.

Table 1. Overall methods and descriptions of our experiments.

Methods			Descriptions
Baselines		TF-IDF+LR	Calculate TF-IDF scores for words, then train a logistic regression classifier
		CNN-W	Train a CNN model over word embeddings. [12]
		CNN-n	Train a CNN model over embeddings of character n-grams (n = 1, 2). [12]
		LSTM-2	[12] evaluates an LSTM trained on bigrams
Our models	CNNs	CNN-WCn	Train a CNN model over embeddings of mixed words and character n-grams (n = 1, 2, 3)
		CNN-WCn+LPS	Combinations of latent posting styles (LPS) with CNN-WCn (n = 1, 2, 3)
	LSTMs	LSTM-WCn	Train a LSTM model over embeddings of mixed words and character n-grams (n = 1, 2, 3)
		LSTM-WCn+LPS	Combinations of latent posting styles (LPS) with LSTM-WCn (n = 1, 2, 3)

WC: mixed words and character n-grams. LPS: latent posting styles.

Table 2. Hyperparameters for CNN and LSTM models.

Layer	Hyperparameters		
		WC	LPS
Embedding	length	140	10
	dimension	300	100
CNN	filter_sizes	[3, 4, 5]	[2, 3]
	num_filters	[128, 128, 128]	[64, 64]
	pooling	max	
LSTM	architecture	bi-directional	
	hidden_dim	128	64
Fully connected	# of units	Depends on the number of authors	

WC: mixed words and character n-grams. LPS: latent posting styles.

4.2 Basic Results

We randomly select 10 groups of datasets containing 50 users and their 1000 tweets each. We evaluate the average accuracy of the models on the 10 groups of datasets with cross validation on training sets. The experimental results are shown in Table 3.

Table 3. Accuracy for 50 authors with 1000 tweets each.

Baselines		Our methods			
		CNNs		LSTMs	
TF-IDF+LR	0.674	CNN-WC1	0.815	LSTM-WC1	0.717
CNN-W	0.548	CNN-WC2	0.828	LSTM-WC2	0.739
CNN-1	0.757	CNN-WC3	0.798	LSTM-WC3	0.701
CNN-2	0.761	CNN-WC1+LPS	0.824	LSTM-WC1+LPS	0.744
LSTM-2	0.645	CNN-WC2+LPS	**0.836**	LSTM-WC2+LPS	0.762
		CNN-WC3+LPS	0.806	LSTM-WC3+LPS	0.725

From the baselines, we can observe that although the traditional machine learning method (TF-IDF+LR) can achieve a good accuracy of 0.674, the deep learning methods have greater potential for improvement. The CNN models far surpass the LSTM models in performance with character embeddings. Besides, the CNN models with character embeddings far outperform those with word embeddings. In the baseline system, CNN-2 achieves the best accuracy of 0.761, which is the state-of-the-art result on this dataset.

Our proposed models contribute to significant improvements over the baselines. Our method of using embeddings of mixed words and character n-grams outperforms the character n-gram embeddings and achieves the best performance when n = 2. In addition, the CNN-based models are far superior to the LSTMs. Also, the method of introducing latent posting styles can effectively improve the models. CNN-WC2+LPS shows the best performance with an accuracy of 0.836, exceeding CNN-2 by 7.5%.

4.3 Varying Numbers of Authors

We further observe the performance of our models in more difficult scenarios, as Schwartz et al. did [11]. To discuss the situation when the number of authors increases, we conduct several series of experiments using the groups of 100, 200, 500, 1000 authors and 200 tweets each. Considering that our models perform obviously worse when n = 3 than when n = 1, 2, we omit experiments when n = 3. The experimental results are presented in Table 4. Although the increase in the number of authors makes AA tasks more difficult, our CNN-based models still have clear advantages over all baselines, and our LSTM-based models are still better than LSTM-2 and CNN-W.

Table 4. Accuracy for varying numbers of authors with 200 tweets each.

Methods			Number of authors			
			100	200	500	1000
Baselines		TF-IDF+LR	0.454	0.453	0.411	0.384
		CNN-W	0.241	0.208	0.161	0.127
		CNN-1	0.508	0.473	0.417	0.359
		CNN-2	0.506	0.481	0.422	0.365
		LSTM-2	0.338	0.335	0.298	0.248
Our models	CNNs	CNN-WC1	0.580	0.556	0.509	0.453
		CNN-WC2	0.598	0.590	0.555	0.489
		CNN-WC1+LPS	0.609	0.590	0.551	0.508
		CNN-WC2+LPS	**0.616**	**0.599**	**0.564**	**0.510**
	LSTMs	LSTM-WC1	0.414	0.338	0.308	0.253
		LSTM-WC2	0.428	0.357	0.324	0.259
		LSTM-WC1+LPS	0.435	0.358	0.321	0.265
		LSTM-WC2+LPS	0.458	0.386	0.339	0.288

5   Conclusion

This paper proposes new approaches for authorship attribution on short texts. The superior performance of the CNN model with character n-gram embeddings has inspired us to propose an improved method that uses mixed words and character n-grams instead of just character n-grams. We set up two sets of comparative experiments to test our ideas on CNNs and LSTMs. Experiments prove that our methods show clear advantages for solving AA problems on short texts. In addition, we capture ten latent posting styles from each tweet and the introduction of the latent posting styles into the network architecture shows further improvements. Our best method achieves an accuracy of 83.6%, which is 7.5% improvement over the state-of-the-art result. Furthermore, as the number of authors increases, the AA tasks become more difficult. Nevertheless, our models have clear advantages.

References

1. Bagnall, D.: Author identification using multi-headed recurrent neural network. arXiv preprint arXiv:1506.04891 (2015)
2. Chen, J., Hu, Y., Liu, J., et al.: Deep short text classification with knowledge powered attention. In: Proceedings of the AAAI Conference on Artificial Intelligence, vol. 33, pp. 6252–6259 (2019)
3. Hua, W., Wang, Z., Wang, H., et al.: Short text understanding through lexical-semantic analysis. In: 31st International Conference on Data Engineering, pp. 495–506. IEEE (2015)

4. Koppel, M., Winter, Y.: Determining if two documents are written by the same author. J. Assoc. Inf. Sci. Technol. **65**(1), 178–187 (2014)
5. Layton, R., Watters, P., Dazeley, R.: Authorship attribution for twitter in 140 characters or less. In: 2nd Cybercrime and Trustworthy Computing Workshop, pp. 1–8. IEEE (2010)
6. Leepaisomboon, P., Iwaihara, M.: Utilizing latent posting style for authorship attribution on short texts. In: Intl Conf CBDCom 2019, pp. 1015–1022. IEEE (2019)
7. Lin, Y., Wang, X., Zhou, A.: Opinion Analysis for Online Reviews, vol. 4. World Scientific (2016)
8. Malik, U.: Python for NLP: introduction to the textblob library. Stack Abuse https://stacka buse.com/python-for-nlp-introduction-to-the-textblob-library/. Accessed 15 Apr 2019
9. Rhodes, D.: Author attribution with CNNs (2015). https://www.semanticscholar.org/paper/ Author-Attribution-with-Cnn-s-Rhodes/0a904f9d6b47dfc574f681f4d3b41bd840871b6f/ pdf. Accessed 22 Aug 2016
10. Ruder, S., Ghaffari, P., Breslin, J.G.: Character-level and multi-channel convolutional neural networks for large-scale authorship attribution. arXiv preprint arXiv:1609.06686 (2016)
11. Schwartz, R., Tsur, O., Rappoport, A., et al.: Authorship attribution of micromessages. In: Proceedings of the 2013 Conference on Empirical Methods in Natural Language Processing, pp. 1880–1891 (2013)
12. Shrestha, P., Sierra, S., González, F.A., et al.: Convolutional neural networks for authorship attribution of short texts. In: Proceedings of the 15th Conference of the European Chapter of the Association for Computational Linguistics, vol. 2, pp. 669–674. Valencia (2017)
13. Stamatatos, E.: A survey of modern authorship attribution methods. J. Am. Soc. Inform. Sci. Technol. **60**(3), 538–556 (2009)
14. Tai, K.S., Socher, R., Manning, C.D.: Improved semantic representations from tree-structured long short-term memory networks. arXiv preprint arXiv:1503.00075 (2015)
15. Tang, D., Qin, B., Liu, T.: Document modeling with gated recurrent neural network for sentiment classification. In: Proceedings of the 2015 Conference on Empirical Methods in Natural Language Processing, pp. 1422–1432 (2015)
16. Wang, J., Wang, Z., Zhang, D., et al.: Combining knowledge with deep convolutional neural networks for short text classification. In: IJCAI, pp. 2915–2921 (2017)

Utilizing BERT Pretrained Models with Various Fine-Tune Methods for Subjectivity Detection

Hairong Huo[✉] and Mizuho Iwaihara[✉]

Graduate School of Information, Production, and Systems, Waseda University,
Kitakyushu 808-0135, Japan
hairong.huo@ruri.waseda.jp, iwaihara@waseda.jp

Abstract. As an essentially antecedent task of sentiment analysis, subjectivity detection refers to classifying sentences to be subjective ones containing opinions, or objective and neutral ones without bias. In the situations where impartial language is required, such as Wikipedia, subjectivity detection could play an important part. Recently, pretrained language models have proven to be effective in learning representations, profoundly boosting the performance among several NLP tasks. As a state-of-art pretrained model, BERT is trained on large unlabeled data with masked word prediction and next sentence prediction tasks. In this paper, we mainly explore utilizing BERT pretrained models with several combinations of fine-tuning methods, holding the intention to enhance performance in subjectivity detection task. Our experimental results reveal that optimum combinations of fine-tune and multi-task learning surplus the state-of-the-art on subjectivity detection and related tasks.

Keywords: Subjectivity detection · Fine-tuning · Multi-task learning · Pretrained language model · BERT

1 Introduction

In natural language processing research, a wide variety of methods have been attempted to interpret information implied in written texts, since knowing the ideas and minds hidden behind the texts is essential to profoundly understand our life in many aspects. Among all the research directions, sentiment analysis, also known as opinion mining, is the study field on estimating people's opinions, sentiments, feelings, as well as attitudes towards objects, news, issues, markets, etc. [9, 29]. Recently, with the dramatic increase of opinionated statements, growing research effort has been paid on sentiment analysis as well as its subtask, subjectivity detection [14]. As an essentially antecedent task of sentiment analysis, subjectivity detection task seeks classifying a sentence into objective and neutral ones without any bias, or instead, subjective and biased ones [15].

© Springer Nature Switzerland AG 2020
X. Wang et al. (Eds.): APWeb-WAIM 2020, LNCS 12318, pp. 270–284, 2020.
https://doi.org/10.1007/978-3-030-60290-1_21

As examples of subjective language introducing bias and objective one, consider the following statements:

- *Scientologists hold the belief that living cells have a memory. This is based on an* **erroneous** *interpretation of the work of Crick and Watson in 1955.* (**opinion, not a fact**)
- *Scientologists hold the belief that living cells have a memory. This is based on an interpretation of the work of Crick and Watson in 1955.* (**fact, not an opinion**)

In the above instances, the word *erroneous* introduces bias, causing the statement being partial.

Generally, one has to classify a sentence as subjective or objective, then the resulting subjective sentence is classified as positive or negative [29]. Also, in collaborative environments where people around the world share information upon, such as Wikipedia, fair-and-square language is desired [6, 8]. Moreover, scenarios like news report will require content to be impartial and deliver objective information to readers. All these reasons make subjectivity detection vital in NLP research.

Although many researches utilize deep learning models to achieve the state-of-art on many NLP tasks as well as subjectivity detection task here, these models require large amounts of datasets, and computational resources to train from scratch. Alternatively, plentiful researches have proven that pretraining language models based on large corpus and fine tuning them on task specific datasets can be beneficial for various NLP tasks including subjectivity detection [5, 7]. The concept and methodology have been widely used in the computer vision (CV) area. By merely fine-tuning the pre-trained model based on a large dataset such as ImageNet can generate great results on a specific task, without training everything from scratch. Inspired by the benefits of pretraining, various carefully designed language models have recently emerged, such as OpenAI GPT [20], UMLFit [7] and BERT [5]. Built on multi-layer bidirectional Transformer [25] blocks, BERT is trained on huge datasets based on two tasks: masked word prediction and next sentence prediction. As the first fine-tuning based representation model, BERT has showed its effectiveness in several NLP tasks. However, there is little research with respect to enhancing performance utilizing BERT further towards target tasks and possible combinations with other strategies. BERT's potential has not been thoroughly explored, which leaves us space to search further.

To this end, the contributions of our paper are as follows:

- We discuss utilizing the standard BERT pretrained language model to fine-tune towards the subjectivity detection and related tasks. We observed that utilizing standard BERT fine-tuning can improve the performance significantly and spared the need of complex neural classifiers.
- We then further explore several fine-tuning strategies with BERT, such as discriminative fine-tuning, multi-task learning, etc. Among our experiments, there is a significant improvement in multi-task learning strategy with shared BERT layers. In fact, by utilizing multi-task learning with 4 tasks and 6 datasets, we can achieve the state-of-the-art result in Wikipedia biased statement dataset, and generalize results close to SOTA on SUBJ dataset.

The rest of this paper is organized as follows: Sect. 2 covers related work. Section 3 describes methodologies. Section 4 shows experimental results, and Sect. 5 is a conclusion.

2 Related Work

2.1 Subjectivity Detection

Although compared to sentiment analysis, researches conducted on subjectivity detection are relatively less, there exists outstanding works regarding the subjectivity task. Chenghua Lin et al. [11] present a hierarchical Bayesian model based on latent Dirichlet allocation (LDA) for subjectivity detection. Instead of designing models based on a pre-labelled dataset or linguistic pattern extraction, they regard subjectivity detection as weakly-supervised generative model learning. Moreover, as the largest collaborative online encyclopedia characterized by free editorial content around the world, there are substantial works [1, 6, 8, 17] conducted on Wikipedia for distinguishing biased statements from impartial language. Desislava et al. [1] propose a multilingual method for detection of biased statements in Wikipedia and creates corpora in Bulgarian, French and English. They utilize a multinomial logistic regression algorithm on top of pretrained word embeddings. Christoph et al. [6] propose a feature-based supervised classification method to detect biased and subjective language in Wikipedia. They achieved detection accuracy of 74% on a dataset consisting of biased and unbiased statements. However, utilizing manually constructed features can be incomprehensive. Christoph et al. [8] present a neural-based model with hierarchical attention mechanism to solve the problem. In their work, they first crawl Wikipedia revision history that have a "POV" flag, that is "point of view," suggesting certain statements containing opinions and subjective ideas towards entities. Additionally, to improve the quality of the original dataset, they use crowdsourcing to filter statements that do not contain bias and subjective information. They finally release the largest corpus of statements annotated for biased language and are able to distinguish biased statements with a precision of 0.917.

2.2 Pretrained Language Model

Although deep neural models can be impressive in the related researches, it demands large labeled datasets to train from scratch [24]. Instead, utilizing pretrained representations and fine-tuning methods can alleviate the problem. Howard et al. [7] propose a universal language model fine-tuning (UMLFit), pretrained on Wikitext-103 consisting of 28,595 Wikipedia articles to capture semantic and syntactic information. Their method significantly surpasses the state-of-art models on six text classification tasks. Meanwhile, Devlin et al. [5] release BERT, the first fine-tuning based representation model that achieves the state-of-the art results on various NLP tasks, making a huge breakthrough in related research areas. Trained on a large cross-domain corpus, BERT is designed for two pretrained tasks: masked language model task and next sentence prediction task. Different from UMLFit, BERT is not limited to a simple combination of two unidirectional language models. Instead, BERT utilizes masked language model to predict words which are masked at random to capture bidirectional and contextual information.

Indeed, BERT is a state-of-art model outperforming in a variety of NLP tasks, demonstrating its effectiveness and potential. In this paper, we aim to explore the fine-tuning methods of BERT for subjectivity detection task, with intention to explore optimum fine-tuning strategies.

3 Methodologies

One of the most remarkable features about BERT is that merely utilizing the released BERT model and fine-tuning it can generate relatively good results, especially on small datasets, like the case in subjectivity detection.

3.1 How to Fine-Tune BERT for Subjectivity Task?

In our work, we utilize BERT-base model released by Google AI as pretrained language model. A BERT-base model consists of a large encoder built with 12 transformer blocks and 12 self-attention heads, with hidden size of 768. The input of BERT Model is a sequence with length no longer than 512 tokens, while the output of BERT is the representation of the whole sequence. Meanwhile, there are two special tokens in BERT: [CLS], which contains the classification embedding information, while token [SEP] is utilized for separating segments of input. Our goal is to separate subjective statements with bias from objective and unbiased ones. For this kind of single sentence classification problem, we can simply plug task-specific inputs into the BERT architecture, and after multi-layer transformer blocks, the final hidden state h of the first token [CLS] in the last layer can be viewed as the ultimate representation of the whole sequence. Then, whether a simple classifier like softmax or other more complicated methods like Long Short Term Memory Network (LSTM) can be added upon the top of BERT to do a classification task.

3.2 Layer-Wise Discriminative Fine-Tuning

In addition to applying a simple classifier like softmax or other more complex ones such as LSTM, we further explore several fine-tuning strategies to help improve the performance. The first method is *layer-wise discriminative fine-tuning* proposed by Howard and Ruder [7]. A BERT model contains a deep encoder consisting of 12 transformer blocks, in other words, the BERT model has 12 layers and each of them is responsible to capture information with different extent. As a matter of course, these layers should be fine-tuned with different extent consistently. To this end, layer-wise discriminative learning rate for each layer is necessary. Instead of allocating all layers with a same learning rate like typical regular stochastic gradient descent (SGD), we choose to give each layer a different learning rate. In regular stochastic gradient descent, the parameters are updated by the following equation:

$$\theta_t = \theta_{t-1} - \eta . \nabla_\theta J(\theta) \tag{1}$$

where η is the learning rate, and $\nabla_\theta J(\theta)$ is the gradient with respect to the model's objective function. As for layer-wise discriminative learning rate, we replace single η with multiple learning rates collection $\{\eta^1, \dots, \eta^L\}$, where η^l denotes the learning rate of l-th layer and L is the total number of the layers. Similarly, we can obtain the parameters $\{\theta^1, \dots, \theta^L\}$, where θ^l consists of the parameters of the l-th layer. By using layer-wise discriminative learning rate, the update of the parameters can be shown as follows:

$$\theta_t^l = \theta_{t-1}^l - \eta^l \nabla_{\theta^l} J(\theta) \tag{2}$$

During the experiment part, we set the initial learning rate as 2e-5 and utilize $\eta^{l-1} = \eta^l/1.1$ as the learning rate for lower layers. Thus, the lower layers tend to have a lower learning rate than higher layers. Intuitively, the lower layers of BERT may contain more general information while higher layer contains more specific information.

3.3 One Cycle Policy

Learning rate is an essential hyperparameter in the neural network, but how to choose an appropriate learning rate can be a subtle and tricky problem, which has perplexed the researchers for a long time. The small learning rate might make the model to converge slowly, leading to a long training time, while a large one may also contribute to diverging.

Leslie N. Smith [23] proposes the strategy *one cycle policy*. In simple terms, one-cycle-policy uses a periodic learning rate. Periodic learning rate here means that firstly starting from a relatively small learning rate, then slowly increases to a higher learning rate, and then decreases. The motivation behind one cycle policy is that during the middle of learning when learning rate is higher, the learning rate works as regularization method to some extent and keep model away from over-fitting. This helps model to avoid steep areas of loss and land better as well as flatter minima. It is a modification of the cyclical learning rate policy [22]. But one cycle policy allows a large initial learning rate (e.g : $LR_{MAX} = 10^{-3}$). This seems to provide greater accuracy.

The schedule of implementing one cycle policy learning rate strategy is described as below:

Initial Learning Rate. We first choose the maximum learning rate according to the LR range test [22]. The idea here is that we need to use a learning rate (lr_{max}) in an order of magnitude lower than the point where the loss of the model starts to diverge. That is, if the learning rate is below 0.01 and the loss of the model starts to diverge, then 0.01 should be the initial learning rate lr_{max}. After choosing the appropriate initial learning rate lr_{max}, we then set the minimum learning rate lr_{min} equal to 1/10 of maximum learning rate lr_{max}.

$$lr_{min} = \frac{1}{10} * lr_{max} \tag{3}$$

Cyclical Momentum. After setting the initial learning rate lr_{max}, we then gradually increase the learning rate from lr_{min} to lr_{max} by utilizing the cyclical momentum. In the experiment part, we pick two values for maximum and minimum momentum: 0.9 and

0.8. As we increase the learning rate from lr_{min} to lr_{max}, the momentum is decreased from mom_{max} to mom_{min} (warm-up step). Then go back to the higher momentum as the learning rate goes down (cool-down step).

Annihilation Phase. The third step is annihilation. As the last part of training, we decrease the learning rate up to a value equal to 1/100 of minimum learning rate and keep the momentum steady at mom_{max}.

$$\begin{cases} lr_{annihilation} = \frac{1}{100} * lr_{min} \\ mom_{annihilation} = mom_{max} \end{cases} \tag{4}$$

The following image shows the one cycle policy learning rate strategy (Fig. 1):

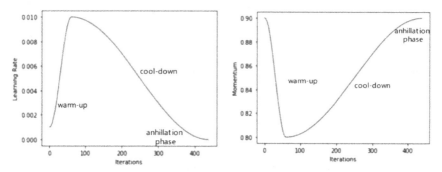

Fig. 1. 1 cycle policy strategy.

3.4 Gradual Unfreezing

In transfer learning, there is a common problem of *catastrophic forgetting*, which refers to the phenomenon such that pretrained knowledge is lessened during the process of learning new knowledge. To overcome this problem, we adopt the strategy called *gradual unfreezing* [7]. For gradual unfreezing, rather than fine-tuning all layers at once, which is likely to lead to catastrophic forgetting, we first unfreeze the last layer of BERT and fine-tune for one epoch, while the remained layers are frozen. Then, we unfreeze the next frozen layer and fine-tune all the unfrozen layers. The rest can be done in the same manner.

3.5 Multi-task Learning

Motivations. In the research field of transfer learning, there has always been a prevalent interest in multi-task learning, since by utilizing multi-task learning instead of training single task separately, the performance has been improved in vast domains from computer vision to natural language processing [3, 28]. With the purpose of improving the performance as well as enhancing the learning efficiency, multi-task learning refers to learning several tasks jointly, so that the knowledge learned in a single task can benefit others. Intuitively, in real life, people often apply the knowledge learned from previous experiences in the new tasks. Generally, as soon as optimizing more than one loss function is done, it is effectively equivalent to do multi-task learning in contrast to single-task learning [19]. The motivations behind multi-task learning can be divided into the following aspects.

Data Augmentation. Traditional supervised neural networks require large amounts of labelled datasets to train from scratch, especially for the deep and complex networks. However, the chances are that such large-scale datasets cannot be always available. By incorporating several tasks as well as datasets, the sample size used for training can be enlarged, which can be helpful for the low-resource task.

Regularization. Multi-task learning can provide the regularization effect to some extent by introducing an inductive bias. Learning single task tends to bear the risk of overfitting, while learning several tasks simultaneously enables levitating the problem, leading to a better universal representation through all the tasks.

In the meanwhile, pretrained language models have proven to be effective in learning universal representations by leveraging plenty of unlabeled data, such as BERT. BERT is built with multi-layer bidirectional transformer blocks trained on two unsupervised objectives: masked word prediction and next sentence prediction. To apply a BERT pretrained language model to a specific task, traditionally, we often fine-tune BERT for each task separately, with task-specific layer and training datasets. There have been several studies [12, 24] arguing that multi-task learning and pretrained language model are complementary technologies and thus, can be combined together to boost the performance and generalize a better universal representation. To this end, we utilize multi-task learning strategy with shared BERT representation layers, with the intention to enhance the performance t our main task: subjectivity detection.

Task. We list several NLP tasks as following as our auxiliary tasks, with the intention to generate a better universal representation and improve the performance towards our main task: subjectivity detection task.

(a) *Pair-wise text similarity task.*
For pair-wise text similarity task, its goal is to determine the similarity of two given texts. As a regression task, the output should be a real-valued score, indicating the semantic similarity of two pieces of texts. Given a pair of texts (x_1, x_2), to apply BERT to the text similarity task, we can take the final hidden state x of token [CLS] in BERT structure, which can be viewed as the representation of the whole sequence pair (x_1, x_2). The similarity score can be computed as follows:

$$SIM_{(x_1, x_2)} = W_{SIM}^T \cdot x \tag{5}$$

where W_{SIM}^T is the task specific parameter matrix. Since the text similarity task is a regression task, we utilize the mean squared error as the loss function:

$$LOSS = \frac{1}{n} \sum_{i=1}^{n} \left(y - SIM_{(x_1, x_2)} \right)^2 \tag{6}$$

(b) *Pair-wise text classification task.*
Pair-wise text classification task refers to predicting the relationship between two texts based on a set of predefined labels. For instance, given a set of premises P and hypothesis H, the goal is to find the logical relationship R (i.e., entailment, neutral, contradiction) between P and H. When applying BERT to this task, given a pair of texts (x_1, x_2) and x denoting the final hidden state of [CLS] token, the probability that x is labeled as class c (i.e., entailment) is predicted by a softmax classifier:

$$P(c|x) = softmax\left(W_{pairwise}^T \cdot x\right) \tag{7}$$

where $W_{pairwise}^T$ is the task-specific parameter matrix. Since this is a classification problem, we utilize cross entropy as the loss function:

$$LOSS = - \sum_i y_i \cdot \log(P(c|x)) \tag{8}$$

(c) *Relevance ranking task.*
Given a query and a list of candidate answers, the goal of relevance ranking task is to rank all the candidates in the order of relevance to the query. When applying BERT to this task, suppose that x denotes the final hidden state of [CLS] token, and the input is a pair of query Q and candidates collection A, the relevance score can be computed as following equation:

$$Relevance(Q, A) = g\left(W_{relevance}^T \cdot x\right) \tag{9}$$

where $W_{relevance}^T$ is the task specific parameter matrix. For a given query, the candidates can be ranked on the basis of relevance score. Following the study of Liu et al. [12], we utilize the pairwise learning-to-rank paradigm [2]. Given a query Q, we can obtain a list of candidate answers A which contains a positive example A^+ that includes the correct answer, and $|A| - 1$ negative examples. We then minimize the negative log-likelihood of the positive example given queries across the training data:

$$LOSS = - \sum_{(Q,A^+)} P_r(A^+|Q) \tag{10}$$

$$P_r\left(A^+|Q\right) = \frac{\exp\left(Relevance(Q, A^+)\right)}{\sum_{A' \in A} \exp(Relevance(Q, A'))} \tag{11}$$

(d) *Single sentence classification task.*
This task refers to classifying a single sentence into a pre-defined label. As an important research branch of single sentence classification, subjectivity detection task is our main task here. We also incorporate biased statement detection task in Wikipedia as a related task to subjectivity detection. To apply BERT to this task, we take the final hidden state x of [CLS] token as the representation of the whole sequence. The probability that x is labeled as class c (i.e., subjective) is predicted by a softmax classifier:

$$P(c|x) = softmax\left(W_{classification}^T \cdot x\right) \tag{12}$$

where $W^T_{classification}$ is the task specific parameter matrix. For the classification problem, we utilize cross entropy as our loss function:

$$LOSS = -\sum_i y_i \cdot \log(P(c|x)) \qquad (13)$$

Multi-task Learning with Shared BERT Layer

(a) *Utilizing BERT-base model as pretrained representation.* The architecture of combining multi-task learning with BERT as shared representation layer is shown in Fig. 2, where the lower layers are shared among four tasks, while the top layers are task-specific layers, corresponding to four tasks. The input of the shared BERT layer can be a single sentence or a pair of sentences, then, the sentences will be first represented as a set of embedding vectors, consisting of the word, position and segment embedding. Then, the main components of BERT, 12 transformer blocks, are responsible for capturing the contextual information, and then the contextual embeddings will be generated.

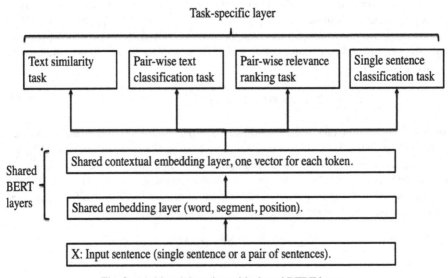

Fig. 2. Multi-task learning with shared BERT layers.

(b) *Multi-task learning upon BERT.* The above shared BERT layers are task-specific layers corresponding to different tasks. Our main task is the single sentence classification. By incorporating BERT with multi-task learning, our goal is to further enhance the performance for subjectivity detection, since compared to other tasks, subjectivity task can be viewed as a task that lacks sufficient labelled samples, where multi-task learning strategy might play a role.

(c) *Further fine-tuning with a task-specific dataset.* In order to improve the performance, we further fine-tune the learned model with a task-specific dataset to generate the final result.

4 Experiments

4.1 Datasets

STS-B Dataset [4]. The Semantic Textual Similarity Benchmark (STS-B) dataset is a collection of sentence pairs drawn from news headlines, video and image captions, and natural language inference data. Given a pair of texts (x_1, x_2), the goal is to compute the similarity between x_1 and x_2, returning a similarity score ranging from 0 to 5. The dataset consists of 8,628 sentences pairs.

SNLI Dataset [21]. The Stanford Natural Language Inference (SNLI) dataset, consisting of 570,152 sentence pairs, is a collection written by human, and is manually labeled with pre-defined three labels: entailment, neutral and contradiction. Given a pair of texts (x_1, x_2), the task is to predict the relationship between them and output the label among entailment, neutral and contradiction.

QNLI Dataset [18]. The Stanford Question Answering (QNLI) dataset is a question-answering dataset consisting of 115,669 question-paragraph pairs. While the question is manually written by an annotator, the paragraph is drawn from Wikipedia containing the answer to the question. Although QNLI is originally defined as a binary classification task to predict whether the paragraph contains the answer to corresponding question or not, following Liu et al. [12], we formulate the problem as pair-wise relevance ranking to evaluate the classification quality. Given a question Q and a set of candidates A containing the correct answer A^+, the goal of the task is to rank the correct answer A^+ higher than the $|A| - 1$ candidates that do not contain the right answers.

SUBJ Dataset [16]. As a specialized dataset for subjectivity detection task, subjectivity dataset (SUBJ) consists of 1346 hand-annotated documents drawn from the top-20 webpages retrieved by the Yahoo! search engine in response to 69 real user queries. The annotations of the dataset indicate whether the statements are subjective or objective. In total, the dataset consists of 5,000 subjective and 5,000 objective sentences.

Wikipedia Biased Statements [8]. This dataset was released by Christoph Hube and Besnik Fetahu. The dataset is constructed with two steps: (1) First they extract POV-tagged statements from Wikipedia, suggesting that the statements are against the "Neutral point of view (NPOV)" principle in Wikipedia. However, the quality of the raw dataset is not satisfying. (2) Then, they utilize crowdsourcing to manually construct ground-truth. Finally, the released dataset consists of 1843 biased statements, 3109 neutral ones, 1843 neutral ones from featured articles in Wikipedia and 1843 neutral ones from featured articles equipped with same type-balanced distribution in biased statements. In the experiment part, we choose biased statements and featured neutral statements with similar type-balanced distribution. In addition to subjectivity detection task, we incorporate Wikipedia biased statement detection task as a related task.

IMDb Dataset [13]. IMDb is a binary sentiment analysis dataset consisting of 50,000 reviews from the Internet Movie Database (IMDb), labeled as positive or negative. The dataset contains an even number of positive and negative reviews.

4.2   Implementation Details

Our experiments are based on PyTorch implementation of BERT. We utilize the BERT-base uncased model consisting of 12 layer transformer blocks and 12 heads as well as 768 hidden units, 110 M parameters in total. As for optimizer, we utilize Adam optimizer [10] with $\beta_1 = 0.9$ and $\beta_2 = 0.99$. We set the batch size to 32, the number of epochs to 5 and dropout probability to 0.1. The base learning rate is 2e−5, while the maximum and minimum momentum are 0.9 and 0.8, respectively (Table 1).

Table 1. Datasets and tasks summary.

Dataset	Dataset size	Label	Task
STS-B	8,628	1	Pair-wise text similarity task
SNLI	570,152	3	Pair-wise text classification task
QNLI	115,669	2	Relevance ranking task
SUBJ	10,000	2	Subjectivity detection task (single sentence classification, main task)
Wikipedia biased statements	3,686	2	Subjectivity detection task (single sentence classification, main task)
IMDb	50,000	2	Single sentence classification

4.3   Results

Since our main task is subjectivity detection task and we incorporate Wikipedia biased statement detection task as a related task, the following experiments and results will focus on the SUBJ and Wikipedia biased statements datasets. In order to evaluate the impact of each fine-tuning strategy on subjectivity detection, three baseline models will be used: (1) Standard BERT-base fine-tuning without applying any fine-tuning strategies. (2) BERT-base model with LSTM network. (3) BERT-base model with Bi-LSTM network.

Moreover, we compare our methods with the current state-of-art models as far as we know for each dataset. For SUBJ dataset, we compare with AdaSent [27]. For Wikipedia biased statement, we compare our model against the neural-based model with hierarchical attention proposed by Hube et al. [8]. Also, although our main task is subjectivity detection, we include IMDb dataset in our experiment result, since it is a single sentence classification task just like SUBJ and Wikipedia biased statements. For the IMDb dataset, we compare our model with XLNet [26].

To keep consistency, we report all results by accuracy. Table 2 shows our experimental results on the three classification tasks.

Impact of Different Classifiers Upon BERT First, we investigate the impact of choosing different classifiers upon BERT. In addition to applying a simple softmax classifier, we choose prevalent neural networks LSTM and Bi-LSTM to see whether

Table 2. Experimental results.

Model	SUBJ	Wikipedia biased statement	IMDb
State-of-art			
AdaSent (Zhao et al. 2015)	95.5	/	/
Neural-based model with attention mechanism (Hube et al. 2019)	/	80.8	/
XLNet (Yang et al. 2019)	/	/	96.21
Baseline models			
BERT-base fine-tuning	94.2	81.56	91.51
BERT-base –LSTM	92.94	80.42	87.4
BERT-base -BiLSTM	92.48	80.94	87.46
Fine-tuning strategies			
BERT-base (Discriminative)	94.18	81.61	91.13
BERT-base (1 cycle policy)	94.53	82.17	91.43
BERT-base (Gradual unfreezing)	93.98	81.29	91.47
BERT-base (MTL, 3 datasets)	95.02	83.04	92.86
BERT-base (MTL, 6 datasets)	**95.23**	83.81	**93.07**
BERT-base (MTL, 6 datasets and 1 cycle policy)	95.18	**84.05**	92.98

choosing a more sophisticated method would boost the performance or not. The result in Table 2 shows that choosing a more complex classifier does not improve the performance. Instead, it would rather decrease the accuracy on the three classification tasks, which makes sense since BERT already consists of deep networks as well as sophisticated training strategies. Adopting a more complex classifier is not a compulsory option.

Impact of Layer-Wise Discriminative Fine-Tuning. To investigate the influence of each fine-tuning strategy on performance, we further utilize the BERT-base model with the combination with each strategy separately. As for discriminative fine-tuning, the result in Table 2 shows that there was no significant improvement in accuracy.

Impact of One Cycle Policy. In applying the one cycle policy, we observe an improvement on the performance. Compared to the basic BERT fine-tuning, utilizing one cycle policy would boost the performance on SUBJ around 0.3% from standard BERT fine-tuning, while 0.6% on Wikipedia biased statement dataset from standard BERT fine-tuning as well. However, one cycle policy does not show improvement on IMDb. Nevertheless, one cycle policy proves to be effective on smaller datasets, suggesting its ability to prevent over-fitting problem.

Impact of Gradual Unfreezing. As for the gradual unfreezing strategy, the result shows that applying gradual unfreezing does not help the model to outperform a standard BERT fine-tuning.

Impact of Multi-task Learning. (1) For the evaluation of multi-task learning, we first utilize three classification datasets: SUBJ, Wikipedia biased statement and IMDb. The result shows that there is a significant improvement on the three classification datasets, suggesting that BERT and multi-task learning can be complementary. (2) To further investigate the influence of choosing a wider range of tasks, we then utilize four tasks and six datasets completely. Not only the result improves compared to standard BERT-base fine-tuning, but also surpasses the result of only utilizing the three classification tasks. In fact, we achieve the best result both on SUBJ and IMDb datasets with accuracy of 95.23% and 93.07%, demonstrating the effectiveness of multi-task learning with using a wider range of tasks.

Impact of the Combination of MTL and 1 Cycle Policy. Since we find that one cycle policy and multi-task learning can both be effective on boosting performance with BERT, how is the case utilizing both of them? The experimental result shows that there is a slight improvement on the Wikipedia biased statement dataset, and we achieve the best accuracy 84.05% on it by combining multi-task learning and one cycle policy, surpassing the best result from [8], while there is no sign of outperforming than merely utilizing multi-task learning on SUBJ and IMDb dataset.

5   Conclusion

In this paper, we first investigated how to utilize a standard BERT fine-tuning for subjectivity detection task, then compared the performance of different classifiers upon BERT, proving that using BERT can spare the need of complex neural classifiers. In addition, we discussed several fine-tuning strategies and conducted experiments on classification task. Among our experiments, there is a significant improvement by the combination of one cycle policy and multi-task learning strategy on Wikipedia biased statement dataset, surpassing the best result from [8], while utilizing multi-task learning with six datasets and four tasks can achieve satisfying results on SUBJ and IMDb datasets. Moreover, experiments prove that choosing a wider range of tasks in multi-task learning can benefit the results more than smaller range of tasks. There are a number of future directions to explore further, including the structure of information sharing mechanism inside multi-task learning.

References

1. Aleksandrova, D., Lareau, F., Ménard, P.: Multilingual Sentence-Level Bias Detection in Wikipedia (2019)
2. Burges, C.J.C., Ragno, R., Le, Q.V.: Learning to rank with nonsmooth cost functions. In: NIPS (2006)
3. Caruana, R.: Multitask learning: A knowledge-based source of inductive bias. Mach. Learn. **28**, 41–75 (1997)
4. Cer, D., Diab, M., Agirre, E., Lopez-Gazpio, I., Specia, L.: SemEval2017 Task 1: Semantic textual similarity multilingual and crosslingual focused evaluation. In: Proceedings f the 11th International Workshop Semantic Evaluation, August 2017, pp. 1–14

5. Devlin, J., Chang, M.-W., Lee, K., Toutanova, K.: Bert: pre-training of deep bidirectional transformers for language understanding (2018)
6. Hube, C., Fetahu, B.: Detecting biased statements in Wikipedia. In: The Web Conference, 1779–1786. International World Wide Web Conferences Steering Committee (2018)
7. Howard, J., Ruder, S.: Universal language model fine-tuning for text classification. In: Proceedings of the 56th Annual Meeting Association Computing Linguistics, vol. 1, pp. 328–339 (2018)
8. Hube, C., Fetahu, B.: Neural based statement classification for biased language. In: Proceedings of the Twelfth ACM International Conference on Web Search and Data Mining, 195–203. ACM (2019)
9. Karamibekr, M., Ghorbani, A.A.: Sentence subjectivity analysis in social domains. In: Proceedings of the IEEE/WIC/ACM International Conference on Web Intelligence (WI 2013), Atlanta, GA, USA (2013)
10. Kingma, D., Ba, J.: Adam: a method for stochastic optimization. In: ICLR (2015)
11. Lin, C., He, Y., Everson, R.: Sentence subjectivity detection with weakly-supervised learning. In: Proceedings of the 5th International Joint Conference on Natural Language Process, pp. 1153–1161, November 2011
12. Liu, X., He, P., Chen, W., Gao, J.: Multi-task deep neural networks for natural language understanding. In: Proceedings of the 57th Annual Meeting Association Computing Linguistics, pp. 4487–4496 (2019)
13. Maas, A.L., Daly, R.E., Pham, P.T., Huang, D., Ng, A.Y., Potts, C.: Learning word vectors for sentiment analysis. In: Proceedings of the 49th Annual Meeting Association Computing Linguistics, Human Language Technology vol. 1, pp. 142–150 (2011)
14. Montoyo, A., Martínez-Barco, P., Balahur, A.: Subjectivity and sentiment analysis: an overview of the current state of the area and envisaged developments. Decis. Supp. Syst. **53**(4), 675–679 (2012)
15. Mäntylä, M.V., Graziotin, D., Kuutila, M.: The evolution of sentiment analysis—a review of research topics venues and top cited papers. Comput. Sci. Rev. **27**, 16–32 (2018)
16. Pang, B., Lee, L.: A sentimental education: Sentiment analysis using subjectivity summarization based on minimum cuts. In: Proceedings of ACL 2004 (2004)
17. Recasens, M., Danescu-Niculescu-Mizil, C., Jurafsky, D.: Linguistic models for analyzing and detecting biased language. In: Proceedings of ACL (2013)
18. Rajpurkar, P., Zhang, J., Lopyrev, K., Liang, P.: Squad: 100,000 + Questions for Machine Comprehension of Text. In: EMNLP (2016)
19. Ruder, S.: An overview of multi-task learning in deep neural networks (2017). http://arxiv.org/abs/1706.05098
20. Radford, A., Narasimhan, K., Salimans, T., Sutskever, I.: Improving language understanding by generative pre-training (2018). https://blog.openai.com/language-unsupervised/
21. Bowman, S.R., Angeli, G., Potts, C., Manning, C,D.: A large annotated corpus for learning natural language inference. In: Proceedings of the 2015 Conference on Empirical Methods in Natural Language Processing, EMNLP 2015, Lisbon, Portugal, 17–21 September 2015, pp. 632–642 (2015)
22. Smith, L.N.: Cyclical learning rates for training neural networks. In: WACV (2017)
23. Smith, L.N.: A disciplined approach to neural network hyper-parameters: Part 1–learning rate, batch size, momentum, and weight decay. arXiv preprint arXiv:1803.09820 (2018)
24. Sun, C., Qiu, X., Xu, Y., Huang, X.: How to fine-tune BERT for text classification? arXiv: 1905.05583 (2019). https://arxiv.org/abs/1905.05583
25. A. Vaswani, N. Shazeer, N. Parmar, J. Uszkoreit, L. Jones, A. N. Gomez, L. Kaiser, I. Polosukhin, "Attention Is All You Need", *CoRR,* vol. abs/1706.03762, 2017

26. Yang, Z., Dai, Z., Yang, Y., Carbonell, J., Salakhutdinov, R., Le, Q.V.: XLNet: generalized autoregressive pretraining for language understanding arXiv:1906.08237 (2019). https://arxiv.org/abs/1906.08237

27. Zhao, H., Lu, Z., Poupart, P.: Self-adaptive hierarchical sentence model (2015). https://arxiv.org/abs/1504.05070

28. Zhang, Y., Yang, Q.: A survey on multi-task learning. arXiv preprint arXiv:1707.08114 (2017)

29. Zhang, L., Wang, S., Liu, B.: Deep learning for sentiment analysis: a survey. In: Wiley Interdisciplinary Reviews: Data Mining and Knowledge Discovery, p. 25, March 2018

A Framework for Learning Cross-Lingual Word Embedding with Topics

Xiaoya Peng and Dong Zhou[✉] [iD]

School of Computer Science and Engineering, Hunan University of Science and Technology,
Xiangtan 411201, Hunan, China
dongzhou1979@hotmail.com

Abstract. Cross-lingual word embeddings have been served as fundamental components for many Web-based applications. However, current models learn cross-lingual word embeddings based on projection of two pre-trained monolingual embeddings based on well-known models such as word2vec. This procedure makes it indiscriminative for some crucial factors of words such as homonymy and polysemy. In this paper, we propose a novel framework for learning better cross-lingual word embeddings with latent topics. In this framework, we firstly incorporate latent topical representations into the Skip-Gram model to learn high quality monolingual word embeddings. Then we use the supervised and unsupervised methods to train cross-lingual word embeddings with topical information. We evaluate our framework in the cross-lingual Web search tasks using the CLEF test collections. The results show that our framework outperforms previous state-of-the-art methods for generating cross-lingual word embeddings.

Keywords: Cross-lingual word embeddings · Topic models · Multilingual web · Cross-lingual web search

1 Introduction

With the increasing amount of multilingual digital content on the World Wide Web, users' demand for information acquisition tends to be diversified and complicated. This puts forward requirements for multilingual information access services. Under this premise, cross-lingual Web search or information retrieval system can help people bridge the language gap, for the quick and accurate retrieving of multilingual information [1]. Recently, cross-lingual word embedding that encodes the syntactic and semantic information of words into continuous vectors has become the most popular technology to implement cross-lingual Web search.

Cross-lingual word embedding models are a natural extension of the monolingual word embedding models. Words in different languages with similar concepts are very close to the word embeddings in the vector space [2, 3]. This enables us to reason about word meanings in multilingual contexts [4]. Cross-lingual representation of words is the key facilitator of cross-lingual transfer when developing related models, especially for low-resource languages. Projection or mapping has shown to be an effective way

© Springer Nature Switzerland AG 2020
X. Wang et al. (Eds.): APWeb-WAIM 2020, LNCS 12318, pp. 285–293, 2020.
https://doi.org/10.1007/978-3-030-60290-1_22

to learn bilingual word embeddings [5]. The underlying idea is to independently train embeddings in two different languages using monolingual corpora, and then map them to a shared space through a linear transformation [6–9]. However, current models learn cross-lingual word embeddings based on projection of two pre-trained monolingual embeddings based on well-known models such as word2vec. This procedure makes it indiscriminative for some crucial factors of words such as homonymy and polysemy. Moreover, it only uses the local context information to learn monolingual embeddings and ignores the global view of the entire corpus.

At the same time, topic models such as Latent Dirichlet Allocation (LDA) model [10] and its variants are widely used in various natural language processing and Web-based tasks [11, 12]. Topic models have proved to be powerful unsupervised tools that rely on word co-occurrences to derive topics from document collections. They usually take a global approach to consider all words equally in a document. On the contrary, word embedding models primarily focus on the word co-occurrences within small sliding windows (i.e. local information). Several researchers have already exploited this complementary representation between word embeddings and topic models [13–15] and achieved great improvements. However, their effectiveness has not been explored in the cross-lingual setting.

In this paper, we propose a novel cross-lingual word embedding learning framework that integrates topics learned by representative latent topic models. In this framework, we firstly incorporate latent topical representations into the well-known Skip-Gram model to learn high quality monolingual word embeddings. Then we use the supervised and unsupervised methods to train cross-lingual word embeddings with topical information.

To verify our proposed framework, we use the well-established CLEF[1] test collections for evaluating our framework. The experimental results show that our framework achieves better results than the baseline models. Our contributions in this paper can be summarized as follows:

- We propose a novel cross-lingual word embedding learning framework that integrates topics learned by representative latent topic models. Our framework outperforms previous state-of-the-art methods for generating cross-lingual word embeddings.
- We propose a novel way to jointly learn LDA model and Skip-Gram model. The new monolingual embeddings are subsequently used to train cross-lingual word embeddings with topical information.
- We present an intensive comparative evaluation where our framework achieves the state-of-the-art performance for many language pairs in cross-lingual Web search tasks.

2 Methodology

In this section, we will present the details of our proposed framework. We firstly introduce a simple but effective modified Skip-Gram model to learn monolingual embeddings. Then we jointly train the LDA model and the modified Skip-Gram model to obtain

---

[1] http://catalog.elra.info/en-us/repository/browse/ELRA-E0008/.

monolingual word embeddings with topical information. Finally, we learn the cross-lingual word embeddings in a supervised or unsupervised way.

2.1 A Modified Skip-Gram Model

Skip-Gram [16] is a state-of-the-art word embedding model for learning word vectors. It aims to predict the context word of a given target word in the sliding window. In this model, each word corresponds to a unique vector. The vector of target word is used as features to predict the context words. Skip-Gram formulates the probability $p(w_{i+c}|w_i)$ using a softmax function as follows:

$$p(w_{i+c}|w_i) = \frac{exp(v_{i+c} \cdot v_i)}{\sum_{j=1}^{|\Lambda|} exp(v_{i+c} \cdot v_j)} \tag{1}$$

Where, v_i and v_{i+c} are vector representations of target words w_i and contextual words w_{i+c} respectively, $|\Lambda|$ represents the vocabulary size of the whole corpus.

However, the size of vocabulary is often large, which makes it more difficult to calculate the probability $p(w_{i+c}|w_i)$. To alleviate this problem, we introduce a novel random negative sampling procedure to form a modified Skip-Gram model. In this modified model, we select N negative samples for each word-context pair and then form $N+1$ labels together with the original label and evaluate the probability only from these training pairs:

$$p'(w_{i+c}|w_i) = \frac{exp(v_{i+c} \cdot v_i)}{exp(v_{i+c} \cdot v_i) + \sum_{k=1}^{N} exp(v_{i+c} \cdot v_k)} \tag{2}$$

Where v_k is a vector representation of the random negative sampled word w_k. Based on the random negative sampling probability $p'(w_{i+c}|w_i)$, the loss function of the modified Skip-Gram model can be defined as:

$$\begin{aligned}
\mathcal{L}_{word} &= - \sum_{-c \leq i \leq c, i \neq 0} log p'(w_{i+c}|w_i) \\
&= - \sum_{-c \leq i \leq c, i \neq 0} v_{i+c} \cdot v_i + \sum_{-c \leq i \leq c, i \neq 0} log\left[exp(v_{i+c} \cdot v_i) + \sum_{k=1}^{N} exp(v_{i+c} \cdot v_i) \right]
\end{aligned} \tag{3}$$

In above way, we still use the complete softmax function. However, the number of negative samples that need to be processed is smaller and the whole procedure is sufficient.

2.2 Jointly Learning Topics and Word Embeddings

Topical Word Embedding (TWE) model [14] is a flexible model for learning topical word embeddings. It uses Skip-Gram model to learn the topic vectors z and word embeddings v separately and then output the final output vectors $v_z = v \oplus z$. In this way, the model allows a word to have different word vectors under different topics. In contrast to the

TWE model, instead of simply concatenating the two sets of vectors together, we jointly learn the LDA model and the Skip-Gram model to generate word embeddings which contain specific topical information for each word.

Due to the space constraint, we omit the description of the training of the LDA in this paper. Readers are referred to their original paper for details. After training, we learn the topics and the words jointly:

$$\mathcal{L} = \mu \mathcal{L}_{word} + (1 - \mu) \mathcal{L}_{topic}$$
$$= - \sum_{-c \leq i \leq c, i \neq 0} log \left[\mu p'(w_{i+c}|w_i) + (1 - \mu) p(t_{i+c}|t_i) \right] \qquad (4)$$

where $\mathcal{L}_{topic}$ represents the loss function of the topic, μ is the weight parameter, $p(t_{i+c}|t_i)$ is similar to $p'(w_{i+c}|w_i)$, and t_i and t_{i+c} are the topic corresponding to the target word w_i and the context word w_{i+c} respectively:

$$p(t_{i+c}|t_i) = \frac{exp(u_{i+c} \cdot u_i)}{exp(u_{i+c} \cdot u_i) + \sum_{k=1}^{N} exp(u_{i+c} \cdot u_k)} \qquad (5)$$

u_{i+c} and u_i are vector representations of topic t_{i+c} and topic t_i respectively, and u_k is vector representations of the random negative sample word t_k. The word embeddings obtained in this way not only contain the global context information, but also fully express the meaning of the words.

2.3 Learning Cross-Lingual Word Embeddings

Typically, projection or mapping-based cross-lingual word embedding models first train two word vector space X_{L1} and X_{L2} in two independent languages, then use a dictionary containing word translations $D = \left\{ w_i^{L1}, w_i^{L2} \right\}_{i=1}^{M}$ to perform the mapping operation. According to [3], all projection-based methods for inducing cross-lingual embedding spaces perform similarly. We opt for the supervised method of Smith et al. [7] and the unsupervised method of Conneau et al. [9] for learning cross-lingual word embeddings due to theirs competitive performance and readily available implementation[2].

Technically, the method of Smith et al. [7] learns two projection matrices W_{L1} and W_{L2} representing the source and target monolingual embedding spaces, to a new shared space by solving the Procrustes problem. Conneau et al. [9] proposed an unsupervised model based on adversarial learning. Their model aligns monolingual word vector spaces in a completely unsupervised manner and automatically constructs a seed bilingual dictionary between two languages without using any parallel corpora.

3 Experimental Setup

We evaluate our framework using three language pairs of varying degree of similarity: English (EN)-{Dutch (NL), Italian (IT), French (FR)}[3]. In all cases we use English (EN)

---

[2] https://github.com/facebookresearch/MUSE.

[3] English and Dutch are Germanic languages, Italian and French are Romance languages.

as source language. For each pair of languages, we adopt DBpedia[4] parallel corpora to jointly train our monolingual word embedding model and the LDA model. We select all NL, IT, and FR document collections from CLEF 2001–2003 and paired them with English queries from the respective year. Following a standard practice [17], queries are created by concatenating the title and the description of each CLEF topic.

In our proposed framework, there are several parameters to be determined. In the joint learning of the Skip-Gram model and the LDA model, the proportional parameter μ of the total loss function is set to 0.5. For all language pairs, the optimal number of LDA training topics is 150 and the dimensions of all word embeddings in the experiment are set to 300.

In this paper, we choose to compare with two baseline cross-lingual search methods using two representative cross-lingual word embeddings: basic Cross-Lingual embeddings (denote as CL) and Cross-Lingual embeddings based on topical word embeddings as introduced (denote as CLTWE). CL does not use the topic information, but it is based on the modified Skip-Gram model. CLTWE is based on the TWE model to learn the cross-lingual word embeddings. For our proposed framework, we denote it as CLBTWE. For all the methods evaluated, two ways are used in mapping the monolingual embeddings, i.e. supervised learning (prefix SU) and unsupervised learning (prefix UN).

In this paper, we use two unsupervised cross-lingual Web search methods proposed by Litschko et al. [18]. Both methods make use of a shared cross-lingual vector space for queries and documents, regardless of which language they belong to. The first method (denote as BWE-AGG) derives the cross-lingual embeddings of queries and documents by aggregating the cross-lingual embeddings of their constituent terms (words). It contains two variants, Agg-Add and Agg-IDF. Agg-Add simply adds the words in the document, that is, $\vec{d} = \sum_{i=1}^{M_d} \vec{w_i^d}$. Agg-IDF uses weighted addition where each word's embedding is weighted with the word's inverse document frequency, that is, $\vec{d} = \sum_{i=1}^{M_d} idf\left(w_i^d\right) \vec{t_i^d}$.

The second method (denote as TbT-QT) performs a term-by-term translation of the query into the language of the document collection relying on the shared cross-lingual space. To make our evaluation more comprehensive, we adopt four evaluation metrics: mean average precision (MAP), normalized cumulative gain (NDCG), mean inverse rank (MRR) and binary preference (Bpref).

4   Results and Discussion

We compare the performance of all models on CLEF 2001-2003 collections. The results are shown in Fig. 1, Fig. 2, Table 1 and Table 2. Figure 1 and Fig. 2 show the performance with the MAP and NDCG metrics. They show the average performance of three years for each language pair in all the CLEF 2001-2003 test collections. Table 1 and Table 2 show the performance with the MRR and Bpref metrics. They show the specific results of each language pair for each individual year of the CLEF 2001–2003 test collections. In two tables, for each retrieval method, the upper half of the dotted line represents supervised learning way and the lower half of the dotted line represents unsupervised learning way for cross-lingual Web search.

---

[4] http://dbpedia.org/resource/.

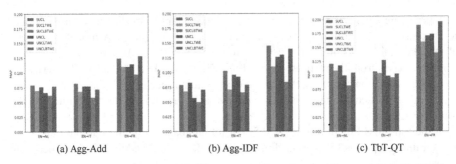

| (a) Agg-Add | (b) Agg-IDF | (c) TbT-QT |

Fig. 1. Average CLIR performance of different cross-lingual embedding models (with MAP).

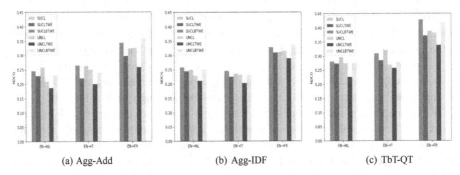

| (a) Agg-Add | (b) Agg-IDF | (c) TbT-QT |

Fig. 2. Average CLIR performance of different cross-lingual embedding models (with NDCG).

Our framework all show competitive performance over all evaluation runs. In Fig. 1 and Fig. 2, we can observe that all of the models have the highest MAP and NDCG values and the best performance is achieved by using the TbT-QT retrieval strategy. This may be because it transforms cross-lingual semantic search to translation-retrieval procedure, which makes the retrieval process more straightforward. Among them, our method is the best no matter which retrieval strategies are used on average performance. The results from Table 1 show that our framework performs better on Agg-Add overall. Among them, Agg-Add + SUCLBTWE and Agg-Add + UNCLBTWE win 7 out of 9 runs compared to various baselines with MRR metric. As can be seen from Table 2, our framework performs well using Agg-IDF as a whole and is superior to the baselines. Among them, Agg-IDF + SUCLBTWE wins 8 out of 9 runs compared to various baselines with Bpref metric, and Agg-IDF + UNCLBTWE performs better than the baselines in all cases. Even though our framework does not outperform every baseline models in every test collection with different evaluation metrics, the overall performance is still very satisfactory. This proves the effectiveness of integrating topics within the cross-lingual word embedding learning framework.

It can be observed from the results, with both supervised and unsupervised way of training, the performance of our proposed framework is very competitive. In general, the supervised methods for learning cross-lingual word embeddings are superior to unsupervised methods, which is in line with the intuition. However, we still observe in some

Table 1. CLIR performance of different cross-lingual embedding models (with MRR).

Retrieval method	Model	EN → NL			EN → IT			EN → FR		
		2001	2002	2003	2001	2002	2003	2001	2002	2003
Agg-Add	SUCL	0.204	0.296	0.308	0.137	0.219	0.278	0.306	0.335	0.351
	SUCLTWE	0.181	0.317	0.293	0.122	0.238	0.222	0.323	0.312	0.348
	SUCLBTWE	0.208	0.323	0.323	0.144	0.227	0.316	0.349	0.306	0.409
	UNCL	0.212	0.238	0.261	0.112	0.264	0.278	0.299	0.342	0.318
	UNCLTWE	0.170	0.175	0.229	0.091	0.162	0.202	0.291	0.293	0.325
	UNCLBTWE	0.176	0.292	0.328	0.126	0.222	0.282	0.377	0.350	0.396
Agg-IDF	SUCL	0.279	0.358	0.259	0.143	0.254	0.297	0.317	0.325	0.342
	SUCLTWE	0.213	0.207	0.296	0.087	0.179	0.188	0.307	0.309	0.313
	SUCLBTWE	0.217	0.285	0.318	0.150	0.298	0.304	0.336	0.365	0.355
	UNCL	0.249	0.199	0.217	0.114	0.285	0.228	0.317	0.344	0.308
	UNCLTWE	0.137	0.128	0.213	0.163	0.155	0.172	0.261	0.268	0.235
	UNCLBTWE	0.236	0.258	0.263	0.135	0.211	0.311	0.348	0.355	0.382
TbT-QT	SUCL	0.305	0.352	0.307	0.254	0.279	0.324	0.296	0.447	0.356
	SUCLTWE	0.274	0.341	0.278	0.220	0.308	0.272	0.219	0.419	0.334
	SUCLBTWE	0.326	0.335	0.316	0.299	0.289	0.245	0.400	0.476	0.392
	UNCL	0.322	0.286	0.242	0.207	0.296	0.230	0.297	0.392	0.344
	UNCLTWE	0.198	0.275	0.174	0.163	0.283	0.222	0.261	0.364	0.312
	UNCLBTWE	0.295	0.321	0.203	0.208	0.301	0.252	0.399	0.398	0.360

cases unsupervised methods work well. For example, from the results in Fig. 1(a), for language pairs EN → NL and EN → IT supervised methods are better than unsupervised methods, but for language pair EN → FR, UNCL and UNCLBTWE perform better than their supervised alternative CL and CLBTWE. Similar results can be observed in Fig. 1(b) and Fig. 1(c). In Fig. 2, again we can discover that in most of cases supervised methods work well. We also notice that the effect of the models based on topical word embeddings (TWE-based) are superior than that of the models that use word embeddings without topical information. This indicates that incorporating topical information into word can indeed improve the performance.

The results imply that the proximity of languages in cross-lingual Web search only has limited compact. Most models exhibit better performance for language pair EN → FR than the other two language pairs. This is actually expected since French is lexically and typologically closer to English than Dutch and Italy. However, even though NL is linguistically closer to EN than IT, for our method we observe better performance for EN → IT than for EN → NL. We speculate that this is due to the compounding phenomenon in word formation [19], which is presented in NL, but is not a property of EN and IT.

Table 2. CLIR performance of different cross-lingual embedding models (with Bpref).

Retrieval method	Model	EN → NL			EN → IT			EN → FR		
		2001	2002	2003	2001	2002	2003	2001	2002	2003
Agg-Add	SUCL	0.134	0.189	0.173	0.089	0.109	0.141	0.185	0.165	0.181
	SUCLTWE	0.123	0.189	0.166	0.086	0.111	0.120	0.188	0.158	0.200
	SUCLBTWE	0.137	0.195	0.174	0.092	0.111	0.121	0.199	0.160	0.232
	UNCL	0.111	0.184	0.147	0.086	0.096	0.122	0.195	0.166	0.191
	UNCLTWE	0.116	0.171	0.150	0.076	0.070	0.052	0.193	0.156	0.201
	UNCLBTWE	0.145	0.188	0.163	0.090	0.111	0.117	0.198	0.166	0.227
Agg-IDF	SUCL	0.143	0.186	0.160	0.095	0.123	0.112	0.210	0.180	0.186
	SUCLTWE	0.142	0.158	0.162	0.098	0.120	0.110	0.216	0.153	0.174
	SUCLBTWE	0.148	0.167	0.165	0.101	0.126	0.117	0.228	0.182	0.215
	UNCL	0.129	0.154	0.141	0.097	0.107	0.096	0.225	0.181	0.198
	UNCLTWE	0.118	0.126	0.140	0.055	0.060	0.055	0.194	0.147	0.145
	UNCLBTWE	0.148	0.155	0.158	0.103	0.127	0.125	0.231	0.184	0.223
TbT-QT	SUCL	0.151	0.207	0.166	0.160	0.190	0.186	0.201	0.248	0.192
	SUCLTWE	0.150	0.179	0.157	0.149	0.177	0.197	0.171	0.220	0.212
	SUCLBTWE	0.151	0.189	0.177	0.175	0.197	0.216	0.217	0.215	0.265
	UNCL	0.137	0.162	0.134	0.149	0.181	0.184	0.210	0.245	0.235
	UNCLTWE	0.101	0.168	0.114	0.069	0.084	0.069	0.174	0.215	0.199
	UNCLBTWE	0.171	0.187	0.109	0.151	0.184	0.193	0.233	0.229	0.259

5 Conclusions

In this paper, we propose a novel cross-lingual word embedding learning framework by incorporating topics that contain global information. We jointly train the LDA model and a modified Skip-Gram model to learn high quality monolingual word embeddings. Then we use the supervised and unsupervised methods to train cross-lingual word embeddings with topical information. We evaluate our embeddings framework in the cross-lingual Web search tasks using CLEF test collections. The results show that our framework achieves the state-of-the-art performance for a number of language pairs. For future work, we will carry out more rigorous and detailed experiments to further improve our framework. We also try to evaluate different topic models and cross-lingual word embedding models under different tasks.

Acknowledgement. This work was supported by the National Natural Science Foundation of China under Project No. 61876062.

References

1. Zhou, D., Truran, M., Brailsford, T., Wade, V., Ashman, H.: Translation techniques in cross-language information retrieval. ACM Comput. Surv. **45**(1), 1–44 (2012)
2. Mikolov, T., Dean, J.: Distributed representations of words and phrases and their compositionality. In: Advances in Neural Information Processing Systems (2013b)
3. Ruder, S., Vulic, I., Søgaard, A.: A survey of cross-lingual word embedding models. Artif. Intell. Res. 1–55 (2018)
4. Upadhyay, S., Faruqui, M., Dyer, C., Roth, D. Cross-lingual models of word embeddings: an empirical comparison. In: Proceedings of the 54th Annual Meeting of the Association for Computational Linguistics (vol. 1: Long Papers), volume 1, pp. 1661–1670 (2016)
5. Lazaridou, A., Dinu, G., Baroni, M.: Hubness and pollution: delving into cross-space mapping for zero-shot learning. In: Proceedings of the 53rd Annual Meeting of the Association for Computational Linguistics and the 7th International Joint Conference on Natural Language Processing (Volume 1: Long Papers), pp. 270–280 (2015)
6. Heyman, G., Verreet, B., Vuli´c, I., Moens, M.F. Learning unsupervised multilingual word embeddings with incremental multilingual hubs. In: Proceedings of the 2019 Conference of the North American Chapter of the Association for Computational Linguistics: Human Language Technologies, pp. 1890–1902 (2019)
7. Smith, S.L., Turban, D.H.P., Hamblin, S., Hammerla, N.Y.: Offline bilingual word vectors, orthogonal transformations and the inverted softmax. In: Proceedings of the 5th International Conference on Learning Representations (2017)
8. Zhang, M., Liu, Y., Luan, H., Sun, M.: Adversarial training for unsupervised bilingual lexicon induction. In: Proceedings of the 53rd Annual Meeting of the Association for Computational Linguistics (2017)
9. Conneau, A., Lample, G., Ranzato, M.A., Denoyer, L., Jégou, H.: Word translation without parallel data. In: Proceedings of the ICLR (2018)
10. Blei, D.M., Ng, A.Y., Jordan, M.I.: Latent dirichlet allocation. Mach. Learn. Res. Archive **3**, 993–1022 (2003)
11. Xu, G., Yang, S.H., Li, H.: Named entity mining from click-through data using weakly supervised latent dirichlet allocation. In: Proceedings of the 15th ACM SIGKDD International Conference on Knowledge Discovery and Data Mining, pp. 1365–1374. ACM (2009)
12. Zhou, D., Wade, V.: Latent document Re-Ranking. In: Proceedings of the 2009 Conference on Empirical Methods in Natural Language Processing (EMNLP), August 2009, Singapore, pp. 1571–1580 (2009)
13. Shi, B., Lam, W., Jameel, S., Schockaert, S., Kwun, P. L.: Jointly Learning Word Embeddings and Latent Topics. J. (2017)
14. Liu, Y., Liu, Z.Y., Tat-Seng, C., Maosong, S.: Topical word embeddings. In: Proceedings of the AAAI, pp. 2418–2424 (2015)
15. Li, C., Wang, H., Zhang, Z., Sun, A., Ma, Z.: Topic modeling for short texts with auxiliary word embeddings. In: Proceedings of the 39th International ACM SIGIR Conference, pp. 165–174. ACM (2016)
16. Mikolov, T., Le, Q.V., Sutskever, I.: Exploiting Similarities among Languages for Machine Translation. arXiv:1309.4168 [cs]. (2013)
17. Vulić, I., Moens, S.: Monolingual and cross-lingual information retrieval models based on (Bilingual) word embeddings. In: Proceedings of the SIGIR, pp. 363–372 (2015)
18. Litschko, R., Glavaš, G., Ponzetto, S. P., Vulić, I.: Unsupervised cross-lingual information retrieval using monolingual data only. In: Proceedings of the SIGIR, pp. 1253–1256 (2018)
19. Hartmann, M., Kementchedjhieva, Y., Søgaard, A.: Why is unsupervised alignment of english embeddings from different algorithms so hard? In: Proceedings of the 2018 Conference on Empirical Methods in Natural Language Processing, pp 582–586 (2018)

Paperant: Key Elements Generation with New Ideas

Xin He[1], Jiuyang Tang[1], Zhen Tan[1(✉)], Zheng Yu[2], and Xiang Zhao[1]

[1] Science and Technology on Information Systems Engineering Laboratory, National University of Defense Technology, Changsha, China
tanzhen08a@nudt.edu.cn
[2] Mininglamp Academy of Sciences, Mininglamp Technology, Beijing, China

Abstract. Long text generation, leveraging one sentence to generate a meaningful paper, is an effective method to reduce repetitive works. Conventional text generation models utilize rule-based and plan-based methods to produce paper, such as SCIgen, which is hard to suit the complex sematic scene. Recently, several neural network-based models, such as Point Network and PaperRobot, were proposed to tackle the problem, and achieve state-of-the-art performance. However, most of them only try to generate part of the paper, and ignore the sematic information of each entity in input sentence. In this paper, we present a novel method named Paperant, which leverage not only multi-sentence features to describe latent features of each entity, but also hybrid structure to generate different parts of the paper. In experiment, Paperant was superior to other methods on each indicator.

Keywords: Long text generation · Background KG construction · Link prediction

1 Introduction

Long text generation refers to generating a meaningful paper from one sentence to reduce a large amount of repetitive work, which is a challenging task. Conventional text generation models use rule-based and plan-based methods to produce paper, which is difficult to adapt to complex semantic scenarios. For example, SCIgen [1], which made a sensation in 2005, only needs to enter the author's name to generate a "quality papers" with many figures and tables. However, all the content in these generated papers did not make any sense, which was unable to replace repetitive labor's work, since many researchers leveraged many methods, such as rule-based and plan-based models, to generate meaningful text. But all the models only generated the content with special form that was difficult to be applied in real scene. Recently, deep neural network-based models are proposed to solve a series of issues, such as image processing [16], natural language processing (NLP) [22], knowledge graph (KG) [15] and so on [18]. Several researchers proposed several neural network-based models such as Seq2seq [24], Pointer Network [17], and PaperRobot [19] to generate papers, which achieved state-of-the-art performance. However, most of methods only generated parts of the paper, what's more,

© Springer Nature Switzerland AG 2020
X. Wang et al. (Eds.): APWeb-WAIM 2020, LNCS 12318, pp. 294–308, 2020.
https://doi.org/10.1007/978-3-030-60290-1_23

they ignored the semantic information of each entity in the input sentence, which is limited for real writing scene. In order to achieve the goal, PaperRobot added the memory network into the pointer network to process unknown words and generate more parts of the paper. However, it still needs a lot of improvements. For better solution, we proposed a novel method named as Paperant, an assistant to help researchers complete their papers. This method not only uses multi-sentence features to describe the latent features of each entity (Sect. 2.2), but also utilizes a hybrid structure to generate different parts of the paper (Sect. 2.3). Our hybrid structure consists of two parts: generation mechanism and extraction mechanism, which are respectively used to produce abstract, conclusion and the future work as well as to produce keywords, related work and references. The detailed processing flow is shown in Fig. 1. In the experiment, we followed the METEOR constructed by Denkowski et al. [23] to measure the relevance between a topic and a given title, and used perplexity to further evaluate the quality of the language model. The experimental results show that Paperant is superior to other methods in each indicator.

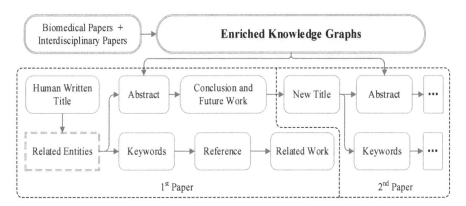

Fig. 1. Paperant processing. The blue double-lined rounded rectangle is the Background KG Construction section and the New Edge Prediction section. Orange single-line rounded rectangles are the paper elements generated by the New Paper Generation section. The blue double dashed rectangle is the middle amount. The black dotted boxes indicate the division of different papers. (Color figure online)

There are two preliminary tasks before generating the key elements of the paper, which is as shown in Fig. 1. First, the background KG is constructed by a large amount of biomedical papers and several interdisciplinary papers, which is corresponding to the process of obtaining basic domain knowledge. The second is to predict new relations on background KG and obtain an enriched KG, which is corresponding to the process of putting forward new ideas based on existing research results in academic research.

The construction of background KG mainly relies on joint knowledge extraction [9]. The previous method used a single- domain paper to construct the domain KG, which might lead to incomplete new ideas. So we added 1/60 interdisciplinary papers to build the background KG, so as to describe the KG more comprehensively. To enrich the KG, we leverage translation-based method to describe the entity and relation features. Besides, compared with previous studies, Paperant used multi-sentence features to describe the latent features of each entity, and combines the features of the graph structure to produce a more accurate representation of the entity.

After we finish the first two steps of the preliminary work, the third one can generate high-quality output, so that the whole process shown in Fig. 1 is closer to the paper completion process. The main contributions of our work include:

- Leveraging multi-sentence features to describe latent features of each entity, so as to improve the ability of link prediction and long text generation.
- Constructing a hybrid structure consisting of a generation mechanism and an extraction mechanism to generate more parts of the paper.
- Combining domain papers and interdisciplinary papers to build a more comprehensive KG.

Organization. We first introduce the Methodology in Sect. 2, followed by experiments in Sect. 3, Afterwards, the related work are discussed in Sect. 4. In the end, we conclude the paper with major findings in Sect. 5.

2 Methodology

The entire framework of Paperant is shown in Fig. 2. For [19], firstly, we obtained a large number of papers in special domains and several interdisciplinary papers to build a more comprehensive background KG; and then combined graphs attention and contextual text attention to predict new links in the background KG, which were used to create new scientific ideas; finally, based on the memory-attention network, some key elements of the new paper were generated. The detailed process is shown as follows:

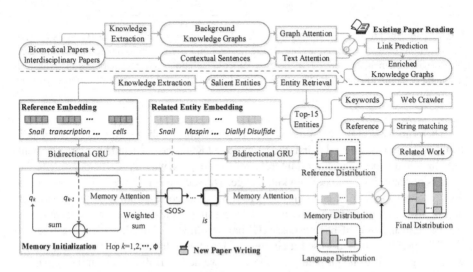

Fig. 2. Paperant architecture overview

2.1 Background KG Construction

Following the advice of biomedical experts, we defined bioinformatics, physics, and chemistry as interdisciplinary subjects.

We collected a large number of biomedical papers, as well as some papers in the fields of bioinformatics, physics, and chemistry, and performed knowledge extraction on these papers to build a background KG. However, the use of multi-domain papers would cause the performance failure of overall model. Hence, how to solve the conflict among papers in different fields is the key. In order to reduce the impact of entities and relations on other fields, we first considered the ratio of biomedical papers to interdisciplinary papers. According to the research of Foster et al. [34], we set the final ratio to 60:1. Then we performed knowledge extraction to extract only the entities and relations in the biomedical domain. In this way, the domain relevance of entities and relations was improved.

Similar to [19], we used the entity mention extraction and linking system proposed by Wei et al. [2] to extract three important types of entities—Disease, Chemical and Gene. Then we obtained the unique ID from Medical Subject Headings (MeSH) mentioned every time and further linked all entities to the Comparative Toxicogenomics Database (CTD), and finally extracted 133 subtypes of relations, such as *Increasing Reaction*, *Affecting Transport*, etc.

2.2 New Edge Prediction

As mentioned above, we constructed a background KG containing interdisciplinary information. In this section, we further enriched it by predicting new links in original KG. Considering that the important role of contextual text information and structural information of the KG on a complete representation of an entity, we used both types of features to better represent each entity in the next step. Under this representation, if the similarity between two entities A and B reaches a certain level, we will determine whether to add a new edge by judging whether an adjacent entity of entity A is sufficiently related to entity B. For example, in Fig. 3, because Na^+ and K^+ are similar both in contextual text information and graph structure, we predicted two new neighbors of Na^+: *Neurotransmitters* and *Kininase 2*, which are neighbors of K^+ in the initial KG.

Then the entire KG can be represented as a series of tuples $\left(e_i^h, r_i, e_i^t\right)$, $i = 0, 1, \cdots, k$. The symbols in parentheses in turn represent the head entity, the relation, and the tail entity. For an entity e_i, it has several neighbor entities, which can be represented by the set $N_{e_i} = n_{i1}, n_{i2}, \cdots$.

Graph Structure Encoder. The entity's graph structure characteristics are derived from all of its neighbor entities. In order to obtain the importance contribution of each neighbor entity to the entity, we used self-attention mechanism to calculate the weight. The calculation formulas are as follows:

$$e_i' = W_e e_i, \; n_{ij}' = W_e n_{ij} \tag{1}$$

$$c_{ij} = \text{LeakyReLU}(W_f(e_i' \oplus n_{ij}')) \tag{2}$$

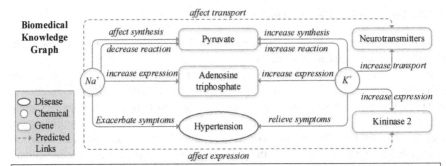

Contextual Sentence: Na^+ and K^+ are charge carriers, can regulate the osmotic pressure of extracellular and internal fluids, are activators of **Adenosine triphosphate**, and participate in the transmission of **Neurotransmitters**. Na^+ and K^+ have different physiological activities. For example, K^+ is an activator of **pyruvate**, which can accelerate the rate of protein synthesis and the respiration of muscle tissue, and Na^+ can hinder both processes.

Fig. 3. Biomedical knowledge extraction and link prediction example

$$c_i' = \text{Softmax}\,(c_i) \tag{3}$$

$$\varepsilon_i = \sigma\left(\sum c_{ij}' n_i'\right) \tag{4}$$

Where W_e is a linear transformation matrix applied to each entity, W_f is a parameter of a single-layer feedforward network, and $\oplus$ represents a concatenation operation between two matrices. ε_i is a structure-based context representation, and the activation function σ is the Sigmoid function. We used multi-head attention for each entity based on multiple linear transformation matrices, and obtained a structure-based context representation $\tilde{e}_i = [\varepsilon_i^0 \oplus \cdots \oplus \varepsilon_i^M]$, where ε_i^M represents the context representation obtained with the m-th head.

Contextual Text Encoder. In such a huge data set, each entity certainly appears more than once. In order to better represent an entity, we randomly selected three sentences $S_i = [w_{1i}, \cdots, w_{li}], i = 1, 2, 3$, which contain the entity e_i, and then passed these three sentences through Bi-LSTM to obtain three hidden states $H_i = [h_{1i}, \cdots, h_{li}]$, where h_{1i} represents the hidden state of w_{1i}. Next, we took S_i as an example, the formulas for calculating the bilinear attention weight of each word in a sentence are as follows:

$$\mu_i = e^T W_s h_i \tag{5}$$

$$\mu' = \text{Softmax}(\mu) \tag{6}$$

Where W_s is a bilinear term. Then the context representation of entity e_i in the S_i sentence can be represented as $\hat{e} = \mu'^T h_i$, and the final context representation of entity e_i can be obtained by averaging the context representations of these three sentences. We designed a gate function to synthesize two types of features, the formulas are as follows:

$$g_e = \sigma(\tilde{g}_e) \tag{7}$$

$$e = g_e \odot \tilde{e} + (1 - g_e) \odot \hat{e} \tag{8}$$

Where g_e is an entity-based gate function, $\tilde{g}_e$ is a different learnable parameter for each entity, the activation function σ denotes sigmod function, and $\odot$ means element-wise multiplication.

Link Prediction. We followed the TransE method proposed by Bordes et al. in 2013 [3] to represent entities and relations. For each tuple, we can calculate its distance score $F(e_i^h, r_i, e_i^t)$. F and the marginal loss used for training are as follows:

$$F(e_i^h, r_i, e_i^t) = \left\| e_i^h + r_i - e_i^t \right\|_2^2 \tag{9}$$

$$Loss = \sum_{(e_i^h, r_i, e_i^t) \in K} \sum_{(\bar{e}_i^h, \bar{r}_i, \bar{e}_i^t) \in \bar{K}} \max(0, \gamma + F(e_i^h, r_i, e_i^t) - F(\bar{e}_i^h, \bar{r}_i, \bar{e}_i^t)) \tag{10}$$

Where (e_i^h, r_i, e_i^t) and $(\bar{e}_i^h, \bar{r}_i, \bar{e}_i^t)$ represent positive and negative tuples, respectively, and γ is a margin. The negative tuple was generated by selecting the positive tuple and replacing its head entity or tail entity with a randomly chosen different entity. After the training, we designed a score y for each pair of indirectly connected entities and a relation type r to calculate the probability that (e_i, r, e_j) is true. Then we get an enriched KG $\hat{K}$.

2.3 New Paper Generation

In this section, our new paper generation module is divided into two parts. The first part is automatic text generation, which includes title-to-abstract, abstract-to-conclusions and future work, conclusions and future work-to-new title. We took title-to-abstract generation as a case to describe the first part. The second part is automatic text extraction, which includes title extracting keywords, keyword generating references, reference extracting related work, and so on.

Automatic Text Generation. For a given title, we first performed entity extraction on it, and for each entity we obtained, we retrieved a series of entities related to it by searching in the enriched KG $\hat{K}$. We sorted the obtained entity set according to the confidence score, and selected the first 15 most related entities, which were used together with the title given as the input of the paper auto-generation model as shown in Fig. 2. This model allows us to balance three types of resource data in each time step of decoding: data generating from the entire vocabulary based on the language model; word copied from reference titles; and data obtained from the incorporation of related entity.

Reference Encoder and Decoder Hidden State Initialization. we randomly embedded each word of the title into a vector and obtain $\tau = [w_1, \cdots, w_l]$, then we put τ into a bidirectional Gated Recurrent Unit (GRU) encoder to produce the encoder hidden state $H = [h_1, \cdots, h_l]$. Since the predicted entities have different correlations with the title, we used memory-attention networks to further filter irrelevant information. The memory-based multihop attention can greatly refine the attention weight of each memory cell, and thereby improve correlation. For a given set of related entities $E = [e_1, \cdots, e_v]$, we randomly initialized their vector representations and stored them in memory. After that, we used the last hidden state h_l of the reference title encoder as the first query vector q_0, and iteratively calculated the attention distribution on all memories and update the query vector:

$$p_{ki} = v_k^T \tanh(W_q^k q_{k-1} + U_e^k e_i + b_k) \tag{11}$$

$$q_k = p_k^T e + q_{k-1} \tag{12}$$

Where k represents the k-th hop during φ hops in total ($\varphi = 3$ in this paper). After the φ hop, we obtained q_φ and use it as the initial hidden state of the GRU decoder.

Memory Network and Reference Attention. We calculated an attention weight for each entity and applied a memory network to optimize this weight, so that we could better capture the contribution of each entity e_j to each decoding output in each decoding step i. We used the hidden state $\tilde{h}_i$ as the initial query vector $\tilde{q}_0$ and iteratively updated it by:

$$\tilde{p}_{kj} = v_k^T \tanh(\tilde{W}_{\tilde{q}}^k \tilde{q}_{k-1} + \tilde{U}_e^k e_j + W_{\hat{c}} \hat{c}_{ij} + b_k) \tag{13}$$

$$u_{ik} = \tilde{p}_k'^T e_j, \quad \tilde{q}_k = u_{ik} + \tilde{q}_{k-1}, \quad \hat{c}_{ij} = \sum_{m=0}^{i-1} \beta_{mj} \tag{14}$$

where $\hat{c}_{ij}$ is an entity coverage vector, $\beta_i = \tilde{p}'_\psi$ is the attention distribution of the last hop and ψ is the total number of hops. Then we obtained a memory-based context vector $x_i = u_{i\psi}$ for related series of entities.

This reference attention aims to capture the contribution of each word in the reference title to the decoded output. In each time step i, the decoder receives the previous word embedding and generates the hidden state of the decoder $\tilde{h}_i$. The attention weight of each reference token is calculated as follows:

$$\alpha_{ij} = \varsigma^T \tanh(W_h \tilde{h}_i + W_\tau h_j + W_{\tilde{c}} \tilde{c}_{ij} + b_r) \tag{15}$$

$$\alpha'_i = \text{Softmax}(\alpha_i); \quad \phi_i = \alpha_i'^T h_j; \quad \tilde{c}_{ij} = \sum_{m=0}^{i-1} \alpha_{mj} \tag{16}$$

where ϕ_i is a reference context vector. $\tilde{c}_{ij}$ is a reference cover vector, which is the sum of the attention distributions of all the previous decoders at each time step.

Text Generator. A particular word w may appear repeatedly in a reference title or in multiple related entities. As thus, at each decoding step i, for each word w, we obtained its final attention weight from the reference attention and memory attention distribution: $P_\tau^i = \sum_{m|w_m=w} \alpha'_{im}$ and $P_e^i = \sum_{m|w\in e_m} \beta_{im}$. In each decoding step i, each word in

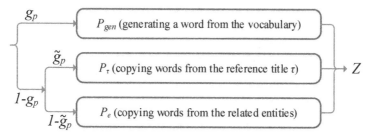

Fig. 4. Relationship between g_p and $\tilde{g}_p$.

the vocabulary may also be generated with a certain probability P_{gen} according to the language model: $P_{gen} = \text{Softmax}(W_{gen}[\tilde{h}_i; \phi_i; x_i] + b_{gen})$, where W_{gen} and b_{gen} are learnable parameters. In order to better combine P_τ, P_e, and P_{gen}, we designed g_p and $\tilde{g}_p$ as soft switches, and their relationship is shown in Fig. 4.

The formulas of g_p and $\tilde{g}_p$ are as follows:

$$g_p = \sigma(W_p^T \tilde{h}_i + W_z^T z_{i-1} + b_p) \tag{17}$$

$$\tilde{g}_p = \sigma(W_\phi^T \phi_i + W_x^T x_i + \tilde{b}_p) \tag{18}$$

where W_p, W_z, W_ϕ, W_x, b_p, and $\tilde{b}_p$ are all learnable parameters. z_{i-1} represents the embedding of token generated in step $i - 1$, and the activation function σ is still sigmod function. The calculation formula for the probability $P(z_i)$ of generating the token z in the decoding step i is:

$$P(z_i) = g_p P_{gen} + (1 - g_p)(\tilde{g}_p P_\tau + (1 - \tilde{g}_p)P_e) \tag{19}$$

Combining with the coverage loss for both reference attention and memory distribution, our loss function is expressed as:

$$Loss = \sum_i -\log P(z_i) + \lambda \sum_i (\min(\alpha_{ij}, \tilde{c}_{ij}) + \min(\beta_{ij}, \hat{c}_{ij})) \tag{20}$$

where λ is a hyperparameter. In addition, 11% of abstract sentences written by human authors contain repetitive entities, which is likely to mislead the language model. Therefore we used coverage loss to avoid any entity from being repeatedly noticed by the attention mechanism in the referenced input text or related entities.

Automatic Text Extraction. This model is mainly composed of three parts: title extracting keywords, keyword generating references, and reference extracting related work. The difference between this module and the previous automatic text generation module is that the sentences obtained by this module are all extracted from the existing papers written by human authors, rather than generated with a certain probability.

Keyword Extraction. We abandoned the original idea of using biomedical domain keyword retraining corpora to build a text keyword extraction model, and instead included all closely related to entities in the expanded KG. Therefore, we directly used the top 5 entities among the top 15 entities with the highest scores obtained in the beginning of Sect. 2.3 as the key words of the paper, and denoted them as $[K_1, \cdots, K_5]$. Their relevance to the subject of the paper decreases in order from K_1 to K_5. We set the correlation value of each keyword K_i to the subject as V_i. Here we set the value of $[V_1, \cdots, V_5]$ to $[5, 4, \cdots, 1]$.

In this way, the overall perplexity of the model is reduced, which saves computing resources and better fits the functional needs of Paperant itself. As for the specific number of keywords output to the paper, it can be set according to the user's requirements for different journals or conferences. Generally, the value range of the number of keywords is 3 to 5. There are also some papers that do not require keywords. At this time, Paperant will not output the extracted keywords, but use them as an intermediate variable to further generate the reference.

Reference Generation. The five keywords $[K_1, \cdots, K_5]$ obtained in the previous step were used as input for this part to obtain references from the keywords. In order to make Paperant more user-friendly, we also provided users with full-text files of all references for their query, study and reference. Generally, in the process of retrieving a paper, one keyword is not enough to search for references with a high degree of matching with the target topic. Usually, it is necessary to enter two or three keywords to obtain satisfactory search results. Consequently, when we searched for references, we selected three $[K_l, K_m, K_n]$ from $[K_1, \cdots, K_5]$ each time. The total subject-related value of each combination is $\sum_{i=l,m,n} V_i$, and the total number of combinations is $C_5^3 = 10$. For each combination, we searched in PubMed Central according to a set of three keywords, and downloaded the first two papers of the output using a crawler, resulting in a citation format of 20 references and their full-text files. The PubMed Central library was chosen because it is the largest free full-text library in the field of biomedicine and can be downloaded anytime.

As for the final ranking of the papers in the reference section, we combined the total subject correlation values and the comprehensive correlation of the PMC library. For example, $[K_1, K_2, K_3]$ has a total topic related value of 12, and its second search result ranks second; while $[K_1, K_2, K_4]$ has a value of 11, its second search result came in fourth. When the values of the two combinations were the same, we compared them one by one from the single keyword with the highest value. For example, the total correlation value of $[K_1, K_2, K_5]$ and $[K_1, K_3, K_4]$ both are 10. First, the keyword K_1 with the highest correlation value in these two groups is the same. Second, the second highest K_2 is higher than K_3. So, $[K_1, K_2, K_5]$ should be ranked before $[K_1, K_3, K_4]$.

Related Work Extraction. Next, the sentences of *Related Work* parts were extracted by the citation format of the references. Because the references are formatted and semi-structured, we used the template method to extract the information needed. The general format of the references generated is shown in Fig. 5 below. This is also one of the common formats in the fields of biomedicine.

Using the template method, we can easily obtain the name of the first author by taking the string before the first symbol, and the first four digits starting with "19" or "20" can be used to obtain the year of publication of the paper. For example, from the first

1. Laskey, R. A., Honda, B. M., Mills, A. D., and Finch, J. T. (1978) Nucleosomes are assembled by an acidic protein which binds histones and transfers them to DNA. *Nature* **275**, 416-420
2. Burgess, R. J., and Zhang, Z. (2013) Histone chaperones in nucleosome assembly and human disease. *Nature structural & molecular biology* **20**, 14-22
3. Mattiroli, F., D'Arcy, S., and Luger, K. (2015) The right place at the right time: chaperoning core histone variants. *EMBO reports* **16**, 1454-1466

Fig. 5. Screenshot of references part.

reference in the figure above, the first author of the paper is Laskey, and the paper was published in 1978. We constructed the string "Laskey et al., 1978" and used this string to match in the *Introduction* dataset because there is no *Related Work* part in biomedical papers. It is possible to obtain multiple matches. We directly extracted the sentence S_1 in which the first result was located to the *Related Work* part. If there were no results, skip to the next paper. The subsequent 19 papers were processed as above, and hence we obtained our *Related Work* part $R_w = [S_1, S_2, \cdots, S_i], i = 0, 1, \cdots, 20$.

3   Experiment

3.1   Datasets

A total of 1,687,000 biomedical papers from PMC Open Access Subset were collected, and separated into four parts: title, abstracts, conclusions and future work, introduction. Then, 28,100 interdisciplinary papers were extracted through Google Scholar which are only used in knowledge graph construction part. To construct a new title prediction part, we assumed that "if a paper A referenced a paper B; then, the title of the paper A would come from the conclusion and future work of the paper B". Extraction and link prediction models were leveraged jointly to extract and enrich triplets from the above papers, separately, and then a background KG with 30,483 entities and 875,964 relations was constructed. Table 1 shows the detailed generation and extraction data statistics.

Table 1. Paper generation and extraction statistics.

Dataset	Number of papers			
	Title-to-abstract	Abstract-to-conclusion and future work	Conclusion and future work-to-title	Related work extraction
Training	24,000	24,000	15,000	800,000
Test	2,000	2,000	2,000	

3.2 Evaluation Metric

We utilized the 1) METEOR [23] to measure the relevance between the title and generated topic; and 2) perplexity to evaluate the quality of the text generation model. The experimental results are shown in Table 2, where **P** denotes to perplexity and **M** to METEOR. On ground of the lack of *Related Work* part in the biomedical paper, the above three methods were not available to generate related work.

Table 2. Automatic evaluation on paper writing for diagnostic tasks (%).

Model	Title-to-abstract		Abstract-to-conclusion and future work		Conclusion and future work-to-title		Extracted related work	
	P	M	P	M	P	M	P	M
Seq2seq	19.6	9.1	44.4	8.6	49.7	6.0		
Editing network [25]	18.8	9.2	30.5	8.7	55.7	5.5		
Pointer network	146.7	8.5	74.0	8.1	47.1	6.6		
Paperant	**11.5**	**13.0**	**18.3**	**11.2**	**14.8**	**8.9**	12.1	14.3

We randomly selected 50 abstracts and 50 related works, then required domain experts to edit the abstracts and the related works until they can be understood easily. Table 3 shows the BLEU [35] and ROUGE [10] scores by comparing the part to be edited and edited part. According to expert feedback, the edited parts in abstracts and related works are stylists, tense (sentence formulation), separately, which is main cause for their different production mechanisms: generation mechanism may generate words with random style while extraction mechanism may extract sentences with different tenses.

Table 3. Evaluation on human post-editing (%).

Edited part	BLEU1	BLEU2	BLEU3	BLEU4	ROUGE
Abstract	60.1	58.9	57.7	57.3	73.9
Related work	66.5	62.4	57.0	61.7	69.1

Table 2 and Table 3 have shown that Paperant has a better performance than other baselines, but it is still need to be improved on generation and extraction parts. For example, the perplexity of related work is higher than abstract, which is contrary to the intuition, where the human-written sentence is better understood than machine-generated one. After analysis, we found that the result is caused by the different written styles or tense with different authors.

In the end, the length statistics of each part of the paper are listed in Table 4.

Table 4. The average number of words of system and human output.

	Title	Abstract	Keywords	Related work	Conclusion and future work	References
Human	13.0	106.5	4.8	Ø	105.5	41.3 papers
System	16.5	112.4	5.0	317.3	88.1	20.0 papers

3.3 Remaining Challenges

Our generation model still relies heavily on the language model and the fact of extraction, making it in absence of knowledge reasoning. In the automatic text generation, on account of the fact that it rarely appears in the training data, the model sometimes generates incorrect abbreviations. Besides, it may generate incorrect numbers or use the wrong pronouns sometimes, such as misusing "it" for "they". All titles generated by the automatic text generation system are standard declarative sentences, while human-written titles are usually more attractive, even include the entity abbreviations newly created. However, these errors do not exist in the automatic text extraction, for the sentences extracted are carefully edited by human researchers. But unsuitable sentences may be extracted from large number of samples.

4 Related Work

Since our work can be divided into three parts: background KG construction, link prediction and text generation, we summarize the related work in these three domains.

KG Construction. KG construction mainly includes artificial construction, construction based on swarm intelligence, and construction based on deep learning. Entity extraction and relation extraction are the most important techniques for constructing a KG. Entity extraction has been developed to a high level and can be performed with named entity recognition and disambiguation [4]. Disambiguation of named entities can be combined with phrase embedding [5]. Relation extraction can be performed by methods such as supervised or distant supervision [6], or combined with the attention to improve it [7]. In addition, many joint entity and relation extraction methods have emerged [8, 9] which is worthy of further research now.

Link Prediction. There are numerous commercial, economic, and biological data that can be represented by complex networks in our world, such as power networks, social networks, the World Wide Web, and so on. Nowadays, the issue of link prediction has received widespread attention in various fields including sociology, information science, and computer science. The main methods of current link prediction cover similarity-based, likelihood-based, and translation-based methods, where translation-based methods [10, 11, 20, 26] are widely utilized. Compared with previous studies, this method involves multi-head graph attention [12, 13] to encourage the model capturing the multi-aspect associations between nodes. We enriched the entity representation by combining context sentences that contain the target entity and its neighbors from the graph [27]. Link prediction is the basis for introducing new ideas into automatic paper writing.

Text Generation. Automatic text generation is an important research direction in the field of NLP, with keyword-based and neural network-based methods being the major ones. Deep neural networks have been used to describe structured knowledge bases [14, 15, 29], attribute-based biographies [30, 31], and image/video captions based on background entities and events [16, 21, 32, 33]. To deal with unknown words, we designed an architecture similar to a pointer-generator network and a copy mechanism. Some of the current interesting applications shall be attributed to the title abstract generation in the field of NLP [25], poster generation [18], or science news blog titles about published papers [22]. This is a cutting-edge work on the automatic writing of key paper elements in the biomedical domain, especially keywords, references and related work.

5 Conclusion

In this paper, we created a Paperant to help researchers speed up scientific discovery and paper output. It first built a comprehensive KG by reading a lot of papers and predicting new links. After that, Paperant predicted the relevant entities for the title entered by human, and then automatically wrote out several important parts of the new paper (abstracts, keywords, related work, conclusions and future work, references). Finally, it generated a new title for the next paper, which indicating the direction of future research. The experimental results show that Paperant is superior to other methods on each indicator. Despite all these above-mentioned advantages, it still has some defects. For example, the constructed KG cannot cover all technical details, the predicted new links need to be verified by domain experts, and the directly produced text has some mistakes. All these defects need to be resolved in the future work.

Acknowledgements. This work was partially supported by NSFC under grants Nos. 61872446, 61701454, 61902417, and 71971212, and NSF of Hunan province under grant No. 2019JJ20024.

References

1. SCIgen. https://pdos.csail.mit.edu/archive/scigen. Accessed 27 Feb 2020
2. Wei, C.H., Kao, H.Y., Lu, Z.: PubTator: a web-based text mining tool for assisting biocuration. Nucleic Acids Res. **41**, 518–522 (2013)
3. Bordes, A., Usunier, N., Duran, A.G., Weston, J., Yakhnenko, O.: Translating embeddings for modeling multi-relational data. In: Advances in Neural Information Processing Systems, pp. 2787–2795 (2013)

4. Luo, G., Huang, X., Lin, C.Y., Nie, Z.: Joint named entity recognition and disambiguation. In: Proceedings of the 2015 Conference on Empirical Methods in Natural Language Processing, pp. 879–888 (2015)
5. Passos, A., Kumar, V., McCallum, A.: Lexicon infused phrase embeddings for named entity resolution. In: Proceedings of the Eighteenth Conference on Computational Language Learning, pp. 78–86 (2014)
6. Mintz, M., Bills, S., Snow, R., Jurafsky, D.: Distant supervision for relation extraction without labeled data. In: Proceedings of the 47th Annual Meeting of the ACL and the 4th IJCNLP of the AFNLP, pp. 1003–1011 (2009)
7. Lin, Y., Shen, S., Liu, Z., Luan, H., Sun, M.: Neural relation extraction with selective attention over instances. In: Proceedings of the 54th Annual Meeting of the Association for Computational Linguistics, pp. 2124–2133 (2016)
8. Kate, R.J., Mooney, R.J.: Joint entity and relation extraction using card-pyramid parsing. In: Association for Computational Linguistics, pp. 203–212 (2010)
9. Yang, B., Mitchell, T.: Joint extraction of events and entities within a document context. In: Proceedings of NAACL-HLT 2016, pp. 289–299 (2016)
10. Lin, C.Y.: ROUGE: a package for automatic evaluation of summaries. In: Proceedings of Text Summarization Branches Out, pp. 74–81 (2004)
11. Wang, Z., Zhang, J., Feng, J.: Knowledge graph embedding by translating on hyperplanes. In: Proceedings of the 28th AAAI Conference on Artificial Intelligence, pp. 1112–1119 (2014)
12. Sukhbaatar, S., Weston, J., Fergus, R.: End-to-end memory networks. In: Advances in Neural Information Processing Systems, pp. 2440–2448 (2015)
13. Madotto, A., Wu, C.S., Fung, P.: Mem2Seq: effectively incorporating knowledge bases into end-to-end task-oriented dialog systems. In: Proceedings of the 56th Annual Meeting of the Association for Computational Linguistics, pp. 1468–1478 (2018)
14. Konstas, I., Lapata, M.: A global model for concept-to-text generation. J. Artif. Intell. Res. **48**, 305–346 (2013)
15. Xu, K., Wu, L., Wang, Z., Feng, Y., Sheinin, V.: SQL-to-text generation with graph-to-sequence model. In: Proceedings of the 2018 Conference on Empirical Methods in Natural Language Processing, pp. 931–936 (2018)
16. Lu, D., Whitehead, S., Huang, L., Ji, H., Chang, S.F.: Entity-aware image caption generation. In: Proceedings of the 2018 Conference on Empirical Methods in Natural Language Processing, pp. 4013–4023 (2018)
17. See, A., Liu, P.J., Manning, C.D.: Get to the point: summarization with pointer generator networks. In: Proceedings of the 55th Annual Meeting of the Association for Computational Linguistics, pp. 1073–1083 (2017)
18. Qiang, Y., Fu, Y., Guo, Y., Zhou, Z., Sigal, L.: Learning to generate posters of scientific papers. In: Proceedings of the 30th AAAI Conference on Artificial Intelligence, pp. 155–169 (2016)
19. Wang, Q., et al.: PaperRobot: incremental draft generation of scientific ideas. In: Proceedings of the 57th Annual Meeting of the Association for Computational Linguistics, pp. 1980–1991 (2019)
20. Lin, Y., Liu, Z., Sun, M., Liu, Y., Zhu, X.: Learning entity and relation embeddings for knowledge graph completion. In: Proceedings of the 39th AAAI Conference on Artificial Intelligence, pp. 2181–2187 (2015)
21. Krishnamoorthy, N., Malkarnenkar, G., Mooney, R.J., Saenko, K., Guadarrama, S.: Generating natural-language video descriptions using text-mined knowledge. In: Proceedings of the 27th AAAI Conference on Artificial Intelligence, pp. 10–19 (2013)
22. Vadapalli, R., Syed, B., Prabhu, N., Srinivasan, B.V., Varma, V.: When science journalism meets artificial intelligence: an interactive demonstration. In: Proceedings of the 2018 Conference on Empirical Methods in Natural Language Processing, pp. 163–168 (2018)

23. Denkowski, M., Lavie, A.: Meteor universal: language specific translation evaluation for any target language. In: Proceedings of the 9th Workshop on Statistical Machine Translation, pp. 376–380 (2014)
24. Bahdanau, D., Cho, K., Bengio, Y.: Neural machine translation by jointly learning to align and translate. In: Proceedings of the 5th International Conference on Learning Representations. arXiv:1409.0473 (2015)
25. Wang, Q., et al.: Paper abstract writing through editing mechanism. In: Proceedings of the 56th Annual Meeting of the Association for Computational Linguistics, pp. 260–265 (2018b)
26. Ji, G., He, S., Xu, L., Liu, K., Zhao, J.: Knowledge graph embedding via dynamic mapping matrix. In: Proceedings of the 53rd Annual Meeting of the Association for Computational Linguistics and the 7th International Joint Conference on Natural Language Processing, pp. 687–696 (2015a)
27. Wang, Z., Li, J.Z.: Text-enhanced representation learning for knowledge graph. In: Proceedings of the 25th International Joint Conference on Artificial Intelligence, pp. 1293–1299 (2016)
28. Xu, J., Chen, K., Qiu, X., Huang, X.: Knowledge graph representation with jointly structural and textual encoding. In: Proceedings of the 26th International Joint Conference on Artificial Intelligence, pp. 1318–1324 (2017)
29. Duma, D., Klein, E.: Generating natural language from linked data: unsupervised template extraction. In: Proceedings of the 10th International Conference on Computational Semantics, pp. 83–94 (2013)
30. Lebret, R., Grangier, D., Auli, M.: Neural text generation from structured data with application to the biography domain. In: Proceedings of the 2016 Conference on Empirical Methods in Natural Language Processing, pp. 1203–1213 (2016)
31. Chisholm, A., Radford, W., Hachey, B.: Learning to generate one-sentence biographies from Wikidata. In: Proceedings of the 15th Conference of the European Chapter of the Association for Computational Linguistics, pp. 633–642 (2017)
32. Wu, Q., Shen, C., Wang, P., Dick, A., Hengel, A.: Image captioning and visual question answering based on attributes and external knowledge. In: Proceedings of the 2018 IEEE Transactions on Pattern Analysis and Machine Intelligence, pp. 1367–1381 (2018)
33. Whitehead, S., Ji, H., Bansal, M., Chang, S.F., Voss, C.: Incorporating background knowledge into video description generation. In: Proceedings of the 2018 Conference on Empirical Methods in Natural Language Processing, pp. 3992–4001 (2018)
34. Foster, J.G., Rzhetsky, A., Evans, J.A.: Tradition and innovation in scientists research strategies. Am. Sociol. Rev. **80**, 875–908 (2015)
35. Papineni, K., Roukos, S., Ward, T., Zhu, W.: BLEU: a method for automatic evaluation of machine translation. In: Proceedings of the 40th Annual Meeting of the Association for Computational Linguistics, pp. 311–318 (2002)

Turn-Level Recurrence Self-attention for Joint Dialogue Action Prediction and Response Generation

Yanxin Tan, Zhonghong Ou$^{(\boxtimes)}$, Kemeng Liu, Yanan Shi, and Meina Song

Beijing University of Posts and Telecommunications, Beijing, China
tobytyx@gmail.com
{zhonghong.ou,liukemeng,apilis,mnsong}@bupt.edu.cn

Abstract. In task-oriented dialogue systems, semantically controlled natural language generation is the procedure to generate responses based on current context information. Seq2seq models are widely used to generate dialogue responses and achieve favorable performance. Nevertheless, how to effectively obtain the dialogue's key information from history remains to be a critical problem. To overcome this problem, we propose a Turn-level Recurrence Self-Attention (TRSA) encoder, which effectively obtains progressive structural relationship in turn-level from conversation history. Moreover, we propose a novel model to predict dialogue actions and generate dialogue responses jointly, which is different from the separate training model used in previous studies. Experiments demonstrate that our model alleviates the problem of inaccurate attention in dialogue history and improves the degree of dialogue completion significantly. In the large-scale MultiWOZ dataset, we improve the performance by 3.9% of inform rate and 3.4% of success rate, which is significantly higher than the state-of-the-art.

Keywords: Self-attention · Dialogue system · Response generation.

1 Introduction

Task-oriented conversational artificial intelligence is a critical research field in artificial intelligence, and has achieved ever-increasing attention [3,7] in recent years. With the rapid development of deep learning, corpus-based semantically controlled response generation models have been proposed [6,11]. These methods usually use a semantic representation to control the generation progress, and employ a seq2seq generation model to splice the whole dialogue history into a long history statement and generate responses [2,6,11].

However, this simplified operation may make the attention matrix evenly distributed throughout the conversation. Tokens for turn i are supposed to focus on turns before i. Nevertheless, due to the operation, part of the attention is diverted to turns after i, where they are not supposed to see. Moreover, existing studies usually do not consider the association between the dialogue action

© Springer Nature Switzerland AG 2020
X. Wang et al. (Eds.): APWeb-WAIM 2020, LNCS 12318, pp. 309–316, 2020.
https://doi.org/10.1007/978-3-030-60290-1_24

prediction task and the generation task. Some studies only represent dialogue actions implicitly without a specific prediction component [12], whilst others separate them apart [2], making it essentially a two-stage model and not able to leverage joint features from the two stages consequently.

To resolve the issues mentioned above, we **first** propose a Turn-level Recurrence Self-Attention (**TRSA**) encoder to encode the dialogue history turn by turn. We **then** propose a **joint model** for dialogue action prediction and response generation with the shared TRSA encoder. Compared with separate training, the joint model with shared encoder is more robust and effective due to the extra supervised signals introduced. In particular, the proposed TRSA encoder effectively improves the capability on dialogue history parsing, which helps accomplish the dialogue task more accurately.

The contributions are summarized as follows:

- We propose a TRSA encoder which effectively models the dialogue progressive structural relationship and improves the distribution of attention.
- We propose a joint learning model which effectively utilizes extra supervised information to train encoder and has a better performance on completing tasks.
- We conduct extensive experiments on a large multi-domain datasets Multi-WOZ [1]. Experiments demonstrate that our model outperforms the state-of-the-art by 3.9% of inform rate and 3.4% of success rate.

2   Related Work

Following the nomenclature proposed in [12], semantically controlled Natural Language Generation is a more comprehensive component which contains Dialogue Action Prediction and Natural Language Generation, assuming that the ground truth belief state and database records are available [2,11]. When dealing with entities in responses, a regular approach is to generate delexicalized sentences with placeholders like "hotel-reference", and then post-process the sentences by replacing the placeholders with database records [10].

Existing models usually use seq2seq structure with various kinds of modules for specific implementation like LSTM [6] and CNN. They concatenate history and dialogue actions together and treat them as a long sentence, which is usually simplistic and ineffective [1,2,6].

Chen et al. [2] proposed a graph-structured representation and a HDSA decoder to alleviate the scalability problem in face of growing number of domains. They use the action feature effectively. Nevertheless, compared with continuous improvement on decoder, not much effort has been spent on encoder.

In this paper, we propose a TRSA encoder to acquire distinct characteristic information and progressive structural relationship of turn-level by utilizing recurrent self-attention architecture. This new architecture is the significant difference between our work and the previous ones. Moreover, in order to enhance the shared encoder by extra supervised signals and promote their mutual influence, we propose a joint model for both dialogue action prediction and response generation with a shared TRSA encoder.

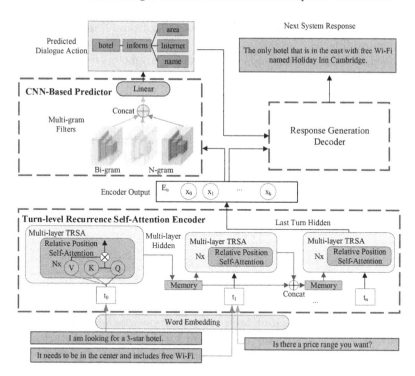

Fig. 1. The overall figure of our model. The component below is TRSA encoder, the one at top left is the CNN-Based dialogue action predictor and the rest is the response generation decoder.

3 Architecture of the Proposed Model

Our model consists of three components: a shared TRSA encoder, a dialogue action predictor, and a response generator. The architecture of our model is illustrated in Fig. 1. We proceed to give detailed description of each component below.

3.1 The TRSA Encoder

Denote the dialogue D with n turns as D_n. We define the n-th layer hidden state representation from the t-th turn r_n by $h_t^n \in R^{L \times d}$, where L is the length of tokens, and d is the hidden dimension of the model. We first concatenate the memory with no gradient m_t^{n-1} and the turn's hidden state h_t^{n-1} from the last layer to acquire the whole context, shown as follows:

$$\tilde{h}_t^{n-1} = [m_t^{n-1} \circ h_t^{n-1}] \tag{1}$$

wherein the notation $[m_t^{n-1} \circ h_t^{n-1}]$ indicates the concatenation of the memory m_t^{n-1} and the current turn's hidden state representation h_t^{n-1}. When embedding the position, we apply relative position embedding from [4] instead of absolute position embedding.

As shown in Eq. 3 and 4, u and v are trainable parameters for position relative to itself, and R_{i-j} means the position embedding from i to j. R is the sinusoid encoding matrix without learnable parameters [9]. Unlike existing studies which leverage the entire context to "query" itself, our keys and values contain memory and current hidden, but the queries are from the current hidden only. This emphasizes the importance of the current turn, and insures that the hidden state of each position can only "query" the preceding turns and the turn which it belongs to. The relative position self-attention is calculated as follows:

$$q_t^n, k_t^n, v_t^n = \mathbf{W_q}^T h_t^{n-1}, \mathbf{W_k}^T \tilde{h}_t^{n-1}, \mathbf{W_v}^T \tilde{h}_t^{n-1} \tag{2}$$

$$r_{i,j}^n = \mathbf{W_R}^T R_{i-j} \tag{3}$$

$$a_{t,i,j}^n = \mathbf{q_{t,i}^n}^T k_{t,j}^n + \mathbf{q_{t,i}^n}^T r_{i,j}^n + \mathbf{u}^T k_{t,j}^n + \mathbf{v}^T r_{i,j}^n \tag{4}$$

$$attn_t^n = Masked - Softmax(a_t^n)v_t^n \tag{5}$$

After self-attention, a linear layer and a residual structure is placed in the model. Following a normalization layer and a position-wise feed-forward layer, we add a masked layer masking the positions of padding to avoid disturbance. We mainly focus on the hidden states from the latest user sentence, which contains attention information to the entire history. Thus, removing the previous gradient helps our model avoid gradient explosion.

3.2 CNN-Based Dialogue Action Predictor

Dialogue actions are a set of triplet actions (domain-action-slot) representing the system's current actions. The triplet action is converted into a binary vector where each position determines whether the node of the action has been activated. Then the predicting task can be considered as a multi-label classification task.

Assume the length of history's representation is L and the hidden dimension is d, we denote the representation as $h_n = [u_0, u_1, u_{L-1}]$, $u \in R^d$. Each convolution filter is parameterized as $W \in R^{n \times d}$, wherein n is the filter size. With k filters, the convolution kernel can be expressed as $K \in R^{k \times n \times d}$. With each kernel, the convolution procedure is presented as follows:

$$c_j = f(W_j \times U + b) \tag{6}$$

$$\tilde{c} = MaxPooling([c_0, c_1, \ldots, c_k]) \tag{7}$$

After performing the same operation in all channels, we repeat the convolution operation m times with different sizes of filters, which focuses on different granularity of sentence characteristics. v_{kb} is the vector of knowledge base, and v_{bs} is the vector of belief state, which we follow the dataset benchmark [1]. The output signals become $\mathbf{o} \in R^{mkd}$, and the probability vector $A \in R^{H_o}$ is shown as follows:

$$\mathbf{o} = [\tilde{c}_0, \tilde{c}_1, \ldots, \tilde{c}_m] \tag{8}$$

$$\tilde{A} = \mathbf{W_a}^\mathrm{T} \sigma(\mathbf{W_o}^\mathrm{T} o + \mathbf{W_b}^\mathrm{T}[v_{kb} : v_{bs}] + b) \tag{9}$$

$$A = Sigmoid(\tilde{A}) \tag{10}$$

3.3 Joint Model for Dialogue Action Prediction and Response Generation

Our decoder uses a similar structure as HDSA [2]. To keep consistent with the position embedding of our TRSA encoder, we modify HDSA model from absolute position embedding to relative position embedding. The decoder consists of three layers of disentangled self-attention modules corresponding to three levels, i.e., domains, actions, and slots. Each layer is controlled by the corresponding action position like a switch. The top layer is the relative Transformer decoder to generate each token. The relative position embedding disentangled self-attention procedure is shown as follows:

$$Q, K, V, R = \mathbf{W_q}^\mathrm{T} h_n, \mathbf{W_k}^\mathrm{T} h_n, \mathbf{W_v}^\mathrm{T} h_n, \mathbf{W_R}^\mathrm{T} R \tag{11}$$

$$attn\_score = \mathbf{Q}^\mathrm{T} \cdot K + \mathbf{Q}^\mathrm{T} \cdot R + \mathbf{u}^\mathrm{T} \cdot K + \mathbf{v}^\mathrm{T} \cdot R \tag{12}$$

$$attn_n = Softmax(attn_score)V \tag{13}$$

$$h_{n+1} = \sum_{i=0}^{X-1} attn_n^i \times da^i \tag{14}$$

Two loss functions are used to train the joint model, i.e., binary cross-entropy loss for dialogue action prediction task (*cls_loss*), and a typical cross-entropy loss to generate responses (*bce_loss*). We join the two loss functions by a hyperparameter α to acquire the general loss:

$$general\_loss = (1 - \alpha)cls\_loss + \alpha(gen\_loss) \tag{15}$$

4 Performance Evaluation

We use a large multi-domain task-oriented dataset MultiWOZ [1] to evaluate performance. The benchmark has richer domain categories and more complex dialogue structures. We follow the dataset benchmark to build validation set and test set with 1000 dialogues each. We conduct contrasted experiments with ablation analysis on two tasks to evaluate the performance of our model.

4.1 Dialogue Action Prediction

We use precision, recall, and F1 score to evaluate performance. The network models we used for comparison are listed as follows: 1) Bi-LSTM 2) 3-layer Transformer encoder 3) 3-layer TRSA encoder 4) **3-layer TRSA encoder & Joint** 5) 12-layer BERT [5]. To provide an apples-to-apples comparison, we use the same configurations for all the network models in addition to Bert. The word-embedding dimension is set as 128, the hidden dimension is set as 128. The optimizer is Adam [8], with the learning rate of $1e^{-3}$ and a warm up stage in 10% epochs.

Table 1. Performance of dialogue action prediction on MultiWOZ.

Method	F1	Precision	Recall
Bi-LSTM	71.4	72.4	70.5
3-layer Transformer encoder	72.3	80.8	65.6
12-layer BERT	77.5	77.4	77.3
3-layer TRSA encoder	73.4	80.1	68.0
3-layer TRSA encoder & Joint	76.7	75.6	78.1

The detailed performance of dialogue action prediction on MultiWOZ is presented in Table 1. From the table, we can see that both our prediction models (3-layer TRSA and 3-layer TRSA & Joint) can improve the prediction performance. Although BERT performs the best, it is mainly because of its large number of parameters (110M) and the corpus consisting of millions of words. On the other hand, we achieve comparable performance with BERT, but with significantly less parameters, i.e., only 4M parameters.

4.2 Dialogue Response Generation

Several metrics are used to evaluate language fluency and task completion, including BLEU-4, entity F1 value, inform rate, and success rate. Amongst them, BLEU and entity F1 are related to fluency and accuracy of the generated responses, while inform rate and success rate are relevant to the dialogue task completion level. The inform & success rate evaluation metrics we use is the same as the dataset benchmark[1] and BLEU metrics we use is from NLTK[2].

We choose four baseline models to compare against ours:

- LSTM: the dataset baseline which the encoder and decoder are both LSTM. We use the official result for comparison [1].
- Standard Transformer: a standard Transformer with a 3 layer self-attention encoder and a 3 layer decoder [9].

---

[1] https://github.com/budzianowski/multiwoz.
[2] http://www.nltk.org/.

- Transformer+DA: 3 layer encoder & decoder standard Transformer with next dialogue actions(DA). The next DA is predicted by Bert model which is introduced earlier.
- HDSA: the model proposed in [2] which is the main reference model of ours.

Table 2. Performance of dialogue response generation on MultiWOZ. "rHDSA" means HDSA with relative position embedding and "Joint" means joint learning mentioned above.

Method	BLEU	Inform rate	Success rate	Entity F1
LSTM	18.9	71.3	60.9	54.8
Standard Transformer	20.0	76.7	60.8	63.3
Transformer+DA	21.7	80.4	65.1	64.6
HDSA	23.1	82.9	68.9	65.7
TRSA+HDSA	22.5	83.1	70.1	68.0
TRSA+rHDSA+Joint	22.6	86.6	70.4	67.4
4Layer+TRSA+rHDSA+Joint	22.6	**86.8**	**72.3**	**67.4**

The performance of dialogue response generation on MultiWOZ is illustrated in Table 2. Compared with HDSA [2], our approach improves 3.9% on inform rate, 3.4% on success rate, and 1.7% on entity F1, which reflects that our improvements are beneficial in completing the dialogue tasks.

Our approach effectively improves the completion on long conversation. Our best model completes 4% of middle length and 8.5% of long dialogues more than HDSA model [2]. These remarkable improvements are probably due to TRSA encoder which avoids model distraction during long conversations and brings key structural relationship into the context representation more directly. Correspondingly, it improves both the success rate and inform rate remarkably.

In order to explain the influence of each improvement on the experimental result, we set an ablation experiments to remove all improvements and append them separately. The models we experiment are listed as follows and the results of ablation experiments are shown in Table 2.

The experiments show that both of joint learning and TRSA has positive effects on the dialogue completion, whether the decoder is HDSA or standard self-attention.

5   Conclusion

In this paper, we proposed a TRSA encoder which effectively reduces the unfavorable attention on history and helps complete the dialogue task. We then proposed a joint model for semantically controlled natural language generation task. It uses a shared TRSA encoder and successfully takes advantage of the information between each task. Experiments on real-world dataset demonstrates effectiveness of our proposed scheme.

The current TRSA focuses on the progressive structural relationship in the dialogue history. In the future, we will try to extract more complicated relationship in the dialogue conversation.

Acknowledgments. This work is supported in part by the National Key R&D Program of China(Grant No.2017YFB1400800). Engineering Research Center of Information Networks, Ministry of Education.

References

1. Budzianowski, P., et al.: Multiwoz-a large-scale multi-domain wizard-of-oz dataset for task-oriented dialogue modelling. arXiv preprint arXiv:1810.00278 (2018)
2. Chen, W., Chen, J., Qin, P., Yan, X., Wang, W.Y.: Semantically conditioned dialog response generation via hierarchical disentangled self-attention. arXiv preprint arXiv:1905.12866 (2019)
3. Chen, X., Xu, J., Xu, B.: A working memory model for task-oriented dialog response generation. In: Proceedings of the 57th Annual Meeting of the Association for Computational Linguistics, pp. 2687–2693 (2019)
4. Dai, Z., Yang, Z., Yang, Y., Cohen, W.W., Carbonell, J., Le, Q.V., Salakhutdinov, R.: Transformer-xl: attentive language models beyond a fixed-length context. arXiv preprint arXiv:1901.02860 (2019)
5. Devlin, J., Chang, M.W., Lee, K., Toutanova, K.: Bert: Pre-training of deep bidirectional transformers for language understanding. arXiv preprint arXiv:1810.04805 (2018)
6. Dušek, O., Jurčíček, F.: A context-aware natural language generator for dialogue systems. arXiv preprint arXiv:1608.07076 (2016)
7. Gao, J., Galley, M., Li, L.: Neural approaches to conversational AI. In: Proceedings of ACL 2018, Tutorial Abstracts, pp. 2–7 (2018)
8. Kim, Y.: Convolutional neural networks for sentence classification. arXiv preprint arXiv:1408.5882 (2014)
9. Vaswani, A., et al.: Attention is all you need. In: Advances in Neural Information Processing Systems, pp. 5998–6008 (2017)
10. Wen, T.H., et al.: Multi-domain neural network language generation for spoken dialogue systems. In: Proceedings of the 2016 Conference of the North American Chapter of the Association for Computational Linguistics: Human Language Technologies, pp. 120–129 (2016)
11. Wen, T.H., Gasic, M., Mrksic, N., Su, P.H., Vandyke, D., Young, S.: Semantically conditioned LSTM-based natural language generation for spoken dialogue systems. arXiv preprint arXiv:1508.01745 (2015)
12. Wen, T.H., et al.: A network-based end-to-end trainable task-oriented dialogue system. arXiv preprint arXiv:1604.04562 (2016)

Mining Affective Needs from Online Opinions for Design Innovation

Danping Jia[ID] and Jian Jin[(✉)] [ID]

Department of Information Management, Beijing Normal University, Beijing 100875, China
jinjian.jay@bnu.edu.cn

Abstract. Innovative product features may gain higher brand reputation with lower cost for companies. Besides functional features, products having differential advantages on aesthetic design are acknowledged to be attractive in the market. As a result, exploring customer affective needs plays a critical role in product design innovation. In this paper, a hybrid method is proposed to reveal and classify customer affective needs from online opinions, including customer affective emotions and related product features. Firstly, inspired by Kansei engineering (KE), a knowledge-based method is presented to extract customer affective emotions. Then, enlightened by Kano model which determines the priorities of product features based on their abilities in satisfying customers, affective features are automatically extracted and classified into Kano categories. Finally, empirical studies are investigated to evaluate the effectiveness of the proposed framework. Compared with others, this method achieves higher F-measure scores in different domains. It highlights that a data-driven integration of KE and Kano model brings novel ideas and advanced suggestions for product design and marketing management in the view of designers and managers.

Keywords: Customer affective needs · Product design · Kano model · KE · Online review · Text mining

1 Introduction

Motivated by the increasing customer requirements and the shortened product life cycle, the customer-oriented product is focused by companies. Customer needs are complex. Besides rational evaluation based on the individual knowledge, customers are unconsciously in the process of evaluating product through all senses, including sight, hearing, taste, smell, and touch. People may be attracted by fancy appearance, scientific ergonomics structure, good sense of touch or other affective features easily. These features reflect the aesthetic, artistic, culturistic, symbolic and ethical meaning of companies [1]. Moreover, customer affective needs have been emphasized because of the functional homogenization. As a result, affective needs are supposed to be explored to keep a high user loyalty for companies. However, many studies [2, 3] are chiefly focused on product functional needs, whereas affective features are neglected.

Kansei Engineering (KE) is widely used to capture customer affective needs, where "Kansei" refers to affective, emotional and sensitive. The theory translates customer's

© Springer Nature Switzerland AG 2020
X. Wang et al. (Eds.): APWeb-WAIM 2020, LNCS 12318, pp. 317–324, 2020.
https://doi.org/10.1007/978-3-030-60290-1_25

intangible psychological feelings into tangible Kansei words and matching them with product features without distinction [4]. However, product features are not treated equally by customers [5]. For instance, people may be attracted by unexpected innovation in exterior colors rather than few improvement in system performance. Accordingly, exploring relations between customer satisfaction and feature fulfillment is important. Kano model brings insight into this problem, where features are classified into 5 Kano categories based on their abilities in satisfying customers, including Must-be (M), One-dimensional (O), Attractive (A), Indifference (I) and Reverse(R).

Traditionally, questionnaire method is widely used in collecting customer needs, but the analysis may be constrained by experts' knowledge. Benefiting from the information technology, reviews contain rich, real, and timely customer feedback. However, affective needs are seldom discussed. Accordingly, this paper probes Kansei feature design for companies. Firstly, customer Kansei needs are identified from reviews; then, Kano model is applied to prioritize affective features; finally, empirical cases are analyzed. The remainder of this paper is organized as follows. Relevant literature is reviewed in Sect. 2. The proposed method is discussed in Sect. 3. A case study is presented in Sect. 4, and in Sect. 5, contributions are discussed.

2 Literature Review

2.1 Customer Needs Mining

At the beginning, customer opinions are collected through qualitative methods. Later, under the background of e-commerce, the attitude of review texts [7], sentences [6] and features [8] are explored. However, affective requirements are less considered. KE is used in affective product design, integrated with psychology, neuropsychology, and manufacturing [9]. Usually, Kansei words and related features are generated by questionnaires [3, 10]. However, the reality of received answers or the limited number of interviewees may lead to marketing blunders. Online opinions can explore affective needs. N-gram language model was introduced to catch Kansei emotions [9]. Wang et al. [11] probed a multiple classification approach based on affective sentiments using deep learning algorithm. Wang et al. [12] used WordNet to enlarge the Kansei space. However, Kansei is context-dependent, which means same Kansei words may represent totally different attitudes in diverse domains. To fill this gap, a context-based method is proposed here to discover Kansei emotions from online reviews.

2.2 User-Centered Product Design in Kano

Companies need to keep a balance between customers and cost through the product feature design. Kano model reveals the ability of features in satisfying customers.

The Kano process is normally standardized into three steps: (1) product features are predefined by experts; (2) for each feature in presence and absence, participants are asked to response by: L (Like), M (Must-be), N (Neutral), W (Live-with), and D (Dislike); (3) based on the Kano evaluation table, every feature is mapped into one Kano category, namely M, O, A, I, and R. Among these categories, (1) M: customers are very displeased when it is done poorly, whereas its fulfillment won't lead to satisfaction; (2) O: it is uphill and linearly related to customer sentiments; (3) A: people may pay for it with great joy, whereas a lack of it won't lead to any dissatisfaction; (4) I: people pay little attention to it; (5) R: it provokes utter horror when met. Additionally, if consumers take a dislike attitude no matter being present or absent, this feature belongs to Q (Questionable) [13]. Inspired by Kano, researchers prioritize features with qualitative methods [14, 15], where innovative features may not be fully covered. Later, the data-driven Kano analysis became a hot focus [16–18]. However, little literature takes notice at affective features' Kano classification. Accordingly, in this study, product design is discussed in a novel perspective to meet customer affective needs with a trade-off idea.

3   A Hybrid Framework for Product Design Innovation

Illustrated in Fig. 1, a hybrid research framework integrating KE and Kano model is proposed to explore customer affective needs from reviews for product innovation.

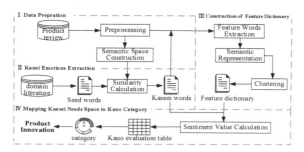

Fig. 1. The research framework

3.1   Data Preparation

A set of preprocessing tasks are conducted, including sentence segmentation, tokenization, Part-of-Speech (POS) tagging, stop words removal, lemmatization and syntactic parsing. Additionally, contextual words semantics is learned by word2vec[1].

3.2   Kansei Emotions Extraction

Kansei emotions are context-dependent. For example, the polarity of "fast" in "phone runs out of battery so fast" and "I love to drive fast cars" are distinct. Moreover, some Kansei words may not be covered in sentiment dictionaries, like "five stars". Accordingly, Kansei words are extracted by collecting seed words, and selecting Kansei words.

Firstly, Kansei words that have been defined by experts in previous studies are taken as seed words. They are selected from the literature in the same domain because of

---

[1] https://pypi.org/project/gensim/.

domain specificity. The sentiment value of seed words are set as 1 or -1 indicating whether positive or negative. Secondly, adjectival tokens and adverbial tokens that are close to seed words are selected as Kansei candidates. The word2vec model mentioned in Sect. 3.1 is used to get words semantics and phrases is represented by the average vectors of words in the phrase. For each token, the semantic similarities between itself and every seed words are calculated. Later, in order to select proper Kansei words from candidates, (1) the maximum similarity is picked out for this candidate; (2) considering the positive candidate may be related to negative the seed word and vice versa, SentiWordNet[2] is used to help filter out terms with misjudged polarities. Moreover, the sentiment score of Kansei words is the determined by related seed words and the similarities. Following [19], every Kansei word is divided into one emotion response based on the sentiment scores, namely L, M, N, W, and D, using a thresholding method.

3.3 The Construction of Product Feature Dictionary

Kansei features are explored by feature words extraction, vectorization, and clustering. Firstly, Nouns having an "amod" or "advmod" dependency relation with Kansei words is selected as candidates. Moreover, inspired by [20], words are concretized using Noun phrases identified by a toolkit[3]. Furthermore, the status of feature word is also judged, i.e., functional present or dysfunctional absent. Secondly, customers talk about same features by varied words, like phone outer covering could be described as "casing", "shell". Hence, feature words should be vectorized and clustered for understanding.

3.4 Mapping Kansei Needs Space to Kano Category

In this Section, Kano model is used to prioritize Kansei features, shown in Fig. 2.

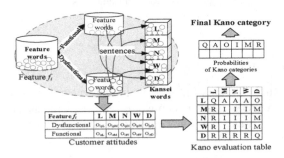

Fig. 2. Kano evaluation for feature f_i

Take feature f_i for instance, as mentioned in Sect. 3.2 and Sect. 3.3, related feature phrases can be tracked based on syntactic structures and every phrase consists in a specific status s_j, i.e., presence or absence; the Kansei word is classified into different response groups g_k based on its sentiment score, i.e., L, M, N, W, and D.

---

[2] https://github.com/aesuli/sentiwordnet.

[3] https://spacy.io/.

Then, customer attitudes towards f_i with status s_i and response group g_k, which are represented as o_{ijk}, can be estimated as the averaged sentiment value of Kansei words belonging to the same status and the same response group. More specifically, for feature f_i, two vectors $\overrightarrow{v_{ip}}$ and $\overrightarrow{v_{ia}}$ are inferred to describe customer attitudes in two states separately, presence and absence. Next, inspired by Kano model, these two vectors are multiplied to map with the Kano evaluation table, represented as:

$$\left(\overrightarrow{v_{ip}}\right)^T \times \overrightarrow{v_{ia}} = \begin{pmatrix} w_{iQ} & w_{iA} & w_{iA} & w_{iA} & w_{iO} \\ w_{iR} & w_{iI} & w_{iI} & w_{iI} & w_{iM} \\ w_{iR} & w_{iI} & w_{iI} & w_{iI} & w_{iM} \\ w_{iR} & w_{iI} & w_{iI} & w_{iI} & w_{iM} \\ w_{iR} & w_{iR} & w_{iR} & w_{iR} & w_{iQ} \end{pmatrix} \tag{1}$$

Each element w_{ic} in the matrix represents the weight of f_i referring to Kano category, c. The sum of elements with same c is the probability of f_i belonging to this category. The category with maximum possibility is the final choice for f_i.

4 Empirical Study

Empirical studies are performed to evaluate the effectiveness and the utility of the proposed method based on customer reviews.

4.1 Evaluation Method

To evaluate the performance of the proposed method, two parts are reckoned, i.e., to identify Kansei words and to associate Kansei words with product features. For the former part, a comparative analysis about three schemes is represented: (1) Seed words + WordNet; (2) Seed words + BOW; (3) Seed words + Cbow. For the latter part, four integrated methods are drawn for feature matching and clustering, including (1) Dependency parsing + Kmeans; (2) Dependency parsing + Hierarchical clustering; (3) Sliding Windows + Kmeans; (4) Sliding Windows + Hierarchical clustering.

The performance of two parts is evaluated separately. 11,542, 8,621 reviews of smartphones and cameras are crawled from Amazon.com. 200 sentences are randomly selected as test corpus. The ground truth is constructed manually by two undergraduate students. The performance is evaluated by precision, recall and F-measure.

4.2 Classifying Kansei Sensitive Features into Kano Categories

10 Seed words are collected, including 5 positive words, i.e. attractive, elegant, reliable, like, professional, and 5 negative words, i.e. stupid, awful, bad, dislike, useless. Later, 100-dimensional vector spaces trained from corpuses are applied to represent tokens. The token with similarity scores within the top 1,000 is selected. After the filter process, 852 Kansei words are identified in smartphone domain, i.e. state of the art, highly recommended, normal style, functionality similarly, and joke absolutely.

Based on the parsed syntax structures in sentences and the transformation process, 832 phrases for smartphone and 527 phrases for camera are identified. Later, a 300-dimensional word embedded model[4] was loaded for phrases representation. In total, there are 14 smartphone feature groups, namely quality, brand, line, signal, shape, camera, material, aesthetic design, safety, service, physical interface, performance, price, and theme.

Inspired by Kano model, affective design features are mapped into 6 Kano categories, namely M, O, A, I, R, and Q. For smartphone features, M category includes quality; I category includes shape; O category includes signal; Q category includes brands, lines, theme, performance; and the others belong to A category, namely camera, aesthetic design, material, safety, service, price, physical interface.

4.3   Performance Comparison Among Benchmarked Approaches

The performances of different approaches on identifying affective emotions are described in Fig. 3 (a). It is found that word2vec model is more appropriate to seek affective sentiment phrases with higher F-measure scores. Not only unigrams, bigrams, i.e. adjectival tokens, adverbial tokens, do represent extensive emotional implications, whereas they may not be well covered in dictionaries or Bow model.

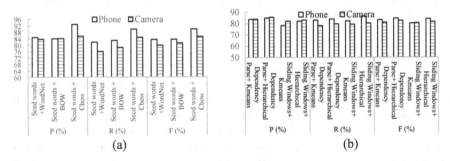

Fig. 3. The evaluation results of Kansei emotion extraction and design feature recognition

The comparative performances of diverse schemes in extracting Kansei features are shown in Fig. 3 (b). It implies that there are losses while seeking Kansei features through dependency parsing even though it has higher precision scores, because some features cannot be searched by "amod" or "advmod" relations derived from Kansei words. Additionally, Kmeans actually did slightly worse in clustering which may be caused by its high sensitivity to outliers. In general, the scheme with dependency parsing and hierarchical clustering performs better than others. The result proves that our method is applicable in Kansei word extracting and design feature summarization.

---

[4] https://spacy.io/models/en#en_core_web_lg.

4.4 Practical Affective Needs in Smartphone

In this section, aesthetic design is analyzed to highlight the practical contributions of the proposed approach in discovering affective needs for companies. The following text in italics are mined by our method, whereas some may not be revealed by others.

The aesthetic design of smartphones often includes case color, sense of touch, and others. The aesthetic design idea includes: (1) it is a tough job for customers to accept a *sharply fresh* color. For example, some people consider the *extraordinary blue* color as an innovation, whereas it is *inconvenient* for seeing flashing light; *classy-looking* colors remain a fundamental focus. (2) Consumers care about body size, smooth edges shape, balanced body thick, together with luxury textures. However, bigger size is *difficult* for pocketing. Keeping balance between convenient operation, excellent visual effects, and *convenient carrying* is important. (3) A good product design ought to cover as much customer behavioral differences as possible. For example, icon layout is supposed to not be *bothersome* for both left-handed person and right-handed person; the differences of different product versions should be noted strikingly. Take camera shutter sound of smartphone as an example, it cannot be turned off in Japanese version, which is *embarrassing* in other countries.

5 Conclusion

Affective features are crucial in delighting customers. In this paper, customer affective needs are explored from customer reviews integrating KE and Kano model.

On the one hand, the theoretical contributions are three-fold: (1) contextual customer affective needs are extracted based on knowledgeable value of the literature and the informative value of customer reviews; (2) the scope of Kansei words is extended automatically; (3) the gap between affective emotions and feature design is shorten using a data-driven method. On the other hand, this paper also has great practical contributions. Basically, an innovative design perspective related to affective needs is provided for designers. In addition, an active mechanism is introduced to prioritize product features for cost management. The main limitation of this study is Kansei words are classified roughly based on a thresholding method.

Acknowledgments. The work was supported by a Grant from the National Nature Science Foundation of China (project no. NSFC 71701019/G0114) and National Social Science Foundation of China (Grant. 19ATQ005).

References

1. Gagliardi, M.: Alchemy of cultures: from adaptation to transcendence in design and branding. Des. Manag. Rev. **12**(4), 32–39 (2001)
2. Archak, N., Ghose, A., Ipeirotis, P.G.: Deriving the pricing power of product features by mining consumer reviews. Manag. Sci. **57**(8), 1485–1509 (2011)
3. Wang, C.H., Chin, H.T.: Integrating affective features with engineering features to seek the optimal product varieties with respect to the niche segments. Adv. Eng. Inform. **33**, 350–359 (2017)

4. Yanagisawa, H., Tamotsu, M., et al.: A proposal of Kansei database framework and Kansei modelling methodology for the delight design platform. J. Integr. Des. Process Sci. **20**(2), 73–84 (2016)

5. Aspect-based Kano categorization: Anna Martí Bigorra, Ove Isaksson, and Magnus Karlberg. Int. J. Inf. Manage. **46**, 163–172 (2019)

6. Hu, Y., Chen, Y., Chou, H.: Opinion mining from online hotel reviews – a text summarization approach. Inf. Process. Manag. **53**(2), 436–449 (2017)

7. Jin, J., Liu, Y., Ji, P., Kwong, C.K.: Review on recent advances of information mining from big consumer opinion data for product design. J. Comput. Inf. Sci. Eng. **19**(1), 1024–1043 (2019)

8. Anand, K., Dewangan, N., Kumar, N., et al.: Aspect ontology-based review exploration. Electron. Commer. Res. Appl. **30**(62), 62–71 (2018)

9. Hsiao, Y.-H., Chen, M.-C., Liao, W.-C.: Logistics service design for cross-border E-commerce using Kansei engineering with text-mining-based online content analysis. Telemat. Inform. **34**, 284–302 (2017)

10. Hartono, M.: The extended integrated model of Kansei engineering, Kano, and TRIZ incorporating cultural differences into services. Int. J. Technol. **7**(1), 97–104 (2016)

11. Wang, W.M., Wang, J., Li, Z., et al.: Multiple affective attribute classification of online customer product reviews: a heuristic deep learning method for supporting Kansei engineering. Eng. Appl. Artif. Intell. **85**, 33–45 (2019)

12. Wang, W.M., Li, Z., Tian, Z.G., et al.: Extracting and summarizing affective features and responses from online product descriptions and reviews: a Kansei text mining approach. Eng. Appl. Artif. Intell. **73**, 149–162 (2018)

13. Chai, C., Defu, B., et al.: The relative effects of different dimensions of traditional cultural elements on customer product satisfaction. Int. J. Ind. Ergon. **48**, 77–88 (2015)

14. Wang, C.H., Wang, J.: Combining fuzzy AHP and fuzzy Kano to optimize product varieties for smart cameras: a zero-one integer programming perspective. Appl. Soft Comput. **22**, 410–416 (2014)

15. Tontini, G., Bento, G.D.S., Milbratz, T.C., et al.: Exploring the impact of critical incidents on customers' general evaluation of hospitality services. Int. J. Hosp. Manag. **66**, 106–116 (2017)

16. Qi, J., Zhang, Z., Jeon, S., et al.: Mining customer requirements from online reviews: a product improvement perspective. Inf. Manag. **53**(8), 951–963 (2016)

17. Xiao, S., Wei, C.P., Dong, M.: Crowd intelligence: analyzing online product reviews for preference measurement. Inf. Manag. **53**(2), 169–182 (2016)

18. Hou, T., Yannou, B., Leroy, Y., et al.: Mining changes in user expectation over time from online reviews. J. Mech. Des. **141**(9), 1–10 (2019)

19. Hartono, M., Santoso, A., Prayogo, D.N.: How Kansei engineering, Kano and QFD can improve logistics services. Int. J. Technol. **8**(6), 1070–1081 (2017)

20. Jin, J., Ji, P., Liu, Y.: Translating online customer opinions into engineering characteristics in QFD: a probabilistic language analysis approach. Eng. Appl. Artif. Intell. **41**, 115–127 (2015)

Spatial, Temporal and Multimedia Databases

Multi-grained Cross-modal Similarity Query with Interpretability

Mingdong Zhu[1(✉)], Derong Shen[2], Lixin Xu[1], and Gang Ren[1]

[1] School of Computer Science and Technology, Henan Institute of Technology, Xinxiang, China
{zhumingdong,l.xu,rengang}@hait.edu.cn
[2] School of Computer Science and Engineering, Northeastern University, Shenyang, China
shenderong@ise.edu.cn

Abstract. Cross-modal similarity query has become a highlighted research topic for managing multimodal datasets such as images and texts. Existing researches generally focus on query accuracy by designing complex deep neural network models, and hardly consider query efficiency and interpretability simultaneously, which are vital properties of cross-modal semantic query processing system on large-scale datasets. In this work, we investigate multi-grained common semantic embedding representations of images and texts, and integrate interpretable query index into the deep neural network by developing a novel Multi-grained Cross-modal Query with Interpretability (MCQI) framework. The main contributions are as follows: (1) By integrating coarse-grained and fine-grained semantic learning models, a multi-grained cross-modal query processing architecture is proposed to ensure the adaptability and generality of query processing. (2) In order to capture the latent semantic relation between images and texts, the framework combines LSTM and attention mode, which enhances query accuracy for the cross-modal query and constructs the foundation for interpretable query processing. (3) Index structure and corresponding nearest neighbor query algorithm are proposed to boost the efficiency of interpretable queries. Comparing with state-of-the-art methods on widely-used cross-modal datasets, the experimental results show the effectiveness of our MCQI approach.

Keywords: Cross-modal · Interpretability · Multi-grained · Similarity query

1 Introduction

With rapid development of computer science and technology, multimedia data including images and texts, have been emerging on the Internet, which have become the main form of humans knowing the world. Consequently, cross-modal similarity query has been an essential technique with wide applications, such as search engine and multimedia data management. Cross-modal similarity query [1] is such an effective query paradigm that users can get the results of one type by submitting a query of the other type. In this work, we mainly focus on queries between images and texts. For instance, when one user submits a piece of textual description of one football game, most relevant images in datasets can be fetched, and vice versa. Cross-modal similarity query should discover

© Springer Nature Switzerland AG 2020
X. Wang et al. (Eds.): APWeb-WAIM 2020, LNCS 12318, pp. 327–341, 2020.
https://doi.org/10.1007/978-3-030-60290-1_26

latent semantic relationships among different types, it has attracted great interests from researchers.

Due to the significant advantage of deep neural networks (DNN) in feature extraction, DNN models are utilized for cross-modal similarity query [2]. The complex structure and high-dimensional feature maps equip the deep neural networks with considerable power of learning non-linear relationships, however, at the same time complex models introduce some drawbacks. First, numerous parameters of deep neural networks make query process and results difficult to be explained. That is, those models have weak interpretability, which is an important property for general and reliable cross-modal query system. Second, in order to find the most similar data objects, typically the cosine similarity between the high-dimensional feature vector of query object and that of each object in the whole dataset should be computed. Hence, for a large-scale dataset, the computation cost is so high that the query response time will be obnoxious. Existing researches tend to focus on designing complicated composite models to enhance query accuracy, and hardly take account of query interpretability and efficiency at the same time.

To this end, we propose a novel efficient and effective cross-modal query framework with interpretability. In order to ensure the adaptability and generality of our framework, during training common feature vectors for different types we first capture coarse-grained and fine-grained semantic information by designing different networks and then combine them. And in order to discover the latent semantic relations between images and texts, we integrated LSTM model and attention model, besides, the data foundation of cross-modal correlative information is constructed in this way. In addition, for the sake of query efficiency, we built an index supporting interpretable query. At last, to confirm the efficiency and effectiveness of our approach, we systematically evaluate the performances of the approach by comparing with 8 state-of-the-art methods on 5 widely-used multi-modal datasets.

The remainder of this paper is organized as follows. Section 2 briefly reviews related work. In Sect. 3, we introduce definitions of problems and then describe in detail our MCQI framework and a kNN query algorithm in Sect. 4. Section 5 provides experimental results and analysis on five datasets, and we conclude in Sect. 6.

2   Related Work

In this section, we briefly review the related researches for cross-modal query, including cross-modal retrieval, latent semantic alignment and cross-modal hashing.

Cross-modal Retrieval. Traditional methods mainly learn linear projections for different data types. Canonical correlation analysis (CCA) [3] is proposed to learn cross-modal common representation by maximizing the pairwise correlation, which is a classical baseline method for cross-modal measurement. Beyond pairwise correlation, joint representation learning (JRL) [4] is proposed to make use of semi-supervised regularization and semantic information, which can jointly learn common representation projections for up to five data types. S2UPG [5] further improves JRL by constructing a unified hypergraph to learn the common space by utilizing the fine-grained information. Recent years, DNN-based cross-modal retrieval has become an active research topic. Deep canonical correlation analysis (DCCA) is proposed by [6] with two subnetworks, which combines DNN with CCA to maximize the correlation on the top of two subnetworks. UCAL [7] is an unsupervised cross-modal retrieval method based on adversarial learning, which takes a modality classifier as a discriminator to distinguish the modality of learned features. DADN [8] approach is proposed for addressing the problem of zeroshot cross-media retrieval, which learns common embeddings with category semantic information. These methods mainly focus on query accuracy rather than query efficiency and interpretability.

Latent Semantic Alignment. Latent semantic alignment is the foundation for interpretable query. [9] embeds patches of images and dependency tree relations of sentences in a common embedding space and explicitly reasons about their latent, inter-modal correspondences. Adding generation step, [10] proposes a model which learns to score sentence and image similarity as a function of R-CNN object detections with outputs of a bidirectional RNN. By incorporating attention into neural networks for vision related tasks, [11, 12] investigate models that can attend to salient part of an image while generating its caption. These methods inspire ideas of achieving interpretable cross-modal query, but neglect issues of query granularity and efficiency.

Cross-modal Hashing. Deep cross-modal hashing (DCMH) [13] combines hashing learning and deep feature learning by preserving the semantic similarity between modalities. Correlation auto-encoder hashing (CAH) [14] embeds the maximum cross-modal similarity into hash codes using nonlinear deep autoencoders. Correlation hashing network (CHN) [15] jointly learns image and text representations tailored to hash coding and formally controls the quantization error. Pairwise relationship guided deep hashing (PRDH) [16] jointly uses two types of pairwise constraints from intra-modality and inter-modality to preserve the semantic similarity of the learned hash codes. [17] proposes a generative adversarial network to model cross-modal hashing in an unsupervised fashion and a correlation graph-based learning approach to capture the underlying manifold structure across different modalities. For large high-dimensional data, hashing is a common tool, which can achieve sub-linear time complexity for data retrieval. However, after constructing a hash index on hamming space, it is difficult to obtain flexible query granularity and reasonable interpretability.

3   Problem Description

For cross-modal similarity query, given a query object of one type, most similar objects of the other type in the dataset should be returned. The formal definition is shown below.

The multi-modal dataset consists of two modalities with m images and n texts, which is denoted as $D = \{D^t, D^i\}$. The texts are encoded as a one hot code originally, and in the set D the data of text modality are denoted as $D^t = D^t = \{x_k^t\}_{k=1}^n$, where the k-th text object is defined as $x_k^t \in \mathbb{R}^{l_k * c}$ with the sentence length l_k and the vocabulary size c. The data of image modality are denoted as $D^i = \{x_k^i\}_{k=1}^n$, where the k-th image instance is defined as $x_k^i \in \mathbb{R}^{w * h * c'}$ with image resolution $w * h$ and color channel number c'. Besides, the pairwise correspondence is denoted as $\left(x_k^t, x_k^i\right)$, which means that the two instances of different types are strongly semantically relevant. Cross-modal similarity query means that given one query object it's to find similar objects of the other modality which share relevant semantics with the given one, kNN query is a classical type of similarity query, the definition is given as follows.

Definition 1 (kNN Query). Given an object q, an integer $k > 1$, dataset D and similarity function SIM, the k nearest neighbors query kNN computes a size-k subset $S \subseteq D$, s.t. $\forall o_i \in S$, $o_j \in D - S$: $\mathrm{SIM}(q, o_i) \geq \mathrm{SIM}(q, o_i)$. In this work, we set cosine similarity as similarity function.

Table 1 lists the used notations throughout this paper. The list mainly consists of the notations which are mentioned far from their definitions.

Table 1. Used notations

Notation	Description
SIM	Similarity function
(x_k^t, x_k^i)	The k-th matched pair of images and texts
d_l	Dimension of local common embedding space
d_g	Dimension of global common embedding space
TU	The set of patch relation tuples between images and texts
Ins_i	The i-th data instance in the dataset
$CFVF_i$	The i-th common fine-grained semantic feature
$CFVC_i$	The i-th common coarse-grained semantic feature
δ	Weight factor to balance fine-grained and coarse-grained features
σ	Probability of weight factor can be omitted

4   Proposed Model

In this section, we describe the proposed MCQI framework in detail. As shown in Fig. 1, MCQI framework consists of two stages. The first stage is the learning stage, which models common embedding representation of multi-modal data by fusing coarse-grained and fine-grained semantic information. The second stage is the index construction stage, in which M-tree index and inverted index are integrated to process efficient and interpretable queries. In the following paragraphs, we introduce it in the aspects of embedding representations of multi-modal data and interpretable query processing.

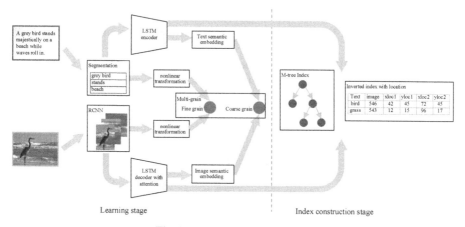

Fig. 1. The framework of MCQI

4.1 Embedding Representations of Multi-modal Data

In the first stage, MCQI learns the embedding representation of multi-modal data by fusing coarse-grained and fine-grained semantic information.

Fine-grained Embedding Learning with Local Semantics. Different methods are used to extract local semantic features for texts and images. For texts, EmbedRank [18] is utilized to extract keyphrases. Then a pretrained model Sent2vec [19] is chosen for computing the embedding of each keyphrase. Then by three-layer fully-connected neural network we map each keyphrase into the common embedding space with dimension d_l, denoted as ts_{pq}, which means the embedding representation of the q-th keyphrase of the p-th text description.

For images, Region Convolutional Neural Network (RCNN) [20] is utilized to detect objects in images. We use top detected locations of the entire image as local semantic features, and then compute the common embedding vectors based on the visual matrix in each bounding box by a pretrained convolutional neural network, and by transition matrix transform the vector to common space with dimension d_l, lastly we get is_{uv}, which means the embedding representation of the v-th bounding box of the u-th image.

Typically, for a pair of matched text and image, at least one of keyphrases in the text is semantically relevant with a certain bounding box in the image instance, that is, at least one common embedding vector of the text instance is close to a certain common embedding vector of the image instance. Base on this intuitiveness, according to hinge rank loss function, we set the original objective of fine-grained embedding learning as follows:

$$C_b(ts_{pq}, is_{uv}) = \sum_q \sum_v (\frac{pnum}{Anum})^{I(p \neq u)}(1 - \frac{pnum}{Anum})^{I(p = u)} \max(0, \ M - (-1)^{I(p \neq u)} \frac{ts_{pq} \cdot is_{uv}}{|ts_{pq}| \cdot |is_{uv}|}) \quad (1)$$

Here, *Pnum* is the number of matched pairs in the training sample set, and *Anum* is the training sample capability. $(\alpha \frac{pnum}{Anum})^{I(p = u)}(1 - \alpha \frac{pnum}{Anum})^{I(p \neq u)}$ is utilized to balance positive and negative samples. $\frac{ts_{pq} \cdot is_{uv}}{|ts_{pq}| \cdot |is_{uv}|}$ is the cosine similarity of two embedding vectors.

M is the margin constant, which defines the tolerance of true positive and true negative. The more M is close to 1, the stricter it is about semantically recognizing true positive and true negative.

C_b cost is computed over all pairs of local features between text instances and image instances. However, in many cases, for two semantically relevant instances only few parts of local features are matched, and similar pairs are difficult to be acquired by computation over all pairs. To address this problem, according to MILE [9], we make a multiple instance learning extension of formula (1) as shown in formula (2). For each text instance, local features of matched image are put into a positive bag, while local features in other image are treated as negative samples.

$$C_P = \min_{k_{qv}} \sum_q \sum_v (\frac{Pnum}{Anum})^{I(p \neq u)} (1 - \frac{Pnum}{Anum})^{I(p = u)} \max(0, M - k_{qv} \frac{ts_{pq} \cdot is_{uv}}{|ts_{pq}| \cdot |is_{uv}|})$$

$$s.t. \sum_{v \in B_q} (k_{qv} + 1) \geq 2 \forall v, \quad k_{qv} = \begin{cases} 1, & p = u \\ -1, & p \neq u \end{cases}. \tag{2}$$

Here, B_q is the positive bag of the q-th feature vector, k_{qv} is the correlation index which indicates whether the corresponding text instance and image instance are matched. It is worth notice that each feature vector is_{uv} and the corresponding bounding box are stored in the storage system for processing interpretable queries.

Coarse-grained Embedding Learning with Global Semantics. Coarse-grained embedding network tries to capture global common semantics between texts and images. For texts, Universal Sentence Encoder [21] is utilized to extract feature vectors of texts, and by fully connected layers the feature vectors are transformed into the global common embedding space with dimension d_g.

For images, inspired by [11] that pretrained LSTM with soft attention model is integrated to translate images into sequential representation. For an image, feature maps before classification in a pretrained R-CNN network and the whole image's feature maps before fully connected layers in pretrained CNN network are combined into feature vectors, denoted as $a = \{a_i\}_{i=1}^{LV}$, and LV is the number of the feature vectors.

Our implementation of LSTM with soft attention is based on [11]. a_i is the input, y and α_{ti} are outputs, y is the generated sequential text and α_{ti} represents importance of feature vector a_i when generating the t-th word. please note that each word y_t has an attention weight α_{ti} for each feature vector a_i, and each tuple $tu_t = <y_t$, imageID, α_{ti}, $xloc_i$, $xloc1_i$, $xloc2_i$, $yloc1_i$, $yloc2_i>$ is stored for answering future queries, where imageID is the image's unique identifier, $xloc_i$, $xloc1_i$, $xloc2_i$, $yloc1_i$, $yloc2_i$ are the corresponding coordinate position of a_i in the image. We collect all tuples as set $TU = \{tu_t\}$.

For generated sequential text y, Universal Sentence Encoder is utilized to generate the coarse-grained representative vector of y, denoted as GIV. While the coarse-grained representative vector of original paired training text by Universal Sentence Encoder is denoted as OTV.

Intuitively, global training objective function is shown as follows.

$$C_G = GIV \cdot OTV \tag{3}$$

Multi-grained Objective Function. We are now ready to formulate the multi-grained objective function. The objective function is designed by two criteria. First, it's likely that matched pairs of images and texts have similar patches, which applies to C_P. Second, matched pairs of image and text probably have similar global semantics, which applies to C_G. By integrating C_P and C_G, the objective function is defined as follows.

$$C(\theta) = \alpha C_P + \beta C_G(\theta) + \gamma |\theta|_2^2, \tag{4}$$

where θ is a shorthand for parameters of our model, and α, β, γ are hyperparameters which are computed by cross-validation. $|\theta|_2^2$ is the regularization.

Optimization. The proposed model consists of two branches, which are designed for common fine-grained semantic and coarse-grained semantic, respectively. Naturally the training process is divided into two stages, i.e., branch training and joint training. Both training processes are based on stochastic gradient descent (SGD) with a batch size of 32, a momentum of 0.9 and a weight decay of 0.00005.

Stage 1: In this stage, branches for common fine grained semantic and coarse grained semantic are trained in turn, taking formula (2) and formula (3) as loss functions respectively. In the fine-grained branch, pretrained Sent2Vec model and RCNN model are utilized, while in the coarse-grained branch, pretrained several pre-trained Universal Sentence Encoder model and LSTM model are utilized. The default parameters in those pretrained models are utilized and its parameters are kept fixed at this stage. The other parameters of our model, including the attentional mechanism, are automatically initialized with the Xavier algorithm [22].

Stage 2: After all branch networks are trained, we jointly fine tune the entire model parameters by combining the loss terms over all granularities in formula (4).

4.2 Interpretable Query Processing

In MCQI framework, images and texts can be represented by high-dimensional feature vectors, which include fine-grained and coarse-grained semantic features. Denote IFV_i as feature vectors of the i-th instance Ins_i, then $IFV_i = \{CFVF_i, CFVC_i\}$, where $CFVF_i$ and $CFVC_i$ mean the corresponding common fine-grained semantic feature and the coarse-grained semantic feature of Ins_i respectively. Given a query instance, i.e., an image or text instance, in order to find the matched cross-modal instance, i.e., the most relevant text or image instance, the similarity between two cross-modal instances can be computed by cosine similarity shown in formula (5) as follows.

$$
\begin{aligned}
SIM(Ins_i, Ins_j) &= \delta \frac{CFVF_i \cdot CFVF_j,}{|CFVF_i| * |CFVF_j|} + (1 - \delta) \frac{CFVC_i \cdot CFVC_j,}{|CFVC_i| * |CFVC_j|} \\
&= \delta \mathrm{Cosine}(CFVF_i, CFVF_j) + (1 - \delta)\mathrm{Cosine}(CFVC_i, CFVC_j)
\end{aligned}
\tag{5}
$$

Here Ins_i and Ins_j are two cross-modal instances, δ is the weight factor, Cosine is the cosine similarity function.

A naive method to obtain the matched cross-modal instances is pair-wise computation, however, this method is inefficient. Especially when the dataset is large and the dimension of vectors is high, the computation is nontrivial. To address this, an inverted index and an M-tree index are integrated into MCQI model. The M-tree index increases the efficiency of queries and the inverted index enhances the interpretability of queries. Index construction and query processing method based on the indices are discussed separately as follows.

Index Construction. It is shown in formula (5) the similarity between two instances mainly is calculated by the cosine similarity of two types of feature vectors. By assuming that variables obey uniform distribution, we get Observation 1 in the following. Observation 1 shows that cosine similarity between the whole feature vectors of Ins_i and Ins_j is close to $SIM(Ins_i, Ins_j)$.

Observation 1. For random variable $\delta \in [0.2, 0.8]$, $\exists \varepsilon, \sigma \in [0, 1]$,
s.t. $P\left(\left| \left(\delta \frac{CFVF_i \cdot CFVF_j}{|CFVF_i| * |CFVF_j|} + (1 - \delta) \frac{CFVC_i \cdot CFVC_j}{|CFVC_i| * |CFVC_j|} \right) - \frac{IFV_i \cdot IFV_j}{|IFV_i| * |IFV_j|} \right| < \varepsilon \right) > \sigma$,
i.e., $P\left(\left| SIM\left(Ins_i, Ins_j\right) - Cosine(Ins_i, Ins_j) \right| < \varepsilon \right) > \sigma$

This Observation is obtained by statistical hypotheses testing method, which will be illustrated in the experiments. By setting $DIF = \left| SIM\left(Ins_i, Ins_j\right) - Cosine(Ins_i, Ins_j) \right|$, we get $P(DIF < \varepsilon)) > \sigma$. In experiments, when set $\varepsilon = 0.05$, we have $\sigma = 0.9$ and when set $\varepsilon = 0.1$, we have $\sigma = 0.98$.

It's known that the M-tree is an efficient structure for NN queries in metric spaces. In order to use M-tree index, cosine distance should be transformed to angular similarity (AS) which is metric. The angular similarity between Ins_i and Ins_j is defined in formula (6) in the following.

$$AS\left(Ins_i, Ins_j\right) = 2 \frac{\arccos(Cosine(Ins_i, Ins_j))}{\pi} \tag{6}$$

Lemma 1. For any instance q, the nearest neighbor of q by angular similarity is also the nearest neighbor of q by cosine similarity.

Lemma 1 can be easily proved by contradiction, which is omitted for simplicity.

Based on Lemma 1 and formula (6), an M-tree is constructed on the data set of feature vectors. And then M-tree is augmented with an inverted index of semantic relationship tuple set TU, which is mentioned in Sect. 4.1.

Interpretable kNN Query. For processing similarity queries efficiently, we adopt a filter-and-fine model. Our method first obtains candidates of matched objects by M-tree, and then verifies the candidates and identifies the final answers.

The M-tree inherently supports range query, denoted as Range (Ins_i, r), where Ins_i is the query instance and r is the query range. In our algorithm the kNN candidates can be efficiently obtained by two range queries on M-tree. To verify the candidates, formula (5) is utilized, and for the verified objects, Inverted index is accessed to give reasons why the objects are relevant to the query. The detailed query processing is shown in algorithm 1 as follows. Specifically, at first we use range query Range $(Ins_i, 0)$ to find the closest index node, and read all the objects in the node(line 2). If the number of objects is less than k, we read its sibling nodes through its parent node, recursively, until we obtain k objects (line 3). And then we use the k-th farthest distance r from the query instance to issue the second range query by setting range as r and get the candidates. Finally, we utilized formula (5) to verify the candidates and each matched pair is augmented with the relationship interpretation through inverted index (line 6-8).

Algorithm 1: kNN Query Processing

Input: NN(Ins_i, k)
Output: Result set R
1    $R = \emptyset$
2   cn= Range(Ins_i, 0)
3   Get at least k objects from in or siblings or parents recursively
4   Set r to the farthest distance
5   S= Range(Ins_i, r+0.1)
6   Verify S by formula (5)
7   Set R to top k similar instances of verified objects
8   Augmented R with interpretation by inverted index
9   Return R

As for complexity, considering the first range query with range zero, the cost of processing a query is $O(H)$, where H is the height of the M-tree. As for the second range query the selectivity of a range query is se, the cost of each level of index nodes can be approximated as a geometric sequence with common ratio, $cr * se$, where cr is the capacity of index node. Hence the average cost is:

$$\frac{cr * se * (1 - (cr * se)^H)}{1 - cr * se} \tag{7}$$

As for query accuracy, by Observation 1 and Lemma 1, it's easy to prove Observation 2 as follows.

Observation 2. Algorithm 1 can obtain kNN instances of the query instances with probability more than σ.

5   Experiment

5.1   Experiment Setup

We evaluate our cross-modal query performance on Flickr8K [23], Flickr30K [24], NUS-WIDE [25], MS-COCO [26], and a synthetic dataset Synthetic9K in our experiments. Flickr8K consists of 8096 images from the Flickr.com website and each image is annotated by 5 sentences by Amazon Mechanical Turk. Flickr30K is also a cross-modal dataset with 31,784 images including corresponding descriptive sentences. NUS-WIDE dataset is a web image dataset for media search, which consists of about 270,000 images with their tags, and each image along with its corresponding tags is viewed together as an image/text pair. MS-COCO contains 123,287 images and each image is also annotated by 5 independent sentences provided by Amazon Mechanical Turk. By extracting 2000 image/text pairs from each above dataset, we obtain a hybrid dataset, denoted as Synthetic9K. For each data set, 10% data are used as testing set and validation set, while the rest are training set.

We compare our approach with 8 state-of-the-art cross-modal retrieval methods, including CCL [27], HSE [28], DADN [8], SCAN [29], DCMH [13], LGCFL [30], JRL [4], KCCA [31]. CCL learns cross-modal correlation by hierarchical network in two stages. First, separate representation is learned by jointly optimizing intra-modality and inter-modality correlation, and then a multi-task learning is adopted to fully exploit the intrinsic relevance between them. HSE proposes a uniform deep model to learn the common representations for four types of media simultaneously by considering classification constraint, center constrain and ranking constraint. DADN proposes a dual adversarial distribution network which takes zero-shot learning and correlation learning in a unified framework to generate common embeddings for cross-modal retrieval. SCAN considers the latent alignments between image regions and text words to learn the image-text similarity. DCMH combines hashing learning and deep feature learning by preserving the semantic similarity between modalities. LGCFL uses a local group based priori to exploit popular block based features and jointly learns basis matrices for different modalities. JRL applies semi-supervised regularization and sparse regularization to learn the common representations. KCCA follows the idea of projecting the data into a higher-dimensional feature space and then performing CCA. Some compared methods rely on category information for common representation learning, such as CCL and HSE, however the datasets have no label annotations available. So, in our experiments first keywords are extracted from text descriptions by TF-IDF method, and seen as labels for corresponding images.

Following [27], we apply the mean average precision (MAP) score to evaluate the cross-modal query performance. We first calculate average precision (AP) score for each query in formula (8), and then calculate their mean value as MAP score.

$$AP = \frac{1}{|R|} \sum_{i=1}^{k} p_i * rel_i, \tag{8}$$

where $|R|$ is the number of ground-truth relevant instances, k is from the kNN query, p_i denotes the precision of the top i results and rel_i is the indicator whether the i-th result is relevant.

We adopt TensorFlow [32] to implement our MCQI approach. In the first stage, we take 4096 dimensional feature extracted from the image inside a given bounding box from RCNN. For the nonlinear transformation model, we use three fully connected layers with 1,024 dimensions and set the dimension of common embedding space d_l and d_g as 1024. The Sent2vec for fine-grained semantics has 700 dimensions, which is pretrained on Wikipedia, and Universal Sentence Encoder for coarse-grained semantics has 512 dimensions. All the experiments are conducted on a server with Intel E5-2650v3, 256 GB RAM, NVIDIA V100 and Ubuntu 16.04 OS.

5.2 Verification of Observation 1

Figures 2 and 3 show the accuracy of $DIF < 0.05$ and $DIF < 0.1$ respectively, with different sample size. δ is randomly generated from 3 different ranges, i.e., [0.2, 0.8], [0.3, 0.7], [0.4, 0.6], and for different varying ranges, it can tell that when δ is closer to 0.5 the accuracy is higher. In the situation of DIF < 0.05, with the increasing of sample size, the accuracy is steadily more than 0.9. And for DIF < 0.1, with the increasing of sample size, the accuracy is steadily more than 0.99. Through this experiment result and statistical hypotheses testing method, it's easy to verify Observation 1.

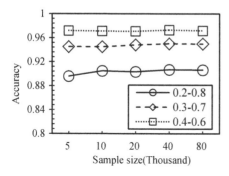

Fig. 2. Accuracy of DIF < 0.05

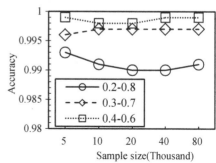

Fig. 3. Accuracy of DIF < 0.1

5.3 Performance of Query Accuracy

We present query accuracy of our MCQI approach as well as all the compared methods in this part. Table 2 shows the MAP scores for 30NN query. As shown in the table, the accuracies of DNN-based methods like DADN and CCL are higher than traditional methods on average. Due to the fusion of multi-grained semantic feature and transfer learning embedding, MCQI approach steadily achieves the best query accuracies. The number of data categories in Sythetic9K is more than other datasets, and comparatively learning common semantic embeddings are more dependent on the quantity of training data. So, under the same condition the accuracy is impacted relatively.

Table 2. MAP scores of MCQI and compared methods for 30NN query

	Flickr8K	Flickr30K	NUS-WIDE	MS-COCO	Synthetic9K
MCQI	0.534	0.683	0.712	0.702	0.528
CCL	0.518	0.566	0.649	0.623	0.423
HSE	0.527	0.526	0.596	0.677	0.452
DADN	0.615	0.412	0.438	0.692	0.341
SCAN	0.223	0.191	0.218	0.254	0.136
DCMH	0.509	0.432	0.487	0.488	0.392
LGCFL	0.457	0.424	0.495	0.369	0.346
JRL	0.421	0.543	0.583	0.576	0.339
KCCA	0.367	0.394	0.421	0.345	0.306

5.4 Performance of Query Time

As shown in Fig. 4, we measure the query time for our proposed MCQI approach as well as two representative methods on 5 datasets. CCL is a DNN-based method and DCMH is a hash-based method. Intuitively query times are proportional to the size of the datasets. As CCL and DCMH are not very sensitive to k of kNN queries, we show query time of only 30NN queries on each dataset. From 30NN queries to 5NN queries, filtering effect of M-tree index enhances, consequently query times decrease. In all cases, MCQI is fastest among the methods. Especially for 5NN, average running times for MCQI are about 13 times faster than that of CCL and 20 times faster than DCMH, i.e., our approach on average outperforms CCL and DCMH by an order of magnitude.

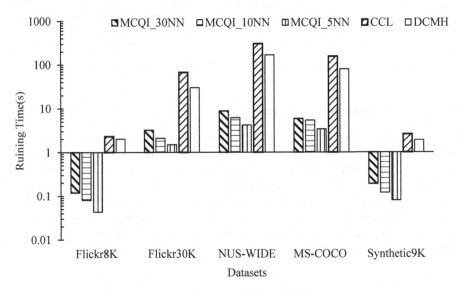

Fig. 4. Performance of query time

5.5 Query Interpretability

Figure 5 shows some examples of cross-modal similarity query results. Because MCQI not only contains the latent semantic common embedding of two types, but also has explicit alignment information. As shown in Fig. 5, for kNN queries, MCQI can return similar objects in datasets, and further gives a reason why those objects are semantically related, which is very important for serious applications.

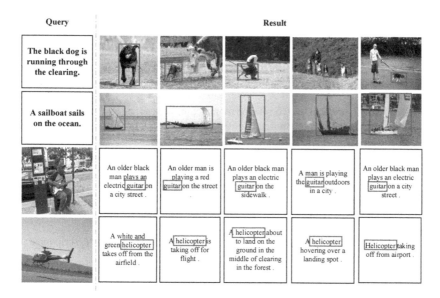

Fig. 5. Examples of processing cross-modal similarity queries by MCQI

6   Conclusion

In this paper, we proposed a novel framework for Multi-grained Cross-modal Similarity Query with Interpretability (MCQI) to effectively leverage coarse-grained and fine-grained semantic information to achieve effective interpretable cross-modal queries. MCQI integrates deep neural network embedding and high-dimensional query index, and also introduces an efficient kNN similarity query algorithm with theoretical support. Experimental results on widely used datasets prove the effectiveness of MCQI. In our future work, we will study more reinforcement learning based cross-modal query approaches for reducing dependence on large training data of certain area.

Acknowledgements. This work is supported by the National Natural Science Foundation of China (61802116), the Science and Technology Plan of Henan Province (192102210113, 192102210248), and the Key Scientific Research Project of Henan Universities (19B520005).

References

1. Peng, Y., Huang, X., Zhao, Y.: An over view of cross-media retrieval: concepts, methodologies, benchmarks, and challenges. IEEE Trans. Circuits Syst. Video Technol. **28**(9), 2372–2385 (2018)
2. He, X., Peng, Y., Xie, L.: A new benchmark and approach for fine-grained cross-media retrieval. In: 27th ACM International Conference on Multimedia, pp. 1740–1748. ACM (2019)
3. Rasiwasia, N., Pereira, J., Coviello, E., et al.: A new approach to cross-modal multimedia retrieval. In: 18th International Conference on Multimedia, pp. 251–260. ACM (2010)

4. Zhai, X., Peng, Y., Xiao, J.: Learning cross-media joint representation with sparse and semisupervised regularization. IEEE Trans. Circuits Syst. Video Technol. **24**(6), 965–978 (2014)

5. Peng, Y., Zhai, X., Zhao, Y., Huang, X.: Semi-supervised cross-media feature learning with unified patch graph regularization. IEEE Trans. Circuits Syst. Video Technol. **26**(3), 583–596 (2016)

6. Yan, F., Mikolajczyk, K.: Deep correlation for matching images and text. In: IEEE Conference on Computer Vision and Pattern Recognition, pp. 3441–3450. IEEE (2015)

7. He, L., Xu, X., Lu, H., et al.: Unsupervised cross-modal retrieval through adversarial learning. In: IEEE International Conference on Multimedia and Expo, pp. 1153–1158. IEEE (2017)

8. Chi, J., Peng, Y.: Zero-shot cross-media embedding learning with dual adversarial distribution network. IEEE Trans. Circuits Syst. Video Technol. **30**(4), 1173–1187 (2020)

9. Andrej, K., Armand, J., Li, F.: Deep fragment embeddings for bidirectional image sentence mapping. In: 27th International Conference on Neural Information Processing Systems, pp. 1889–1897, ACM (2014)

10. Andrej, K., Li, F.: Deep visual-semantic alignments for generating image descriptions. IEEE Trans. Pattern Anal. Mach. Intell. **39**(4), 664–676 (2017)

11. Xu, K., Ba, J., Kiros, R., et al.: Show, attend and tell: neural image caption generation with visual attention. In: 2015 International Conference on Machine Learning, pp. 2048–2057. IEEE (2015)

12. Wang, X., Wang, Y., Wan, W.: Watch, listen, and describe: globally and locally aligned cross-modal attentions for video captioning. In: Proceedings of 2018 Conference of the North American Chapter of the Association for Computational Linguistics, pp. 795–801. ACL (2018)

13. Jiang, Q., Li, W.: Deep cross-modal hashing. In: 2017 IEEE Conference on Computer Vision and Pattern Recognition, pp. 3270–3278. IEEE (2017)

14. Cao, Y., Long, M., Wang, J., et al.: Correlation autoencoder hashing for supervised cross-modal search. In: International Conference on Multimedia Retrieval, pp. 197–204. ACM (2016)

15. Cao, Y., Long, M., Wang, J.: Correlation hashing network for efficient cross-modal retrieval, In: 28th British Machine Vision Conference, pp. 1–12. BMVA (2017)

16. Yang, E., Deng, C., Liu, W., et al.: Pairwise relationship guided deep hashing for cross-modal retrieval. In: 31st Conference on Artificial Intelligence, pp. 1618–1625. AAAI (2017)

17. Zhang, J., Peng, Y., Yuan, M., et al.: Unsupervised generative adversarial cross-modal hashing. In: 32nd Conference on Artificial Intelligence, pp. 539–546. AAAI (2018)

18. Bennanismires, K., Musat, C., Hossmann, A., et al.: Simple unsupervised keyphrase extraction using sentence embeddings. In: Conference on Computational Natural Language Learning, pp. 221–229. ACL (2018)

19. Shen, Y., He, X., Gao, J., et al.: A latent semantic model with convolutional-pooling structure for information retrieval. In: Conference on Information and Knowledge Management. pp. 101–110. ACM (2014)

20. Cheng, B., Wei, Y., Shi, H., et al.: Revisiting RCNN: on awakening the classification power of faster RCNN. In: Ferrari, V., Hebert, M., Sminchisescu, C., Weiss, Y. (eds.) ECCV 2018. LNCS, vol. 11219, pp. 473–490. Springer, Cham (2018). https://doi.org/10.1007/978-3-030-01267-0_28

21. Cer, D., Yang, Y., Kong, S., et al.: Universal sentence encoder. arXiv: Computation and Language, https://arxiv.org/abs/1803.11175v2. Accessed 12 Apr 2018

22. Glorot, X., Bengio, Y.: Understanding the difficulty of training deep feedforward neural networks. In: 13th International Conference on Artificial Intelligence and Statistics, pp. 249–256 JMLR (2010)

23. Hodosh, M., Young, P., Hockenmaier, J.: Framing image description as a ranking task: data, models and evaluation metrics. J. Artif. Intell. Res. **47**(1), 853–899 (2013)
24. Young, P., Lai, A., Hodosh, M., et al.: From image descriptions to visual denotations: new similarity metrics for semantic inference over event descriptions. Trans. Assoc. Comput. Linguist. **7**(2), 67–78 (2014)
25. Chua, T., Tang, J., Hong, R., et al.: NUS-WIDE: a real-world web image database from national university of Singapore. In: 8th Conference on Image and Video Retrieval, pp. 1–9. ACM (2009)
26. Lin, T., Maire, M., Belongie, S.: Microsoft COCO: common objects in context. In: Fleet, D., Pajdla, T., Schiele, B., Tuytelaars, T. (eds.) ECCV 2014. LNCS, vol. 8693, pp. 740–755. Springer, Cham (2014). https://doi.org/10.1007/978-3-319-10602-1_48
27. Peng, Y., Qi, J., Huang, X., et al.: CCL: cross-modal correlation learning with multigrained fusion by hierarchical network. IEEE Trans. Multimedia **20**(2), 405–420 (2018)
28. Chen, T., Wu, W., Gao, Y., et al.: Fine-grained representation learning and recognition by exploiting hierarchical semantic embedding. In: 26th ACM Multimedia, pp. 2023–2031. ACM (2018)
29. Lee, K., Chen, X., Hua, G., et al.: Stacked cross attention for image-text matching. In: Ferrari, V., Hebert, M., Sminchisescu, C., Weiss, Y. (eds.) ECCV 2018. LNCS, vol. 11208, pp. 212–228. Springer, Cham (2018). https://doi.org/10.1007/978-3-030-01225-0_13
30. Yan, F., Mikolajczyk, K.: Deep correlation for matching images and text. In: 2015 Computer Vision and Pattern Recognition, pp. 3441–3450. IEEE (2015)
31. Kang, C., Xiang, S., Liao, S., et al.: Learning consistent feature representation for cross-modal multimedia retrieval. IEEE Trans. Multimedia **17**(3), 370–381 (2015)
32. Abadi, M., Barham, P., Chen, J., et al.: TensorFlow: a system for large-scale machine learning. In: 12th USENIX Conference on Operating Systems Design and Implementation, pp. 265–283. ACM (2016)

Efficient Semantic Enrichment Process for Spatiotemporal Trajectories in Geospatial Environment

Jingjing Han, Mingyu Liu, Genlin Ji, Bin Zhao[✉], Richen Liu, and Ying Li

School of Computer Science and Technology, Nanjing Normal University, Nanjing, China
hanjingjingsarah@163.com, 924686743@qq.com, glji@niju.edu.cn,
{zhaobin,richen.liu,ying.li}@njnu.edu.cn

Abstract. The existing semantic enrichment process approaches which can produce semantic trajectories, are generally time consuming. In this paper, we propose a semantic enrichment process framework for spatiotemporal trajectories in geospatial environment. It can derive new semantic trajectories through the three phases: pre-annotated semantic trajectories storage, spatiotemporal similarity measurement, and semantic information matching. Having observed the common trajectories in the same geospatial object scenes, we propose an algorithm to match semantic information in pre-annotated semantic trajectories to new spatiotemporal trajectories. Finally, we demonstrate the effectiveness and efficiency of our proposed approach by using the real dataset.

Keywords: Semantic trajectories · Semantic enrichment process · Semantic information matching

1 Introduction

Semantic enrichment process is a key stage in semantic modeling [1], which can generate semantic trajectories. It can annotate appropriate semantic information in spatiotemporal trajectories. Semantic enrichment process annotates appropriate semantic information in spatiotemporal trajectories. With different types of semantic information, the existing semantic enrichment process approaches can be divided into three categories: (1) Early approaches directly annotate velocity and direction in spatiotemporal trajectories, which have a low semantic interpretation. (2) Part approaches annotate domain knowledge in spatiotemporal trajectories through ontology. However, these approaches transform semantic trajectories into RDF graph description, which cause the finding and reasoning semantic trajectories time consuming. (3) The typical approaches annotate geographical objects information through Spatial Join [2] algorithm and Map-Matching [3] algorithm. The execution time of [2, 3] are linearly correlated with the number of geospatial objects, which result in high time consumption. It can be seen that the existing semantic enrichment process approaches have the disadvantage of high time consumption.

© Springer Nature Switzerland AG 2020
X. Wang et al. (Eds.): APWeb-WAIM 2020, LNCS 12318, pp. 342–350, 2020.
https://doi.org/10.1007/978-3-030-60290-1_27

On the other hand, giving movement trajectories limited by the topological relationship of urban road networks, there are common movement trajectories in the same geospatial object scenes. For example, commuters departing from the Tsinghua Park residential usually take Metro Line 4 to Beijing Zhongguancun SOHO Building. Due to traffic restrictions, it is easy to collect a large number of identical commuting trajectories. Obviously, the new commuting trajectory information can directly adopt to historical commuting trajectories. Similarly, it is possible to directly annotate the semantic information in the pre-annotated semantic trajectories to new spatiotemporal trajectories, which may avoid inefficient semantic enrichment process.

In this paper, we propose a new semantic enrichment process approach named Efficient Semantic Enrichment Process for Spatiotemporal Trajectories based on Semantic Information Matching (SEPSIM), which firstly use semantic information in pre-annotated semantic trajectories for annotating spatiotemporal trajectories. We propose a new algorithm named Semantic Information Matching Algorithm based on Similar Episodes (SESIM), which can match semantic information of episodes to new trajectory. In order to reduce the search cost of metrics and matching, we build a spatial index to store pre-annotated semantic trajectories. Experiments results prove the high effectiveness and efficiency of SEPSIM approach.

2 Related Work

Early semantic enrichment process approaches directly annotate velocity and direction in spatiotemporal trajectories, which generate semantic trajectories as stop and move sub-trajectories sequences. Ashbrook [4] calculated the moving speed to identify the stop sub-trajectory. Krumm [5] annotated the speed and direction; Palma [6] set the stop sub-trajectory which is below the average speed; In addition to the moving speed, Zheng [7] also calculated the acceleration and speed change rate to discover the move sub-trajectories.

Part semantic enrichment process approaches annotate domain knowledge as semantic information through ontology by transforming semantic trajectories into RDF graphical descriptions, which result time consumption. Modeling semantic trajectories through ontology was first proposed by Baglioni [8]. Based on the concepts of "stop" and "move", Baglioni's ontology was used to define the semantic trajectory. After this, Baglioni's ontology is getting more and more attention and improvement such as Core Ontology [9], QualiTraj ontology [10], and FrameSTEP ontology [11].

The typical semantic enrichment process approaches mainly annotate geographical objects and corresponding topological relationships [12] information, including ROIs, LOIs, and POIs. The typical approaches usually use the *Spatial Join* algorithm [2] to annotate ROIs, which have topological relationships with the spatiotemporal trajectories. For POIs, Yan used Markov model to annotate the POIs categories for the stop sub-trajectories. For LOIs, *Map-Matching* algorithm [3] was used to determine the locations of the move sub-trajectories.

3 Preliminaries

Definition 1 *(Trajectory). A trajectory T is a sequence of sampling points, i.e. $T = \{p_1, p_2, \cdots p_{|T|}\}$, $p_i = (tid, x_i, y_i, t_i)$, where tid is an object identifier and x, y and t are respectively spatial coordinates and a time stamp.*

Definition 2 *(Sub-trajectory). A sub-trajectory is a substring of a trajectory, i.e. $T_s = \{p_{i+1}, p_{i+2}, p_{i+3}, \ldots, p_{i+m}\}$, where $0 \leq i \leq |T| - m, m \geq 0$.*

Definition 3 *(Stop sub-trajectory and Move sub-trajectory). Given the distance threshold ε and the number of point threshold minPts, DBSCAN cluster analysis trajectory T. If each Pi in $T_s = \{p_{i+1}, p_{i+2}, p_{i+3}, \ldots, p_{i+m}\}$ is an outlier, Ts is a stop sub-trajectory (stop Ts). If point Pi in the end of a stop sub-trajectory, point Pi + m+1 in the begin of another stop sub-trajectory, $i + m < |T|$, Ts is a move sub-trajectory (move Ts).*

Definition 4 *(Geospatial Object). A geospatial object Go is a uniquely identified specific space site (e.g., a park, a road or a cinema). A Go is a quad (id, cat, loc, con), where id denotes a geospatial object identifier and cat denotes the category of it (e.g., ROI, LOI, POI) and loc denotes its corresponding location attribute in terms of longitude and latitude coordinates and con denotes its name.*

Definition 5 *(Topological Relation). The topological relationships are defined as the following seven types: Ts pass by Go (Go is a LOI), Ts pass by Go (Go is a POI), Ts pass by Go (Go is a ROI), Ts across Go (Go is a ROI), Ts enter Go (Go is a ROI), Ts leave Go (Go is a ROI), Ts stop inside Go (Go is a ROI).*

Definition 6 *(Episode). An episode is a multi-layered semantic sequence aligned in accordance with the time of the sub-trajectory. i.e. episode =< Ts, sp, dir, geoinf >, where Ts denotes the episode corresponding to the trajectory segment and sp denotes the average speed of the episode and dir denotes the direction of the episode and geoinf denotes the episode corresponding geospatial information.*

Definition 7 *(Semantic Trajectory). A semantic trajectory ST is a sequence of episodes in spatiotemporal order of a moving object. i.e. $ST = \{Episode_1, Episode_2, \ldots, Episode_{|ST|}\}$.*

Problem Definition. Given a trajectory T, a pre-annotated semantic trajectory dataset *OST*, two clustering thresholds ε and *minpts*, four radius r_1, r_2, r_3, r_4 and a similarity threshold σ, the output is a semantic trajectory ST, which annotates semantic information of pre-annotated semantic trajectories in trajectory T.

4 Framework

In this section, we will present *SEPSIM* framework proposed in this paper. As illustrated in Fig. 1, this framework first store and segment the pre-annotated semantic trajectories into a set of stop/move episodes. In the spatiotemporal similarity measurement phase, it measures the spatiotemporal similarity between the given trajectory T and the stop/move episodes, which satisfy the specified similarity condition. In the third phase, it matches semantic information of similar stop/move episodes to trajectory T. Finally, we can get semantic trajectories.

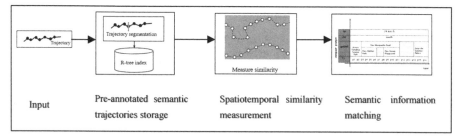

Fig. 1. The framework of SEPSIM

4.1 Pre-annotated Semantic Trajectories Storage

When we get the pre-annotated semantic trajectory dataset *OST*, the first task is to store them for matching phase. We choose to store all pre-annotated semantic trajectories in the form of episodes, which can improve the matching accuracy. However, episode can only be obtained through trajectory segmentation. So, we segment the trajectory by the moving state of the moving object. For the reason that the stop of moving object produces trajectory points gathering, we segment pre-annotated semantic trajectories into stop/move episodes by *DBSCAN* clustering.

4.2 Spatiotemporal Similarity Measurement

For an incoming trajectory T, we compare it with episodes to find similar episodes. Once we find the similar episodes, we can match the semantic information of episodes to trajectory T. Giving the limitation of topological relationship of urban road networks, there are many similar or same trajectory segmentations. So, we first segment trajectory T into stop/move Ts by *DBSCAN* clustering. Then, there are problems to be solved: the similarity between stop sub-trajectory and stop episodes determination and the similarity between move sub-trajectory and move episodes determination. Next, we will discuss the solutions for these two problems respectively in the following.

We view each stop trajectory, which is a stop Ts or a stop episode, as a point set. We convert the stop Ts to a point set P. According to the minimum circumscribed point o in point set P and the given radius r_1, we draw a circular area $Circle_1$ as the similar region of the stop Ts. Each stop episode, which intersects with or is inside $Circle_1$, will be extracted for similarity measurement in the form of the point set Ps. Then, we calculate the *Hausdorff* distance between P and Ps in similar region. The point set Ps with the minimum *Hausdorff* distance to P, is the most similar episode to the stop Ts.

Giving a move Ts, we use the same way to draw the similar region $Circle_2$ of it. For each move episode in $Circle_2$, we draw two circular area $Circle_3$, $Circle_4$ with the given radius r_3, r_4 and two circle points o_1, o_2, which are the begin and end point of the move episode. The part of trajectory T, which is tangent to $Circle_3$, $Circle_4$ is the measurement range corresponding to the move Ts. Finally, we calculate the similarity $simSed(move\ episode, part\ trajectory\ T)$ based on the Longest Common Subsequence(LCS) [13] method. If the $simSed$ is greater than or equal to the given similarity threshold σ, the move episode is similar to the part trajectory T.

4.3 Semantic Information Matching

Given a trajectory T and a set of similar episodes, the episodes corresponding to T have different matching ways. Obviously, there is a problem need to be solved: how to determine if the selected episodes are the best combination in the similar episode set for matching T to ST, which has the most semantic information.

To solve the problem, we propose a Semantic Information Matching Algorithm based on Similar Episodes (*SESIM*). The detailed description, see Algorithm 1.

Algorithm 1. SESIM: Semantic Information Matching Algorithm based on Similar Episodes

---

Input: *trajectory T, a set of similar episodes e {episode₁, episodes₂, ..., episodeₙ}*

Output: *a semantic trajectory ST*

1: for $i = 1$ *to* n do

2:    $P_{begin}, P_{end}, V(i), L(i)$ <- *Measurement (episodeᵢ, T)*

3:    *Insert* $P_{begin}, P_{end}, V(i)$ *into* *Episodeᵢ*

4: return *Epiosdeᵢ (episodeᵢ, $P_{begin}, P_{end}, L(i), V(i)$)*

5:    set E = *sortByTrajSpatial(Epiosdeᵢ)*

6: for $i = 0$ *to* $|T|$ in T do

7:    $SemScore(0) = 0$

8:    if P_{end} *in Episodeᵢ is equal to* P_{end} *in Trajectory T*

9: $SemScore(|T|)=Max(SemanticScore(|T|-1), SemanticScore(|T|-L(i))+V(i))$

10: return *episodes contained in* $SemScore(|T|)$

11:    ST <- *MatchSemanticInf(episodes)*

12: return ST

We first measure the similar range of the trajectory T corresponding to similar episodes as the measurement ranges determination in second phase. In this step, we convert the set of similar episodes to the candidate set $E(Epiosde_1, Epiosde_2, ..., Epiosde_n)$, $Epiosde_i$ (*episodeᵢ, $P_{begin}, P_{end}, L(i), V(i)$*), where P_{begin}, P_{end} is the begin and end point of Ts corresponding to *episodeᵢ*, $L(i)$ is the number of sampling points in Ts, and $V(i)$ is the number of geospatial information in *episodeᵢ*. Then, we sort the set E by the position of P_{begin} in trajectory T. Next, we select the best combination of episodes in set E for matching the semantic trajectory with most semantic information. We analog knapspack algorithm, considering the number of sampling points of the trajectory T as the capacity of the backpack W, and the number of geospatial information in $episode_i$ as the value of episode. Start matching from the end sampling point P_{end} of the trajectory T, we aim to maximize the total value of the entire backpack. Given the candidate set $E(Epiosde_1, Epiosde_2, ..., Epiosde_n)$, $Epiosde_i$ $(episode_i, P_{begin}, P_{end}, L(i), V(i))$, We define the value of the trajectory T using the following formula: $SemScore(|T|) = Max(SemScore(|T| - 1), SemScore(|T| - L(i)) + V(i))$.

4.4 Spatial Index Establishment

To quickly get the pre-annotated episodes similar to trajectory T, we create and maintain a spatial index of pre-annotated episodes. Common spatial index includes R-tree index, Quad-tree index and grid index. The elements stored in the spatial index are episodes, which is essentially trajectory edge data. Quad-tree index is only adapted to query trajectory point. The large number of unevenly distributed geospatial objects causes the grid index to be inefficient. Meanwhile, the R-tree index can be efficient in the unevenly distributed dataset in this paper by ensuring the balance of the tree. Therefore, we create and maintain an R-tree index for pre-annotated episodes. With this index, we can compare an incoming sub-trajectory Ts with pre-annotated episodes in the index, which are inside or intersect with the sub-trajectory Ts.

5 Experiments

In order to verify the performance of SEPSIM, we evaluate the experiments on the Geolife dataset, which was collected in GeoLife project by 182 users in a period of over five years. It contains trajectories with a total distance of 1,292,951 km by different GPS loggers in Beijing, China, and the data size is 1.87 GB. In this paper, all the pre-annotated semantic trajectories are generated by the typical approach. Both algorithms are implemented in Java and run on computers with Intel(R) Xeon(R) CPU E5-2620 (2.10 GHz) and 32 GB memory.

5.1 Effectiveness

In this paper, we propose a new standard to measure the effectiveness of SEPSIM. For a trajectory T, we view the semantic trajectory ST_1 generated by the typical approach as the standard one, and compare the semantic trajectory ST_2 generated by *SEPSIM* with its difference. We compared the accuracy of each pair of sub-trajectories Ts_1 and Ts_2 between ST_1 and ST_2. The effectiveness of ST_2 is the average accuracy of matched semantic information.

$$Effictiveness(ST_2) = \frac{\sum Ts_2.Accuracy * Ts_2.Count}{ST_2.Count} \tag{1}$$

$$Ts_2.Accuracy = \frac{matchedGeoInf\ of\ Ts_2.Count}{standardGeoInf\ of\ Ts_1.Count} \tag{2}$$

Where $Ts_2.Accuracy$ is the correct matched semantic information accuracy of the sub-trajectory Ts_2 compared to corresponding sub-trajectory Ts_1 in ST_1, it is the ratio of correct matched semantic information quantity in $Ts_2(matchedGeoInf\ of\ Ts_2.Count)$ to the standard semantic information quantity in $Ts_2(standardGeoInf\ of\ Ts_1.Count)$, $Ts_2.Count$ and $ST_2.Count$ represent the number of sampling points contained in Ts_2 and semantic trajectory ST_2. Obviously, the higher the average accuracy of a matched sub-trajectory, the more effectiveness of our proposed algorithm will be.

Figure 2(a) shows the change in the effectiveness with the increasing of pre-annotated trajectories. Obviously, after processing more and more pre-annotated trajectories, the effectiveness of trajectories that need to be enriched is gradually increasing. When the number of pre-annotated trajectories reaches 4000, the effectiveness exceeds 90% and keeps increasing steadily. Figure 2(b) shows the change in the effectiveness with the increasing of test trajectories. It can be seen that the effectiveness of test trajectories keeps above 90%.

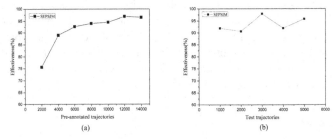

Fig. 2. The effectiveness of SEPSIM approach

5.2 Efficiency

To evaluate the efficiency of SEPSIM, we compare it with the typical approach and the LCS approach, which can annotate the semantic information on the similar trajectories. The results of comparison are shown in Fig. 3(a). We can see that the typical approach and the LCS approach spends more time annotating the same number of test trajectories than the SEPSIM approach. With the increasing of the test trajectories, the time spent by the typical approach and the LCS approach and the time spent by the SEPSIM approach gradually become more time-consuming.

Figure 3(b) shows the efficiency of the SEPSIM with different spatial indexes. Obviously, the time spent by the SEPSIM with the R-tree index is much less than the other two spatial indexes in the SEPSIM approach, which means the R-tree index is appropriate to the dataset in this paper. Meanwhile, the SEPSIM approaches with the three indexes are faster than the typical approach and the LCS approach, which represents the high efficiency of our proposed SEPSIM approach.

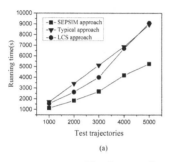
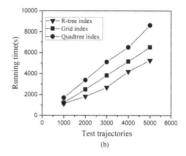

Fig. 3. The efficiency of SEPSIM approach

6 Conclusion

In this paper, we study the problem of semantic enrichment process for spatiotemporal trajectories in geospatial environments. We firstly use semantic information in preannotated semantic trajectories for annotating spatiotemporal trajectories by the *SEPSIM* framework. Extensive experiments over the real dataset verify the superiority of SEPSIM in terms of effectiveness and efficiency. Our future work will study how to mine patterns in semantic trajectories generated by SEPSIM approach.

Acknowledgements. This work is supported by the National Natural Science Foundation of China No. 41971343 and NSFC.61702271.

References

1. Zhixian Y.: Towards semantic trajectory data analysis: a conceptual and computational approach. In: VLDB 2009, Lyon, France (2009)
2. Zhixian, Y., Dipanjan, C., Christine, P., Stefano, S., Karl, A.: Semantic trajectories: mobility data computation and annotation. ACM TIST **4**(3), 1–38 (2013)
3. Christine, P., et al.: Semantic trajectories modeling and analysis. ACM Comput. Surv. **45**(4), 1–32 (2013)
4. Daniel, A., Thad, S.: Using GPS to learn significant locations and predict movement across multiple users. Pers. Ubiquit. Comput. **7**(5), 275–286 (2003). https://doi.org/10.1007/s00779-003-0240-0
5. Krumm, J., Horvitz, E.: Predestination: inferring destinations from partial trajectories. In: Dourish, P., Friday, A. (eds.) UbiComp 2006. LNCS, vol. 4206, pp. 243–260. Springer, Heidelberg (2006). https://doi.org/10.1007/11853565_15
6. Andrey, T., Vania, B., Bart, K., Luis O.: A clustering-based approach for discovering interesting places in trajectories. In: SAC 2008, pp. 863–868, Fortaleza, Ceara, Brazil (2008)
7. Yu, Z., Lizhu, Z., Zhengxin, M., Xing, X., Wei-Ying, M.: Recommending friends and locations based on individual location history. TWEB **5**(1), 1–44 (2011)
8. Stefano, S., Christine, P., Maria, L., Jose, A., Fabio, P., Christelle, V.: A conceptual view on trajectories. Data Knowl. Eng. **65**(1), 126–146 (2008)
9. Miriam, B., Jose, A., Chiara, R., Roberto, T., Monica, W.: Towards semantic interpretation of movement behavior. In: AGILE 2009, pp. 271–288. Hannover, Germany (2009)

10. Nogueira, T.P., Martin, H.: Qualitative representation of dynamic attributes of trajectories. In: Agile Conference on Geographic Information Science (2014)
11. Tales, P., Reinaldo, B., Carina, T., Herve, M., Fabio, P., Christelle, V.: Framestep: a framework for annotating semantic trajectories based on episodes. Expert Syst. Appl. **92**, 533–545 (2018)
12. Longgang, X., Tao, W., Jianya, G.: A geo-spatial information oriented trajectory model and spatio-temporal pattern quering. Acta Geodactica et Catographica Sin. **43**(9), 982–988 (2014)
13. Kima, J., Mahmassanibhan, S.: Spatial and temporal characterization of travel patterns in a traffic network using vehicle trajectories. In: 21st International Symposium on Transportation and Traffic Theory, pp. 164–184 (2015)

On the Vulnerability and Generality of K−Anonymity Location Privacy Under Continuous LBS Requests

Hanbo Dai[1], Hui Li[2(✉)] (iD), Xue Meng[2], and Yingxue Wang[3]

[1] Hubei University, Wuhan, China
[2] Xidian University, Xi'an, China
`hli@xidian.edu.cn`
[3] National Engineering Laboratory for Public Safety Risk Perception
and Control by Big Data, Beijing, China

Abstract. With the development of personal communication devices, location-based services have been widely used. However, the risk of location information leakage is a fundamental problem that prevents the success for these applications. Recently, some location-based privacy protection schemes have been proposed, among which K-anonymity scheme is the most popular one. However, as we empirically demonstrated, these schemes may not preserve satisfactory effect in trajectory-aware scenarios. In particular, we propose a new attack model using public navigation services. According to the empirical results, the attack algorithm correlates a series of snapshots associated with continuous queries, eliminating some of the less likely routes, and seriously undermining the anonymity of the query, thereby increasing the probability of attack. In order to defend against the proposed attacks, two enhanced versions of K-anonymity mechanism are proposed for this attack model, which further protects the user's trajectory privacy.

Keywords: Location privacy · Location-based services · Attack · K-anonymity

1 Introduction

Thanks to the development of mobile computing and correlated technologies, mobile users are now able to query location service providers (LSPs) [9,15] and enjoy a variety of location-based services (LBSs), e.g., map and navigation services. However, when users share their locations directly to untrusted third-party

Hanbo Dai and Hui Li are co-first authors and contribute equally to this work. This work is granted by National Natural Science Foundation of China (No. 61672408, 61972309) and National Engineering Laboratory (China) for Public Safety Risk Perception and Control by Big Data (PSRPC).

X. Wang et al. (Eds.): APWeb-WAIM 2020, LNCS 12318, pp. 351–359, 2020.
https://doi.org/10.1007/978-3-030-60290-1_28

Fig. 1. Framework of current K-anonymity location privacy. KNN is the K-nearest neighbor query, ASR is anonymous spatial region.

applications, their sensitive information will inevitably suffer from a risk of disclosure, which is vital for the success of LBSs. Thus, location privacy [2] is a core concern for public LBSs.

To guarantee location privacy, [7] proposed the concept of location K-anonymity. Since then, many other K-anonymity solutions have been developed afterwards [1,10,11,16]. These methods are specifically designed for privacy-preserving of *independent* locations, we argue that they may not provide satisfactory efficacy in light of correlated locations. In particular, for trajectory-aware scenarios where continuous locations shall be anonymized, we show that the location information can be acquired by the attacker even if some K-anonymity schemes have already been applied. We present an attack model by utilizing a public navigation services. Through the model, we are able to quantitatively analyze the risk of privacy disclosure in the K-anonymity scheme. We also show the effectiveness of the attack model both theoretically and empirically. Moreover, in order to address the privacy leakage due to the proposed attack model, we further present a pair of advanced K-anonymity mechanisms.

2   Preliminaries and Related Works

Location-based privacy protection mechanism can be classified into two categories: trusted third party (TTP)-free schemes [4,5] and TTP-based schemes [6,8]. In TTP-free schemes, users query the LSP directly. In order to protect the real location from the untrusted LSP, users either obfuscate their locations and send the fake ones to the LSP or cloak location by their peers' locations. In TTP-based schemes, a trusted entity, called the *Anonymizer*, is introduced [3,14], acting as an intermediate tier between the users and the LSP.

One of the most typical TTP-based scheme was presented in [12], this paper proposed a user-centric $K-$anonymity privacy protection scheme for both snapshot and continuous queries. Firstly, the MCC algorithm is used to collect valuable information from multi-hop peers and fulfil user's requirement locally. Secondly, the CPPQ algorithm enables the user to issue either a fake query to confuse the adversary or a real query while privacy is preserved. The TTP-based schemes require a trusted Anonymizer (see Fig. 1), which has the knowledge about all users' locations. Thus, the security of the location information after being anonymized depends to a large extent on the Anonymizer. Once the Anonymizer is attacked by a strong attack model, it will pose a serious threat to privacy and may put the user information in high risk. To facilitate the following discussion, we introduce a pair of basic concepts in the follows.

Definition 1 (Location-aware K-anonymity). *[13] Assuming that the LBS requests sent by a user at different moments $t_1, \ldots, t_n$ are respectively $r_1, \ldots, r_n$, the request processed by a LTS (Location-tracking system) anonymously is $r'_1, \ldots, r'_n$, at any time t_i $(1 < i < n)$, the corresponding anonymous set of r'_i is denoted as $S(r'_i)$, if and only if $2^{E_s(r'_i)} \geq K$, where $S = \bigcap_{i=1}^{n} S(r'_i)$, then it is considered that this continuous LBS request satisfies K-anonymity.*

Definition 2 (Spherical distance). *The distance between two points of the sphere is the length of the round arc of the two points:*

$$d = R \cdot \arccos(\cos(latA)\cos(latB)\cos(lngB - lngA) + \sin(latA)\sin(latB)). \qquad (1)$$

R is the radius of the earth, i.e., $R = 6371.012KM$; $lngA$ and $latA$ are the longitude and latitude of position A, respectively.

3   The Vulnerability of K-Anonymity Location in Trajectory-Aware Scenario

3.1   The Anonymous Model Assumption

As shown in Fig. 1, the user sends a query request to the anonymous device, which uses the period τ to collect the query sent by the user. In each iteration, each user sends up to only one query request. Anonymous device uses the Clocking algorithm to process the query request and send it to the LSP. The message received by the anonymous device is: $Inquire = (ID, lng, lat, t, C)$ where ID indicates the identity of the user, t refers to the query timestamp, lat and lng are the exact location where the user sends the query, C indicates the content of the query. The anonymous device removes the user ID and generalizes its location into an area containing K different locations, and finally sent to the LSP. That is, the LSP receives the information for K different (lng, lat, t, C).

Assuming that as the user moves, she sends four requests in different timestamps, and formed four anonymous areas accordingly, namely A, B, C and D. Assuming K is set to 4, so there exist $4^4 = 256$ possible routes for the user.

3.2   The Adversary Model

The Knowledge of the Adversary. In the above assumption, if a route is randomly selected, the probability of the user's real route being compromised is $\frac{1}{K^n}$, where n denotes the number of LBS requests for the user. However, when the anonymized location is not independent to each other, e.g., trajectories, the privacy guarantee cannot be satisfied. In particular, hereby we propose an attack model by utilizing the public navigation service that returns route planning distance and travel time (e.g., RouteMatrix[1]), with following assumptions:

---

[1] http://lbsyun.baidu.com/index.php?title=webapi/route-matrix-api-v2.

- LBS is curious-but-honest or compromised, it can get all the snapshots of the anonymous device, that is, an adversary can get all the query requests (lng, lat, t, C).
- The adversary knows the user's dwell time T at each location.
- The adversary does not know what specific algorithm is used by the Anonymizer.

3.3   The Attack Algorithm

Algorithm 1 shows the pseudo code of our attack algorithm. According to all the assumptions above, we can get a series of information using RouteMatrix API between a pair of arbitrary positions (e.g., a, e), including the distance, expected traveling time (e.g., driving, riding and walking time) between each pair of given locations. Assuming that the driving, riding and walking time between a and e is $t_{d(a \to e)}$, $t_{r(a \to e)}$, $t_{w(a \to e)}$, respectively. Besides, we refer to the eventual time as $t_{true(a \to e)} = t_e - t_a$. As there exist a bias between the ideal and eventual time, we need to set a tolerant range to allow impact of the external environment, assume that the tolerant range is $\lambda \times t_{true(a \to e)}$. The core idea of the attack algorithm is that if the ideal time of the position pair in the adjacent area is within the tolerant period, the route between the location pairs is considered to be a real one. e.g., if one of $t_{d(a \to e)}$, $t_{r(a \to e)}$ and $t_{w(a \to e)}$ is within the real time range $[t_{true(a \to e)} - \lambda_1 \times t_{true(a \to e)}, t_{true(a \to e)} + \lambda_2 \times t_{true(a \to e)}]$, the route from a to e is considered to be the user's real route. Accordingly, we get some possible routes for target user and increasing the probability for identifying the real routes by the attacker. In addition, we can also perform the following for all trails that are not excluded: assuming that location a to e and location e to i are two possible routes, we can get the spherical distance between two points by Eq. 1. If $d_{(a \to e)} + d_{(e \to i)} - d_{(a \to i)} \leq Z$ (Z is a pre-defined distance threshold), the distance from position a to i via e and the distance from position a to i are treated as equal to each other. Notably, the expected distance and travel time returned by public navigation services may not accurately reflect real scenario, so we have to carefully set the tolerant parameters to allow such deviations. The difficulty of this algorithm lies in the selection of λ and Z. When λ and Z are set too large, the attack model may not meet the high quality requirements, then there will be a lot of interference routes. On the other hand, when λ, Z is too small, the actual route of the target user may be falsely eliminated.

We conduct experimental study for the proposed attack model with a real-world LBSs data provided by Didi[2]. We adopt the algorithm proposed in [13] as the privacy protection algorithm to process the locations and ensure K-anonymity. The experimental study is implemented as follows. Firstly, based on the dataset, users' latitude and longitude information is passed through the anonymous device, which is running the anonymous model proposed in [13]. Then, we implement our attack model over the anonymized data that is generated. Finally, we analyze the performance of the attack model. We evaluate

---

[2] http://www.didichuxing.com/.

Algorithm 1. Trajectory-aware attack algorithm

Require: $p_1(lng_1, lat_1, t_1), p_2(lng_2, lat_2, t_2)$
Ensure: Keep or delete the route between these two points
1: **function K-AnnAttack**(p_1, p_2)
2:     $t_{d(1\rightarrow2)}, t_{r(1\rightarrow2)}, t_{w(1\rightarrow2)} \leftarrow$ **Call RouteMatrix API**$(lng_1, lat_1, lng_2, lat_2)$
3:     $t_{true(1\rightarrow2)} \leftarrow t_2 - t_1$, $min \leftarrow (1 - \lambda_1)t_{true(1\rightarrow2)}$, $max \leftarrow (1 + \lambda_2)t_{true(1\rightarrow2)}$
4:     **if** $max \geq (t_{d(1\rightarrow2)} \| t_{r(1\rightarrow2)} \| t_{w(1\rightarrow2)}) \geq min$ **then**
5:         Keep the route between these two points
6:     **else**
7:         Delete the route between these two points
8:     **end if**
9: **end function**

---

the performance of the attack by the ratio of successfully identified number of real sender query divided by the number of all inquiries, the higher the recognition rate, the more serious the damage to anonymity. According to the results, traffic lights and other environmental effects, the actual time the taxi arrives at the destination is always inaccurate with the theoretical time calculated using RouteMatrix API, so when the theoretical time calculated by RouteMatrix API is within $[t_{true} - \lambda_1 \times t_{true}, t_{true} + \lambda_2 \times t_{true}]$, the target user's track will not be deleted, and while the attack algorithm delete 15 false trajectory in the adjacent areas, the probability of successful attack increased from $\frac{1}{16}$ to $\frac{1}{1}$.

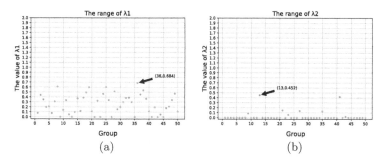

Fig. 2. The values of λ_1 (a) and λ_2 (b) that satisfy the difference between user's real travel time and expected travel time after Algorithm 1.

Besides, most of the users' actual driving time is close to the theoretical time, which shows that it is feasible to use RouteMatrix API to calculate the user's real driving time. However, there are often many external environmental impacts in reality, such as traffic congestion, red lights, navigation errors, etc., therefore, theoretical time is often less than eventual time, as shown in Fig. 2(a) and (b). In order to make the theoretical time within the fault tolerance range, it can be seen from Fig. 2(a) and (b) that the value of λ_1 and λ_2 should be the maximum of all its values. As analyzed above, since the theoretical time is often less than actual travel time, most of λ_2's values are 0. In particular, when K is 2, 3, 4, 5, 6, respectively, the theoretical values of the routes are 4, 9, 16, 25, 36, respectively. After applying Algorithm 1, for each value of K, the average number of remaining routes for randomly selected 10 adjacent anonymous location pairs after Algorithm 1 is less than $\frac{K}{2}$, which justifies our attack algorithm.

Since the choice of anonymous algorithms is not unique, we must take two special cases into account. The first is that the timestamps of K users in each anonymous area are equal, and the performance of Algorithm 1 in this case may not be ideal. The second is that the timestamp of the target user in each anonymous area and the timestamps of the other $K-1$ users are different in hours, in this case, the performance of Algorithm 1 is optimal and can uniquely identify the target user's track. As existing K-anonymity schemes divide the whole space using latitude and longitude, the above two extremes seldom appear in practice, in other words, Algorithm 1 can effectively exclude many fake locations, so as to improve the probability of recognizing the target user's track.

4   Advanced Models Against the Attack

4.1   An Iterative Approach

Since the attack algorithm can effectively improve the probability that the target user's track is identified by the attacker, it greatly reduces the number of interference routes. In order to protect the target user's trajectory privacy, we must seek an advanced anonymous algorithm in light of this attack. To this end, we present a pair of new privacy preserving solutions to overcome the risk brought by the attack model in last section. The first algorithm is an improved version of the K-anonymity location privacy protection mechanism, namely IterAnn (Iterative K-Anonymizer), which is illustrated in detail in Algorithm 2.

Algorithm 2. IterAnn	**Algorithm 3.** K*Ann
Require: $tr' = \{S(r_1'), ..., S(r_n')\}$, K	**Require:** $tr' = \{S(r_1'), ..., S(r_n')\}$, K
Ensure: $tr'' = \{S(r_1''), ..., S(r_n'')\}$	**Ensure:** $tr'' = \{S(r_1''), ..., S(r_n'')\}$
1: **for** each p_j in $S(r_i')$, q_j in $S(r_{i+1}')$ **do**	1: **for** each p_j in $S(r_i')$, q_j in $S(r_{i+1}')$ **do**
2: $tr'' \leftarrow$ **K-AnnAttack**(p_j, q_j)	2: $tr'' \leftarrow$ **K-AnnAttack**(p_j, q_j)
3: **end for**	3: **end for**
4: **while** $minRoutes(tr'') < K^2$ **do**	4: **while** $minRoutes(tr'') < K_1^2$ **do**
5: $tr''^* \leftarrow$ **IterAnn**(tr'^*, K)	5: $K^* \leftarrow K^* + 1$
6: $tr'' \leftarrow tr'' \bigcap tr''^*$	6: $tr' \leftarrow$ **K-anonymity**(K^*)
7: **end while**	7: **K*Ann**(tr', K_1, K^*)
8: **return** tr''	8: **end while**
	9: **return** tr''

Raw LBS data is passed through [13] and forms the K-anonymity trajectory dataset, denoted by $tr' = \{S(r_1'), ..., S(r_n')\}$, the elements in tr' are the target user's anonymous areas at each timestamp, each of which contains K different location points. Afterwards, tr' is visible to the attack algorithm proposed in this paper, we generate the fragile trajectory dataset $tr'' = \{S(r_1''), ..., S(r_n'')\}$, the elements in tr'' are the target user's $K - x_1, ..., K - x_n$ anonymous areas, $x_1, ..., x_n$ are the number of interference traces that the attack algorithm excludes in each anonymous region. Now we start the first round of iteration, sends initial general LBS data to the K-anonymity model along with the target user's trajectory data denoted by tr'^*, then passes them to the attack algorithm. Then we have a second set of fragile trajectory dataset tr''^*, the elements in tr''^* are the target user's $K - y_1, ..., K - y_n$ anonymous area at each time, $y_1, ..., y_n$ are the number of interference traces that the attack algorithm excludes in each anonymous region. The results of the two rounds are integrated to obtain a new trajectory dataset, and the iteration will not terminate until K-anonymity is satisfied. For the case where the number of routes of the adjacent anonymous area is larger than K^2, the $K^2 - 1$ routes of the time spend closest to the target position at the time spend can be selected directly from the routes after the iterative approach, thus ensuring the location K-anonymity. It can be seen from Fig. 3(a) that in order to satisfy K-anonymity, the average number of iterations is empirically $2K$.

However, the iterative method is extremely demanding for the selection of iterative data. When the degree of similarity of the iterative data is large, the iterative method will be very expensive as the data needs to be deduplicated while consolidated. In order to overcome the problem of obtaining iterative data, we present another solution in next part.

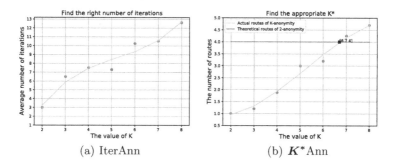

(a) IterAnn   (b) K^*Ann

Fig. 3. Effectiveness for both approaches

4.2 K^* Anonymizer

Since the K-anonymity location privacy mechanism is vulnerable to the attack algorithm and can not meet the K-anonymity requirements (eventually satisfy K^--anonymity, $K^- < K$), we can increase the value of K to meet the original privacy requirements. Based on this idea, we present a second solution, namely K^*Ann (K^*-anonymizer), by modifying K as shown in Algorithm 3.

As shown in Fig. 3(b), the X-axis indicates the total number of routes between adjacent anonymous regions after the attack algorithm. The Y-axis corresponds to the abscissa of the polyline obtained by averaging the total number of routes of 10 randomly selected adjacent anonymous regions. The straight line shows that the total number of theoretical routes that should be reached for adjacent anonymous regions under 2-anonymity mechanism is $2^2 = 4$. As can be seen from the figure, as K is an integer and the experimental result must reach the ideal state after the attack algorithm, so when K^* is set to 7, the new mechanism can meet the original 2-anonymity requirements. The figure shows that K has an approximate linear relationship with the actual number of routes when K is taken as a small value, we can therefore infer other K^* that satisfy the K-anonymity mechanism, for example, $K^* = 15$ mechanism can meet the original 3-anonymity requirements. Compared to the iterative method mentioned above, this method does not require de-duplication of the dataset, therefore, the time complexity and space complexity of Algorithm 3 are lower than those of Algorithm 2 in practical applications.

5   Conclusion

In this paper, a continuous query attack algorithm and two advanced K-anonymity defense schemes against the attack are proposed. In our implementation, the attack algorithm uses a public navigation service to calculate the theoretical time between two points, thus is able to eliminate many interference routes and reducing the effectiveness of privacy protection algorithm. Simulation results show that the continuous query attack algorithm has obvious effect on snapshot anonymity. To overcome the problem introduced by our proposed attack model, we further present two solutions towards K-anonymity schemes. Our proposed advanced K-anonymity solutions can effectively resist this attack algorithm, thus protecting the target user's track privacy. In general, between the two solutions, we believe that K^*-anonymity model is more suitable for general LBS dataset because it is not sensitive to the selection of dataset, so that it can work well in the scenarios where the time complexity and space complexity are too high.

References

1. Anthony, D., Henderson, T., Kotz, D.: Privacy in location-aware computing environments. IEEE Pervasive Comput. **6**(4), 64–72 (2007)
2. Beresford, A.R., Stajano, F.: Location privacy in pervasive computing. IEEE Pervasive Comput. **2**(1), 46–55 (2003)
3. Gedik, B., Liu, L.: Location privacy in mobile systems: a personalized anonymization model. In: ICDCS, pp. 620–629. IEEE Computer Society (2005)
4. Ghinita, G., Kalnis, P., Khoshgozaran, A., Shahabi, C., Tan, K.: Private queries in location based services: anonymizers are not necessary. In: SIGMOD, pp. 121–132. ACM (2008)
5. Ghinita, G., Kalnis, P., Skiadopoulos, S.: MobiHide: a mobilea peer-to-peer system for anonymous location-based queries. In: Papadias, D., Zhang, D., Kollios, G. (eds.) SSTD 2007. LNCS, vol. 4605, pp. 221–238. Springer, Heidelberg (2007). https://doi.org/10.1007/978-3-540-73540-3_13

6. Gkoulalas-Divanis, A., Kalnis, P., Verykios, V.S.: Providing k-anonymity in location based services. SIGKDD Explor. **12**(1), 3–10 (2010)
7. Gruteser, M., Grunwald, D.: Anonymous usage of location-based services through spatial and temporal cloaking. In: MobiSys, pp. 31–42. USENIX (2003)
8. Khoshgozaran, A., Shahabi, C.: Blind evaluation of nearest neighbor queries using space transformation to preserve location privacy. In: Papadias, D., Zhang, D., Kollios, G. (eds.) SSTD 2007. LNCS, vol. 4605, pp. 239–257. Springer, Heidelberg (2007). https://doi.org/10.1007/978-3-540-73540-3_14
9. Kido, H., Yanagisawa, Y., Satoh, T.: An anonymous communication technique using dummies for location-based services. In: ICPS, pp. 88–97. IEEE Computer Society (2005)
10. Liu, H., Li, X., Li, H., Ma, J., Ma, X.: Spatiotemporal correlation-aware dummy-based privacy protection scheme for location-based services. In: INFOCOM, pp. 1–9. IEEE (2017)
11. Niu, B., Li, Q., Zhu, X., Cao, G., Li, H.: Enhancing privacy through caching in location-based services. In: INFOCOM, pp. 1017–1025. IEEE (2015)
12. Peng, T., Liu, Q., Meng, D., Wang, G.: Collaborative trajectory privacy preserving scheme in location-based services. Inf. Sci. **387**, 165–179 (2017)
13. Song, D., Park, K.: A privacy-preserving location-based system for continuous spatial queries. Mob. Inf. Syst. **2016**(1), 1–9 (2016)
14. Vu, K., Zheng, R., Gao, J.: Efficient algorithms for k-anonymous location privacy in participatory sensing. In: INFOCOM, pp. 2399–2407. IEEE (2012)
15. Yiu, M.L., Jensen, C.S., Huang, X., Lu, H.: SpaceTwist: managing the trade-offs among location privacy, query performance, and query accuracy in mobile services. In: ICDE, pp. 366–375. IEEE Computer Society (2008)
16. Zheng, X., Cai, Z., Li, J., Gao, H.: Location-privacy-aware review publication mechanism for local business service systems. In: INFOCOM, pp. 1–9. IEEE (2017)

Fine-Grained Urban Flow Prediction via a Spatio-Temporal Super-Resolution Scheme

Rujia Shen⬤, Jian Xu⁽✉⁾⬤, Qing Bao⬤, Wei Li⬤, Hao Yuan⬤,
and Ming Xu⬤

Computer Science and Technology, Hangzhou Dianzi University, Hangzhou, China
{rujiashen,jian.xu,qbao,wei.li,harvey,mxu}@hdu.edu.cn

Abstract. Urban flow prediction plays an essential role in public safety and traffic scheduling for a city. By mining the original granularity flow data, current research methods could predict the coarse-grained region flow. However, the prediction of a more fine-grained region is more important for city management, which means cities could derive more details from the original granularity flow data. In this paper, given the future weather information, we aim to predict the fine-grained region flow. We design Weather-affected Fine-grained Region Flow Predictor (WFRFP) model based on the super-resolution scheme. Our model consists of three modules: 1) *Key flow maps selection* module selects key flow maps from massive historical data as the input instance according to temporal property and weather similarity; 2) *Weather condition fusion* module processes the original weather information and extracts weather features; 3) *Fine-grained flow prediction* module learns the spatial correlations by wide activation residual blocks and predicts the fine-grained region flow by the upsampling operation. Extensive experiments on a real-world dataset demonstrate the effectiveness and efficiency of our method, and show that our method outperforms the state-of-the-art baselines.

Keywords: Deep learning · Spatio-temporal data · Prediction

1 Introduction

The urban flow prediction system is crucially essential to urban planning, public safety and various applications such as bike-sharing platforms. The current research methods could approximate the future urban flow [21,22]. However, their predicting area is coarse due to the limitation of sparse sensors deployed over the city. Predicting the fine-grained region flow (*e.g.*, crowd flow and traffic flow) under the future weather conditions is important for a city, which can improve traffic management and guarantee public safety.

For instance, as shown in Fig. 1 left, the area is divided into 8×8 grid regions, and we can only obtain the flow of the coarse-grained regions (*e.g.*, R_1) from the sensors deployed over the city. For bike-sharing platforms like Hellobike and

X. Wang et al. (Eds.): APWeb-WAIM 2020, LNCS 12318, pp. 360–375, 2020.
https://doi.org/10.1007/978-3-030-60290-1_29

Mobike, they launch bikes based on the crowd flow of region R_1. However, region R_1 is large and the crowd flow is unevenly distributed. Magnifying region R_1, we will find that the crowd flow is more concentrated in fine-grained region r_1 (outdoor region) on a sunny day, but more concentrated in region r_2 (indoor region) on a cloudy day. If people could predict the fine-grained regions flow (*e.g.*, r_2) with future weather conditions, bike-sharing platforms could allocate bike resources reasonably and provide better service for consumers.

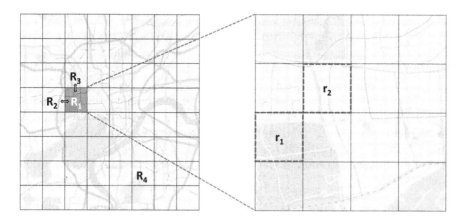

Fig. 1. Left: an area is divided into 8×8 coarse-grained grid region. We can obtain coarse-grained crowd flow of each region by CCTVs and loop detectors. Right: the corresponding fine-grained grid regions of region R_1. We aim to predict the crowd flow of a more precise region (*e.g.*, r_1).

In this paper, our goal is predicting the spatially fine-grained flows from the observed coarse-grained data when the future weather condition is given. Predicting the weather-affected fine-grained region flow means to explore the relationship between the flow distribution and the weather, and reduce the scope of the predicting area to obtain details from coarse-grained flow. However, the prediction is challenging due to the following complex factors:

- **Redundant Input Data.** For the weather-affected fine-grained region flow prediction problem, the input will be a very long historical data sequence, which is difficult for model training. Besides, some historical data is less relevant to the future weather condition, and even bring negative impact for prediction.
- **Spatial Dependencies.** On one side, the flow of a region can be affected by the surrounding regions. A shown in Fig. 1, the outflow from region R_1 affects the region flow of R_2 and R_3. Likewise, outflows from surrounding regions and distant regions (*e.g.*, R_4) will affect the flow of region R_1. On the other side, the corresponding fine-grained flow distribution of a coarse-grained region will change over time and weather conditions.

To tackle these challenges, we propose a deep neural network model, Weather-affected Fine-grained Region Flow Predictor (**WFRFP**), which could predict the future fine-grained region crowd flow when the future weather condition is available. WFRFP is inspired by the solutions for single image super-resolution (SISR) problem [3, 10, 12], which aims at the recovery of a high resolution (HR) image from its low resolution (LR) counterpart. Solutions for SISR problem have motivated applications in other fields, such as satellite [15], medical imaging [17], meteorology [14] and flow inferring [11]. Particularly, Liang et al. [11] firstly proposed the fine-grained urban flow inferring model, which maps coarse-grained flow to fine-grained flow based on super-resolution scheme. Please note that our work is different from the work of Liang et al. [11]. The work of Liang et al. aims to use the flow data that has already been obtained to learn high-resolution mapping, while our work aims to predict the future fine-grained flow from massive historical flow data according to the future weather condition.

In this paper, we adopt the similar idea of SISR and design an appropriate model to predict the weather-affected fine-grained region flow. Specifically, WFRFP first selects weather-similar and time-series data, and then learns weather features and spatial features from these data. Finally, it performs the upsampling operation to obtain the fine-grained region flow. Our contributions are as follows:

- We present the idea to predict the weather-affected fine-grained region flow. And we design the WFRFP model, which can capture weather and spatial impacts on crowd flow, and predict the fine-grained region flow of a more precise region.
- We design a method to select key flow data from massive historical data, which both remains time-series property and has high a correlation with the future weather condition. Our structure reduces the amount of data input while improving the training efficiency.
- We performed experiments and evaluate our framework on a real-world dataset with baselines. And the experimental results proved that our method is superior to other baseline methods.

The rest of this paper is organized as follows. In Sect. 2, we define notations and formalize the problem of weather-affected fine-grained region flow prediction. In Sect. 3, we introduce our prediction method in detail. In Sect. 4, we show the process and the algorithm of model training. In Sect. 5, we describe our experiment settings and analyze the experimental results. Section 6 reviews the related work and Sect. 7 concludes our work.

2   Formulation

In this section, we first define notations in this paper and then formulate the problem of Weather-affected Fine-grained Region Flow Prediction (**WFRFP**). We give the notations used in this paper in Table 1.

Table 1. Notations and meanings

Notations	Meanings
$\mathbf{C}_t$	The coarse-grained flow map at t-th time slot
$\mathbf{F}_t$	The fine-grained flow map at t-th time slot
$\mathbf{M}_t$	The weather condition at t-th time slot
$m_{(q,i)}$	The q-th weather variable of a weather condition at t-th time slot
N	The upsampling factor
$\mathbf{M}^c$	The coarse-grained weather feature map
$\mathbf{M}^f$	The fine-grained weather feature map
$\mathbf{m}_{con}$	Vector of continuous weather variables
$\mathbf{m}_{disc}$	Vector of discrete weather variables
$\mathcal{C}$	The set of historical coarse-grained flow maps
$\mathcal{M}$	The set of historical weather conditions

Definition 1 (Region). As shown in Fig. 1, given the latitude and longitude of an area of interest (*e.g.*, a city, a district, etc.), we divide it into an $I \times J$ grid map. Each grid corresponds to a region [21]. Partitioning the city into smaller regions suggests that we can obtain flow data with more details, which produces a more fine-grained flow map.

Definition 2 (Flow Map). Each divided grid region has a certain region flow, and we define flow maps to describe the flow distribution in grid regions. Let $\mathbf{C}_t \in \mathbb{R}_+^{I \times J}$ represent a coarse-grained crowd flow map at the t-th time slot. $\mathbb{R}_+$ denotes the flow class (*e.g.*, crowd flow, traffic flow, etc.). Given an upsampling factor N, we represent a fine-grained crowd flow map at the t-th time slot as $\mathbf{F}_t \in \mathbb{R}_+^{NI \times NJ}$. Figure 2 shows an example when upsampling factor N is 2. Each coarse-grained grid in Fig. 2 left is divided into 2×2 fine-grained grids in Fig. 2 right.

Definition 3 (Weather Condition). Let $\mathbf{M}_t$ represents the weather condition at the t-th time slot. Each $\mathbf{M}_t$ contains several weather variables m. According to whether the value of the variable is continuous, we divide those weather variables into two categories: discrete and continuous weather variables. Continuous weather variables include temperature, rainfall and wind speed. Discrete weather variables include weather categories (*e.g.*, sunny, cloudy) and time information. We will process those variables into an embedding vector for model training.

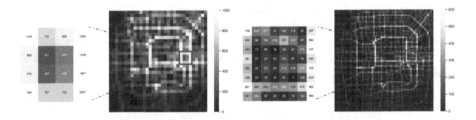

Fig. 2. An example when upsampling factor N is 2. Left: a 32×32 coarse-grained flow map. Right: a 64×64 fine-grained flow map. Each coarse-grained grid is divided into 2×2 fine-grained grids.

Problem Statement (WFRFP). Given the historical coarse-grained region flow maps $\mathcal{C} = \{\mathbf{C}_0, \mathbf{C}_1, \cdots, \mathbf{C}_t\}$, the historical weather conditions $\mathcal{M} = \{\mathbf{M}_0, \mathbf{M}_1, \cdots, \mathbf{M}_t\}$, the future weather condition $\mathbf{M}_{t+\Delta t}$ and an upsampling factor N, predict the future fine-grained region crowd flow map $\mathbf{F}_{t+\Delta t}$.

3   Methodology of WFRFP Model

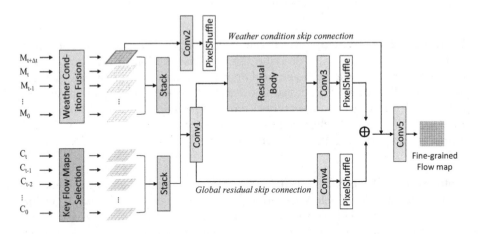

Fig. 3. The architecture of our model. Our model consists of three modules: *key flow maps selection* module, *weather condition fusion* module and *fine-grained flow prediction* module.

Figure 3 shows the architecture of our model, which consists of the following three parts: key flow maps selection, weather condition fusion and fine-grained flow prediction.

Key Flow Maps Selection. This part aims to select key flow maps from the massive historical data as the input sequence for model training. Our method depicts temporal correlations by time-series method, and takes the impact of the future weather condition into account by selecting weather-similar flow data, which reduces the amount of data input and improves training efficiency.

Weather Condition Fusion. Original weather condition information cannot be fed to neural networks directly, thus we process original information before model training. We first transform weather variables into low-dimension vectors, and then we obtain weather feature maps though weather feature extraction network. The weather feature maps will be concatenated with the key flow maps as the input for model training.

Fine-Grained Flow Prediction. This module learns the spatial correlations and predicts the fine-grained region flow. We first use wide activation residual blocks to extract spatial correlation features, which allow more low-level information to pass through. Then, we perform the upsampling operation with a global residual skip connection to obtain fine-grained flow maps.

3.1   Key Flow Maps Selection

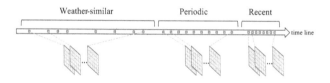

Fig. 4. Method proposed to select key flow maps. We divide the time line into three parts, and select the high-relevant flow maps according to temporal property and weather similarity of each part.

Due to such a long sequence of historical urban flow data, feature learning and model training become very challenging. In addition, there are two kinds of flow maps more relevant and significant than others for prediction: 1) flow maps with similar weather conditions to the future condition; 2) flow maps at similar times to the prediction target. For instance, if tomorrow is rainy and the goal is to predict the region flow at 8 p.m., historical flow maps at 8 p.m. with rainy weather condition own a higher correlation than others for prediction. Therefore, we propose an effective method to select these higher-relevant flow maps to reduce the input size, while the generated input sequence still preserves temporal property. Figure 4 depicts the method of key flow maps selection.

We first select the key flow maps according to temporal property, and divide them into two categories: recent flow maps $\mathcal{C}^r = \{\mathbf{C}_t, \mathbf{C}_{t-1}, \cdots, \mathbf{C}_{t-(l_r-1)}\}$, and periodic flow maps $\mathcal{C}^p = \{\mathbf{C}_{t+\Delta t-p}, \mathbf{C}_{t+\Delta t-2p}, \cdots, \mathbf{C}_{t+\Delta t-l_p \cdot p}\}$. l_r and l_p are the length of recent flow map sequence and periodic flow map sequence separately.

p is the period interval (*e.g.*, 24 h), and $t + \Delta t$ is the predicting target time. The recent flow sequence and periodic flow sequence maintain the temporal property, which captures the mobility trend over the predicting area.

Second, we select the weather-similar flow maps from the remaining historical data. We still select periodic flow maps from the remaining historical data, and each flow map owns corresponding weather condition. We normalize the weather conditions data so that those weather variables are scaled to the same range. Then we calculate the similarity between the future weather condition $\mathbf{M}_{t+\Delta t}$ and the weather conditions of these historical periodic flow maps:

$$sim(\mathbf{M}_{t+\Delta t}, \mathbf{M}_q) = \frac{1}{\sqrt{\sum_{i=1}^{N}\left(m_{(t+\Delta t,i)} - m_{(q,i)}\right)^2}} \tag{1}$$

$$s.t. \ q = t + \Delta t - k \cdot p, k \in \mathbb{Z}^+.$$

We select the top-k periodic flow maps $\mathcal{C}^s = \{\mathbf{C}_{q_1}, \mathbf{C}_{q_2}, \cdots, \mathbf{C}_{q_k}\}$ with higher *sim* as the weather-similar flow maps. We will feed weather-similar flow maps $\mathcal{C}^s$ with recent flow maps $\mathcal{C}^r$ and periodic flow maps $\mathcal{C}^p$ as input instance. We obtain the input instance with the consideration of the temporal property and the weather condition similarity, which reduces input size while improving the training efficiency.

3.2 Weather Condition Fusion

Weather conditions have a complicated and significant influence on region flow distribution over the fine-grained regions. For example, even if the total population in a coarse-grained region remains stable over time, under storming weather people tend to move from outdoor regions to indoor regions, which results in the change of flow distribution in the fine-grained regions. Thereby, we design a subnet to handle those implicit weather impacts on flow distribution all at once.

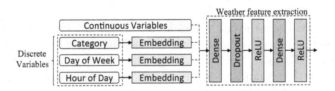

Fig. 5. The structure of weather condition fusion module.

For each flow map selected in Sect. 3.1, we process corresponding weather conditions inspired by [11], and Fig. 5 shows the architecture of the weather condition fusion module. We have divided weather variables into discrete and continuous variables in Sect. 2. For continuous weather variables, we directly concatenate them to a vector $\mathbf{m}_{con}$. And for discrete weather variables, we feed them into different embedding layers separately and obtain low-dimensional vectors, and we concatenate those vectors to a vector $\mathbf{m}_{disc}$. Then, the concatenation of $\mathbf{m}_{con}$ and $\mathbf{m}_{disc}$ gives the final embedding vector for weather conditions $\mathbf{m} = [\mathbf{m}_{con}; \mathbf{m}_{disc}]$.

We feed the concatenated vector $\mathbf{m}$ into the weather feature extraction sub-network whose structure is depicted in Fig. 5. By using dense layers, different external impacts are compounded to construct a hidden representation, which models the complicated interaction. The set of coarse-grained weather feature maps $\mathcal{M}^c$ can be obtained though weather feature extraction subnetwork.

Intuitively, the future weather condition is more influential on the future flow distribution than other historical weather conditions. However, as the neural network goes deeper, future weather information becomes weaker. To avoid the perishing of future weather information, we apply a 3×3 kernel size convolutional layer followed by a PixelShuffle layer [16] to obtain the fine-grained future weather feature map $\mathbf{M}^f$, and $\mathbf{M}^f$ will directly carry the future weather information to the later stage of model training, which plays a similar role as skip connection in Residual Network.

3.3   Fine-Grained Flow Prediction

Fine-grained Flow Prediction module extracts high-level features, which describe not only the citywide flow distribution, but also the weather influences, and finally output the fine-grained flow maps.

For SISR problem, it has been demonstrated that with same parameters and computational budgets, models with wider features before activation have significantly better performance [20]. Considering the similarity between SISR and WFRFP, we adopt the wide activation strategy in our network.

After obtaining the key flow maps and weather feature maps as we described in Sect. 3.1 and 3.2, we stack them into a tensor separately. And then the two tensors concatenated together, which is represented by $\mathbf{X}^{(0)}$ will be fed into flow prediction module. Convolutional layer is widely used to capture the correlations between an image pixel and the surrounding pixels. Like pixels in image, the crowd flow of a region is also affected by surrounding regions. So we use a convolutional layer with 5×5 kernel size to extract low-level features. The convolutional layer *Conv1* is defined as follows:

$$\mathbf{X}^{(1)} = f\left(W^{(1)} * \mathbf{X}^{(0)} + b^{(1)}\right) \tag{2}$$

where $*$ denotes the convolution operation, f is an activation function, $W^{(1)}$ and $b^{(1)}$ are the learnable parameters of the convolutional layer *Conv1*. Then we feed the fused feature maps into the residual body, which contains R residual blocks to extract high-level features. Figure 6 shows the structure of wide activation residual block.

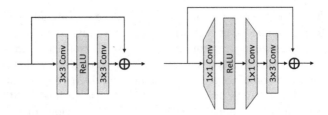

Fig. 6. Left: the structure of vanilla residual block. Right: the structure of residual block with wide activation.

The vanilla residual block (*e.g.*, used in EDSR and MDSR [12]) usually consists of two convolutional layers, *i.e.*, one 3×3 before ReLU activation and another 3×3 after. Both layers produce the same number of feature maps. Different from the vanilla residual block, the wide activation residual block expands the features before activation to let more low-level information pass through ReLU activation and produce more feature maps. Specifically, to reduce the computational cost, we first slim the features of residual identity mapping pathway. Then, a 1×1 convolution layer with more channel numbers (*e.g.*, 256 channels) is used to expand the features. After ReLU, two convolutional layers with fewer features are applied sequentially: one 1×1 convolutional layer for reducing the number of features to 64 and the other 3×3 convolutional layer for further spatial-wise feature extraction.

Since we utilize a fully convolutional residual architecture, the reception field grows larger as the network goes deeper. In other words, each pixel at the high-level feature map will be able to capture distant or even citywide spatial correlations. After extracting the high-level features though residual blocks, we perform the upsampling operation. We use a 3×3 convolutional layer and a PixelShuffle layer [16] to rear-range and upsample the feature maps to $N \times$ size with the number of channels unchanged, and output $NI \times NJ$ fine-grained flow feature map $\mathbf{F}'$.

We take the low-level flow feature as input, and use the same upsampling structure (a convolution layer followed by a PixelShuffle layer) as the global residual skip connection, which building an information highway skipping over the residual blocks to allow efficient gradient back-propagation. We obtain the fine-grained flow feature map $\mathbf{F}''$ by this way. Finally, we add $\mathbf{F}'$ and $\mathbf{F}''$, and concatenate them with fine-grained weather feature map $\mathbf{M}^f$ obtained in Sect. 3.2. Then we use a 9×9 convolution layer to map the concatenated feature to a tensor $\mathbf{F}$.

4 Model Training

Our WFRFP model can be trained to predict future fine-grained flow from historical region flow data and weather conditions data by minimizing Mean Squared Error (MSE) between the predicted flow matrix $\hat{\mathbf{F}}_t$ and the true flow matrix $\mathbf{F}_t$:

Algorithm 1. WFRFP Training Algorithm

Input: Historical flow maps and weather conditions: $\{\mathbf{C}_0, \mathbf{C}_1, \cdots, \mathbf{C}_t\}$, $\{\mathbf{M}_0, \mathbf{M}_1, \cdots, \mathbf{M}_t\}$;
lengths of recent, periodic, weather-similar sequences: l_r, l_p, l_s;
future weather condition $\mathbf{M}_{t+\Delta t}$; period: p; target time: $t + \Delta t$; upsampling factor N.
Output: Learned WFRFP model

1: $\mathcal{Q} \leftarrow \emptyset$
2: **for** $i \in [0, l_r - 1]$ **do**
3:     $\mathcal{Q} \leftarrow \mathbf{C}_{t-i}$;
4: **end for**
5: **for** $i \in [1, l_p]$ **do**
6:     $\mathcal{Q} \leftarrow \mathbf{C}_{t+\Delta t - i \cdot p}$;
7: **end for**
8: **for** $i \in [1, l_s]$ **do**
9:     Compute $sim(\mathbf{M}_{t+\Delta t}, \mathbf{M}_{t+\Delta t - l_r - p \cdot (l_p + i)})$ with Eq. 1
10:     **if** $sim(\mathbf{M}_{t+\Delta t}, \mathbf{M}_{t+\Delta t - l_r - p \cdot (l_p + i)}) < \alpha$ **then**
11:         $\mathcal{Q} \leftarrow \mathbf{M}_{t+\Delta t - l_r - p \cdot (l_p + i)}$;
12:     **end if**
13: **end for**
14: **for** $i \in [0, length(\mathcal{Q})]$ **do**
15:     Select corresponding weather conditions and obtain weather feature maps $\mathbf{M}$ though weather feature extraction module;
16:     Select corresponding $\mathcal{Q} \leftarrow \mathbf{M}$;
17: **end for**
18: initialize all learnable parameters θ in WFRFP
19: **repeat**
20:     randomly select a batch of instances $\mathcal{Q}_b$ from $\mathcal{Q}$
21:     find θ by minimizing the objective $L(\theta)$ in Eq. 3 with $\mathcal{Q}_b$
22: **until** *stopping criteria is met*
23: **return**

$$L(\theta) = \left\| \mathbf{F}_t - \hat{\mathbf{F}}_t \right\|_F^2 \tag{3}$$

where θ denotes the set of parameters in WFRFP.

Algorithm 1 outlines the training process. We first construct the training instances from the original flow data and weather conditions data (lines 1–17). Then, our model is trained via backpropagation and Adam [9] (lines 18–23).

5   Experiments

In this section, we evaluate the performance of our WFRFP model. We conduct experiments on a real-world dataset and compare 2 evaluation scores between 4 baselines and our proposed model. Besides, we also discuss the performance of different variants of our model.

5.1 Experimental Setting

Dataset. We evaluate our model on TaxiBJ dataset, which contains weather conditions and crowd flows information. Table 2 shows more details about TaxiBJ dataset.

- Weather Conditions: This part records the weather conditions in Beijing during 7/1/2013 to 10/31/2013, which contains 16 types weather category (*e.g.*, sunny), temperature, wind speed, and holiday information.
- Crowd flows: This part records the taxi flows traveling through Beijing during 7/1/2013 to 10/31/2013. The studied area is split into 32×32 grids, where each grid reports the coarse-grained flow information every 30 min. The data format is a 32×32 matrix, and each value in the matrix represents the flow of a grid region. Here, we utilize the coarse-grained taxi flows to predict fine-grained flows with $2\times$ resolution ($N = 2$) and $4\times$ resolution ($N = 4$).

Table 2. Dataset description

TaxiBJ	Value
Time span	7/1/2013–10/31/2013
Time interval	30 min
Coarse-grained size	32×32
Upsampling factor (N)	2, 4
Fine-grained size	64×64, 128×128
Weather data	Value
Category	16 types (*e.g.*, Sunny)
Temperature/°C	$[-24.6,\ 41.0]$
Wind speed/mph	$[0,\ 48.6]$
Holidays	41

Training Details and Hyper-parameters. In our experiment, we partition the data into non-overlapping training, validation and test data by a ratio of 2:1:1 respectively. Conv1 uses a convolutional layer with 64 filters of kernel size 5×5. Conv2, Conv3 and Conv4 uses a convolutional layer with 64 filters of kernel size 3×3. Conv5 uses a convolutional layer with 1 filters of kernel size 9×9. The settings of 3 convolutional layers in wide activation residual block are 256 filters of kernel size 1×1, 64 filters of kernel size 1×1 and 64 filters of kernel size 3×3. The number of residual block is set to 16 and the batch size is 16. l_r, l_p and l_s are set to 2, 3 and 3 respectively. The period interval p is 24 h.

Evaluation Metrics. We use RMSE (Root Mean Square Error), MAE (Mean Absolute Error) as the evaluation metrics for each model:

$$RMSE = \sqrt{\frac{1}{T} \sum_{t=1}^{T} \left\| \mathbf{F}_t - \hat{\mathbf{F}}_t \right\|_2^2} \tag{4}$$

$$MAE = \frac{1}{T} \sum_{t=1}^{T} \left\| \mathbf{F}_t - \hat{\mathbf{F}}_t \right\|_1 \tag{5}$$

where $\mathbf{F}$ and $\hat{\mathbf{F}}_t$ are the ground truth and the prediction of the fine-grained flow map at t-th time slot, and T is the total number of test samples. In general, RMSE favors spiky distributions, while MAE focuses more on the smoothness of the outcome. Smaller metric scores indicate better model performances.

Baselines

- Linear Interpolation Scaling (LIS): Linear interpolation is widely used in image upsampling. we first utilize linear interpolation to upsample the flow maps and compute the flow ratio of each fine-grained region to corresponding coarse-grained region. Then we obtain the fine-grained flow by the Hadamard product of the flow ratio and coarse-grained flow maps.
- SRCNN [3]: SRCNN presented the first successful introduction of convolutional neural networks (CNNs) into the SISR problems. It consists of three layers: patch extraction, non-linear mapping and reconstruction.
- VDSR [8]: SRCNN has several drawbacks such as slow convergence speed and limited representation ability owing to the three-stage architecture. Inspired by the VGG-net, VDSR model adopts Very Deep neural networks architecture with depth up to 20. This study suggests that a large depth is necessary for the task of SR.
- EDSR [12]: By applying the residual architecture [5] and removing unnecessary modules from residual architecture, EDSR achieve improved results while making model compact. EDSR also employs residual scaling techniques to stably train large models.
- WFRFP-p: To evaluate the key flow maps selection module, we also compare it with WFRFP-p, which trains WFRFP model with only periodic flow map sequences.

5.2   Experiment Result

Table 3. Comparison among baselines and our method for two upsampling factor.

Method	2		4	
	RMSE	MAE	RMSE	MAE
LIS	16.458	6.874	11.652	4.279
SRCNN	12.759	7.686	8.336	4.792
VDSR	11.032	7.105	8.159	4.513
EDSR	10.601	6.930	7.973	4.380
WFRFP	**10.316**	**6.629**	**7.730**	**4.273**
WFRFP-p	11.351	6.775	7.995	4.324

Study on Model Comparison. Table 3 depicts the experiment result of baselines and our method. According to the results, our fine-grained flow prediction model advances baseline methods, which brings 2.7%–59.6% improvement under two upsampling factors ($N = 2$ and $N = 4$). Moreover, several important observations are as follows:

- All deep neural network approaches have lower RMSE and MAE than the interpolation method, which verifies that convolutional architecture could learn correlations with spatial features by extracting high-level information.
- The framework obtains about 1.2%–2.2% and 3.4%–10.0% enhancement on two metrics respectively after employing wide activation residual blocks. Experiment result demonstrates the advantage of expand the features before activation, which could allow more low-level information to pass though and capture spatial correlations more effectively.
- The advance of WFRFP over WFRFP-p proves that key flow maps selection module plays a significant role in our method. Constructing the input instance by selecting high-relevant data could improve the prediction performance and reduce the input size.
- For each model, the performance of $N = 2$ has higher RMSE and MAE than $N = 4$. This may be because the spatial feature becomes complex and vague when the predicting region gets larger. But we lake of different sizes of flow data to confirm the supposition.

Study on Number of Residual Blocks. Figure 7 depicts the the variation of accuracy and training time with the increase of the number of residual blocks. At first, as the number of residual block increases, the value of RMSE decreases. This is because deep network could capture more distant spatial dependence and learn flow distribution features better. However, when the number of residual block increases to more than 16, the performance of our model starts to decline. The reason is that when the neural network stacks too deep, the probability of model overfitting increases. After many experiments, we found that when the number of residual block is 16, models has the best performance.

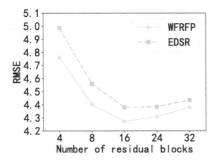
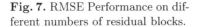
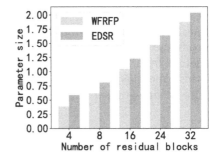

Fig. 7. RMSE Performance on different numbers of residual blocks.

Fig. 8. Parameter size on different numbers of residual blocks.

Study on Parameter Size. Figure 8 shows the parameter size of baseline methods and our method as the number of residual blocks grows. The default upsampling factor N is 4. Result shows that WFRFP outperforms baseline method, which demonstrates that our method save more memory space without performance decline by applying wide-activation residual block.

6 Related Work

We review some previous works on urban flow prediction. Urban flow prediction problem is typically spatio-temporal series prediction problems. In earlier time, classical time-series models including Autoregressive Moving Average (ARMA) model [4] and its integrated version such as Vector ARMA model [7] and Integrated Moving Average (ARIMA) model [2] were used to solve urban flow prediction problem. Those classical time-series methods can capture temporal correlations from historical data, however they can not capture the spatial correlations of urban flow distribution.

Later, some machine learning methods were applied to forecast urban flow. Support vector machines have greater generalization ability and guarantee global minima for given training data, and it has proved that SVR performs well for urban flow prediction [18]. Alternatively, STW-KNN [19] is an improved KNN (K-nearest neighbor algorithm) model which enhances forecasting accuracy of urban flow based on the spatio-temporal correlation.

Recently, due to the powerful expressive capabilities of deep neural networks, researchers have started to focus on predicting urban flow by deep learning methods. Deep-ST [22] firstly utilized a convolutional network to capture spatial correlations and forecasted region flow. Further, ST-ResNet [21] was proposed by employing an advanced residual neural network instead of the general convolution operation. By combining the pyramidal ConvGRU model [1] with periodic representations, Periodic-CRN [23] was designed to model the periodic nature of crowd flow explicitly. STRCNs [6] and DeepSTN+ [13] explored the combination of convolution and LSTM to predict long-term urban flow. All of these deep-learning-based methods have noticed the temporal and spatial dependence of urban flow and tried to find better structures to depict it. However, none of them constructed a special structure for fine-grained flow prediction to capture more details from flow maps.

In this paper, inspired by the solutions for SISR problem, we construct a new structure for fine-grained flow prediction with future weather conditions.

7   Conclusion

In this paper, we formalize the Weather-affected Fine-grained Region Flow Prediction problem and propose WFRFP model, which adopts the idea used in image super-resolution and predict the flow of a more precise region range. Moreover, WFRFP addresses the two challenges, *i.e.*, redundant input data and the spatial dependence by selecting high-relevant flow data and applying the fully convolutional residual architecture. The experiments on the real-world dataset confirm that our method is more effective than other baseline methods for fine-grained region flow prediction. In the future, we will explore the solution for long-term fine-grained flow prediction and take more data sources (*e.g.*, point of interest) into consideration.

Acknowlededgments. This work is supported by the National Natural Science Foundation of China (No. 61572165) and the National Natural Science Foundation of China (No. 61806061).

References

1. Ballas, N., Yao, L., Pal, C., Courville, A.: Delving deeper into convolutional networks for learning video representations. arXiv preprint arXiv:1511.06432 (2015)
2. Box, G.E., Jenkins, G.M., Reinsel, G.C., Ljung, G.M.: Time Series Analysis: Forecasting and Control. Wiley, Hoboken (2015)
3. Dong, C., Loy, C.C., He, K., Tang, X.: Image super-resolution using deep convolutional networks. IEEE Trans. Pattern Anal. Mach. Intell. **38**(2), 295–307 (2015)
4. Hamilton, J.D.: Time Series Analysis. Economic Theory. II, pp. 625–630. Princeton University Press, Princeton (1995)
5. He, K., Zhang, X., Ren, S., Jian, S.: Deep residual learning for image recognition. In: 2016 IEEE Conference on Computer Vision and Pattern Recognition (CVPR) (2016)
6. Jin, W., Lin, Y., Wu, Z., Wan, H.: Spatio-temporal recurrent convolutional networks for citywide short-term crowd flows prediction. In: Proceedings of the 2nd International Conference on Compute and Data Analysis, pp. 28–35. ACM (2018)
7. Kamarianakis, Y., Prastacos, P.: Forecasting traffic flow conditions in an urban network: comparison of multivariate and univariate approaches. Transp. Res. Rec. **1857**(1), 74–84 (2003)
8. Kim, J., Lee, J.K., Lee, K.M.: Accurate image super-resolution using very deep convolutional networks
9. Kingma, D.P., Ba, J.: Adam: a method for stochastic optimization. arXiv preprint arXiv:1412.6980 (2014)

10. Ledig, C., et al.: Photo-realistic single image super-resolution using a generative adversarial network. In: Proceedings of the IEEE Conference on Computer Vision and Pattern Recognition, pp. 4681–4690 (2017)

11. Liang, Y., et al.: UrbanFM: inferring fine-grained urban flows. arXiv preprint arXiv:1902.05377 (2019)

12. Lim, B., Son, S., Kim, H., Nah, S., Mu Lee, K.: Enhanced deep residual networks for single image super-resolution. In: Proceedings of the IEEE Conference on Computer Vision and Pattern Recognition Workshops, pp. 136–144 (2017)

13. Lin, Z., Feng, J., Lu, Z., Li, Y., Jin, D.: DeepSTN+: context-aware spatial-temporal neural network for crowd flow prediction in metropolis. In: Proceedings of the AAAI Conference on Artificial Intelligence, vol. 33, pp. 1020–1027 (2019)

14. Liu, N., Ma, R., Wang, Y., Zhang, L.: Inferring fine-grained air pollution map via a spatiotemporal super-resolution scheme. In: Adjunct Proceedings of the 2019 ACM International Joint Conference on Pervasive and Ubiquitous Computing and Proceedings of the 2019 ACM International Symposium on Wearable Computers, pp. 498–504 (2019)

15. Peled, S., Yeshurun, Y.: Superresolution in MRI: application to human white matter fiber tract visualization by diffusion tensor imaging. Magn. Reson. Med.: Off. J. Int. Soc. Magn. Reson. Med. **45**(1), 29–35 (2001)

16. Shi, W., et al.: Real-time single image and video super-resolution using an efficient sub-pixel convolutional neural network. In: Proceedings of the IEEE Conference on Computer Vision and Pattern Recognition, pp. 1874–1883 (2016)

17. Thornton, M.W., Atkinson, P.M., Holland, D.: Sub-pixel mapping of rural land cover objects from fine spatial resolution satellite sensor imagery using super-resolution pixel-swapping. Int. J. Remote Sens. **27**(3), 473–491 (2006)

18. Wu, C.H., Ho, J.M., Lee, D.T.: Travel-time prediction with support vector regression. IEEE Trans. Intell. Transp. Syst. **5**(4), 276–281 (2004)

19. Xia, D., Wang, B., Li, H., Li, Y., Zhang, Z.: A distributed spatial-temporal weighted model on MapReduce for short-term traffic flow forecasting. Neurocomputing **179**, 246–263 (2016)

20. Yu, J., et al.: Wide activation for efficient and accurate image super-resolution. arXiv preprint arXiv:1808.08718 (2018)

21. Zhang, J., Zheng, Y., Qi, D.: Deep spatio-temporal residual networks for citywide crowd flows prediction. In: Thirty-First AAAI Conference on Artificial Intelligence (2017)

22. Zhang, J., Zheng, Y., Qi, D., Li, R., Yi, X.: DNN-based prediction model for spatio-temporal data. In: Proceedings of the 24th ACM SIGSPATIAL International Conference on Advances in Geographic Information Systems, p. 92. ACM (2016)

23. Zonoozi, A., Kim, J.J., Li, X.L., Cong, G.: Periodic-CRN: a convolutional recurrent model for crowd density prediction with recurring periodic patterns. In: IJCAI, pp. 3732–3738 (2018)

Detecting Abnormal Congregation Through the Analysis of Massive Spatio-Temporal Data

Tianran Chen[1,2], Yongzheng Zhang[1,2(✉)], Yupeng Tuo[1], and Weiguang Wang[1]

[1] Institute of Information Engineering,
Chinese Academy of Sciences, Beijing, China
{chentianran,zhangyongzheng,tuoyupeng,wangweiguang}@iie.ac.cn
[2] School of Cyber Security,
University of Chinese Academy of Sciences, Beijing, China

Abstract. The pervasiveness of location-acquisition technologies leads to large amounts of spatio-temporal data, which brings researchers opportunities to discover interesting group patterns like congregation. Typically, a congregation is formed by a certain number of individuals within an area during a period of time. Previous work focused on discovering various congregations based on real-life scenarios to help in monitoring unusual group activities. However, most existing research didn't further analyze these results due to the consideration that the congregation is an unusual event already. In this article, firstly, we propose a group pattern to capture a variety of congregations from trajectory data. Secondly, congregations are separated into unexpected congregations and periodic congregations by extracting spatio-temporal features from historical trajectories. Thirdly, we further investigate the intensity of periodic congregation and combine environmental factors to dynamically identify anomalies within it, together with previously obtained unexpected congregations to form abnormal congregations. Moreover, incremental update techniques are utilized to detect abnormal congregations over massive-scale trajectory streams online, which means it can immediately respond to the updated trajectories. Finally, based on real cellular network dataset and real taxi trajectory dataset, our approach is evaluated through extensive experiments which demonstrate its effectiveness.

Keywords: Abnormal congregation detection · Trajectory mining · Spatio-temporal data

1 Introduction

Trajectory mining has received great attention in recent years. Many applications, including community recommendation [13], traffic prediction [5,19], group pattern discovery [3,4,8,10,11,20] etc. benefit from trajectory mining. In this

X. Wang et al. (Eds.): APWeb-WAIM 2020, LNCS 12318, pp. 376–390, 2020.
https://doi.org/10.1007/978-3-030-60290-1_30

work, we focus on efficiently discovering a group pattern called *congregation*, and further exploring congregation results by proposing a novel anomaly detection method based on historical spatio-temporal features to capture *abnormal congregations* from trajectory streams.

Detecting congregations can help in monitoring a variety of unusual group events (e.g., celebrations, parades, business promotions, traffic jams and other significant happenings), which is of great importance to public safety and traffic management. To capture desired congregation, we propose a pattern that should be satisfying the following requirements: 1) A congregation should consist of a certain number of objects who form a dense group of any sharp and extent for at least a period of time. 2) It allows members to join or leave group at any time, but a certain number of *core members* stay in the group is required to maintain the congregation. 3) Core members should be dedicated members who commit to participate the group event *recently*.

Besides, most existing research didn't further analyze congregation results due to the consideration that the congregation is an unusual event already. However, for example, traffic jams frequently take place at some certain main roads at rush hours, people would like to gather in malls at night and weekends, etc. Compared to these regular or periodic congregations, the aforementioned celebrations, parades, and traffic jams caused by accidents anywhere are more likely sudden events, which are regarded as unexpected congregations and worth more attention. Moreover, some of periodic congregations are still noteworthy. If there are much more people congregated in shopping mall or scenic spot than usual, indicating that some events happened and deploying more police to maintain security might be necessary. If more vehicles congregated at some roads longer than usual, indicating that situation deteriorated and it requires manual intervention to recover. Therefore, employing a method to detect such abnormal congregations is valuable for various applications, such as transportation management, public safety monitoring and emergency response in smart city.

To the best of our knowledge, this is the first attempt to further analyze long-period congregation results for differentiating abnormal congregations from normal ones based on spatio-temporal data. To achieve this goal, we have developed a novel method for abnormal congregation detection. To summarize, the major contributions of this paper are as follows.

- We propose a group pattern which captures congregations formed by connected objects who share common purposes or behaviors.
- We develop a novel abnormal congregation detection method by further exploring long-period congregation results. Eventually, all unexpected congregations, and periodic congregations with anomalous intensity form the updated abnormal congregations.
- Incremental update optimizations are utilized in each phase to detect abnormal congregations over massive-scale trajectory streams online, which means it can immediately respond to the updated trajectories.
- We evaluate the effectiveness of our proposed model with extensive experimental study on real cellular network data and taxi trajectory data [12,17].

Indeed, by visualizing the results obtained from our system, we can successfully detect abnormal congregations from spatio-temporal data.

2   Related Work

Over past years, many group patterns have been proposed in previous work. Flock [3], convoy [8], swarm [11] required the same set of individuals in the group during its lifetime, which is unrealistic since members frequently change in real word scenarios. Gathering [20] adopted participator(dedicated member who can stick to the group for a long time) to allow ordinary members join or leave the group event at any time but maintain its stability simultaneously. However, a participator holds dedicated title forever, resulting in it insensitive to rapid changes. Evolving group [10] discovered objects that share common behaviors in most of the time instead of consecutive timestamps. Congregate group [4] was capable of detecting rapid change of unusual events and yielding more reasonable results by ensuring its members change gradually over time. In terms of abnormal congregation detection, most work mainly focused on addressing congestion-related problems. Kong et al. [9] proposed a long-term traffic anomaly detection based on crowdsourced bus trajectory data. Anbaroglu et al. [1] proposed a non-recurrent congestion detection method by clustering link journey time estimates. Sun et al. [15] proposed a deep neural network-based method to explain non-recurring traffic congestion. Wang et al. [16] proposed an error-feedback recurrent convolutional neural network structure for continuous traffic speed prediction and congestion sources exploration. Anwar et al. [2] utilized physical and logical layers to capture congestion evolution. Mondal et al. [14] proposed a neural network-based system to estimate and classify the traffic congestion state from inroad stationary sensors.

However, these group patterns and traffic jams discovered by existing research are only a part of unexpected or periodic congregations. Therefore, further research into a more fine-grained abnormal congregation detection is urgently needed, which motivates our work. Moreover, the above detected congestion is limited to address traffic problems, while our work is also applicable to other spatial temporal domains.

3   Problem Definition

The goal of this paper is to detect abnormal congregations from spatial-temporal data. To do this, we need to discover congregation first. As shown in Fig. 1, we generate snapshot cluster, an area consists of density-reachable objects with arbitrary shape by adopting a density-based clustering algorithm [6], then obtain crowds [20] to connect snapshot clusters in temporal aspect.

Definition 1 (Crowd, Cr). *Given snapshot clusters for a certain period of time, the lifetime threshold k_c, object threshold m_c, distance threshold δ_c, a crowd Cr is a sequence of snapshot clusters at consecutive timestamps $Cr = \langle C_i, C_{i+1}, ..., C_j \rangle$ satisfying the following conditions:*

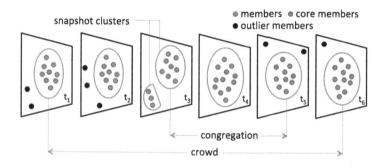

Fig. 1. Illustration of snapshot cluster, crowd and congregation.

- *The lifetime of Cr is $j - i + 1 \geq k_c$.*
- *Cr contains at least m_c objects at any time.*
- *The distance between consecutive pair of snapshot clusters C_i and C_{i+1} is not greater than δ_c.*

Now, the concept of *core member* is defined to address over-involvement problem of previous patterns. Then, we introduce *congregation* that should contain a certain number of ordinary and core members at any time.

Definition 2 (Core Member, CM). *Given a crowd $Cr = \langle C_i, C_{i+1}, ..., C_j \rangle$, lifetime threshold of a participator k_p, a sliding window W, the occurrence threshold of a core member w_p, an object o is qualified for core member only if:*

- *o appears in at least k_p clusters of Cr.*
- *o has appeared in W for at least w_p timestamps.*

Definition 3 (Congregation, CG). *Crowd Cr evolves to congregation if there are at least m_p participators and m_{cm} core members in each snapshot cluster of Cr, i.e., $\forall o_i \in O_{DB}, |\{o_i|o_i(t) \in Par_t\}| \geq m_p, |\{o_i|o_i(t) \in CM_t\}| \geq m_{cm}$.*

Next, we need to detect abnormal congregations from results. Intuitively, we separate nearby congregations as periodic congregation candidates from isolated congregations, then extract periodic congregations from the candidate sets.

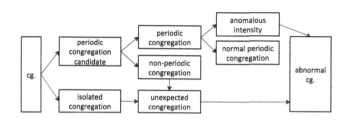

Fig. 2. Illustration of unexpected, periodic and abnormal congregations.

Definition 4 (Periodic Congregation, PCG). *Given candidates PCG_{pre}, time interval difference δ_t. PCG is a subset of PCG_{pre} where the interval T of consecutive pair is similar. $PCG = \langle Cg_1, Cg_2, ..., Cg_t \rangle \subseteq PCG_{pre}$ satisfying $\forall Cg_i, Cg_{i+1}, Cg_{i+2} \in PCG, |T_{Cg_{i+2},Cg_{i+1}} - T_{Cg_{i+1},Cg_i}| \leq \delta_t$.*

Definition 5 (Unexpected Congregation). *Given a congregation Cg, congregation set $CG = \langle Cg_t^1, ..., Cg_t^k, Cg_{t+1}^1, ..., Cg_{t+1}^k, Cg_{t+n}^1, ..., Cg_{t+n}^k \rangle$, distance threshold δ_{cg}. Cg is an unexpected congregation: $\nexists Cg_t^i \in CG$ satisfying Hausdorff distance $Haus(Cg_t^i, Cg) \leq \delta_{cg}$ within periodic time interval.*

The detection process is illustrated in Fig. 2. All unexpected congregations, both isolated congregations and non-periodic congregations, belong to abnormal congregations because there is no other congregation with spatial and temporal similarity exists, which is consistent with the features of aforementioned sudden events. Also, periodic congregations with anomalous intensity, either member number or duration significantly exceed threshold, will be considered as abnormal congregations.

Definition 6 (Problem Statement). *Given a trajectory set of moving objects O_{DB}, our goal is to find all isolated congregations, non-periodic congregations and periodic congregations with anomalous intensity from O_{DB} to form the abnormal congregations.*

4   System Framework

In this section, we will elaborate system framework and methods to detect abnormal congregations. As illustrated in Fig. 3, our system consists of four stages: trajectory preprocessing, congregation discovery, congregation classification and abnormal congregation detection.

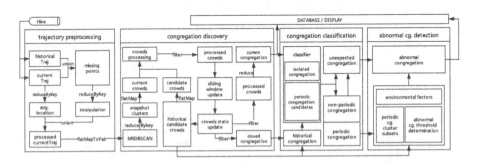

Fig. 3. System framework of abnormal congregation detection.

4.1 Congregation Discovery

First of all, we apply linear interpolation and map-matching prediction algorithm for objects based on their speed or data source during trajectory preprocessing. The details of this phase are omitted due to the space limitation. Then we adopt MRDBSCAN [7], a parallelized density-based clustering algorithm, to obtain snapshot clusters, which are combined with historical crowds to generate updated crowds in parallel. As a consequence, a historical crowd either evolves to at least one candidate crowd, or permanent break due to no snapshot cluster is available to be appended to the crowd. Finally, a congregation is formed if a crowd contains enough core members at any time.

Table 1. Illustration of incremental update of congregation discovery

t_1	t_2	t_3	t_4	t_5	t_6	t_7	t_8	t_9
o_1	o_1	o_1		o_1				o_1
o_2	o_2	o_2	o_2	o_2		o_2	o_2	
o_3			o_3		o_3	o_3	o_3	
		o_4	o_4	o_4	o_4		o_4	
			o_5		o_5	o_5		
				o_6	o_6		o_6	
						o_7		
c_1	c_2	c_3	c_4	c_5	c_6	c_7	c_8	c_9

time	Par	CanCM	Cr^{bit}	Congregation
t_1	$\emptyset$	$\emptyset$	0	$\emptyset$
t_2	$\emptyset$	o_1, o_2	00	$\emptyset$
t_3	o_1, o_2	o_1, o_2, o_4	111	$\langle c_1, c_2, c_3 \rangle$
t_4	o_1, o_2, o_4	o_1, o_2, o_4	1111	$\langle c_1, c_2, c_3, c_4 \rangle$
t_5	o_1, o_2, o_4	o_2, o_4, o_5	11111	$\langle c_1, c_2, c_3, c_4, c_5 \rangle$
t_6	$o_1, ..., o_4$	o_2, o_3, o_4	111110	$\langle c_1, c_2, c_3, c_4, c_5 \rangle$
t_7	$o_1, ..., o_5$	o_2, o_3, o_5, o_6	1111101	$\langle c_1, c_2, c_3, c_4, c_5 \rangle$
t_8	$o_1, ..., o_5$	o_2, o_3, o_6	11111011	$\langle c_1, c_2, c_3, c_4, c_5 \rangle$
t_9	$o_1, ..., o_6$	o_2, o_3, o_6	111111110	$\langle c_1, ..., c_8 \rangle$

We use an example to illustrate the discovery progress of a congregation. Table 1 presents a gathering scenario and the process of incremental update. Let $k_c = m_c = k_p = 3$, $m_p = m_{cm} = w_p = 2$, $W = 3$. At t_3, cluster c_3 consists of enough candidate core members $\{o_1, o_2, o_4\}$ and participators $\{o_1, o_2\}$. It is easy to observe that there are two core members($CanCM \cap Par \cap \{o_i | o_i \in c_3\}$), satisfying the requirements for a crowd to be a congregation $\langle c_1, c_2, c_3 \rangle$. At t_6, the congregation is suspended since there is only one core member o_3 appears in the cluster. However, o_6 becomes a candidate core member at t_7 and has appeared in k_p historical clusters during $[t_1, t_9]$, which is qualified for a core member. Therefore, we set the cluster c_6 as valid and update congregation as $\langle c_1, c_2, c_3, c_4, c_5, c_6, c_7, c_8 \rangle$ at t_9. The progress illustrates that an invalid cluster might support the crowd to be a congregation later even if it has been moved out of the sliding window. On the contrary, an out-of-sliding-window cluster containing inadequate candidate core members will lead to the crowd break immediately since the cluster remains invalid permanently. Assume the number of candidate core members in c_9 is inadequate when t_{11} arrives, we truncate the longest qualified sequence of clusters before c_9, i.e., $\langle c_1, c_2, c_3, c_4, c_5, c_6, c_7, c_8 \rangle$, and convert it into a closed congregation. Meanwhile, the clusters after c_9, i.e., $\langle c_{10}, c_{11}, ... \rangle$ will be re-evaluated to update the bit vector of crowd.

4.2 Abnormal Congregation Detection

Congregation Classification. First, we introduce a classification algorithm, which divides congregations into three categories, i.e., isolated congregation, non-periodic congregation from candidate sets and periodic congregation. As shown in Fig. 4, we cluster nearby congregations to obtain raw periodic congregation candidates, while outliers will be regarded as isolated congregations because there is no historical congregation located around. A periodic congregation is a subset from the candidate set, which has similar time interval between every two consecutive congregations. Intuitively, we check the multiple of time slot to capture congregations with arbitrary period, which is time-consuming and unnecessary. Instead, we adopt an interval examination method to do this. Figure 6(a) presents a five-day congregation at same location scenario. Usually, $PCG = \langle Cg_1, Cg_2, Cg_3, Cg_4, Cg_5 \rangle$ is a strict periodic congregation since there is a time overlap among all congregations. However, it might be problematic since it requires a new congregation to overlap with all old periodic congregations. As shown in Fig. 6(b), the earlier end of congregation on day2 leads to the periodic congregation candidate set is divided into three subsets, namely $PCG_1 = \langle Cg_1, Cg_2, Cg_3, Cg_4 \rangle, PCG_2 = \langle Cg_1, Cg_3, Cg_5 \rangle, PCG_3 = \langle Cg_3, Cg_4, Cg_5 \rangle$. In fact, they belong to the same periodic congregation, unequivocally. Therefore, we improve the model by allowing a later congregation to have overlap with most prior congregations, which is more common in real scenarios. Meanwhile, a parameter δ_{ppcg} is designed to deal with limited lack of congregations.

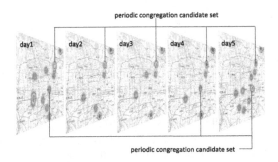

Fig. 4. Periodic congregation candidate set.

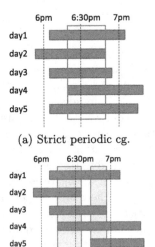

(a) Strict periodic cg.

(b) Improved periodic cg.

Fig. 6. Periodic congregation.

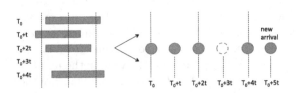

Fig. 5. Eliminating impact of occasional absence.

As shown in Fig. 5, the interval of periodic congregations has been extended to $2t$ due to the missing congregation at $T_0 + 3t$. With applying δ_{ppcg}, system will fill a virtual congregation to maintain original interval, which makes the new arrival be correctly classified as periodic congregation.

Moreover, we optimize this process by designing an incremental update algorithm to process streaming data. As shown in Fig. 7, prior candidates formed by location-nearby congregations will be saved. When an updated congregation arrives, we calculate the distance between it and each periodic congregation candidate to determine if a new arrival is an extend of previous congregations or an outlier, instead of re-cluster all historical and current congregations. If a congregation belongs to an existing periodic congregation candidate set, we further explore the time interval between the new congregation and periodic congregations. As a consequence, an updated congregation would be 1) an extend of an/multiple existing periodic congregation(s) and inserted to the rear of set(s), 2) a non-periodic congregation from periodic congregation candidate set which might evolve to a periodic congregation later, 3) forming a new periodic congregation candidate set with prior isolated congregation, or 4) an isolated congregation due to no previous congregation located around.

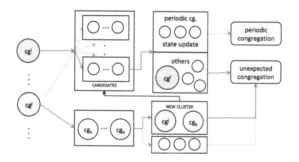

Fig. 7. Illustration of incremental update of congregation classification.

Eventually, the process illustrates that a potential periodic congregation might be marked as unexpected congregation first due to lack of historical information. However, the follow-up nearby congregations with appropriate time interval will be correctly determined as periodic congregation, which means it can update the state of various periodic congregation gradually and dynamically.

Abnormal Congregation Detection. We need to further validate a congregation is abnormal or not after it has been determined as an extend of periodic congregation. Intuitively, we set intensity threshold like what we did in the process of congregation discovery. However, the popularity is not evenly distributed over the whole urban area. A congregation located at transportation hubs is usually more serious than those around CBDs or residential areas. The system will fail to obtain reasonable results if we use same thresholds to determine anomaly.

A large value of threshold will lead to the missing of detecting abnormal congregation while a small one may result in raising too many false alerts. To address this problem, we try to set various threshold for each periodic congregation based on its own historical intensity. As Formula 1 shown, the threshold is adaptively adjusted according to the latest j timestamps, and latter congregations weight more on the threshold-deciding process by shrinking $weight_i$ of earlier ones.

$$\delta_{pcg_n} = \frac{1 + H(\delta_{env_n}) \cdot \delta_{env_n}}{j} \sum_{i=n-j}^{n-1} |pcg_i| \cdot weight_i \tag{1}$$

$$H(x) = \begin{cases} 0 & x < \delta_{env} \\ 1 - \frac{\delta_{env}}{x} & x \geq \delta_{env} \end{cases}$$

$$\delta_{env_n} = \frac{1}{m} \sum_{k=0}^{m-1} \frac{|pcg_n^k|}{\frac{1}{j}\sum_{i=n-j}^{n-1} |pcg_i^k|} - 1 \tag{2}$$

Besides, some external factors might result in the total number of people gathering, such as slow traffic on rainy days or increased human activities during holidays. We believe that the impact should be properly taken into account if most congregation deteriorated. Although the system is not exactly aware of what happened in the real world, it should have ability to self-correct by identifying whether such a situation has occurred through anomalous change of most congregations. To do this, we add an environmental parameter δ_{env_n} to automatically adjust the threshold, which is decided by the differences between historical and current congregations situation. If the number of congregations and the average of participants in a single congregation are both significantly above normal situation, threshold will be increased appropriately to reduce false positives. As shown in Formula 2, we should calculate the mean of intensity increase in each historical periodic congregation. If the average growth of δ_{env_n} is greater than δ_{env}, the threshold for abnormal congregation determination is increased. Otherwise, we believe that the impact of environmental factors can be ignored.

Compared with abnormal increase of congregation participants, longer duration is mainly influenced by the characteristics of the congregation rather than external factors, which makes it relatively simpler to deal with. Therefore, we only need to calculate the average duration of each periodic congregation. A periodic congregation will be warned only if the number of participants in a new congregation is not lower than those in its history, while the duration is significantly longer than the historical average.

5   Experimental Results

In this section, we conduct extensive experiments to evaluate the effectiveness of our proposed system based on real trajectory dataset.

5.1   Experiment Settings

We use two real trajectory data sources:

- Cellular Data. The dataset is a sample of signaling data from the cellular network of Beijing provided by a network operator. It contains trajectories of 7,416 persons during the period of September 15 to December 3, 2017. To protect users' privacy, all phone numbers have been mapped to unique ids.
- Taxi Data. It contains two taxi datasets. One is from T-Drive project [17,18] collected by Microsoft Research Asia. It contains GPS trajectories of 10,357 taxis during the period of February 2 to February 8, 2008 in Beijing. The total number of points in this dataset is about 17.66 million and the average sampling interval is about 3 min. The other dataset contains a one-month taxi trajectory of Beijing in May 2009 [12]. Each day has records of 6000 to 8000 taxis. The trajectories cover main urban area of Beijing in weekdays, weekends and public holidays, which has good spatial and temporal coverage.

First, proposed congregation is evaluated based on the Cellular Data and T-Drive Data [17,18]. Then, we validate the effectiveness of anomaly detection based on Beijing Taxi Data [12], which is sufficient for long-period analysis.

5.2   Effectiveness of Congregation Discovery

Firstly, we compare congregation pattern against gathering pattern on cellular network data with settings $MinPts = 5$, $\epsilon = 250$ m, $k_c = k_p = m_c = 5$, $m_p = m_{cm} = 3$, $w_p = 3$, $\delta_c = 500$ m. Figure 8 shows that the number of congregation is more than the number of gathering, while the duration is shorter. The gap between two patterns during day time is more obvious than night, which is caused by some core members in an area have left the group for a long time and returned later. A typical scenario is illustrated in Fig. 8(c), a gathering is formed during the whole time. However, all members at t_{20} are changed compared to t_{19}, but the gathering is sustained by old participators o_2 and o_6. The similar situation occurs more frequently as the number of participators grows over time, which leads to a gathering insensitive to rapid changes. However, our pattern can detect such change and capture two anticipated congregations. Each one consists of connected members who share common purposes or behaviors.

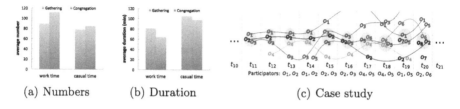

(a) Numbers   (b) Duration   (c) Case study

Fig. 8. Effectiveness study of two patterns

Then, we further validate the effectiveness and scalability of our proposed pattern on T-driver data [17,18]. The congregations have been discovered for a week with settings $MinPts = 10$, $\epsilon = 300$ m, $k_c = k_p = 3$, $m_c = 10$, $m_p = m_{cm} = 5$, $w_p = 3$, $\delta_c = 1000$ m. A day has been divided into 24 slots, and average number of congregations in each slot is calculated by applying multiple counting, which means that a congregation starts at 6:30 and ends at 8:30 will be counted each time for slot 6, 7 and 8, respectively. Moreover, we take samplings density into account due to the fact that abundant objects will easily form more clusters. Therefore, we adjust results by Formula 3.

$$Cg_{t_i}^* = Cg_{t_i}^{raw} \cdot \frac{\min(\sum_{d=0}^{j}|O(points)_{d.t_0}|, ..., \sum_{d=0}^{j}|O(points)_{d.t_{23}}|)}{\sum_{d=0}^{j}|O(points)_{d.t_i}|} \tag{3}$$

As shown in Fig. 9, surprisingly, the revised congregations reach its peak in the early morning. We manually inspect distribution of these congregations and find that a part of them is located around car rental companies and residential areas. This is because most taxi drivers park their vehicles at night, and the vehicles stationed in the area tend to form congregations. In other time slots, the congregation changes are relatively stable, and distributions are also consistent with human activities. Moreover, we compare the number of congregations with relative clusters for further exploration. Usually, only a small part of clusters can form congregations, while less clusters evolve to more congregations in the midnight and morning. On the one hand, it is consistent with the rest time of taxi drivers, and on the other hand, the increase of the number of morning congregations cancels out the effect of the decrease of night congregations, thus maintaining the high number.

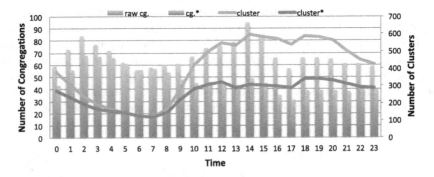

Fig. 9. Effectiveness of case study

After that, the total number falls to normal. Besides, there is no significant increase in the number of congregations at evening rush hours, indicating that the traffic in the evening are better during the week.

We further conduct analysis on one-week congregations obtained from two perspectives regarding to intensity.

Participants. Figure 10(a) shows larger congregations tagged with start time and object number. Note that there are several congregations with more than 100 participants, which are significantly above most congregations. Further study conclusively shows that these congregations distributed around railway station and airport where taxi waiting areas are located. A congregation is easily formed if taxi drivers spend more time waiting for passengers, which leads to the increasing of the number of core members. We believe that long-period congregation results associated with traffic information can help in optimizing taxi dispatching, which is beneficial to enhance transport efficiency and reduce waiting time.

Duration. Figure 10(b) shows longer congregations tagged with end time and duration. We manually inspect the distribution of these congregations and find that their locations can be divided into three categories. 1) Car services such as taxi rental companies and automobile repair centers. Most congregations around rental companies started at midnight and ended in the morning, which coincide with human daily activity. However, there is no pattern detected on congregations located around repair centers because it is unpredictable. 2) Transportation hubs. This kind of congregation with long duration often occurs at night because it takes more time to wait for passengers. 3) Hospital and residential areas. It is interesting that these congregations are easily formed by less objects with longer duration compared to those located around airport or railway station.

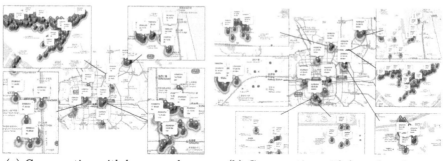

(a) Congregation with large number.   (b) Congregation with long duration.

Fig. 10. Further study of congregation case.

5.3   Effectiveness of Abnormal Congregation Detection

Next, we validate the effectiveness of congregation classification and abnormal congregation detection based on one-month taxi trajectory data set [12]. To the best of our knowledge, there is no publicly available benchmark model for the

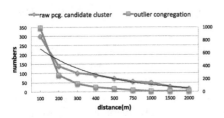

Fig. 11. Number of pcg. w.r.t δ_{cg}

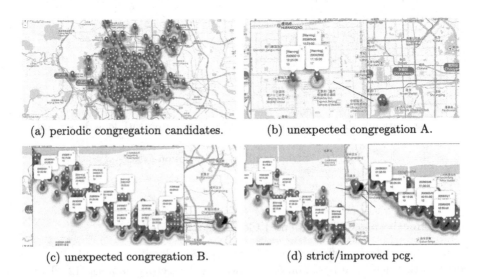

Fig. 12. Distribution of outlier cg.

task of predicting abnormal congregations. Therefore, our method will be verified through the analysis of several typical scenarios in real world.

By applying aforementioned congregation discovery algorithm, we obtain 468,094 clusters, and 50,050 eligible crowds, which form 10,042 congregations. Then, we perform location-based clustering on these congregations to generate periodic congregation candidates. In terms of parameter selection, we first conduct study on correlation between distance threshold δ_{cg} and number of periodic congregation candidate sets. As shown in Fig. 11, the number of candidates decreases significantly at first since more congregations are clustered into same raw periodic congregation candidate cluster. It can be easily seen that change tends to be slower when the distance is within the range of 500–1000. Based on real situation, we set δ_{cg} to 500 m and obtain 158 periodic congregation candidates, as well as 1 outlier cluster. Figure 12 presents all 46 outlier congregations, which are distributed all over the whole urban area. They are not only isolated, but also formed at random time, which is consistent with the definition of unexpected congregation.

(a) periodic congregation candidates.   (b) unexpected congregation A.

(c) unexpected congregation B.   (d) strict/improved pcg.

Fig. 13. Classifying periodic congregation candidates as different results.

Figure 13(a) shows the distribution of obtained candidates. Then, we try to extract non-periodic congregations from these sets. Fig. 13(b) shows a sparse periodic candidate set containing several congregations with random occurrences, which are considered as unexpected congregations. Figure 13(c) presents another example of unexpected congregation, which is located around periodic congregation. The relative scenario in reality is that, for instance, many people gather at a bar street every night, while a congregation is worth more attention if it occurs in the region at afternoon someday. Besides, Fig. 13(d) demonstrates the effect of improved periodic congregation algorithm. The left figure shows a strict method is utilized to detect periodic congregation. Some prior congregations occurred during 0:00–1:00 and 0:40–1:40, resulting in false positives of latter congregations due to the overlap time window is reduced. After applying the improved model, the latter ones can be correctly identified as periodic congregations.

When a congregation becomes a periodic congregation, we need to further determine if it is anomalous by comparing its intensity with historical results. Figure 14(a) and Fig. 14(b) present that some periodic congregations are considered as abnormal congregations because the number of participants or duration significantly exceeds their history, which means there are some unusual events in the region.

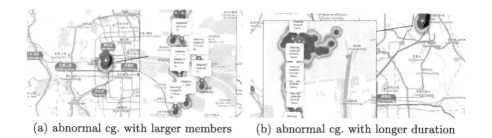

(a) abnormal cg. with larger members   (b) abnormal cg. with longer duration

Fig. 14. Example of abnormal congregation detection from periodic congregations.

6 Conclusion

In this paper, we introduce a systematic study on abnormal congregation detection through the analysis of massive spatio-temporal data. Specifically, we first focus on discovering congregation pattern, which is more sensitive to continuous change. Then, we propose a novel classification model to divide congregations into unexpected congregations and periodic congregations. After that, we develop an anomaly detection method to further explore periodic congregations with anomalous intensity. Finally, we validate the effectiveness of our approach by conducting extensive experiments on real world datasets.

Acknowledgements. This work is supported by the National Natural Science Foundation of China under Grant No. U1736218 and the Beijing Municipal Science & Technology Commission under Grant No. Z191100007119005.

References

1. Anbaroglu, B., Heydecker, B., Cheng, T.: Spatio-temporal clustering for non-recurrent traffic congestion detection on urban road networks. Transp. Res. Part C: Emerg. Technol. **48**, 47–65 (2014)
2. Anwar, T., Liu, C., Vu, H.L., Islam, M.S., Sellis, T.: Capturing the spatiotemporal evolution in road traffic networks. IEEE Trans. Knowl. Data Eng. **30**(8), 1426–1439 (2018)
3. Benkert, M., Gudmundsson, J., Hübner, F., Wolle, T.: Reporting flock patterns. Comput. Geom. **41**(3), 111–125 (2008)
4. Chen, T., Zhang, Y., Tuo, Y., Wang, W.: Online discovery of congregate groups on sparse spatio-temporal data. In: PIMRC, pp. 1–7 (2018)
5. Deng, D., Shahabi, C., Demiryurek, U., Zhu, L.: Situation aware multi-task learning for traffic prediction. In: ICDM, pp. 81–90 (2017)
6. Ester, M., Kriegel, H., Sander, J., Xu, X.: A density-based algorithm for discovering clusters in large spatial databases with noise. In: KDD 1996, pp. 226–231 (1996)
7. He, Y., Tan, H., Luo, W., Feng, S., Fan, J.: MR-DBSCAN: a scalable MapReduce-based DBSCAN algorithm for heavily skewed data. Front. Comput. Sci. **8**(1), 83–99 (2014). https://doi.org/10.1007/s11704-013-3158-3
8. Jeung, H., Shen, H.T., Zhou, X.: Convoy queries in spatio-temporal databases. In: ICDE, pp. 1457–1459 (2008)
9. Kong, X., Song, X., Xia, F., Guo, H., Wang, J., Tolba, A.: LoTAD: long-term traffic anomaly detection based on crowdsourced bus trajectory data. World Wide Web **21**(3), 825–847 (2018). https://doi.org/10.1007/s11280-017-0487-4
10. Lan, R., Yu, Y., Cao, L., Song, P., Wang, Y.: Discovering evolving moving object groups from massive-scale trajectory streams. In: MDM, pp. 256–265 (2017)
11. Li, Z., Ding, B., Han, J., Kays, R.: Swarm: mining relaxed temporal moving object clusters. PVLDB **3**(1), 723–734 (2010)
12. Lian, J., Zhang, L.: One-month Beijing taxi GPS trajectory dataset with taxi ids and vehicle status. In: DATA@SenSys, pp. 3–4 (2018)
13. Liu, S., Wang, S.: Trajectory community discovery and recommendation by multi-source diffusion modeling. IEEE Trans. Knowl. Data Eng. **29**(4), 898–911 (2017)
14. Mondal, M.A., Rehena, Z.: Intelligent traffic congestion classification system using artificial neural network. In: WWW, pp. 110–116. ACM (2019)
15. Sun, F., Dubey, A., White, J.: DxNAT - deep neural networks for explaining non-recurring traffic congestion. In: IEEE BigData, pp. 2141–2150 (2017)
16. Wang, J., Gu, Q., Wu, J., Liu, G., Xiong, Z.: Traffic speed prediction and congestion source exploration: a deep learning method. In: ICDM, pp. 499–508 (2016)
17. Yuan, J., Zheng, Y., Xie, X., Sun, G.: Driving with knowledge from the physical world. In: ACM SIGKDD, pp. 316–324 (2011)
18. Yuan, J., et al.: T-drive: driving directions based on taxi trajectories. In: ACM-GIS, pp. 99–108 (2010)
19. Zhan, X., Zheng, Y., Yi, X., Ukkusuri, S.V.: Citywide traffic volume estimation using trajectory data. IEEE Trans. Knowl. Data Eng. **29**(2), 272–285 (2017)
20. Zheng, K., Zheng, Y., Yuan, N.J., Shang, S.: On discovery of gathering patterns from trajectories. In: ICDE, pp. 242–253 (2013)

SSMDL: Semi-supervised Multi-task Deep Learning for Transportation Mode Classification and Path Prediction with GPS Trajectories

Asif Nawaz[1](✉), Zhiqiu Huang[1,2,3], and Senzhang Wang[1]

[1] College of Computer Science and Technology, Nanjing University of Aeronautics and Astronautics (NUAA), Nanjing 211106, People's Republic of China
{asifnawaz,zqhuang,szwang}@nuaa.edu.cn
[2] Key Laboratory of Safety-Critical Software, NUAA, Ministry of Industry and Information Technology, Nanjing 211106, People's Republic of China
[3] Collaborative Innovation Center of Novel Software Technology and Industrialization, Nanjing 210093, People's Republic of China

Abstract. The advancement of positioning technology enables people to use GPS devices to record their location histories. The patterns and contextual information hidden in GPS data opens variety of research issues including trajectory prediction, transportation mode detection, travel route recommendation and many more. Most existing studies have been performed to address these individual issues, but they have the following limitations. 1) Single task learning does not consider the correlations among the correlated tasks. 2) A large number of training samples are required to achieve better performance. In this paper, we propose a semi-supervised multi-task deep learning model to perform the tasks of transportation mode classification and path prediction simultaneously with GPS trajectories. Our model uses both labelled and unlabeled dataset for model training dataset, and concurrently perform both tasks in parallel. Experimental results over a large trajectory dataset collected in Beijing show that our proposal achieves significant performance improvement in terms of all evaluation metrics by comparison with baseline models.

Keywords: GPS Trajectory · Semi-supervised learning · Multi-task learning

1 Introduction

In recent years, due to the continuous improvement of location acquisition technology, especially global positioning system technology, a large number of trajectory data has been used in several spatiotemporal data mining applications [1,2], such as behavior prediction [3], location-based services [4], transportation management [5] and many more. Lots of useful information can be achieved and

© Springer Nature Switzerland AG 2020
X. Wang et al. (Eds.): APWeb-WAIM 2020, LNCS 12318, pp. 391–405, 2020.
https://doi.org/10.1007/978-3-030-60290-1_31

utilized by analyzing these trajectories. Typically, a GPS trajectory consists of a sequence of the spatiotemporal points, each of which is formatted as a tuple (latitude, longitude, timestamp). One of the important application of trajectory mining is intelligent transportation [6], which is a complex system composed of roads, pedestrians, and vehicles.

With the improvement of living standards and rapid growth of population, traffic congestions is becoming a big global issue worldwide [7]. To address such issues, it is critically important to understand the movements of human beings and their mobility modes in large-scale transportation network for effective congestion control and traffic planning. Anticipating the future situation by analyzing the patterns in existing data is also the key perception challenge for traffic congestion control and autonomous vehicles driving. Therefore, accurate classification and prediction of GPS trajectories has becoming more important problems that provides the basis to achieve high level tasks such as urban planning, location based services, congestion control etc.

With more applications and services depending on trajectory data analysis, it is vital for us to consider how these new issues influence the new applications. Existing studies solved many trajectory mining tasks like human mobility [8], trajectory prediction [9], travel route planning [10] etc. using several state of the art machine learning and deep learning based approaches. Human mobility mode detection and path prediction are among the most important problems in trajectory data mining tasks, that provides the basis for many different application like route planning [10], traffic estimation [11]. All existing studies used these models to solve single task at a time. Supervised learning based problems like mobility detection only used the labelled data, whereas most of the trajectories in the dataset are unlabeled, so most of hidden patterns in unlabeled trajectories remain undetected. Therefore, it becomes essential to make use of unlabeled data to learn distinct complex patterns. Multi-task learning in our context is a useful approach to address this issue, that is able to optimize model parameters using both labelled and unlabeled trajectories for multiple heterogeneous tasks.

Many trajectory mining tasks like mode detection, path prediction uses the common behaviors and underlying structures in the trajectories to achieve the desired tasks. Multi-task learning is a useful approach to solve different kinds of similar problems using the common underlying structure and shared knowledge representation, even the tasks with sparse labelled data can be learnt effectively. In addition, it also supports implicit data augmentation and eavesdropping as well [12]. Multi-task learning achieved great success across wide range of applications ranging from speech recognition, computer vision, natural language processing and many more [12]. Inspiring from the success of multiple language translation [13] that uses multi-task learning to translate to different languages from the common source language using a common architecture. Based on the similarities of sequential data properties of trajectories data and language modeling, we propose a multi-task learning approach to perform transportation mode classification and trajectory path prediction simultaneously, as both of these tasks shares common underlying structures. Under classical machine learning models, it is difficult to share information across multiple tasks, and inference quality decreases if the size of training corpus is smaller for some task, therefore; we choose path prediction problem that uses unlabeled trajectories in addition to the labelled trajectories and supports implicit data augmentation. All tasks in multi-task learning support each other by sharing the learnt parameters to optimize the performance of the model [12], meanwhile, it is also challenging to optimize model parameters considering both tasks in parallel.

GPS trajectory prediction and trajectory classification are different tasks but they use similar underlying structure. In this study, our effort is to adopt common underlying structure to model both of these tasks using deep neural net based multi-task learning. The input to both of these tasks is the sequence of GPS points, which are encoded using common layers of deep neural net, the encoded vectors are then processed using task specific decoders to achieve the required tasks. The task specific decoders aims to optimize the parameters of their respective tasks.

Following are the key contributions in our work:

- We for the first time propose a semi-supervised learning framework to use both labelled and unlabelled trajectories for transportation mode classification and travel path prediction.
- Based on the shared similar latent patterns in trajectories, we propose a multi-task learning model to solve the two tasks in parallel using the shared layers in the proposed deep learning model.
- We evaluate the proposed model SSMDL on microsoft geolife trajectories dataset. The result shows that the performance of SSMDL is significantly improved as compared to all baseline methods.

The rest of the paper is organized as follows. The Sect. 2 briefly introduces the relevant work. In Sect. 3, multi-task learning for heterogeneous tasks is elaborated with detail. Detailed analysis of the results of multi-task learning are discussed in Sect. 4, and conclusion of our work is given in Sect. 5.

2   Related Work

In recent years, mining of GPS trajectories has gained a lot of attention. Several methods have been proposed to solve many transportation problems. Zheng et al. [14] proposed change point based segmentation algorithm to identify single mode segments, and identify kinematic features like velocity, acceleration, heading change rate. These features are passed to machine learning methods like Hidden Markov Model, K-Nearest Neighbors, Support Vector Machines, Decision Trees and Random Forest to classify transportation modes of the segments. Wang et al. [15] extracts traffic events from twitter and integrates with GPS data, and uses hidden markov model to estimate traffic conditions. The limitations in these techniques are that these techniques require human intelligence and domain expertise to extract the features. The traditional machine learning methods are shallow models, and it is difficult to deal with big data using these approaches [16]. In recent years, the proliferation of mobile phone data, GPS trajectories data and location-based online social networks data has become easily accessible. These fast-growing human mobility data is the "big data" of today, which provides a new gateway to address the problems faced by previous large-scale traffic planning and human mobility research. Deep learning technology is an effective learning approach to deal with big data, and demonstrated superior performances in wide range of application domains.

Deep learning is state of the art technology that achieved the great success in many applications domain; including computer vision, speech recognition, biomedical imaging [16]. It imitates the way the human brain perceives and organizes, and makes decisions based on data input. When the neural network processes the input, the neural network can automatically extract features from the original data. A neural network consists of a large number of simple processors that uses mathematical formulas to learn complex functions [2]. Deep learning in recent era achieved great success in solving many transportation problems including transportation mode inference [17,18], and trajectory prediction [9,19] etc. All existing approaches addresses these issues as standalone problem. Predicting and classifying the trajectories at the same time using the common set of trajectories is a challenging task. Under the current conventional machine learning approaches, it is hard to share information across different set of similar trajectories. The prediction quality of the task also decreases if the training size of one task is smaller. To address such issues, multi-task learning is more effective and powerful approach to gain the advantages by utilizing the information from other similar task by supporting implicit data augmentation and eavesdropping.

Multi-task learning (MTL) has been used successfully across wide range of applications ranging from speech recognition, natural language processing, and drug discovery [12]. MTL trains the multiple tasks in parallel while sharing the underlying network structure. We can generalize our model better for each individual task using the shared representation of data between related tasks. Compared to single-task learning, where each task is carried out separately without considering the correlations among peer tasks, MTL is able to consider these correlations using shared representation of data for all tasks. As a result, MTL often leads to better generalization ability than single-task learning approaches [20]. For learning new tasks, we often apply the knowledge we have acquired by learning related tasks. The basic assumptions of our problem is also similar, underlying tasks differ by objective but are closely related to each other in modeling perspective. We explore such correlation across different tasks and realize it under a multi-task learning framework.

3   Multi-task Learning for Trajectory Classification and Prediction

This section provides the details of our semi-supervised multi-task deep learning architecture (SSMDL) for GPS trajectories mode classification and path prediction. Our proposed approach SSMDL works as follows. First, raw GPS trajectories are collected through multiple sensors like mobile phones, GPS trackers etc.

over a period of time. Due to measurement errors by these devices, the collected trajectories are usually not precise. For this purpose, these trajectories need to be refined before being further processed. In preprocessing step, noisy data is discarded to refine the trajectories, as it affects the performance of learning algorithms [14]. Next, all GPS trajectories are divided into equal size segments, so that deep learning models can be applied. These segments are feed into the training models, that gives inference for two different tasks.

3.1 Definitions and Problem Statement

Prior to the formal description of our problem in hand, the concepts of GPS trajectories and GPS segments are defined as follows.

GPS Trajectory (_Tra_): A user's GPS trajectory Tra is the sequence of GPS points such that $p_i \epsilon Tra$, $Tra = [p_1, p_2, ..., p_N]$. where N is the number of points in trajectory Tra. Each GPS point p_i is represented by latitude, longitude, and timestamp, $p_i = [lat, lon, t]$, that determines the geospatial location of point p_i at time t.

Trip (_TR_): We divide a trajectory Tra into trips Tr based on the preset time interval threshold between the consecutive GPS points [22].

Segment (_SE_): Segment is defined as a part of trip that has only one transportation mode $y \epsilon Y$, Y is the set of transportation modes (walk or bus etc.). A GPS segment is represented as $SE = [p_1, p_2, ..., p_M]$, where M is the number of GPS points in segment SE.

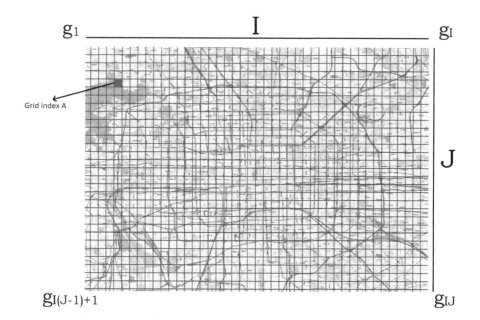

Fig. 1. Map grid representation

Map Grid (G): A geographical space is divided into two-dimensional grid G having $I \times J$ grid cells of equal size based on latitude and longitude, as shown in Fig. 1. All GPS trajectories Tra and segments SE are represented with sequence of grid indices g_{ij}, such that $i \epsilon I^j \epsilon J$ denoted by $G = [g_1, g_2, ..., g_{ij}]$.

Problem Statement: Given a set of user's GPS trajectories $Tra = [tra_1, tra_2, ..., tra_n]$, in G. Our goal is to simultaneously classifying the transportation mode of a trajectory tra_i and predict its future path.

3.2   Preliminaries

GPS data is spatiotemporal time series data. Convolutional neural networks (CNN) are good to deal with spatial dependencies in the data, recurrent neural networks (RNN) are more capable to deal with temporal dependencies in the data. Due to spatiotemporal nature of GPS data, we used Convolutional LSTM (ConvLSTM) architecture [21], that is able to capture both spatial and temporal correlations in GPS trajectories data. Differency between Fully Connected Long Short Term Memory (FC-LSTM) and ConvLSTM is that input and state at the timestep is 1D vector, dimensions of the state can be permuted without affecting the overall structure. Whereas in ConvLSTM input and state at a timestep is 3D for a single channel, thus capable of dealing with both spatial and temporal correlations using convolution and temporal operations. The structure of ConvLSTM cell is shown in Fig. 2.

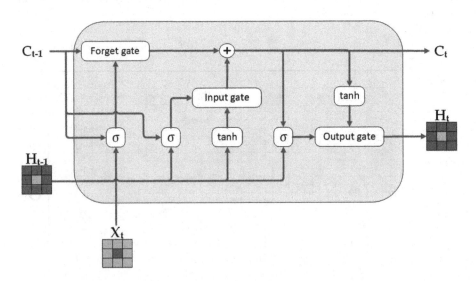

Fig. 2. ConvLSTM cell structure

Convolution is used for both input-to-state and state-to-state connection instead of vector multiplication in FC-LSTM. It uses hamadard product to keep the constant error carousel (CEC) property of the cell. The key equations of ConvLSTM are given in Eq. 1.

$$i_t = \sigma(W_{xi} * X_t + W_{hi} * H_{t-1} + W_{ci} \circ C_{t-1} + b_i)$$
$$f_t = \sigma(W_{xf} * X_t + W_{hf} * H_{t-1} + W_{cf} \circ C_{t-1} + b_f)$$
$$C_t = f_t \circ C_{t-1} + i_t \circ tanh(W_{xc} * X_t + W_{hc} * H_{t-1} + b_c) \quad (1)$$
$$o_t = \sigma(W_{xo} * X_t + W_{ho} * H(t-1) + W_{co} \circ C_t + b_o)$$
$$H_t = o_t \circ tanh(C_t)$$

Where $*$ is the convolutional operator; i, f and o are input gate, forget gate and output gate respectively. Similarly, C and H represents the cell states and hidden states respectively. Padding is also applied to keep the same dimensions for input and the states.

3.3   Input Features

Inspired from the study [17], we extract the following point level features given two consecutive GPS points p_i and p_{i+1}.

$$D_{p_i} = Vincenty(p_i, p_{i+1}) \quad (2)$$

$$\Delta t_{p_i} = t_{p_{i+1}} - t_{p_i} \quad (3)$$

$$V_{p_i} = \frac{D_{p_i}}{\Delta t} \quad (4)$$

$$A_{p_i} = \frac{V_{p_{i+1}} - V_{p_i}}{\Delta t} \quad (5)$$

$$J_{p_i} = \frac{A_{p_{i+1}} - A_{p_i}}{\Delta t} \quad (6)$$

where $D_{p_i}, V_{p_i}, A_{p_i}, J_{p_i}$ are the vincenty distance, velocity, acceleration and jerk of point p_i, computed in equations (2) to (6). Δt_{p_i} is the time difference between points p_i and p_{i+1}. t_{p_i} represents the timestamp of point p_i at time t. Bearing rate is calculated from the given set of equations.

$$y = sin[p_{i+1}(long) - p_i(long)] * cos[p_{i+1}(lat)],$$
$$x = cos[p_i(lat)] * sin[p_{i+1}(lat)] - sin[p_i(lat)] * cos[[p_{i+1}(lat)]*$$
$$cos[[p_{i+1}(long) - p_i(long)], \quad (7)$$
$$Bearing_{p_i} = tan^{-1}(y, x),$$
$$BR_{p_i} = |Bearing_{p_i} - Bearing_{pi+1}|$$

$p_i(lat), p_i(long)$ are the latitude and longitude of point p_i, BR_{pi} is the bearing rate of point p_i, which is the absolute difference of bearings between two consecutive points. In addition to these features, we also introduced the region index by dividing the whole region into two dimensional grid G having I columns and J rows of equal sizes. All latitude and longitude values are associated with their respective row and column number in the grid. The two dimensional grid values are converted to single dimension attribute using the equation (8) below.

$$g_i = (j - 1) \times I + j \tag{8}$$

where i and j are the specific row and column number of GPS point on a 2D grid G, I is the total number of columns in a 2D grid. In addition to these features, we also used external auxiliary features like day of the week, timeslice of the day, and weather features including temperature, visibility, wind speed and humidity.

3.4   Proposed Approach Architecture

The core concept of multi-task learning is to learn several tasks at the same time in order to achieve the mutual benefit [23], and it can be used to improve learning performance while using the shared representation. As shown in Fig. 3, the architecture is based on deep learning based shared encoder and task specific decoders. The shared encoder uses set of deepnet layers that processes the input trajectories for both the tasks, that are passed to task specific decoder to predict the respective task. The encoder's hidden layers share the same parameters among both tasks. In a typical deep neural network architecture, earlier layers in the network identifies simpler structures in the data, later layers identify more complex patterns [23]. Based on this property of neural network, we make earlier layers common for both tasks, that are responsible to learn simple patterns from data for both tasks, whereas the later layers in our architecture are task specific that learn more specialized patterns related to the specific task.

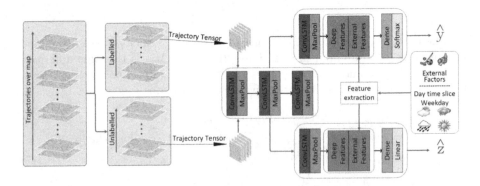

Fig. 3. Multi-task deep learning architecture of SSMDL

To train our model, we used ConvLSTM architecture [21] to model the input trajectories. Most of existing studies in trajectory mining either used CNN or LSTM architecture to model the trajectory. CNN models are better to cope with spatial correlations, where LSTM performs better on data having temporal relationships [24]. GPS trajectories data is spatiotemporal in nature. ConvLSTM is the variations of recurrent neural network based LSTM architecture, that is able to deal with both spatial and temporal correlations in the data.

The GPS trajectories dataset contains both labelled and unlabeleld GPS trajectories. Path inference is unsupervised task, we make use of unlabeled trajectories for this task. Whereas, mode inference is supervised learning task, therefore we can only use labelled data in our dataset. However, it takes advantage of parameters learnt by unsupervised task through unlabeled trajectories. The ConvLSTM layers in encoder module are shared among both the tasks and process the labelled and unlabeled trajectories. The layers in decoder module are task specific, that takes their respective processed trajectories from the encoder and predict their task specific output, using the set of layers shown in Fig. 3. It is important to mention that the movement patterns of trajectories are also influenced by some external factors; for example, the velocity of vehicles varies during peak and non-peak hours of the day and sometimes is equivalent to walk mode. Traffic conditions may change on weekends and weekdays, and also dependent of weather conditions. These external factors like week day, timeslice or outside temperature remains the same throughout all timesteps in a trajectory. Therefore, we do not input these points as the model input, instead we merge these external features with the deep features produced in the task decoder, that in result reduces overall model complexity. The combined set of features are then passed to fully connected layer using their respective activation function to produce task-specific output as shown in Fig. 3.

The model is optimized using two different loss functions for both the tasks; cross-entropy-loss-function is used for mode classification shown in Eq. 9, whereas mean-squared-error is used for path inference shown in Eq. 10. The output of mode classification task interprets the probability of membership in the indicated class, whereas for path inference problem, which is regression problem, mean-squared-error is considered as cross-entropy between distributions of model predictions and distribution of target variable under the framework of maximum likelihood estimation. The overall loss is the sum of losses for both of these tasks as shown in Eq. 11. Our objective is to minimize the joint loss occurred by these two tasks. Adam optimizer of the stochastic gradient descent is used to update the parameters and adjust the learning rate to minimize the losses. ReLU (Rectified Linear Unit) is used as activation function to introduce non-linearity in the model, except the last layer in which softmax activation function is used for classification task, and linear activation function is used for path prediction. It is important to mention that it is difficult to optimize the common loss parameters for both tasks at the same time, because the optimal parameters for one task may not be optimal for another. Therefore, it is non-trivial to optimize the parameters for both tasks at the same time. For this purpose, we use task specific layers in our model so that task specific parameters can be optimized in their respective decoder layers. This way parameters for both the tasks can be optimized at the same time, thus overall loss of the model can be minimized as well. In our models, we optimize two losses in parallel for both tasks, the overall loss is the sum of the losses for both tasks as shown in Eq. 11.

$$L_1(y, \hat{y}) = -\frac{1}{m} \sum_{i=1}^{m} y_i log \hat{y}_i \qquad (9)$$

$$L_2(z, \hat{z}) = \frac{1}{N} \sum_{i=1}^{N} (z_i - \hat{z}_i) \qquad (10)$$

$$L(\theta, \hat{\theta}) = L_1(y, \hat{y}) + L_2(z, \hat{z}) \qquad (11)$$

The parameters y and $\hat{y}$ of loss function L_1 are the ground truth and predicted output for task 1, similarly the parameters z and $\hat{z}$ of loss function L_2 are ground truth and predicted output for task 2. θ and $\hat{\theta}$ represents the combined ground truth and predicted output parameters of joint loss function L.

4   Experiments

In this section, we will start with the description of GPS dataset, and evaluation metrics used to analyze the performance of our approach SSMDL. Next we will discuss the configurations used for our model. Finally, we will explain the results obtained by our experiments. For all these experiments, we used python version 3.8, scikit learn version 0.21.0 and deep learning library keras v.2.2.5 using tensor flow at backend. For analysis of GPS data we used open source GIS software QGIS version 3.10.2-A.

4.1   Dataset Description and Evaluation Metric

We present our experiments using publically available Microsoft geolife GPS trajectory dataset [1, 22, 25]. The data is collected in 30 cities of China, and 70% of overall data is collected in capital of China, Beijing. The city has complex transportation network, and after the detailed analysis of data, we have found that the Beijing city has densed representation of data. The deep learning algorithm give reliable estimation, when these are trained on big dataset having densed representation [16]. Therefore, we only consider data from Beijing city in our study. We consider four different types of transportation modes, i.e. walk, bike, bus and driving, as there is enough data available for all these modes to train the model. In addition to labelled data, we also used unlabeled data that is used to train the same multi-task model and used for path prediction task. We prepared two datasets for two different tasks. For classification task we used labelled data, whereas for path prediction we use unlabeled data. The distribution of labelled

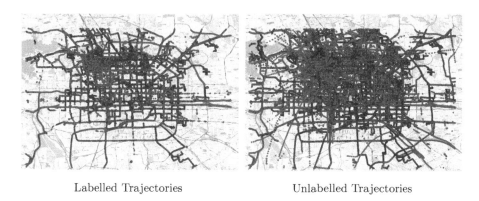

Labelled Trajectories   Unlabelled Trajectories

Fig. 4. Geolife GPS trajectories dataset for Beijing city

and unlabeled data in Beijing city is shown in Fig. 4(a) and Fig. 4(b) respectively. For weather features, we used global weather dataset MIDAS [26], which is recorded from year 1974 till present with an interval of 3 h.

For the transportation mode identification task, we use precision, recall, f-score and accuracy as the benchmark metric, Whereas we use the evaluation metric of Average Displacement Error (ADE) and Final Displacement Error (FDE) from trajnet challenge [27] to predict the Euclidean distance between ground truth and predicted trajectory.

4.2 Parameter Settings

Input to deep neural networks is of fixed length, for this purpose, a single user's trajectory is breaks into trips, when the time difference between two consecutive GPS points exceeds 20 min [28]. A trip is divided into fixed length segments, each of size 200 GPS points, which is median length of a GPS segment [17]. The geospatial region of the city is divided into two-dimensional grid; size of each grid is taken $5\,m^2$. In case of trajectory path prediction, if a predicted points lies on same grid cell as its ground truth, this will be considered as true. In our experiments, we used different settings for number of layers and filters to optimize the parameters. In the encoder module, we used 3 ConvLSTM layers having 32, 64 and 128 filters respectively, the decoder's used 1 ConvLSTM layer followed by 1 fully connected dense layer for each task. 1×3 filter is used for all ConvLSTM layers with maxpooling layers. We trained our model at 100 epochs, which is a standard in most of deep net studies. L2 regularization is set to 0.01 and 0.5 dropout rate is also used to avoid overfitting.

4.3 Performance Evaluation

In this section, we compare the performance of our multi-task approach and baseline models for both the tasks, using the evaluation metrics described earlier. Conventional machine learning methods like SVM and DT uses hand-crafted features, so for this purpose we used the feature set in study [22]. Table 1 summarizes the performances of all the models for classifying transportation modes. We can see from the table that our proposed model SSMDL performs better than the reference models. Conventional approaches have shallow models and do not have enough capabilities to handle the complexities in mobility patterns. Meanwhile, we can see that our multi-task approach achieved better performance than standalone tasks using multiple baseline deep net architectures. Table 1 shown the results of classifying transportation modes. The results are also presented visually in Fig. 5.

We also compare the performance of our second task trajectory path prediction for varying lengths ranging from 10 timesteps to 30 timesteps using ADE

Table 1. Comparison of Transportation mode classification

Method	Avg. Precision	Avg. Recall	Avg. FScore	Accuracy
SVM	67.42	64.67	66.72	65.35
DT	69.63	69.82	72.34	69.71
MLP	56.73	54.07	54.16	55.60
GRU	75.04	73.40	73.37	73.64
LSTM	74.94	73.57	73.42	74.67
CNN	76.58	76.01	76.15	75.75
ConvLSTM	78.14	77.81	77.89	77.65
SSMDL	**79.55**	**80.09**	**79.81**	**79.37**

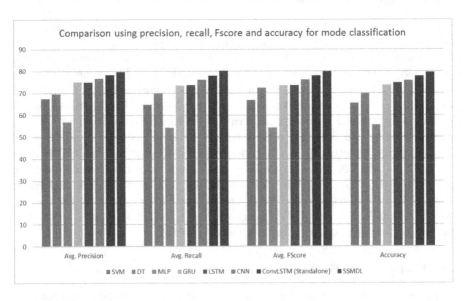

Fig. 5. Comparison of Task 1 using precision, recall, Fscore and accuracies

and FDE loss metric describes above. Table 2 shows the comparison of our model SSMDL with various baseline methods. It can be seen from Table 1 and Table 2 that the performance of multi-task learning is better as compared to the standalone baseline methods.

Table 2. Comparison of ADE and FDE predictions @10, @20, @30 timesteps

Method	ADE Predictions			FDE Predictions		
	@10 ts	@20 ts	@30 ts	@10 ts	@20 ts	@30 ts
Linear Regression	12.91	15.73	21.69	35.24	42.95	59.21
SVR	12.20	15.86	21.78	32.57	42.34	58.15
MLP	10.60	14.21	18.69	27.45	36.81	48.40
RNN	9.12	9.79	14.73	23.53	25.25	38.00
CNN	6.83	9.97	16.01	17.55	25.62	41.15
GRU	5.46	8.29	16.10	14.03	21.31	41.37
LSTM	5.28	6.82	11.73	13.31	17.19	29.56
ConvLSTM	4.77	5.43	8.36	11.88	13.53	20.83
SSMDL	**3.65**	**4.14**	**8.09**	**8.50**	**9.65**	**18.85**

5 Conclusion

A novel semi-supervised multi-task learning based method for transportation mode detection and future path prediction using GPS trajectories is proposed. Most of existing studies have solved these problems independently. Single task learning ignores the possible relationship between tasks, whereas multi-task learning takes into account the differences and the similarities between tasks. The existing approaches on mode classification only used the labelled data, while ignoring the unlabeled data. GPS data is spatiotemporal time series having both spatial and temporal relationships between consecutive GPS points. We make use of ConvLSTM model that is able to deal with both spatial and temporal structures in the spatiotemporal GPS data. We used shared encoder for both the tasks in hand to process the input trajectories, and used the task specific decoders to deal with their respective outputs. Experimental results show that our multi-task learning based method outperforms all other single-task learning methods over all the evaluation metrics for the tasks.

References

1. Zheng, Y., Zhang, L., Xie, X., Ma, W.Y.: Mining interesting locations and travel sequences from GPS trajectories. In: Proceedings of the 18th International Conference on World Wide Web 2009 Apr 20, pp. 791–800 (2009)

2. Wang, S., Cao, J., Yu, P.S.: Deep learning for spatio-temporal data mining: a survey. CoRR abs/1906.04928 (2019)

3. Shalev-Shwartz, S., Ben-Zrihem, N., Cohen, A., Shashua, A.: Long-term planning by short-term prediction. arXiv preprint arXiv:1602.01580 Feb 4 2016

4. Symeonidis, P., Ntempos, D., Manolopoulos, Y.: Location-based social networks. Recommender Systems for Location-based Social Networks. SECE, pp. 35–48. Springer, New York (2014). https://doi.org/10.1007/978-1-4939-0286-6_4

5. Wang, S., He, L., Stenneth, L., Yu, P.S., Li, Z.: Citywide traffic congestion estimation with social media. In: Proceedings of the 23rd SIGSPATIAL International Conference on Advances in Geographic Information Systems, 3 Nov 2015, pp. 1–10 (2015)

6. Lin, H., Lv, J., Yang, C., Deng, M., Wang, K., Wang, X.: GPS trajectory mining: a survey. J. Comput. Inf. Syst. **10**(16), 6947–56 (2014)

7. Wang, S., et al.: Computing urban traffic congestions by incorporating sparse GPS probe data and social media data. ACM Trans. Inf. Syst. (TOIS) **35**(4), 1–30 (2017)

8. Gonzalez, M.C., Hidalgo, C.A., Barabasi, A.L.: Understanding individual human mobility patterns. Nature **453**(7196), 779–82 (2008)

9. Mohajerin, N., Rohani, M.: Multi-step prediction of occupancy grid maps with recurrent neural networks. In: Proceedings of the IEEE Conference on Computer Vision and Pattern Recognition 2019, pp. 10600–10608

10. Xu, J., et al.: DTRP: a flexible deep framework for travel route planning. In: Bouguettaya, A., et al. (eds.) WISE 2017. LNCS, vol. 10569, pp. 359–375. Springer, Cham (2017). https://doi.org/10.1007/978-3-319-68783-4_25

11. Wang, S., He, L., Stenneth, L., Philip, S.Y., Li, Z., Huang, Z.: Estimating urban traffic congestions with multi-sourced data. In: 2016 17th IEEE International Conference on Mobile Data Management (MDM), 13 June 2016, vol. 1, pp. 82–91. IEEE (2016)

12. Ruder, S.: An overview of multi-task learning in deep neural networks. arXiv preprint arXiv:1706.05098 (2017)

13. Dong, D., Wu, H., He, W., Yu, D., Wang, H.: Multi-task learning for multiple language translation. In: Proceedings of the 53rd Annual Meeting of the Association for Computational Linguistics and the 7th International Joint Conference on Natural Language Processing (Volume 1: Long Papers), July 2015, pp. 1723–1732 (2015)

14. Zheng, Y., Chen, Y., Li, Q., Xie, X., Ma, W.Y.: Understanding transportation modes based on GPS data for web applications. ACM Trans. Web (TWEB) **4**(1), 1–36 (2010)

15. Wang, S., Zhang, X., Li, F., Philip, S.Y., Huang, Z.: Efficient traffic estimation with multi-sourced data by parallel coupled hidden Markov model. IEEE Trans. Intell. Transp. Syst. **20**(8), 3010–23 (2018)

16. LeCun, Y., Bengio, Y., Hinton, G.: Deep learning. Nature **521**(7553), 436–44 (2015)

17. Dabiri, S., Heaslip, K.: Inferring transportation modes from GPS trajectories using a convolutional neural network. Transp. Res. Part C: Emerg. Technol. **1**(86), 360–71 (2018)

18. Wang, H., Liu, G., Duan, J., Zhang, L.: Detecting transportation modes using deep neural network. IEICE Trans. Inf. Syst. **100**(5), 1132–5 (2017)

19. Pecher, P., Hunter, M., Fujimoto, R.: Data-driven vehicle trajectory prediction. In: Proceedings of the 2016 ACM SIGSIM Conference on Principles of Advanced Discrete Simulation, 15 May 2016, pp. 13–22 (2016)

20. Wang, F., Han, H., Shan, S., Chen, X.: Deep multi-task learning for joint prediction of heterogeneous face attributes. In: 2017 12th IEEE International Conference on Automatic Face & Gesture Recognition (FG 2017) 30 May 2017, pp. 173–179. IEEE (2017)

21. Xingjian, S.H., Chen, Z., Wang, H., Yeung, D.Y., Wong, W.K., Woo, W.C.: Convolutional LSTM network: a machine learning approach for precipitation nowcasting. In: Advances in Neural Information Processing Systems 2015, pp. 802–810 (2015)

22. Zheng, Y., Li, Q., Chen, Y., Xie, X., Ma, W.Y.: Understanding mobility based on GPS data. In: Proceedings of the 10th International Conference on Ubiquitous Computing, 21 September 2008, pp. 312–321

23. Ngiam, J., Khosla, A., Kim, M., Nam, J., Lee, H., Ng, A.Y.: Multimodal deep learning. In: Proceedings of the 28th International Conference on Machine Learning, ICML 2011, pp. 689–696 (2011)

24. Nawaz, A., Zhiqiu, H., Senzhang, W., Hussain, Y., Khan, I., Khan, Z.: Convolutional LSTM based transportation mode learning from raw GPS trajectories. IET Intell. Transp. Syst. **14**(6), 570–577 (2020). https://doi.org/10.1049/iet-its.2019.0017

25. Zheng, Y., Xie, X., Ma, W.Y.: GeoLife: a collaborative social networking service among user, location and trajectory. IEEE Data Eng. Bull. **33**(2), 32–9 (2010)

26. Office, Met: MIDAS: Global Weather Observation Data. NCAS British Atmospheric Data Centre (2006). https://catalogue.ceda.ac.uk/uuid/0ec59f09b3158829a059fe70b17de951

27. Sadeghian, A., Kosaraju, V., Gupta, A., Savarese, S., Alahi, A.: Trajnet: towards a benchmark for human trajectory prediction. arXiv preprint (2018)

28. Zheng, Y., Liu, L., Wang, L., Xie, X.: Learning transportation mode from raw GPS data for geographic applications on the web. In: Proceedings of the 17th International Conference on World Wide Web, 21 April 2008, pp. 247–256 (2008)

Database Systems

GHSH: Dynamic Hyperspace Hashing on GPU

Zhuo Ren$^{(\boxtimes)}$, Yu Gu, Chuanwen Li, FangFang Li, and Ge Yu

School of Computer Science and Engineering, Northeastern University,
Liaoning 110819, China
1801807@stu.neu.edu.cn

Abstract. Hyperspace hashing which is often applied to NoSQL databases builds indexes by mapping objects with multiple attributes to a multidimensional space. It can accelerate processing queries of some secondary attributes in addition to just primary keys. In recent years, the rich computing resources of GPU provide opportunities for implementing high-performance HyperSpace Hash. In this study, we construct a fully concurrent dynamic hyperspace hash table for GPU. By using atomic operations instead of locking, we make our approach highly parallel and lock-free. We propose a special concurrency control strategy that ensures wait-free read operations. Our data structure is designed considering GPU specific hardware characteristics. We also propose a warp-level pre-combinations data sharing strategy to obtain high parallel acceleration. Experiments on an Nvidia RTX2080Ti GPU suggest that GHSH performs about 20–100X faster than its counterpart on CPU. Specifically, GHSH performs updates with up to 396 M updates/s and processes search queries with up to 995 M queries/s. Compared to other GPU hashes that cannot conduct queries on non-key attributes, GHSH demonstrates comparable building and retrieval performance.

1 Introduction

NoSQL databases such as key-value stores are increasingly prevalent in big data applications for their high throughput and efficient lookup on primary keys. However, many applications also require queries on non-primary attributes. For instance, if a tweet has attributes such as tweet id, user id, and text, then it would be useful to be able to return all tweets of a user. But supporting secondary indexes in NoSQL databases is challenging because secondary indexing structures must be maintained during writes. To solve this issue, hyperspace hashing is proposed in HyperDex system [1] for distributed key-value stores that supports retrieving partially-specified secondary attribute searches in addition to primary keys. Compared to the method of stand-alone secondary indexes (e.g. table-based secondary index in Hbase [2]), hyperspace hashing can greatly save storage space, which is particularly important for in-memory databases. Compared to the method of embedded secondary indexes like KD-tree [3], hyperspace hashing can quickly locate the hash bucket where the data is located, without

© Springer Nature Switzerland AG 2020
X. Wang et al. (Eds.): APWeb-WAIM 2020, LNCS 12318, pp. 409–424, 2020.
https://doi.org/10.1007/978-3-030-60290-1_32

judging each layer in order. Hyperspace hashing represents each table as an independent multidimensional space, where the dimension axis directly corresponds to the attributes of the table. An object is mapped to a deterministic coordinate in space by hashing each attribute value of the object to a location on the corresponding axis. As shown in Fig. 1, one plane represents the plane perpendicular to the axis of the query for a single attribute through all points of last name = 'Smith', and the other plane through all points of first name = 'John'. Together, they represent a line formed by the intersection of two search criteria, meaning "John Smith". So one can find "John Smith" by looking up the number of John Smith in the hash bucket that intersects this line.

HyperDex is a distributed system which can relieve the performance issue of hyperspace hashing. But in a centralized enviorment, GPU-accelerated implementation is imperative. In this paper, we aim to crack the nut of improving the performance of hyperspace hashing on GPU for the first time. By using the traditional hyperspace hash structure, it is difficult to maximize memory throughput on GPU as the number of queried attributes can not be previously determined. Two concurrently executed queries may need to be performed in different hash buckets or need to query different attributes. It will lead to branch divergence, which will decrease the query performance tremendously when processed in the same GPU warp. Moreover, updating indexable attribute values will cause data relocation, which will further increase the complexity of concurrency. All these characteristics of HyperSpace hash mismatch the features of GPU, which impedes the performance of Hyperspace hash on GPU.

Based on this observation, we propose a new hyperspace hash data structure (GHSH) to make hyperspace hashing better adapted to GPU. In GHSH, we use structure-of-arrays instead of array-of-structures data layouts, in which keys, second attributes, and values are stored separately. The novel data structure is more suitable for GPU's thread execution model and memory hierarchy. Furthermore, for batch queries, we devise a warp-level pre-combination data sharing strategy that uses query classifications to reduce branch divergence. To further improve the performance of GHSH, we explore two other tailored optimizations, i.e., atomic operations instead of locking and a new concurrency control strategy.

The experiments performed on an Nvidia RTX2080Ti (Turing) GPU suggest that GHSH has advantages in both flexibility and performance. Compared with the CPU version hyperspace hashing, GHSH outperforms it by 20–100 times. Compared to other GPU hashes that cannot conduct queries on non-key attributes, GHSH demonstrates comparable building and retrieval performance and achieves full concurrency. Our contributions are summarized as follows:

- We focus on the GPU-based hyperspace hashing technique for the first time and propose a novel hyperspace hash data structure that is well adaptive with the GPU memory hierarchy with the superior locality.
- We propose a warp pre-combination data sharing strategy to minimizes divergences, and we also propose a method of using atomic operations instead of locking and a temporary repeated read strategy to improve the performance of GHSH to achieve lock-free full concurrency.

- Based on the above design, we further describe how GHSH handles common operations in a batch update scenario, including bulk-build, search by key, search by secondary attribute, modify, insert and delete.

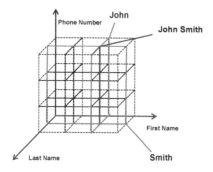

Fig. 1. Three-dimensional space hash

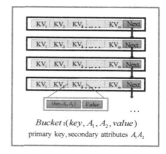

Fig. 2. Traditional data strucure

2 Background and Realted Work

General-Purpose GPUs. GPUs are massively parallel processors with thousands of active threads. The threads in a warp are executed in a single instruction multiple thread manner, and thus any branch statements that cause threads to run different instructions are serialized (branch divergence). A group of threads (multiple warps) is called a thread block and is scheduled to be run on different streaming processors (SMs) on the GPU. Maximizing achieved memory bandwidth requires accessing consecutive memory indices within a warp (coalesced access). NVIDIA GPUs support a set of warp-wide instructions (e.g., shuffles and ballots) so that all threads within a warp can communicate with each other.

Secondary Index. Several NoSQL databases have added support for secondary indexes. Mohiuddin et al. [4] perform a comparative study of secondary indexing techniques in NoSQL databases showing that the stand-alone indexes have higher maintenance cost in terms of time and space, and embedded indexes have slower query time. But hyperspace hashing devised in HyperDex [1] can better balance the maintenance cost and query efficiency as an embedded secondary index. Nuno Diegues et al. [5] explore a performance model and propose a method for adaptively selecting best solutions based on changing workloads. But it is also designed for the distributed implementation.

GPU Hash. With the popularity of parallel hardware, significant efforts have been made to improve the insert and query performance of hash. There are multiple GPU based static hash tables. Alcantara et al. [6] propose Cuckoo hashing which has good performance in batch construction and retrieval stages. It is adopted in the implementation of the CUDA data-parallel primitives library (CUDPP) [7]. However, for a large load factor requirements, the batch construction is likely to fail. Garcia et al. [8] propose a Robin hood-based hashing, focusing on higher load factors and take advantage of the spatial locality of graphics applications, but the performance of this method is impacted. Khorasani et al. [9] propose Stadium Hashing (Stash), by extending the Cuckoo hashing for large hash tables. The key focus of Stash is to design an out-of-core hash table for the case that the data cannot be completely accommodated into a single GPU memory. In the research of GPU's fully concurrent and dynamically updateable hash table, Misra and Chaudhuri [10] evaluate the acceleration of several lock-free data structures transplanted from CPU to GPU. However, the implementation is not completely dynamic. We can see from the experiments that node resource arrays are pre-allocated for future insertions (i.e., it must be known at compiling time), and cannot be dynamically allocated and released at runtime. One main objective of our proposed GHSH is to conquer this problem. Cederman et al. [11] perform similar experiments on various known lock-based and lock-free Queue implementations. They find that the parallel optimization of Queues on GPU is beneficial to performance improvement. Multi-core GPU technology can further improve data parallelism. Maksudul Alam et al. [12] propose a novel parallel algorithms for fast Multi-GPU-Based generation of massive networks. Inspired by [10], Moscovici et al. [13] propose a GPU-friendly skip list (GFSL) based on fine-grained locks, mainly considering the preferred coalesced memory accesses of the GPU. Recently, Ashkiani et al. [14] propose a fully concurrent dynamic lock-free chained hash table on GPU named Slab Hash.

3   GHSH Structure

In this study, we represent the element N as $(key, A_1, A_2, ..., A_p, value)$, where key is the primary key, $A_1, A_2, ..., A_p$ are indexable secondary attributes with the number of p, and $value$ is a location ID or value. We build a hyperspace hash to assist the query processing of secondary attributes. Here, p secondary attributes require a hyperspace hash of $p + 1$ dimensions.

3.1   Data Structure

We adopt a linked list to handle hash collisions. Due to the variability of p, it is difficult for the accesses to be as coalesced as in traditional methods (see Fig. 2). In this paper, we propose a new data structure – super node. As shown in Fig. 3, a super node contains a key node, p attribute nodes, and a value node. Each node in a super node stores corresponding portions of multiple data for data alignment. We set pointers for each queryable attribute node and key node so that we can quickly traverse between them to find querying targets. For a query task, we search in the hash buckets where the target may be stored based on our hash function. Each thread traverses the corresponding attribute chain in a hash bucket that it is responsible for, and finds the corresponding value from the corresponding value node after finding the target. To maximize memory throughput, the size of each node is set as 128 bytes, which is same as the size of a cache line on NVIDIA GPUs. Thus a warp of 32 threads can access the entire contents of a node at once. We assume that each element and pointer take a memory space with a size of $(p+2)x$ and y bytes. Therefore, the number of elements stored in each super node is $M = \lfloor \frac{128-y}{x} \rfloor$.

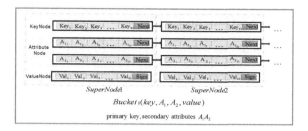

Fig. 3. GHSH data structure

We use a universal hash function on each dimension, $h(k; a, b) = ((ak + b) \bmod q) \bmod B$, where a, b are random arbitrary integers and q is a random prime number. As a result, elements are expected to be distributed uniformly among B^{p+1} buckets with an *average super node count* of $\beta = \lceil \frac{n}{MB^{p+1}} \rceil$ super nodes per bucket, where n is the total number of elements in GHSH. When searching a secondary attribute, we perform $\beta + F (0 \leq F \leq \beta)$ memory accesses, where F is the number of fetches required to read the values in a bucket. Processing queries of keys (recall that keys are unique) can achieve slightly better performance, but have similar asymptotic behavior. In that case, we perform $\lceil \frac{n}{B^{p+1}} / \lfloor \frac{128-y}{(p+2)x} \rfloor \rceil$ memory accesses with the traditional data structure. It can be deduced from Eq. 1 that when $n > B^{p+1} \cdot (p+1)$, our data structure can reduce the number of memory accesses. In our application scenarios, $n \gg B^{p+1} \cdot (p+1)$, so the proposed data structure is theoretically effective, in that it maximizes the throughput.

$$\zeta_{optimized}(x, y, p, B, n, F) = \lceil \frac{n/B^{p+1}}{\lfloor \frac{128-y}{x} \rfloor} \rceil + F < \lceil \frac{n/B^{p+1}}{\lfloor \frac{128-y}{(p+2)x} \rfloor} \rceil \qquad (1)$$

For open addressing hash tables, the memory utilization is equal to the load factor, i.e., the number of stored elements divided by the table size. In order to be able to compare our memory usage with open-addressing hash tables that do not use any pointers, we define the memory utilization to be the amount of memory actually used to store the data over the total amount of used memory (including pointers and unused empty slots), which is shown in Eq. 2. Assume k_i denotes the number of super nodes for bucket i. The maximum memory utilization can reach $\frac{Mx}{(Mx+y)}$. Intuitively, this case happens when all nodes in GHSH are full. According to Eq. 2, we can calculate the memory utilization of GHSH by the number of buckets, and set various memory utilization in the experiments in Sect. 5.

$$\eta(x,y,B,p) = \frac{(p+2)x}{\lfloor\frac{128-y}{x}\rfloor(p+2)x+(p+2)y} \cdot \frac{n}{\sum\limits_{i=1}^{B^{p+1}} k_i} \leq \frac{\lfloor\frac{128-y}{x}\rfloor(p+2)x}{\lfloor\frac{128-y}{x}\rfloor(p+2)x+(p+2)y}$$

(2)

3.2   Supported Operations in GHSH

Suppose our GHSH maintains a set of tuples represented by S. We allow the secondary attributes to be non-unique, but the primary key is unique. We support the following operations. More details will be introduced in Sect. 4.2.

- Insert($key, A_1, A_2, ...A_p, value$) : $S \leftarrow S \cup < key, A_1, A_2, ...A_p, value >$, which represents inserting a tuple into GHSH.
- Search($key, val(key)$): Returning $< key, A_1, A_2, ...A_p, value >\in S$, or $\emptyset$ if not found.
- Search($A_i, val(A_i)$): Returning all found instances of A_i in the data structure ($\{< *, A_i = val(A_i), * >\} \in S$), or $\emptyset$ if not found.($1 \leq i \leq p$)
- Modify($key, A_1, A_2, ...A_p, value$) : $S \leftarrow (S - \{< key, * >\}) \cup \{< key, A_1, A_2, ...A_p, value >\}$, which represents inserting a new tuple and deleting the old one.
- Delete(key) : $S \leftarrow S - \{< key, A_1, A_2, ...A_p, value >\}$, which represents deleting the tuple $< key, A_1, A_2, ...A_p, value >$.

4   Implementation Details

4.1   Optimizations

Warp Pre-combination Data Sharing Strategy. Assume that the batch size of queries is b and there are $p + 1$ query types. We denote queries as $Q = \{key : val(key), A_1 : val(A1), ..., A_p : val(A_p)\}$, where $val(key)$ denotes the value of the key and $val(A_i)$ denotes the value of the secondary attribute A_i. GPU organizes threads in units of warps. Different query paths may incur warp divergence (see Fig. 4). A traditional solution is the warp-cooperative work sharing (WCWS) strategy [14], which forms a work queue of arbitrary requested operations from different threads within a warp. All threads within a warp cooperate to process these operations one at a time. However, a query operation of a hyperspace hash maps multiple query paths, which results in a sharp increase in the number of query tasks. The serialization of threads in a warp in WCWS severely hinders operation efficiency in hyperspace hashing. Considering the characteristics of our new hyperspace hash data structure, in this paper, we propose a new approach where threads in a warp read corresponding data of nodes to shared memory. All threads in a warp can compare in parallel whether the current node has its target. We call this strategy warp pre-combination data sharing (WPDS). WPDS is particularly suitable in following scenarios: 1) threads are assigned to independent and different tasks, which can avoid divergence within a warp; 2) each task requires an arbitrarily placed but vectorized memory access (accessing consecutive memory units); 3) it is possible to process each task in parallel within a warp using warp-wide communication (warp friendly). It is worth mentioning that WPDS is not suitable for situations where the branch divergence in a warp cannot be avoided through previous operations.

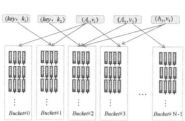

Fig. 4. Query divergence

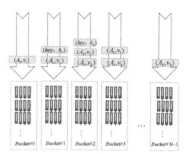

Fig. 5. Classify by BucketID

In our data structure context, query classifications are combined to reduce branch divergence. Take a secondary attribute query as an example. A query $(A_i, val(A_i))$ may exist in B^p buckets. Since the results are not unique, we need to traverse all nodes in these hash buckets. For query tasks of number b, classification is performed in two steps: *classify by BucketID* (CBB) and *pre-combining by query type* (PBQ). Each bucket i maintains a task queue TQ_i. In the CBB step, each task is parsed into p subtasks and added to the corresponding TQ_i (see Fig. 5). This can be performed in parallel on GPU. The variety of query types in a warp makes memory divergence (see Fig. 6(a)), which would greatly impede the GPU performance. To eliminate the divergence, in the PBQ step, threads in each TQ_i are grouped in a warp according to A_i (see Fig. 6(b)).

The total amount of time required for searching a batch of b elements in GHSH (n elements are stored in GHSH) is $T^b_{Search}(n, p) = T^b_{CBB} + T^b_{PBQ} + T^b_{Tra}$, where T^b_{CBB} is the time spent to classify a size b batch by *bucketID*, T^b_{PBQ} is the time spent to pre-combinate a size b batch by query type, and T^b_{Tra} is the time spent to traversal in buckets. The time complexity is $O(\frac{n/B^{p+1}}{\lfloor (128-y)/x \rfloor})$. Recall that the time complexity is $O(n/B^{p+1})$ without using WPDS strategy.

Global Memory with CUDA Atomic Operations. The GPU memory structure is divided into three levels: global memory that can be accessed by all threads in the device, smaller but faster shared memory per thread block, and local registers for each thread in the thread block. The shared memory is small and partitioned, so threads in different blocks cannot access the shared memory of other blocks. Due to the limited number of SMs, thread blocks need to be queued for SM. Therefore, there is no way to synchronize all threads globally except when the kernel function ends. In order to achieve full concurrency between warps, GHSH uses global memory to ensure the sharing of all data states by each thread. GHSH controls concurrency optimistically. Common lock-free algorithms are generally based on atomic operations. For multiple atomic operations in GHSH, we set lock tag on data items, and use atomic operations to change the lock tag to make the locking of data items atomic.

(a) Queries   (b) Pre-combination queries

Fig. 6. An example of memory access pattern for queries

Temporary Repeated Read Strategy. The existing method employs reader-writer locks to allow concurrent read to hash table, which may cause conflicts to increase latency. In order to make GHSH free of structural locks, we design a "temporary repeated read" strategy. We first put new data into a new hash bucket, and then delete the data in the old bucket. This ensures all existing data will be read. Although it will cause a short term duplication, it guarantees the valid values stored in the table can be read. If the query result for a key returns two values, either can be used. The "temporary repeated read" strategy guarantees the no-wait feature of reading operations, which can greatly improve the efficiency of reading operations in a concurrent situation.

4.2 Operation Details

We use WPDS for bulk query and deletion concurrency. But we still use WCWS [14] for full concurrency of all operations of different types. Because branch divergence here is caused not only by query path divergence but also by different instruction types. We design the node size as 128 B, so that when a warp accesses a node each thread has exactly 1/32 of the node's content. We use the term "lane" to denote the portion of a node that is read by the corresponding warp's thread, and we denote *lane 31* as *ADDRESS_LANE*. We assume that the key and the secondary attributes each take 4 bytes, and the value takes 4 bytes. For a node, we also need a 4-byte space to store a pointer. The remaining 124 bytes can be used to store a total number of 31 of keys or secondary attributes. Obviously, the spatial complexity of these operations is $O(n)$.

A. Insertion

Bulk-Build. The batch building operation constructs a hyperspace hash directly from the batch input of tuples. We first sort tuples by *bucketID* to ensure that data from a warp is most likely to be inserted into the same hash bucket. The first 31 threads in a warp are responsible for writing the corresponding part of the data, and the 32nd thread is responsible for putting the node into the linked list of the corresponding bucket. We assign a lock tag for each bucket. Only when a thread modifies the lock tag through atomic operations can it chain its data block into the bucket by header interpolation. The different tasks of the last thread will cause divisions, which is inevitable because the link operation must be executed after applying for memory. The first 31 threads can be parallelized, which is faster than the 32 thread tasks serialized in Slab hash.

Incremental Insertion. As shown in Algorithm 1, any thread that has an inserting operation to perform will set *is_active* to true. Following WCWS introduced earlier, all threads read the corresponding part of the target super node, and search for the empty point in the key node of the super node. If found, the thread uses an atomicCAS operation to insert its key, secondary attributes and value address into the corresponding node of the super node (Line 6). If the insertion succeeds, the thread marks its operation as resolved. If fails, it means that some other warps have been inserted into that blank spot. Then the whole process should be restarted. If no empty point is found, all threads will obtain the address of the next super node from the ADDRESS_LANE. If the address is not empty, we should read a new super node and repeat the insertion process. Otherwise, a new super node should be allocated. Then, the source thread uses `atomicCAS` to update the pointer of the previous super node. If `atomicCAS` succeeds, the entire insertion process is repeated using the newly allocated super node. If not, it means that another warp has allocated and inserted a new super node. Then the super node allocated by this warp should be reassigned and the process should be restarted with the new super node.

B. Search and Deletion

Search by Key. Algorithm 2 shows the pseudocode of searching in GHSH. We use WPDS to reduce query divergence with high concurrency. During the query process, we first parse the query tasks and distribute the results to the queue to be queried for the corresponding hash bucket (Line 1). Query tasks with the same query attributes are aggregated (Line 3), and organized into warps, and query paths are shared to avoid warp divergence. Each thread in a warp determines

---

Algorithm 1: Incremental Insertion

 Input: $HashTable, data\_list$
 Output: Hash Table after insertion
 1 $src\_bulk \leftarrow$ hash$(key, A_1, ..., A_p)$;
 2 $src\_lane \leftarrow next\_task(workqueue)$;
 3 $dest\_lane \leftarrow$ ffs(ballot $(ReadData == EMPTY))$;
 4 **if** $dest\_lane$ *is valid* **then**
 5 $\quad$ old=atomicCAS(GetAdd$(bulk\_table(src\_bulk))$,EMPTY,$<$ $key, A_1, ..., A_p, value >)$;
 6 $\quad$ **if** $src\_lane == laneID$ **then**
 7 $\quad\quad$ **if** $old==EMPTY$ **then**
 8 $\quad\quad\quad$ $is\_active \leftarrow false$;

 9 **else**
 10 $\quad$ next_ptr=shfl$(read\_data, ADDRESS\_LANE)$;
 11 $\quad$ **if** $next\_ptr==NULL$ **then**
 12 $\quad\quad$ new_SuperNode_ptr==allocate();
 13 $\quad\quad$ **if** $laneID==Address\_LANE$ **then**
 14 $\quad\quad\quad$ Temp=atomicCAS(GetAdd$(ADDRESS\_LANE)$,EMPTY_POSTION,
 15 $\quad\quad\quad$ new_SuperNode_ptr);
 16 $\quad\quad\quad$ **if** $Temp!=EMPTY\_POSTION$ **then**
 17 $\quad\quad\quad\quad$ deallocate$(new\_SuperNode\_ptr)$;

 18 $\quad\quad$ next=next_ptr;

---

the part of the data it should read according to the *laneID* it carries. Although the reading positions are different, each thread needs to make a conditional judgment on the data in the node, and thus it uses shuffle instruction. The address read by the first thread is distributed to other threads (Lines 5–6). When GHSH performs a search operation, it reads the corresponding position of the linked list node. When checking whether there is data equal to the target key, the ballots and ffs instructions are used to make a parallel judgment on the data held by all threads in the warp (Line 7). If the target is found, we read the corresponding value into *myValue* and mark the corresponding task as resolved (Lines 8–12). Otherwise, each thread reads the pointer marked by ADDRESS_LANE and finds the next key node until the pointer is empty (Lines 14–19).

Search by Secondary Attribute. The secondary attribute query is similar to the key query, except that since the second attribute is not unique, a query may correspond to multiple values. Therefore, we need to traversal all the super nodes stored in a bucket. Without accessing other attribute nodes, we can just query a linked list of the query attribute.

Deletion. Deletion is similar to search. If valid (matching found), we use $DELETEDKEY$ to overwrite the corresponding element. If not found, the

---

Algorithm 2: Search by Key

Input: $HashTable, query\_list$
Output: value list

1 $work\_queue \leftarrow hash(querylist)$;
2 $src\_lane \leftarrow next\_task(workqueue)$;
3 G=CoalescedThreads();
4 hash=**hash**($srcKey$);
5 *position=HashTable[hash];
6 *pos= **shfl**(*$position,0$);
7 found_lane=**ffs**(**ballot**($read\_data==srcKey$));
8 **if** $found\_lane$ is valid **then**
9 $\quad$ found_value=the corresponding part of the corresponding value node;
10 $\quad$ **if** $lane\_ID == src\_lane$ **then**
11 $\quad\quad$ myValue=**FoundValue**($lane\_ID$);
12 $\quad\quad$ $is\_active \leftarrow false$;
13 **else**
14 $\quad$ next_ptr=**shfl**($read\_data, ADDRESS\_LANE$);
15 $\quad$ **if** $next\_ptr == NULL$ **then**
16 $\quad\quad$ **if** $lane\_ID==src\_lane$ **then**
17 $\quad\quad\quad$ myValue=NotFound;
18 $\quad\quad\quad$ is_active=false;
19 $\quad\quad$ *pos=next_ptr;
20 **return** myValue;

---

next pointer is updated. If the end of the list is reached, the target does not exist and the operation terminates successfully. Otherwise, we load the key node of the next super node and restart the process. In particular, if the data being modified is found, there may be two values returned, and both are deleted.

C. Modification. In GHSH, the modification is divided into two types. One is to change the non-queryable attribute value, and the other is to change the secondary attribute value. The former is relatively simple, whose operation process is similar to a query, except that when the key value is found, the corresponding value is modified by using an atomic operation. The latter is more complicated. According to the updated value, the modified data may be or not be in the same hash bucket. If it involves a bucket change operation, we use the temporary repeated read strategy introduced earlier. Specifically, the data in the original bucket needs to be deleted, and the new value needs to be inserted into a new hash bucket. These two operations should be performed in an atomic fashion. Otherwise, data errors will occur. So we design a lock tag on the data item, namely $swap\_lock$, and modify it through atomic operations to ensure that data is not modified by other tasks while it is being modified. For a modification $(key, A_1, A_2, ...A_p, value)$, we first search for key, and if not found, it returns invalid task. If found without $swap\_lock$, we mark $swap\_lock$ before inserting the new value with *swap_lock*. Afterward, we delete the found data and erase the lock tag. Otherwise, we need to wait until *key*'s lock tag is erased.

5   Evaluation

We use an Nvidia RTX2080Ti (Turing) GPU for all experiments on an 8-core server (Intel Xeon CPU Silver 4110 @ 2.1 GHz, 64G host memory). It has 68 SMs and an 11GB GDDR6 memory with a peak bandwidth of 616 GB/s. All results are harmonic averages of rate or throughput. Our implementation is compiled by CUDA 10 on Ubuntu 16.04 using O3 optimization option. Because the existing GPU-based index studies 4-byte keys and values for benchmarking and large batches for scalability tests [3,14], we follow the convention and employ similar simulation patterns and parameter settings. Our experiment additionally sets two secondary attributes.

Figure 7 shows the building rate and query rate of several hash methods for various memory utilization. $n = 2^{22}$ elements are stored in the table. At about 60% memory utilization there is a sudden drop in performance for both bulk building and searching operations. Our experimental scenarios below using uniform distributions as input data set with 60% memory utilization based on this result and existing work [14]. In the concurrent benchmark, we set the initial memory utilization to 50% because of the insertions in concurrent workload.

5.1   Baseline: CPU Hyperspace Hash

We compare the speed of GHSH with its counterpart on CPU. Since there is no existing open-sourced concurrent CPU hyperspace hashing in the centralized envioroment, we implemented one based on openMP [15]. Experimental results show that the building performs best with 8 threads and the searching for secondary attributes performs best with 12 threads on CPU. Thus, we use these settings as benchmarks to compare with GHSH. We choose an initial number of buckets so that its final memory utilization is 60%. The means of all operation

Table 1. Rates (M Operation/s) for different bath-sized put and get on GPU and CPU

Bath size	GPU (put)	CPU (put)	GPU (get)	CPU (get)
2^{10}	6.81	1.02	9.72	0.30
2^{11}	14	1.23	17	0.27
2^{12}	26	1.23	40	0.23
2^{13}	47	1.17	69	0.25
2^{14}	86	1.05	146	0.27
2^{15}	151	0.9	211	0.28
Mean	20.24	1.09	28.17	0.26

rates for a given batch size of b is reported in Table 1. The mean of bulk building rates on GPU is 20.24M elements/s, which is 20x of CPU. The mean of searching rates on GPU is 28.17M elements/s, which is 100x of CPU.

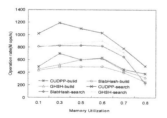

Fig. 7. Impact of memory utilization

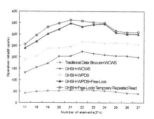

Fig. 8. Modification rate

5.2 Impact of Different Design Choices

We evaluated the basic query operation with WCWS, CBB, and WPDS (CBB+PBQ). The results are shown in Fig. 11. We find that search efficiency can be greatly enhanced with CBB, but CBB is more time consuming as a pre-processing. Only with PBQ can a better optimization effect be achieved, which accelerates 1.25x on average. It is worth mentioning that branch divergence in a warp cannot be avoided, if directly perform PBQ without CBB and hence threads in a warp cannot be parallelized. Figure 8 shows the effectiveness of our novel data structure and three techniques. Assume that all modifications need bucket changing. We find that GHSH data structure can achieve performance improvement by 3.92X. Based on our data structure, after replacing the locking with global memory and atomic operation, the bucket changing rate of GHSH increases significantly, by 27% on average. This is because atomic operations greatly reduce the locking cost. Adding the temporary repeat read strategy to the lock-free version, the two techniques can improve the modification rate by 34%. However, with the increase in the number of elements, the acceleration effect is not obvious due to the limitation of the SM's number.

5.3 Baseline: Operations of GPU Hash for Keys

We compared GHSH with CUDPP (the most representative static hash) and Slab Hash (the most advanced dynamic hash). Figure 9 shows the building rate (M elements/second) versus the total number of elements (n) in table. We can see that when the table size is very small, CUDPP's building performance is particularly high, since most atomic operations can be done at cache level. Static data structures often sustain considerably better bulk-building and querying rates when compared to structures that additionally support incremental mutable operations. However, the cost of these additional operations in GHSH is modest.

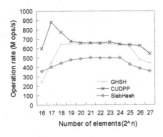

Fig. 9. Build rate

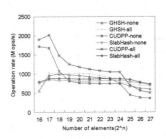

Fig. 10. Search rate

Slab hash and GHSH will make GPU resources reach $2^{20} \leq n \leq 2^{24}$. The build rate of GHSH is up to 1.32x that as those on Slab hash, since the basic nodes of GHSH store almost twice the data of Slab hash. Besides, data allocation in GHSH can be performed in parallel, which improves data parallelism.

For key search queries, we generate two sets of random queries: 1) all queries exist in GHSH; 2) none of the queries exist. The two scenarios are important as they represent the best and worst case. The harmonic averages are 838 M/s and 732 M/s for search-all and search-null (see Fig. 10). The speedups of CUDPP over the GHSH are 1.27x, 1.16x, and 0.86x for bulk building, search-all, and search-none, respectively. The speedups of Slab hash over the GHSH are 0.84x, 1.01x, and 1.02x for bulk building, search-all, and search-none, respectively. GHSH's key query speed is slightly lower than Slab hash, which is the cost of supporting non-key queries. It is necessary for secondary attribute queries to traverse the complete linked list, which is equivalent to the worst case of key queries.

5.4   Concurrency Performance of GHSH

A significant feature of GHSH is that it can perform true concurrent query and update operations without dividing different operations into different calculation stages. To evaluate the concurrency characteristics, we design the following benchmarks. We perform operations in one of the following four categories: a) inserting a new element, b) deleting a previously inserted element, c) searching for an existing element by secondary attribute, d) modifying a element to a new bucket. We define an operation distribution $\Gamma = (a, b, c, d)$, such that every item is nonnegative and $a + b + c + d = 1$. Given any Γ, we can construct a random workload where, for instance, a denotes the fraction of new insertions compared to all other operations. Operations are run in parallel and randomly assigned to each thread (one operation per thread) such that all four operations may occur within a single warp. We consider three scenarios as shown in Table 2. In order to evaluate the value range of keys and secondary attributes, four different integer ranges, $[0, 100]$, $[1]$, $[0, 10000]$, and $[0, 100000]$, are designed for each operation combination. The total number of operations is fixed at 100,000. The operation data are randomly generated from the range being evaluated.

Table 2. three scenarios of Concurrent benchmarks

Name	Workload	Operation Distribution
A	100%updates,0%searches	$\Gamma_0 = (0.4, 0.4, 0, 0.2)$
B	50%updates,50%searches	$\Gamma_1 = (0.2, 0.2, 0.5, 0.1)$
C	30%updates,70%searches	$\Gamma_2 = (0.1, 0.1, 0.7, 0.1)$

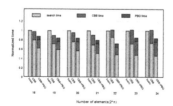

Fig. 11. Impact of WPDS

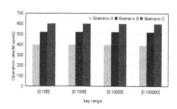

Fig. 12. Concurrency performance of GHSH

Figure 12 shows performance of GHSH for three scenarios and different key ranges. Since updates are computationally more expensive than searches, given a fixed memory utilization, performance becomes better with fewer updates $(\Gamma_0 < \Gamma_1 < \Gamma_2)$. From the experimental results, we can see that the key range does not have much impact on performance. Comparing against bulk benchmark in Fig. 12, it is clear that GHSH performs slightly worse in our concurrent benchmark (e.g., Γ_0 in Fig. 9 and 12). There are two main reasons: (1) We assign multiple operations per thread and hide potential memory-related latencies, as it is assumed that in static situations all operations are available, and (2) we run four different procedures (one for each operation type) in concurrent benchmarks, but the bulk benchmark runs just one.

6 Conclusion

Through a comprehensive analysis of the characteristics of hyperspace hashing and the features of GPU, we identify some gaps between hyperspace hashing and GPU, such as the gap in memory access requirement, memory divergence, and query divergence. Based on the analysis, we propose a novel hyperspace hash data structure, where the query attributes are stored separately. Hence, GHSH can make full use of the GPU memory hierarchy to reduce the number of high-latency memory accesses via cache access on GPU. We also propose three optimizations in GHSH to alleviate the different divergences on GPU to improve resource utilization: warp pre-combination data sharing strategy, a method of using atomic operations instead of locking and temporary repeated read strategy. Experimental results suggest that our dynamic hyperspace hash table for GPU can gain advantages in both flexibility and performance.

Acknowledgements. This work is supported by the National Key R&D Program of China (2018YFB1003400), the National Natural Science Foundation of China (U1811261, 61872070), the Fundamental Research Funds for the Central Universities (N180716010) and Liao Ning Revitalization Talents Program (XLYC1807158).

References

1. Escriva, R., Wong, B., Sirer, E.G.: Hyperdex: a distributed, searchable key-value store. In: PrACM SIGCOMM, pp. 25–36. ACM (2012)
2. D'silva, J.V., Ruiz-Carrillo, R., Yu, C.: Secondary indexing techniques for key-value stores: two rings to rule them all. In: DOLAP (2017)
3. Holanda, P., Nerone, M., de Almeida, E.C.: Cracking KD-tree: the first multidimensional adaptive indexing (position paper). In: EDDY (2018)
4. Qader, M.A., Cheng, S.: A comparative study of secondary indexing techniques in LSM-based NOSQL database. In: SIGMOD, pp. 551–566 (2018)
5. Diegues, N., Orazov, M., Paiva, J., Rodrigues, L., Romano, P.: Optimizing hyperspace hashing via analytical modelling and adaptation. ACM SIGAPP Appl. Comput. Rev. **14**(2), 23–35 (2014)
6. Alcantara, D.A., et al.: Real-time parallel hashing on the GPU. ACM Trans. Graph. (TOG) **28**(5), 154 (2009)
7. Harris, M., Owens, J., Sengupta, S., Zhang, Y., Davidson, A.: Cuda data parallel primitives library. In: CUDPP (2007)
8. García, I., Lefebvre, S., Hornus, S., Lasram, A.: Coherent parallel hashing. In: TOG, vol. 30, p. 161. ACM (2011)
9. Khorasani, F., Belviranli, M.E., Gupta, R.: Stadium hashing: scalable and flexible hashing on GPUs. In: PACT, pp. 63–74. IEEE (2015)
10. Misra, P., Chaudhuri, M.: Performance evaluation of concurrent lock-free data structures on GPUs. In: ICPADS, pp. 53–60. IEEE (2012)
11. Cederman, D., Chatterjee, B., Tsigas, P.: Understanding the performance of concurrent data structures on graphics processors. In: Kaklamanis, C., Papatheodorou, T., Spirakis, P.G. (eds.) Euro-Par 2012. LNCS, vol. 7484, pp. 883–894. Springer, Heidelberg (2012). https://doi.org/10.1007/978-3-642-32820-6_87
12. Alam, M., Perumalla, K.S., Sanders, P.: Novel parallel algorithms for fast multi-GPU-based generation of massive scale-free networks. Data Sci. Eng. **4**(1), 61–75 (2019)
13. Moscovici, N., Cohen, N., Petrank, E.: Poster: a GPU-friendly Skiplist algorithm. PPOPP **52**(8), 449–450 (2017)
14. Ashkiani, S., Farach-Colton, M., Owens, J.D.: A dynamic hash table for the GPU. In: IPDPS, pp. 419–429. IEEE (2018)
15. Chandra, R., Dagum, L., Kohr, D., Menon, R., Maydan, D., McDonald, J.: Parallel Programming in OpenMP. Morgan Kaufmann, San Mateo (2001)

A Unified Framework for Processing Exact and Approximate Top-k Set Similarity Join

Cihai Sun[1,2], Hongya Wang[1(✉)], Yingyuan Xiao[3], and Zhenyu Liu[4]

[1] School of Computer Science and Technology, Donghua University, Shanghai, China
sun8421@gmail.com, hywang@dhu.edu.cn
[2] School of Statistics and Information, Shanghai University of International Business and Economics, Shanghai, China
[3] School of CSE, Tianjin University of Technology, Tianjin, China
[4] Shanghai Key Laboratory of Computer Software Testing and Evaluation, Shanghai, China

Abstract. An interesting observation was made that only a few (far shorter than the prefix) low-frequency tokens are enough to help finding similarity pairs for processing top-k set joins. This phenomenon is ubiquitous in all real datasets we have experimented with, covering domains as varied as text, social network, protein sequence data. Possible explanations are discussed. Based on this observation, we propose an algorithm called AEtop-k for processing both approximate and exact top-k similarity join in a unified framework. Comprehensive experiments demonstrate that, compared with the state-of-the-art algorithm on a large collection of real-life datasets, the approximate version of our algorithm can achieve up to 10000× speedup with little sacrifice on accuracy and the exact version runs up to 5× faster than the existing algorithm.

Keywords: Shoft-prefix phenomenon · Top-k · Unified framework

1 Introduction

Set similarity join is a fundamental problem. Given two collections of sets, each of which contains a set of elements, set similarity join finds all similar set pairs from the collections. It have a wide range of applications, including data cleaning [8], data integration [5], data mining [4], personalized recommendation [6], community mining [14], and near duplicate web page detection [7].

Generally speaking, similarity joins are often solved using the threshold-driven paradigm, which consists of three steps: (1) select a similarity function (like Jaccard, Cosine or Dice). (2) choose a threshold (like 0.8). (3) design an algorithm to find all object pairs whose similarities are no less than the threshold.

The work reported in this paper is partially supported by NSFC under grant number 61370205.

X. Wang et al. (Eds.): APWeb-WAIM 2020, LNCS 12318, pp. 425–440, 2020.
https://doi.org/10.1007/978-3-030-60290-1_33

Step (1) and (2) are usually left to the users as some hyperparameters to choose. However, selecting an appropriate threshold is often a non-trivial issue. It is extremely difficult for humans to figure out the impact of different thresholds on result quality. Choosing a good threshold depends on not only the specified similarity function but also the underlying data distributions. For example, a reasonable threshold of a STACK-OV dataset is 0.95, which differs a lot from the threshold 0.6 on the WIKI dataset to get the same number of results. Instead, the top-k similarity join solves these problems by only yielding out k pairs with highest similarity. Many studies [9,19] have mentioned its benefits and a lot of related researches have been done.

Motivation. A few efficient exact top-k similarity set join algorithms have been proposed [9,12,19] for different scenarios such as single machine, distributed computing and streaming processing. However, little work is known to handle the approximate version of this problem although approximate algorithm is widely used to process other types of top-k queries [3,16]. To this end, it is highly desirable to design a unified framework to process top-k similarity set join and produce approximate and exact answers in an interactive fashion. In the data exploration stage, one may expect to find approximate top-k similarity pairs in a short amount of time. If the user is satisfied with the result quality (the increase of the kth highest similarity pair is very small), then it is done. If not, the user may decide to continue the computation (no waste of the previous computation) and get the exact results.

Contributions. To achieve this goal, we propose a novel algorithm AEtop-k based on an interesting observation and the contributions of this paper are listed as follows:

(1) Short-prefix phenomenon. By increasing the length of the prefix one by one, both in threshold-driven and top-k similarity join methods, we observed the short-prefix phenomenon that most results are already yielded using very short prefix. We tested a large collection of data sets and found that this phenomenon exists in all these real-life data sets.

(2) Analysis of the phenomenon. We try to explore the rationale behind this phenomenon by testing three synthetic datasets (ZIPF, D-RANKING, and S-WORLD). According to the results, it does not occur in ZIPF and D-RANKING datasets while appears for S-WORLD dataset. We also give plausible reasons why this phenomenon exists for real-life data sets.

(3) Processing approximate and exact similarity join in a unified framework. Based on this phenomenon, we propose a unified framework called AEtop-k for processing both approximate and excat top-k similarity join. AEtop-k pauses when no new similarity pairs are generated while processing a column of tokens and report the results as approximate answers. If the user chooses to continue, AEtop-k is able to output the exact results by examining remaining prefixes.

(4) Extensive experimental comparison. We have tested a large collection of datasets, covering domains as varied as text, social network and protein sequence data. Experimental results show that even the approximate version obtains very high accuracy and achieves up to 10000× speedup compared with the

state-of-the-art algorithm. For the exact version, AEtop-k runs up to $5\times$ faster than the existing algorithm.

2   Preliminaries

2.1   Problem Definition

Given two sets of records, X and Y, a similarity function $sim()$, and a similarity threshold t, the similarity join problem is to find all pairs of records from each set, $\langle x, y \rangle$, such that their similarities are no less than the given threshold t, i.e, $\{\langle x, y \rangle | sim(x, y) \geq t, x \in X, y \in Y\}$ [4]. A Top-k similarity join returns k pairs of records from each set, and their similarities are the highest among all possible pairs [19]. For the ease of exposition, we will focus on self-join case in this paper.

A similarity function, $sim(x, y)$, returns a similarity value in $[0, 1]$ for these two records. This means they are just the same when $sim(x, y) = 1$, and totally different when $sim(x, y) = 0$. There are several commonly used similarity functions $sim()$ for sets and vectors:

- Overlap similarity: $sim_O(x, y) = |x \cap y|$
- Cosine similarity: $sim_C(x, y) = \frac{x \cdot y}{\|x\| \cdot \|y\|} = \frac{|x \cap y|}{\sqrt{|x|} \cdot \sqrt{|y|}}$
- Jaccard similarity: $sim_J(x, y) = \frac{|x \cap y|}{|x \cup y|} = \frac{|x \cap y|}{|x| + |y| - |x \cap y|}$
- Dice similarity: $sim_D(x, y) = \frac{2 \cdot |x \cap y|}{|x| + |y|} = \frac{2 \cdot |x \cap y|}{|x| + |y|}$

For example, consider two text records R_x ="**The deep says it is not in me**" and R_y = "**The sea says it is not with me**", which can be tokenized as some tokens: $x = \{A, B, C, D, E, F, G, H\}$ and $y = \{A, I, C, D, E, F, J, H\}$ with the following word-to-token mapping table:

Word	the	deep	says	it	is	not	in	me	sea	with
Token	A	B	C	D	E	F	G	H	I	J
Frequency	2	1	2	2	2	2	1	2	1	1

Then, every record's token can be sorted by the global frequency ascending order into the following ordered sequences: $x = [B, G, A, C, D, E, F, H]$ and $y = [I, J, A, C, D, E, F, H]$. The Overlap similarity of x and y is $|x \cap y| = |\{A, C, D, E, F, H\}| = 6$, the Jaccard similarity is $\frac{|x \cap y|}{|x \cup y|} = \frac{6}{10} = 0.6$, and the cosine similarity is $\frac{x \cdot y}{\|x\| \cdot \|y\|} = \frac{6}{\sqrt{8} \cdot \sqrt{8}} = 0.75$. If the threshold $t = 0.5$ and similarity function is Jaccard, $\langle x, y \rangle$ will be selected since $0.6 \geq 0.5$.

2.2 Prefix Filtering

Prefix filtering is a pruning strategy that ignores those pairs who have no common token from their prefix. For example, in Jaccard similarity, we should find all pairs $\langle x, y \rangle$ that $sim_J(x, y) \geq t$ should match the equation $\frac{|x \cap y|}{|x|+|y|-|x \cap y|} \geq t \Rightarrow$

$$|x \cap y| \geq \frac{t}{1+t} \cdot (|x| + |y|) \tag{1}$$

Suppose $|x| \leq |y|$, then the maximum of $|x \cap y|$ is $|x|$, and the maximum of $sim_J(x, y)$ is $\frac{|x|}{|x|+|y|-|x|} = \frac{|x|}{|y|}$. If $sim_J(x, y) \geq t$ then $\frac{|x|}{|y|}$ must $\geq t$, therefore

$$|x| \geq t \cdot |y| \tag{2}$$

and by applying Eqs. (1) and (2), we have $|x \cap y| \geq \frac{t}{1+t} \cdot (|x| + |y|) \geq \frac{t}{1+t} \cdot (t \cdot |y| + |y|) = t \cdot |y|$, therefore

$$|x \cap y| \geq \lceil t \cdot |y| \rceil \tag{3}$$

Then, we define a prefix length $p_y = |y| - \lceil t \cdot |y| \rceil + 1$ for each record, and let x be any record that its length is shorter or equal than y. This x still has its own prefix $p_x = |x| - \lceil t \cdot |x| \rceil + 1$, and store every token in p_x into a $\boldsymbol{I}$ (inverted index [1]).

By using Eq. (3), we know that if $sim_J(x, y) \geq t$, their overlap $|x \cap y| \geq \lceil t \cdot |y| \rceil$. Suppose all the overlap locate at the end of the record (high-frequency tokens). The rest part of y plus one word: $|y| - \lceil t \cdot |y| \rceil + 1$ (blue part in Fig. 1), must have at least one common word with the rest part of x plus one word: $|x| - \lceil t \cdot |y| \rceil + 1$ (green part in Fig. 1). And since we have already store the p_x in $\boldsymbol{I}$, we can increase the green part to red part, to prune the pairs if x and y have no common tokens in their own prefix. (Because $|x| - \lceil t \cdot |x| \rceil + 1 \geq |x| - \lceil t \cdot |y| \rceil + 1$, if the red part has no common tokens, the green part will also have no common tokens). So, we can sort all the records in the dataset by their length from short to long, and check every record's prefix to find out whether there is a common token with the previous records, and calculate the real similarity from them. This pruning process is the main strategy in all-pairs [4], ppjoin+[20], adapt-join [17] etc.

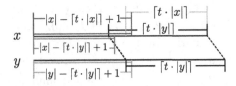

Fig. 1. Prefix filtering

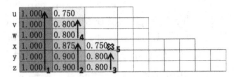

Fig. 2. The working principle of Top-k Join

2.3   Top-k Join

Prefix filtering algorithm can get all pairs of records $\langle x, y \rangle$, such that $sim_J(x, y) \geq t$. But in some cases, users only concern about top-k similarity results. Top-k join [19] algorithm aim to generate the answers from highest similarity pair to k^{th} highest similarity pair.

According to [19], the maximal value of $sim_J(x, y)$ is the follow equation if a token w at $y[i]$ (where i is from 1 to p_y) find a common token in x's prefix.

$$M_{sim} = \frac{|y| - i + 1}{|y|} \qquad (4)$$

Now if we have a priority-queue which stores the temporary top-k similarity pairs, and sim_k is the smallest similarity in this queue. Then, we can traverse all tokens from high to low order by their M_{sim}. And check these token in I (inverted index) and push the pair into the priority-queue if $sim_J(x, y) > sim_k$. Finally we can stop the whole process as soon as the current $M_{sim} \leq sim_k$.

Figure 2 shows the main process of the top-k join algorithm. Suppose there are 6 records (R_i from u to z, length from 4 to 10) in dataset. Set an empty priority-queue with a capacity of k to store the maximum k similarity pairs and an empty I to store the R_i for each token e_i. Then calculate each token's M_{sim} value (eg, 1.000, 0.900, 0.750) based on its position (Eq. 4) in each record, and visit them from high to low. If the token was previously stored in I and the M_{sim} value of the token (eg, 0.8) is greater than the kth similarity value (returns 0 if it does not exist) in the priority-queue (eg, 0.77), then calculated the real similarity of these two records and push the pair to the priority-queue if needed and insert the token to I. If the M_{sim} value of the token (eg, 0.75) is less or equal than the kth similarity value in the priority-queue (eg, 0.77), it means that the maximum value of the two records similarity is less than sim_k, the algorithm can stop here.

Top-k algorithm has to check $\langle x, y \rangle$ whether has been duplicate visited, because one pair may be calculated multiple times in difference prefix length. More optimizations and details can be found in [19] for further study.

3   Short-Prefix Phenomenon

3.1   Observation

The threshold-driven (prefix filtering) and top-k algorithm both traverse the whole prefix of every record to generate exact results. **But what will happen when executing the program with a fixed length which is shorter than the whole prefix?** We randomly selected a threshold t (like 0.84), and fixed the length of each record's prefix to a constant p_f (shorter than the original prefix). The p_f will be increased one by one, we calculate the number of results ($sim_J(x, y) \geq t$) by each p_f, and write the increments of them.

For example in Table 1's DBLP data set, we increase the p_f from 1 to 9. When $p_f = 1$, there are 7669 pairs whose similarities are greater or equal than

Table 1. Observation when prefix length increasing, $t = 0.84$

Prefix length	DBLP	WIKI3	SEQ.5gram	JD-VIEW	ENRON.5gram	BIBLE
1	7669	23	64314	90	1095	105
2	1182	39	42103	340	988	15
3	54	1	13691	34	1309	1
4	0	0	4789	8	1162	0
5	0	0	2214	2	2321	3
6	0	0	1062	0	24167	0
7	0	0	626	0	2019	0
8	0	0	355	0	1418	0
9	0	0	143	0	914	0
...	...	...	...	...	...	...
Max prefix	42	6572	1127	359	28827	26
Last non-zero	3	3	19	5	419	5
First zero	4	4	15	6	104	4

0.84. And 1182 new pairs are found when p_f is increased from 1 to 2, which means there are totally 8851 pairs when $p_f = 2$.

An interesting phenomenon is that after p_f is greater or equal to 4, the increments are all 0. This means no more pairs can be found satisfying the threshold no matter how the prefix increasing, while the longest record's prefix length in DBLP is 42. In WIKI3 data set, the increments become 0 when prefix length is from 4 to 6572, and in SEQ.5gram data set, the increments become 0 when prefix is from 20 to 1127.

In a similar way, we can also fix the range of positions in top-k algorithm to p_f, and count the number of 'push' operation increment on priority-queue when p_f is increased by 1 (count the number of better pairs whose similarity are greater than the current sim_k). Figure 3 shows the phenomenon of this idea, it's clearly that those real data sets are very quickly down to 0 within 20 prefix length.

3.2 Exploration and Discussion

What is the interesting point in this phenomenon? Suppose we use the most extreme data set WIKI3 as an example. The average length of WIKI3 is about 2644. When $k = 5000$, the similarity of the kth pair is about 0.583 (these data are shown in Table 2), meanwhile its average prefix length is about 1102. Surprisingly, all the results were found within 10 prefixes, using only 1% of the original prefix. This is a bit like taking out a random ball from 100 balls, and each time you take out the No.1 ball. What is even stranger is that because all tokens are sorted by their frequency ascend, the No. 1 ball will have the lowest probability of being taken out of all the balls.

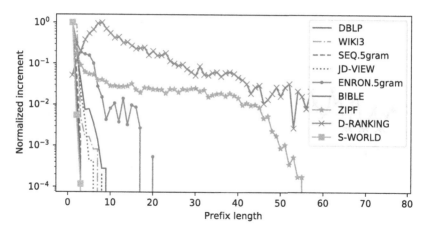

Fig. 3. A comparison between real data sets and simulated data sets, $k = 1000$ (ZIPF, D-RANKING and S-WORLD are simulated data sets) by top-k algorithm.

The phenomenon tells us if two records are similar, their very low-frequency tokens must have one overlap. A basic question is whether this phenomenon is general in all text data sets? We generate 3 simulated data sets to test this question:

(1) ZIPF simulated dataset. The zipfian distribution is widely considered to be the distribution of natural language [2]. We use numpy.random.zipf package of python to generate a 100000 records data set (ZIPF in Fig. 3) with 83793 tokens in total and each record has 100 tokens.

(2) D-RANKING simulated dataset. Another more complex generation model is dynamic ranking (D-RANKING in Fig. 3)[13] which uses the zipfian distribution first but reorder the ranking by their counts if the token already appear. This will cause the tokens that have been already used to appear more times in the same record.

(3) S-WORLD simulated dataset. Furthermore, we use the NSW (navigable small world [10]) to generate a simulated social network, and use this network to generate a text model (S-WORLD in Fig. 3). The algorithm can be summarized in two steps: 1) Insert random points to a space one by one. 2) For every new inserted point, connect it to k-nearest points as its friends in the current space. After n points have been inserted to the space, many early points will be the key persons who have many friends (edges), and the whole network will become a navigable small world [10] graph which can find nearest neighbor with logarithmic scalability of the greedy search algorithm. Then we transform every point's friends to a token by their point ID, and make the whole network to a data set: one point's friends represent one record.

Figure 3 depicts the number of top-1000 similar pairs identified as the prefix length increases. One can see that a large proportion of top-1000 results are found within short prefix length for real-life datasets. For synthetic datasets, ZIPF and D-RANKING do not exhibit such a property while S-WORLD fits much better than them. Then we explore these results and try to give possible reasons:

Reason 1. Many high-similar records have their special purpose, they are born to be similar. For example, in the BIBLE data set, high-similar pairs mostly occurs in repeated or parallel sentences. This is a rhetorical technique to express emphasis. After we ignore these pairs which have 100% similarity, the high similairty pairs mostly appeared in the Old Testament: like Isaiah ↔ 2 Kings, 2 Samuel ↔ 1 Chronicles etc. Actually, one is another's collection part, such as Kings and Chronicles are the collections of those Prophets. For they are meant to express the same meaning, only some minor words (high-frequency words) can be changed. Such as:

- 2Kings 20:1 ...And the prophet Isaiah the son of Amoz came **to** him...
- Isaiah 38:1 ...And Isaiah the prophet the son of Amoz came **unto** him...

Also in WIKI datasets, if some pages represent the similar meaning, they will redirect to the same page:

- Sep 11, 2001 terrorist attack *redirect* 9/11 conspiracy theories
- Sep 11, 2001 terrorist attack **and rumors** *redirect* 9/11 conspiracy theories

Reason 2. One of the original purposes of checking high-similar records is for data cleaning, and the high similarity often represent some mistakes. For example, in DBLP dataset, many high-similar pairs are caused by wrong submission:

- David Harel, Some Thoughts on Statecharts, 13 Years Later **(Abstract)**.
- David Harel, Some Thoughts on Statecharts, 13 Years Later.

The first submission includes the wrong token: Abstract. Submission errors or misspellings are often associated with only a small number of tokens. So they may always have some low frequency tokens that are common.

Reason 3. Let us think about the problem from another angle. A low-frequency token usually express a special meaning and will generally bring a specific cluster of correlative tokens. Let's take **Harry** and **Kedavra** for an example: 1) **Harry** is a high-frequency token which usually represents a name like '**Harry** Potter'. 2) **Kedavra** is a low-frequency token which only used in the phrase: 'Avada **Kedavra**', a spell name in '**Harry** Potter'. When the **Harry** appears, the topic of the record may talk about million **Harry**s, such as Prince Harry, Harry & David, Harry's Shaving etc. And every field carve up the probability so that it's difficult to forecast the content of the record by this high-frequency token. But when the **Kedavra** appears, the paragraph must talk about some magic in '**Harry** Potter', so there is a high possibility that a cluster of tokens like 'killing', 'curse', 'wizard', 'magic' will also appear. This cause the high similarity of two records if they have the same low-frequency tokens.

In the S-WORLD social network dataset, a low-frequency token means a lonely point who has few friends. If two points both have this lonely friend as their k-nearest friends, the distance between these two points may very close (far less than the average distance of all points in experiments actually) and have many common friends near by. But in ZIPF and D-RANKING data sets, low-frequency tokens have no relationship with other tokens, they are isolated and only generated by the probability. This is the reason why they have no this phenomenon.

4   Algorithm

By using the phenomenon shown above, we established a unified framework called AEtop-k to speeding up the process, and handle both approximate and excat top-k similarity join. When in the original top-k process, we sort all the M_{sim} descend from data sets and calculate them while $M_{sim} > sim_k$. In Fig. 2, every block represents a token and every M_{sim} inside the block was calculated by the Eq. 4. Since Top-k will calculate those M_{sim} from high to low, it's a bit like a back-to-back running from bottom left to top right and stop the whole world if 0.750 appears when sim_k supposed to 0.751 right now.

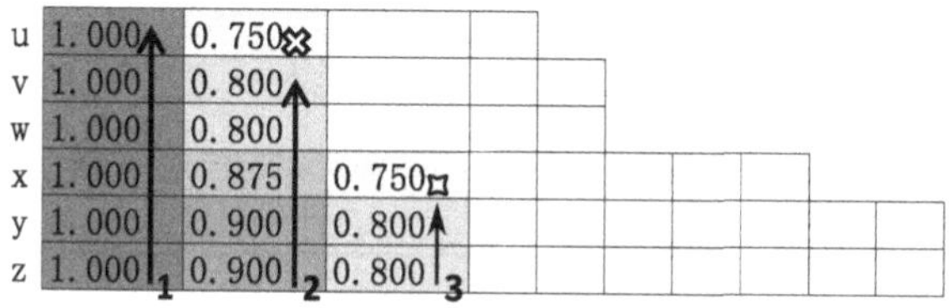

Fig. 4. The working principle of AEtop-k

But since we fix the prefix (column) and increase it one by one, there is no need to sort the whole M_{sim} any more. In Fig. 4, M_{sim} in the same column must be ascending when record's ID ascending because the records were sorted by their length ascending. We can just calculate the block from bottom to top for the descending M_{sim}, and still stop the current column loop when $M_{sim} < sim_k$. Then continue the new column from bottom to top as the Fig. 4 shows.

In algorithm 1, we make i to be the column index from left to right, and make h to be the row index from bottom to top. A variable Δ to record the priority-queue changes on every column. The algorithm will stop when the first bottom $M_{sim} < sim_k$, or just inquire user whether to stop when first 0 change happens.

In fact, there are more stop strategys to stop the algorithm. For example, we can compare the sim_k of this column to the sim_k of last column, if the difference between them is less than a given ε, we can stop the precess either. But since the distribution is mostly obey the power-law in Fig. 3, we can assume that there is a low possibility to find more results after the first 0 appears, so for the simple purpose, we just stop the stop the precess when first 0 appears.

Algorithm 1: AEtop-k join algorithm

Input: R is a collection of records; n is the number of R; k is a user-specified parameter; m is the total count of tokens from R

Output: Top-k similar pairs

1   $result \leftarrow$ an empty priority-queue with k capacity and sort by M_{sim} descending;
2   $list \leftarrow \emptyset,\ visited \leftarrow \emptyset,\ I_i \leftarrow \emptyset (1 \leq i \leq m),\ y_{max} \leftarrow R[n]$;
3   **for** $i = 1$ **to** $|y_{max}|$ **do**
4      $\Delta \leftarrow 0$;
5   **for** $h = n$ **to** 1 **do**
6         $y \leftarrow R[h]$;
7   **break if** $i > |y|$;
8         $M_{sim} \leftarrow \frac{|y|-i+1}{|y|}$;
9         $sim_k \leftarrow result[k].sim$ **or** (0 **if** $result.length < k$);
10   **break if** $M_{sim} < sim_k$;
11        $w \leftarrow y[i]$;
12        $M \leftarrow$ empty map;
13   **for** $j = 1$ **to** $|I_w|$ **do**
14           $x \leftarrow I_w[j]$;
15   **if** $|x| \geq t \cdot |y|$ **and** $|x| \leq \frac{|y|}{t}$ **and** $\langle x, y \rangle \notin visited$ **then**
16             $M[x] \leftarrow M[x] + 1$;
17        $I_w \leftarrow I_w \cup \{y\}$;
18   **foreach** x such that $M[x] > 0$ **do**
19   **if** $sim_J(x, y) \geq sim_k$ **then**
20             $result.push(\langle x, y \rangle)$;
21             $visited \leftarrow visited \cup \{\langle x, y \rangle\}$;
22             $\Delta \leftarrow \Delta + 1$;
23   **break if** $\Delta == 0$ **and** user doesn't want to coninue;
24 **return** $result$

---

5   Performance Evaluation

5.1   Data Sets

We tested a lot of data sets to check whether this phenomenon is ubiquitous and the performance of the AEtop-k. Due to space reasons, we list only part of the data sets below. Table 2 shows the statistics of datasets, like record size, max length, average length, and token size. Furthermore, when $k = 5000$, Table 2 also shows the max prefix length, first zero prefix length, and kth similarity. In general these data sets are divided into 4 categories:

   (1) Normal text Datasets: DBLP*[1], ENRON*[2], WIKI*[3], BIBLE[4], PARADISE[5].

---

[1] http://dblp.uni-trier.de/db/, a snapshot of the bibliography records from the DBLP web site, contains about 0.9M records (author names + title).

[2] http://www.cs.cmu.edu/enron, about 0.25M ENRON emails from about 150 users.

[3] http://ftp.acc.umu.se/mirror/wikimedia.org/dumps/, picked from enwiki-*-pages-articles*.xml (title + content).

[4] BIBLE is a KJV version bible, and take one verse to one record.

[5] PARADISE is from Paradise Lost by the poet John Milton (1608–1674).

(2) Social network Datasets: TWITTER[6], STACK-OV[7].
(3) Simulated Datasets: ZIPF[8], D-RANKING[9], S-WORLD*[10].
(4) Miscellaneous Datasets: SEQ*[11], JD-VIEW[12].

Table 2. Data statistics

Datasets	Records	MaxLen	AvgLen	Tokens	MaxPref	First0	sim_k
Normal text Datasets							
DBLP	854k	258	12.792	359k	33	4	0.875
DBLP.3gram	854k	256	10.795	6664k	81	11	0.684
DBLP.5gram	847k	254	8.872	6839k	105	11	0.588
ENRON	244k	180171	158.498	2078k	3964	12	0.978
ENRON.3gram	242k	180169	157.723	19416k	8108	31	0.955
ENRON.5gram	237k	180167	159.286	23074k	9189	45	0.949
WIKI2	10k	39685	2877.244	2964k	24486	9	0.383
WIKI3	20k	41069	2643.974	6555k	17126	10	0.583
WIKI12	204k	125486	747.119	9017k	7404	11	0.941
BIBLE	25k	158	14.921	17k	98	16	0.385
PARADISE	11k	9	4.311	9k	7	7	0.286
Social network Datasets							
TWITTER	95k	250	2.651	81k	126	3	0.5
STACK-OV	66369k	393	15.16	10039k	13	5	0.968
Simulated Datasets							
ZIPF	100k	100	99.859	84k	76	58	0.25
D-RANKING	10k	7070	168.283	441k	6668	146	0.057
S-WORLD	100k	2412	599.097	100k	140	4	0.942
S-WORLD2	9987k	101	10.006	10000k	17	3	0.833
Miscellaneous Datasets							
SEQ.3gram	462k	11738	125.242	61k			
SEQ.5gram	462k	7043	75.344	2814k	148	5	0.979
JD-VIEW	42k	2238	50.927	239k	746	12	0.667

---

[6] http://snap.stanford.edu/data, Social circles from Twitter. It take every node as a record and every edge connected by this node as its tokens.
[7] https://archive.org/download/stackexchange, Stack Overflow collections.
[8] ZIPF is generated by python's numpy.random.zipf package.
[9] D-RANKING refers to [13], and described in Sect. 3.2.
[10] S-WORLD* refer to [10], and described in Sect. 3.2.
[11] http://www.uniprot.org/downloads, protein sequence datas from the UniProt.
[12] A customer's product views from jd.com's data-mining contest.

5.2 Environment and Preprocessing

All algorithms were implemented in C++. To make fair comparisons, all algorithms use Google's dense_hash_map class for accumulating overlap values for candidates, as suggested in [4]. And all experiments were carried out on a workstation with Intel(R) Xeon(R) CPU E5-2667 3.20 GHz, and 256 GB memory. The operating System is Ubuntu 16.04 LTS. All algorithms were implemented in C++ and compiled using GCC 6.3.0 with -O3 flag.

In the preprocessing of data sets, letters are converted into lowercase, and remove the stop words and duplicate records. Then we count every token's frequency and sort them ascending which is mentioned in Sect. 2.1. The running time does not include loading, tokenizing of datasets and output of the results.

5.3 Comparison

We use the top-k similarity set join algorithm proposed in [19] as the baseline method because it is the state-of-the-art algorithm in the single machine setting. Other top-k similarity set join algorithms are targeted for different application scenario such as Map-reduce platform and streaming environment, and thus are not comparable with our algorithm.

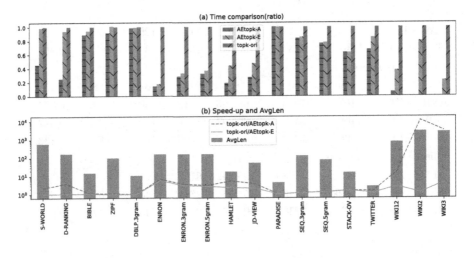

Fig. 5. Time comparison, $k = 5000$

Figure 5(a) shows the running time comparison of each algorithm when $k = 5000$. In this figure, *(1) AEtopk-A* is an approximate version of AEtop-k, stop the process when first 0 appears (zero push operation on priority-queue). *(2) AEtopk-E* is an exact version of AEtop-k, stop the process until current $M_{sim} < sim_k$. *(3) topk-ori* is the state-of-the-art top-k similarity join algorithm [19].

Figure 5(b) shows the relationship between the average length of the data set and the speedup of the algorithm.   *(1) topk-ori/AEtopk-A* represents the speedup achieved by the approximate version of AEtop-k compared to topk-ori.

(2) topk-ori/AEtopk-E represents the speedup achieved by the exact version of AEtop-k compared to topk-ori. We can observe the longer the average length is, the better AEtopk performs in general. When processing the WIKI2 dataset and $k = 5000$, the AEtopk-A can accelerate upto 11592.52× comparing to the topk-ori algorithm. And when processing the ENRON dataset the AEtopk-E can accelerate upto 5.75× comparing to the topk-ori algorithm.

Figure 6 shows the comparisons from a series of datasets, with k increasing from 500 to 5000. Each dataset is associated with two graphs, the upper graph shows the running time of the 3 algorithms, the lower graph shows the sim_k of the results from 3 algorithms and the difference between the sim_k of AEtopk-A and AEtopk-E. As you can see, instead of using the value of recall, we compare the value of sim_k directly because the answer is not unique, there will be multiple pairs with the same similarity. Here are some important remarks that are worth mentioning according to Fig. 5 and 6:

(1) The 'first 0 stop' strategy is good enough. In our whole experiments, only 13.3% of results' sim_k minus the true sim_k is greater than 0, and only 8.6% of results' sim_k minus the true sim_k is greater than 0.001.

(2) Long record data sets own a significant speed-up. For example, WIKI2 and WIKI3 data sets can get more than 3000×–10000× speed-up when using the approximate AEtop-k algorithm and most of them have no loss of precision. But some short record data sets like DBLP have only a small amount of improvement.

(3) The exact AEtop-k can also beat the top-k join in most data sets. In some data sets (like ENRON*, WIKI*, SEQ, JD-VIEW etc.), the exact AEtop-k still runs faster than the original top-k join. This may be caused by two reasons: 1) there is no need to sort the M_{sim} in top-k algorithm. 2) it is a faster way to reduce the sim_k by vertical traversal of the prefix as shown in Fig. 4.

(4) Miscellaneous data sets also have this phenomenon. For example, the SEQ* data set represents the protein sequence, the JD-VIEW data set represents the user's product browsing record, and the TWITTER data set represents the social network's two-way relationship. They all have nothing to do with the text, but still have this phenomenon.

(5) D-RANKING data sets is special. Although the phenomenon of the D-RANKING data set is not obvious in Fig. 3, the experimental results show that the AEtop-k can still find the results quickly. It can be seen from Table 2 that First0 is much less than MaxPrefix, but the similarities between those records are very low. This is due to D-RANKING's mechanism: when a token appears once, it will appear more, so there will be some very high-frequency tokens. For those same tokens, the preprocessing will separate them to different tokens. For example a token ID e_{34} appearing 5 times in one record, then assign them the number $e_{34}^1\ e_{34}^2, ..., e_{34}^5$, so the e_{34}^5 becomes a low-frequency word. Once e_{34}^5 becomes a overlap word, the two records will have at least 5 overlaps. Other data sets basically do not have this phenomenon.

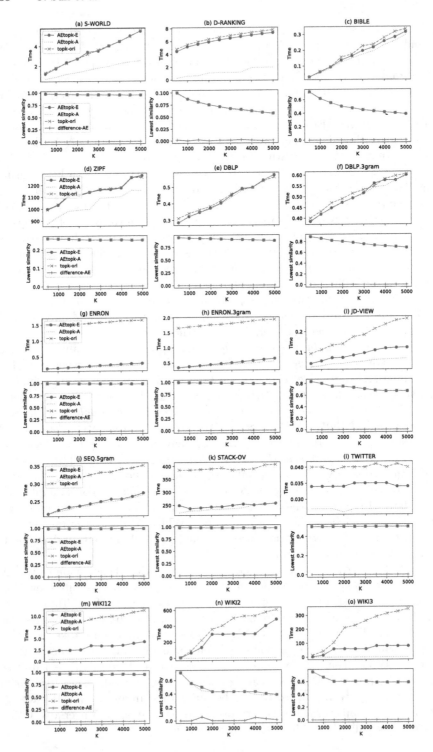

Fig. 6. Comparison between AEtop-k and original top-k

(6) The Cosine function has a similar result to the Jaccard funciton. We also tested the cosine function from datasets and found that it is not much different from the jaccard function. Due to space limitations, figures will not be displayed in this paper.

6 Related Works

Set similarity joins have received much attention in recent years. Willi Mann et al. [11] compared 7 threshold-driven set similarity join algorithms such as ALL, PPJ, PPJ+, MPJ, PEL, ADP, GRP. Rafael David Quirino et al. Xubo Wang et al. [18] leveraging set relations to speed up similarity search algorithms. However, all of them belong to the threshold-driven join algorithms. In the top-k similarity join topic, there are mostly application papers, such as [12,15]. These papers show the algorithm has a broad applications in practice.

7 Conclusions

In this paper, we propose a unified framework similarity join algorithm by using the short-prefix phenomenon. The algorithm provide efficient solution for both approximate and exact top-k join. We show a lot experiments from data sets in different fields, including (1) normal text data sets (2) social network data sets (3) simulated data sets and (4) miscellaneous data sets, and most of them have a significant improvement when using the approximate method, and some of them have a small progress when using the exact method. Especially when the data set is very long, like WIKI* and ENRON* data sets, the unified framework will reduce a lot of work and have a huge advantage in approximate similarity join.

References

1. Inverted index. Wikipedia. https://en.wikipedia.org/wiki/Inverted_index
2. Zipf's law. Wikipedia. https://en.wikipedia.org/wiki/Zipf%27s_law
3. Angiulli, F., Pizzuti, C.: An approximate algorithm for top-k closest pairs join query in large high dimensional data. Data Knowl. Eng. **53**(3), 263–281 (2005)
4. Bayardo, R.J., Ma, Y., Srikant, R.: Scaling up all pairs similarity search. In: Proceedings of the 16th International Conference on World Wide Web, pp. 131–140 (2007)
5. Cohen, W.W.: Integration of heterogeneous databases without common domains using queries based on textual similarity. In: Proceedings of the 1998 ACM SIGMOD International Conference on Management of Data, pp. 201–212 (1998)
6. Das, A.S., Datar, M., Garg, A., Rajaram, S.: Google news personalization: scalable online collaborative filtering. In: Proceedings of the 16th International Conference on World Wide Web, pp. 271–280 (2007)
7. Henzinger, M.: Finding near-duplicate web pages: a large-scale evaluation of algorithms. In: Proceedings of the 29th Annual International ACM SIGIR conference on Research and Development in Information Retrieval, pp. 284–291 (2006)

8. Hernández, M.A., Stolfo, S.J.: Real-world data is dirty: data cleansing and the merge/purge problem. Data Mining Knowl. Disc. **2**(1), 9–37 (1998)
9. Kim, Y., Shim, K.: Parallel top-k similarity join algorithms using mapreduce. In: 2012 IEEE 28th International Conference on Data Engineering, pp. 510–521 (2012)
10. Malkov, Y., Ponomarenko, A., Logvinov, A., Krylov, V.: Approximate nearest neighbor algorithm based on navigable small world graphs. Inf. Syst. **45**, 61–68 (2014)
11. Mann, W., Augsten, N., Bouros, P.: An empirical evaluation of set similarity join techniques. Proc. VLDB Endowment **9**(9), 636–647 (2016)
12. Mann, W., Augsten, N., Jensen, C.S.: Swoop: Top-k similarity joins over set streams. arXiv preprint arXiv:1711.02476 (2017)
13. Serrano, M.Á., Flammini, A., Menczer, F.: Modeling statistical properties of written text. PLoS ONE **4**(4), e5372 (2009)
14. Spertus, E., Sahami, M., Buyukkokten, O.: Evaluating similarity measures: a large-scale study in the orkut social network. In: Proceedings of the Eleventh ACM SIGKDD International Conference on Knowledge Discovery in Data Mining, pp. 678–684 (2005)
15. SriUsha, I., Choudary, K.R., Sasikala, T., et al.: Data mining techniques used in the recommendation of e-commerce services. ICECA **2018**, 379–382 (2018)
16. Theobald, M., Weikum, G., Schenkel, R.: Top-k query evaluation with probabilistic guarantees. In: Proceedings of the Thirtieth International Conference on Very Large Data Bases, vol. 30, pp. 648–659 (2004)
17. Wang, J., Li, G., Feng, J.: Can we beat the prefix filtering? an adaptive framework for similarity join and search. In: Proceedings of the 2012 ACM SIGMOD International Conference on Management of Data, pp. 85–96 (2012)
18. Wang, X., Qin, L., Lin, X., Zhang, Y., Chang, L.: Leveraging set relations in exact set similarity join. In: Proceedings of the VLDB Endowment (2017)
19. Xiao, C., Wang, W., Lin, X., Shang, H.: Top-k set similarity joins. In: 2009 IEEE 25th International Conference on Data Engineering, pp. 916–927 (2009)
20. Xiao, C., Wang, W., Lin, X., Yu, J.X., Wang, G.: Efficient similarity joins for near-duplicate detection. ACM Trans. Database Syst. (TODS) **36**(3), 1–41 (2011)

Quantitative Contention Generation for Performance Evaluation on OLTP Databases

Chunxi Zhang[1], Rong Zhang[1(✉)], Weining Qian[1], Ke Shu[2], and Aoying Zhou[1]

[1] East China Normal University, Shanghai 200000, China
cxzhang@stu.ecnu.edu.cn
{rzhang,wnqian,ayzhou}@dase.ecnu.edu.cn
[2] PingCAP Ltd., Beijing 100000, China
shuke@pingcap.com

Abstract. Although we have achieved significant progress in improving the scalability of transactional database systems (OLTP), the presence of contention operations in workloads is still the fundamental limitation in improving throughput. The reason is that the overhead of managing conflict transactions with concurrency control mechanism is proportional to the amount of contentions. As a consequence, contention workload generation is urgent to evaluate performance of modern OLTP database systems. Though we have kinds of standard benchmarks which provide some ways in simulating resource contention, e.g. skew distribution control of transactions, they can not control the generation of contention quantitatively; even worse, the simulation effectiveness of these methods is affected by the scale of data. So in this paper we design a scalable quantitative contention generation method with fine contention granularity control, which is expected to generate resource contention specified by contention ratio and contention intensity.

1 Introduction

Massive scale of transactions with critical requirements becomes popular for emerging businesses, especially in E-commerce. One of the most representative applications is promotional events run in Alibaba's platform, widely expected by global customers. For example, on November 11, the Singles' Day, global shopping festival runs annually, where large promotions lauched by almost all vendors start exactly at midnight. It has been found that it suffers 122 times of workload increasing in transactions per second (TPS) suddenly, compared to stable response time observed in an online database [8], called the tsunami problem named as "SecKill". Such transactions have two major characteristics which can choke databases (DB):

- High Concurrency: "SecKill" promotion events generate massive concurrent access to DBs. During promotions, it attracts huge vertical spikes. One of the possible ways to alleviate the stress is to construct distributed databases.

X. Wang et al. (Eds.): APWeb-WAIM 2020, LNCS 12318, pp. 441–456, 2020.
https://doi.org/10.1007/978-3-030-60290-1_34

It may work but it will cost a lot on hardware deployment and maintenance. And the most terrible thing is introducing distributed transactions will greatly dwarf such a distributed architecture.

– High Contention: Workload distribution is drastically unbalanced. Hot/ popular items attract the majority of workloads especially writings. This kind of fierce contention on resources can suffer database instantaneously. Additionally, large amount of hot records can easily overwhelm system buffers, which requires swift I/O ability between memory hierarchies.

Then the ability to resolve resource contention is the supreme evaluation metric to transaction processing (TP) DBs. Simulating access contention to databases explicitly and quantitatively is of the most importance to expose database ability [2, 10, 14].

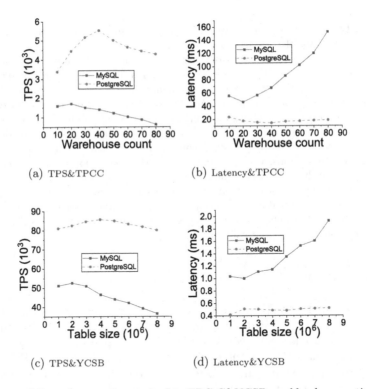

(a) TPS&TPCC

(b) Latency&TPCC

(c) TPS&YCSB

(d) Latency&YCSB

Fig. 1. Effect of contention control in TPC-C&YCSB workload generation

However, contention generation method has not been explicitly declared by most of the benchmarks. For example, TPC-C [4] simply tones down contentions by increasing the number of warehouses or decreasing the number of concurrent posts; YCSB [6] controls contention intensity by changing the size of data tables accessed by workloads. As shown in Fig. 1, by increasing data size (i.e. add more warehouses in TPC-C or increase table size in YCSB), system performance is expected to keep increasing. Though PeakBench [5] is the first work which proposes to control the contentions quantitatively, it has a serious drawback in scalability of contention generation, for it takes the block-based method and has strong dependence on the number of free threads.

In this paper, we design a new scalable way to simulate contentions from the perspective of iteratively adjusting contention data or contention generation threads in a non-block way. We propose two kinds of contention generation modes. In a *global* mode, we can promise the final contention status as defined; in a *local* mode, we can guarantee the runtime contention status as expected. By each generation mode, we design and implement three levels of contention granularity. In the experiment, we demonstrate the excellent performance of our method by comparing with the state-of-the-art related work.

2   Related Work

High contentions result in serious impact to performance in OLTP databases (DB) [1,7,8]. It has been mentioned that multi-core and new OLTP engines can improve database scalability in some way [2,10,14], but they can not deal with the drawbacks caused by high contentions effectively. However, there are more and more new applications, which require the ability to handle high contentions, such as "black friday" in USA and "11·11" in Alibaba's platform. Then the way to simulate contentions is an urgent requirement for driving the development of databases.

Tranditional benchmarks for transaction processings describe the general business procedure with abstracted workloads in some representative application scenario, e.g. TPC-C [4], YCSB [6] and TATP [13]. They can only simuate contentions in a coarse way. TPC-C adjusts the number of warehouses (i.e. data size) or the number of concurrency to change the contentions. YCSB adopts the Zipfan functions to control workload distributions on dataset for different contentions. SmallBank [3] can only coarsely change contentions by adjusting workload proportions. In TATP and DebitCredit [12], they don't considered about contention generation intentionally. However, those traditional benchmarks have not a strict defintion to contentions and can not control the generation of contentions. In PeakBench [5], it provides detailed defintion to contentions using contention ratio and contention intensity, and intends to make contention generation controllable. But the contention generation method takes a block-based way, which makes the test client have to wait for a bunch of free threads declared by contention intensity to simulate resource contention. For simulating high contention, it can easily bottleneck the simulator itself instead of databases. So PeakBench has serious problem of generation scalability. Contention generation in a scalable and controlable way is still a tough work.

3   Problem Definition

3.1   Notations and Problem Definition

Contention status can be described by Contention Ratio CR and Contention Intensity CI as defined in PeakBench [5]. CR is the ratio of contention transactions to the whole transction set. CI is the number of transactions contending to each other for the same resource at the same time. For contention status, we can specify it from two types of modes, called *global* mode ($gMode$) and *local* mode ($lMode$). In $gMode$, CR/CI is an average value calculated by the number of contention transactions to the whole workload set; while in $lMode$, CR/CI is calculated by the number of real-time contention transactions to current transaction set. All notations used for our paper are defined in Table 1.

Based on the contention granularities among transactions, we conduct three levels of contentions, i.e. $lev1$-$lev3$, defined as follows:

- **Lev1: Contention on Table** (CoB). Transactions on the same table have the same contention status, if they generate contentions.
- **Lev2: Contention on Transaction** (CoT). One type of transactions has the same contention status on the same table, even if they conflict with different transactions.
- **Lev3: Contention on Transaction to Transaction** (CoT^2). Even the same type of transactions has different contention status on the same table, if they conflict with different transactions.

Table 1. Common notations

N	The size of nodes
T	The collection of threads, $|\mathbb{T}| = M$
TB	The collection of tables, $|\mathbb{TB}| = b$
TX	The collection of transactions, $|\mathbb{TX}|=m$
TXR	Transaction ratio,$|\mathbb{TXR}| =m.$ $\forall \, txr_i \in \mathbb{TXR},\ 0 \leq txr_i \leq 1$ && $\sum_1^m txr_i = 1$
$\mathbb{C}_{m,b}$	Access status matrix between transactions TX and tables TB. If tx_i accesses tb_j, $c_{i,j} = 1$, or else $c_{i,j}=0$, $tx_i \in \mathbb{TX}$ && $tb_j \in \mathbb{TB}$
$\mathbb{LX}_{m,b}$	Transaction latency matrix of TX on TB. $L1_{i,j}$ ($L0_{i,j}$) represents the processing latency of contention (non-contention) transaction tx_i on table tb_j, $tx_i \in \mathbb{TX}$ && $tb_j \in \mathbb{TB}$
$\mathbb{CR}$	3-dimension contention ratio matrix between transactions TX on TB with $cr_{i,j,k}$ as contention ratio between tx_i and tx_j on table tb_k, $|\mathbb{CR}|= m^2 \cdot b$ && $0 \leq cr_{i,j,k} \leq 1$
$\mathbb{CI}$	3-dimension contention intensity matrix between transactions TX on TB, with $ci_{i,j,k}$ as contention intensity between tx_i and tx_j on table tb_k, $|\mathbb{CI}|=m^2 \cdot b$ && $0 \leq ci_{i,j,k} \leq M$

Table 2. Transaction distribution

$\mathbb{C}_{tx,tb}$	tb_1	tb_2	tb_3
tx_1	1	1	0
tx_2	0	1	1

Table 3. Contention transaction latency on tables

$\mathbb{L}1_{tx,tb}$	tb_1	tb_2	tb_3
tx_1	$l1_{1,1}$	$l1_{1,2}$	–
tx_2	–	$l1_{2,2}$	$l1_{2,3}$

Table 4. Non-contention transaction latency on tables

$\mathbb{L}0_{tx,tb}$	tb_1	tb_2	tb_3
tx_1	$l0_{1,1}$	$l0_{1,2}$	–
tx_2	–	$l0_{2,1}$	$l0_{2,3}$

Definition 1. Contention Generation: Using the collection of threads $\mathbb{T}$ on tables $\mathbb{TB}$ to generate contentions, it satisfies contention status (i.e. CR and CI) with granularity specified on $CoB/ CoT/ CoT^2$. □

3.2 Examples

In Table 2, 3, and 4, we give a transaction execution example by using the notations defined in Table 1. Two transactions $\mathbb{TX} = \{tx_i\}(i=1,2)$ operate on three tables $\mathbb{TB} = \{tb_k\}$ ($k=1,2,3$). Supposing tx_1 and tx_2 have the execution probabilities of $txr_1 = 40\%$ and $txr_2 = 60\%$ respectively. In Table 5, we show the most strict contention status settings (i.e. $Lev3$) formatted as $cr : ci$ between transactions on tables. For example, tx_1 conflicts with itself on tb_1 with 0.6:3, that is $cr = 0.6$ and $ci = 3$.

We can accumulate the coarser contention status for $Lev1$ and $Lev2$ based on the data of $Lev3$. For example, contention status is specified as $cr_{tb}{:}ci_{tb}$. Supposing the contention ratio caused by tx_i on table tb_k is $cr_{i,k}$ ($Lev2$), it is calculated by accumulating the contentions from all tx_j (to tx_i) as $cr_{i,k} = \sum_{j=1}^{m} cr_{i,j,k} \cdot c_{i,k}$. For example in Table 6, $cr_{tx_1,tb_2} = \sum_{j=1}^{2}(cr_{tx_1,tx_1,tb_2} \cdot 1 + cr_{tx_1,tx_2,tb_2} \cdot 1) = 0.3 + 0.4 = 0.7$, with $c_{tx_1,tb_2} = 1$. For any transaction tx, its contention intensity on a table tb is the maximum intensity caused by tx on tb, which is 4 for tx_1 on tb_2 in Table 6. For $Lev1$, the contention ratio of tb_k, i.e. cr_{tb_k}, is accumulated from all transaction contention status on tb_k, i.e. $cr_{i,k}$, of $Lev2$ by Eq. 1

$$cr_{tb_k} = \frac{\sum_{i=1}^{m} cr_{i,k} \cdot txr_i}{\sum_{i=1}^{m} txr_i \cdot c_{i,k}} \tag{1}$$

Contention intensity on table tb is set as the maximum ci caused by any transaction tx on tb. For example, the $Lev1$ contention ratio of tb_2 is 0.64, calculated by $cr_{tb_2} = \frac{cr_{tx_1,tb_2} \cdot txr_1 + cr_{tx_2,tb_2} \cdot txr_2}{txr_1 \cdot c_{tx_1,tb_2} + txr_2 \cdot c_{tx_2,tb_2}} = \frac{0.7 \cdot 40\% + 0.6 \cdot 60\%}{40\% \cdot 1 + 60\% \cdot 1} = 0.64$; its cotention intensity ci_{tb_2} is 4 caused by tx_1, as shown in Table 7.

Theorem 1. For given thread set $\mathbb{T}$, $\forall ci_{i,j,k} \in CR, ci_{i,j,k} \leq |\mathbb{T}|$. □

Proof 1. Since workloads/queries are distributed and assigned by threads, parallel data operations can not be larger than the total number of threads $\mathbb{T} = M$. □

Table 5. Contention status CoT^2 (tx_i operates on tb_k is $tx_i^{tb_k}$)

$\mathbf{CR}_{tx,tx,tb} : \mathbb{CI}_{tx,tx,tb}$	$tx_1^{tb_1}$	$tx_2^{tb_1}$	$tx_1^{tb_2}$	$tx_2^{tb_2}$	$tx_1^{tb_3}$	$tx_2^{tb_3}$
tx_1	0.6 : 3	–	0.3 : 3	0.4 : 4	–	–
tx_2	–	–	0.4 : 4	0.2 : 2	–	0.5 : 4

Table 6. Contention status CoT

$\mathbf{CR}_{tx,tb} : \mathbb{CI}_{tx,tb}$	tb_1	tb_2	tb_3
tx_1	0.6 : 3	0.7 : 4	–
tx_2	–	0.6 : 3	0.5 : 4

Table 7. Contention tatus CoB

	tb_1	tb_2	tb_3
$\mathbf{CR}_{tb} : \mathbb{CI}_{tb}$	0.6 : 3	0.64 : 4	0.5 : 4

4   Adaptive Contention Generation on Different Granularities

The main task for contention generation is to find the size of threads th assigned simultaneously on a part of contention data CD, with $\|CD\| = \delta$ for a predefined contention status on any table. We design two methods to generate contentions for different contention granulartiy, i.e. $Lev1 \sim Lev3$, in *global* and *local* modes.

4.1   Contention Control on Tables CoB

For $Lev1$, transactions on the same table have the same transaction status. Since the size of threads $|\mathbb{T}| = M$, the maximum locks can be assigned to one item is M, which is the maximum contention intensity. For tb_k, in order to generate cr_k contention transactions, the size of threads th_k configured for it is calculated by Eq. 2, where the total threads assigned for table tb_k is $M \cdot \sum_{i=1}^{m} txr_i \cdot c_{i,k}$ and the ratio of contention transactions is cr_k.

$$th_k = M \cdot cr_k \cdot \sum_{i=1}^{m} txr_i \cdot c_{i,k} \tag{2}$$

We need to decide the contention data set CD_k in tb_k sized δ_k to promise contention intensity ci_k. In $Lev1$, contention status is supposed to be the same on the same table for all transactions. Supposing t among th_k threads conflict on data x ($x \in CD_k$, $ci_k = t$), the probability of x visisted currently by t threads are:

$$p(t) = c_{th_k}^{t} \cdot (\frac{1}{\delta_k})^t \cdot (\frac{\delta_k - 1}{\delta_k})^{th_k - t} \tag{3}$$

Since the contention expection on x is ci_k, it satisfies:

$$E(x) = \sum_{k=0}^{th_k} t \cdot p(t) = ci_k \tag{4}$$

$$\overline{L1}_k = \sum_{i=1}^{m} txr_i \cdot \overline{L1}_{i,k} \cdot c_{i,k}; \qquad \overline{L0}_k = \sum_{i=1}^{m} txr_i \cdot \overline{L0}_{i,k} \cdot (1 - c_{i,k}); \qquad (5)$$

Based on th_k with the predefined ci_k, it is easy to calculate δ_k by Eq. 3 and 4. But usually contention transaction will cause larger lantency than non-contention ones. If we take the threads assignment method in Eq. 2, threads concurrently accessing CD_k will increase to be larger than th_k, for contention transactions can not be completed as fast as non-contention ones, and then threads assigned for contention generation cause the piling. So contention status can not be promised but will be larger than expection during running of workloads, calculated by Eq. 5. We design two ways to adatively manage contention generations, which act in *global* mode (*gMode*) and *local* mode (*lMode*) respectively. In *gMode*, it guarantees the average contention status as specified, which is the target for contention simulation in previous work by adjusting the conflicted data size. However, until now, previous work is either too rough to be used or has the scalability problem in generation as in PeakBench. *lMode* is a new design by guaranteeing the runtime contention status consistent to the specified one.

– Global Contention Control of *Lev*1 (*gMode*[1]): In Eq. 6, the thread proportion assigned to contention transactions is *ratio* by taking into account the latency difference of contention and non-contention transactions with $\overline{L1}_k$ and $\overline{L0}_k$. But contention status will be more severe, for usually $\overline{L1}_k > \overline{L0}_k$. In order to keep ci unchanged, we enlarge the candidate data CD_k assigned for contention generation to relax contentions by lowing $\overline{L1}_k$.

$$ratio = \frac{cr_k \cdot \overline{L1}_k}{cr_k \cdot \overline{L1}_k + (1 - cr_k) \cdot \overline{L0}_k}; \qquad th_k = M \cdot ratio \qquad (6)$$

– Local Contention Control of *Lev*1 (*lMode*[1]): If we want to guarantee cr_k value along the whole execution procedure, we need to decrease the real-time execution contention ratio to cr'_k as explained previously, shown in Eq. 7. Since $\overline{L1}_k > \overline{L0}_k$ leading to the pile of concurrency threads, decreasing the contention ratio to cr'_k is a possible way.

$$cr_k = \frac{cr'_k \cdot \overline{L1}_k}{cr'_k \cdot \overline{L1}_k + (1 - cr'_k) \cdot \overline{L0}_k} \qquad (7)$$

4.2 Contention Control on Transactions *CoT*

We have introduced the adjust intuition for generating coarse *Lev*1 contentions. It does not consider the difference of transaction contention status on tables, which is not true actually. We discriminate contention status for different transactions on tables in *Lev*2. On table tb_k, the size of threads assigned for transaction tx_i to generate its contention is $th_{i,k}$. We initialize $th_{i,k}$ in Eq. 8 by using

$cr_{i,k}$ instead of cr_k in Eq. 2. Together with Eq. 3 and 4 in which we use $ci_{i,k}$ to replace ci_k, we can get the initial contention data size $\delta_{i,k}$.

$$th_{i,k} = M \cdot txr_i \cdot cr_{i,k} \cdot c_{i,k} \tag{8}$$

In Lev2, $\overline{L1}_{i,k}$(resp. $\overline{L0}_{i,k}$) is the average latency for contention transaction (resp. non-contention transaction) tx_i on tb_k.

- Global Contention Control of Lev2 ($gMode^2$): $th_{i,k}$ is then calculated by Eq. 9, in which $M \cdot txr_i$ is the total number of threads assigned for transaction tx_i. It adjusts the proportion of threads for contention generation on table tb_k by ratio, which considers the difference of transaction execution on tables by latencies $\overline{L1}_{i,k}$ and $\overline{L0}_{i,k}$. it then takes the same method to enlarge the contention data size $\delta_{i,k}$ to guarantee contention status.

$$ratio = \frac{cr_{i,k} \cdot \overline{L1}_{i,k}}{cr_{i,k} \cdot \overline{L1}_{i,k} + (1 - cr_{i,k}) \cdot \overline{L0}_{i,j}}; \quad th_{i,k} = M \cdot txr_i \cdot ratio \tag{9}$$

- Local Contention Control of Lev2 ($lMode^2$): By $\overline{L1}_{i,k}$ and $\overline{L0}_{i,k}$, we adjust the real-time execution contention ratio $cr'_{i,k}$ to promise the required $cr_{i,k}$, as shown in Eq. 10.

$$cr_{i,k} = \frac{cr'_{i,k} \cdot \overline{L1}_{i,k}}{cr'_{i,k} \cdot \overline{L1}_{i,k} + (1 - cr'_{i,k}) \cdot \overline{L0}_{i,k}} \tag{10}$$

4.3   Contention Control Among Transactions CoT^2

Transaction latency can be affected by the transaction it conflicts with. For example, tx_1 probably may have different performance influence by conflicting with tx_2 and tx_3, which may have totally different operations. In Lev3, we define fine contention status between transactions (e.g. tx_i an tx_j) on a table (e.g. tb_k), where contention ratio and contention intensity are represented by $cr_{i,j,k}$ and $ci_{i,j,k}$. In such a case, the initial threads $th_{i,j,k}$ assigned to generate contentions for tx_i (resp. tx_j) are calculated as in Eq. 11 by using $cr_{i,j,k}$. Then the initial contention dataset size $\delta_{i,j,k}$ for tx_i and tx_j is fixed. We differentiate the latencies generated by different transaction pairs. $\overline{L1}_{i,j,k}$ (resp. $\overline{L0}_{i,-,k}$) is the average latency between contention transaction tx_i and tx_j on tb_k (resp. latency with no contention for tx_i on tb_k).

$$th_{i,j,k} = M \cdot txr_i \cdot cr_{i,j,k} \cdot c_{i,k} \tag{11}$$

- Global Contention Control of Lev3 ($gMode^3$): Threads assigned to tx_i is calculated by Eq. 12. It is affected by three elements. One is contention between tx_i and tx_j, which is $cr_{i,j,k} \cdot \overline{L1}_{i,j,k}$; the second one is the contention between tx_i and tx_l ($l \neq j$), which is $\sum_{l \neq j}^{m} \overline{L1}_{i,l,k} \cdot cr_{i,l,k}$; the third one is the non-contention transactions, which is $\overline{L0}_{i,-,k} \cdot (1 - \sum_{p=0}^{m} cr_{i,p,k})$.

$$th_{i,j,k} = \frac{M \cdot txr_i \cdot cr_{i,j,k} \cdot \overline{L1}_{i,j,k}}{cr_{i,j,k} \cdot \overline{L1}_{i,j,k} + \sum_{l \neq j}^{m} \overline{L1}_{i,l,k} \cdot cr_{i,l,k} + \overline{L0}_{i,-,k} \cdot (1 - \sum_{p=0}^{m} cr_{i,p,k})} \tag{12}$$

– Local Contention Control of $Lev3$ ($lMode^3$): By adjusting $cr'_{i,j,k}$ periodically in Eq. 13, we expect to generate the expected contention status $cr_{i,j,k}$.

$$cr_{i,j,k} = \frac{cr'_{i,j,k} \cdot \overline{L1}_{i,j,k}}{cr'_{i,j,k} \cdot \overline{L1}_{i,j,k} + \sum_{l \neq j}^{m} \overline{L1}_{i,l,k} \cdot cr_{i,l,k} + \overline{L0}_{i,-,k} \cdot (1 - \sum_{p=0}^{m} cr_{i,p,k})} \quad (13)$$

5 Implementation Architecture

The implementation architecture is shown in Fig. 2. It includes six modules: **Schema Interpreter, Transaction Interpreter, Workload Generator, Contention Controller, Workload Executor** and **performance Monitor**.

Schema Interpreter: It reads the configuration $config$ and extracts data characteristics in $DBschematemplate$ to generate database schema used for data and workload generation. The main schema items are shown in Table 8 (i.e. **Schema**), which includes information for tables (TB) and attributes (Attr).

Table 8. Transaction information ($*$ is multiple occurrency).

Name	Characteristics	
Schema	TB name, TB size, key, foreign key; Attr name, Attr type, domain	
Transaction	*Basic Info*	transID, transRatio, compile mode
	Contention	contentionGeMode, contentionGranularity
	*Operation**	contentionorNot, contentionParaPos, contentionTB,$[tx,\ cr,\ ci]*$

Transaction Interpreter: It interprets information from transaction (trans) template, including three parts of information (Info):

– *Basic Info*: It covers $tranID$, $transRatio$ and $compilemode$ (i.e. prepare or non-prepare execution mode).
– *Contention*: It contains the specification to contention generations. $ContentionGeMode$ declares to guarantee contention status in $gMode$ or $lMode$. $ContentionGranularity$ selects contention generation granularity.
– *Operation**: Each transaction may have more than one operations. We label whether it conflicts with others ($contentionorNot$). If it has multiple predicate prarameters, we shall point out the prararameter generating contentions by $contentionParaPos$ with transaction tx on table $contentionTB$ by setting its contention status as cr and ci.

Contention Controller: After **Transaction Interpreter** gets all the contention specifications, we can calculate to generate different levels of contention status, e.g. $Lev1$. The contention information is transfered to **Workload Generator** to control the workload generation. During the running of workloads, **Performance Monitor** collects the running performance (i.e. latency) as a feedback to **Contention Controller**. We draw the contention generation algorithms for $ContentionGeMode = global$ and $local$ in Algorithm 1 and Algorithm 2, respectively.

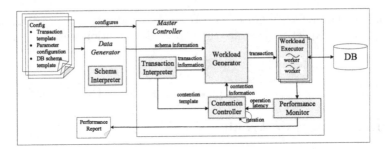

Fig. 2. System architecture

In Algorithm 1, we promise the contention status satisfied the requirement after a period of running by adjusting the contention data size δ iteratively. In line 2–3, we initialize the thread size th and data size δ. For different contention granularity declared by $ContentionGranularity$, we select different initialization method, which have been introduced in Sects. 4.1, 4.2 and 4.3. In $gmode$, the smaller the δ, the more intensive the contention and the lower the throughput. Initialization to δ does not taken into account the latency difference between contention transactions and non-contention transactions.

In Algorithm 2, we guarantee the same contention status in $lMode$ during the real-time execution by adjusting the execution cr' iteratively. Intuitively, the larger the cr, the more intensive the contention and the lower the throughput. We first initialize parameters in line 2. During iteration (line 4–20), we select the perfect cr by binary search bounded in $minRatio$ and $maxRatio$. Algorithm 2 will not stop until the calculated $cr' == lastcr$ (line 14).

Algorithm 1: Global Contention Control

Input: contention status cr, ci on tb,
 th contention thread size, transaction ratio set TXR,
 $C_{m,k}$ transaction access status matrix.
Output: δ: data size on tb for contention generation

1 Initialize :
2 th; δ=adjustCDsize(th, ci, cr);
3 $last\delta \leftarrow 0$; $minSize \leftarrow \delta$; $maxSize \leftarrow 10000$; $flag \leftarrow 1$;
4 $iterationContentionData(\delta)$
5 {
6   $last\delta = \delta$;
7   set $\overline{L1}$ and $\overline{L0}$ values;
8   update th according to $\overline{L1}$ and $\overline{L0}$ values;
9   **if** $flag == 1$ **then**
10    $maxSize$ = adjustCDsize(th, ci, cr);
11    $flag = 0$;
12 **else**
13   **if** $adjustCDsize(th,ci,cr) == last\delta$ **then**
14   return $last\delta$;
15   **else if** $adjustCDsize(th,ci,cr) > last\delta$ **then**
16      $minSize = last\delta$;
17   **else**
18      $maxSize = last\delta$;
19    $\delta = (maxSize + minSize)/2$;
20 }
21 return null ;

Algorithm 2: Local Contention Control

Input: cr, ci contention status on tb, cr' adjusted
 contention ratio,
 TXR transaction ratio set, $C_{m,k}$ transaction access status
 matrix.
Output: cr' expected contention ratio

1 Initialize :
2 $lastcr \leftarrow 0$; $minRatio \leftarrow 0.0$; $maxRatio \leftarrow cr$; $flag \leftarrow 1$;
 $cr' \leftarrow cr$;
3 $iterationContenionRatio$
4 {
5   $lastcr = cr'$;
6   set $\overline{L1}$ and $\overline{L0}$ values;
7   update cr';
8   **if** $flag == 1$ **then**
9     $minRatio = cr'$;
10    $cr' = (maxRatio + minRatio)/2$;
11    $flag = 0$;
12 **else**
13   **if** $cr' == lastcr$ **then**
14   return cr' ;
15   **else if** $cr' > lastcr$ **then**
16      $minRatio = lastcr$;
17   **else**
18      $maxRatio = lastcr$;
19    $cr' = (maxRatio + minRatio)/2$;
20 }
21 return null;

6   Experimental Results

Experimental Setting: Our experiments are conducted on a cluster with 4 nodes configured in RAID-5 on CentOS v.6.5. We demonstrate the effectiveness of our contention generation method by running it on two popularly used open sourced database systems MySQL (v. 14.14) [11] and PostgreSQL (v. 9.5.1). [9] (PG for short). The iteration period is configurable. We set the iteration period as 10 s, while performance metrics are output every 5 s (e.g. TPS).

Compared Work and Workloads: YCSB is the most popular benchmark designed for I/O performance evaluation, which is selected to demonstrate the effectiveness of our work ($tx_0 \sim tx_2$ in Table 9). tx_0 is a single line update; tx_1 includes two writes op_1 and op_2; tx_2 has one write op_3 and one read op_4. Usually, tx_1 has longer execution time than tx_2, so tx_1 is a long transaction compared to tx_2. The contentions are caused by $tx_0.op_0$, $tx_1.op_1$ and $tx_2.op_3$, where $contention = 1$ in Table 9. PeakBench [5] is the first work which proposes to control contention simulation in fine granularities, which is selected as our comparison work. Among workloads of PeakBench, during second kill, only *submit order* (i.e. tx_3 in Table 9) causes severe contentions. Notice that, our contention control method can be applied to other benchmarks too.

Table 9. Experimental workloads

Id	txr	oID	Workload setting	Contention	Type
tx_0	1	op_0	update usertable set $field1 = ?$ where $ycsb_{key} = ?;$	1	$YCSB$
tx_1	0.5	op_1	update usertable set $field1 = ?$ where $ycsb_{key} = ?;$	1	
		op_2	update usertable set $field1 = ?$ where $ycsb_{key} = ?;$	0	
tx_2	0.5	op_3	update usertable set $field1 = ?$ where $ycsb_{key} = ?;$	1	
		op_4	select $*$ from usertable where $ycsb_{key} = ?$;	0	
tx_3	1	op_5	select sl_{price} from seckillplan where $sl_{skpkey} = ?$;	0	$PeakBench$
		op_6	update seckillplan set $sl_{skpcount} = sl_{skpcount} + 1$ where $sl_{skpkey}= ?$ and $sl_{skpcount} < sl_{plancount};$	1	
		op_7	replace into orders ($o_{orderkey}$, $o_{custkey}$, o_{skpkey}, o_{price}, $o_{orderdate}$, o_{state}) values (?, ?, ?, ?, ?, 0) ;	0	
		op_8	replace into orderitem ($oi_{orderkey}$, $oi_{itemkey}$, oi_{count}, oi_{price}) values (?, ?, 1, ?) ;	0	

In Sect. 6.1, we demonstrate our work by collecting performance during adjustion in both $gMode$ and $lMode$ as well as algorithm convergences. In Sect. 6.2, we compare our work with PeakBench.

6.1 Contention Simulation by Different Granularity

Lev1: Contention on Tables. In $Lev1$,transactions on a table are supposed to have the same transaction status (if any). In Fig. 3, we run tx_0 by changing cr and ci. Our method is effective in contention control on both DBs, which has obvious variations with the change of cr and ci. Since in $gMode$ we guarantee the final contention ratio cr as expected, its real-time contention (i.e. ci_{gMode} or cr_{gMode}) is usually severer than expected. But in $lMode$ (i.e. ci_{lMode} or cr_{lMode}), the run-time contention status is supposed to be guaranteed. In this way, $gMode$-based method will have lower performance (TPS/Latency) than $lMode$-based one during the testing. When we increase ci, performance keeps decreasing until it comes to system performance limitation, i.e. $ci = 15$ in Fig. 3(e).

Lev2: Contention on Transactions. In $Lev2$, we generate contentions between two types of transactions, i.e. tx_1 and tx_2. In order to compare the difference between $Lev2$ and $Lev1$, we draw the base lines labeled by $base_{lev1}$ for $Lev1$ contention control by $cr_{tb} = 0.5$ and $ci_{tb} = 5$, and $txr_1 = txr_2 = 0.5$. In Fig. 4, $TPS(tx_i)$ represents throughput for tx_i, and $TPS(tx) = \sum_{i=1}^{2} TPS(tx_i)$. We adjust contention ratio between tx_1 and tx_2 to check performance variations. Notice that contention ratio for tx_2 is $cr_{tx_2} = 1 - cr_{tx_1}$. So when we increase cr_{tx_1}, cr_{tx_2} will decrease correspondingly.

In MySQL, resources are usually assigned to transactions with high contentions and also to short transactions (i.e. tx_2). In $gMode$, when increasing cr_{tx_1} to 0.5, tx_1 meets more contentions but tx_2 gets more resources. so tx_1 (tx_2) has higher (lower) latency shown in Fig. 4(a) and 4(b). When $cr_{tx_1} > 0.5$, its performance receding affects MySQL more than the performance improving from tx_2. So the global peformance becomes worse. But its runtime contention ratio is always severer than the expected one, so its average performance is worse than the baseline $base_{Lev1\_gMode}$. MySQL reaches its performance peak when $cr_{tx_1} = cr_{tx_2} = 0.5$. But in $lMode$,runtime contention is actually lower than the specified one and that in $gMode$, and then the total performance is better compared with baseline $base_{Lev1\_lMode}$. As increasing cr_{tx_1}, system performance keeps increasing, because tx_2 is getting more resources while for less contentions during the runtime. Additionally, when $cr_{tx_1} > 0.5$, its latency becomes less worse than in $gMode$, for the local adjustion decreases a lot of contentions; the latency of tx_2 becomes better for it has less contentions and it is the perfered short transactions in MySQL.

For PG, Performance changes in TPS are similar to MySQL as shown in Fig. 4(c). But PG usually assigns resources to transactions with high contentions. In $gMode$, when starting to increase cr_{tx_1}, tx_2 holds more resources for cr_{tx_2} is much bigger though it is decreasing. Latency for tx_1 (resp. tx_2) has a short-time increasing (resp. decreasing). When we keep increasing cr_{tx_1} from 0.2, tx_1

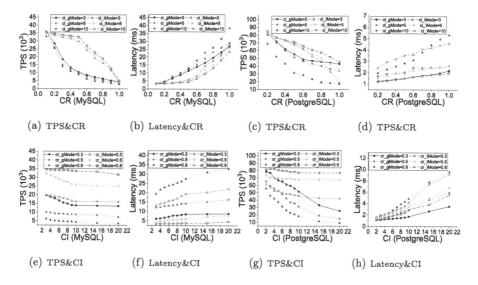

Fig. 3. *Lev*1: Contention simuation on table with tx_0

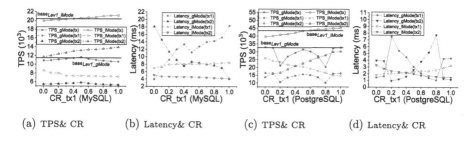

Fig. 4. *Lev*2: Contention simulation on transactions tx_1 and tx_2

are gathering resources, and then its latency keeps decreasing, but latency of tx_2 becomes larger. When $cr_{tx_1} < 0.1$ or $cr_{tx_1} > 0.9$, PG meets its processing bottleneck for contentions and then performance will not change much when we vary the contention status. In *gMode*, it meets much more contentions than expected and has sharp performance changes than in *lMode*. In *lMode*, when increasing cr_{tx_1}, latency of tx_1 will be a little larger. Latency changes are shown in Fig. 4(d). According to our *lMode* adjusion method, if we have higher contentions, it will generate a smaller cr' to implement runtime contentions. Since tx_1 has longer latency than tx_2, contention relaxation to tx_1 benefits the whole system and finally we get better performance than the baseline $base_{Lev1\_lMode}$ as shown in Fig. 4(c).

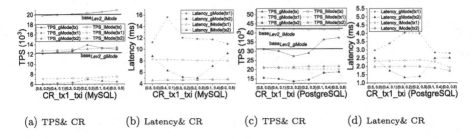

(a) TPS& CR   (b) Latency& CR   (c) TPS& CR   (d) Latency& CR

Fig. 5. $Lev3$: Contentions between transactions tx_1 and tx_2

Lev3: Contention Among Transactions. tx_1 and tx_2 have $txr = 0.5$, and contention status on table in $Lev2$ are set to $cr_{tx,tb} = 0.5$ and $ci_{tx,tb} = 5$ which generates $base_{lev2}$ in Fig. 5. Each pair of x-axis represents the contention ratio of tx_1 to tx_1 and to tx_2 respectively, and the sum value in each pair equals to cr_{tx_tb} (i.e. 0.5). For example, (0.4,0.1) represents that tx_1 generates 40% contentions to itself and the other 10% to tx_2. In Fig. 5(a) and 5(b), when contention between tx_1 and tx_2 starts to increase, the short transaction tx_2 can apply more resources in MySQL. Then tx_2 (resp. tx_1) has lower (resp. higher) latency in $gMode$. It is the same for PG as shown in Fig. 5(d). When contentions between tx_1 and tx_2 is larger than 0.3, the severe (resp. softer) contention status makes tx_2 (resp. tx_1) increase (resp. decrease) its latency. However, in $lMode$, when tx_1 increases contentions from tx_2, it will not generate too much runtime additional contentions, and then its latency is stably increasing. But when tx_1 decreases contention from tx_1, the global performance $TPS(tx)$ increases for both $gMode$ and $lMode$, for contention latency caused by tx_1 is bigger than tx_2. However, in PG, the contention from long transaction tx_1 affects performance more, so TPS is increasing in $lMode$ when contentions from tx_1 reduces. In $gMode$, its performance is still affected much by the accumulate additional contentions, which leads to a little lower performance than the baseline $base_{Lev2\_gMode}$. When contention from tx_2 increases, it then has more advantage in applying resource and its TPS increases, shown in Fig. 5(c). Compared to $gMode$, performance is more sensitive to $lMode$-based adjustion.

Alogrithm Convergency. We run the fine granularity contention generation in $Lev3$ by specifying the contention pairs between tx_1 and tx_2 with the same settings as in Fig. 5. In Fig. 6, either in $gMode$ or in $lMode$, we find that our algorithm will stop in less than 10 iterations.

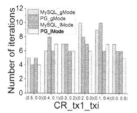

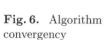

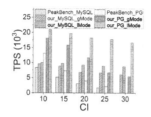

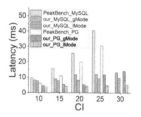

Fig. 6. Algorithm convergency

Fig. 7. Compare with Peak-Bench of TPS

Fig. 8. Compare with PeakBench of Latency

6.2 Compare with PeakBench

PeakBench guarantees the global transaction contention status by block-based method, which will not generate contention until it collects all the execution threads specified by ci. We run PeakBench and our methods on both $MySQL$ and PG (i.e. Ours_MySQL and Ours_PG) by adjusting the contention intensity for workloads (ci between 10 and 30). Contention ratio on table is $cr = 0.3$ and the workload threads are 100. The result is shown in Fig. 7 and Fig. 8. When ci is small, i.e. $ci = 10$, PeakBench has almost the same performance as our methods. But when we increase ci, e.g. $ci = 30$, PeakBench can not simulate high contentions any more. Even when $ci = 25$, the block-based contention generation in PeakBench makes the client as bottleneck (sharp drop of TPS), for it has to wait until get the specified free threads ($=ci$). Then Peakbench causes CPU idling in clients and block the workloads assignments, which starves the DBs and leads to low TPS or high Latency. So PeakBench has severe scalability problem in contention simulation. Our method has solved this problem well. And our work in $lMode$ always has better performance than that in $gMode$, for it has better contention simulation ability.

6.3 Summary

Previous work tries to get contention status in $gMode$, such as PeakBench, but they are not scalabe to generate intensive contentions quantitatively, which has been solved in our work. $lMode$ guarantees the runtime contention status, which can simulate contentions more accurately and improve the usability. From the experimental results in $Lev1 \sim Lev3$, we find that performance in both MySQL and PG is sensitive to high contention workloads; MySQL is easily affected by the contention changes of short transcations but PG is affected by contention changes of long transactions. In summary, contention generation in $lMode$ is better than in $gMode$, but both are better than previous work.

7 Conclusion

We have designed two iterative algorithms to quantitatively simulate transaction contentions. Our method can be widely used for OLTP database testing and performance evaluation or optimization. Compared with the latest related work PeakBench, it has the advantage of high scalability in contention generation, which improves its usability. We also provide extensive experiments to highlight the importance of our work and demonstrate that fine granularity contention control can expose the process details in different databases.

Acknowledgment. This work is partially supported by National Key Research and Development Plan Project (No. 2018YFB1003404). Ke Shu is supported by PingCAP.

References

1. Aditya, G., Dheren, G., Fei, Z., Amit, P., Zhan, F.M.: Btrim: hybrid in-memory database architecture for extreme transaction processing in VLDBS. In: VLDB, pp. 1889–1901 (2018)
2. Appuswamy, R., Anadiotis, A.C., Porobic, D., Iman, M.K., Ailamaki, A.: Analyzing the impact of system architecture on the scalability of oltp engines for high-contention workloads. VLDB **11**(2), 121–134 (2017)
3. Cahill, M.J., Röhm, U., Fekete, A.D.: Serializable isolation for snapshot databases. TODS **34**(4), 20 (2009)
4. Chen, S., Ailamaki, A., Athanassoulis, M., et al.: TPC-C: characterizing the new TPC-E benchmark via an I/O comparison study. SIGMOD **39**(3), 5–10 (2011)
5. Chunxi, Z., Yuming, L., Rong, Z., et al.: Benchmarking on intensive transaction processing. Front. J. Higher Educ. Press, **14**, 145–204 (2019)
6. Cooper, B.F., Silberstein, A., Tam, E., Ramakrishnan, R., Sears, R.: Benchmarking cloud serving systems with YCSB. In: Proceedings of the 1st ACM Symposium on Cloud Computing, pp. 143–154. ACM (2010)
7. Harding, R., Aken, D.V., Pavlo, A., Stonebraker, M.: An evaluation of distributed concurrency control. VLDB **10**(5), 553–564 (2017)
8. Huang, G., et al.: X-engine: an optimized storage engine for large-scale e-commerce transaction processing. In: SIGMOD, pp. 651–665. ACM (2019)
9. PostgreSQL. https://www.postgresql.org/ddl-partitioning.html/
10. Ren, K., Faleiro, J.M., Abadi, D.J.: Design principles for scaling multi-core OLTP under high contention. In: SIGMOD, pp. 1583–1598. ACM (2016)
11. Ronstrom, M., Thalmann, L.: Mysql cluster architecture overview. MySQL Technical White Paper (2004)
12. Stonebraker, M.: A measure of transaction processing power. In: Readings in Database Systems, pp. 442–454 (1994)
13. Wolski, A.: TATP benchmark description (version 1.0) (2009)
14. Zhou, N., Zhou, X., Zhang, X., Du, X., Wang, S.: Reordering transaction execution to boost high-frequency trading applications. Data Sci. Eng. **2**(4), 301–315 (2017)

Pipelined Query Processing
Using Non-volatile Memory SSDs

Xinyu Liu, Yu Pan, Wenxiu Fang, Rebecca J. Stones, Gang Wang$^{(\boxtimes)}$,
Yusen Li, and Xiaoguang Liu$^{(\boxtimes)}$

College of CS, TJ Key Lab of NDST, Nankai University, Tianjin, China
{liuxy,panyu,fangwx,becky,wgzwp,liyusen,liuxg}@nbjl.nankai.edu.cn

Abstract. NVM Optane SSDs are faster than traditional flash-based SSDs and more economical than DRAM main memory, so we explore query processing with the inverted index on NVM aiming at reducing costs, but this leads to NVM-to-DRAM I/O which negatively affects the search engine's responsiveness. To alleviate this problem, we propose a pipelining scheme to overlap CPU computation with NVM-to-DRAM I/O. We further propose some optimizations: variable coalesced block size, data prefetching, and block skipping.

The experiments on the Gov2 and ClueWeb document corpuses indicate a reduction in CPU waiting time caused by NVM-to-DRAM I/O by around 85% for Maxscore, Wand, and BlockMaxWand queries vs. not using pipelining, while maintaining comparable query throughput (loss within 6%) vs. an in-memory inverted index (DRAM-based scheme). For RankAnd queries, we occupy 3% of the inverted index in memory for caching to achieve similar query efficiency (within 6%) vs. the DRAM-based scheme.

Keywords: NVM Optane SSD · Query processing · Pipeline · Prefetch

1 Introduction

The *inverted index* [4,12] is the most commonly used data structure for current search engines [5,15] consisting of *posting lists* for terms in the document corpus. Commercial search engines incur storage cost challenges [19,24], so if the inverted index is entirely maintained in the DRAM main memory, storage cost issues become problematic. However, query responsiveness is a concern if the inverted index is stored on disk, SSD, or other low-cost storage devices.

The emerging Non-volatile Memory Optane SSD (NVM) compensates for the read latency and bandwidth shortcomings of traditional SSDs. To illustrate,

This work is partially supported by National Science Foundation of China (61872201, 61702521, U1833114); Science and Technology Development Plan of Tianjin (17JCY-BJC15300, 18ZXZNGX00140, 18ZXZNGX00200).

X. Wang et al. (Eds.): APWeb-WAIM 2020, LNCS 12318, pp. 457–472, 2020.
https://doi.org/10.1007/978-3-030-60290-1_35

Fig. 1 plots the differences in bandwidth and latency between a traditional flash-based SSD (480 GB Intel SATA SSD) and the NVM device described in Sect. 4.1 for random read. We use the widely used workload generator, Fio, with single-threaded, libaio I/O engine with various read block sizes.

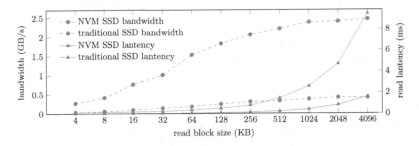

Fig. 1. Bandwidth and read latency of random read on traditional flash-based SSD (with 70k IOPS) and NVM Optane SSD (with 230k IOPS).

Motivated by the bandwidth advantage (vs. traditional SSDs) and the price advantage [10] (vs. DRAM) of NVM Optane SSD, we manage to migrate the inverted index from DRAM to the NVM (i.e., the entire inverted index is stored on the NVM). So a naive scheme is, when a search engine executes a query, it reads the corresponding posting lists from the NVM into DRAM, then performs the computations for returning the top K scored docIDs. We call this the *NVM baseline*.

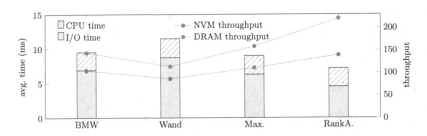

Fig. 2. The average query execution time and query throughput of the NVM baseline and DRAM-based schema on the Gov2 corpus for the MillionQuery set (execution time broken down in I/O and CPU computation).

For the NVM baseline, Fig. 2 breaks down the average query response time and plots the query throughput difference between NVM baseline and DRAM-based schema on the Gov2 corpus for BlockMaxWand [8] (BMW), Wand [3], Maxscore [18], and RankAnd queries. The I/O time is the read latency for all relevant posting lists, while the CPU time is the time spent on computation. We observe that compared with the DRAM-based scheme, the query response time increases by around 30% to 60%. Figure 2 indicates that I/O time is significant, negatively affecting the query response time and query throughput. The result is mainly because of the synchronous nature of I/O and computation: prior to performing CPU computation, the CPU waits until all the relevant posting lists are read into DRAM completely.

To address this issue, we propose using pipelining: each query initiates two threads, an I/O thread which reads data from NVM and a CPU thread which performs computation processes (decoding, intersection/union, scoring, etc.), whereby reading occurs in parallel with computation. Ideally, the reading speed matches the computation speed, whereby we minimize idleness.

The major contributions of this paper are as follows:

1. For the NVM Optane SSD, we propose pipelined query processing, and model the query response time.
2. In order to achieve an approximately ideal pipeline, we propose some optimizations: variable reading block size, data prefetching, and skipping unnecessary coalesced blocks.
3. We experimentally test various coalesced block sizes, integer encodings, query algorithms, and the number of recalled documents on the proposed pipeline method. We also investigate pipelining with caching and on traditional SSDs.

2   Background and Related Work

There are two query types: (1) conjunctive (i.e., intersection), where we return the docIDs containing all the query terms and (2) disjunctive (i.e., union), where we return the docIDs containing at least one of the query terms. Disjunctive queries involve more documents, so scoring is more time-consuming. Thus to reduce the query response time, researchers proposed Maxscore [18], Wand [3], and BlockMaxWand [8] which use score upper bound data to skip low-quality documents, each of which we also investigate.

Posting lists are divided into fixed-length blocks [11,14] (e.g., 128 docIDs per block), which are individually compressed and decompressed. We record the maximum docID of each block, which facilitates skipping irrelevant blocks during query processing. Posting lists also record the term frequencies.

A variety of integer encodings are used to reduce storage, such as VByte [7,17], PforDelta [11,22,25], Simple [1,23], and interpolative coding [13]. Nevertheless with insufficient memory, researchers store the inverted index on a low-cost storage device such as SSDs [19], resulting in SSD-to-memory transfer costs. To alleviate these transfer costs, some cache strategies have been proposed [19,24] to retain frequently accessed data in memory. However, the I/O delay issue (that our pipeline strives to solve) cannot be eliminated by cache, since reading data from SSD to DRAM is inevitable when there is a cache miss.

NVM has been attracting attention recently since they are more economical than DRAM while its read latency and bandwidth are far better than traditional SSDs (as per Fig. 1). Researchers have proposed different storage schemes and reading strategies using NVM as a substitute for DRAM for various applications, such as databases [9], byte-addressable file systems with DIMM form NVM memory [20,21], and recommendation systems [10]. However there is no research for applying NVM to search engines.

3   Pipelined Query Processing

We store the inverted index on the NVM Optane SSD instead of in DRAM. When receiving a user query, we *read* the relevant posting lists, i.e., transfer them from the NVM to DRAM. Excluding the cache, once the query finishes, the memory space is freed.

We begin with a *basic pipeline* which reads blocks individually using one CPU thread (the *I/O thread*), while a second CPU thread processes the blocks in the DRAM (the *CPU thread*), i.e., it performs decoding, intersection/union, and scoring. Vitally, the CPU is able to process available blocks regardless of whether subsequent blocks are available. This pipeline method overlaps I/O reading and CPU computation, thereby mitigating the read I/O latency.

In query processing, the basic unit is a compressed block b consisting of 128 docIDs which is generally around 100 bytes. However, to make better use of the NVM read bandwidth, the I/O thread reads a *coalesced* block B (over 4 KB, consisting of several hundreds to thousands of compressed blocks b) before making it available. In this paper, we consider document-at-a-time (DAAT) computation. Thus, the I/O thread sequentially reads the first coalesced blocks Bs of each posting list, and then reads the second Bs, and so on. The I/O thread fetches index data to the memory buffer and the CPU thread only reads this buffer.

In the ideal case, the CPU only waits for the first coalesced block B to be read by the I/O thread, and afterwards whenever the CPU thread requires any block b for decoding and processing, the I/O thread has already read b into memory. Otherwise, at some point the CPU thread requires an unread block b, but needs to wait for the I/O thread to make b available, thereby decreasing query efficiency.

To analyze the effect of various factors for pipelined query processing and further optimize the pipeline method, we model the query processing time in detail as follows. For a query set $\mathcal{Q}$, the *average query execution time* is

$$\frac{\sum_{q \in \mathcal{Q}} T_q}{|\mathcal{Q}|},$$

and we split the *query response time* for query q into

$$T_q = t_{\text{decode}} + t_{\text{operate}} + t_{\text{wait}}, \tag{1}$$

which consists of the decoding time t_{decode}, the operation time t_{operate} (including the time spent on intersection/union and scoring), and the CPU waiting time t_{wait}. In this work, we mainly aim to minimize t_{wait}.

Because of skipping irrelevant blocks using block meta data, the CPU thread may only accesses a proportion $S_{\text{access}}/S_{\text{total}}$ of the coalesced blocks B, where

S_{access} is the total size of coalesced blocks accessed by the CPU and S_{total} is the total size of all coalesced blocks. Define $\ell = S_{\text{total}}/S_{\text{access}}$ and note that $\ell \geq 1$. For this model, we assume every ℓ-th coalesced block is accessed.

We define the *CPU access speed*

$$V_{\text{CPU}} = S_{\text{access}}/(t_{\text{decode}} + t_{\text{operate}}),$$

and the *I/O bandwidth*

$$V_{\text{IO}} = S_B/\text{lat}_B, \tag{2}$$

where S_B is the size of a coalesced block B and lat_B is the read latency of B. Note that the I/O bandwidth only varies with size of B, but not the specific query. Define $k = V_{\text{IO}}/V_{\text{CPU}}$.

Having the previous definitions, we model the CPU waiting time by

$$t_{\text{wait}} = \begin{cases} \text{lat}_B + C_b\gamma & \text{if } \ell \leq k \\ \text{lat}_B + (\ell - k)\text{lat}_B \frac{S_{\text{total}}}{S_B \ell} + C_b\gamma & \text{otherwise,} \end{cases} \tag{3}$$

where C_b is the total number of accessed 128-docID blocks during query processing and γ is the average check time per block.

We justify Eq. (3) as follows. To begin, the CPU thread waits for the I/O thread to read the first coalesced block. Each time the CPU thread accesses a block b (i.e., it decodes b) the CPU thread needs to check the last read position of the I/O thread to determine whether b is available, so there is a check overhead $C_b\gamma$.

If $\ell \leq k$, the I/O thread keeps pace with the CPU thread (i.e., the ideal situation), so the CPU waiting time is as given as $\text{lat}_B + C_b\gamma$. We now treat the case of $\ell > k$. We illustrate this case using a toy example in Fig. 3. During the time the CPU thread takes to process a coalesced block, the I/O thread reads $k < \ell$ coalesced blocks in parallel (noting that k might be less than one, which occurs when the I/O bandwidth V_{IO} is smaller than CPU access speed V_{CPU}). Recall that the CPU thread accesses every ℓ-th coalesced block, so the I/O thread reads $\ell - k$ further coalesced blocks while the CPU thread waits. Thus, prior to accessing the next coalesced block, the CPU thread waits time $(\ell - k)\text{lat}_B$. On average, the CPU thread accesses $S_{\text{total}}/(S_B\ell)$ coalesced blocks, and thus we obtain the result for $\ell > k$.

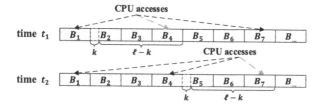

Fig. 3. A toy example illustrating Eq. (3) where the CPU accesses B_4 (top) and later accesses B_7 (bottom) and $\ell = 3$. Shaded coalesced blocks have been read.

Equation (3) indicates that an important parameter for optimization is the coalesced block size S_B. If S_B is small, then we do not benefit as much from the NVM's read bandwidth (around 4 KB, as per Fig. 1). Moreover, a small S_B results in small I/O bandwidth V_{IO} in Eq. (2) and thus small k. However, if S_B is large, then the read latency lat_B increases, accounting for the main part of CPU waiting time, and V_{IO} also peaks (at around 1024 KB, as per Fig. 1).

Section 4.2 experimentally analyzes the effect of various coalesced block sizes S_B and we find that 256 KB is a suitable choice which balances I/O bandwidth and latency. The NVM baseline is equivalent to when the size of B is equal to the size of corresponding posting lists.

We expect that the pipeline approach is also applicable to the scenario that multiple queries are processed concurrently, because if the pipeline is not used, each query can only be processed after all its required data is read from NVM to DRAM, which would cause a long response time (I/O waiting time plus CPU computation time). We regard investigating the impact of multithreading on the proposed pipeline method as future work.

3.1   Optimizations

Although the above basic pipeline overlaps I/O reading with CPU computation, it still encounters some challenges.

1. Posting list length varies greatly, so if the coalesced block size is fixed, unnecessary data may be read in advance, while the data needed by the CPU thread is not read in advance.
2. For computation-heavy queries, the I/O thread finishes before the CPU thread, resulting in an idle I/O thread.
3. We do not need the whole posting lists as we can skip unneeded blocks, but the basic pipeline simply reads all blocks.

There, we try to optimize the pipeline method from these aspects.

Variable Coalesced Block Size. Queries with posting-list length differences exceeding 8 MB account for 22% of the MillionQuery query set using the Gov2 corpus. Consider a short posting list l_1 and a long posting list l_2, both containing docID d. Since l_2 is longer, there tends to be more docIDs preceding d in l_2 than in l_1. Thus with a fixed block size, there tends to be more blocks preceding d need to be read for l_2 than for l_1. Figure 4 illustrates how, for the basic pipeline, this imbalance leads to the I/O thread reading blocks unnecessarily in advance, while the CPU thread is waiting for other blocks.

In Fig. 4, with a fixed coalesced block size S_B, when the CPU thread needs to locate docID d in all posting lists, it waits for the I/O thread to read it into memory. While the CPU thread is waiting, the I/O thread is also reading blocks from l_1 succeeding d. However, these blocks are not usable by the CPU thread until it finishes processing docID d.

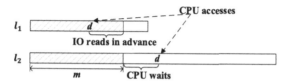

Fig. 4. Basic pipeline: The CPU thread waits to access the docID d while the I/O thread reads coalesced blocks from the short posting list that proceed d. Shaded parts indicate read coalesced blocks.

Assuming docIDs are distributed evenly throughout posting lists, a docID d will occur in the same relative position in a posting list (e.g., at 10% of the length of the posting list) regardless of the length of the posting list (assuming a fixed number of documents). Thus, we investigate assigning larger I/O coalesced block sizes S_B to longer posting lists, so that all lists are read proportionally, thereby prioritizing reading blocks that the CPU thread can actually process.

Data Prefetching. For some queries the I/O thread completes reading while the CPU thread is still computing; this occurs when the I/O read bandwidth is larger than CPU access speed. In this case, when the I/O thread completes one query, it then prefetches the posting list data for the next query instead of idling. This is realistic, with mass user queries there are always to-be-processed queries in queue [2]. Prefetching is performed exploiting the idle time of the I/O thread with two double buffering technology and will stop just after the CPU computation of the current query completes, therefore it does not hurt the processing time of the current query. If the CPU thread ends before I/O thread, prefetching will not not be triggered. Prefetching not only hides the latency of reading first block lat_B in Eq. (3), but also indirectly reduces the CPU waiting time, thereby improving the query efficiency.

Coalesced Block Skipping. Ordinarily in query processing, the CPU uses block skipping (utilizing maximum docID information) and score skipping (utilizing score upper bound information), and thus often does not require the entire posting lists. For Maxscore, on average the access data only accounts for around 50% of the total data when S_B is equal to 256 KB (Gov2 corpus and Million-Query). Thus we reduce the time that the CPU waits for unneeded data by skipping blocks.

Whether a block is accessed is determined by the block access pattern of the user query, and we do not know the access pattern in advance. Therefore, we propose in-process skipping, in which the CPU thread and the I/O thread interact to skip (i.e., forego reading) unneeded coalesced blocks. Specifically, when the CPU thread requires access to an unavailable block in a posting list l, it notifies the I/O thread of the read start position of l. This optimization incurs some communication overhead.

For queries that access a small proportion of the corresponding index data, the benefits of skipping blocks outweigh the communication overhead. In terms of Eq. (3), we wait around for $2 - k$ coalesced blocks to be read instead of $\ell - k$. In preliminary experiments, we find that queries with large differences in posting-list length lead to many skips. To increase the amount of data skipped, we decrease the coalesced block size in experiments (see Sect. 4.4).

4   Experimental Results

We implement the proposed pipeline scheme with the aforementioned optimizations. Motivated by the analytical model proposed in Sect. 3, we optimize the coalesced block size. We explore the effect of pipelining on various query algorithms, integer encodings, and varying the number of recalled documents. We also explore block skipping strategies (Sect. 3.1) for Maxscore; investigate query throughput with various cache sizes; and test the application of the pipeline scheme on traditional SSDs. We verify that the proposed optimized pipeline method achieves a comparable query efficiency for Maxscore, Wand and BMW queries with almost no memory overhead (only several MBs memory buffer).

4.1   Experiment Setup

We conduct the experiments using the public widely used Gov2 (containing 25 million documents) and ClueWeb09B (containing 50 million documents) datasets. We retain the title and body without extra information (e.g. HTML tags) and do not remove any stop words. We reorder the docIDs according to URL. For the query set, we use public queries from the 2007, 2008, and 2009 TREC Million Query tracks (named MillionQuery). In the MillionQuery query set, the terms which do not exist in the Gov2 (resp. ClueWeb) corpus are filtered out and 58,506 (resp. 59,413) queries remain. We do not remove one-term queries.

All experiments are run on a machine equipped with a eighteen-core CPU (Xeon Gold 5220) and 128 GB RAM, running CentOS 7.4 with Linux kernel 3.10.0. All code is written in C++11 and complied using g++ 4.8.5 with the −O3 optimization flag. The NVM device is an Intel Optane SSD 900P with 3D XPoint. For traditional flash-based SSD, we use a 480 GB Intel SATA SSD.

We conduct DAAT RankAnd, Maxscore [18], Wand [3], BlockMaxWand (BMW) [8] which return the top-10 highest scored docIDs using BM25 [16]. On average, each query requires several MBs of index data. We use a block size of 128 docIDs. The block metadata and the upper bound of the scores are stored in memory. Except for Sect. 4.5, for the proposed pipeline methods and the NVM baseline, the inverted indexes are stored on the NVM Optane SSD with only in-memory buffer. We also avoid the impact of system page caching through DirectIO.

4.2 Model Analysis

We analyze the effect of various coalesced block sizes, integer encodings, query algorithms, and the values of K on the proposed pipeline method through the model proposed in Sect. 3. We randomly sample 10% of the queries to estimate the average query execution time of the entire MillionQuery set using Eq. (1). We record the estimated CPU execution time and waiting time and the statistics after query measurement of the entire MillionQuery set. In this section we use the Gov2 corpus with the basic pipeline (see Sect. 3), i.e., without the variable length block size, prefetching, and skip block optimizations.

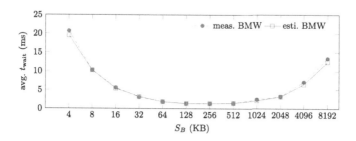

Fig. 5. The estimated and measured CPU waiting time t_{wait} on MillionQuery under various coalesced block size S_B for BMW algorithm.

Coalesced Block Size. We explore the impact of coalesced block size S_B on the basic pipeline. For inverted-index compression we use SIMDNewPfor. Figure 5 plots the estimated average CPU waiting time t_{wait} using Eq. (3) and measured value of the entire query set under various coalesced block sizes for the BlockMaxWand algorithm (other query algorithms are similar).

Observed that the estimated results are coincident with the empirical results, which affirms the accuracy of Eq. (3). We find that an optimal block size of 256 KB, which balances I/O bandwidth V_{IO} and read latency lat_B. In the subsequent experiments in this section, the coalesced block size S_B is set to 256 KB.

Integer Encoding. We investigate various integer encodings with the basic pipeline. Figure 6 plots the measured average query execution time (for BMW queries) vs. the compressed index size. Figure 7 breaks down the measured average query execution time under the five integer encodings where I/O time is the CPU waiting time t_{wait} caused by NVM-to-memory I/O and CPU time is the computation time $t_{\text{decode}} + t_{\text{operate}}$.

Due to byte alignment, VarintG8IU [17] inherits fast decoding of the traditional VByte [7], and using SIMD further accelerates decoding. However, byte alignment compression also leads to a poor compression ratio. Binary interpolative encoding [13] compresses and decompresses recursively, resulting in the best compression ratio but poor decoding efficiency. SIMDNewPfor and SIMDOptP-for [11,22] are optimized versions of PforDelta, offering a trade-off between the

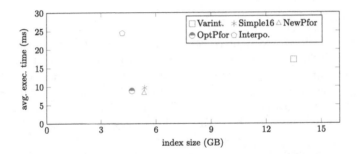

Fig. 6. Measured average query execution time and index size for BMW queries under various integer encodings.

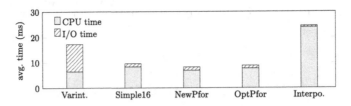

Fig. 7. Break down of the average query execution time for BMW queries under various integer encodings.

two extremes. Simple16 [23] is a word-alignment compression method which aims to densely pack integers into words.

From Eq. (1), vs. maintaining index in memory, the performance loss of the pipeline is concentrated on the CPU wait time t_{wait} which is directly related to the CPU access speed V_{CPU} and the amount of data accessed S_{access}. The pipeline most benefits algorithms for which the CPU accesses data at a slower speed (k in Eq. (3) is larger).

For VarintG8IU, the huge index and faster decoding leads to insufficient I/O bandwidth to match the CPU access speed. For binary interpolative encoding, the CPU accesses data slowly leading to minor CPU waiting time, and query efficiency is hindered by decoding time. Simple16, SIMDNewPfor and SIMDOptPfor strike a balance between decoding time and CPU waiting time. Thus, subsequent experiments are performed using SIMDNewPfor for compression. Compared with NVM baseline (see Fig. 2), even basic pipeline significantly decreases the CPU waiting time.

Query Algorithm. We focus on the effects on the pipeline of various query algorithms. Figure 8 plots the average CPU waiting times (measured and estimated), for BlockMaxWand, Wand, Maxscore, and RankAnd queries.

We observe that pipelining results in the smallest CPU waiting times for Wand and BlockMaxWand, while the greatest is for RankAnd. The analysis in Sect. 4.2 indicates pipelining most benefits the query algorithm with the slower

CPU access speed. From Fig. 2, we observe that the RankAnd computation times are shorter, while Wand and BlockMaxWand computation times are longer. For Maxscore the CPU only accesses around 50% of the corresponding index, while V_{CPU} is slightly slower than Wand, the greater ℓ leads to a slightly longer CPU waiting time than Wand.

Number of Recalled Documents. We explore varying the number of recalled documents (top-K) on basic pipeline method. Figure 9 plots average CPU waiting time t_{wait} for BMW queries under various values of K (we also plot average t_{wait} of NVM baseline described in Sect. 1). We observe that larger K leads to smaller CPU waiting time, since as K increases, the CPU takes more calculations (smaller V_{CPU}) and accesses more data (larger S_{access}) which results in shorter CPU waiting time, as per Eq. (3). We observe that basic pipeline always outperforms NVM baseline. Subsequent experiments are performed with top-10. (Note that larger K leads to better pipelining performance while it has no effect on NVM baseline.)

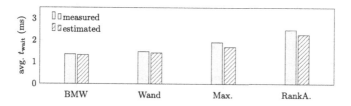

Fig. 8. The estimated and measured CPU waiting time t_{wait} for BMW, Wand, Maxscore and RankAnd queries.

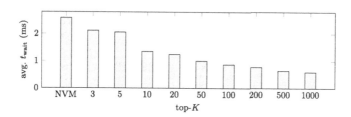

Fig. 9. The measured CPU waiting time t_{wait} for BMW queries under various top-K.

4.3   Pipelining and Optimizations

In this section we test pipelining and optimizations (using SIMDNewPfor for compression). We compare the following setups.

1. DRAM-based scheme (DRAM): The inverted index resides in memory.
2. NVM baseline (NVM): The naive NVM scheme described in Sect. 1.

3. Pipeline256 (P256): The basic pipeline described in Sect. 3 where S_B is set to 256 KB.
4. PVari.: Variable coalesced block size optimization described in Sect. 3.1. We segment the posting-list length into four buckets: less than 500 KB, from 500 KB to 1000 KB, from 1000 KB to 2000 KB, and greater than 2000 KB. For these buckets, the coalesced block size S_B is respectively set to 64 KB, 128 KB, 256 KB, and 512 KB.
5. PPref.: PVari. with the prefetching optimization described in Sect. 3.1.

Table 1 lists the query throughput (no. of queries completed per second) of the above methods on Gov2 and ClueWeb corpuses with top-10. The DRAM-based scheme gives an upper bound on the throughput, and ideally the pipeline method achieves a throughput close to the DRAM throughput.

We can see that the variable coalesced block size optimization increases throughput by up to 6%, while data prefetching further increases throughput by up to 15% which indicates some wastefulness of the I/O thread in the basic pipeline. The optimized pipeline (PPref.) only suffers a throughput degradation (vs. DRAM) less than 6% with Wand and BMW (up to 14% with Maxscore), which is the expense of reducing memory requirements by 5.4 GB for Gov2 and 20 GB for ClueWeb. Compared with the NVM baseline, the optimized pipeline saves up to 87% (from 2.58 ms to 0.34 ms) and 93% (from 7.71 ms to 0.56 ms) CPU waiting time per query on the Gov2 and ClueWeb corpuses respectively (omitted from Table 1).

We also test top-100 queries for comparison. Compared the DRAM baseline, the optimized pipeline decreases throughput by less than 3% with Wand and BMW. (Varying top-K has no effect on RankAnd; it scores all intersection documents regardless of K.) Compared with the NVM baseline, pipelining saves up to 98% CPU waiting time, further verifying the pipeline efficiency for larger top-K.

Table 1. Query throughput of the proposed pipeline with various optimizations on the Gov2 and ClueWeb corpuses.

	DRAM	NVM	P256	PVari.	PPref.
Gov2 corpus					
BMW	144.61	105.30	120.95	125.66	137.75
Wand	114.21	87.07	97.72	100.56	107.41
Maxscore	158.81	111.13	121.93	125.65	136.07
RankAnd	220.91	139.30	142.84	151.06	172.38
ClueWeb corpus					
BMW	45.09	33.46	38.35	39.72	43.99
Wand	33.12	26.25	29.08	29.72	31.97
Maxscore	41.29	31.14	34.43	35.28	38.48
RankAnd	56.08	38.36	39.10	41.23	47.43

4.4 Skipping Unnecessary Blocks

For Maxscore queries with a small amount of data S_{access} accessed by the CPU, we propose skipping blocks to avoid unnecessary reads during computation. Since skipping introduces a communication overhead, we apply skipping only for queries with posting-list length differences exceeding 8MB. To increase the amount of skipped data, for these queries, we reduce the variable coalesced block size to the range 8 KB to 64 KB, rather than 64 KB to 512 KB.

Table 2 records the average CPU execution time without including the prefetching time in the previous query, for the Gov2 and ClueWeb corpuses according to the number of terms contained in the query. We observe that the skipping optimization has a positive effect on the Maxscore algorithm especially for long queries (up to 12% improvement). The query efficiency is almost identical to the DRAM baseline on ClueWeb corpus while the whole index is maintained on NVM instead of in DRAM. The skipping optimization reduces unnecessary data reads, and the prefetch optimization hides the first block reading latency.

Table 2. Average CPU execution time (ms) of MillionQuery for various query lengths on the Gov2 and ClueWeb corpuses (Maxscore top-10 queries).

| | Number of query terms |||||| avg. |
	1	2	3	4	5	6_+	
Gov2 PPref.	3.7	4.0	6.0	8.6	11.3	18.4	7.3
Gov2 PSkip	3.7	3.8	5.5	7.7	10.0	16.3	6.7
Clue. PPref.	12.0	17.2	24.0	30.7	37.1	55.3	26.0
Clue. PSkip	11.9	16.1	22.3	28.7	34.5	51.2	24.3

4.5 Cache Size

In this section, we explore the impact of static cache on the proposed pipeline. Specifically, we cache the longest inverted lists [6] and occupy the amount of memory to use for the cache.

Figure 10 plots the optimized pipeline (PPref.) and NVM baseline throughput for various cache sizes for RankAnd queries on Gov2 corpus (this is the "most challenging case" because the other query algorithms have at most 6% throughput degradation using PPref. or PSkip even without caching). We observe that as the size of the cache increases, the throughput of the pipeline and the NVM baseline increases sharply first and then stabilizes. The pipeline method always outperforms the NVM baseline. Although the pipeline method uses 2% of the memory space of the DRAM-based scheme, we are able to achieve comparable throughput (within 6%) for RankAnd queries. The experimental results on the ClueWeb corpus are not substantially different (only needing 3% of the memory space).

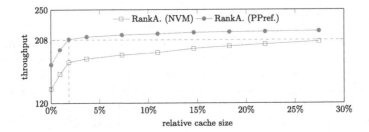

Fig. 10. Query throughput of NVM base and optimized pipeline using various relative cache sizes for RankAnd top-10 queries. We also indicate 94% throughput of the DRAM baseline using dashed lines. Note the y axis does not start at 0.

4.6   Traditional SSD

In this section, we apply the pipeline method (PPref.) to traditional SSDs. For the Gov2 corpus, when applying pipelining to the traditional SSD, the CPU thread wastes on average 14 ms per query for BMW, while in comparison NVM just uses 0.4 ms. The query efficiency on the traditional SSD is far worse than on NVM. As per Fig. 1, because of the low read bandwidth and high read latency of traditional SSDs, the I/O bandwidth is outpaced by the CPU access speed which leads to CPU always waiting for the I/O thread (as per Eq. 3). Thus, we consider the proposed pipeline method to be better suited to fast storage devices. We learn that there are some fast NVMe SSDs and flash based SSDs which have similar read performance with NVM Optane SSDs. We expect that the proposed pipeline method will have positive effects on such fast devices.

5   Conclusion

This paper focuses on migrating the search-engine inverted index from memory to NVM Optane SSD, thereby reducing the memory storage overhead at the cost of introducing NVM-to-memory I/O. To diminish the I/O costs, we propose a pipeline query process, along with various optimizations, whereby I/O occurs in parallel with CPU computation. We also model the query efficiency for further analysis. Experimental results show that pipelining reduces up to 90% of the time lost due to using the NVM. Compared with query processing where the index is maintained in memory, the storage cost is significantly reduced, and for the Maxscore, Wand, and BlockMaxWand query algorithms, the degradation of query throughput is small (within 6%).

In the future, it would be interesting to explore: (a) designing a cache strategy tailored to the pipeline method; (b) better utilizing the idle resources when the CPU waits for I/O; and (c) investigating the impact of multithreading on the pipeline method.

References

1. Anh, V.N., Moffat, A.: Index compression using 64-bit words. Softw. Pract. Exp. **40**(2), 131–147 (2010)
2. Ao, N., et al.: Efficient parallel lists intersection and index compression algorithms using graphics processing units. PVLDB **4**(8), 470–481 (2011)
3. Broder, A.Z., Carmel, D., Herscovici, M., Soffer, A., Zien, J.Y.: Efficient query evaluation using a two-level retrieval process. In: Proceedings of CIKM. pp. 426–434 (2003)
4. Büttcher, S., Clarke, C.L.A., Cormack, G.V.: Information Retrieval-Implementing and Evaluating Search Engines. MIT Press, Cambridge (2010)
5. Cambazoglu, B.B., Baeza-Yates, R.A.: Scalability challenges in web search engines. Synth. Lect. Inf. Concepts Retr. Serv. **7**, 1–138 (2015)
6. Cambazoglu, B.B., Kayaaslan, E., Jonassen, S., Aykanat, C.: A term-based inverted index partitioning model for efficient distributed query processing. TWEB **7**(3), 15:1–15:23 (2013)
7. Cutting, D.R., Pedersen, J.O.: Optimizations for dynamic inverted index maintenance. In: Proceedings of SIGIR, pp. 405–411 (1990)
8. Ding, S., Suel, T.: Faster top-k document retrieval using block-max indexes. In: Proceedings of SIGIR, pp. 993–1002 (2011)
9. Eisenman, A., et al.: Reducing DRAM footprint with NVM in Facebook. In: Proceedings of EuroSys, pp. 42:1–42:13 (2018)
10. Eisenman, A., et al.: Bandana: using non-volatile memory for storing deep learning models. CoRR arxiv:1811.05922 (2018)
11. Lemire, D., Boytsov, L.: Decoding billions of integers per second through vectorization. Softw. Pract. Exp. **45**(1), 1–29 (2015)
12. Liu, X., Peng, Z.: An efficient random access inverted index for information retrieval. In: Proceedings of WWW, pp. 1153–1154 (2010)
13. Moffat, A., Stuiver, L.: Binary interpolative coding for effective index compression. Inf. Retr. **3**(1), 25–47 (2000)
14. Ottaviano, G., Tonellotto, N., Venturini, R.: Optimal space-time tradeoffs for inverted indexes. In: Proceedings of WSDM, pp. 47–56 (2015)
15. Risvik, K.M., Chilimbi, T.M., Tan, H., Kalyanaraman, K., Anderson, C.: Maguro, a system for indexing and searching over very large text collections. In: Proceedings of WSDM, pp. 727–736 (2013)
16. Robertson, S.E., Jones, K.S.: Relevance weighting of search terms. JASIS **27**(3), 129–146 (1976)
17. Stepanov, A.A., Gangolli, A.R., Rose, D.E., Ernst, R.J., Oberoi, P.S.: SIMD-based decoding of posting lists. In: Proceedings of CIKM, pp. 317–326 (2011)
18. Turtle, H.R., Flood, J.: Query evaluation: strategies and optimizations. Inf. Process. Manag. **31**(6), 831–850 (1995)
19. Wang, J., Lo, E., Yiu, M.L., Tong, J., Wang, G., Liu, X.: The impact of solid state drive on search engine cache management. In: Proceedings of SIGIR, pp. 693–702 (2013)
20. Xia, F., Jiang, D., Xiong, J., Sun, N.: HIKV: a hybrid index key-value store for DRAM-NVM memory systems. In: Proceedings of USENIX, pp. 349–362 (2017)
21. Xu, J., Swanson, S.: NOVA: a log-structured file system for hybrid volatile/non-volatile main memories. In: Proceedings of FAST, pp. 323–338 (2016)
22. Yan, H., Ding, S., Suel, T.: Inverted index compression and query processing with optimized document ordering. In: Proceedings of WWW, pp. 401–410 (2009)

23. Zhang, J., Long, X., Suel, T.: Performance of compressed inverted list caching in search engines. In: Proceedings of WWW, pp. 387–396 (2008)
24. Zhang, R., Sun, P., Tong, J., Stones, R.J., Wang, G., Liu, X.: Compact snippet caching for flash-based search engines. In: Proceedings of SIGIR, pp. 1015–1018 (2015)
25. Zukowski, M., Héman, S., Nes, N., Boncz, P.A.: Super-scalar RAM-CPU cache compression. In: Proceedings of ICDE (2006)

Sorting-Based Interactive Regret Minimization

Jiping Zheng$^{(\boxtimes)}$ (iD) and Chen Chen

College of Computer Science and Technology,
Nanjing University of Aeronautics and Astronautics,
Nanjing, China
{jzh,duplicc}@nuaa.edu.cn

Abstract. As an important tool for multi-criteria decision making in database systems, the regret minimization query is shown to have the merits of top-k and skyline queries: it controls the output size while does not need users to provide any preferences. Existing researches verify that the regret ratio can be much decreased when interaction is available. In this paper, we study how to enhance current interactive regret minimization query by sorting mechanism. Instead of selecting the most favorite point from the displayed points for each interaction round, users sort the displayed data points and send the results to the system. By introducing sorting mechanism, for each round of interaction the utility space explored will be shrunk to some extent. Further the candidate points selection for following rounds of interaction will be narrowed to smaller data spaces thus the number of interaction rounds will be reduced. We propose two effective sorting-based algorithms namely Sorting-Simplex and Sorting-Random to find the maximum utility point based on Simplex method and randomly selection strategy respectively. Experiments on synthetic and real datasets verify our Sorting-Simplex and Sorting-Random algorithms outperform current state-of-art ones.

Keywords: Regret minimization query · Utility hyperplane · Conical hull frame · Skyline query · Top-k query

1 Introduction

To select a small subset to represent the whole dataset is an important functionality for multi-criteria decision making in database systems. Top-k [11], skyline [3,7] and regret minimization queries [14–16,20,21] are three important tools which were fully explored in the last two decades. Given a *utility* (*preference* or *score* are another two concepts interchangeably used in the literature) function, top-k queries need users to specify their utility functions and return the best k points with the highest utilities. Skyline queries output the points which are not dominated by any other points in the database. Here, domination means two points are comparable. A point p is said to dominate another point q if p is not worse than q in each dimension and p is better than q in at least one dimension.

© Springer Nature Switzerland AG 2020
X. Wang et al. (Eds.): APWeb-WAIM 2020, LNCS 12318, pp. 473–490, 2020.
https://doi.org/10.1007/978-3-030-60290-1_36

However, both queries suffer from their inherent drawbacks. For skyline queries, the results cannot be foreseen before the whole database is accessed. In addition, the output size of skyline queries will increase rapidly with the dimensionality. Top-k queries ask users to specify their utility functions, but the user may not be able to clearly know what weight each attribute should be, which brings a big challenge to top-k queries. Regret minimization queries return a subset of data points from the database under a required size k that minimizes the maximum regret ratio across all possible utility functions. Here regret ratio of a subset is defined as the relative difference in utilities between the top-1 point in the subset and the top-1 point in the entire database.

The regret minimization query has the merits of both top-k and skyline queries, *i.e.*, the output size (k) can be controlled while it does not need users to specify the utility functions. Moreover, it has been verified that small regret ratio can be achieved by presenting only a few tuples [15]. For example, when there are 2 criteria (dimensions/attributes), 10 points are presented to guarantee a maximum regret ratio of 10% in the worst case, and the same number of points still make the maximum regret ratio below 35% for 10 criteria. But the regret ratios shown above cannot make users satisfied. If we want to achieve 1% maximum regret ratio with 10 criteria, we have to show about 1,000 points to the user [15]. Fortunately, it has shown that interaction is much helpful to reduce the user's regret ratio [14,21]. In [14,21], the interaction worked as follows which requires little user effort. When presenting a screen of points, the user chooses his/her favorite point. Based on the user's choice, the system modifies the simulated user's utility function and shows another screen of points for next round of interaction until the user has no regret in front of the displayed points or the regret ratio of the user is below a small threshold ϵ. The aim of each interaction round is to approach the user's true utility function which he/she cannot specify. However, the main drawback of existing methods [14,21] is that they need too many rounds of interaction to achieve a low regret ratio. For example, for a 4-dimensional anti-correlated dataset with 10,000 points generated by the data generator [3], the method proposed in [14] needs 21 rounds of interaction when displaying 5 points a time to achieve 0.1% regret ratio. For the algorithms proposed in [21], 9 rounds of interaction are needed when displaying 4 points a time to find the user's favorite point. Too many interaction rounds of the existing methods take too much effort of the user. In this paper, we propose sorting-based interaction mechanism to reduce the rounds of users' interaction. Instead of pointing out the favorite point among the displayed points at each interaction, the user sorts the displayed points according to his/her utility function. As we know that for s data points, the time complexity of choosing the best point is $O(s)$ while the time complexity of sorting s data points is $O(s \log_2 s)$ on average and $O(s)$ in the best case. If s is small, that is, only displaying several points, the time complexities of finding the maximum utility point and sorting have little difference. Thus sorting the displayed points does not increase user's effort. Also, when a user points out the best point, at the same time he/she has browsed all the points which makes him/her easily sort these points, especially in front of only several points. By sorting, our proposed method will need few rounds of interaction because our sorting mechanism can help to shrink the utility function space rapidly. Following is an example to show the pruning power of our sorting-based interactive regret minimization method. Suppose there are 3 points $p_1(10, 1)$, $p_2(9, 2)$ and $p_3(8, 5)$ displayed to the user and the utility space is composed by three utility functions $\{f_1, f_2, f_3\}$ as shown in Table 1. The utility is the inner product of point p and utility function f, e.g., $f_1(p_1) = 10 \times 0.8 + 1 \times 0.2 = 8.2$. Without sorting, when the user points out p_1 is his/her favorite point, utility function f_3 will not be considered because $f_3(p_3) > f_3(p_1) > f_3(p_2)$ and f_1, f_2 are both possible user's utility functions. If the user sorts the 3 points with $p_1 > p_2 > p_3$, utility functions f_2, f_3 are pruned (f_2 is pruned because $f_2(p_1) > f_2(p_3) > f_2(p_2)$). We can see that our sorting based method can faster approach user's actual utility function with fewer rounds of interaction.

Table 1. Utilities for different utility functions of three points p_1, p_2 and p_3

p	A_1	A_2	$f_1(p)$ $f_1 = <0.8, 0.2>$	$f_2(p)$ $f_2 = <0.7, 0.3>$	$f_3(p)$ $f_3 = <0.6, 0.4>$
p_1	10	1	8.2	7.3	6.4
p_2	9	2	7.6	6.9	6.2
p_3	8	5	7.4	7.1	6.8

In summary, the main contributions of this paper are listed as follows.

- We propose a sorting-based pruning strategy, which can shrink user's utility space more quickly than existing interactive regret minimization algorithms.
- Based on the utility space after pruning, we prune the candidate set by utility hyperplanes to ensure that the displayed points in the next round of interaction are more reasonable and close to the user's favorite point. Two sorting-based interactive regret minimization algorithms, namely Sorting-Random and Sorting-Simplex are proposed based on random and Simplex strategies respectively for displayed points selection.
- Extensive experiments on both synthetic and real datasets are conducted to verify efficiency and effectiveness of our sorting-based algorithms which outperform the existing interactive regret minimization algorithms.

Roadmap. Related work is described in Sect. 2. We provide some basic concepts of the regret minimization query as well as some geometric concepts and our interactive framework in Sect. 3. Our sorting-based technique is introduced in Sect. 4. In Sect. 4, the utility function space pruning strategies via sorting as well as the candidate points selection are detailed. Experimental results on synthetic and real datasets are reported in Sect. 5. Section 6 concludes this paper.

2   Related Work

Top-k [11] and skyline [3,7] queries are two popular tools for multi-criteria decision making in database systems. However, top-k query requires users to specify their utility functions and it is usually difficult for users to specify their utility functions precisely while skyline query has a potential large output problem which may make users feel overwhelmed. There are several efforts to control skyline output size, such as k-dominant skyline queries [5], threshold-based preferences [8], top-k representative skyline [13], distance-based representative skyline [19] etc. To bridge the gap of top-k query for specifying accurate utility functions and skyline query for outputting too many results, regret-based k representative query which was proposed by Nanongkai et al. [15] tries to output a specified size $e.g.$, k while minimizing user's maximum regret ratio.

Following researches are along with the regret minimization query [15] from various aspects. Peng et al. [16] introduce the concept of $happy\ points$ in which the final k points included to speed up the query process. Approximate solutions in polynomial time with any user-specified accurate thresholds are proposed in [1,2] or with asymptotically optimal regret ratio in [22]. [14,21] investigate how interaction is helpful to decrease users' regret ratios. Chester et al. [6] relax regret minimization queries from top-1 regret minimization set to top-k minimization set which they call k-RMS query. Further, coreset based algorithms [1,4,12] or hitting set based algorithms [1,12] are developed to solve the k-RMS problem efficiently and effectively. Faulkner et al. [10] and Qi et al. [17] extend linear utility functions used in [14–16,21,22] to CONVEX, CONCAVE and CES utility functions and multiplicative utility functions respectively for k-regret queries. Zeighami and Wong [24] propose the metric of average regret ratio to measure user's satisfaction against output results and further develop efficient algorithms to solve it [23].

From the variants of the regret minimization query listed above, the most related to our research is [14] and [21]. Nanongkai et al. [14] first enhance traditional regret minimization sets by user interaction. At each round of interaction, the user is presented a screen of artificial data points which have the great possibility to attract user's attentions for next interaction. Then the system asks the user to choose his/her favorite point. Based on the user's choice, the system learns user's utility function implicitly. With limited number of interaction rounds, the user may find his/her favorite point or the point within a specified small regret ratio. Xie et al. [21] argue that displaying fake points to users [14] makes users disappointed for they are not indeed inside the database. Also the number of interaction rounds for the proposed method in [14] is a little large. In this paper, we follow the paradigm of interactive regret minimization. Instead of pointing out the most favorite point at each round of interaction, we sort the displayed data points and fully exploit the pairwise relationship among displayed points of each interaction to narrow the utility space. Thus our proposed sorting-based interactive regret minimization which needs much less rounds of interaction than existing approaches [14,21].

3   Preliminaries

Before we give our interaction framework (Sect. 3.3), we first introduce some basic concepts for the regret minimization query (Sect. 3.1). Then useful geometric concepts such as boundary points, convex hull and conical hull frame etc. are listed in Sect. 3.2.

3.1   Regret Minimization Query

Let D be a set of n d-dimensional points over positive real values. For each point $p \in D$, the value on the ith dimension is represented as $p[i]$. Related concepts of the regret minimization query are formally introduced as follows [15].

Utility Function. A user utility function f is a mapping $f \colon \mathbb{R}_+^d \to \mathbb{R}_+$. Given a utility function f, the utility of a data point p is denoted as $f(p)$, which shows how satisfied the user is with the data point p.

Obviously, there are many kinds of utility functions, such as convex, concave, constant elasticity of substitution (CES) [10] and multiplicative [17] etc. In this paper, we focus on linear utility functions which are very popular to model users' preferences [14–16,21,22].

Linear Utility Function. Assume there are some nonnegative real values $\{v_1, v_2, \cdots, v_d\}$, where v_i denotes the user's preference for the ith dimension. Then a linear utility function can be represented by these nonnegative reals and $f(p) = \sum_{i=1}^{d} v_i \cdot p[i]$. A linear utility function can also be expressed by a vector[1], i.e., $v = <v_1, v_2, ..., v_d>$, so the utility of point p can be expressed by the dot product of v and p, i.e., $f(p) = v \cdot p$.

Regret Ratio. Given a dataset D, a subset S of D and a linear utility function f, the regret ratio of S, represented by $rr_D(S, f)$, is defined as

$$rr_D(S, f) = 1 - \frac{\max_{p \in S} f(p)}{\max_{p \in D} f(p)}$$

Since S is a subset of D, given a utility function f, it is obvious that $\max_{p \in S} f(p) \leq \max_{p \in D} f(p)$ and the $rr_D(S, f)$ falls in the range $[0, 1]$. The user along with utility function f will be satisfied if the regret ratio approaches 0 because the maximum utility of S is close to the maximum utility of D.

Maximum Regret Ratio. Given a dataset D, a subset S of D and a class of utility functions $\mathcal{F}$. The maximum regret ratio of S, represented by $rr_D(S, \mathcal{F})$, is defined as

$$rr_D(S, \mathcal{F}) = \sup_{f \in \mathcal{F}} rr_D(S, f) = \sup_{f \in \mathcal{F}} \left(1 - \frac{\max_{p \in S} f(p)}{\max_{p \in D} f(p)} \right)$$

To better understand above concepts, we present a concrete car-selling example for illustration. Consider a car database containing 5 cars with two attributes

---

[1] In the following, we use utility function and utility vector interchangeably.

namely miles per gallon (MPG) and horse power (HP) whose values are normalized as shown in Table 2. Let a linear utility function $f = <0.7, 0.3>$. The utilities of 5 cars under the utility function f are shown in the 4th column of Table 2. We can see that the point with the maximum utility 0.69 is p_5. If we select p_2, p_4 as the result set, that is, $S = \{p_2, p_4\}$, we can obtain the regret ratio $rr_D(S, f) = 1 - \frac{\max_{p \in S} f(p)}{\max_{p \in D} f(p)} = 1 - \frac{0.61}{0.69} = 11.6\%$.

Table 2. Car database and the utilities under f

Car	MPG	HP	$f(p)$
p_1	0.4	0.8	0.52
p_2	0.6	0.5	0.57
p_3	0.3	0.6	0.39
p_4	0.7	0.4	0.61
p_5	0.9	0.2	0.69

3.2 Geometric Concepts for Interactive Regret Minimization

Similar to [21], interesting geometric properties can be exploited to prune the utility space and compute the maximum regret ratio of a given subset more easily. Before we define our problem, we provide useful geometric concepts for our interactive regret minimization.

Boundary Point. Given a d-dimensional dataset D of n points, a point $p \in D$ is said to be an ith ($i \in [1, d]$) dimension boundary point of D if $p[i]$ is the largest value among all points in D in ith dimension. Consider our example in Fig. 1 showing a set D of 7 data points, namely $p_1, p_2, \ldots, p_7$ in a 2-dimensional space with two dimensions A_1, A_2. We can see that p_5, p_1 are the boundary points corresponding to A_1, A_2 respectively. When the values of all the points in each dimension are normalized to $[0, 1]$ and let $b_i[j] = 1$ if $j = i$, and $b_i[j] = 0$ if $j \neq i$ where $i, j = 1, ..., d$, we say that b_is are boundary points of $D \cup \{b_1, b_2, ..., b_d\}$. Next important geometric concept is convex hull in which points have great possibility to be included in the result set of the regret minimization query [2, 16].

Convex Hull. In geometry, the convex hull of D, denoted by $Conv(D)$, is the smallest convex set containing D. A point p in D is a vertex of $Conv(D)$ if $p \notin Conv(D/\{p\})$. In 2-dimensional space, let $O = (0, 0)$ be the origin and b_1, b_2 are two boundary points of $D \cup \{b_1, b_2\}$. Figure 1 shows the convex hull of points set $D \cup \{b_1, b_2, O\}$, denoted as $Conv(D \cup \{b_1, b_2, O\})$. Note that for any linear utility function, the point in D with the maximum utility must be a vertex of $Conv(D \cup \{b_1, b_2, O\})$. Here, we say a point in $Conv(D \cup \{b_1, b_2, O\})$ to be a vertex of the hull.

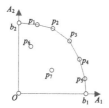

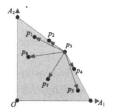

Fig. 1. Convex hull with boundary points

Fig. 2. Conical hull

Although the maximum utility point for each linear utility function lies in the convex hull of $D \cup \{b_1, b_2, O\}$, investigating each point in the convex hull to find the point with maximum utility is too time-consuming because the number of points in a convex hull is usually very large. Even in 2-dimensional case, the convex hull can be as large as $O(n^{1/3})$ and for a database with 5 dimensions, the convex hull can often be as large as $O(n)$ [2]. Thus instead of the convex hull, the concept of conical hull frame [9] helps to find a small subset of the convex hull for the maximum utility point investigation. Following are three geometric concepts to find this kind of subset.

Conical Hull. Given a vertex p in $Conv(D)$, we let vector set $V = \{q - p | \forall q \in D/\{p\}\}$. The conical hull of a point p w.r.t. V is defined to be $C_{p,V} = \{q \in \mathbb{R}^d | (q - p) = \sum_{v_i \in V} w_i \cdot v_i\}$ where $w_i \geqslant 0$ [9] and the conical hull $C_{p,V}$ is also a convex cone with apex p [18]. Figure 2 shows an example of a conical hull in 2-dimensional space. In Fig. 2, the conical hull of point p_3 is $\{p_2 - p_3, p_1 - p_3, p_6 - p_3, p_7 - p_3, p_5 - p_3, p_4 - p_3\}$ which is the shaded region in Fig. 2.

Conical Hull Frame. A set $V_F \subseteq V$ is defined to be a conical hull frame of a vector set V if V_F w.r.t. a point p is the minimal subset of V such that V_F and V have the same conical hull of p, i.e., $C_{p,V} = C_{p,V_F}$. It is obvious that for each vector $v \in V_F$, we have $v \notin C_{p,V/\{v\}}$. In Fig. 2, for point p_3 and vector set $V = \{p_i - p_3 | \forall p_i \in D/\{p_3\}\}$, the conical hull frame of V w.r.t. p_3 is $V_F = \{p_2 - p_3, p_4 - p_3\}$ which is the frame of V since it is the minimal subset of V such that $C_{p_3,V} = C_{p_3,V_F}$.

Neighbouring Vertex. As the name suggests, the neighbouring vertex set N_p of a point p is composed of the neighbors of p in the convex hull. For the example in Fig. 2, the neighbouring vertexes of p_3 in $Conv(D)$ are p_2 and p_4. For a utility function f and a point $p \in Conv(D)$, either p is the maximum utility point to f or there exists a vertex in N_p whose utility is larger than that of p [21]. Based on this, if p is not the maximum utility point, we can find a better one in N_p. Intuitively, N_p can be selected after the computation of the whole convex hull. As mentioned above, computing the whole convex hull is time-consuming. Fortunately, [21] shows that the conical hull frame of V is close to N_p, i.e., $q \in N_p$ if and only if $q - p \in V_F$ which makes it efficient to be calculated.

3.3   Sorting-Based Interaction

Our sorting-based interaction framework works as follows. Initially, the system interacts with a user *w.r.t.* an unknown utility function, displaying s points for the user to sort. We restrict s to be a small integer not bigger than 10 to alleviate the burden of sorting. After the user's feedback, *i.e.*, returning the sorting list to the system, we shrink the utility space which the user's utility function may be in and prune the non-maximum utility points in the candidate set. After certain rounds of interaction like this, the system returns a point with the regret ratio below a predefined value ϵ. Here, ϵ ranges from 0% to 100%. If $\epsilon = 0$, it means that the user has no regret on the point returned by the system.

The main problem is the rounds of the user's interaction needed for our interaction framework. Comparing to the existing methods which only select the favorite point at each interaction round, by introducing sorting mechanism we can fully exploit the information the user has provided and quickly find the favorite point in the database D. Next section we show how sorting can help to reduce rounds of interaction for regret minimization queries.

4   Sorting-Based Interaction for Regret Minimization Queries

In this section, we first illustrate sorting is helpful to shrink the utility space which the user's unknown utility function falls in. Then, we provide the strategies to select the points for next round of interaction.

4.1   Utility Space Shrinking via Sorting

In each iteration, when the displayed s points are sorted and returned to the system, the system will shrink the utility function space $\mathcal{F}$ to some extent. We first define the concept of utility hyperplane then illustrate our utility space pruning procedure. Given two points p and q, we define a utility hyperplane, denoted by $h_{p,q}$, to be the hyperplane passing through the origin O with its normal in the same direction as $p - q$. The hyperplane $h_{p,q}$ partitions the space $\mathbb{R}^d$ into two halves. The half space above $h_{p,q}$ is denoted by $h_{p,q}^+$ and the half space below $h_{p,q}$ is denoted by $h_{p,q}^-$. The following lemma from [21] shows how we can shrink $\mathcal{F}$ to be a smaller space based on utility hyperplane.

Lemma 1. *Given utility space $\mathcal{F}$ and two points p and q, if a user prefers p to q, the user's utility function f must be in $h_{p,q}^+ \bigcap \mathcal{F}$.*

We can find that the half space $h_{p,q}^+$ represents the range of all possible utility functions for p is prior to q. For example in Fig. 3, the system presents three points in 3-dimensional space to the user, $p = (\frac{1}{2}, 0, \frac{1}{2})$, $q = (0, \frac{1}{2}, \frac{1}{2})$ and $r = (\frac{1}{2}, \frac{1}{2}, 0)$, the user sorts p, q, r based on his/her unknown utility function. The region of $\triangle ABC$ represents all possible values of utility functions, $\sum_{i=1}^{d} f[i] = 1$. Sorting information can be fully exploited as follows.

- According to $f(p) > f(q)$, the utility hyperplane $Om_1n_1p_1$ (the blue rectangle in Fig. 3(a)) is constructed. The part where the hyperplane intersects with the $\triangle ABC$ is a straight line Ar, where the region of $\triangle ABr$ contains all possible utility functions that satisfy $f(p) > f(q)$, and the region of $\triangle ACr$ contains all possible utility functions that satisfy $f(p) < f(q)$. So the utility space $\triangle ABr$ is reserved.
- For $f(p) > f(r)$ and $f(r) > f(q)$, similar to the above analysis, only the regions of $\triangle ABq$ and $\triangle BCp$ are reserved.

After this interaction round, the utility space $\mathcal{F}$ containing the user's utility function shrinks from $\triangle ABC$ to $\triangle Bpt = \triangle ABC \cap \triangle ABr \cap \triangle ABq \cap \triangle BCp$ (Fig. 4(a)). As a contrast, if only selecting the favorite point p at this round, i.e., without (WO) sorting, it implies $f(p) > f(q)$ and $f(p) > f(r)$, the utility space only shrinks from $\triangle ABC$ to $\triangle AtB = \triangle ABC \cap \triangle ABr \cap \triangle ABq$ as Fig. 4(b) shows. It is obvious that the shrunk utility space $\mathcal{F}_{sorting}$ belongs to the shrunk utility space $\mathcal{F}_{nosorting}$ without sorting, i.e., $\mathcal{F}_{sorting} \subseteq \mathcal{F}_{nosorting}$. The idea shown here can be naturally extended to high dimensional data space, thus our sorting-based interactive regret minimization is superior to existing methods [14,21].

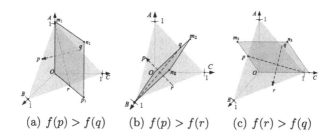

(a) $f(p) > f(q)$ (b) $f(p) > f(r)$ (c) $f(r) > f(q)$

Fig. 3. Utility space shrinking via sorting (Color figure online)

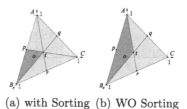

(a) with Sorting (b) WO Sorting

Fig. 4. Shrunk utility space

When the system gets the feedback from the user, it prepares to select specified s points presenting to the user for next round of interaction. Since the utility space has been shrunk to a smaller space, correspondingly, the candidate set for selecting points displayed to the user will also be reduced. In the literature, the skyline of the dataset D is initially regarded as the candidate set C. We provide a strategy named utility hyperplane based candidate set pruning to reduce the size of the candidate set C by removing non-maximum utility points in C. From Lemma 1, if a utility function f falls in $h_{p,q}^+ \bigcap \mathcal{F}$, we can say that the user prefers p to q. That is, we can safely prune q if there is a p in C when f is the user's utility function from $h_{p,q}^+ \bigcap \mathcal{F}$. We summarize utility hyperplane based candidate set pruning by Lemma 2.

Lemma 2. *Given the utility space $\mathcal{F}$, a point q can be pruned from C if there exists a point p in C such that $h_{q,p}^+ \bigcap \mathcal{F} = \phi$.*

4.2 Displayed Points Selection

There are two strategies to select s points from C presenting to the user, namely *random* and *Simplex*. The idea of random strategy is to randomly select s points from the candidate set C to the user. The Simplex approach, based on the conical hull frame, according to the user's favorite point p in the previous interaction round, uses Simplex method to pick neighbouring points of p in the convex hull and displays them to the user. The idea of the Simplex strategy is borrowed from the Simplex method for Linear Programming (LP) problems [9,21]. Note that the maximum utility point must be a vertex in $Conv(D)$. It is time-saving to interactively check if there is a vertex in $Conv(D)$ with a higher utility than p by displaying p and at most $s - 1$ neighboring vertices in $Conv(D)$ represented as N_p to the user at each round. So we just present points in C which are also vertices in N_p, *i.e.*, the vertex set $\{p \in C \bigcap N_p\}$ to the user. Instead of obtaining N_p from $Conv(D)$ which is time-consuming to compute it for high dimensional dataset, we compute N_p by p's conical hull frame. Similar to [21], we use the algorithm in [9] to compute the conical hull frame. Based on above analysis, we provide our sorting-based interactive regret minimization algorithm Sorting-Simplex as shown in Algorithm 1. Also, we propose our Sorting-Random algorithm using random points selection strategy instead of Simplex method (in line 9).

In Algorithm 1, we first initialize the candidate set C to be the skyline of D and the utility space $\mathcal{F}$ to be the whole linear utility space (lines 1–2). Then we choose a point in the convex hull of D (line 3). If not satisfying the stop condition (below a small regret ratio with $||\mathcal{F}||_1 > \frac{\epsilon}{2d}$ [21] or C has only one point, line 4), Algorithm 1 will choose s points presented to the user (line 5) and the user sorts the s points in descending order of their utilities (line 6). The system exploits Simplex method to obtain the neighbouring vertexes in the convex hull (line 7–9). Then the system shrinks the utility space $\mathcal{F}$ with C_s^2 utility hyperplanes (lines 10–13) and reduces the size of the candidate set C with utility hyperplane pruning (line 14–20). At length, the system returns the user's favorite point or the point with the regret ratio no larger than ϵ.

Following we present the lower bound of the number of interaction rounds needed to return the user's favorite point.

Algorithm 1: Sorting-Simplex Algorithm

Input: dataset D, a regret ratio ϵ, displayed points per interaction s, an unknown utility
vector f, displayed point set T
Output: a point p in D with $rr_D f(p) \leqslant \epsilon$

1 Initially, $\mathcal{F} \leftarrow f \in \mathbb{R}_+^d \mid \sum_{i=1}^d f[i] = 1$;
2 $C \leftarrow$ the set of all skyline points $\in D$;
3 $p \leftarrow$ a vertex of $Conv(D)$;
4 **while** $\|\mathcal{F}\|_1 > \frac{\epsilon}{2d}$ *and* $|C| > 1$ **do**
5 | $T \leftarrow$ display p and $s-1$ points in $N_p \cap C$;
6 | $L \leftarrow$ sort the points in T with $f(L[1]) > f(L[2]) > ... > f(L[s])$;
7 | **if** $L[1] \neq p$ **then**
8 | | $p \leftarrow L[1]$;
9 | | Use Simplex method to choose the neighboring vertices of p in $Conv(D)$ to N_p;
10 | **for** $i = 0, i < s, i++$ **do**
11 | | **for** $j = 0, j < s, j++$ **do**
12 | | | **if** $i \neq j$ *and* $i < j$ **then**
13 | | | | $\mathcal{F} = \mathcal{F} \cap h_{L[i], L[j]}^+$;
14 | **for** $i = 0, i < |C|, i++$ **do**
15 | | **for** $j = 0, j < |C|, j++$ **do**
16 | | | **if** $i \neq j$ *and* $i < j$ **then**
17 | | | | **if** $h_{C[i], C[j]}^+ \cap \mathcal{F} = \emptyset$ **then**
18 | | | | | remove $C[i]$;
19 | | | | **if** $h_{C[i], C[j]}^- \cap \mathcal{F} = \emptyset$ **then**
20 | | | | | remove $C[j]$;

21 **return** $p = \arg\max_{q \in C} f \cdot q$ where $f \in \mathcal{F}$;

Theorem 1. *For any d-dimensional dataset, there is an algorithm that needs $\Omega(log_{C_s^2} n)$ rounds of interaction to determine the user's favorite point.*

Proof. The step of determining the user's favorite point in the interaction can be simulated in the form of a tree. Consider an s-ary tree with height r where r represents the rounds of interaction and each leaf node of the s-ary tree represents the data point in D. If we show the s points in each interaction round, the user sorts the s points, and we can get C_s^2 comparison information, similar to in the case of no comparison showing 2 points a time for C_s^2 rounds. Since it is an s-ary tree with n leaves, the height of the tree is $\Omega(log_{C_s^2} n)$. In other words, any algorithm needs $\Omega(log_{C_s^2} n)$ rounds of interaction to identify the maximum utility point in the worst case.

In order to describe the advantage of our Sorting-Simplex algorithm, we take the 4-dimensional NBA dataset as an example, and the four dimensions represent a play's statistics on *points*, *rebounds*, *steals*, and *assists* respectively. The method proposed in [21] named the UH-Simplex algorithm corresponds to Table 3 and our algorithm refers to Table 4. We assume the user's utility function f is (0.3, 0.3, 0.2, 0.2). In the process of interaction, the maximum regret ratio between the point shown by the Sorting-Simplex algorithm and the user's favorite point is 35.31%, and that of the UH-Simplex algorithm is 58.63%. UH-Simplex needs 6 rounds of interaction but our Sorting-Simplex only needs 2 rounds. We can see

Table 3. UH-Simplex example with utility function $f = <0.3, 0.3, 0.2, 0.2>$

Round	Player name	season	points	rebound	steals	assists	utility	regret ratio
1	**Wilt Chamberlain**	1961	4029	2052	0	192	1862.7	0%
	Michael Jordan	1988	2633	652	234	650	1162.3	37.60%
	Michael Jordan	1987	2868	449	259	485	1143.9	38.59%
2	**Wilt Chamberlain**	1961	4029	2052	0	192	1862.7	0%
	Mike Conley	2008	2505	251	354	276	952.8	48.85%
	Tiny Archibald	1972	2719	223	0	910	1064.6	42.86%
3	**Wilt Chamberlain**	1961	4029	2052	0	192	1862.7	0%
	John Stockton	1988	1400	248	263	1118	770.6	58.63%
	Wilt Chamberlain	1960	3033	2149	0	148	1584.2	14.95%
4	**Wilt Chamberlain**	1961	4029	2052	0	192	1862.7	0%
	Wilt Chamberlain	1967	1992	1952	0	702	1323.6	28.94%
	Isiah Thomas	1984	1720	361	187	1123	886.3	52.42%
5	**Wilt Chamberlain**	1961	4029	2052	0	192	1862.7	0%
	Oscar Robertson	1961	2432	985	0	899	1204.9	35.31%
	Michael Jordan	1986	3041	430	236	377	1163.9	37.52%
6	**Wilt Chamberlain**	1961	4029	2052	0	192	1862.7	0%
	McGinnis George	1974	2353	1126	206	495	1183.9	36.44%

Table 4. Sorting-Simplex example with utility function $f = <0.3, 0.3, 0.2, 0.2>$

Round	Player name	season	points	rebound	steals	assists	utility	regret ratio
1	Wilt Chamberlain ①	1961	4029	2052	0	192	1862.7	0%
	Oscar Robertson ③	1961	2432	985	0	899	1204.9	35.31%
	Wilt Chamberlain ②	1967	1992	1952	0	702	1323.6	28.94%
2	Wilt Chamberlain ①	1961	4029	2052	0	192	1862.7	0%
	Wilt Chamberlain ②	1960	3033	2149	0	148	1584.2	14.95%

that at each interaction round Wilt Chamberlain in 1961 season is with the best performance *w.r.t.* the user's utility function (denoted as p, the user's favorite point). Even we add other players in different seasons (vertexes in N_p) for the user to choose, this record is still the user's favorite. For the Sorting-Simplex algorithm there are only two points displayed for the last interaction round. Since the whole candidate set C only has two points left, they are both taken out for the user to choose from, and the one that the user chooses is his/her favorite point.

5   Experimental Results

In this section, we verify the efficiency and effectiveness of our algorithms on both synthetic and real datasets.

5.1   Setup

We conducted experiments on a 64-bit machine with 2.5 GHz CPU and 8G RAM on a 64-bit whose operating system is the Ubuntu 16.04 LTS. All programs were implemented in GNU C++. The synthetic datasets were generated by the dataset generator [3]. The anti-correlated datasets all contain 10,000 points with 4, 5 and 6 dimensions. For real datasets, we adopted Island, NBA and Household datasets. Island is 2-dimensional, which contains 63,383 geographic positions [19]. NBA dataset[2] contains 21,961 points for each player/season combination from year 1946 to 2009. Four attributes are selected to represent the performance of each player, *i.e.*, *total scores*, *rebounds*, *assists* and *steals*. Household[3] is a 7-dimensional dataset consisting of 1,048,576 points, showing the economic characteristics of each family of US in 2012. All the attributes in these datasets are normalized into $[0, 1]$. Unless specified explicitly, the number of displayed points s is 4.

Our algorithms were compared with previous UH-Simplex algorithm [21], UH-Random algorithm [21], and the UtilityApprox algorithm [14]. Moreover, like studies in the literature [10,14–16,22], we computed the skyline first and then identified the user's favorite point from it.

5.2   Results on Synthetic Datasets

In Fig. 5, above 5 mentioned algorithms were run on the Anti-5d dataset with the final regret ratio not more than 2%. We varied the number of displayed points s from 3 to 6 and used the number of total displayed points during the interaction to measure the performances of these 5 algorithms. In order to ensure that the user's regret ratio cannot exceed 2%. In Fig. 5(a), the UtilityApprox algorithm needs to present about 112 points to the user. When $s = 3$, we find that our Sorting-Simplex algorithm finally presents only 24 points to the user, meeting the 2% regret ratio. And the last point displayed is the user's favorite point. However, UtilityApprox needs to show 105 points and require 35 rounds of interaction to meet the requirement of the regret ratio. The UH-Simplex algorithm requires 14 rounds to meet the user's regret ratio. We observe that the Sorting-based algorithms *i.e.*, Sorting-Random and Sorting-Simplex can reduce the rounds of user interaction. Although the algorithms which exploit random point selection strategy do not provide provable guarantees on the number of interaction rounds, they are a little better than Simplex-based algorithms in rounds of interaction. Also, they need less time to execute due to their randomness (Fig. 5(b)). We also observe that as the number of points for each round increases, the total number of interaction rounds along with the total number of displayed points decreases. For example, when $s = 3$, we need 8 rounds of interaction, showing a total of 24 points. But when $s = 6$, only 3 rounds of interaction are needed, and the total number of displayed points is 18.

---

[2] https://www.rotowire.com/basketball/.
[3] http://www.ipums.org.

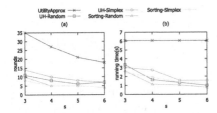
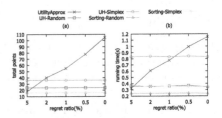

Fig. 5. vary s on the Anti-5d dataset

Fig. 6. Vary regret ratio ($d = 4$, $s = 4$, $n = 10,000$)

In Fig. 6, we compared the performances of the 5 algorithms under different regret ratios. The regret ratio ranges from 5% to 0%, and the smaller value is better. Although we set the required regret ratio is not larger than 5%, the regret ratios of the result sets returned by the 4 algorithms, Sorting-Simplex, Sorting-Random, UH-simplex, UH-Random are all 0% (they are flat lines in Fig. 6(a)). But the regret ratio of UtilityApprox is 4.87%, which performs worse than the other algorithms. We observe that the Sorting-based algorithms are better than the other algorithms, either in the number of displayed points or in the running time. And the Sorting-Simplex algorithm takes less time than UH-Simplex and UtilityApprox. The total number of displayed points of Sorting-Simplex is less than that of the UH-Simplex algorithm, because when s points are shown, the UH-Simplex algorithm can only get the $s - 1$ comparisons for the candidate set pruning. As a contrast, our Sorting-Simplex algorithm can get C_s^2 comparisons which are exploited to delete larger amount of the data points having no possibility to be the maximum utility point from the candidate set. Also, Sorting-Simplex only needs to show half number of the points of UH-Simplex to achieve the same regret ratio. If the user wants to choose his/her favorite point, UtilityApprox needs to show 105 points compared with the other 4 algorithms. We know that the more points shown to the user, the more effort he/she will take to browse them. So UtilityApprox wastes a lot of the user's effort and takes up too much time of the user (as shown in Fig. 6(b)). This leads to the worst performance of UtilityApprox against the other 4 algorithms.

We also evaluated the scalability of our Sorting-based algorithms in Fig. 7 and Fig. 8. In Fig. 7, we studied the scalability of each algorithm on the dataset size n. Our Sorting-Simplex algorithm scales well in terms of the running time while showing the smallest amount of points to the user. In particular, to guarantee a 0.1% regret ratio on a dataset with 20,000 points, the number of points we display is half of that of UH-Simplex and one sixth of that of UtilityApprox (Fig. 7(a)). Besides, the other 4 interactive algorithms are significantly faster than UtilityApprox (Fig. 7(b)). In Fig. 8, we studied the scalability of each algorithm on the dimensionality d. Compared with UH-Simplex and UtilityApprox, Sorting-Simplex and Sorting-Random consistently show fewer points in all dimensions, verifying the usefulness of sorting points in reducing the rounds of interaction.

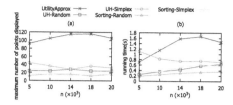

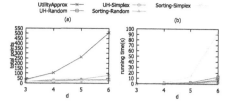

Fig. 7. Vary n ($d = 4$, $s = 4$, $\epsilon = 0.1\%$)

Fig. 8. Vary d ($n = 10,000$, $s = 4$, $\epsilon = 0.1\%$)

5.3   Results on Real Datasets

We studied the effects of the algorithms on the 3 real datasets in terms of the regret ratio, candidate set size and running time of each algorithm. Note that our sorting-based algorithms perform very efficiently on real datasets. This is because that sorting the displayed points can generate more information for learning user's utility function and reducing the candidate set size. Note that when the running time remains unchanged (Fig. 9(c), Fig. 10(c)), it means the points displayed in the previous interaction round satisfy the user's requirement, there is no need to present more points to the user. The random algorithms, *i.e.,* UH-Random and Sorting-Random with unstable tendency are due to the randomness for the displayed point selection.

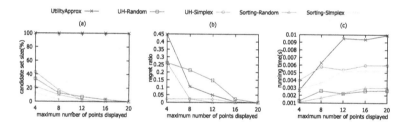

Fig. 9. Vary maximum number of points displayed on NBA

The results on the NBA and Household datasets are shown in Fig. 9 and Fig. 10 where we varied the maximum number of points displayed. Our sorting-based algorithms effectively reduce the candidate set size and take only a few seconds to execute. The Sorting-Simplex algorithm reached 0% regret ratio in the 3rd round. When the Sorting-Simplex algorithm is executed, the candidate set size is reduced rapidly. In particular, after 2 rounds (*i.e.,* total 8 points presented to the user since $s = 4$), we prune 98%, 50% of data points in the candidate set on NBA and Household as shown in Fig. 9(a) and Fig. 10(a), respectively.

When the system required the same regret ratio of result set for each algorithm, we found that our Sorting-Simplex algorithm performs best among all the algorithms as shown in Fig. 6. Moreover for smaller target regret ratios,

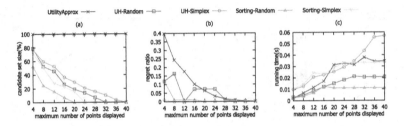

Fig. 10. Vary maximum number of points displayed on household

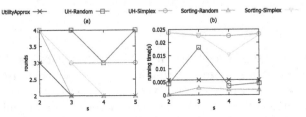

Fig. 11. vary s on island ($d = 2$, $\epsilon = 0\%$)

Sorting-Simplex clearly outperforms UH-Simplex and UtilityApprox. The same phenomenon occurs when we increase the number of points shown to the users, as shown in Fig. 9(b), Fig. 10(b). This confirms that the idea of sorting is crucial in reducing the rounds of interaction. The results on the Island dataset are shown in Fig. 11 where we vary the number of displayed points. In Fig. 11(a), we find that only 3 or 4 rounds needed for interaction due to low dimensionality. From Fig. 9(c), Fig. 10(c) and Fig. 11(b), our sorting-based algorithms are competitive over other algorithms in running time. However, the time spent by the UtilityApprox algorithm is not longer than the UH-based algorithms due to the fact that the points presented by the UtilityApprox algorithm are artificial/fake points. These points do not take time to select from the dataset.

6   Conclusion

In this paper, we present sorting-based interactive framework for regret minimization query. With the help of nice properties of geometric objects describing multidimensional data points, such as boundary point, hyperplane, convex hull, conical hull frame, neighbouring vertex etc., we fully exploit the pairwise relationship of the sorted points to shrink the user's possible utility space greatly and reduce the size of the candidate set which has a consequence that our proposed method requires less rounds of interaction. Experiments on synthetic and real datasets verify our proposed Sorting-Random and Sorting-Simplex algorithms are superior to existing algorithms in terms of interaction rounds and running time.

Acknowledgments. This work is partially supported by the National Natural Science Foundation of China under grants U1733112, 61702260 and the Fundamental Research Funds for the Central Universities under grant NS2020068.

References

1. Agarwal, P.K., Kumar, N., Sintos, S., Suri, S.: Efficient algorithms for k-regret minimizing sets. In: Proceedings of the 16th International Symposium on Experimental Algorithms (SEA) (2017)
2. Asudeh, A., Nazi, A., Zhang, N., Das, G.: Efficient computation of regret-ratio minimizing set: a compact maxima representative. In: SIGMOD (2017)
3. Börzsöny, S., Kossmann, D., Stocker, K.: The skyline operator. In: ICDE (2001)
4. Cao, W., et al.: k-regret minimizing set: efficient algorithms and hardness. In: ICDT (2017)
5. Chan, C.Y., Jagadish, H.V., Tan, K.L., Tung, A.K.H., Zhang, Z.: Finding k-dominant skylines in high dimensional space. In: SIGMOD (2006)
6. Chester, S., Thomo, A., Venkatesh, S., Whitesides, S.: Computing k-regret minimizing sets. In: VLDB (2014)
7. Chomicki, J., Ciaccia, P., Meneghetti, N.: Skyline queries, front and back. SIGMOD Rec. **42**(3), 6–18 (2013)
8. Das Sarma, A., Lall, A., Nanongkai, D., Lipton, R.J., Xu, J.: Representative skylines using threshold-based preference distributions. In: ICDE (2011)
9. Dulá, J.H., Helgason, R.V., Venugopal, N.: An algorithm for identifying the frame of a pointed finite conical hull. INFORMS J. Comput. **10**(3), 323–330 (1998)
10. Faulkner, T.K., Brackenbury, W., Lall, A.: k-regret queries with nonlinear utilities. In: VLDB (2015)
11. Ilyas, I.F., Beskales, G., Soliman, M.A.: A survey of top-k query processing techniques in relational database systems. CSUR **40**(4), 11:1–11:58 (2008)
12. Kumar, N., Sintos, S.: Faster approximation algorithm for the k-regret minimizing set and related problems. In: Proceedings of the 20th Workshop on Algorithm Engineering and Experiments (ALENEX) (2018)
13. Lin, X., Yuan, Y., Zhang, Q., Zhang, Y.: Selecting stars: the k most representative skyline operator. In: ICDE (2007)
14. Nanongkai, D., Lall, A., Das Sarma, A., Makino, K.: Interactive regret minimization. In: SIGMOD (2012)
15. Nanongkai, D., Sarma, A.D., Lall, A., Lipton, R.J., Xu, J.: Regret-minimizing representative databases. In: VLDB (2010)
16. Peng, P., Wong, R.C.W.: Geometry approach for k-regret query. In: ICDE (2014)
17. Qi, J., Zuo, F., Samet, H., Yao, J.: K-regret queries using multiplicative utility functions. TODS **43**(2), 10:1–10:41 (2018)
18. Rockafellar, R.: Convex Analysis. Princeton University Press, Princeton (2015)
19. Tao, Y., Ding, L., Lin, X., Pei, J.: Distance-based representative skyline. In: ICDE (2009)
20. Xie, M., Wong, R.C.W., Lall, A.: An experimental survey of regret minimization query and variants: bridging the best worlds between top-k query and skyline query. VLDB J. **29**, 147–175 (2019)
21. Xie, M., Wong, R.C.W., Lall, A.: Strongly truthful interactive regret minimization. In: SIGMOD (2019)
22. Xie, M., Wong, R.C.W., Li, J., Long, C., Lall, A.: Efficient k-regret query algorithm with restriction-free bound for any dimensionality. In: SIGMOD (2018)

23. Zeighami, S., Wong, R.C.W.: Finding average regret ratio minimizing set in database. In: ICDE (2019)
24. Zeighami, S., Wong, R.C.W.: Minimizing average regret ratio in database. In: SIG-MOD (2016)

Tool Data Modeling Method Based on an Object Deputy Model

Qianwen Luo, Chen Chen, Song Wang, Rongrong Li, and Yuwei Peng[✉]

School of Computer Science, Wuhan University, Wuhan, Hubei, China
{qwluo17,chenchen33,xavierwang,rrli,ywpeng}@whu.edu.cn

Abstract. With the development of intelligent manufacturing industry, the management of tool data in machine tool processing is becoming more and more important. Due to the richness of machine tool data and the complexity of relationships in them, it's hard for a traditional relational database to manage the tool data. Therefore, a new method should be proposed to manage these data in a better way. In this work, we propose a tool data modeling method based on the object deputy model, which utilizes the characteristics of the class and the objects to express the meaning of the tool data and the various semantic constraints on them. Unlike the traditional relational model, objects are connected with a two-way pointer in the object deputy model where an object can have one or more deputy objects that inherit the properties and methods of the source object, and the deputy objects can have their own properties and methods. Besides, the two-way pointer between the source class and its deputy class makes the cross-class query easier in two aspects: One is to make complex queries expressed in intuitive statements, and the other is to improve query efficiency. We implemented and evaluated our model on an object deputy database. Experiments show that our method is better than the traditional relational ones.

Keywords: Object deputy model · Tool data · Data modeling · Database

1 Introduction

In traditional metal manufacturing, the reasonable use of various tools is of great significance to improve production efficiency, product quality, and process safety, and reduce costs. In today's large-scale use of NC machining, the use of tool data in the programming process is particularly important. Especially the selection of tools and the recommended cutting parameters of the tool when processing the workpieces are of decisive significance. In detail, the tool data has two main characteristics. Firstly, the tool data have rich meanings, including the geometric parameters of the tool, such as diameter, included Angle, cutting edge length, programming length, and material of the tool, such as tool material, tool coating material, and description information of the tool, i.e. tool type, scope of application. Secondly, the tool data contains complex relations, such as the machining

© Springer Nature Switzerland AG 2020
X. Wang et al. (Eds.): APWeb-WAIM 2020, LNCS 12318, pp. 491–499, 2020.
https://doi.org/10.1007/978-3-030-60290-1_37

of the tool, which needs to consider the parameters of the tool, the processing technology, the workpiece material, and the cutting speed of the tool. According to Sandvik's statistics, machine tool operators spend 20% of their time finding suitable tools in the manufacturing process which is a high percentage. Therefore, if the time required to find a suitable tool is reduced, the machining efficiency will be greatly improved. Advanced manufacturing countries attach great importance to tool data management and have successively developed their own tool management software, such as AutoTas tool management system developed by Sandvik of Sweden, TDM Systems developed by Walter Information System of Germany, TMS developed by Zoller of Germany, WinTool system developed by WinTool of Switzerland. The mature tool management system is still absent in China. The existing tool management systems are developed by different enterprises according to their own requirements. Consequently, they lack uniform standards. This situation is incompatible with China's status as the world's largest manufacturing country. Therefore, our work focused on the organization of tool data and the construction of the tool management model on the basis of industrial data processing and industrial Internet technology.

In view of the above data characteristics, all of the above-mentioned foreign tool management systems adopt the relational data model to represent tool entities and their relationships. Since the relational data model is simple and clear [1]. It has a solid mathematical theoretical foundation, and the operating language is descriptive, which greatly improves the efficiency of data storage and system development. However, there are still some shortcomings. We begin with a careful exploration of the tool data model and discuss the limitations of the relational data model concerning the characteristics of the tool data listed above. First, the semantic expression is foggy. In the tool processing scenario, the completion of the workpiece is related to many factors such as the workpiece material and processing use cases. No matter what kind of relationship between entities is connected by the join in the relational data model, the semantic expression is foggy. Second, it's hard for the relational data model to maintain data consistency. During the use of the tool, the life cycle of the tool is limited, so the tool will be updated frequently. Finally, the query efficiency of the relational model in our scenario is low. A large number of join operations are required to determine the information to be found. As we all know, the join operation takes a lot of time. Therefore, to address these problems, we propose a tool data modeling method based on the object deputy model [3]. The object deputy model [2] is a new data model based on the traditional object-oriented model, which enhances the flexibility and modeling ability of the object-oriented model. There are four kinds of relationship types in the object deputy model, namely select, group, union, and join, which make the semantic relation between tool data express accurately and abundantly. The select deputy class indicates whose deputy objects are selected from a class according to a select predicate. The join deputy class indicates that the deputy objects are derived from the results of several classes connected according to a combination predicate, so a join deputy object corresponds to a source object in each source class. The group deputy class indicates whose deputy objects are derived from a class according to a grouping predicate, so a group deputy object corresponds to a set of source objects. The union deputy class indicates that the source objects of several classes of the same type are merged into one deputy class. When the attribute values of the tool are modified, our object deputy model provides the update propagation mechanism to maintain their consistency. In addition, the cross-class query supported by the object deputy model avoids a large number of join operations in the relational data model. In order to verify the effectiveness of our modeling method, we used the actual tool data to make a comparative experiment between the object deputy model and the relational model, the results of which show our data model is more efficient than the relational data model.

In summary, our contribution are as follows.

- We propose a semantic analysis method for tool application scenarios. We use classification to represent all objects in the tool scene. We use a classification method to represent all objects in the tool scene according to the object characteristics.
- We propose the tool data modeling method based on an object deputy model, which effectively manages the tool data while meeting the most important requirements in machine tool processing.
- We conduct experimental evaluations for our tool data model and existing model based on the relational model. We evaluated the models from both storage space and retrieval time.

The remainder of this paper is organized as follows. We introduce our Tool Data modeling based on the Object Deputy Model in Sect. 2. Section 3 describes our modeling method implementation and evaluates its efficiency, before concluding the paper in Sect. 4.

2   Tool Data Modeling Method

In this section, we introduce the semantics of the tool data, illustrate the specific Tool Data Modeling Method based on the Object Deputy Model, and give cross-class query statements for the tool data scenarios.

2.1   Semantic Analysis

In our tool data model, we use a classification method to analyze data semantics. According to the processing technology, the tools are divided into four categories which are Drill, Mill Cutter, Boring Cutter, and Turning Tool. So we define four source classes to represent the four types of tools in the tool processing scene. In details, a class named Drill is used to define common drill objects which have basic attributes, such as drillid which is the unique identifier of the object, description which is recording the main purpose of the tool, material, Tconnection to describe the interface of the drill, and some geometric parameters that are diameter, included angle, programming length, cutting edge length and total length. The other three almost have the same attributes as the drill. Therefore, only the drill is used as an example to describe the scene in the following. What's more, when the tools are installed on the machine, they need to be connected to the machine through a tool holder. So we need to design a tool holder source class to describe the tool holder interface information. In tool processing, if the interface of the tool and the interface of the holder are matched, they can be successfully paired and used. The workpiece to be processed is the most important part of tool processing, and the material characteristics of the workpiece play a decisive role in determining the processing parameters. We define a PartMaterial class to record material information. And the use case also affects the choice of cutting parameters, so we define a UseCase class to record the descriptions, indicating roughing or finishing.

2.2 Tool Data Modeling

In the previous chapter, we have introduced several important source classes. We present the complete model in this subsection. As shown in Fig. 1, the model contains four different deputy relationships, covering the main application scenarios of tool processing. Next, we will introduce specific modeling schemes for different data association relationships in the actual tool machining scene. We have adopted the classification standard of tools in the manufacturing field according to processing technology. Actually, each type of tool can be subdivided according to its material. Machine managers usually want to see as few unrelated tools as possible when looking for suitable tools. So we use the select operation to derive a deputy class which only includes the deputy objects of the instances of the source class that satisfy a selection predicate. Take Drill source class as an example, the drill contains many instances including high-speed steel drills, carbide drills, and so on. While processing a workpiece, the managers usually need to find a class of tools for its purpose, so the construction of the select deputy class can make it more convenient and express the relationship of different types of tools accurately. In Fig. 1, the select deputy class depicts the relationship of this situation.

When a tool is selected to machine a workpiece, it needs to be installed on the machine tool via a tool holder. However, the tool and tool holder are paired by the value of Tconnection, an attribute that records the interface criterion of the tool and tool holder. So we also construct a join deputy class to record the paired tools and tool holders. Further, looking up the suitable cutting speed is a very common scenario in tool machining when the other factors such as use case, material, and tool are exact. Therefore, we need to use these factors as filter conditions to query the cutting speed. We use the join operation to derive a deputy class that can store the relationship between them in order to express this relationship. In this way, we can find the cutting speed we need to find through this join deputy class. In Fig. 1, the join deputy class depicts the relationship of this situation. The Tool deputy class is defined with SQL-like statements as:

```
CREATE JOINDEPUTYCLASS Tool  AS (
SELECT  spiraldrill.id, toolholder.id,
toolholder.MConnection as MConnection
FROM spiraldrill, toolholder
WHERE spiraldrill.Tconnection=toolholder.TConnection)
```

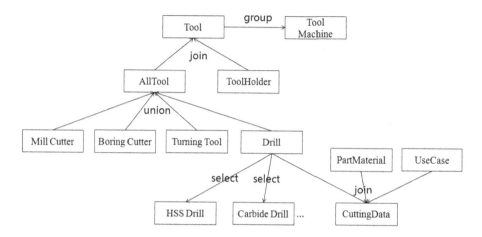

Fig. 1. The tool data model

As mentioned above, we represented four different tools as four different source classes, but we need to check all the tools during the inventory check, so we have to put all the tools together so that the type of tools is no longer single. The union operation in object deputy model can derive a deputy class of which extension consists of deputy objects of instances of more than one source class. Therefore, we use the union deputy class to describe the collection of four different types of tools. In Fig. 1, the union deputy class depicts the relationship of this situation.

During tool processing, the tool needs to be replaced frequently due to wear, and the interface for installing the tool on the machine tool is fixed. In a real-life scenario, when replacing the tools, we need to find the applicable tools for the machine tool through the interface information. Therefore, in order to facilitate the subsequent procurement of tools that can match the specific machine tool, we can know the number of tools applicable to each machine tool in the tool magazine through the tool interface information. The group operation of the object deputy model can derive a deputy class which only includes the deputy objects of the instances of the source class that have the same features. So we need to use the group deputy class to show this message.

2.3   Cross Class Query

In the previous part, we stored the tool data according to their semantic relationships. In the actual application scenario, machine operators hope to quickly retrieve the tool data that they want to query, so we can take advantage of the cross-class query feature in our model. Cross-class query refers to finding an object in a source class or deputy class based on the related information of the other source classes or deputy classes. The objects and their deputy objects are linked in two directions through pointers. So there is a path between any two objects in our model to link them. For example, in the tool data scenario, we usually need to find the optimal cutting speed of the tool when we already know the type of tool, the material of the workpiece, and so on. We can define the following cross-class query:

```
SELECT (spiraldrill{diameter='16.0'}->cuttingdata).cuttingspeed
FROM drill WHERE cuttingspeed IN
(SELECT(usecase{description='roughing'}->cuttingdata).cuttingspeed
FROM usecase WHERE cuttingspeed IN
(SELECT(partmaterial{description='GG'}->cuttingdata).cuttingspeed
FROM partmaterial);
```

In this cross-class query, we can see that using arrows to represent associations between classes is very simple and intuitive. The system will first scan the CuttingData class, and then check its connected source objects in the source class Drill, and see whether its diameter is equal to 16. If the filter condition is satisfied, then the system will judge whether the next filter condition is met until all filter conditions are met, and its attribute cuttingid will be returned, along with the value of its local attribute cutting speed. So the result of this query will be cutting speed. The cross-class queries use bidirectional pointers to find information in associated classes avoiding a large number of join operations in relational types. In general, the cross-class query makes the complex queries involving many filter conditions be presented clearly and executed efficiently.

2.4   Consistence Maintenance

In this section, we introduce how to achieve consistency maintenance by the update propagation mechanism [5]. The update propagation mechanism is that when an object is modified, the modification is automatically reflected its deputy object through a switching operation. There are usually three types of modifications in the tooling scenario. First, when a tool object is added, its deputy objects may be created automatically which satisfies the selection predicate so that the tools can be presented in different machining applications. Second, when an old tool is damaged, that is, a tool object is deleted, its deputy objects will also be deleted. Third, when a tool object is modified, some of its deputy objects may be deleted and some other deputy objects may be added. Thus, our tool data model can maintain the consistency of the tool data by the update propagation mechanism.

3   Experiments

In this section, we introduce our performance testing experiments on the model from three aspects: platform, data set, and experimental results.

3.1   Platform

We report the different experiments we run to evaluate the performance of our tool data model. We evaluate the performance of each data model when processing the queries. We execute the query on two databases: Totem as a representative for the object deputy model, and PostgreSQL represents the relational model. Totem has been developed as a database management system (DBMS) based on the object deputy model [4]. In Totem, queries are expressed with a declarative query language which is named object deputy query language (ODQL) [6]. A query is executed on both of them, and meanwhile, the retrieval time and storage space are recorded. The experiments were performed using object deputy database Totem and relational database PostgreSQL under such a platform: Intel(R)Core(TM)i7-2320 3.0 GHz CPU with 4 GB memory, 500 GB hard disk and Ubuntu16.04.

3.2   Data Set

In the experiments, we used two types of data to evaluate the tool data models. One type was collected from the tool catalog which is from real-world use cases. But there are only a few hundred of such data. The other type was generated by simulation based on the attribute type of the real data. In this way, we get the data sets of different orders of magnitude. Every record in each data set represents a tool application instance which includes the unique identifier of the tool and its cutting speed corresponding to different machining conditions. We choose the main application scenario of tool data, namely query cutting speed, as our experimental scenario. We will compare the storage space of the tool data and the retrieval time needed when querying the same amount of tool objects between two data models based on two databases. We have done several tests with the different data sets. The test results of the response time and storage size are shown in Fig. 2. From the figures, we can see that the response time and the consumed storage spaces in Totem outperform the PostgreSQL.

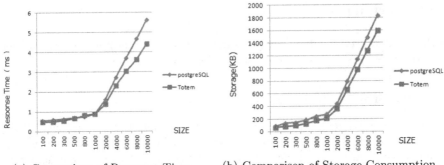

(a) Comparison of Response Time.   (b) Comparison of Storage Consumption.

Fig. 2. The experimental results

4   Conclusion

We presented the tool data modeling method based on the object deputy model. To the best of our knowledge, this model is the first implemented and evaluated in tool data management. And the results of the experiments show that the performance of the object deputy model is better compared to the relational model in the retrieval time and consumed storage space. We also achieved consistency maintenance of the tool data by the update propagation mechanism to make the tool management efficient. As future work, we will further improve query performance and optimize our model to meet more scenarios.

Acknowledgement. This work is supported by the Key Research and Development Program of China (2016YFB1000701) and the key projects of the National Natural Science Foundation of China (No. U1811263).

References

1. Codd, E.F.: A relational model of data for large shared data banks. Commun. ACM **13**(6), 377–387 (1970)
2. Kambayashi, Y., Peng, Z.: Object deputy model and its applications. In: Proceedings of the 4th International Conference on Database Systems for Advanced Applications (DASFAA), Singapore, pp. 1–15 (1995)
3. Peng, Z., Kambayashi, Y.: Deputy mechanisms for object-oriented databases. In: Proceedings of the Eleventh International Conference on Data Engineering, pp. 333–340 (1995)
4. Peng, Z., Peng, Y., Zhai, B.: Using object deputy database to realize multi-representation geographic information system. In: Proceedings of the 15th ACM International Symposium on Geographic Information Systems, ACM-GIS 2007, Seattle, Washington, USA, 7–9 November 2007, pp. 43–46 (2007)

5. Wang, L., Wang, L., Peng, Z.: Probabilistic object deputy model for uncertain data and lineage management. Data Knowl. Eng. **109**, 70–84 (2017)
6. Zhai, B., Shi, Y., Peng, Z.: Object deputy database language. In: Fourth International Conference on Creating, Connecting and Collaborating through Computing, C5 2006, Berkeley, California, USA, 26–27 January 2006, pp. 88–95 (2006)

Unsupervised Deep Hashing with Structured Similarity Learning

Xuanrong Pang[1], Xiaojun Chen[1(✉)], Shu Yang[1], and Feiping Nie[2]

[1] College of Computer Science and Software, Shenzhen University, Shenzhen 518060, Guangdong, China
{pangxuanrong2018,yangshu2018}@email.szu.edu.cn, xjchen@szu.edu.cn
[2] School of Computer Science and Center for OPTical IMagery Analysis and Learning (OPTIMAL), Northwestern Polytechnical University, Xi'an 710072, Shaanxi, China
feipingnie@gmail.com

Abstract. Hashing technology, one of the most efficient approximate nearest neighbor searching methods due to its fast query speed and low storage cost, has been widely used in image retrieval. Recently, unsupervised deep hashing methods have attracted more and more attention due to the lack of labels in real applications. Most unsupervised hashing methods usually construct a similarity matrix with the features extracted from the images, and then guide the hash code learning with this similarity matrix. However, in unsupervised scenario, such similarity matrix may be unreliable due to the affect of noise and irrelevant objects in images. In this paper, we propose a novel unsupervised deep hashing method called Deep Structured Hashing (DSH). In the new method, we first learn both continuous and binary structured similarity matrices with explicit cluster structure to better preserve the semantic structure, where the binary one preserves the coarse-grained semantic structure while the continuous one preserves the fine-grained semantic structure. And then jointly optimize three kinds of losses to learn high quality hash codes. Extensive experiments on three benchmark datasets show the superior retrieval performance of our proposed method.

Keywords: Deep hashing · Image retrieval · Binary codes

1 Introduction

With the explosive growth of social data such as images and videos, exact nearest neighbor searching has become time-consuming and inefficient. Instead, approximate nearest neighbor (ANN) searching has attracted more and more attention due to its high search efficiency. Among the existing ANN technologies [1,8], hashing technology is a popular and efficient one due to its fast query speed and low storage cost [25].

© Springer Nature Switzerland AG 2020
X. Wang et al. (Eds.): APWeb-WAIM 2020, LNCS 12318, pp. 500–514, 2020.
https://doi.org/10.1007/978-3-030-60290-1_38

Generally speaking, hashing methods can be divided into two main categories: data-independent hashing methods and data-dependent hashing methods. The hash function of data-independent hashing methods [1,2,5,11] is usually generated by manually construction or random projection, independent of the specific data. Locally sensitive hashing (LSH) [5] is one of the classic algorithms for data-independent hashing methods, which can make similar data share similar binary codes in the Hamming space with high probability. However, data-independent hashing methods need longer binary codes to achieve high accuracy, which also means more storage cost. Recently, data-dependent hashing methods had attracted more and more attention since it can learn more compact hash codes from the specific data. Existing data-dependent hashing methods can be further summarized into supervised hashing methods and unsupervised hashing methods. Supervised hashing methods [3,7,9,10,16,20,29] use labeled information to learn hash codes and hash functions, and have shown satisfactory performance. However, with the rapid increase of the data size, it is often costly to obtain labeled data [17]. Manually labeling the data is not only time-consuming and expensive, but also limits the performance of the supervised hashing method. Therefore, researchers have turned their attention to unsupervised hashing, which is also the focus of this paper.

Representative unsupervised hashing methods include stochastic generative hashing (SGH) [4], iterative quantization (ITQ) [6], spectral hashing (SH) [26], hashing with graphs (AGH) [15], etc. ITQ first maps data to low-dimensional space through PCA, and then reduces quantization error through orthogonal rotation. Both SH and AGH are manifold-based hashing methods, which first construct a similarity matrix and then learn hash codes to preserve the manifold structure of the original data. SGH is a generative method that uses the minimum description length principle to compress data into hash codes. Although the aforementioned unsupervised hashing methods have made progress in this field, they are all traditional shallow architecture hashing methods which depends heavily on the hand-crafted features. More recently, deep neural networks have been used for hashing due to their powerful feature learning ability, e.g., deep binary descriptors (DeepBit) [14], greedy hash(GH) [23], semantic structure-based unsupervised deep hashing (SSDH) [28] and binary generative adversarial hashing (BGAN) [22]. DeepBit treats the image and its corresponding image after rotation as similar pairs, and maintains this similarity in hash code learning. GH uses the greedy principle to deal with the gradient vanishing problem of the sign function during the back propagation process. SSDH first learns the semantic structure of the original data based on pairwise distance and Gaussian estimation, and then uses it to guide the hash code learning. BGAN limits the input noise variable of the generative adversarial networks to be binary, and then learns binary hash codes in an unsupervised way.

Most unsupervised hashing methods use similarity matrix to guide the hash code learning, e.g., SH, AGH and BGAN. With the extracted features from the images, they usually construct the similarity matrix according to some specific criterias (such as k nearest neighbors). However, in unsupervised scenario, due

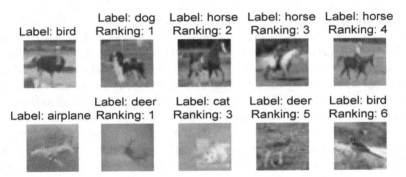

Fig. 1. Irrelevant nearest neighbors calculated from the extracted deep features on the CIFAR-10 dataset. **Label** indicates the category of image, and the number after **Ranking** indicates their ranking in the k nearest neighbors.

to the affect of noise and irrelevant objects in images, the calculated k nearest neighbors may not be accurate, which in turn cause the similarity matrix to be unreliable. For example, Fig. 1 shows irrelevant nearest neighbors (in different classes) calculated from the fc-7 layer features in VGG19 [24] on the CIFAR-10 dataset. Obviously, the similarity matrix they constructed will mislead the hash code learning so that the images in different classes have similar hash codes. To overcome this problem, in this paper, we propose a novel unsupervised deep hashing framework Deep Structured Hashing (DSH). The new method learns two structured similarity matrices which only consists of a desired number of connected components, and then uses these structured similarity matrices to learn the hash codes. Our main contributions are summarized as follows:

- We propose to learn structured similarity matrix which only consists of a desired number of connected components, by globally cutting off the connections between some irrelevant images (setting their similarities to zeros). The motivation behind this is that the cost of cutting off the images in different classes should be smaller than the cost of cutting off the images in the same class. Different from the existing methods which only learn a continuous similarity matrix (e.g., SH and AGH) or binary similarity matrix (e.g., BGAN), we propose to learn both continuous and binary structured similarity matrices to better preserve the semantic structure, where the continuous one preserves the fine-grained semantic structure while the binary one preserves the coarse-grained semantic structure.
- We propose to learn binary hash codes by jointly optimizing three losses, i.e., the similarity loss, the reconstruction loss and the hash loss. In the similarity loss, we propose to use both continuous and binary similarity matrices to guide the hash code learning since these two similarity matrices can help each other to learn better hash codes together.
- Extensive experiments on three widely-used benchmark datasets show that our proposed method outperforms the state-of-the-art unsupervised hashing methods.

2 Notations and Problem Definition

Let us introduce some notations for this paper, we use boldface uppercase letters like $\mathbf{A}$ to represent the matrix, $\mathbf{a}_i$ represents the i-th row of $\mathbf{A}$, a_{ij} represents the i-th row and the j-th column element of $\mathbf{A}$, and $\mathbf{A}^T$ denotes the transpose of $\mathbf{A}$. $\mathbf{I_r}$ represents $r \times r$ identity matrix. $\mathbf{1}$ represents the vector with all elements is one. $\| \cdot \|_F$ represents the Frobenius norm of the matrix. $sgn(\cdot)$ is the sign function, which outputs 1 for positive numbers, or -1 otherwise. $tanh(\cdot)$ is the hyperbolic tangent function. $\cos(\mathbf{x}, \mathbf{y})$ represents the cosine similarity between vector $\mathbf{x}$ and vector $\mathbf{y}$.

Suppose we have a training set $\mathbf{X} = \{\mathbf{x}_i\}_{i=1}^n$ that contains n images without labeled information. The goal of unsupervised hashing is to learn a set of compact binary hash codes $\mathbf{B} = \{\mathbf{b}_i\}_{i=1}^n \in \{-1, 1\}^{n \times r}$ for $\mathbf{X}$ and a hash function, where r represents the length of hash codes.

3 Proposed Method

In this section, we present our new method. We first introduce the network architecture in Sect. 3.1. In Sects. 3.2 and 3.3, we show how to learn structured similarity matrices and binary hash codes. Finally, we show network training and hash code generation in the last two subsections, respectively.

3.1 Network Architecture

Our network, as shown in Fig. 2, consists of four modules: Encoder, Decoder, Similarity Learning and Hash Code Learning. The Encoder generates the hash codes and the Decoder generates images from the hash codes. To learn high quality hash codes, we propose to learn two structured similarity matrices with the Similarity Learning module and learn the binary hash codes with the Hash Code Learning module.

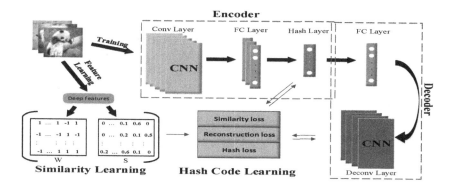

Fig. 2. The framework of Deep Structured Hashing.

In the Encoder, we use VGG19 [24] as its basis model, which contains five convolutional layers and three fully-connected layers. Here, we replace the last layer of VGG19 with a new fully-connected layer with 1000 hidden units and followed by a hash layer (the size of the hash layer is the length of hash codes). Since our goal is to learn hash codes, a commonly-used approach is to use $sgn(\cdot)$ as the activation function of the hash layer such that the output $\mathbf{B} \in \{-1,1\}^{n \times r}$ will be the desired hash codes. However, the ill-posed gradient problem of $sgn(\cdot)$ will make it intractable to train the network with back propagation algorithm. Therefore, we use $tanh(\cdot)$ to approximate $sgn(\cdot)$ as the activation function of the hash layer. We represent the Encoder as $E(\cdot; \Theta)$ where Θ is the set of network parameters, and the output of the hash layer in the Encoder as $\mathbf{H} = E(\mathbf{X}; \Theta)$.

The Decoder generates images from $\mathbf{H}$ with one fully-connected layer and four deconvolutional layers. The size of the fully-connected layer is $8 \times 8 \times 64$. The kernel size of the four deconvolutional layers are $5 \times 5, 5 \times 5, 5 \times 5, 1 \times 1$, and the number of kernels is $128, 64, 32, 3$, respectively. We represent the Decoder as $G(\cdot; \Psi)$, where Ψ is the set of network parameters.

3.2   Structure Similarity Learning

Without labeled information, most unsupervised hashing methods [12,13,15,21] first compute a similarity matrix, and then perform the hash code learning with this similarity matrix. However, as shown in Fig. 1, such similarity matrix may be unreliable in unsupervised scenario and thus lead to undesired hash codes. In this paper, inspired by the work in [19], we propose to learn both continuous and binary structured similarity matrices with explicit cluster structures to better preserve the semantic structures, where the binary one $\mathbf{W}$ preserves the coarse-grained semantic structure while the continuous one $\mathbf{S}$ preserves the fine-grained semantic structure. We hope that the graph with $\mathbf{S}$ or $\mathbf{W}$ as affinity matrix consists of only c connected components in order to globally cut off some irrelevant connections by setting their similarities to zeros.

We first use VGG19 [24] to extract deep features from the training images and obtain features $\mathbf{Z}$ as the output of the seventh fully-connected layer in VGG19. Then we use the CAN in [19] to learn the desired continuous similarity matrix $\mathbf{S}$ from $\mathbf{Z}$, in which each row contains k positive values for k nearest neighbors. However, CAN is not able to learn the binary matrix $\mathbf{W}$, so we propose a new method to learn it. To improve the quality of $\mathbf{W}$, we propose to learn $\mathbf{W}$ from $\mathbf{S}$ instead of $\mathbf{Z}$. Specifically, we treat each row of $\mathbf{S}$ as a new feature for each image and compute the cosine similarity matrix $\mathbf{A}$ in which $a_{ij} = \cos(\mathbf{s}_i, \mathbf{s}_j)$. The motivation behind this is that two semantically related images should have similar similarities with other images. It can be verified that $\mathbf{A} \in [0,1]^{n \times n}$ since $\mathbf{S} \in [0,1]^{n \times n}$. Intuitively, we hope to learn w_{ij} from a_{ij}. So we form the following objective function for $\mathbf{W}$

$$\min_{\mathbf{W} \in \{0,1\}^{n \times n}, \; rank(\mathbf{L}_W) = n-c} \|\mathbf{W} - \gamma \mathbf{A}\|_F^2 \qquad (1)$$

where γ is a parameter, $rank(\mathbf{L}_W) = n - c$ is the structural constraint, which will make the graph with $\mathbf{W}$ as affinity matrix consists of only c connected components.

Similar to the CAN in [19], solving problem (1) is equivalent to solving the following problem

$$
\min \| \mathbf{W} - \gamma \mathbf{A} \|_F^2 + 4\lambda Tr(\mathbf{F}^T \mathbf{L}_W \mathbf{F})
$$
$$
s.t. \mathbf{W} \in \{0,1\}^{n \times n}, \mathbf{F} \in \mathbf{R}^{n \times c}, \mathbf{F}^T \mathbf{F} = \mathbf{I}
$$
(2)

where λ is a parameter, $\mathbf{L}_W = \mathbf{D}_W - \frac{\mathbf{W} + \mathbf{W}^T}{2}$ is the Laplacian matrix, $\mathbf{D}_W$ is a diagonal matrix and the i-th diagonal element is defined as $\sum_j \frac{w_{ij} + w_{ji}}{2}$.

Problem (2) can be solved with the alternative optimization method. If $\mathbf{W}$ is fixed, according to Algorithm 1 in [19], the optimal solution of $\mathbf{F}$ is formed by the c eigenvectors of $\mathbf{L}_W$ corresponding to its c smallest eigenvalues. If $\mathbf{F}$ is fixed, the optimal solution of $\mathbf{W}$ can be obtained by solving the following problem

$$
\min_{\mathbf{W} \in \{0,1\}^{n \times n}} \left\| \mathbf{W} - (\gamma \mathbf{A} - \lambda \mathbf{D}^f) \right\|_F^2
$$
(3)

where $\mathbf{D}^f$ is a distance matrix in which $d_{ij}^f = \| \mathbf{f}_i - \mathbf{f}_j \|_2^2$. It can be verified that its optimal solution is as follows

$$
w_{ij} = \begin{cases} 1 & if \ \gamma a_{ij} - \lambda d_{ij}^f \geq 0.5 \\ 0 & otherwise \end{cases}
$$
(4)

3.3   Hash Code Learning

To learn high quality hash codes, we introduce three kinds of loss, i.e., similarity loss, reconstruction loss and hash loss. We will show the details of the three losses below.

Similarity Loss. With the learned structured similarity matrices $\mathbf{S}$ and $\mathbf{W}$, we impose the following loss on the $\mathbf{H}$ to preserve the semantic structure in both matrices

$$
\mathcal{L}_s = \frac{1}{n^2} \left(\sum_{i,j=1}^n \| \mathbf{h}_i - \mathbf{h}_j \|_2^2 \, s_{ij} + \sum_{i,j=1}^n (\frac{1}{r} \mathbf{h}_i^T \mathbf{h}_j - w_{ij}')^2 \right)
$$
(5)

where $\mathbf{h}_i \in [-1,1]^r$ is the relaxed hash codes of the image $\mathbf{x}_i$, and

$$
w_{ij}' = \begin{cases} 1 & if \ w_{ij} = 1 \\ -1 & if \ w_{ij} = 0 \end{cases}
$$
(6)

Here, we replace '0' in $\mathbf{W}$ as '-1' since we hope that $\mathbf{H} \in [-1,1]^{n \times r}$. The first item in Eq. (5) is to learn H according to the continuous similarity $\mathbf{S}$, and the second item in Eq. (5) is to learn H such that the similarity between $\mathbf{h}_i$ and $\mathbf{h}_j$ approximates the discrete similarity matrix $\mathbf{W}'$.

Reconstruction Loss. In unsupervised scenarios, the reconstruction criterion is used as an indirect method to preserve semantic structure, which is the same as the goal of similarity loss, that is, it encourages (dis) similar data to be mapped to (dis) similar hash codes. We introduce the reconstruction loss to learn high quality hash codes, by minimizing the widely-used pixel-level MSE between the generated images and the original images

$$\mathcal{L}_r = \frac{1}{n|\mathbf{x}_i|} \sum_{i=1}^{n} \left\| \mathbf{x}_i - \mathbf{x}_i^R \right\|_F^2 \tag{7}$$

where $|\mathbf{x}_i|$ is the size of image $\mathbf{x}_i$, $\mathbf{x}_i^R = G(\mathbf{h}_i; \Psi)$ represents the reconstructed image for $\mathbf{x}_i$.

Hash loss. We further impose the following two regularization terms to improve the quality of $\mathbf{H}$

$$\mathcal{L}_h = \left\| \mathbf{H}^T \mathbf{1} \right\|_2^2 + \left\| \frac{1}{n} \mathbf{H}^T \mathbf{H} - \mathbf{I}_r \right\|_F^2 \tag{8}$$

where the first term is the balanced loss that improves the usage of each bit in the hash codes by using the maximum information entropy criterion, and the second term is the uncorrelated loss that forces each bit of the hash codes to be independent of each other.

Finally, we reach the overall objective function as follow

$$\min_{\Theta, \Psi} \mathcal{L} = \mathcal{L}_s + \mu_1 \mathcal{L}_r + \mu_2 \mathcal{L}_h \tag{9}$$

where μ_1 and μ_2 are two weight parameters.

3.4 Network Training

We use VGG19 pre-trained on ImageNet to initialize the first seven layers in the Encoder and the rest parameters in Θ and Ψ are randomly initialized. Then we use back propagation (BP) to train the Encoder and Decode networks. In each iteration, we first sample a mini-batch of the training set, obtain the value of the loss $\mathcal{L}$ through the forward propagation, and then update the network parameters Θ, Ψ as follows

$$\begin{cases} \Theta \leftarrow \Theta - \alpha \nabla_\Theta(\mathcal{L}) \\ \Psi \leftarrow \Psi - \alpha \nabla_\Psi(\mathcal{L}) \end{cases} \tag{10}$$

where α is the learning rate. The details of our method is summarized in Algorithm 1.

3.5 Hash Code Generating

With the trained network parameters Θ, the hash codes $\mathbf{b}_q$ for a query image $\mathbf{q}$ can be obtained as follow

$$\mathbf{b}_q = sgn(E(\mathbf{q}; \Theta)) \tag{11}$$

Algorithm 1. Deep Structured Hash

Input: Training set $\mathbf{X}$, hash code length r, learning rate α, weight coefficients (μ_1, μ_2), k, c, γ and λ for learning $\mathbf{S}$ and $\mathbf{W}$, mini-batch size b.
Output: Hash codes $\mathbf{B}$ and hash function $h(\mathbf{q})$.
Procedure:
1: Initialize network parameters Θ and Ψ.
2: Extract deep features $\mathbf{Z}$ from $\mathbf{X}$.
3: Given $\mathbf{Z}$ as input, update $\mathbf{S}$ via CAN [19].
4: Randomly initialize $\mathbf{W}$.
5: **repeat**
6:    Update $\mathbf{F}$ by the c eigenvectors of $\mathbf{L}_W$ corresponding to its c smallest eigenvalues.
7:    Update $\mathbf{W}$ by by solving problem (3).
8: **until** problem (2) converges
9: **repeat**
10:    Randomly select b samples $\mathcal{Q}$ from $\mathbf{X}$.
11:    Update Θ and Ψ by Eq. (10) with the samples in $\mathcal{Q}$.
12: **until** convergence
13: **return** $\mathbf{B} = sgn(E(\mathbf{X}; \Theta))$ and $h(\mathbf{q}) = sgn(E(\mathbf{q}; \Theta))$.

4   Experimental Results and Analysis

In this section, we report the experimental result on three popular benchmark datasets to evaluate the performance of our proposed method.

4.1   Benchmark Datasets

We conduct empirical evaluation on the following three benchmark datasets: **CIFAR-10**, **FLICKR25K** and **NUS-WIDE**. CIFAR-10 contains $60,000$ color images in 10 classes, where each class contains $6,000$ images of size 32×32. FLICKR25K contains $25,000$ images collected from Flickr, each image in which is labeled with at least one of 24 unique provided labels. NUS-WIDE contains 269,648 images downloaded from Flickr, which contains 81 ground-truth concepts and each image in which is tagged with multiple semantic labels. Following the setting in [30], we chose the 21 most frequent classes from the dataset and each class contains at least $5,000$ related images.

For the CIFAR-10 dataset, we randomly selected 100 images per class as the query set and used the remaining images as the retrieval set. In the retrieval set, we also randomly selected $1,000$ images per class as the training set. For the FLICKR25K and NUS-WIDE datasets, we randomly selected $1,000$ and $2,100$ images, respectively, as the query sets and used the remaining images as the retrieval sets. In the retrieval sets, we also randomly selected $10,000$ and $10,500$ images, respectively, as the training sets.

4.2   Implementation Details

We first used VGG19 [24] to extract features $\mathbf{Z}$ from the training images, and then learn structured similarities matrices $\mathbf{S}$ and $\mathbf{W}$ from $\mathbf{Z}$. For all datasets, we set the number of nearest neighbors k to $1,000$, the number of connected components c to 10. γ and λ were set to 0.96 and 0.1. When training network, training image are resized to 224×224 as the input. We set both μ_1 and μ_2 to 1. The mini-batch size b and learning rate α were set to 50 and 0.0001, respectively.

4.3   Evaluation Metrics and Baseline Methods

We used three evaluation metrics to evaluate the retrieval performance of our proposed method: Mean Average Precision (MAP), precision of the top N retrieved images (Precision@N), and precision-recall curves. For the multi-label dataset, the retrieved image is considered to be related to the query image if they shares at least one label.

We compared our method with several unsupervised hashing methods, including LSH [5], SH [26], ITQ [6], AGH [15], SP [27], SGH [4], GH [23], SSDH [28] and BGAN [22], where LSH, SH, ITQ, AGH, SP and SGH are traditional hashing methods, GH, SSDH and BGAN are deep hashing methods. The parameters of the comparison methods are set according to the original papers.

To perform fair comparison, we used the fc7-layer feature of VGG19 pretrained on ImageNet for all traditional hashing methods, and directly used the original datasets as input for all deep hashing methods.

Table 1. MAP@all for 10 methods with different number of bits on CIFAR-10.

Method	16bits	32bits	64bits	128bits
LSH+VGG	0.1561	0.1606	0.2158	0.2391
SH+VGG	0.2203	0.2022	0.1838	0.2017
ITQ+VGG	0.2364	0.2529	0.2678	0.2911
AGH+VGG	0.3213	0.2857	0.2452	0.2233
SP+VGG	0.2796	0.2886	0.3144	0.3417
SGH+VGG	0.2683	0.2855	0.2777	0.2919
GH	0.2594	0.3225	0.3219	0.3189
SSDH	0.2172	0.2193	0.2109	0.2070
BGAN	0.4122	0.4305	0.4465	0.4617
Ours	**0.4606**	**0.5068**	**0.5354**	**0.5446**

4.4   Results and Analysis

We report the MAP@all results of all 10 hashing methods on three benchmark datasets in Tables 1, 2 and 3. A careful examination of Tables 1, 2 and 3 shows that our method (DSH) significantly outperforms all baseline methods on the three datasets, especially on the CIFAR-10 dataset. Specifically, on the CIFAR-10 dataset, our method achieves 7.63% (32 bits), 8.89% (64 bits), and 8.29% (128 bits) improvements over the best baseline. On the FLICKR25K dataset, our

Table 2. MAP@all for 10 methods with different number of bits on FLICKR25K.

Method	16bits	32bits	64bits	128bits
LSH+VGG	0.5901	0.6099	0.6205	0.6367
SH+VGG	0.6173	0.6022	0.5923	0.5927
ITQ+VGG	0.6636	0.6653	0.6640	0.6810
AGH+VGG	0.6861	0.6687	0.6582	0.6218
SP+VGG	0.6717	0.6677	0.6830	0.6966
SGH+VGG	0.6663	0.6555	0.6407	0.6411
GH	0.6401	0.6605	0.6773	0.6803
SSDH	0.6724	0.6818	0.6846	0.6923
BGAN	0.6632	0.6615	0.6767	0.6855
Ours	**0.6992**	**0.7048**	**0.7120**	**0.7153**

Table 3. MAP@all for 10 methods with different number of bits on NUS-WIDE.

Method	16bits	32bits	64bits	128bits
LSH+VGG	0.3586	0.3778	0.3970	0.4453
SH+VGG	0.4073	0.3771	0.3660	0.3752
ITQ+VGG	0.4693	0.4877	0.4673	0.5031
AGH+VGG	0.5078	0.4604	0.4414	0.4051
SP+VGG	0.5023	0.4974	0.5087	0.5192
SGH+VGG	0.4785	0.4610	0.4437	0.4418
GH	0.4352	0.4778	0.5181	0.5326
SSDH	0.5097	0.5294	0.5267	0.5360
BGAN	0.5020	0.5217	0.5408	0.5498
Ours	**0.5410**	**0.5753**	**0.5851**	**0.6015**

method achieves 2.3% (32 bits), 2.74% (64 bits), and 1.87% (128 bits) improvements over the best baseline. On the NUS-WIDE dataset, our method achieves 4.59% (32 bits), 4.43% (64 bits), and 5.17% (128 bits) improvements over the best baseline. With the increase of hash code length, the performance of most hashing methods is improved accordingly. However, some traditional methods, including SH, AGH and SGH, show no improvement with the increase of code length on some datasets. In summary, deep hashing methods perform better than the traditional hashing methods. Due to the introduction of two learned structured similarity matrices, our method significantly outperforms all methods, especially on the CIFAR-10 dataset which is of lower image resolution and contains more noise. The superiority of our proposed method in these experiments indicates the effectiveness of the structured similarity matrix learning.

We select the CIFAR-10 dataset to show the precision-recall and precision@N curves in Fig. 3. Figure 3(a), Fig. 3(b) and Fig. 3(c) plot the precision-recall

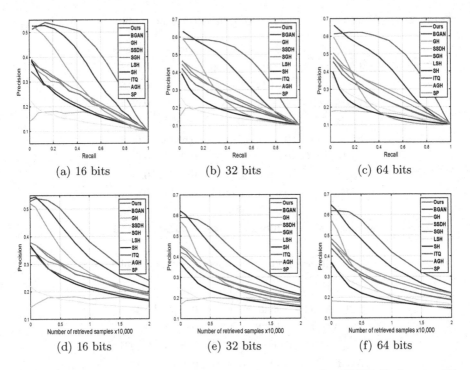

(a) 16 bits   (b) 32 bits   (c) 64 bits

(d) 16 bits   (e) 32 bits   (f) 64 bits

Fig. 3. Precision-recall curves and Precision@N curves on the CIFAR-10 dataset with different number of bits.

curves of all hashing methods and Fig. 3(d), Fig. 3(e) and Fig. 3(f) show the precision curves with top 20,000 retrieved images of all hashing methods, with hash code lengths of 16, 32 and 64 bits. BGAN outperforms our method when retrieving a small number of samples (or with small recall), however, our method soon significantly outperforms BGAN (and all other methods) with the increase of the number of retrieved samples (or recall). Besides BGAN and our method, the other two deep hashing methods GH and SSDH do not show superiority in comparison with traditional hashing methods. SSDH even underperforms all hashing methods with the small number of retrieved samples (or low recall). Therefore, much effort should be devoted for deep hashing methods in order to further improve their performances. In summary, our method always yields the best results in almost all cases, indicating its stable performance.

4.5   Similarity Matrices and Hash Codes

Given a similarity matrix $S \in R^{n \times n}$, we wish the sum of the inner-class weights to be large, while the sum of inter-class weights to be small. To this end, we define the following metric to measure the quality of S

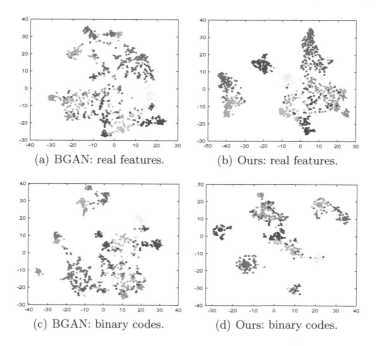

(a) BGAN: real features. (b) Ours: real features.

(c) BGAN: binary codes. (d) Ours: binary codes.

Fig. 4. Visualization of the learned real features (before binarizing) and binary hash codes by t-SNE. Different colors represent different classes. (Color figure online)

$$
QOS(\mathbf{S}) = \begin{cases} \dfrac{1}{n} \displaystyle\sum_{i=1}^{n} \dfrac{\sum\limits_{j \in \Omega_s(i)} s_{ij}}{\epsilon + \sum\limits_{j \in \Omega_d(i)} s_{ij}} & if \ \mathbf{S} \in [0,1]^{n \times n} \\[2em] \dfrac{1}{n} \displaystyle\sum_{i=1}^{n} \dfrac{count_s(\mathbf{s}_i, 1)/|\Omega_s(i)|}{(count_d(\mathbf{s}_i, 1)+1)/|\Omega_d(i)|} & if \ \mathbf{S} \in \{\pm 1\}^{n \times n} \end{cases} \tag{12}
$$

where $\epsilon = 10^{-10}$ is a small number to avoid divide-by-zero problem, $\Omega_s(i)$ denotes the index set of the samples in the same class as the i-th sample, $\Omega_d(i)$ denotes the index set of the samples in the different class from the i-th sample, $count_s(\mathbf{s}_i, 1)$ returns the number of assigned '1' to the same class in the i-th sample, and $count_d(\mathbf{s}_i, 1)$ returns the number of assigned '1' to the different class in the i-th sample. Higher $QOS(\mathbf{S})$ indicates better local structure preserved in $\mathbf{S}$.

Although many baseline methods involve similarity matrix computing, we only compare our method with BGAN (with binary similarity matrix) and AGH (with continuous similarity matrix) due to their better performance among the baselines. On the CIFAR-10 dataset, the QOS results of BGAN and $\mathbf{W}$ in our method are 16.57 and 41.06, and the QOS results of AGH and $\mathbf{S}$ in our method are 2.4347 and 1.3×10^8. Clearly, our method learns much better continuous and binary similarity matrices than existing methods.

Figure 4 shows the t-SNE visualization [18] of both real features and binary hash codes learned by our method and BGAN on the query set of the CIFAR-10 dataset, where the length of both real features and hash codes is 64 bits. An examination of these figures show that the binary hash codes learned by our method best preserve the local neighborhood structure, especially with smaller inner-class distances and larger inter-class distances.

4.6 Parameter Sensitivity

Figure 5 shows the retrieval performance of our method on the CIFAR-10 dataset with different parameters, where the hash code length is fixed at 32 bits. The results in Fig. 5(a) indicates that increasing the number of nearest neighbors k and c improves the performance first, but causes performance degradation if they are too large. In real applications, we have to carefully set k and c according to the images. The results in Fig. 5(b) indicates that the performance of our method is not sensitive to both μ_1 and μ_2.

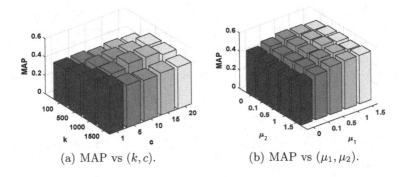

(a) MAP vs (k, c).   (b) MAP vs (μ_1, μ_2).

Fig. 5. Parameter sensitivity analysis results.

5 Conclusion

In this paper, we propose a novel unsupervised deep hashing method DSH to learn compact binary hash codes. Different from existing unsupervised hashing methods, we propose to learn both continuous and binary structured similarity matrices with explicit cluster structured by adaptively reducing the irrelevant similarities to zeros. Both similarity matrices are used to guide the hash code learning. Extensive experiments on three benchmark datasets show better retrieval performance of DSH in comparison with the state-of-art unsupervised hashing methods.

In this version, both similarity matrices are initially learned and fixed during the network training process. The concerns behind this include: 1) it is time consuming to adaptively update the similarity matrix during the network training process, 2) our experimental results show that updating the similarity matrices during the network training process will cause the whole training process unstable and result in poor performance. However, intuitively, adaptively updating the similarity matrix during the network training process may result in better hash codes. In the future work, we will try to solve this problem.

Acknowledgments. This research was supported by Major Project of the New Generation of Artificial Intelligence(No. 2018AAA0102900), NSFC under Grant no. 61773268, Natural Science Foundation of SZU (no. 000346) and the Shenzhen Research Foundation for Basic Research, China (Nos. JCYJ20180305124149387).

References

1. Andoni, A., Indyk, P.: Near-optimal hashing algorithms for approximate nearest neighbor in high dimensions. In: 2006 47th Annual IEEE Symposium on Foundations of Computer Science (FOCS 2006), pp. 459–468. IEEE (2006)
2. Bentley, J.L.: Multidimensional binary search trees used for associative searching. Commun. ACM **18**(9), 509–517 (1975)
3. Chen, Y., Lai, Z., Ding, Y., Lin, K., Wong, W.K.: Deep supervised hashing with anchor graph. In: Proceedings of the IEEE International Conference on Computer Vision, pp. 9796–9804 (2019)
4. Dai, B., Guo, R., Kumar, S., He, N., Song, L.: Stochastic generative hashing. In: Proceedings of the 34th International Conference on Machine Learning-Volume 70, pp. 913–922. JMLR. org (2017)
5. Gionis, A., Indyk, P., Motwani, R., et al.: Similarity search in high dimensions via hashing. In: Vldb, vol. 99, pp. 518–529 (1999)
6. Gong, Y., Lazebnik, S., Gordo, A., Perronnin, F.: Iterative quantization: a procrustean approach to learning binary codes for large-scale image retrieval. IEEE Trans. Pattern Anal. Mach. Intell. **35**(12), 2916–2929 (2012)
7. Gui, J., Liu, T., Sun, Z., Tao, D., Tan, T.: Fast supervised discrete hashing. IEEE Trans. Pattern Anal. Mach. Intell. **40**(2), 490–496 (2017)
8. Indyk, P., Motwani, R.: Approximate nearest neighbors: towards removing the curse of dimensionality. In: Proceedings of the 30th Annual ACM symposium on Theory of computing, pp. 604–613 (1998)
9. Jiang, Q.Y., Li, W.J.: Asymmetric deep supervised hashing. In: 32nd AAAI Conference on Artificial Intelligence (2018)
10. Kang, W.C., Li, W.J., Zhou, Z.H.: Column sampling based discrete supervised hashing. In: 30th AAAI Conference on Artificial Intelligence (2016)
11. Kulis, B., Grauman, K.: Kernelized locality-sensitive hashing for scalable image search. In: 2009 IEEE 12th International Conference on Computer Vision, pp. 2130–2137. IEEE (2009)
12. Lai, Z., Chen, Y., Wu, J., Wong, W.K., Shen, F.: Jointly sparse hashing for image retrieval. IEEE Trans. Image Process. **27**(12), 6147–6158 (2018)
13. Li, X., Hu, D., Nie, F.: Large graph hashing with spectral rotation. In: 31st AAAI Conference on Artificial Intelligence (2017)
14. Lin, K., Lu, J., Chen, C.S., Zhou, J.: Learning compact binary descriptors with unsupervised deep neural networks. In: Proceedings of the IEEE Conference on Computer Vision and Pattern Recognition, pp. 1183–1192 (2016)
15. Liu, W., Wang, J., Kumar, S., Chang, S.F.: Hashing with graphs. In: Proceedings ICML, pp. 1–8 (2011)

16. Luo, X., Nie, L., He, X., Wu, Y., Chen, Z.D., Xu, X.S.: Fast scalable supervised hashing. In: The 41st International ACM SIGIR Conference on Research & Development in Information Retrieval, pp. 735–744. ACM (2018)

17. Luo, Y., Tao, D., Xu, C., Li, D., Xu, C.: Vector-valued multi-view semi-supervised learning for multi-label image classification. In: Proceedings of the 27th AAAI Conference on Artificial Intelligence, pp. 647–653. AAAI 2013 (2013)

18. Maaten, L.V.D., Hinton, G.: Visualizing data using t-SNE. J. Mach. Learn. Res. 9(Nov), 2579–2605 (2008)

19. Nie, F., Wang, X., Huang, H.: Clustering and projected clustering with adaptive neighbors. In: Proceedings of the 20th ACM SIGKDD International Conference on Knowledge Discovery and Data Mining, pp. 977–986. ACM (2014)

20. Shen, F., Shen, C., Liu, W., Tao Shen, H.: Supervised discrete hashing. In: Proceedings of the IEEE Conference on Computer Vision and Pattern Recognition, pp. 37–45 (2015)

21. Shen, F., Xu, Y., Liu, L., Yang, Y., Huang, Z., Shen, H.T.: Unsupervised deep hashing with similarity-adaptive and discrete optimization. IEEE Trans. Pattern Anal. Mach. Intell. 40(12), 3034–3044 (2018)

22. Song, J., He, T., Gao, L., Xu, X., Hanjalic, A., Shen, H.T.: Binary generative adversarial networks for image retrieval. In: 32nd AAAI Conference on Artificial Intelligence (2018)

23. Su, S., Zhang, C., Han, K., Tian, Y.: Greedy hash: towards fast optimization for accurate hash coding in cnn. In: Advances in Neural Information Processing Systems, pp. 798–807 (2018)

24. Szegedy, C., et al.: Going deeper with convolutions. In: Proceedings of the IEEE Conference on Computer Vision and Pattern Recognition, pp. 1–9 (2015)

25. Wang, J., Zhang, T., Song, J., Sebe, N., Shen, H.T.: A survey on learning to hash. IEEE Trans. Pattern Anal. Mach. Intell. 40(4), 769–790 (2017)

26. Weiss, Y., Torralba, A., Fergus, R.: Spectral hashing. In: Advances in Neural Information Processing Systems, pp. 1753–1760 (2009)

27. Xia, Y., He, K., Kohli, P., Sun, J.: Sparse projections for high-dimensional binary codes. In: Proceedings of the IEEE Conference on Computer Vision and Pattern Recognition, pp. 3332–3339 (2015)

28. Yang, E., Deng, C., Liu, T., Liu, W., Tao, D.: Semantic structure-based unsupervised deep hashing. In: IJCAI, pp. 1064–1070 (2018)

29. Zhang, Z., et al.: Scalable supervised asymmetric hashing with semantic and latent factor embedding. IEEE Trans. Image Process. 28(10), 4803–4818 (2019)

30. Zhu, H., Long, M., Wang, J., Cao, Y.: Deep hashing network for efficient similarity retrieval. In: 30th AAAI Conference on Artificial Intelligence (2016)

A New CPU-FPGA Heterogeneous gStore System

Xunbin Su, Yinnian Lin, and Lei Zou[⊠]

Peking University, Beijing, China
{suxunbin,linyinnian,zoulei}@pku.edu.cn

Abstract. In this demonstration, we present a new CPU-FPGA heterogeneous gStore system. The previous gStore system is based on CPU and
has low join query performance when the data size is too big. We implement a FPGA-based join module to speed up join queries. Furthermore,
we design a FPGA-friendly data structure called FFCSR to facilitate
it. We compare our new system with the previous one on the LUBM2B
dataset. Experimental results demonstrate that the new CPU-FPGA heterogeneous system performs better than the previous one based on CPU.

Keywords: gStore · FPGA · FFCSR · Join query acceleration

1 Introduction

Recently in large-scale data retrieval and query, graph database has been applied
in a wide range of fields. gStore [3] is a graph-based RDF data management
system on multi-core CPU that supports SPARQL 1.1 standard query language
defined by W3C. It stores RDF data as a labeled directed graph G (called
RDF graph), where each vertex represents a subject or an object and each edge
represents a predicate. Given a SPARQL query, we can also represent it as a
query graph Q. Then gStore employs subgraph matching of Q over G to get
query results. Specific technical details of gStore have been published before [6]
and [7].

Though gStore can already support the storage and query of billions of RDF
triples, the query performance significantly decreases as the data size increases,
especially join queries (SPARQL queries involving join process). Two main performance bottlenecks for join queries are a large number of list intersections and
too many reading Key-Value store operations from the external storage.

To overcome the two problems above and improve the overall performance
of gStore, we introduce the field-programmable gate array (FPGA). A FPGA
has many advantages including low energy consumption, high concurrency, pro-
grammability and simpler design cycles. In recent years, not only has GPU been
widely used in graph computation [1] but also using FPGAs for hardware acceleration has gradually become a trend. For example, FPGAs are often used for
accelerating some common graph algorithms like breadth-first search (BFS) and
single-source shortest path (SSSP) [5].

© Springer Nature Switzerland AG 2020
X. Wang et al. (Eds.): APWeb-WAIM 2020, LNCS 12318, pp. 517–522, 2020.
https://doi.org/10.1007/978-3-030-60290-1_39

In this demo, we design and implement a new CPU-FPGA heterogeneous gStore system that has a FPGA-based join module and a FPGA-friendly data structure called FFCSR, which can accelerate join queries and improve the overall performance of gStore.

We conduct a comparative experiment on the previous and the new version of gStore on LUBM2B dataset. Experimental results demonstrate that the new CPU-FPGA heterogeneous gStore system performs better compared with the previous one on CPUs.

2   System Overview

The whole gStore system consists of an offline part and an online part. The offline part consists of a build module and a load module, for data preprocessing. The online part consists of a SPARQL parser, a filter module and a join module, handling a SPARQL query. We depict the system architecture in Fig. 1.

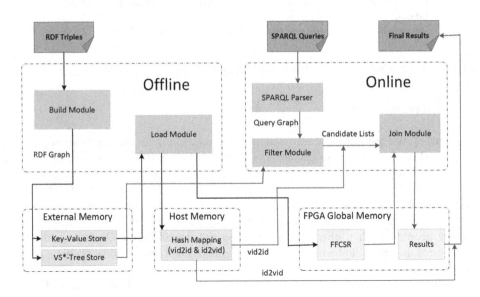

Fig. 1. The system architecture

Build Module. In the offline phase, gStore first accepts an RDF file and converts it to RDF triples. Then the build module uses adjacency list representation to build a RDF graph. The RDF graph is stored in external memory in the form of a Key-Value store and a VS*-tree store.

Load Module. GSI [4] proposes a GPU-friendly data structure to represent an edge-labeled graph, called PCSR. Inspired by [4], we build a FPGA-friendly Compressed Sparse Row during the load module, which we call FFCSR. Additionally, two sets of hash mappings are created to facilitate FPGA random access to the FFCSR. We describe them in Fig. 2. Hash mappings are stored in host memory and the FFCSR is transferred to the FPGA's global memory (DRAM).

There are three components in the FFCSR: an index list, k offset lists and k adjacency lists, where k is the number of DDRs in DRAM. The index list has p triples, where p is the number of predicates. The first element of the i-th triple represents a DDR number. The second and the third are an out-edge offset initial position and an in-edge offset initial position. The i-th offset list and adjacency list are stored on the i-th DDR, which could be favorable for FPGA reading operations in parallel. The mapping $vid2id$ converts the discrete but ordered vertex ids (vid) to the consecutive offset ids (oid) and the mapping $id2vid$ is just opposite.

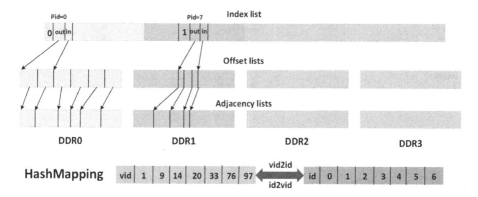

Fig. 2. The structure of FFCSR and corresponding hash mappings

SPARQL Parser. In the online phase, the SPARQL parser converts a SPARQL query given by a user to a syntax tree and then builds a query graph based on the syntax tree. The query graph is encoded into a signature graph with the similar encoding strategy that encodes RDF graphs.

Filter Module. After the SPARQL parser, the filter module uses the VS*-tree store to generate an ordered candidate list for each query node. This step is necessary to reduce the size of the input to the join module.

Join Module. The join module can be divided into two parts: a CPU host and a set of FPGA kernels. We adopt multi-step join [2] in the join module. The order which query node should be added in each step is determined by its priority. The priority of each query node is inversely proportional to the size of its candidate list because the smaller size leads to fewer intermediate results and a faster join. Then the host generates two types of candidate lists for FPGA kernels. One is mapped using the mapping $vid2id$, which we call CLR (candidate list for reading). The other is converted to a bitstring where the i-th bit represents whether $vid = i$ exists, which we call CLS (candidate list for searching). Finally,

FPGA kernels perform specific computational tasks to get results. Note that results should be restored using the mapping *id2vid*.

3   FPGA Kernel

A set of FPGA kernels are designed for computation of intersection among multiple candidate lists. They are controlled by the host. A FPGA kernel is designed as a 4-stage pipeline consisting of reading FFCSR and CLR, intersection computing, searching in CLS and writing back, as shown in Fig. 3.

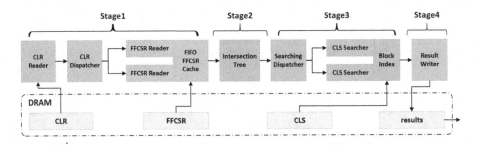

Fig. 3. The pipeline overview of a FPGA kernel

Reading FFCSR and CLR. A CLR reader reads one set of k elements at a time and passes them to a dispatcher for FFCSR reading. A dispatcher decides to assign tasks to FFCSR reading threads according to the *oid*. As soon as a thread gets an *oid*, it accesses the FFCSR in DRAM for corresponding adjacency list and stores it in a buffer in BRAM for the next stage.

Intersection Computing. We implement a merge-based intersection tree whose leaf nodes correspond to original adjacency lists, to find the common elements among all k adjacency lists in a bottom-up manner. At every cycle an intersection is conducted between each 2 sibling nodes. Because the BRAM is faster than the DRAM, we design a simple FIFO cache shared by the threads. Before a thread accesses the DRAM, it first searches in the cache in BRAM to see if the needed list is already cached to avoid unnecessary IO.

Searching in CLS and Writing Back. The *vids* generated by the intersection tree are sent to another dispatcher. This dispatcher conducts Round-Robin Scheduling and allocates a *vid* to a searching thread each cycle. Then each thread searches a given *vid* in the CLS. If the corresponding bit of the CLS is equal to one, the result will be written to the output buffer.

Optimization. We design a smaller in-BRAM block index for searching to reduce DRAM access. Note that in most cases the CLS is very sparse with many continuous zeros. Therefore, we use a bitstring index where one bit represents a fixed-length block of the CLS. The size of the block index is small enough to be put in BRAM. A searching thread first checks the block index to determine whether a given *vid* is valid. The CLS in DRAM is searched only when the *vid* is valid.

4   Demonstration

In this demo, we use the famous Lehigh University Benchmark (LUBM) for evaluating the efficiency of our new gStore system. We choose the LUBM2B dataset with 2136214258 triples for our experiments. The host system is a supermicro 7046GT-TRF (Intel Xeon E5-2620 v4 2.10 GHz, 256 GB memory) which is equipped with a Xilinx alevo-u200 FPGA board (64GB global memory, 35 MB BRAM) via PCIe 3.0 with 16 lanes. The design on the FPGA is clocked with 330 MHz.

In Fig. 4(a), we input a join query and execute it with gStore on CPU and CPU-FPGA heterogeneous gStore, respectively. The performance comparison histogram is below to validate the effectiveness. In Fig. 4(b), the visual query results are shown to validate the correctness. Experimental results demonstrate that CPU-FPGA heterogeneous gStore can achieve up to 3.3× speedup for join queries.

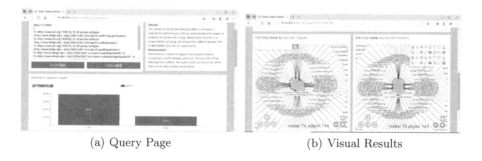

(a) Query Page   (b) Visual Results

Fig. 4. Demonstration of gStore

Acknowledgment. This work was supported by The National Key Research and Development Program of China under grant 2018YFB1003504 and NSFC under grant 61932001.

References

1. Alam, M., Perumalla, K.S., Sanders, P.: Novel parallel algorithms for fast multi-GPU-based generation of massive scale-free networks. Data Sci. Eng. **4**(1), 61–75 (2019). https://doi.org/10.1007/s41019-019-0088-6
2. Ngo, H.Q., Porat, E., Ré, C., Rudra, A.: Worst-case optimal join algorithms. J. ACM (JACM) **65**(3), 16 (2018)

3. Shen, X., et al.: A graph-based RDF triple store. In: 2015 IEEE 31st International Conference on Data Engineering, pp. 1508–1511. IEEE (2015)
4. Zeng, L., Zou, L., Özsu, M.T., Hu, L., Zhang, F.: GSI: GPU-friendly subgraph isomorphism. arXiv preprint arXiv:1906.03420 (2019)
5. Zhou, S., Prasanna, V.K.: Accelerating graph analytics on CPU-FPGA heterogeneous platform. In: 2017 29th International Symposium on Computer Architecture and High Performance Computing (SBAC-PAD), pp. 137–144. IEEE (2017)
6. Zou, L., Mo, J., Chen, L., Özsu, M.T., Zhao, D.: gStore: answering SPARQL queries via subgraph matching. Proc. VLDB Endow. 4(8), 482–493 (2011)
7. Zou, L., Özsu, M.T., Chen, L., Shen, X., Huang, R., Zhao, D.: gStore: a graph-based SPARQL query engine. VLDB J.-Int. J. Very Large Data Bases 23(4), 565–590 (2014)

Euge: Effective Utilization of GPU Resources for Serving DNN-Based Video Analysis

Qihang Chen, Guangyao Ding, Chen Xu$^{(\boxtimes)}$, Weining Qian, and Aoying Zhou

School of Data Science and Engineering, East China Normal University,
Shanghai 200062, China
{qhchen,gyding}@stu.ecnu.edu.cn, {cxu,wnqian,ayzhou}@dase.ecnu.edu.cn

Abstract. Deep Neural Network (DNN) has been widely adopted in video analysis application. The computation involved in DNN is more efficient on GPUs than on CPUs. However, recent serving systems involve the low utilization of GPU, due to limited process parallelism and storage overhead of DNN model. We propose Euge, which introduces multi-process service (MPS) and model sharing technology to support effective utilization of GPU. With MPS technology, multiple processes overcome the obstacle of GPU context and execute DNN-based video analysis on one GPU in parallel. Furthermore, by sharing the DNN-based model among threads within a process, Euge reduces the GPU memory overhead. We implement Euge on Spark and demonstrate the performance of vehicle detection workload.

Keywords: GPU · DNN · MPS · Model sharing

1 Introduction

Deep Neural Network (DNN) technology has been widely adopted for the intelligent analysis of video data, such as vehicle and pedestrian detection, face recognition and family safety monitoring [4]. However, adopting DNN technology causes a lot of computation. Employing only CPU to make a DNN-based prediction obtains a high latency [5]. It is common to accelerate the computation of DNN by GPU. The acceleration of GPU depends on the utilization of GPU resources [1]. The utilization of GPU is the proportion of resources being used in the whole available computing resources. In general, the higher the utilization of GPU is, the better the acceleration we get.

Significant efforts have been made to improve the utilization of GPU computing resources. Tensorflow-Serving [2] and Nexus [6] schedule different jobs employing the same GPU in a round-robin mode. Both of them improve the utilization of GPU resources by switching jobs quickly and reasonably. However, there is only one job running on a GPU at the same time and the single job is not able to utilize all the compute capacity available on the GPU. Spark-GPU [7]

X. Wang et al. (Eds.): APWeb-WAIM 2020, LNCS 12318, pp. 523–528, 2020.
https://doi.org/10.1007/978-3-030-60290-1_40

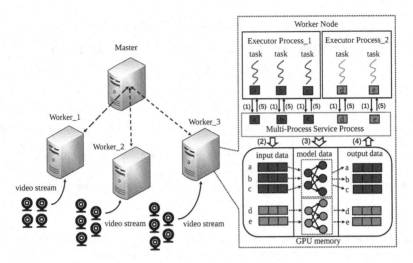

Fig. 1. Euge system overview

improves the utilization of GPU computing resources through sharing the GPU among multiple CPU threads or processes. However, due to the obstacle of the GPU context, it executes multiple processes concurrently on the GPU instead of in parallel. In addition, it considers a general workload rather than the DNN-based video analysis. In DNN-based applications, the model often consumes a large memory size. Hence, it is crucial to reduce the GPU memory overhead.

To enable effective utilization of GPU resources, there are two challenges: *1) How to enable multiple CPU processes to employ GPU resources in parallel?* Each process obtains its own GPU context. Kernel functions in different contexts cannot run on one GPU in parallel, which makes it difficult for multiple processes to employ the GPU in parallel. *2) How to reduce the GPU memory overhead when serving DNN-based video analysis?* Each analysis thread requires a same and read-only DNN model to make a prediction, and the model takes up a large amount of GPU memory. Hence, it causes a waste of GPU memory which is a limitation of parallelism. To address these challenges, we propose Euge which employs *MPS technology* [1] as well as a *model sharing* strategy. In particular, we implement Euge based on Spark [8] and demonstrate the performance of Euge during the execution of video analysis application.

2 Euge Overview

Euge inherits the master-slave architecture of Spark. There are two different types of nodes, i.e., master node and worker nodes, in the cluster. The master node is responsible for the management of cluster resources while the worker node is responsible for the execution of tasks. Each worker node launches one or more executor processes and each executor process issues one or more threads to execute video analysis tasks. As shown in Fig.1, Euge executes video analysis

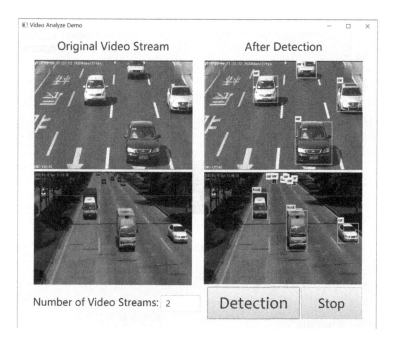

Fig. 2. Video analysis result

applications (e.g., vehicle detection) in the following five steps. (1) The task sends its memory copy requests or kernel function requests to MPS. (2) The MPS loads video data from CPU memory into GPU memory. (3) The MPS calls kernels to make a prediction employing the DNN model. (4) The MPS pulls the results of prediction from GPU memory and copies them into CPU memory. (5) The task receives the results returned by MPS. In particular, we employ the following two technologies in Euge to overlap multiple processes on GPU and reduce the waste of GPU memory.

2.1 MPS in Euge

As shown in Fig. 1, the kernel functions of task a, b, c, d and e from the two processes cannot run on one GPU in parallel without MPS technology. The processes employ GPU by switching context, which causes additional switching time and context storage overhead. In addition, there is only a single process running on the GPU at the same time which is not able to utilize all the compute capacity available on the GPU. The obstacles above results in a low utilization of GPU. To improve the utilization of GPU, as shown in Fig. 1, Euge employs the MPS technology which starts a service process on the GPU. The service process schedules GPU requests from all processes in parallel in one context (process). This avoids context switching and storage overhead and allows the leftover GPU capacity to be occupied with kernel functions from different processes. Clearly, Euge significantly improves the utilization of GPU resources.

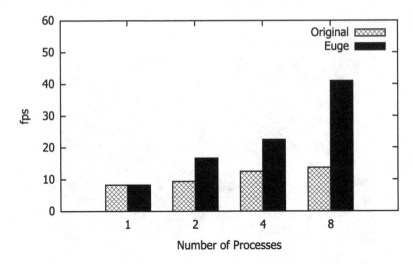

Fig. 3. Prediction ability

2.2 Model Sharing

The DNN-based model takes up a large amount of GPU memory. However, as shown in Fig. 1, each task such as a, b, c, d and e requires a model to make a prediction. There are five models in GPU memory which may exceed the capacity of GPU memory and limits the parallelism. Euge shares the model among parallel tasks within a process. As shown in Fig. 1, task a, b and c from process 1 share the same model, and task d and e from process 2 share the same model. There are five parallel tasks in execution, but only two models in the GPU memory, which effectively reduces the waste of GPU memory. Model sharing alleviates the limitation of GPU memory size on parallelism, so as to improve the utilization of GPU.

3 Demonstration

We firstly run the workload of DNN-based [3] vehicle detection application using traffic video stream on the Euge and show the result on the client GUI. Then, we demonstrate the effectiveness of Euge through performance evaluation tool.

3.1 Video Analysis Result

As shown in Fig. 2, we show the original traffic video stream on the left window and the result traffic video stream on the right window. Euge supports the use of multiple GPUs in the cluster, and makes full use of the computing resources in each GPU. Euge achieves significant speedups for large-scale traffic video stream data analysis and shows the results in real time.

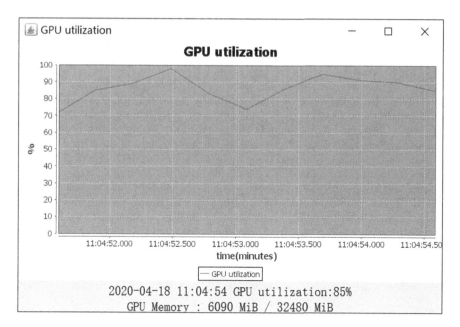

Fig. 4. Utilization and GPU memory

3.2 Performance Evaluation

Euge is built on Spark 2.4.3 and implemented for NVIDIA Tesla V100 platform running CentOS 7. As shown in Fig.3, with the increase number of processes running on one GPU, the prediction ability of Euge scales well, while the system without employing MPS technology obtains a low performance improvement. The result demonstrates the effectiveness of Euge. As shown in Fig.4, we measure the utilization of GPU computing resources and GPU memory by NVIDIA System Management Interface and show them on a GUI in real time. We can see that Euge achieves significant improvement in the utilization of GPU computing resources with less GPU memory. We are also able to get more detailed performance data in the dashboard of the nvidia visual profiler.

Acknowledgment. This work has been supported through grants by the National Key Research & Development Program of China (No. 2018YFB1003400), National Natural Science Foundation of China (No. 61902128, 61732014) and Shanghai Sailing Program (No. 19YF1414200).

References

1. Multi-Process Service. https://docs.nvidia.com/deploy/mps/index.html
2. Baylor, D., Breck, E., Cheng, H., Fiedel, N., Foo, C.Y., et al.: TFX: a tensorflow-based production-scale machine learning platform. In: Proceedings of the 23rd ACM International Conference on Knowledge Discovery and Data Mining (SIGKDD), pp. 1387–1395 (2017)

3. Redmon, J.: Darknet: open source neural networks in C (2013–2016). http://pjreddie.com/darknet/
4. Redmon, J., Farhadi, A.: YOLOv3: an incremental improvement. CoRR abs/1804.02767 (2018)
5. Ruvo, P.D., Distante, A., Stella, E., Marino, F.: A GPU-based vision system for real time detection of fastening elements in railway inspection. In: Proceedings of the 16th International Conference on Image Processing (ICIP), pp. 2333–2336 (2009)
6. Shen, H., Chen, L., Jin, Y., Zhao, L., Kong, B., et al.: Nexus: a GPU cluster engine for accelerating DNN-based video analysis. In: Proceedings of the 27th ACM Symposium on Operating Systems Principles (SOSP), pp. 322–337 (2019)
7. Yuan, Y., Salmi, M.F., Huai, Y., Wang, K., Lee, R., Zhang, X.: Spark-GPU: an accelerated in-memory data processing engine on clusters. In: Proceedings of the 4th IEEE International Conference on Big Data (BigData), pp. 273–283 (2016)
8. Zaharia, M., Chowdhury, M., Franklin, M.J., Shenker, S., Stoica, I.: Spark: cluster computing with working sets. In: Proceedings of the 2nd USENIX Workshop on Hot Topics in Cloud Computing (HotCloud) (2010)

Blockchain PG: Enabling Authenticated Query and Trace Query in Database

Qingxing Guo, Sijia Deng, Lei Cai, Yanchao Zhu, Zhao Zhang$^{(\boxtimes)}$, and Cheqing Jin

School of Data Science and Engineering, East China Normal University,
Shanghai, China
{qingxingguo,sjdeng,leicai,yczhu}@stu.ecnu.edu.cn,
{zhzhang,cqjin}@dase.ecnu.edu.cn

Abstract. Blockchain comes under the spotlight for successfully implementing a tamper-resistant ledger among multiple untrusted participants. The widespread adoption of blockchain in data-intensive applications has led to the demand for querying data stored in blockchain databases. However, compared to traditional databases, current blockchain systems cannot offer efficient queries. Moreover, migrating the original business supported by traditional databases to blockchain systems takes a long time and costs a lot. Motivated by this, we design and implement Blockchain PG, a novel data management system built on a legacy system. The system architecture applies to most databases system. By establishing a trusted relationship between the database and the client, Blockchain PG not only guarantees that the existing legacy system will not be greatly affected, but also achieves the data integrity and correctness by authenticated query, and the traceability of data by trace query.

Keywords: Blockchain · Authenticated query · MBtree · Trace query.

1 Introduction

The centralized database might be compromised and authorized users can abuse privileges to disguise the identity of others to maliciously operate data, making data security becomes a serious problem [6]. Recently, the appearance of blockchain offers a promising direction for protecting data. As a distributed append-only ledger maintained by multiple parties, Blockchain provides reliable data storage service in a potentially hostile environment [1].

When blockchain is widely used by many applications in various fields, query requests are growing in number and complexity [8]. So far many efforts have been devoted to improving data management of blockchain [2,7,9]. By integrating the blockchain technique and database characteristics, the blockchain database has been optimized to support rich queries. For example, SEBDB [10] achieves the APIs interface of SQL-like language by adding relational semantics

© Springer Nature Switzerland AG 2020
X. Wang et al. (Eds.): APWeb-WAIM 2020, LNCS 12318, pp. 529–534, 2020.
https://doi.org/10.1007/978-3-030-60290-1_41

to blockchain systems. However, when the business involves more complex functions that blockchain systems do not support, like aggregate queries, it will be tricky to migrate them from a traditional database to blockchain systems without changing the original functions. Besides, current blockchain platforms run in a distributed environment, resulting in low efficiency in submitting transactions through a consensus protocol.

This paper proposes Blockchain PG modified based on PostgreSQL. The system architecture is also applicable to other databases. Firstly, we build Authenticated Data Structure(ADS)[5] on tuples to ensure that client can verify the integrity and correctness of data through authenticated query. Then, the history table is designed to track user operation and table rows are chained through cryptographic hashes to ensure tamper-evident data. The history table empowers trace queries to detect illegal behaviors of authorized users. Finally, establishing a trusted relationship between the system and the client without consensus protocol can greatly improve query performance.

2   System Overview

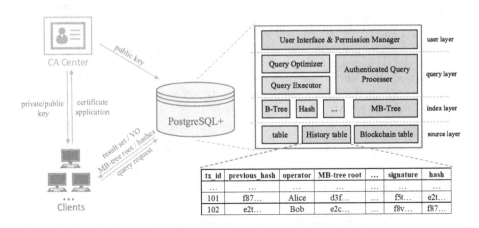

Fig. 1. System architecture.

As shown in Fig. 1, Blockchain PG consists of three parts, CA center, client, and PostgreSQL+. The CA center is responsible for distributing certificates that can prove the client's identity. PostgreSQL+ is a database system divided into four layers: (i) user layer works to process user request and verify the user's identity with the public key; (ii) query layer generates a plan for authenticated query or normal query; (iii) index layer performs as data retrieval, and MB-tree [4] is built as an authenticated index structure at this layer; and (iv) source layer works to store table files, including blockchain tables and history tables. Compared with an ordinary table, the blockchain table is a new type with an MB-tree index.

The history table is insert-only and highly tamper-resistant. Table rows are chained by cryptographic hashes based on previous row hash and current row data.

2.1 Identity Management

CA Center provides stronger database security against user fraud. It will generate a pair of public and private keys upon receipt of the client's certificate request, and then send the private key to the client and broadcast the public key to other clients and PostgreSQL+. Message signed by the client's private key can be decrypted and its owner will be verified by the corresponding public key stored on others [3].

2.2 Maintaince of Verification Information

If a client successfully connects to PostgreSQL+, it will synchronize the MB-tree root and hashes taken from the history table at specific intervals, including the latest hash value, to the client as initial verification information.

Once the client initiates update requests along with the message signature through the user's private key, the MB-tree index in PostgreSQL+ will be updated and generate the newest hash root. Next, PostgreSQL+ inserts the update operation into the history table and calculates a new row hash. Finally, the newest MB-tree root and row hash are synchronized to all clients for a basis for the client to verify the query result. Expired hashes left on clients are not discarded completely, but stored by clients at certain intervals. For example, the hash column in the history table of Postgresql+ is (h0, h1, h2, ..., h102), while the client stores (h0, h10, h20, ..., h100, h101, h102).

2.3 Queries

As a centralized database might be untrusted, we proposed authenticated query and trace query in Blockchain PG for clients to verify the correctness and completeness of the data and tracking the illegal behavior of authorized users. Now we detail authenticated query and trace query procedures.

Authenticated Query. When Blockchain PG receives an authenticated query request, it generates an authenticated query plan that allows the executor to obtain tuples of the blockchain table through the MB-tree index in the query layer. As suggested in Fig. 2(a), Query executor accesses nodes in the MB-tree from root to leaf and appends hashes of sibling nodes to verification objects(known as VO), and then sends VO and query result to the client. The client calculates a new MB-tree root hash from VO and result set as demonstrated in Fig. 2(b). We can judge whether the result set is correct and complete by comparing the calculated hash value with the latest MB-tree root saved locally on the client.

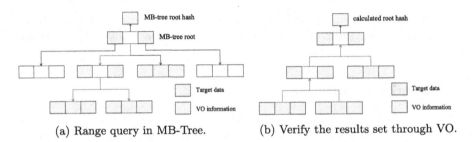

(a) Range query in MB-Tree.   (b) Verify the results set through VO.

Fig. 2. Query and verification of Authenticated query.

Trace Query. Trace query provides an approach to track user behavior. Since the client stores the hash column of the history table at intervals, our query strategy does not need to return the whole data of the history table to determine whether the table has been changed. If the client wants to know data changes of blockchain tables in a certain period, it first finds two boundary hash values containing the query target in the local hash set, and then query all data in the boundary interval from the history table of PotsgreSQL+. After the client receives the query result, it will hash the data and reorganize them into a hash chain. We know whether the log record has been modified by comparing the two ends of the hash chain with the previous boundary hashes. Moreover, the signature bound to the user's private key in the history table provides identity fraud protection.

Blockchain PG

AUTHSELECT * FROM userinfo WHERE user_id < 8 AND user_id > 5:   Search

Results

userinfo

user_id	name	age	signup_date
6	Bob	22	2019-07-20
7	Alice	18	2019-09-13

Verification information

error : The root hash calculated from VO and result set is different from the one stored by the client

local latest MB-tree root hash : **f53ed063e82ebc2f78af3434df1c0dc9**
root hash : **3bd0bf8739d69ec61278d42a773514cb**
+ root node
  - leaf node [Keys: {1,4}, Hash: {2f4c7f892a70e324f1bb3d161e05ca1b}]
  + branch node
    - leaf node [Keys: {5}, Hash: {7cd454c137d2910ea3333d2167b89f24}]
    - leaf node [Keys: {8}, Hash: {4C6E15fdce99e0a7ab05387f181b4a2p6}]

Fig. 3. The interface of Authenticated Query. (Color figure online)

3   Demonstration and Evaluation

Blockchain PG is implemented on the basis of PostgreSQL which is an excellent open-source database. The system architecture is also applicable to other databases. The whole system runs on Ubuntu 16.04 OS. The client protocol has been modified to accommodate authenticated and trace queries. Figure 3 and Fig. 4 show the response results when the client sends authenticated query and trace query requests, respectively. We create a userinfo table containing name, age, and other fields in PostgreSQL+, and implement a data generator which supports uniform and Gaussian distribution of data to simulate the real scenario. In Fig. 3, The VO structure, including leaf node and branch node, marked in blue font is presented in the form of a tree. We can calculate a root hash value through VO and the result set of the query, and then compare the hash value with local root hash to check whether the query result set is correct and complete. As the data in the blockchain table is maliciously modified by other authorized user, the client find that the data is wrong when verifying the query set. In addition, we can track user behavior through trace queries illustrated in Fig. 4. Since target records that the client wants to find is in the hash interval marked in red font, the client only needs to look up the records in the hash interval to prove that the records have not been modified, thus correctly tracks the user's behavior.

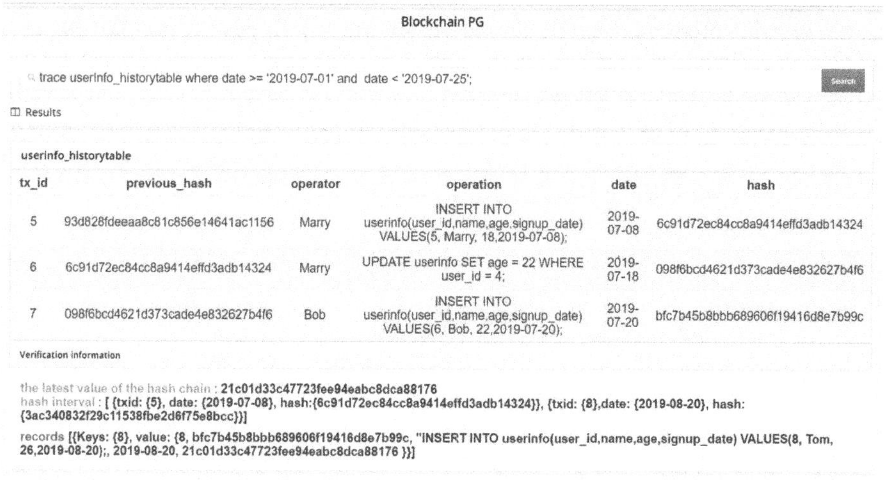

Fig. 4. The interface of Trace Query.

Acknowledgments. This research is supported by in part by National Science Foundation of China under grant number U1811264, U1911203, 61972152 and 61532021.

References

1. Chitti, P., Murkin, J., Chitchyan, R.: Data management: relational vs blockchain databases. In: Advanced Information Systems Engineering Workshops - CAiSE 2019 International Workshops, pp. 189–200 (2019)
2. El-Hindi, M., Binnig, C., Arasu, A., Kossmann, D., Ramamurthy, R.: Blockchaindb - A shared database on blockchains. In: Proceedings VLDB Endowment, pp. 1597–1609 (2019)
3. Hyla, T., Pejas, J.: Long-term verification of signatures based on a blockchain. Comput. Electr. Eng. **81**, 106523 (2020)
4. Li, F., Hadjieleftheriou, M., Kollios, G., Reyzin, L.: Dynamic authenticated index structures for outsourced databases. In: Proceedings of the ACM SIGMOD International Conference on Management of Data, pp. 121–132. ACM (2006)
5. Martel, C.U., Nuckolls, G., Devanbu, P.T., Gertz, M., Kwong, A., Stubblebine, S.G.: A general model for authenticated data structures. Algorithmica **39**(1), 21–41 (2004)
6. Mathew, S., Petropoulos, M., Ngo, H.Q., Upadhyaya, S.J.: A data-centric approach to insider attack detection in database systems. In: RAID, pp. 382–401 (2010)
7. Ruan, P., Chen, G., Dinh, A., Lin, Q., Ooi, B.C., Zhang, M.: Fine-grained, secure and efficient data provenance for blockchain. In: Proceedings VLDB Endowment, pp. 975–988 (2019)
8. Xu, C., Zhang, C., Xu, J.: vchain: enabling verifiable boolean range queries over blockchain databases. In: Proceedings of the 2019 International Conference on Management of Data, pp. 141–158. ACM (2019)
9. Zhang, C., Xu, C., Xu, J., Tang, Y., Choi, B.: Gem2-tree: a gas-efficient structure for authenticated range queries in blockchain. In: ICDE, pp. 842–853 (2019)
10. Zhu, Y., Zhang, Z., Jin, C., et al.: SEBDB: semantics empowered blockchain database, pp. 1820–1831. IEEE (2019)

PHR: A Personalized Hidden Route Recommendation System Based on Hidden Markov Model

Yundan Yang, Xiao Pan[✉], Xin Yao, Shuhai Wang, and Lihua Han

Shijiazhuang Tiedao University, Shijiazhuang 050043, Hebei, China
smallpx@163.com

Abstract. Route recommendation based on users' historical trajectories and behavior preferences is one of the important research problems. However, most of the existing work recommends a route based on the similarity among the routes in historical trajectories. As a result, hidden routes that also meet the users' requirements cannot be explored. To solve this problem, we developed a system PHR that can recommend hidden routes to users employing the Hidden Markov Model, where a route recommendation problem is transformed to a point-of-interested (POI) sequence prediction. The system can return the top-k results including both explicit and hidden routes considering the personalized category sequence, route length, POI popularity, and visiting probabilities. The real check-in data from Foursquare is employed in this demo. The research can be used for travel itinerary plan or routine trip plan.

Keywords: Hidden Markov Model · Route recommendation · Hidden routes · Trajectory big data

1 Introduction

With the increasing popularity of Location-based Social Network (LBSN), the dissemination and sharing of information becomes much more convenient. A large amount of user-generated content information including reviews, photos, check-in data, travel notes, GPS tracks, etc., has been accumulated. By analyzing these user-generated contents, users' preferences and behaviors can be obtained, making it possible to recommend personalized travel routes for users and better meet user needs and preferences. On the other hand, it is time-consuming and difficult to plan a qualified route since the travel information is numerous and jumbled. Most of the existing work recommends a route through comparing the similarities between the user's historical trajectories and other users' travel records. Thus, only explicit routes can be returned, while the new hidden routes, that meet user requirements, cannot be explored.

For example, Alice issues a query for requesting a path from the airport to her hotel. She also wants to pass by an art gallery, a café, and a bookstore. The route is expected to be short and with high popularity. Figure 1 shows two historical routes, which is in a blue dash line and a green solid line respectively (i.e., R_1 and R_2). We use a round

© Springer Nature Switzerland AG 2020
X. Wang et al. (Eds.): APWeb-WAIM 2020, LNCS 12318, pp. 535–539, 2020.
https://doi.org/10.1007/978-3-030-60290-1_42

rectangle to represent a POI whose category is shown in the rectangle. We observe that R_1 covers an art gallery and a café except a bookstore, and R_2 goes through both a café and a bookstore except an art gallery. None of the existing historical routes contains all the required POIs. However, a hidden route (*i.e.*, R' in a red line), that is combined from part of R_1 and part of R_2, can satisfy all the requirements.

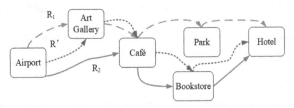

Fig. 1. Illustration for hidden routes (Color figure online)

Users' historical travelling routes can be regarded as POIs visiting sequences. We organized historical travelling routes by a Hidden Markov Model. The POIs are the unobservable hidden states, and the POI categories are observable states. Then, a route recommendation problem is transformed to a POIs sequence prediction. When a user issues a query with (origin, destination, a category sequence), an improved Viterbi algorithm is used to generate multiple POI sequence candidates. Next, the sequence candidates are ranked by the balanced scores, which consider the route length, POI popularity and the visiting probability. Finally, the top-k routes are displayed and returned to users. With the help of the Hidden Markov Model, both explicit and hidden routes can be found out.

2 PHR Overview

Figure 2 gives an overview of PHR. PHR is mainly composed of four modes: (1) data preprocessing; (2) Hidden Markov Model; (3) route generation; (4) route ranking and visualization. The first two modes operate offline and the last two modes is running online.

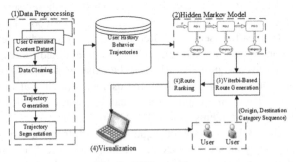

Fig. 2. PHR overview

2.1 Offline Operation Modes

Data Preprocessing. We clear the dirty data by deleting the duplicate records and the records with null values (i.e., without locations or timestamps). After data cleaning, a trajectory is generated for each user by sorting the points timestamps. Then, the trajectories are partitioned by a fixed time interval, e.g., a day, a month or a year.

Modeling. Hidden Markov Model consists of two state sets (i.e., observation state set and hidden state set) and three probability matrices λ (initial hidden state probability matrix, hidden state transition probability matrix and emission matrix). The system sets the POI categories as observation states and the POIs as the hidden states. The three probability matrices are calculated using the users' historical routes. Readers can refers to the specific computation methods in our paper [1].

2.2 Online Operation Modes

Route Generation. When a user issues a query in the form (origin, destination, a category sequence), the query is sent to the route generation mode. Given a category sequence, the route generation mode aims to find an existing or hidden POI sequences. This problem is similar to the existing sequence prediction on Hidden Markov Model [2], where Viterbi algorithm is the well-known method. Thus, we employ the improved Viterbi algorithm to generate several candidate POI sequences.

Route Ranking. The candidate POI sequences, generated in the route generation mode, have not consider the locations of the origin and the destination and users' preferences. As a result, the returned routes could be far from the origin and the destination, or the POIs in the returned routes are not popular. Thus, we fuse the distances between the first point (the last point) in the candidate route and the origin (destination), POI popularity, and the access probability of the route into a balanced score. Readers can refer to paper [1] for more computation detail as well. The candidate routes are ranked by the balance scores and the top-k routes are returned to users.

Visualization. The top-k (i.e., $k = 3$) routes are visualized and returned to users as shown in Fig. 3. User can choose the checkbox to display the route on the map. Different colored solid lines are used to indicate differently ranked routes. For instance, the blue line indicates the highest rank. Each point on the route has a label. The labels with {first, second, third} indicate the visiting order. The straight line between two consecutive points indicates the direction, which is not the navigation path.

3 Demonstration Outline

PHR is implemented using Java, SQL Server 2017 and Baidu map API. The real check-in data from New York and Los Angeles captured on the Foursquare website [3, 4] were used as experimental datasets. We generated 26,748 trajectories including 50,143 points. We use the real historical trajectories to measure the accuracy of the result, the recommendation routes' accuracy can reach more than 90% when $k = 3$ [1].

In particular, Fig. 3 shows the hidden route recommendation. Users can click the "Category Sequence" textbox to choose categories, and click the venue in the map (blue heart label) to choose origin(destination). After clicking "Submit", the top-1 route is displayed on the map by default. The top-3 routes are displayed below the map, and users can click the checkbox to show the route in the map. In addition, the route lengths are also displayed.

Besides hidden routes recommendation, PHR also supports "shortest route recommendation", "route recommendation based on Markov model" [5] and "Comparison and Statistics". This system can be extended to be used in travel itinerary plan or routine trip plan.

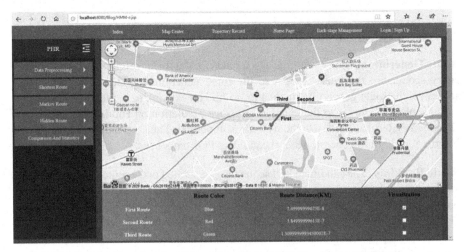

Fig. 3. Demonstration for hidden route recommendation (Color figure online)

Acknowledgment. This research was partially supported by the Natural Science Foundation of Hebei Province (F2018210109), the Key projects from the Hebei Education Department (No. ZD2018040), the Foundation of Introduction of Oversea Scholar (C201822), the Basic Research Team Project from Science and Technology Department (2019JT70803), the Fourth Outstanding Youth Foundation of Shijiazhuang Tiedao University.

References

1. Pan, X., Yang, Y.D., Yao, X., et al.: Personalized hidden route recommendation based on Hidden Markov Model. J. Zhejiang Univ. (Eng. Sci.) **54**(9), 1736–1745 (2020). (in Chinese)
2. Qiao, S.J., Shen, D.Y., et al.: A self-adaptive parameter selection trajectory prediction approach via Hidden Markov Models. IEEE Trans. Intell. Transp. Syst. **16**(1), 284–296 (2015)

3. Jie, B., Yu, Z., et al.: Location-based and preference-aware recommendation using sparse geo-social networking data. In: Proceedings of ACM GIS, pp. 199–208 (2012)
4. Wei, L.Y., Zheng, Y., Peng, W.: Constructing popular routes from uncertain trajectories. In: Proceedings of SIGKDD Annual Conference of ACM, pp. 195–203 (2012)
5. Chen, D.W., Ong, C.S., et al.: Learning points and routes to recommend trajectories. In: Author Proof Proceedings of CIKM, pp. 2227–2232 (2016)

JoyDigit NexIoT: An Open IoT Data Platform for Senior Living

Kai Zhao[1(✉)], Peibiao Yang[1], Peng Zhang[1], Sufang Wang[1], Feng Wang[1], Xu Liu[1], and Hongyan Deng[2]

[1] JoyDigit, Beijing, China
{zhaokai,yangpeibiao,zhangpeng,wangsufang,wangfeng,liuxu}@joydigit.com
[2] Zaozhuang University, Shandong, China
denghongyan@uzz.edu.cn

Abstract. The senior care service plays an important role in senior living industry. With the unprecedented increasing of the seniors and the demanding activities of daily living (ADL) service, caregiver's workload and community's operational cost grow dramatically which lead tremendous challenges. From both caregivers and community operators' perspective, we developed an open IoT data platform for senior living named JoyDigit NexIoT to solve above problems. Multidimensional open IoT data from smart home, health care equipment and security monitoring devices are integrated and processed in real-time on the platform to build dynamical profiles for both seniors and communities, and it also provides open data APIs for customized senior living applications. Together with the novel JoyDigit Intelligent Action Adviser (JIAA), the platform outputs the recommended service or management actions to caregivers and operators, which could greatly reduce the caregiver's daily workload and increase community operator's management efficiency. In this paper, we describe JoyDigit NexIoT platform's features, architecture and JIAA, and also present the practical scenarios to be demonstrated.

Keywords: Data platform · Internet of Things · Intelligent Action Adviser

1 Introduction

The senior care service occupies most of workloads in senior living communities. The utilization of IoT technologies [4] and applications, like bed exit alarm [5], sleep analysis [6] and etc., relieves the caregiver's stress and workload. And IoT platforms are used for connecting heterogeneous IoT devices and building own applications. Comparing with general IoT platforms [1,2] which emphasizes on Platform as-a Service (PaaS), the IoT platform for senior living is much more care operation oriented. AIP (aging in place) service platform [3] that allows people to use composition tool to build medication reminder together with light and sound. HABITAT [7] monitors the daily behaviors of people by

© Springer Nature Switzerland AG 2020
X. Wang et al. (Eds.): APWeb-WAIM 2020, LNCS 12318, pp. 540–544, 2020.
https://doi.org/10.1007/978-3-030-60290-1_43

embedding the IoT devices in everyday life objects like wall light, armchair, belt and wall panel etc. The IoT silos are built for individual scenarios and not integrated. More importantly, except for the routine service plan, caregivers and operators need intelligent action adviser based on comprehensive data insight from multidimensional IoT data, senior's profile and community regulations.

We implemented an open IoT data platform called JoyDigit NexIoT for senior living. It has following features:

Open IoT Management. Adaptor technology is used for IoT data connection via third party IoT vendor cloud and APIs. Multidimensional IoT data are transformed and indexed in the hierarchy of locations like building, floor, area, room, senior and device which facilitate the further data access and analysis for certain layer directly and easily.

Open Data Application Builder and Marketplace. The building blocks like authorized public open data APIs and interactive data visualization are supported in the platform, and customization of IoT application is developer friendly.

Novel Intelligent Action Adviser (JIAA). Based on adaptive rule engine and user profiling, JIAA provides the recommended actions for caregivers and operators for better service management and regulation compliance.

2   Platform Architecture and Implementation

JoyDigit NexIoT's platform architecture is shown in Fig. 1. IoT Adaptor module is the open wrapper that customized to connect the devices via device cloud or APIs. The multidimensional IoT data from multiple devices are merged and stored according to the location of hierarchy. The platform provides building blocks like open data APIs and powerful interactive data visualization tool. Based on the building blocks, senior living IoT applications could easily constructed and released to Marketplace. Both the Building Blocks and applications in Marketplace act as the inputs for the JoyDigit Intelligent Action Adviser, JIAA, which outputs the proper actions to caregivers and operators according to the Adaptive Rule Engine algorithm and User Profiling. The action's positive feedback loop will greatly reduce the front-line caregiver's workload and work pressure, and improve the senior's service quality.

3   JoyDigit Intelligent Action Adviser and Algorithm

JIAA is built upon the adaptive rule engine and user profiling.

3.1   Definitions

Definition 1 (Rule). *Rule: ActivityPattern(AP) → Action where AP = ActivitySteps(S) × Time(T) × Locality(L), and ActivitySteps(S) are derived from multidimensional IoT data within specific time T and locality L.*

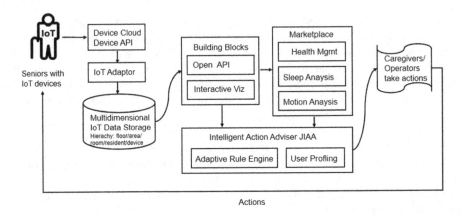

Fig. 1. JoyDigit NexIoT platform architecture.

e.g. the $AP_{insomnia}$ can be simply characterized by fail to fall asleep during the night time. $S_{insomnia} = (BodyMovment|BedExit)^*$ as regular expression which generated from IoT data from smart mattress. $T_{insomnia} = \{time| 21{:}00 \leq time \leq 05{:}00\}$ as configuration parameters. $L_{insomnia} = \{locality| locality \text{ is bed room}\}$ as the location enumeration.

Definition 2 (UserProfile). *The UserProfile(UP) for $senior_i$ is Rule set for $senior_i$. $UP_{seniori} = \{Rule \mid Rules \text{ on } senior_i \text{ should be checked}\}$.*

e.g. $UP_{Jim} = (AP_{insomnia} \rightarrow MedicineAction, AP_{bedexit} \rightarrow Assistance Action)$

3.2 JIAA Algorithm

We briefly introduce the JIAA algorithm, and it has three parts, the rule initialization, adaptive rule generation and rule check on user profile. As rule check is almost self-explained, we will focus on the first two parts.

Rule Initialization. Some initial rules are mandatory rules according to regulations and globally effective, called GlobalProfile. Other rules are manually built according $senior_i$'s care assessment and care plans, and tagged in corresponding $UP_{seniori}$.

Adaptive Rule Generation. Take all senors' daily activity steps as input, JIAA uses hybrid methods to generate the rule in adaptive ways.

a. Common activity pattern generation. We use the association rule algorithms like Apriori to discover the frequent activity patterns. These common patterns indicate we should provide standard service and work flow to reduce operation cost.

b. Outlier activity pattern generation. With predefined high-risk activities (e.g. falling, lost), we use statistic and data visualization (e.g. sankey diagram [8]) to get the preceding abnormal activities (called outliers) which lead to those predefined high-risk activities. The caregivers and operators should place more attentions and timely actions to these outlier patterns, because if not handled properly, they will lead the occurrences of the high-risk activities and high work pressure for caregivers and operators.

4   Demonstration Scenarios

Following scenarios will be demonstrated:

Platform's Open Capability. Take senior living health management as example to show the platform's open capability to IoT devices and data applications.

JoyDigit Intelligent Action Adviser. The IoT environment for insomnia rule detection as mentioned in Sect. 3.1 is setup with smart mattress and motion sensors. The end-to-end work flow of JIAA from rule definition, match and medication action triggered are demonstrated (in Fig. 2).

Fig. 2. JIAA with insomnia rule demonstration.

5   Conclusion

In this paper, JoyDigit NexIoT, an open IoT platform for senior living with novel Intelligent Action Adviser (JIAA) embedded, is introduced. The platform was deployed in some of senior living communities in China and received positive feedback with the caregiver's daily workload reduced and community operator's management efficiency increased.

References

1. Amazon IoT. http://aws.amazon.com/iot. Accessed 1 May 2020
2. GE Predix. www.ge.com/digital/iiot-platform. Accessed 1 May 2020

3. Fattah, S., Sung, N.-M., Ahn, I.-Y., Ryu, M., Yun, J.: Building IoT services for aging in place using standard-based IoT platforms and heterogeneous IoT products. Sensors **17**, 2311 (2017)
4. Maskeliūnas, R., Damaaeviius Damaševičius, R., Segal, S.: A review of Internet of Things technologies for ambient assisted living environments. Future Internet **11**, 259 (2019)
5. Jähne-Raden, N., Kulau, U., Marschollek, M., Wolf, K.-H.: INBED: a highly specialized system for bed-exit-detection and fall prevention on a geriatric ward. Sensors **19**, 1017 (2019)
6. Roebuck, A., et al.: A review of signals used in sleep analysis. Physiol. Meas. **35**, 1 (2014)
7. Borelli, E., et al.: HABITAT: an IoT solution for independent elderly. Sensors **19**, 1258 (2019)
8. Sankey Diagram. https://developers.google.com/chart/interactive/docs/gallery/sankey. Accessed 1 May 2020

Epidemic Guard: A COVID-19 Detection System for Elderly People

Wenqi Wei, Jianzong Wang$^{(\boxtimes)}$, Ning Cheng, Yuanxu Chen, Bao Zhou,
and Jing Xiao

Ping An Technology(Shenzhen) Co., Ltd., Shenzhen, China
jzwang@188.com

Abstract. The global outbreak of the COVID-19 in the worldwide has drawn lots of attention recently. The elderly are more vulnerable to COVID-19 and tend to have severe conditions and higher mortality as their immune function decreased and they are prone to having multiple chronic diseases. Therefore, avoiding viral infection, early detection and treatment of viral infection in the elderly are important measures to protect the safety of the elderly. In this paper, we propose a real-time robot-based COVID-19 detection system: Epidemic Guard. It combines speech recognition, keyword detection, cough classification, and medical services to convert real-time audio into structured data to record the user's real condition. These data can be further utilized by the rules engine to provide a basis for real-time supervision and medical services. In addition, Epidemic Guard comes with a powerful pre-training model to effectively customize the user's health status.

Keywords: COVID-19 · Automatic Speech Recognition · Cough classification · Few-shot learning · Attention similarity

1 Introduction

Since the first outbreak of COVID-19 in China in December 2019, this virus has rapidly spread worldwide and turned into a global pandemic. As of May 21th 2020, there were in total 5147966 confirmed cased worldwide [1]. Early symptoms of COVID-19 infection assembles a common flu such as cough, fever and sometimes dyspnea [2,3], but could developed into an acute respiratory distress syndrome. As shown in the current researches, elder people infected by COVID-19 tend to have worse outcomes [4]. Therefore, it is necessary to identify COVID-19 infection at early stage and take effective measures in time when the elderly show initial symptoms. In this paper, we developed a cough-based COVID-19 detection system for the elderly aiming to identify COVID-19 infection at early stage. The system has been deployed in community robots to assist self diagnose and could assist remote diagnose without physical contact. In a real world setting, we collected data from several elderly people and developed a visualization interface of our system with the realworld data. A comprehensive diagnose conclusion are given by the system with regarding to users' information including chronic medical history, geographical location, and cough recording.

© Springer Nature Switzerland AG 2020
X. Wang et al. (Eds.): APWeb-WAIM 2020, LNCS 12318, pp. 545–550, 2020.
https://doi.org/10.1007/978-3-030-60290-1_44

2   Overview of Epidemic Guard

We obtained data from some seniors who volunteered for Epidemic Guard program in the elder community. The basic information of the elders will be utilized for electronic medical records. In addition, we will ask the elder key questions through online phone service or oine intelligent servicing robot, i.e. *Have you ever been to a high risk area in the last 14 days, Have you shown fever, cough and other symptoms in the last 14 days.* Eventually, we asked the respondent to cough three times and record it. The cough audio will be compared with a large number of different types of cough according to our algorithm, and then the diagnosis result will be drawn and display on the interaction screen of the Epidemic Guard.

Epidemic Guard can be placed in elderly communities, parks, pharmacies and other places to achieve contactless COVID-19 diagnosis. The Epidemic Guard system is connected to the hospital to provide medical assistance to patients with the possibility of infection in time.

2.1   The Capabilities of Epidemic Guard

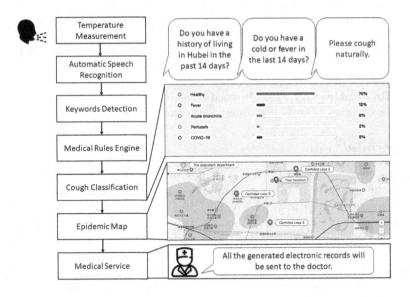

Fig. 1. The Architecture of Epidemic Guard

The main functional modules and processes of Epidemic Guard are shown in Fig. 1. The conversation between the user and our robot will be passed to several modules in order to obtain the basic information of the user and diagnose the disease by coughing. Specifically, we will introduce each capability in Epidemic Guard in detail:

Temperature Measurement. Epidemic Guard uses infrared imaging technology to achieve non-contact temperature measurement, and the measurement results will also serve as an important reference for diagnosis.

Automatic Speech Recognition. Our Kaldi-based ASR system [5] has the ability to handle thousands of concurrent requests at a time with low latency and low word error rate. The health-related information from the text transcripts mentioned in our ASR system will be added to electronic health records during human-robot conversations.

Keywords Detection. Through the way of online phone or offline robot, the elderly will be asked some key questions. After recording the answers, we use neural network model to extract key words from the answers, so as to help the system to evaluate the situation of the elderly more comprehensively.

Cough Classification. In the database, we classify and mark each cough data for each new cough record, we compare it with coughs from multiple diseases in the database and calculate the attention similarity. The current database contains cough data for various conditions including acute bronchitis, chronic pharyngitis, whooping cough, fever, and COVID-19. Here we combine the attention method with the few shot learning. In our experiment, the attention method is helpful to improve the accuracy of the few-shot sound recognition. The attention similarity of COVID-19 is named the COVID-19 index and will provide an important reference for doctors. Our system can help doctors to give a comprehensive evaluation standard considering the previous medical history, body temperature, COVID-19 index and other indicators.

Medical Rules Engine. This model can define complex triggers for call events. For example, if the system finds that the respondents give sensitive answers to some questions after keyword extraction, the system will give real-time early warning.

Medical Service. All the generated electronic medical records will be sent to the doctor, and the doctor will select the abnormal medical records for further consultation. If necessary, the doctor will arrange the user to perform medical CT imaging or nucleic acid detection.

2.2   Cough Classification Algorithm

Because COVID-19 patients need to take strict isolation measures, the number of coughs from COVID-19 patients is small. For model training, a small amount of data will cause serious overfitting problems. In addition, the cough duration of different users is inconsistent, which makes it impossible to directly compare the similarity between two coughs.

In order to address the above problem, we introduce a few-shot learning method [6], namely *c-way k-shot learning*, which leverage small amount of samples to complete a brand new classication task. The training strategy of the introduced approach is made up of multiple iterations, so as to approximate the final classification result in a loop. The characteristics of this paradigm are highly compatible with COVID-19's disease detection tasks. Inspired by this, the experimental method we adopted when pre-training the model is consistent with [7]. Each iteration randomly selects c categories from all categories, each category contains k samples, and selects one category from each of the c categories as the test set. Due to multiple iterations, all data will be used.

Based on the training strategy of few-shot learning, we introduce an attention similarity to complete the task of cough classification [7]. Unlike the previous method of calculating similarity by pooling to the same length, it can directly receive input features of different lengths and calculate the attention similarity between the input features and a certain type of features. The input feature X is a cough recording collected by the robot, where the length of time for each input X varies with different coughs. The input feature X will calculate the attention similarity with the average cough sound of several diseases in the database, and select the result with the highest attention similarity as the output (Figs. 2 and 3).

3 Demonstration

● Electronic Case of Cough

The user can log in through the mobile number to view the electronic medical record already stored in the system.

● Cough Classification

The robot provides the API interface of cough detection. Users can perform cough classification detection through the robot. In addition, the system will customize basic diagnosis suggestions for users according to the results.

● Epidemic Map

According to the location of the robot, the system will generate an epidemic map to help users identify the nearby risk areas.

Fig. 2. Functions of offline robots

Fig. 3. Examples of electronic medical record and epidemic maps

We design COVID-19 detection robots and put them into various communities. The elderly nearby can use the robots to detect the possibility of COVID-19 infection. This application is easy to operate and reduces human contact. At the same time, a demo video is available[1].

3.1   Electronic Medical Record of Cough

The elderly can log in to the system to view the electronic medical record through the mobile phone number. Electronic medical records include basic information, cough detection history, etc. During the detection, if the elderly is identified as high risk, he/she will receive the highlight (yellow or red frame) of the system in this interface.

Our system also has the ability of resource management. Medical s will be automatically allocated to corresponding staff in hospitals. Once abnormal records are noticed, the corresponding person will receive a phone call from doctors for further treatment.

3.2   Cough Classification

The system provides real-time cough detection function. The elderly will be asked to cough naturally after answering the key questions. The system records the coughing sound, quickly analysis, and recommends the basic diagnosis to the user according to the results. As for the COVID-19 infection, the system will also report to the community related epidemic prevention personnel, and provide more epidemic prevention services.

3.3   Epidemic Map

The location of COVID-19 confirmed cases will be marked in the epidemic map and their scope of activities will be marked as the risk area, so as to remind

---

[1] https://v.douyin.com/TVnpDB/.

the elderly to avoid risks and reduce the possibility of individual infection. In addition to the risk areas, we also label nearby pharmacies and fever clinics. When the elderly use our robot for cough detection, it will generate epidemic map according to the location and situation of the community. In addition, we also provide the elderly with the epidemic map by SMS, the map will update at 8:00 every morning.

4   Discussion

In this article, we design a COVID-19 detection system for the elderly, which extracts cough audio through human-robot conversation for disease detection. The generated electronic medical record and epidemic map can help doctors to conduct crowd screening in an orderly manner, thereby preventing the problem of running out of medical resources. The system we proposed can effectively avoid cross-infection caused by person-to-person contact and relieve medical pressure.

Acknowledgements. This paper is supported by National Key Research and Development Program of China under grant No.2018YFB1003500, No.2018YFB0204400 and No.2017YFB-1401202. Corresponding author is Jianzong Wang from Ping An Technology (Shenzhen) Co., Ltd.

References

1. Dong, E., Du, H., Gardner, L.: An interactive web-based dashboard to track COVID-19 in real time. Lancet Infectious Diseases (2020)
2. Guan, W., et al.: Clinical characteristics of 2019 novel coronavirus infection in China. medRxiv (2020)
3. Joseph,W., Leung, K., Leung, G.: Nowcasting and forecasting the potential domestic and international spread of the COVID-19 outbreak originating in Wuhan, China: a modelling study. The Lancet (2020)
4. Huang, C., et al..: Clinical features of patients infected with 2019 novel coronavirus in Wuhan, China. The Lancet (2020)
5. Povey, D., Ghoshal, A., Boulianne, G.: The Kaldi Speech Recognition Toolkit. IEEE automatic speech recognition and understanding workshop (2011)
6. Oriol, V., Charles, B., Timothy, L., Daan, W.: Matching networks for one shot learning. In: Advances in Neural Information Processing Systems (2016)
7. Chou, S., Cheng, K., Jang, J., Yang, Y.: Learning to match transient sound events using attentional similarity for few-shot sound recognition. In: IEEE International Conference on Acoustics, Speech and Signal Processing (ICASSP) (2019)

Automatic Document Data Storage System Based on Machine Learning

Yu Yan[1], Hongzhi Wang[1,2(✉)], Jian Zou[1], and Yixuan Wang[1]

[1] Harbin Institute of Technology, Harbin, China
{yuyan0618,wangzh,1180300918,1180300929}@hit.edu.cn
[2] Peng Cheng Laboratory, Shenzhen, China

Abstract. Document storage management plays a significant role in the field of database. With the advent of big data, making storage management manually becomes more and more difficult and inefficient. There are many researchers to develop algorithms for automatic storage management(ASM). However, at present, no automatic systems or algorithms related to document data has been developed. In order to realize the ASM of document data, we firstly propose an automatic document data storage system (ADSML) based on machine learning, a user-friendly management system with high efficiency for achieving storage selection and index recommendation automatically. In this paper, we present the architecture and key techniques of ADSML, and describe three demo scenarios of our system.

Keywords: Automatic management · Index recommendation · Storage selection · Machine learning

1 Introduction

Managing document data is one of the most important tasks in many applications such as library management system, document retrieval and so on. A vital part of document management is storage management which determines the storage selection and index configuration. Traditionally, experienced engineers make the storage decision relying on so-called design consulting tools [1,4,5], which provide some statistical data to express data features. However, with the rapid growth in document data quantity and diversity, it becomes more and more difficult for engineers to make the best choice based solely on experience.

Currently, researchers propose many algorithms [2,3,6] for managing data automatically. However, most of existing algorithms focus on the research of relational database. There is no systems or algorithms to study automatic storage management on document data. And with large amounts of document data, the traditional methods based on experience which rely on statistical data is very expensive and usually do not get good result. So, achieving automatic document management has become a new important research direction.

X. Wang et al. (Eds.): APWeb-WAIM 2020, LNCS 12318, pp. 551–555, 2020.
https://doi.org/10.1007/978-3-030-60290-1_45

In order to solve these problems, we firstly design an automatic document data storage system to achieve the intelligent storage management. The main features of our system are summarized as follows:

- *Automatic Management.* Our system realizes the automatic storage management of document data such as achieving storage intelligent decision and generating efficient index recommendations which greatly accelerate the workload execution.
- *Friendly UI.* ADSML provides friendly user interface. In our system, users only need to upload document data, workloads and configure some parameters, then they can view and edit these data easily through our graphical interface to complete automatic management.

Our paper is organized as follows. In Sect. 2, we introduce the architecture and implementation of ADSML in detail. After knowing how the modules of ADSML work together, in Sect. 3, we demonstrate two key technologies (storage selection and index recommendation) which support the core function of our system. Finally, the demonstration plan of ADSML will be shown in Sect. 4.

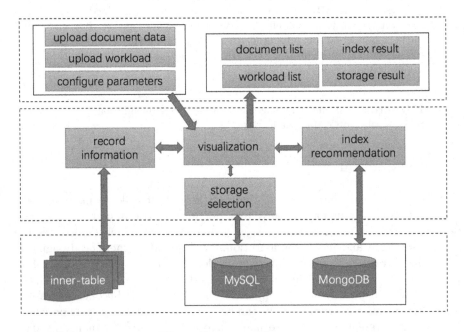

Fig. 1. System architecture

2   System Architecture and Implementation

In this section, we introduce the architecture and implementation of our ADSML as shown in Fig. 1. The *Visualization* module is the core of our system. Users could view and process these source data (document and workloads) easily through the *Visualization* module, such as delivering source data to other modules, recording the introduction of source data by calling the *Record Information* module, getting storage scheme by calling the *Storage Selection* module, making efficient index recommendations by the *Index Recommendation* module and saving the decision-making outcomes to database. Taking the uploading data as a specific example, after users provide the directory of source data, our system delivers these massege to *Record Information* module through the *Visualization* module and constructs the inner-table to save the directory and other details of these data. Then, our system shows the document list and workload list through the *Visualization* module. The *Storage Selection* module and the *Index Recommendation* module are similar to *Record Information* module in terms of module invocation relationships.

Considering that Python integrates many machine learning libraries which helps to build our model, our system is mainly constructed in Python and Java based on C/S structure. And we choose the well-known NoSQL (MongoDB) and MySQL as the storage basement.

3   Key Technologies

In this section, we would introduce the key technologies in ADSML. We divide the automatic management process into two phases, one is to select the appropriate database, and the other is to recommend the best index configuration on the basis of checked database. Then, we will describe the technologies related to these two phases separately.

3.1   Storage Selection

We would start with the first step of automatic management, storage selection. The first thing to know is that document can be stored in document databases and relational databases, because of document can be organized as tree and complex parent-child relationship. Nowadays, there are variable kinds of databases, such as MySQL, MongoDB, Neo4J. These databases are suitable for different scenarios. Our model is the first one which considers the automatic database selection. In this paper, we design a classifier for document data based on logistic regression(LR) to achieve automatic selection between MySQL and MongoDB. We take height, width, number of nodes, number of leaf nodes of the document tree which can reflect the complexity of tree structure as the input of our model. And then ADSML can get the classification result quickly by calling the LR algorithm. Our model is very efficient in extracting document tree features and is able to respond in milliseconds.

3.2   Index Recommendation

After deciding which database to store the documents, we looked at how to recommend index automatically for accelerating workload execution. In this section,

Table 1. Configuration of recommendation model

Layers	Configuration	Output shape
Input layer		[None, 30000, 7, 26]
Convolution layer	[5, 7, 26]*2, [10, 7, 26]*2, [20, 7, 26]*2, [30, 7, 26]*2, [50, 7, 26]*2	[None, 6000, 1, 1, 2], [None, 3000, 1, 1, 2], [None, 1500, 1, 1, 2], [None, 1000, 1, 1, 2], [None, 600, 1, 1, 2]
Max-pooling layer	[60, 1, 1], [30, 1, 1] [15, 1, 1], [10, 1, 1] [6, 1, 1]	[None, 100, 2], [None, 100, 2] [None, 100, 2],[None, 100, 2] [None, 100, 2]
Flatten layer		[None, 1000]
Full connected layer	64, dropout = 0.1, relu	[None, 64]
Output layer	4, dropout = 0.1, sigmoid	[None, 4]

we study the index recommendation on the condition that the data is stored in MongoDB. We innovatively transfer the index recommendation problem to a multi-class task. We define the document data and workloads as the input of this task. And we use the character-level coding method [7] to encoding the input data. The output of this task is the index classes supported by MongoDB, we use one-hot coding to vectorized these index classes. We propose a multi-class model based on convolutional neural network to achieve the above multi-class task. Our model realizes the high-quality knowledge representation by using the strong learning ability of multi-core CNN. This model consists of five layers as shown in Tab. 1. The convolution layer has multiple convolution kernels in order to increase the feature diversity. Designing the max-pooling layer can quickly reduce the feature dimension to facilitate the reduction of network parameters. At the end of network, we use the sigmoid as the activation function to get index class vector. Then, ADSML parses the output vector to the index configuration and presents it in system interface.

4   Demonstration Scenario

We plan to demonstrate our ADSML from the following three parts.

- *Upload Source Data.* As shown in Fig. 2a, after just scaning the directory of source data (document data and workloads), users can view and edit source data easily through our graphical interface.
- *Storage Selection.* as depicted in Fig. 2b, users first check the document dataset which uploaded by themselves. After calling our model, ADSML shows the result of automatic storage selection and give some examples of storage scheme. And then, users decide whether to apply this result or not.

– *Index Recommendation.* As Fig. 2c presents, ADSML expresses the best index configuration of all items automatically, just after users check the data list and workload list. Similar to storage selection, we provide three choices (save, apply and abandon) to users.

(a) Upload Source Data   (b) Storage Selection   (c) Index Recommendation

Fig. 2. System demonstration

Acknowledgement. This paper was partially supported by NSFC grant U1866602, 61602129, 61772157.

References

1. Toolpark.de Alle Rechte vorbehalten: The website of powerdesigner. http:// powerdesigner.de (2016)
2. Chaudhuri, S., Narasayya, V.R.: An efficient, cost-driven index selection tool for Microsoft SQL server. In: VLDB, vol. 97, pp. 146–155. Citeseer (1997)
3. Ding, B., Das, S., Marcus, R., Wu, W., Chaudhuri, S., Narasayya, V.R.: AI meets AI: leveraging query executions to improve index recommendations. In: Proceedings of the 2019 International Conference on Management of Data, pp. 1241–1258 (2019)
4. IDERA, I.L.P.S.G.: The website of er/studio. https://www.idera.com (2004–2020)
5. S.S.P. Ltd.: The website of sparx enterprise architect. https://sparxsystems.com (2000–2020)
6. Sharma, A., Schuhknecht, F.M., Dittrich, J.: The case for automatic database administration using deep reinforcement learning. arXiv preprint arXiv:1801.05643 (2018)
7. Zhang, X., Zhao, J., Lecun, Y.: Character-level convolutional networks for text classification. In: ADVANCES IN NEURAL INFORMATION PROCESSING SYSTEMS 28 (NIPS 2015). vol. 28 (2015), 29th Annual Conference on Neural Information Processing Systems (NIPS), Montreal, CANADA, 07–12 December 2015 (2015)

A Meta-Search Engine Ranking Based on Webpage Information Quality Evaluation

Yukun Li[1,2(✉)], Yunbo Ye[1], and Wenya Xu[1]

[1] Tianjin University of Technology, Tianjin 300384, China
liyukun_tjut@163.com
[2] Tianjin Key Laboratory of Intelligence Computing and
Novel Software Technology, Tianjin, China

Abstract. This paper demonstrates a meta-search engine developed by the authors, which ranks the results based on web page information quality evaluation algorithm. The web page information quality score is calculated based on the title of the web page, the abstract of the web page and the source of the web page. The quality of web page can be evaluated by these factors. When a user submits an input, the proposed meta-search engine system collects the results from some general search engines like Baidu, Bing, Sogou and so on, and rank the web pages according to their information quality scores. Because we do not need a local database to store a large amount of data, all operations are completed in the cache, which greatly reduces system consumption. The system is evaluated by three kinds of representative queries, and the results show that its search accuracy and user experience are obviously better than the current general search engines.

Keywords: Meta-search engine · Web information quality evaluation algorithm · Result ranking

1 Introduction

In the era of big data, a large amount of information appears in front of users. Only in China, the number of search engine users has reached 681.32 million [1]. However, due to low accuracy and low recall rate [2], a single search engine sometimes leads to low user satisfaction. Therefore, a meta-search is proposed to expand the coverage of information retrieval and improve the recall rate. The most critical technology of the meta-search engine is to re-synthesize the results of existing search engines like Baidu, Google and so on. The quality of ranking results directly affects the performance of the entire meta-search engine.

Direct merge is the naive ranking method of meta-search engine, which directly merges the results of sub-search engines. Yuan [3] proposed a result sorting algorithm based on web page summary and location, and determined the priority according to the number of returned results. Jitendra Kumar [4] used the genetic algorithm to calculate the retrieved web pages and sorted the web pages, but the stability of the algorithm was poor. These methods pay little attention to the quality of the web pages, and we develop a prototype meta-search engine based on web page quality.

© Springer Nature Switzerland AG 2020
X. Wang et al. (Eds.): APWeb-WAIM 2020, LNCS 12318, pp. 556–560, 2020.
https://doi.org/10.1007/978-3-030-60290-1_46

2 System Architecture

The meta-search engine designed in this demonstration mainly includes four modules, and the system framework is shown in Fig. 1.

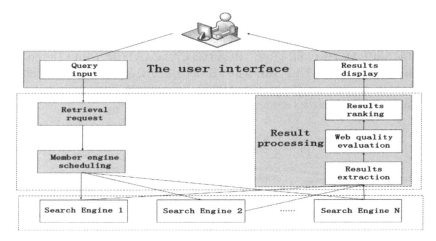

Fig. 1. The architecture of system

The user interface module mainly includes user input and query result display. This system provides a friendly interactive interface, it provides user input form, general search column (like news, map, library, etc.) and current search hotpots.

The retrieval request module is mainly to receive the user's search request and analyze the processing parameters. The search parameters required by different member search engines are not the same, so the request parameters need to be converted into the parameters required by the corresponding member search engines. Then the parameters are submitted to the member search engines.

The member engine scheduling module adopts a multi-threaded parallel working mode, and simulates a synchronization stack to ensure synchronization among threads. All operations are completed in the cache, without the need for a local database, which greatly reduces the system overhead.

The result processing module includes three parts: retrieval result extraction, webpage quality evaluation, and result ranking. It is responsible for obtaining the query results returned by each sub-search engine, and obtaining the webpage quality score through the web information quality evaluation algorithm. Finally, the ranking are sorted in descending order based on the scores.

3 Web Information Quality Evaluation Algorithm

This demonstration proposes a web page quality evaluation algorithm based on three factors: web page title, web page abstract and web page source.

The webpage title score is obtained by calculating the cosine similarity between the query sentence and the webpage title. we segment the query and webpage title, count the word frequency vector. Then calculate the cosine, we denote it as $Score_t$. The web page abstract is a short article concisely and accurately describes the important content of a web page. The abstract score is denoted as $Score_d$, and is decided by computing the common largest sequential segment of user input and web page abstract. For example, the user input can be segmented to three sequential parts denoted as A, B and C. The results of permutation and combination of the strings connected by ABC are: A | AB | AC | ABC | ACB | B | BA | BC | BAC | BCA | C | CA | CAB | CB | CBA |.The positive sequential ones include: A | AC | AB | ABC | B | BC | C |.The abstract scores calculating method to this example are illustrated in Table 1. For example, if the abstract of a web page include ABC,its abstract score is 10.

Table 1. The scoring process of largest participle matching

The cases of segment positive distribution in webpage abstract	Positive sequential combination of segments in abstract	Abstract score processing
...ABC...	ABC, AB, BC, A, B, C	$3 + 2 + 2 + 1 + 1 + 1 = 10$
...AB...C...	AB, A, B, C	$2 + 1 + 1 + 1 = 5$
...A...BC...	BC, A, B, C	$2 + 1 + 1 + 1 = 5$
...AB...	AB, A, B	$2 + 1 + 1 = 4$
...BC...	BC, B, C	$2 + 1 + 1 = 4$
...A...B...C...	A, B, C	$1 + 1 + 1 = 3$
...A...	A	1
...B...	B	1
...C...	C	1

Determination of Weight Coefficient. We take well-accepted information retrieval metrics nDCG(Normalized Discounted cumulative gain) [5] to compute the weight coefficient of title score and abstract score and they are denoted as α and β. They are computed by independently running title-based method and abstract-based method based on the same search samples.

The Calculation of Webpage Source Score. We take a voting method to compute the data source-based weight of a web page, and denote it as $Score_f$. It equals to the number of the member search engines whose results include the web page. For example, if the webpage appeared in three member search engines, its $Score_f$ is 3. The web page quality-based score is computed with the formula as below.

$$Score_{wq} = (\alpha \times Score_t + \beta \times Score_d) \times Score_f \qquad (1)$$

4   Evaluation and Demonstration

We use three representative queries to evaluate our system with Baidu and Google search engines by nDCG measure. The nDCG measure is a retrieval measure devised specifically for web search evaluation, and its value depends on not only the top k results, but also their sequence. The queries include: Website of Sina(Q1); Java learning route(Q2); Free music download(Q3). The ground truth of the queries is generated by the expert's analysis of the web page. The results are shown in Fig. 2. It can be found that our demo system is relatively stable, and the search quality of our system is significantly improved compared to Baidu and Google. Figure 3. shows the graphical interface of the system.

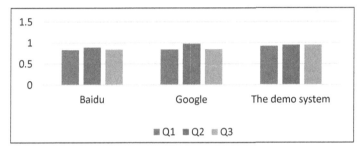

Fig. 2. The evaluation result of nDCG

Fig. 3. User interface

The demo system has the following features: (1) Good recall and precision, It can help people search expected information efficiently; (2) Compared with existing meta search engines, our system returns better results in less time; (3) It proposes some columns to help people to quickly locate frequently-used websites, like dictionary, map, translation, video, music, email and so on; (4) It provides people some hotpots to help people explore latest hotpot information easily.

References

1. CNNIC Internet research. The 43rd CNNIC China Internet Report Released. China Broadcasting, 4 (2019)

2. Sahoo, P., Parthasarthy, R.: An efficient web search engine for noisy free information retrieval. Int. Arab J. Inf. Technol. **15**(3), 412–418 (2018)
3. FuYong, Y., JinDong, W.: An implemented rank merging algorithm for meta search engine. In: International Conference on Research Challenges in Computer Science, pp. 191–193. IEEE Computer Society (2009)
4. Kumar, J., Kumar, R., Dixit, M.: Result merging in meta-search engine using genetic algorithm. In: International Conference on Computing, Communication and Automation, ICCCA 2015, pp. 299–303. IEEE (2015)
5. Järvelin, K., Kekäläinen, J.: IR evaluation methods for retrieving highly relevant documents. In: SIGIR, pp. 41–48 (2000)

Author Index

.

Printed in the United States
By Bookmasters